Sixth Edition
Global Edition

MANAGING QUALITY

INTEGRATING THE SUPPLY CHAIN

S. Thomas Foster
Brigham Young University

PEARSON

Boston   Columbus   Indianapolis   New York   San Francisco
Amsterdam   Cape Town   Dubai   London   Madrid   Milan   Munich   Montréal   Paris   Toronto
Delhi   Hong Kong   Mexico City   São Paulo   Seoul   Singapore   Sydney   Taipei   Tokyo

Vice President, Business Publishing: Donna Battista
Editor-in-Chief: Stephanie Wall
Acquisitions Editor: Daniel Tylman
Editorial Assistant: Linda Albelli
Associate Acquisitions Editor, Global Edition:
  Ananya Srivastava
Assistant Project Editor, Global Edition:
  Saptarshi Deb
Vice President, Product Marketing: Maggie Moylan
**Director of Marketing, Digital Services and
  Products:** Jeanette Koskinas
Field Marketing Manager: Lenny Ann Raper
Product Marketing Assistant: Jessica Quazza
Team Lead, Program Management: Ashley Santora
Program Manager: Claudia Fernandes

Team Lead, Project Management: Jeff Holcomb
Project Manager: Nicole Suddeth
Project Manager, Global Edition: Nitin Shankar
**Senior Manufacturing Controller, Global
  Edition:** Angela Hawksbee
Operations Specialist: Carol Melville
Creative Director: Blair Brown
Art Director: Janet Slowik
**Vice President, Director of Digital Strategy and
  Assessment:** Paul Gentile
Manager of Learning Applications: Paul DeLuca
**Full-Service Project Management and
  Composition:** Integra
Cover Designer: Lumina Datamatics, Inc
Cover Art: © Robert Adrian Hillman/Shutterstock

Microsoft and/or its respective suppliers make no representations about the suitability of the information contained in the documents and related graphics published as part of the services for any purpose. All such documents and related graphics are provided "as is" without warranty of any kind. Microsoft and/or its respective suppliers hereby disclaim all warranties and conditions with regard to this information, including all warranties and conditions of merchantability, whether express, implied or statutory, fitness for a particular purpose, title and non-infringement. In no event shall Microsoft and/or its respective suppliers be liable for any special, indirect or consequential damages or any damages whatsoever resulting from loss of use, data or profits, whether in an action of contract, negligence or other tortious action, arising out of or in connection with the use or performance of information available from the services.

The documents and related graphics contained herein could include technical inaccuracies or typographical errors. Changes are periodically added to the information herein. Microsoft and/or its respective suppliers may make improvements and/or changes in the product(s) and/or the program(s) described herein at any time. Partial screen shots may be viewed in full within the software version specified.

Microsoft® and Windows® are registered trademarks of the Microsoft Corporation in the U.S.A. and other countries. This book is not sponsored or endorsed by or affiliated with the Microsoft Corporation.

Pearson Education Limited
Edinburgh Gate
Harlow
Essex CM20 2JE
England

and Associated Companies throughout the world

Visit us on the World Wide Web at: www.pearsonglobaleditions.com

© Pearson Education Limited 2017

ISBN 10: 1-292-15421-7
ISBN 13: 978-1-292-15421-3

British Library Cataloguing-in-Publication Data
A catalogue record for this book is available from the British Library

Typeset in Times LT Pro

Printed and bound by Vivar in Malaysia.

To Camille: You Rock!

BRIEF CONTENTS

CONTENTS

PREFACE

Welcome to the sixth edition of *Managing Quality: Integrating the Supply Chain*. We are using the theme of supply chain management as a unifying theme for quality improvement. Previous adopters of *Managing Quality* will note that the coverage of quality topics is just as comprehensive as ever. We simply adopt the unifying theme of the supply chain to enhance our emphasis on the integration of systems with customers, suppliers, technology, and people. We think you will find that your customers—the students—will find this quality management course ever more relevant and interesting. Of course, the new edition of the text has been updated with many changes to keep our coverage of quality topics on the cutting edge.

NEW TO THIS EDITION

- The acceptance sampling supplement to Chapter 9 is back. It provides coverage of important quality management tools.
- We have added coverage of process chain network (PCN) diagramming. This little-known tool provides an excellent way to redesign services processes.
- The main theme for this update is *currency*. We have worked hard to update vignettes and references to keep the book state-of-the-art.
- Many references have been updated to reflect the state of the art in research.
- This book includes the ISO 9000:2015 standard and the most recent Baldrige criteria available at the time of publication.
- All Excel templates (and MS Project) have been updated to the most recent version.
- There is increased focus on lean in this edition.
- Many other changes, too numerous to mention, have been incorporated into this book. However, while adding new content, we have not added to the bulk of the book. This allowed us to keep our focus on a lean and mean book that will hold the interest of students.

MAJOR THEMES

Supply Chain as a Unifying Theme

Today's firms are ever more focused on improving supply chain performance, and key to this improvement is quality management. As we look upstream, we need to develop our suppliers. Downstream, we focus on customer service and after-sales service. Implicit in this process is service design. In your classes, you can drive these concepts home by emphasizing the systems view implicit in supply chain management. This unifying theme provides a linkage between the roots of quality management (Shewhart and Deming) and new developments such as Six Sigma and service quality. *For clarification, this is not a supply chain management text. This is a quality management text that uses supply chain management as a unifying theme.*

Integrative Approach

Workers and managers in organizations are somewhat limited by their particular functional preparation and specialization (going back to their educational training). This narrow presentation filter is how they analyze and cognitively interpret information. However, quality management has emerged as a discipline that is not owned by any of the functional areas such as operations management, supply chain management, human resources, or marketing. We all have to work together to satisfy customers.

Contingency Approach

This is a concept we have emphasized for a long time that is gaining traction in the research and practitioner literature. We passionately believe that the future of quality management will involve learning the contingencies associated with managing quality. There is no "one way" or "magic pill" that companies can implement to improve quality. Therefore, the contingency approach is used to instruct students how to assess the current position of the firm and identify an effective strategy for improvement based on a profound understanding of their company, market, customers, and so on. Thus improvement is based on the contingent variables that are operative in the firm as it exists. This contingency approach is introduced in Chapter 1 and permeates the rest of the text.

The author and more than 300 universities around the world have successfully taught quality management using this contingency approach. This approach, coupled with the unifying theme of the supply chain, makes it pedagogically even more powerful. To manage quality effectively, a few conditions must be present: Students must understand their businesses, understand the quality body of knowledge, understand the available tools, and have a method for planning quality based on this knowledge. This text provides a basis for accomplishing this—when combined with an instructor's insight.

SUPPORT FOR THIS EDITION

Active Models

There are interactive Excel spreadsheets located at **www.pearsonglobaleditions.com/Foster** that correspond to examples in Chapter 12 and Chapter 13 and allow the student to explore and better understand important quantitative concepts. Students or instructors can adjust inputs to the model and, in effect, they can answer a whole series of "what if" questions that are provided (e.g., What if variation in the process changes? What if the process indicates changes are needed? What if we change the sample size?). These Active Models are great for classroom presentation and/or homework.

FOR THE INSTRUCTOR

Besides the changes and additions to the text, we've made substantial revisions to the support materials for this book.

Instructor's Resource Center

At the Instructor Resource Center, **www.pearsonglobaleditions.com/Foster**, instructors can easily register to gain access to a variety of instructor resources available with this text in downloadable format. If assistance is needed, our dedicated technical support team is ready to help with the media supplements that accompany this text. Visit **https://support.pearson.com/getsupport/s** for answers to frequently asked questions and toll-free user-support phone numbers.

The following supplements are available with this text

- Companion Website
- Instructor's Resource Manual
- Test Bank
- TestGen® Computerized Test Bank
- PowerPoint Presentation

ACKNOWLEDGMENTS

I wish to first thank my family for putting up with the fences left unmended, the mountains not explored, the rivers not rafted, the snow unskied, the music not played, and the many hours spent in front of a computer screen over the last years writing and updating this book. It has truly been a labor of love for me. I believe that these concepts are important for the future of the world.

I would like to thank my parents, who always emphasized the importance of education as a means of achieving a happy life. I thank Everett E. Adam Jr. for mentoring me. I would like to acknowledge my colleagues at Brigham Young University for providing encouragement for this project. Thanks to all my students and those individuals who have hired me as a consultant. These people have helped me pursue lifelong learning.

Dan Tylman, my editor at Pearson, deserves recognition for the great encouragement he has given to me. Finally, I am thankful for my faith, which keeps me progressing eternally.

GLOBAL EDITION ACKNOWLEDGEMENTS

Pearson would like to thank and acknowledge James Corbett, Galway-Mayo Institute of Technology; and Kate Dunne, Galway-Mayo Institute of Technology for their contributions to this Global Edition.

We would also like to thank Andreas Kakouris, American College of Greece; Ramin A., Khazar University; Bjorn Samuelsson, Luleå University of Technology; and Rene Claus Larsen, VIA University College, for reviewing the global content and sharing useful suggestions to help improve the Global Edition content.

ABOUT THE AUTHOR

Dr. Tom Foster is a professor, researcher, and consultant in the field of quality management. Among his areas of expertise are strategic quality planning, service quality, Six Sigma, government quality, and the role of technology in improving quality. Tom is the Donald L. Staheli Professor of quality and global supply chain management in the Marriott School of Management at Brigham Young University. He has also taught at Pennsylvania State University and Boise State University. He received his Ph.D. from the University of Missouri–Columbia.

Tom has professional experience in manufacturing, financial services operations, and international oil exploration. He has consulted for more than 30 companies, including Trus Joist MacMillan, the U.S. Department of Energy, Hewlett-Packard, Heinz Frozen Food, and Cutler Hammer/Eaton Corporation. Tom recently served on the 12-person Board of Overseers for the Malcolm Baldrige Award and has served as a judge for state awards.

Tom is on the editorial boards of the *Journal of Operations Management,* the *Quality Management Journal,* and *Decision Sciences*. He has published more than 80 quality-related research articles in journals such as *The Journal of Operations Management, Decision Sciences*, the *International Journal of Production Research*, the *Quality Management Journal*, and *Quality Progress*. He is listed in *Who's Who in America* and *Who's Who in the World*.

Tom is the founder of www.freequality.org, was awarded the ASBSU Outstanding Faculty Award, and served as guest editor for the *Journal of Operations Management* and *Quality Management Journal* special issue on supply chain quality. In addition, he was the winner of the 2002 Decision Sciences Institute Innovative Education Award. Tom is coauthor of *Managing Supply Chain and Operations*, published by Pearson.

Tom has ten children and fourteen grandchildren, and is married to the former Camille Curtis. In his spare time, he skis, enjoys the Rocky Mountains, and plays his Gibson Les Paul Custom.

Understanding Quality Concepts

To understand quality in the supply chain, we need a common language. In the general public, the language of quality is imprecise and inconsistent. The language of quality professionals is much more precise and consistent.

To understand the advanced concepts in the later chapters, in Chapters 1 through 3 we build a conceptual foundation of quality theory. This forms the basis of the contingency approach. To apply quality improvement on a contingent basis, you need to understand the foundation that has been laid by leaders in the quality movement such as W. Edwards Deming, Joseph Juran, Philip Crosby, Kaoru Ishikawa, and others. These people have made huge contributions to the world of quality and a knowledge of their teachings and ideas is necessary for quality application.

In Chapter 3, we consider important frameworks, such as ISO 9000, the Deming Prize, and the Baldrige criteria. They provide models for improvement that are being used in many countries around the world.

Differing Perspectives on Quality

Chapter Objectives

After completing this chapter, you should be able to:

1. Recognize that different dimensions of quality.
2. Be able to discuss quality dimensions.
3. Communicate the seven different functional perspectives on quality.
4. Understand why it is important to know that the different perspectives exist.
5. Define a quality system using the three spheres.
6. Understand how the three spheres complement each other.
7. Understand the value-added perspective on quality.
8. Discuss differing cultural perspectives on quality.

Quality management involves flows. There are process flows, information flows, material flows, and flows of funds. Each of these flows has to operate effectively, efficiently, and with outstanding quality. Like a river, we refer to these as upstream and downstream flows. The sums of these flows comprise the supply chain.

Considering the **supply chain** causes us to think about quality differently. One of the problems with quality efforts has been that they tend to be too internally oriented. The supply chain causes us to expand our vision as we *externalize* processes that had previously been *internalized*. They include **upstream** processes relating to our dealing with suppliers—negotiating, selecting, and improving supplier performance—and **downstream** processes—delivering products and services and serving customers.

The supply chain encompasses many differing functions and processes. It includes all the core activities from the raw materials stage to after-sale service. To execute all of these processes correctly involves integrating differing functions, expertise, and dimensions of quality. This need for integration increases the requirement for flexible, cross-functional problem solving and employees who can adapt to rapidly changing markets.

There are many different definitions and dimensions of quality in the supply chain. We present several of these definitions and dimensions in this chapter. For the present, you can view quality as a measure of goodness that is inherent to a product or service. Employees working for the same firm often view quality differently. Think of the different functions involved in creating

A CLOSER LOOK AT QUALITY 1-1   Buying Clothing in Asia

One of the benefits of the global supply chain has been the opening of new markets in places such as China and India. A recent study by PwC[1] shows that Asian preferences for apparel among affluent shoppers are very different from the United States and Europe. It is fair to say that wealthy Asian shoppers are addicted to luxury-brand products. Affluent Asian shoppers are four times more likely to pay high prices for luxury brands such as Gucci, Prada, and Hermes than U.S. and European consumers. Why is this true? In Asian cultures, these name-brand products signal a shopper's wealth or social status. Affluent Asians crave conspicuous consumption.

In developing Asia, product quality and guaranteed authenticity are more important than price. In developed countries, price is considered a much more important purchase criterion. In developing countries, upward mobility is a newer reality, and luxury products are seen as a method for moving up the social ladder and tapping into the newest fashions. Asians are twice as likely as developed country people to use the Internet and social media to identify which brands are currently the hottest.

As a result, retailers moving into Asian countries can maximize their success by building brand equity, using web-based brand advocates, and tapping celebrities to advertise their products. Using social media in this way can influence perceptions of quality in these rapidly growing markets.

---

[1]Based on Shah, S., et al., "The Rise of the Affluent Asian Shopper," PwC's Experience Radar 2013, PwC, 2013.

---

products and services. They include design engineering, marketing, operations, cost accounting, financial management, and others throughout the supply chain. A product design engineer might feel that customer satisfaction is mostly influenced by product design and product attributes, and take great pains to design a product that satisfies the customer. However, the product also needs to satisfy marketing's need for quick design cycle times and accounting's need for low-cost products. So perceptions differ on a variety of levels, including what our goals for the product or service are. A Closer Look at Quality 1-1 illustrates this point by comparing Asian perceptions concerning apparel purchases.

Perceptions affect every aspect of our world—including the business world. To communicate effectively about quality, managers need to recognize that differences in perceptions of quality exist. Although this observation may not seem too startling, many managers have strong opinions about what quality is. Sometimes these opinions can be at variance with the beliefs of the majority of their customers, which may hurt the competitiveness of a firm. For that reason, in this chapter we study quality from a variety of perspectives. Later we provide a means for recognizing and resolving differences in perception. Finally, we introduce the contingency view of quality management that we emphasize throughout this book.

WHAT IS QUALITY?

If you ask 10 people to define quality, you probably will probabily get 10 different definitions.

Product Quality Dimensions

There are several definitions of quality, or **quality dimensions.** One of the most respected collections of quality dimensions was compiled by David Garvin[2] of the Harvard Business School (see Table 1-1).

Garvin developed a list of eight quality dimensions (see Table 1-1). These dimensions describe product quality specifically in the following paragraphs.

---

[2]Garvin, D., "What Does 'Product Quality' Really Mean?" *Sloan Management Review* (Fall 1984): 25–43.

TABLE 1-1	Product Quality Dimensions

Performance
Features
Reliability
Conformance
Durability
Serviceability
Aesthetics
Perceived quality

Source: © 1984 from MIT Sloan Management Review/
Massachusetts Institute of Technology.

Performance refers to the efficiency with which a product achieves its intended purpose. This might be the return on a mutual fund investment, the fuel efficiency of an automobile, or the acoustic range of a pair of stereo speakers. Better performance is usually synonymous with better quality.

Features are attributes of a product that supplement the product's basic performance. They include many of the "bells and whistles" contained in products. A visit to any television or computer retail store will reveal that features such as surround sound, HDTV capability, 3-D, and size are powerful marketing tools for which customers will pay a premium. A full-line television retail store may carry televisions priced from $200 to $12,000. This range represents a 6,000% price premium for additional features!

Reliability refers to the propensity for a product to perform consistently over its useful design life. A subfield in quality management has emerged, called *reliability management,* based on the application of probability theory to quality. A product is considered reliable if the chance that it will fail during its designed life is very low. For example, if a refrigerator has a 2% chance of failure in a useful life of 10 years, we say that it is 98% reliable.

Conformance is perhaps the most traditional dimension of quality. When a product is designed, certain numeric dimensions for the product's performance are established, such as capacity, speed, size, durability, or the like. These numeric product dimensions are referred to as *specifications.* The number of ounces of pulp allowed in a half-gallon container of "pulp-free" orange juice is one example. Specifications typically are allowed to vary a small amount called *tolerance.* If a particular dimension of a product is within the allowable range of tolerance of the specification, it conforms.

The advantage of the conformance definition of quality for products is that it is easily quantified. However, it is often difficult for a service to conform to numeric specifications. For example, imagine trying to measure the quality of a counselor's work versus that of a carmaker. Because counseling is intangible, it is almost impossible to measure.

Durability is the degree to which a product tolerates stress or trauma without failing. An example of a product that is not very durable is a lightbulb. Lightbulbs can be damaged easily and cannot be repaired. In contrast, a trash can is a very durable product that can be subjected to much wear and tear.

Serviceability is the ease of repair for a product. A product is very serviceable if it can be repaired easily and cheaply. Many products require service by a technician, such as the technician who repairs your personal computer. If this service is rapid, courteous, easy to acquire, and competent, the product generally is considered to have good serviceability. Note that different dimensions of quality are not mutually exclusive.

Aesthetics are subjective sensory characteristics such as taste, feel, sound, look, and smell. Although vinyl interiors in automobiles require less maintenance, are less expensive, and are more durable, leather interiors are usually considered more aesthetically pleasing. We measure aesthetic quality as the degree to which product attributes are matched to consumer preferences.

Perceived quality is based on customer opinion. As we said in the beginning of this chapter, quality is as the customer perceives it. Customers imbue products and services with their understanding of their goodness. This is perceived quality. We can witness an example of the effect of perceived quality every year in college football polls that rank teams. In many cases, the rankings are based on past records, team recognition, university tradition, and other factors that are generally poor indicators of team quality on a given Saturday. In the same way that these factors affect sportswriters' perceptions, factors such as brand image, brand recognition, amount of advertising, and word of mouth can affect consumers' perceptions of quality.

The Garvin list of quality dimensions, although it is the most widely cited and used, is not exhaustive. Other authors have proposed lists of additional quality measures, such as safety. Carol King[3] identified dimensions of service quality such as *responsiveness, competence, access, courtesy, communication, credibility, security,* and *understanding.* Allowed time, you probably could think of additional dimensions as well.

Service Quality Dimensions

Service quality is even more difficult to define than product quality. Although services and production share many attributes, services have more diverse quality attributes than products. This often results from wide variation created by high customer involvement. For example, the consumer of a fountain pen probably will not care that the factory worker producing the pen was in a foul mood (as long as the quality of the pen is good). However, excellent food served in a restaurant generally will not suffice if the server is in a foul mood. In addition, a consumer probably will not consider a pen poor quality if he or she is in a bad mood when using the pen. However, food and service in a restaurant could be excellent and still be perceived poorly if the patron is feeling bad.

Parasuraman, Zeithamel, and Berry (PZ&B), three marketing professors from Texas A&M University, published a widely recognized set of service quality dimensions. These dimensions have been used in many service firms to measure quality performance. The PZ&B dimensions are defined here (see Table 1-2).

Tangibles include the physical appearance of the service facility, the equipment, the personnel, and the communication materials. For example, a hotel with yellowed linens will be rated low for quality. Hair salons catering to an elite clientele might invest in ambient lighting and employ only well-dressed hairstylists. That the hairstylist is dressed well does not affect the service being provided; however, clients believe that their hair will be better styled by someone who is dressed stylishly.

Service reliability differs from product reliability in that it relates to the ability of the service provider to perform the promised service dependably and accurately. For example, a firm might hire a consultant based on reputation alone. If the consultant delivers what the customer wants, the customer will be satisfied and pay the consultancy fee. If the consultant delivers something other than what the customer expects, the customer will not pay the consultancy fee.

TABLE 1-2	PZ&B's Service Quality Dimensions
Tangibles	
Service reliability	
Responsiveness	
Assurance	
Empathy	

Adapted from Parasuraman, A., Zeithamel, V., and Berry, L., "A Conceptual Model of Service Quality" (Report No. 84–106). Copyright © 1984 by Marketing Science Institute. Reprinted by permission.

[3]King, C., "A Framework for a Service Quality Assurance System," *Quality Progress* 20, 9 (1987): 27–32.

Responsiveness is the willingness of the service provider to be helpful and prompt in providing service. When you last called your bank for service, how long did it take for a response? Were your problems taken care of quickly, or did you have to wait while you listened to "elevator music" for an hour? Does your service provider always respond to you within three rings of the phone—without forwarding your call to another location?

Assurance refers to the knowledge and courtesy of employees and their ability to inspire trust and confidence. If you needed heart surgery, you probably would not opt for a doctor who appeared forgetful and disorganized during an office consultation. Rather, you would want assurance that the doctor is competent.

Finally, consumers of services desire **empathy** from the service provider. In other words, the customer desires caring, individualized attention from the service firm. A maxim in the restaurant industry is that "if you are in it for the money, you probably won't survive." A restaurant in which the employees are constantly focused on efficiency will not give the customers the feeling that their needs are important. Therefore, no empathy will be shared, and restaurant employees will not adequately provide service that will make customers want to return again and again.

Just as there are many quality dimensions relating to production, there are several other dimensions of service quality, such as *availability, professionalism, timeliness, completeness*, and *pleasantness*. Note that service design strives to address these different service dimensions simultaneously. It is not sufficient for a services firm to provide only empathy if responsiveness and service reliability are inadequate.

Why Does It Matter That Different Definitions of Quality Exist?

One problem with having multiple dimensions of quality is communication. It is difficult to devise a coherent strategic plan relating to quality when communication is imprecise. One important attribute of a strategic plan is functional alignment or consistency. If different departments in a company understand quality differently, the strategic plan will not be in alignment. Understanding that different definitions and dimensions of quality exist allows measures to be taken to provide a good basis for communication and planning. By sharing a common definition of quality, each department within a company can work toward a common goal. In addition, understanding the multiple dimensions of quality desired by consumers can lead to improved product and service design. Hewlett-Packard Corporation, a producer of laser printers, understands this concept very well. Early in its quality journey, Hewlett-Packard developed products that consistently conformed to specifications. This involved years of product design, process control, and process improvement. Once the printers conformed to specifications, the company emphasized reliability. After the printers were found to be reliable, the company was able to improve the aesthetics of its printers. After years of working on these different quality dimensions, Hewlett-Packard embarked on a "customer one-on-one" program that emphasized customer interaction with production workers. In this program, Hewlett-Packard production workers take time to call customers on the phone to assess and improve the "relationship" that the customer has with a printer.

DIFFERING FUNCTIONAL PERSPECTIVES ON QUALITY

One of the important determinants of how we perceive quality is the functional role we fulfill organizationally. Just as artists and scientists process information differently, so do employees who perform different functions in an organization.

Differences between artists and scientists are only one instance of different perspectives created by functional differences. Accountants are interested in information for accounting and tax purposes, operations people want information for process control and scheduling, finance people need information to manage cash, and marketing needs information to see whether sales quotas are being met.

The **organic view of the organization**[4] sees the whole as the sum of different parts uniting to achieve an end. The heart and the liver do not perform the same function in a body, but they each perform processes that are necessary for survival of the whole. Just as the body is subject to breakdown when different parts do not perform properly, so are organizations. Unfortunately, firms do not have the magnificent communication network (i.e., the central nervous system) to coordinate activities that human bodies have. For this reason, firms must constantly improve their communication. Recognizing fundamental differences between how different functions view quality is an important first step in understanding and resolving problems associated with mismatches of quality perceptions within organizations.

As organizational processes become more cross-functional, many of these communications issues will find resolution. However, experience with cross-functional teams has been difficult for many firms because of poor communication skills among team members. Therefore, it is expected that cognitive differences between different functions will continue to be a major problem that firms must overcome.

This section of the chapter views quality management from the perspectives of several different functions. Many of the topics discussed in this chapter are presented in concept only. More in-depth discussions of these topics appear in later chapters. This chapter is designed to lay out the field of quality management from an interdisciplinary, integrative perspective. The functions discussed here include supply chain management, engineering, operations, strategic management, marketing, finance/accounting, and human resources.

A Supply Chain Perspective

Supply chain management grew out of the concept of the value chain, which includes **inbound logistics, core processes,** and **outbound logistics.** Other functions, such as human resources, information systems, and purchasing, support these core processes. Operations, purchasing, logistics, and marketing are the primary participants in the supply chain. In recent years, supply chain management has moved to the forefront in importance. This is largely due to the opportunity for cost savings along with quality and service improvement. There are many important quality-related activities that are part of supply chain management. We discuss these separately as upstream activities, core processes, and downstream activities.

Figure 1-1 shows a global supply chain management model.[5] The two-way arrow at the center is the supply chain with the suppliers upstream and the customers downstream. At the center of the supply chain is operations management, or the transformation of inputs into products and services. (Operations management is discussed later in the chapter.) Upstream is supplier and purchasing management, which is associated with bringing in parts and components used in production. Downstream is marketing and customer relationship management. As is shown at the bottom, logistics and quality management are used to optimize performance throughout the entire supply chain. The entire model is tied together by strategy.

Upstream activities include all those activities involving interaction with suppliers. **Supplier qualification** involves evaluating supplier performance to determine whether they are worthy providers. This often requires grading suppliers using established criteria, such as conformance rates, cost levels, and delivery reliability. Many times, **supplier filters** are used, such as **ISO 9000,** an international standard. This means that you can filter suppliers based on whether they are ISO 9000 registered. **Supplier development** activities include evaluating, training, and implementing systems with suppliers. This often includes the use of **electronic data interchange (EDI)** to link customer purchasing systems to supplier enterprise resource planning systems. **Acceptance sampling** may be needed to determine whether

---

[4]Foster, S. T., Howard, L., and Shannon, P., "The Role of Quality Tools in Improving Satisfaction with Government," *Quality Management Journal* 9, 3 (2002): 20–31.
[5]Holstein, W., "Hyundai's Capability Play," *Strategy and Business* 70 (Spring 2013): 13–18.

FIGURE 1-1   A Global Supply Chain Model   *Source:* Foster, S. Thomas; Sampson, Scott E.; Wallin, Cynthia; Webb, Scott W, Managing Supply Chain And Operations: An Integrative Approach, 1st Ed., © 2016, p.15. Reprinted and Electronically reproduced by permission of Pearson Education, Inc., New York, NY.

supplier products meet requirements. **Global sourcing** is an important supply chain issue with many companies—especially in China. This is discussed in more depth in Chapter 3.

Core process activities include traditional process improvement as well as **value stream mapping.** This requires flowcharting processes to determine where customer value is created as well as identifying non-value-added process steps. Value stream mapping involves analyzing processes from a systems perspective such that upstream and downstream effects of core process changes can be evaluated. **Six Sigma** is a procedure for implementing quality improvement analysis to reduce costs and improve product, service, and process design. Six Sigma black belts become supply chain quality consultants who can lead value-adding improvements. The steps in Six Sigma include **define, measure, analyze, improve, and control (DMAIC)**-related activities. A major tool used in Six Sigma is the **design of experiments (DOE).**

Downstream activities include shipping and logistics, customer support, and focusing on delivery reliability. Supply chain management has also focused more attention on **after-sale service.**

An Engineering Perspective

Engineering is an applied science. As such, engineers are interested in applying mathematical problem–solving skills and models to the problems of business and industry. One outgrowth of this approach is the field of operations research. For example, in the early twentieth century, Sir R. A. Fisher and other researchers in England expanded the field of mathematical statistics to problems related to variation experienced in the production area.

Two of the major emphases in engineering are the areas of product design and process design. **Product design engineering** involves all those activities associated with developing a product from concept development to final design and implementation. Figure 1-2 demonstrates

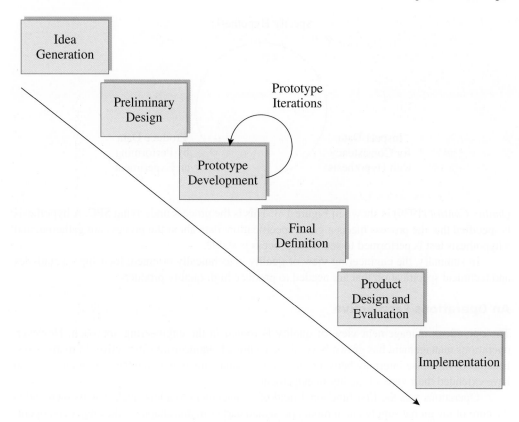

FIGURE 1-2 Design Life Cycle

the six steps in the engineering life cycle for the design of products. The product design process results in a final design, possibly generated using a computer-aided design (CAD) system. Product design is the key because quality is assured at the design stage.

Product and process design are fields of engineering that have experienced major changes in recent years. Whereas traditionally they were considered separate and in most cases sequential activities, **concurrent engineering** has resulted in the simultaneous performance of these activities. Typically, concurrent engineering involves the formation of cross-functional teams, which allow engineers and managers of differing disciplines to work together simultaneously in developing product and process designs. The result of concurrent design has been improved quality and faster speed to market for new products.

Engineers also have applied statistical thinking to the problem of *reliability*. As already discussed, reliability management is concerned with assessing and reducing the propensity of a product to fail. Reliability engineers use probability theory to determine the rate of failure that a product will experience over its useful life. **Life testing** is a facet of reliability engineering that determines whether a product will fail under controlled conditions during a specified life. Also, reliability engineers are interested in knowing whether failure of certain product components will result in failure of the overall product. If a component has a relatively high probability for failure that will affect the overall function of a product, **redundancy** is applied so that a backup system can take over for the failed primary system. Many redundant systems are used on the NASA space shuttle in case of primary system breakdown. After all, if a hard drive crashes in space, it is not easy to find a replacement close by.

Another engineering-related contribution to quality management is **statistical process control (SPC),** which is concerned with monitoring process capability and process stability. If a process is capable, it will consistently produce products that meet specification. If a process is stable, it will only exhibit random or **common cause variation** instead of nonrandom **special cause variation.** This type of variation is often acceptable, if kept within limits. The control process as specified by Walter Shewhart in his book *Statistical Method from the Viewpoint of*

FIGURE 1-3   Shewhart's
Control Process

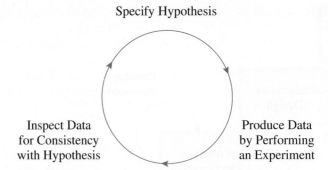

Specify Hypothesis

Inspect Data
for Consistency
with Hypothesis

Produce Data
by Performing
an Experiment

Quality Control (1939) is shown in Figure 1-3. This is the process underlying SPC. A hypothesis is specified that the process meets a given specification, data about the process are gathered, and a hypothesis test is performed to see if the process is stable.

In summary, the engineering view of quality is technically oriented, focusing on statistics and technical specification that are needed to produce high-quality products.

An Operations Perspective

The operations management view of quality is rooted in the engineering approach. However, operations management has grown beyond the technical engineering perspective. In many ways, because of the close interplay between operations management and engineering, engineers also have extended their view of quality management.

Operations was the first functional field of management to adopt quality as its own and is the core of the global supply chain model presented earlier in this chapter. Like engineers, operations managers are concerned about product and process design. However, rather than focusing on only the technical aspects of these activities, operations concentrates on the management of these activities. Initially, operations quality was focused almost entirely on SPC. Later, statistical quality control (SQC) courses became more managerial in nature, including teachings by W. E. Deming, an important quality expert, and others. Today, operations management has developed into an integrative field combining concepts from engineering, operations research, organizational theory, organizational behavior, and strategic management to address quality problems.

Operations management (OM) uses the **systems view** that underlies modern quality management thinking. The systems view involves the understanding that product quality is the result of the interactions of several variables, such as machines, labor, procedures, planning, and management. OM focuses on the management and continual improvement of conversion processes. This systems view focuses on interactions between the various components (i.e., people, policies, machines, processes, and products) that combine to produce a product or service. The systems view also focuses management on the *system as the cause of quality problems.*

In summary, the historically internally focused view of operations managers has become externalized. Still, the customer needs to become more central in the thinking of many operations managers who still tend to be too product focused. This will occur as operations management becomes more service oriented.

A Strategic Management Perspective

Strategy refers to the planning processes used by an organization to achieve a set of long-term goals. The keys here are planning processes and a long-term orientation. Firms establish a planned course of action to attain their objectives. Further, this planned course of action must be cohesive and coherent in terms of goals, policies, plans, and sequencing to achieve quality improvement.

When the concept first arose, practitioners treated quality-related strategic planning as if it were a separate exercise from strategic planning. However, we soon realized that quality management, to become pervasive in a firm, needed to be included in all the firm's business processes, including strategic planning. Thus quality-related goals, tactics, and strategies are becoming more a part of the strategic planning process instead of a separate entity.

Company strategies are rooted in the building blocks of mission and core values. An organization's **mission** states why the organization exists. The **core values** of an organization refer to guiding principles that simplify decision making in that organization. Therefore, if a company states "sustainability" as a core value, it will institute policies leading to practices that favor a clean environment. Companies go to great extents to establish, communicate, and reinforce a sense of mission and values in their organizations because mission and values strongly influence organizational culture. Organizational culture is often seen as a major determinant (and sometimes a roadblock) to the successful implementation of quality improvement.

The quality movement has greatly influenced strategy process in recent years. *Strategy process* refers to the steps an organization uses in the development of its strategic plans. Although we discuss this in greater depth in Chapter 4, strategic planning processes often involve a comprehensive environmental analysis that includes the remote, operating, and external environments that influence quality performance.

Figure 1-4 shows a generic strategic planning process and its components. Based on the analysis of mission, vision, and goals, strategic options and business-level and functional-level strategies are developed.

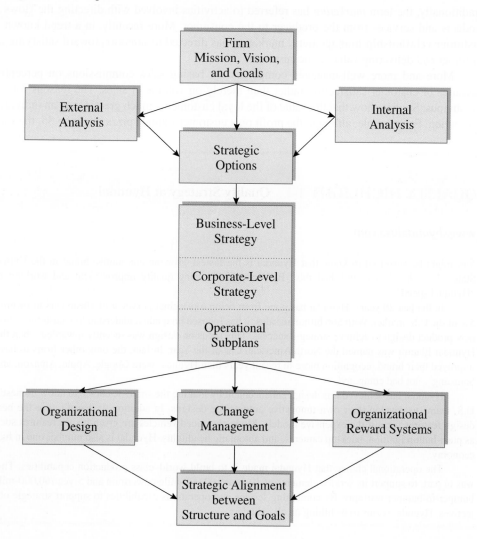

FIGURE 1-4   A Generic Strategic Planning Process

Development of functional-level strategies helps improve the coherence and alignment of strategic plans within an organization. *Alignment* refers to consistency between different operational subplans and the overall strategic plan. For example, if an organization pursues a quality emphasis from a strategic standpoint, the company should pursue supply chain, human resources, budgetary, or marketing courses of action that support a quality emphasis.

The ultimate goal of strategic quality planning is to aid an organization to achieve sustainable competitive advantage. In many markets, such as the auto industry, it is becoming difficult to sustain a competitive advantage based on quality alone. This is also true in many other markets where quality is an order qualifier. In some markets, such as semiconductors, where yield rates are low, competitive advantage in cost can be gained by a quality conformance strategy. Thereby, the quality–cost combination can be used as an order winner.

As quality has become integral to competitiveness, strategic planning for quality has become more important. Research shows that quality is still the major competitive concern of CEOs. Quality Highlight 1-1 shows how Hyundai has made quality a key strategic imperative. This Highlight also demonstrates the interrelatedness among strategy, finance, and operations in achieving strategic objectives.

A Marketing Perspective

Traditionally, the term *marketing* has referred to activities involved with directing the flows of products and services from the producer to the consumer. More recently, in a trend known as **customer relationship management,** marketing has directed its attention toward satisfying the customer and delivering value to the customer.

More and more well-managed companies are basing sales commissions on perceptual measures of customer satisfaction rather than merely on volume of sales. The reasons for this are obvious. Studies show that the value of the loyal customer is much greater than an individual transaction. For example, although the profit on a customer's single pizza might be $5, the same

---

QUALITY HIGHLIGHT 1-1   Quality Strategy at Hyundai

www.hyundaiusa.com

You might be surprised to know that Hyundai is the fastest–growing automotive brand in the United States. How has it accomplished this? By strategically using quality improvement and working at "Hyundai speed."

In the last 20 years, Hyundai has gone from being a marginal purveyor of cheap cars to owning 5% of the U.S. market. With $66 billion in sales, it has focused on quality, understanding customers, and new product design to achieve strategic success. This focus on design was recently rewarded when the Hyundai Elantra was named the North American Car of the Year. In fact, the only other firms to have improved their brand recognition more in recent years than Hyundai were Google, Apple, Amazon, and Samsung—not bad company!

Hyundai has achieved this design enhancement by making the strategic choice to allow domestic U.S. teams to develop their own innovative automobile designs. In addition, it doesn't save the best design features for just the expensive models. Modestly priced vehicles are given luxury features such as push-button ignition, back-up cameras, and automatic headlights. Hyundai is also number one in fuel economy.

The operational choice that Hyundai made is to build world–class production capabilities. This was in part, to support its service elements of 10-year/100,000-mile powertrain and 5-year/60,000-mile bumper-to-bumper warranty. By combining service and operations capabilities to support strategic objectives, Hyundai seems to be hitting on all cylinders.

customer is worth $600 if he or she orders one pizza per month for 10 years. This figure becomes $3,600 if the satisfied customer influences 5 friends to buy one pizza a month over 10 years. If all customers are satisfied, sales increase exponentially! Therefore, more firms are focusing on relationship management, which increases the importance of high levels of customer service and after-sales support.

The marketer focuses on the *perceived quality* of products and services. As opposed to the engineering-based conformance definition of quality, perceived quality means that quality is as the customer views it. Therefore, marketing efforts are often focused on managing quality perceptions.

Although the primary marketing tools for influencing customer perceptions of quality are price and advertising, they are imperfect mechanisms for influencing perceptions of quality. Toothpaste that sells for $4 is not necessarily better than toothpaste that costs $3. The link between price and quality could be significant if all products were priced based on cost of materials and production only. However, not all products are priced this way.

Advertising and quality levels might be related. However, the relationship is not as straightforward as one would hope. Tellis and Johnson[6] proposed a contingency theory of advertising and quality saying that this relationship is "more likely when product quality is produced at lower cost and consumers rely less on advertising for their information." Their research showed that the positive effects of quality also were more pronounced later in the life cycle of a product. In these later stages, products are more likely to be standardized. This would give consumers more time to become informed about products and give firms more time to standardize and control costs.

Marketing is also concerned about systems. The marketing system involves the interactions between the producing organization, the intermediary, and the final consumer (see Figure 1-5). Because of this relationship, it is often very difficult for firms and organizations to agree on who the customer is.

Another important contribution of the marketing perspective has been the focus on service at the time of the transaction and after-sales support.

One of the ways marketing has helped improve product and service quality has been to interact closely with engineering and operations in product design. The role of marketing in design has been to bring the voice of the customer[7] into the design process.

Customer service surveys are important tools for assessing the multiple dimensions of quality. Surveys provide a means for developing multidimensional perceptual measures of quality.

In short, the marketing perspective on quality is unique because the customer is the focus of marketing-related quality improvement. In trying to satisfy customer needs, marketing often wants to develop specialized products for different customers to perfectly satisfy customer needs. This can make life more difficult for producers because operations wants to standardize products to reduce processing complexity. Often, quality strategies result in a compromise between these two polar positions.

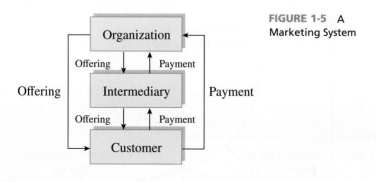

FIGURE 1-5 A Marketing System

[6]Tellis, G., and Johnson, J., "The Value of Quality," *Marketing Science* 26, 6 (2007): 758–773.
[7]Griffin, A., and Hauser, J., "The Voice of the Customer," *Marketing Science* 12, 1 (1993): 1–26.

A Financial Perspective

One of the most commonly asked questions about quality management is "will it pay us financial benefits?" The answer to this question is an unqualified "maybe." Implemented correctly, improved quality reduces waste and can lead to reduced cost and improved profitability. However, these returns tend to be long term rather than short term. W. E. Deming, the influential quality expert, made the first theoretical attempt to link quality improvement to financial results through the "Deming value chain." In his value chain, Deming linked quality improvement to reduction in defects and improved organizational performance. He also stressed quality as a way to increase employment.

The finance function is primarily interested in the relationships between the risks of investments and the potential rewards resulting from those investments. The goal of finance is to maximize return for a given level of risk. A comptroller for a large U.S. corporation stated this as "helping the customer to decide where to buy assets." In this sense, this comptroller viewed his primary customers as the stockholders (i.e., owners) of the corporation.

Communication relating to quality might be made more difficult for comptrollers and treasurers because accounting is the primary language of the financial function. Joseph Juran, another influential quality expert, referred to this communication problem when he stated that "*the language of management is money.*" One way to translate quality concerns is to identify and measure the costs of quality. These quality-related costs can be in lost sales because of a poor reputation for reliability. Also, training and inspection cost money. Therefore, trade-off and break-even analyses can be performed using the various costs of quality. Often what is discovered is that although improving quality seems expensive, the savings from reducing scrap, defects, and rework results in favorable returns on investment. This is why companies such as Motorola, Westinghouse, and GE are willing to pay millions of dollars to pursue quality.

However, the relationship between quality improvement and financial success is confounded by several intervening variables. For example, a firm that invests a great deal of effort and money to establish a quality program for a product in the decline stage of the product life cycle may not receive the expected benefits. Top management involvement that is limited to lip service often results in great expenditure, and great effort, but eventually failure. *The pursuit of quality does not safeguard a company against bad management.*

Another concept that affects financial officers' perceptions of quality improvement is the **law of diminishing marginal returns.** According to this law, there is a point at which investment in quality improvement will become uneconomical. Figure 1-6 shows a quadratic economic quality level model. According to this model, the pursuit of higher levels of quality will result in higher expenditures. So to invest beyond the minimum cost level will result in noneconomic decisions. This view is at odds with the ethic of continual improvement. Such debate has resulted in much controversy in the quality field. Although we save resolution of these issues for Chapter 4,

FIGURE 1-6   Basic Economic Quality Level Model

it should be emphasized that quality evangelizers who claim that the pursuit of quality is eternal and that any investment in quality is always justified will be met with skepticism by financial officers trained in economics.

In summary, the financial perspective on quality relies more on quantified, measurable, results-oriented thinking. This has influenced quality thinking as quality professionals have had to seek approval for funding quality improvement efforts. If the objective of a firm is to return value to its shareholders, the financial view toward quality must be well understood and used.

The Human Resources Perspective

Human resources (HR) managers are involved in enabling the workforce to develop and use its full potential to meet the company's objectives. Understanding the HR perspective on quality is essential because it is impossible to implement quality without the commitment and action of employees. Although leadership is an important antecedent to successful quality efforts, the involvement and participation of employees is just as key. After all, it is the rank and file that implements quality throughout the organization.

Of particular interest to HR managers is **employee empowerment.** Empowering employees involves moving decision making to the lowest level possible in the organization. For example, empowerment can involve something fairly minor, such as allowing employees to replace broken or worn-out tools without management approval. In more spectacular instances, empowerment has resulted in the elimination of management as employees do their own scheduling, design, and performance of work.

The topic of empowerment is closely related to **organizational design.** HR managers are involved in many aspects of organizational design, such as the design of reward systems, pay systems, organizational structure, compensation, training mechanisms, and employee grievance arbitration.

HR balances the needs of the employee and the organization by advocating the employee to management and advocating the company's needs to employees. *Quality management flourishes where the workers' and the company's needs are closely aligned.* When needs are aligned, actions that are good for the company are also good for the employee.

Job analysis is a major function of HR.[8] Job analysis involves collecting detailed information about a particular job. This information includes tasks, skills, abilities, and knowledge requirements that relate to certain jobs. The information then defines a job description that is used in setting pay levels. Job analysis sometimes has limited the capability of organizations to adapt to the flexibility needed for quality management. Important HR functions are recruitment and hiring of employees. A process called **selection** is employed. Traditionally, selection involved finding workers who have the technical preparation to perform the tasks associated with a job. Fast learners are becoming more valued by today's organizations. Of course, this does not mean that nuclear engineers will be replaced by former romance languages majors. However, it could mean that groups of engineers might report directly to a romance languages expert.

HR departments typically administer and oversee performance appraisal and evaluation. Traditionally, these evaluations involved face-to-face reporting sessions with employees and supervisors. Although some critics, such as Deming, have found this system ineffective, many companies believe performance evaluations are a key method for motivating employees. One quality-related approach to improving the process of performance evaluation is the **360-degree evaluation,** in which an employee's peers, supervisors, and subordinates are involved in evaluating the worker's performance. The College of Business at the University of North Carolina at Greensboro performs 360-degree teaching evaluations for its faculty. Each semester, students fill out teaching evaluations. Fellow faculty members attend each other's classes and read each other's student evaluations every semester. A meeting is then held, at which the faculty members

---

[8]Morgeson, F., Spitzmuller, M., and Garza, A., "Pay Attention! The Liabilities of Respondent Experience and Carelessness When Making Job Analysis Judgments," *Journal of Management,* in press.

evaluate and critique the others' teaching performance. In this setting, the focus is on constructive criticism. Finally, the professor's supervisor uses the student and peer input to complete an annual evaluation. This approach seems to be effective in improving teaching performance.

In summary, the focus of quality management is to manage properly the interactions among people, technology, inputs, processes, and systems to provide outstanding products and services to customers. HR managers have been very active in advocating quality approaches to improve organizational performance. Therefore, an HR focus on human performance provides important insights to quality thinking.

Is Quality Management Its Own Functional Discipline?

A quick read of the *Wall Street Journal* in any given week will reveal job openings for quality managers and engineers. The companies that run these ads seek people who, like you, are committed to and interested in quality management. However, the roles of these departments and specialists are changing in the new century of quality.

Historically, the quality management department performed a policing function in the firm. Quality managers were responsible for quality conformance and spent their time ferreting out causes of defects. However, Armand Feigenbaum, a well-known quality consultant who is discussed in Chapter 2, and others showed the limitations of this approach. Thus the movement began toward the total involvement of employees, spawning total quality management (TQM). *TQM* was the 1980s term to describe quality management programs.

With total involvement, the role of the quality department moved from a technical inspection role to a supportive training and coaching role. As a manager or a quality specialist, you will be asked to either arrange or perform quality-related training. Thus the abilities to conduct effective training and to facilitate teams are important tools for the quality professional.

Is quality management its own discipline? Yes and no. Consultants, quality engineers, Six Sigma black belts, trainers, coaches, and managers are still needed. Therefore, the demand for quality specialists persists. However, because the eventual goal is to completely immerse the organization in quality thinking and commitment, the need for the specialist decreases with time. Therefore, a strong knowledge of quality is best coupled with technical expertise in other areas such as materials management, supply chain management, finance, accounting, operations management, HR management, strategy, industrial engineering, or myriad other disciplines. Indeed, the eventual goal of many companies is to completely distribute the quality management function throughout the firm.

In this section of the chapter, we have discussed many different functional perspectives toward quality. Skilled management must recognize that these functional differences exist and provide communication in a way that completely addresses the different perspectives. Recognition that these multiple dimensions exist improves understanding among these disparate coalitions and helps all members of an organization to work toward a common goal.

THE THREE SPHERES OF QUALITY

One way to conceptualize the field of quality management is known as the **three spheres of quality.** These spheres are quality control, quality assurance, and quality management, and their functions overlap, as seen in Figure 1-7.

The first sphere is **quality control.** The control process is based on the scientific method, which includes the phases of analysis, relation, and generalization. In the *analysis* phase, a process is broken into its fundamental pieces. *Relation* involves understanding the relationships between the parts. Finally, *generalization* involves perceiving how interrelationships apply to the larger phenomenon of quality being studied. Activities relating to quality control include the following:

- Monitoring process capability and stability
- Measuring process performance
- Reducing process variability

FIGURE 1-7 Three Spheres of Quality

- Optimizing processes to nominal measures
- Performing acceptance sampling
- Developing and maintaining control charts

Quality assurance refers to activities associated with guaranteeing the quality of a product or service. These activities are often design-related. This view of quality states that quality control is reactive rather than proactive by detecting quality problems after they occur. Given this, the best way to ensure quality is in the design of products, services, and processes. Quality assurance activities include tasks such as

- Failure mode and effects analysis
- Concurrent engineering
- Experimental design
- Process improvement
- Design team formation and management
- Off-line experimentation
- Reliability/durability product testing

The management processes that overarch and tie together the control and assurance activities make up **quality management.** See Quality Highlight 1-2 for an example of a company with

QUALITY HIGHLIGHT 1-2   Federal Express Corporation[9]

www.fedex.com

Federal Express at a Glance

Conceived by Chairman and Chief Executive Officer Frederick W. Smith, Federal Express began operations in 1973. At that time, a fleet of eight small aircraft was sufficient to handle demand. The firm's cargo fleet is now the world's largest—at more than 645.

FedEx's "People–Service–Profit" philosophy guides management policies and actions. The company has a well-developed and thoroughly deployed management evaluation system called

---

[9]Adapted from the Malcolm Baldrige award "Profiles of Malcolm Baldrige Award Winners," National Institute for Standards and Technology, Gaithersburg, MD, 2016.

(continued)

SFA (survey/feedback/action) that involves a survey of employees, analysis of each group's results by the work group's manager, and a discussion between the manager and the work group to develop written action plans for the manager to improve and become more effective. Data from the SFA process are aggregated at all levels in the organization for use in policy making.

Training of frontline personnel is a responsibility of managers, and "recurrency training" is a widely used instrument for improvement. Consistently included in listings of the best U.S. companies to work for, FedEx has a "no-layoff" philosophy, and its "guaranteed fair treatment procedure" for handling employee grievances is used as a model by firms in many industries. Frontline employees can participate in a program to qualify themselves for management positions. In addition, Federal Express has a well-developed recognition program for team and individual contributions to company performance.

Service Quality Indicators

To spur progress toward its ultimate goal of 100% customer satisfaction, FedEx replaced its old measure of quality performance, percentage of on-time deliveries, with a 12-component index that comprehensively describes how its performance is viewed by its customers. Each item in the service quality indicator (SQI) is weighted to reflect how significantly it affects overall customer satisfaction.

To reach its aggressive quality goals, the company has set up one cross-functional team for each service component of the SQI. A senior executive heads each team for each service component of the SQI and ensures the involvement of frontline employees, support personnel, and managers from all parts of the corporation when needed. Two of these corporate-wide teams have a network of more than 1,000 people working on improvements.

Employees are encouraged to be innovative and to make decisions that advance quality goals. FedEx provides employees with the information and technology they need to continuously improve their performance. An example is the Digitally Assisted Dispatch System (DADS), which communicates to some 47,500 couriers through screens in their vans. The system enables quick response to pickup and delivery dispatches and allows couriers to manage their time and routes with great efficiency.

---

effective quality management. The integrative view of quality management supports the idea that quality is the responsibility of all management, not just quality managers. For this reason, a number of managers, supervisors, and employees are involved in quality management activities such as

- Planning for quality improvement
- Creating a quality organizational culture
- Providing leadership and support
- Providing training and retraining
- Designing an organizational system that reinforces quality ideals
- Providing employee recognition
- Facilitating organizational communication

Many quality-related activities can occur simultaneously within the framework of the three spheres of quality. Because these activities overlap, communication between the protagonists performing the different activities becomes key.

OTHER PERSPECTIVES ON QUALITY

Although we have discussed a variety of perspectives on quality, there are a few others.

The Value-Added Perspective on Quality

A customer-based perspective on quality that is used by services, manufacturing, and public sector organizations involves the concept of value. A **value-added** perspective on quality involves a subjective assessment of the efficacy of every step of the process for the customer. A value-added activity can be pinpointed by asking, "Would this activity matter to the customer?" In other words, in most cases, a value-added activity will have economic value to the customer.

Cultural Perspectives on Quality

International marketers have long noted differences in tastes and preferences between cultures and nations. For example, Mexican food sold in the United States by the major restaurant chains is very different from the food sold in Mexico. This is so because American restaurant chains have found that customers prefer the Americanized versions of these foods.

Although it is somewhat obvious that differences in tastes and preferences exist between different cultures, it is not so obvious that approaches to quality improvement may differ according to culture. However, differences do exist. For example, Japanese companies tend to stress conformity and uniformity in producing quality. This results in high consistency among Japanese products. American firms are more likely to favor empowerment approaches that reward creativity and individualism. Certainly, cultures that are more class conscious or command-and-control-oriented might have trouble delegating decision making to lower levels of employees.

Arriving at a Common Understanding of Quality Using a Contingency Perspective of Quality

Businesses differ in key areas such as mission, core competence, customer attributes, target markets, technology deployment, employee knowledge, management style, culture, and myriad other environmental variables. **Contingency theory** presupposes that there is no theory or method for operating a business that can be applied in all instances. A coherent quality strategy will address these key environmental variables. For example, a company that defines part of its mission as "valuing and satisfying our customers through personalized service" likely will pursue a different technological approach toward its customers than a company with the mission of "applying technology to solving customer problems." One approach implies personalized service in interacting with customers, whereas the second company focuses on digital interfaces with the customer. Both companies are focused on satisfying the customer. The difference is that they pursue different paths and strategies to achieve customer service.

The contingency approach to quality also helps settle the different perceptions concerning the definition of quality. By adopting a contingency philosophy, we find that the definitions and dimensions of quality applied within organizations will (and should) vary. The definitions of quality used by the Department of Agriculture, Ford Motor Company, and the University of Colorado at Boulder will not be the same. Different definitions of quality also might exist within an organization, even though their quality definitions should be consistent. In an organization that adopts the contingency approach, the dimensions of quality will depend on the environment in which the company operates. This approach provides useful flexibility to managers in pursuing quality.

Summary

There are many different perspectives on quality management. We found that customers and producers viewed quality differently. A focus on production and a focus on services provide two very different perspectives on quality.

There is even a great deal of disagreement about an appropriate definition of quality. A contingency perspective on quality shows that different definitions of quality are appropriate for different organizations.

The functional perspectives on quality vary greatly. As we understand these different functional perspectives, we form the basis for alignment in strategies and improvement in quality communication.

The fundamental areas of quality control, quality assurance, and quality management within the field of quality focus us on different aspects of quality. By designing plans and systems in each of these areas simultaneously, we develop a robust system of quality improvement that will set the stage for improved competitiveness.

Something else that becomes apparent is that quality improvement, despite the simplicity of many principles, requires a complex mix of systems design, organizational design, rewards design, and process design. As discussed throughout this text, these issues can be tied together in a strategic framework.

Key Terms

Acceptance sampling
Aesthetics
After-sale service
Assurance
Common cause variation
Concurrent engineering
Conformance
Contingency theory
Core processes
Core values
Customer relationship
    management
Define, measure, analyze,
    improve, and control
    (DMAIC)
Design of experiments
    (DOE)

Downstream
Durability
Electronic data interchange
    (EDI)
Empathy
Employee empowerment
Features
Inbound logistics
Global sourcing
ISO 9000
Job analysis
Law of diminishing
    marginal returns
Life testing
Mission
Organic organization
Organizational design

Outbound logistics
Perceived quality
Performance
Product design
    engineering
Quality assurance
Quality control
Quality dimensions
Quality management
Redundancy
Reliability
Responsiveness
Selection
Service reliability
Serviceability
Six Sigma
Special cause variation

Statistical process control
    (SPC)
Strategy
Supplier development
Supplier filters
Supplier qualification
Supply chain
Systems view
Tangibles
360-degree evaluation
Three spheres of quality
Upstream
Value-added
Value stream mapping

Discussion Questions

1. Why is *quality* a difficult term to define? How can we improve our understanding of quality?
2. Briefly discuss Garvin's eight dimensions of quality. Is Garvin's multidimensional approach a step forward in improving our understanding of quality? Why or why not?
3. Why is service quality more difficult to define than product quality?
4. Define the concept of *empathy*. Provide an example of empathy as a dimension of service quality?
5. Why is communication within an organization an important part of the quality improvement process?
6. Compare and contrast the engineering perspective and the marketing perspective of quality. How could an overemphasis on the engineering perspective work to the disadvantage of a business organization?
7. Describe the relevance of the "systems view" to our understanding of quality management.
8. Why is planning an important part of the quality management process? How could a firm's quality management initiatives be adversely affected if planning were not a part of the process?
9. Research has shown that quality is a major competitive concern of CEOs in American corporations. Is this level of concern about quality warranted? Explain your answer.
10. What is meant by the phrase *cost of quality*? How can this phrase help a firm address its quality concerns?
11. What are the major differences between traditional human resource management and total quality human resource management? How does total quality human resource management transcend traditional human resource management in regard to providing an environment that is supportive of quality concerns?
12. Explain the three spheres of quality.
13. Discuss the value-added perspective on quality.

14. How does contingency theory inform decision making when implementing improvement efforts?
15. Should a firm consider the law of diminishing marginal returns when striving to improve quality? Why or why not?
16. Are the perspectives of quality independent of one another? If not, describe ways in which they are interrelated.
17. How can an understanding of the multiple dimensions of quality lead to improved product and service designs?
18. What is your concept of quality? Is it multidimensional, or does it focus on a single dimension such as features, reliability, or conformance? Explain your answer.
19. Describe an instance in which you and a co-worker (or superior) perceived the needs of a customer very differently. How did your differences in perception influence how each of you wanted to meet your customer's needs?

CASES

Case 1-1 FedEx: Managing Quality Day and Night
FedEx Homepage: www.fedex.com

As darkness falls across America and most businesses are locking up for the evening, one company is gearing up for a long night's work. FedEx, the world leader in the overnight package delivery market, delivers more than 7.6 million packages per business day. Most of us know FedEx as the overnight delivery company with white delivery vans, courteous drivers, and the distinctive purple-and-orange FedEx logo. But behind what the casual observer sees is a very complex company with the capacity to deliver millions of packages to millions of addresses around the globe overnight. Throughout the course of virtually every day and night, FedEx mobilizes its army of 165,000 employees, 47,500 vans and trucks, and 647 planes to get the job done.

For FedEx, getting the job done means managing quality 24 hours per day, with a watchful eye on customer expectations. The company's goals are simple: 100% customer satisfaction, 100% on-time deliveries, and 100% accurate information available on every shipment to every location around the world. Although these sound like far-fetched goals, the company goes to great lengths to try to make them a reality. One of the principal weapons that FedEx uses in pursuit of its goals is its total commitment to quality management.

Quality management at FedEx encompasses all its operations. Although the company is the acknowledged leader in the air freight industry, a formal Quality Improvement Process (QIP) plays an integral role in all the company's activities.[10]

At the heart of the QIP program is the philosophy that quality must be a part of the way that FedEx does business, not part of the time, but all the time. As a result, themes such as "Do it right the first time," "Make the first time you do it the only time anyone has to," and "Q = P" (quality = productivity) are important parts of the FedEx culture. To reinforce these themes, the company teaches its employees the 1–10–100 rule. According to the rule, if a problem is caught and fixed as soon as it occurs, it costs a certain amount of time and money to correct. If a mistake is caught later in a different department or location, it may cost 10 times that much to repair. And if a mistake is caught by a customer, it may cost 100 times as much to fix.

A number of substantive strategies have been implemented by FedEx to support its quality efforts. Quality action teams (QATs) design work processes to support new product and service offerings. A set of service quality indicators (SQIs) has been established to determine the main areas of customers' perception of service. Through careful tracking of these indicators, the company generates a weekly summary of how well it is meeting its customer satisfaction targets. An SQI team works through problems revealed by the indicators. For example, if problems were being created by confusion in FedEx labeling instructions, the team would work on improving the clarity of the instructions. Some of the company's tactics to ensure total quality are extraordinary. For example, every night FedEx launches an empty airliner from Portland, Oregon, bound for Memphis. The jet follows a course that brings it close to several FedEx terminal airports. The purpose of the jet is to swoop down and pick up FedEx packages if any of the company's regularly scheduled airplanes is experiencing mechanical difficulty.

---

[10]www.fedex.com.

(continued)

Along with a focus on its external customers, FedEx's approach to quality also involves strengthening the bonds between its internal customers, or employees. To reinforce this notion, the company asks all its employees to ask the following three questions when they interface with a co-worker:

1. What do you need from me?
2. What do you do with what I give you?
3. Are there any gaps between what I give you and what you need?

The company also reaches out to its employees in a number of substantive ways. To do this, the company adopted its People–Service–Profit (PSP) philosophy, which articulates the view that when people are placed first, service and profit follow. An aggressive training program, competitive wages and benefits, profit sharing, bonuses, and a state-of-the-art employee grievance process are all elements of the PSP philosophy. Employee recognition also plays an important role in the company's quality pursuits. For example, each quarter FedEx divisions select their best quality

success story, which is entered in a company-wide competition. Presentations are made by the finalists before the company's CEO, executive vice president, and other top managers. The award for being a finalist is a gold quality pin for each member of the team and the opportunity to be interviewed on the company's internal television network.

The quality efforts practiced by FedEx have paid off. The company has achieved a remarkable 99.7% on-time delivery level. The list of awards the company has won are too numerous to publish. The most impressive are the Malcolm Baldrige award; the AT&T Top Performer award; the Quality Carrier of the Year award, presented by Merck Pharmaceuticals; and the Company of the Year Distinguished Service award, presented by the National Alliance of Businesses. Will FedEx's pursuit of quality end here? Asked if winning the Malcolm Baldrige award signifies that FedEx has achieved the ultimate level of quality, CEO Fred Smith said, "Receipt of the award is simply our license to practice." Apparently, the quest for improved quality at FedEx will continue, day and night.

Discussion Questions

1. What is FedEx's "common language" of quality? Is it important for a company to establish a "common language" of quality? If so, why?
2. There are several different perspectives of quality, including the operations perspective, the strategic perspective, the marketing perspective, the financial perspective, the HR perspective, and the systems perspective. Which of these perspectives are being emphasized by FedEx? Why?
3. Is FedEx's level of emphasis on quality appropriate? Why or why not?

Case 1-2 Graniterock Company: Achieving Quality through Employees
Graniterock Homepage: www.graniterock.com

Graniterock, a California-based mining and construction company, was founded in 1900, but its journey toward improved quality did not start until many decades later. The managers at Graniterock knew that a resulting decline in customer satisfaction was inevitable and responded to this self-assessment by deciding it needed to become more customer focused. At Graniterock, this meant not only learning more about the customer but also providing its employees the training and skills necessary to properly implement the company's new philosophy.

At first, this focus on HR management was emphasized through employee training. As explained by ex-CEO Bruce Woolpert, you can't have employees out telling customers "yes" unless everyone else in the company knows how to follow up on "yes." As a result, an aggressive training program was implemented,

involving on-the-job training and classroom time for a majority of the firm's employees. A program called IPDP (Individual Personal Development Plan) was created to help each employee take responsibility for his or her own training program. As the program gained momentum, remarkable things started to happen. One employee indicated that he wanted to learn to read better. As a result of that request, the company initiated a reading program that has helped a number of Graniterock's employees improve their reading skills. As part of the company's effort to reduce process variability and increase product reliability, many employees were trained in statistical process control, root-cause analysis, and other quality-minded competencies. Today, Graniterock spends up to $1,600 per year for training of each employee, which is more than 10 times the average for the mining and construction industries.

An equally important step in equipping its employees to contribute to the firm's efforts was establishing an atmosphere of trust between management and the rank-and-file employees. That effort has been pursued in a number of ways, and the trust developed throughout the company has resulted in the effective implementation of employee empowerment and teamwork. In addition, the company has done away with its conventional performance-appraisal system (feeling that it was ineffective) and has incorporated performance appraisal into each employee's IPDP. As part of this plan, each employee meets with his or her supervisor at least once per year to discuss job responsibilities, review accomplishments, assess skills, and set skill and career development goals. Although the IPDP is not mandatory for the company's unionized workers, overall participation stands at 83%. Because the IPDP approach to training and appraisal prepares employees to assume greater responsibilities, Graniterock promotes heavily from within.

Graniterock, having won the Malcolm Baldrige award and one of *Fortune* magazine's best 100 companies to work for, is aggressively pursuing its quality initiatives, with the cooperation of its 700 employees.

Discussion Questions

1. Rather than focusing on human resource management (HRM) as a means of supporting its quality initiatives, Graniterock could have chosen another area as its focal point (e.g., marketing, operations, information systems, and so on). How does a focus on HRM support a company's quality initiatives?

2. Discuss the different components of Graniterock's HRM initiatives. How can each of these components support the company's quality efforts?

3. Discuss ex-CEO Woolpert's feelings about communication with the customers (paragraph 2). What happens when others in the company don't know what has been promised to the customer? How can quality management help to overcome this situation?

CHAPTER 2

Quality Theory

Chapter Objectives

After completing this chapter, you should be able to:

1. Integrate theories and concepts from key thought leaders in quality management.

2. Discuss differing ideas from quality management thought leaders to determine the best methods for managing quality.

3. Discuss key quality improvement variables and how they combine to create a quality management system.

4. Assess a quality management system using the theoretical framework for quality management.

For some reason, the word *theory* conjures negative thoughts among many students and businesspeople. There is a supposition that an emphasis on theory will somehow distance us from the real world and what "really works." However, theories form the basis for much of what happens around us, and most of us use them every day without knowing it. For instance, mechanical theories are at work when you drive your car. When you turn on a light, theories are at work, harnessing the power of electricity. The airplanes overhead benefit by Bernoulli's theory. The organizations we work for are based on theories proposed by generations of organizational theorists. The money we spend is managed by macroeconomic theory. Because there can be no understanding of the phenomena that surround us without theory, shouldn't there be a general theory of quality management? In other words, is there a model that explains how organizations such as Federal Express, Apple, and Toyota have achieved such high levels of quality within the past generation?

Several theories on quality improvement are in practice currently. In this chapter we learn about the experts in this field, their theories, and how these theories have been used by various organizations.

WHAT IS THEORY?

The term *theory* is often misused. Generally, theory is a "coherent group of general propositions used as principles of explanation for a class of phenomena."[1] For example, it might have been observed that many companies that have implemented quality improvement have experienced

---

[1]*Random House Webster's College Dictionary* 2011.

FIGURE 2-1   A Theoretical Model Relating
Quality Improvement to Worker Morale

improved worker morale. Therefore, a theoretical model of quality and worker morale might be developed as shown in Figure 2-1.

The model in Figure 2-1 has two variables: quality improvement and worker morale. The arrow implies causality. Because the head of the arrow points to worker morale, this is the *dependent variable*, with quality improvement being the *independent variable*. Thus we can see that our small theoretical model is testable. To test our model, we formulate a hypothesis, gather data under controlled conditions, and analyze the data. There is no way to prove the theory. The results of our statistical research will only support the theory or fail to support the theory.

For a theory to be complete, it must have four elements[2]: what, how, why, and who-where-when. The *what* of the theory involves which variables or factors are included in the model. The variables in Figure 2-1 are the *what* of that model.

The *how* of a theoretical model involves the nature, direction, and extent of the relationship among the variables. For example, in our simple quality/morale model, we posited that quality improvement positively influences worker morale. This is represented by the plus sign in the model.

The *why* of the theory is the theoretical glue that holds the model together. For example, what are the psychological dynamics that could cause quality improvement to increase worker morale? Suppose we theorize that organizations using quality improvement are more organic in nature, stressing worker empowerment. Suppose further that worker empowerment lifts worker self-esteem by stressing increased decision making and control over his or her own job. Finally, we propose that this increase in self-esteem results in improved worker morale.

The *who-where-when* aspects place contextual bounds on the theory. For example, we might add a condition to our model stating that morale is improved only in companies that receive strong leadership by top management to implement quality improvement.

As shown in Figure 2-2, theories are established in one of two ways. A theory generated by observation and description is said to have been developed by the process of **induction.** The process of induction is useful, but it is also subject to observer bias and misperception. Suppose we developed our quality/morale theory after visiting a series of Chicago, Illinois, firms that had implemented quality improvement. During our site visits, we found that employee morale was

Induction

Data ⟶ Generalization

Deduction

Generalization ⟶ Supported by Data

FIGURE 2-2   Inductive versus Deductive
Reasoning

[2]Davis, J., Eisenhardt, K., and Bingham, C., "Developing Theory through Simulation Methods," *Academy of Management Review* 32, 2 (2007): 480–499.

high in all the sites we visited. Our inductive observations of quality influencing morale might be correct. However, as committed researchers, we are so enthralled by our discovery that we fail to notice that the Cubs (the Chicago baseball franchise) just won the World Series. Therefore, our inductively produced model of quality/morale might have been confounded by an intervening variable (the glorious win by the Cubs).

The more common theoretical approach used by researchers is **deduction.** Using deduction, researchers propose a model based on prior research and design an experiment to test the theoretical model. These studies follow the scientific method discussed in Chapter 1.

Many of the concepts and models proposed in this chapter are developed by induction. Therefore, when considering concepts put forth by experts such as Deming, Juran, and Crosby, note that their principles are based on years of experience with a wide variety of firms that have improved quality. Their models and principles are also laden with personal biases, judgments, and values. This is fine, as long as you recognize these limitations to their models.

Is There a Theory of Quality Management?

As yet, there is not a unified theory explaining quality improvement in the supply chain that is widely accepted by the quality community. In fact, as we saw in Chapter 1, the literature concerning quality is contradictory and somewhat confusing. Different theories have been proposed by practitioners and researchers. Some of these theories have been drawn from organizational theory, behavioral theory, and statistical theory.

The differing approaches to quality improvement represent competing philosophies that have sought their places in the marketplace of ideas. Practicing quality managers must become familiar with these philosophies and apply those that are appropriate to their particular situations.

The diversity of approaches to quality contributes to variability in the approaches used by companies and increases the chance for failure in organizations. Some of these approaches are proven, and others aren't. This has spawned myriad consulting firms and consultants. As shown in A Closer Look at Quality 2-1, some of them are legitimate, and some are in it for profit only. In past decades, there has been an explosion of consulting firms around the world that taught a variety of means for achieving quality. In the following sections, we discuss the problem of the fragmentation of the quality message from a managerial point of view.

A CLOSER LOOK AT QUALITY 2-1   Quality and Management Fads[3]

Every holiday season, there are long lines at the toy stores. Everyone is hoping to purchase the popular toy. Walking down the street or in school hallways, people are wearing the same style of clothes. The latest trends are what people think about. But just as quickly as the toy or clothing fad comes, it will go away with the next "it" item. Fads are not confined to the fashion or toy industry, but also exist in the area of business management and quality theories and practices.

Quality management can be a jumble of alphabet soup. Managers say, "We use TQM, lean and MBO" or "We are ISO registered." Some of these programs add value to a company, whereas others may be fads without lasting effects. Danny Miller and Jon Hartwick state, "Fads like TQM can profoundly change companies, for better or for worse."

So how does a firm avoid a fad and select a tool that might endure? Through research, Miller and Hartwick have identified several qualities of business fads. They define fads as simple, prescriptive, falsely encouraging, one-size-fits-all, easy to cut and paste, in tune with the zeitgeist, novel, not radical, and externally legitimized by gurus and disciples. These can serve as a set of criteria for evaluating business and quality programs.

[3]Based on Miller, D., and Hartwick, J., "Spotting Management Fads," *Harvard Business Review* 80, 10 (2002): 26–27.

(continued)

Making changes in a company is not easy. The goal is to make a positive impact. As we discuss in this chapter, quality tools should be assessed based on their effects on the business. Following are some questions to consider:

- Is the approach used in the real world?
- Is the approach a correct fit for or adaptable to the business?
- Does the approach deliver measurable results?
- Does the approach address the root cause of problems?
- Does the approach challenge the status quo?

Proven tools come from responding to economic, social, and competitive challenges. Ultimately, lasting changes to the firm will come from management profoundly understanding the business and adapting quality tools to the particular needs of the business.

There is no perfect test to distinguish fads from proven tools. Some fads will have merit and make a positive lasting change. Management must perform due diligence when selecting tools for the organization. If done correctly, the firm will have its own distinct "style" when it comes to managing quality.

HISTORY OF QUALITY MANAGEMENT

Table 2-1 outlines a brief history of the quality movement. Later in this chapter, we further develop the teachings of many of the key contributors in quality management. From the scientific management movement of the early twentieth century to the present focus on supply chain quality, there has been a continual growth of the field.

LEADING CONTRIBUTORS TO QUALITY THEORY: W. EDWARDS DEMING

W. Edwards Deming (see Figure 2-3) was widely accepted as the world's preeminent authority on quality management. Deming gained credibility because of his influence on Japanese and American industry. When it became apparent that many Japanese products were of better quality than U.S. products, U.S. managers were surprised to learn that the Japanese had learned quality

TABLE 2-1	History of Quality
Early 1900s	Frederick Taylor, Frank and Lillian Gilbreth, and scientific management
1920s	Walter Shewhart and statistical process control
1930s	Dodge and Romig introduce acceptance sampling
1940s	Military standards introduced
1950s	Deming and Juran introduce quality management to Japan
1960s	Taguchi method and other tools developed
1970s	Quality becomes strategic; beginning of major adoption in the United States
1980s	"If Japan Can, Why Can't We?" airs on U.S. TV; introduction of Lean with Schonberger, Shingo, and Hall; TQM and empowerment become watchwords in quality field; Baldrige award program implemented
1990s	Reengineering and Six Sigma become major movements with mixed results; wide dissemination of quality approaches
2000s	Growth of supply chain management and improvement of supplier development; lean Six Sigma becomes popular; contingency theory in quality becomes recognized as important
2010s	Supply chain quality management (SCQM) gains traction as a field
	Innovation in design is emphasized, along with supplier development and customer relationship management

FIGURE 2-3   W. Edwards Deming
© Catherine Karnow/Corbis.

management from W. E. Deming, an American. In fact, the Japanese still use the original lectures given by Deming to train new generations of businesspeople.

Although Deming is best known for his emphasis on the management of a system for improving quality, his thinking was based on the use of statistics for continual improvement. In the 1920s, Deming worked in the Western Electric Hawthorne plant. Trained in engineering and mathematical physics at the University of Wyoming and Yale University, he came to know Walter Shewhart, who influenced his thinking about improving quality through the use of statistics.

After working at the Hawthorne plant, Deming worked in government jobs with the U.S. Department of Agriculture and the Bureau of the Census, at which he helped develop statistical sampling techniques. During World War II, he worked with U.S. defense contractors to use statistics to identify systematic quality problems occurring within defense-related products.

After the war, Deming was sent to Japan by the U.S. secretary of war to work on a population census. During this time, the Japanese Union of Scientists and Engineers asked him to provide lectures on statistical quality control applications. While in Japan, Deming became impressed by the precision and single-mindedness with which the Japanese pursued quality improvement. Late in his life, Deming commented that he had consulted around the world and had found that Japan's commitment to quality was unparalleled. In his mind, this unwavering pursuit of quality improvement was the genius of the Japanese people. When the United States discovered that it was lagging behind the Japanese in quality, large corporations hired Deming to help them develop quality management programs.

Toward the end of his career, Deming gave seminars, wrote books, taught classes, and published articles to explain his approach to quality management. This led to wide dissemination of the Deming approach to quality. In part because of the lack of focus in America, the results have been somewhat mixed.

Deming stressed that consumers are well served by insisting that service and product providers deliver high quality. He believed that the more consumers demand high-quality products and services, the more firms will continually aspire to higher levels of performance. In fact, this has happened in the United States. As opposed to the past, consumers now expect high-quality products at a reasonable cost.

Deming's mantra was "continual never-ending improvement." The goal of higher levels of quality would perhaps never be completely met, but firms would continually exercise themselves to get better and better. This is why quality improvement is often referred to as a journey where the elusive destination is never reached.

Deming's 14 Points for Management

Although Deming espoused the belief that theory was important to the understanding of quality improvement, the closest he ever came to expounding a theory was in his 14 points for management. The foundation for the 14 points was Deming's belief that the historic approach to quality used by American management was wrong in one fundamental aspect: Poor quality was not the fault of labor; it resulted from poor management of the system for continual improvement. Although this might now seem obvious, at the time Deming taught this, it was a revelation to managers. Taken as a whole, the 14 points for management (see Table 2-2) represent many of the key principles that provide the basis for quality management in many organizations.[4]

   1. *Create constancy of purpose toward improvement of product and service with the aim to become competitive, stay in business, and provide jobs.* Constancy of purpose means that management commits resources—over the long haul—to see that the quality job is completed. This is in contrast to managers who want to achieve quick returns and get bottom-line results after embarking on quality "programs." In recent years, more people have come to realize that U.S. management is too short-term-oriented in its thinking. Unfortunately, quality improvement requires time to be effective. The Japanese experience was instructive. Deming helped to begin the Japanese quality revolution in the early 1950s. As already stated, the Japanese displayed remarkable commitment to and focus on quality improvement. Even with all this effort, the Japanese were not really recognized as world leaders in quality until the late 1970s.

   2. *Adopt a new philosophy. We are in a new economic age.* Western management must awaken to the challenge, must learn its responsibilities, and must take on leadership of change. Planned obsolescence was the order of the day when Deming first discussed the new economic age. During this time, automobiles were designed to last 80,000 miles. Deming referred to an age in which Americans would no longer accept defective products. Now that many firms have excellent quality at a reasonable cost, they are turning to service quality to make the next big advances. More and more, specification measurements are being replaced by customer service metrics as the important measures of quality.

   3. *Cease dependence on mass inspection to improve quality.* Eliminate the need for inspection on a mass basis by building quality into the product in the first place. In many companies still, the "quality department" performs in-process and final inspection of a product. In this scenario, responsibility for quality lies with the quality department. However, by the time the

TABLE 2-2 Deming's 14 Points	
1. Create constancy of purpose.	8. Drive out fear.
2. Adopt a new philosophy.	9. Break down barriers between departments.
3. Cease mass inspection.	10. Eliminate slogans.
4. End awarding business on the basis of price tag.	11. Eliminate work standards.
5. Constantly improve the system.	12. Remove barriers to pride.
6. Institute training on the job.	13. Institute education and self-improvement.
7. Improve leadership.	14. Put everybody to work.

Adapted from W. E. Deming, *Out of the Crisis* (Boston: MIT/CAES, 1986), pp. 18–96. © 2000 Massachusetts Institute of Technology, by permission of The MIT Press.

---

[4]Deming, W. Edwards, *Out of the Crisis,* 14 Points, pages 23–24, © 2000 Massachusetts Institute of Technology, by permission of The MIT Press.

quality department inspects the product, either the quality is built in or it is not built in. At this point, it is too late to add quality.

Deming's alternative is **quality at the source.** This means that all workers are responsible for their own work and perform needed inspections at each stage of the process to maintain process control. Of course, this is possible only if management trusts and trains its workers properly.

4. *End the practice of awarding business on the basis of price tag alone.* Instead, minimize total cost. Move toward a single supplier for any one item, based on a long-term relationship of loyalty and trust. Traditionally, U.S. firms maintained many suppliers. The theory behind this approach was that competition among suppliers would improve quality and decrease cost. In reality, however, the existence of many suppliers caused an overemphasis on cost and an increase in variability. For example, if a metal fabrication company has multiple suppliers, the result is great variability in the makeup and consistency of the incoming stock. The alternative supply chain approach used by many firms is **single source purchasing.** This approach minimizes the number of suppliers used, resulting in decreased variability. Also long-term contracts are used that result in the capability to develop and certify suppliers. Often these certifications are based on quality standards such as the Malcolm Baldrige award criteria or the ISO 9000 international standard for quality systems. In other cases, supplier certification is based on an internally developed standard.

5. *Improve constantly and forever the system of production and service to improve quality and productivity, and thus constantly decrease cost.* This point focuses on the management of the system of production.

The system of production includes product design, process design, training, tools, machines, process flows, and myriad other variables that affect the system of production and service. In the final analysis, management is responsible for most of the system design elements because it is management that has the authority and the budget to implement systems. Therefore, the workers can be held responsible only for their inputs to the system. Mediocre or poor performance of a system is most often the result of the poor performance of management.

6. *Institute training on the job.* People must have the necessary training and knowledge to perform their work. Many companies employing laborers have found they must design job-related training. Note that training, although a necessary condition for improvement, is not sufficient to guarantee successful implementation of quality management. The design of effective training is important for quality improvement.

7. *Improve leadership.* The aim of supervision should be to help people, machines, and gadgets to do a better job. The supervision of management and supervision of production workers are in need of overhaul. All quality experts agree that leadership is key to improving quality. If assembly line employees become enthusiastic about quality management, they will be able to make some small improvements to their organization. However, this improvement can occur only within the realm of influence of the employee. For wide-ranging improvements to occur, upper management must be involved. It is upper management that has the monetary and organizational authority to oversee the implementation of quality improvement. Without management support and leadership, quality improvement efforts will fail.

8. *Drive out fear so that everyone may work effectively for the company.* For the most part, Deming was referring to those situations in which employees were fearful to change or even admit that problems existed. Many of these problems still exist. At times, employees who surface problems and seek to create change are considered troublemakers or dissatisfied. It might be true that such employees are dissatisfied. However, does an organization want employees who are satisfied with the status quo? Often, employees who seek to create change should be most prized. Some fear comes from making recommendations for improvement and having those recommendations ignored.

Another type of fear should be recognized by top managers who desire to improve quality. Many employees view process-improvement efforts as disguised excuses for major layoffs. Often, after pursuing the easy solution of downsizing or outsourcing, the same cultural and organizational barriers that impeded improvement are still there. However, the company has lost the capability to be creative and really improve its capability to increase value to the customer. One solution was offered by a major Midwestern defense contractor. It developed a written policy stating that management reserved the right to reduce staffing levels as a result of economic downturns. However, the written policy also stated, "No layoffs will result from productivity or quality improvement projects or efforts."

9. *Break down barriers between departments.* People in research, design, sales, and production must work as a team to foresee problems of production and use that may be encountered with the product or service. In many companies, the time it takes to get design and marketing concepts to market is extremely long. Ingersoll-Rand produces a hand grinder that once required four years to develop a new generation of the product. One employee was quoted as saying, "It took us longer to develop a new generation of the product than it took the Allies to win World War II." In the new competitive environment, such delays in design can jeopardize a company's capability to compete. Honda nearly bankrupted Yamaha because of Honda's capability to introduce new designs to market rapidly. Hyundai competes by quickly designing and introducing new products. One reason for slow design cycles was the **sequential or departmental approach to design.** This approach requires product designers, marketers, process designers, and production managers to work through organizational lines of authority to perform work. The alternative is **parallel processing in focused teams** who work simultaneously on designs.

10. *Eliminate slogans, exhortations, and targets for the workforce that ask for zero defects and new levels of productivity.* Such exhortations only create adversarial relationships because the bulk of causes of low quality and low productivity belong to the system and thus lie beyond the power of the workforce. In Deming's view, exhortations to "get it right the first time" and "quest for perfection" can have the opposite of the intended effect. By pressuring employees to higher levels of productivity and quality, managers place the onus for improvement on the employees. If systems or means for achieving these higher levels of performance are not provided, workers can become jaded and discouraged. Examples of providing systems to employees might be to provide better training, to empower employees to make process decisions, and to provide a strategic structure that ensures alignment of key strategic goals and operational subgoals.

11. *Eliminate work standards on the factory floor.* Eliminate management by objective. Eliminate management by numbers and numeric goals. Substitute leadership. Deming was very much opposed to work measurement standards on the shop floor. Note that work standards are used worldwide, and companies such as Lincoln Electric have been very successful with the skilled use of such standards. However, often work standards are implemented improperly. It is obvious that if quantity becomes the overriding concern, quality suffers. More subtly, if work standards are in place, employees who perform at high levels might lose the impetus to continually improve because they already will have satisfied standards.

Management by objective refers to a process of setting annual goals, typically during a performance appraisal, that are binding on the employee. Although goals are set for employees, systems often are not provided by management to attain these goals. For this reason, Deming disdained performance appraisals.

12. *Remove barriers that rob workers of their right to pride in the quality of their work.* The responsibility of supervisors must be changed from sheer numbers to quality. Too often, hourly laborers are hired to perform only the physical tasks assigned by management. Such workers often suffer from low morale and low commitment to the organization. Unskilled managers often add to this problem by reinforcing the fact that employees cannot be trusted with decisions and self-determination. Once, while discussing self-directed work teams, a manager commented that he feared he was "turning the asylum over to the inmates." Such attitudes were obvious on the shop floor, and employees were very dissatisfied with their work environment. The upside is that after seeing the results of self-directed teams, this same manager became one of the biggest allies of the process of employee empowerment.

13. *Institute a vigorous program of education and self-improvement.* Point 6 referred to training on the job. Point 13 relates to more generalized education. Many quality experts have argued that firms must exhibit the capability to increase and "freeze" learning. Learning in an organization is a function of the creativity of employees and the capability of the organization to institutionalize the lessons learned over time. This is difficult in firms that have high employee turnover. One of the benefits of the ISO 9000 international quality standard is the requirement that firms document their processes and improvements to the processes. Procedure manuals can help make learning permanent. However, this is not enough. Organizational learning requires a structure that reinforces and rewards learning. Such an organization is difficult to create in a command-and-control environment because command-oriented managers will not understand what it takes to allow employees to achieve their best.

14. *Put everybody in the company to work to accomplish the transformation.* The transformation is everybody's job. Point 14 reinforces the fact that everyone in the organization is responsible for improving quality. This again reinforces the fact that a total system for improving quality is needed that includes all the people in the organization.

LEADING CONTRIBUTORS TO QUALITY THEORY: JOSEPH M. JURAN

Joseph Juran, a Romania-born immigrant in 1904, was also responsible for the growth of quality in the past half-century. He visited the Japanese Union of Scientists and Engineers to teach quality concepts. Juran took a more strategic and planning-based approach to improvement than Deming. Juran promotes the view that organizational quality problems are largely the result of insufficient and ineffective planning for quality. He argues that companies must revise strategic planning processes and achieve mastery over these processes. The means proposed by Juran establish specific goals to be reached and plans for reaching those goals. In addition, Juran's process assigns clear responsibility for meeting the goals and bases rewards on results achieved.

The Juran Trilogy

Juran identifies three basic processes that are essential for managing to improve quality. These processes are referred to as the *Juran trilogy*. The points of the Juran trilogy are interrelated. The three aspects of Juran's trilogy are planning, control, and improvement. Juran discusses these as follows:

> It all begins with quality planning. The purpose of quality is to provide the operating forces with the means of producing products that can meet the customer's needs, products such as invoices, polyethylene film, sales contracts, service calls, and new designs for goods.
>
> Once planning is complete, the plan is turned over to the operating forces. Their job is to produce the product. As operations proceed, we see that the process is deficient: 20% of the operating force is wasted, as the work must be redone due to quality deficiencies. The waste then becomes chronic because of quality deficiencies. The waste becomes chronic because it was planned that way.
>
> Under conventional responsibility patterns the operating forces are unable to get rid of that planned chronic waste. What they do instead is carry out quality control to prevent things from getting worse. Control includes putting out the fires, such as sporadic spikes.[5]

---

[5]Juran, J. M., *Juran on Planning for Quality* (Boston: Free Press, 1988), p. 11.

Control versus Breakthrough

Another important Juran concept is *control versus breakthrough*. According to Juran, control is a process-related activity that ensures processes are stable and provides a relatively consistent outcome. Control involves gathering data about a process to ensure the process is consistent. Control is discussed in more depth in Chapters 11 and 12.

Breakthrough improvement implies that the process has been studied and that some major improvement has resulted in large nonrandom improvement to the process. The difference between control and breakthrough can be understood when considering a disease such as polio. Control activities involved improving health by quarantining people who had the disease. Breakthrough improvement occurred with the development of the polio vaccine that eradicated the disease.

It is important to understand that control and breakthrough–related activities should occur simultaneously. This distinction clarifies a false dichotomy sometimes associated with continuous improvement versus reengineering. Some managers believe that continuous improvement prevents companies from pursuing large improvements because the focus on detail may lead to neglect of larger needed changes. However, there is nothing about continuous improvement that precludes large improvements. The optimal set of improvement activities probably involves some mix of continuous improvement and breakthrough improvement activities.

Project-by-Project Improvement

Juran teaches that improvement in organizations is accomplished on a project-by-project basis "and in no other way." The project-by-project approach advocated by Juran is a planning-based approach to quality improvement.

In planning for quality improvements, Juran states that managers must prioritize which projects will be undertaken first. Organizations involve a hierarchy of languages (see Figure 2-4). In this hierarchy, the work that is done operationally at the lowest level is performed by analysts who speak in the language of things. The language of things is typically technical, including jargon and engineering terminology. To help determine what projects should be undertaken, these technical people must use the language of management, that is, money. Therefore, projects identified for possible adoption are prioritized based on financial return. One of the problems many companies experience when implementing quality improvement is showing bottom-line results.

Juran has had a very profound impact on the practice of quality management worldwide. A Closer Look at Quality 2-2 discusses him further.

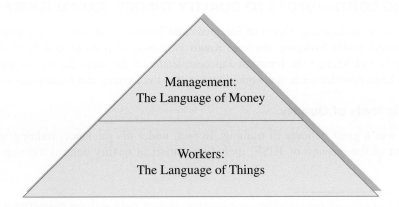

FIGURE 2-4   The Hierarchy of Languages

A CLOSER LOOK AT QUALITY 2-2   Juran on the Past Century of Quality[6]

After the end of World War II, Deming and Juran went to Japan to help rebuild the Japanese economy through quality management. Although "Made in Japan" at one point meant poor quality, it is much different today.

After World War II, Japan sought to increase its exports. With few natural resources, the Japanese had to import their materials, work on them, and then ship them overseas. As a result, Japanese CEOs decided to improve the quality of products produced there. The Keidanren and the Japanese Union of Scientists and Engineers brought in Juran to teach about planning for quality improvement. According to Juran, "Deming's lectures were on statistical methods, especially the Shewhart control chart. My lectures were on managing for quality, especially the concept and methodology of annual quality improvement."

Joseph Juran identified an economic concept that he applied to quality problems. This economic concept is called **Pareto's law** or *the 80/20 rule.* It is named after Vilfredo Pareto (1848–1923), an Italian economist, who modeled income distributions in Milan, Italy. Pareto found that 80% of the wealth in Milan was held by about 20% of the population. Applying Pareto's law to quality problems, imagine a grocer who decides to survey his customers to investigate where quality improvement is needed in his store. He offers a free pound of hamburger to customers who agree to fill out the survey. One of the open-ended questions in the survey asks, "Where do we most need to improve?" Do you suppose that the responses will be uniformly distributed among several problems? No. The majority of the respondents will identify a certain aspect of the grocer's business as the major quality issue. For example, out of 100 respondents, 80 answer, "The meat department needs to be improved." Therefore, in this case, 80% of the dissatisfaction with quality is related to a single area: the meat department.

Using Pareto's law, we see that the majority of quality problems are the result of relatively few causes. Juran dichotomizes the population of causes of quality problems as the "vital few" and the "trivial, but useful, many." Pareto analysis is used as one of the basic seven tools of quality.

Juran Stateside

Back in the states, Juran became a major voice for quality improvement. In addition to his Quality Handbook, he wrote books about his trilogy, consulted with hundreds of companies, and developed a series of influential videos. Probably his greatest contribution was convincing managers of the strategic importance of quality management.

---

[6]Based on Bisgaard, S., "Quality Management and Juran's Legacy," *Quality & Reliability Engineering International* 23 (2007): 665–677.

LEADING CONTRIBUTORS TO QUALITY THEORY: KAORU ISHIKAWA

The founder of the Japanese Union of Scientists and Engineers (JUSE) was the distinguished business leader Ichiro Ishikawa. His son, Kaoru Ishikawa, went on to lead JUSE during its growth years and became the foremost Japanese leader in the Japanese quality movement.[7] Kaoru Ishikawa provided tools that worked well within the Deming and Juran frameworks.

The Basic Tools of Quality

Ishikawa was a great believer in training. In fact, under his guidance, training was a key component of the mission of JUSE, including statistical quality control training. Perhaps

---

[7]Many of the Ishikawa concepts discussed here are derived from his book, *Guide to Quality Control* (White Plains, NY: Quality Resources, 1968).

Ishikawa's greatest achievement was the development and dissemination of the basic seven tools of quality (B7). As the developer of these tools, Ishikawa is credited with *democratizing statistics*. Although statistical quality control traditionally had been the domain of specialized statisticians, Ishikawa felt that to be successful, firms must make everyone responsible for statistical analysis and interpretation.

Although not strictly a theoretical contribution, the tools are presented in Chapter 10 because they are used for continuous improvement. The major theoretical contribution of Ishikawa is his emphasis on total involvement of the operating employees in improving quality. Ishikawa is credited for coining the term *company-wide quality control* in Japan.

LEADING CONTRIBUTORS TO QUALITY THEORY: ARMAND FEIGENBAUM

During the years when quality was overlooked as a major competitive factor in the United States, two books were used by most every quality professional. These books were *Statistical Quality Control*[8] by Eugene Grant and Richard Leavenworth, and *Total Quality Control*[9] by Armand Feigenbaum. Whereas the approach of the former was statistically oriented, Feigenbaum's book studied quality in the context of the business organization. Feigenbaum's primary contribution to quality thinking in America was his assertion that the entire organization should be involved in improving quality. He was the first in the United States to move quality from the offices of the specialist back to the operating workers. This occurred in the 1950s.

Feigenbaum proposes a three-step process to improving quality. These steps involve *quality leadership, quality technology*, and *organizational commitment.* Leadership is the motivating force for quality improvement. Quality technology includes statistics and machinery that can be used to improve technology. Organizational commitment includes everyone in the quality struggle.

Major impediments to improving quality included the four deadly sins of hothouse quality, wishful thinking, producing overseas, and confining quality to the factory. *Hothouse quality* refers to quality programs that receive a lot of hoopla and no follow-through. This is a failing of many firms that do not commit resources *over time. Wishful thinking* occurs with those who would pursue protectionism to keep American firms from having to compete on quality. *Producing overseas* is a panacea sometimes undertaken by managers who wish that out of sight, out of mind could solve quality-related problems. Even well-run companies can fall prey to this thinking. The disk-memory division of Hewlett-Packard offshored its production from the United States to Malaysia in a move to overcome its noncompetitiveness in the market. The move to Malaysia did nothing to solve its problems related to design and process. HP's problems have not gotten better since the move—they have gotten worse. *Confining quality to the factory* means that quality historically has been viewed as simply a shop-floor concern. In actuality, it is everyone's responsibility.

The 19 Steps of TQC

Armand Feigenbaum proposed 19 steps for improving quality (see Table 2-3). These 19 steps outline his approach to the total quality control (TQC) system, which emphasizes organizational involvement in improving quality. In 2008, Feigenbaum was awarded the National Medal of Technology and Innovation by the U.S. president for his work in quality management.

---

[8]Grant, E., and Leavenworth, R., *Statistical Quality Control* (New York: McGraw-Hill, 1988; original 1946).
[9]Feigenbaum, A., *Total Quality Control* (New York: McGraw-Hill, 1983; original 1951).

TABLE 2-3	Feigenbaum's 19 Steps

1. Total quality control is defined as a system of improvement.
2. Big Q quality (company-wide commitment to TQC) is more important than little q quality (improvements on the production line).
3. Control is a management tool with four steps.
4. Quality control requires integration of uncoordinated activities.
5. Quality increases profits.
6. Quality is expected, not desired.
7. Humans affect quality.
8. TQC applies to all products and services.
9. Quality is a total life-cycle consideration.
10. Control the process.
11. A total quality system involves the entire company-wide operating work structure.
12. There are many operating and financial benefits of quality.
13. The costs of quality are a means for measuring quality control activities.
14. Organize for quality control.
15. Managers are quality facilitators, not quality cops.
16. Strive for continuous commitment.
17. Use statistical tools.
18. Automation is not a panacea.
19. Control quality at the source.

Source: Based on A. Feigenbaum, *Total Quality Control* (New York: McGraw-Hill, 1991; original 1951).

LEADING CONTRIBUTORS TO QUALITY THEORY: PHILIP CROSBY

Philip Crosby was the most successful in marketing his quality expertise of all the leading quality authors and thinkers. Although he began his career as a podiatrist (which he disliked), Crosby pursued a career as a reliability engineer with Crosley Corporation in Indiana. Later, he worked for Martin Corporation as a quality manager; he then served as the director for quality at International Telephone and Telegraph. He founded Crosby and Associates of Winter Park, Florida—the world's largest and most successful quality consulting company.

Crosby became very well known for his authorship of the book *Quality Is Free.*[10] The primary thesis of his book is that quality, as a managed process, can be a source of profit for an organization.

Crosby identified a period of enlightenment during which management becomes attuned to the importance of quality. This enlightenment can be achieved through exposure to videos, books, and seminars and by a sense of needing to respond to competitive challenges. A quality improvement team is then established. This team consists of a member from each department within the organization. Organizational quality measures are established and continually reviewed by the team.

Next, quality-related costs are evaluated. This effort is to be coordinated by the controller's office by establishing the location of areas in which corrective action would be most profitable. Quality awareness is emphasized, which addresses the philosophical underpinnings of the Crosby approach. This step addresses the importance of the worker in ensuring quality and demonstrating the need to make the employee aware of the necessity for quality improvement.

The final steps are corrective action, establishing an ad hoc committee for the zero-defects program, supervisory training, the establishment of a zero-defects day, error-cause removal, employee recognition, and the establishment of quality councils. These steps then become ingrained by beginning the process over again.

Although he prescribes quality teams consisting of department heads, Crosby did not promote the same kind of strategic planning proposed by Deming and Juran. Crosby adopted a human resources approach similar to Deming's in that worker input is valued and is encouraged as central to the quality improvement program.

[10]Crosby, P., *Quality Is Free: The Art of Making Quality Certain* (New York: Mentor Executive Library, 1979).

LEADING CONTRIBUTORS TO QUALITY THEORY: GENICHI TAGUCHI

The Taguchi method was first introduced by Dr. Genichi Taguchi to AT&T Bell Laboratories in the United States. Because of its increased acceptance and utilization, the Taguchi method for improving quality is now believed to be comparable in importance to the Deming approach and to the Ishikawa concept of total quality control. Taguchi's method is a continuation of the work in quality improvement that began with Shewhart's work in statistical quality control and Deming's work in improving quality. Objectives of the Taguchi method are synopsized in Table 2-4.

Among the unique aspects of the Taguchi method are the Taguchi definition of quality, the quality loss function (QLF), and the concept of robust design.

Definition of Quality

The traditional definition of quality was conformance to specifications. However, as discussed in Chapter 1, in recent years this narrow definition of quality has been extended.

Taguchi diverges from the traditional definition of quality. In Taguchi's terms, *ideal quality* refers to a reference point for determining the quality level of a product or service. This reference point is expressed as a target value. Ideal quality is delivered if a product (or a service tangible) performs its intended function throughout its projected life under reasonable operating conditions without harmful side effects. In services, because of increased customer interaction, ideal quality is a function of customer perceptions and satisfaction. Taguchi measures service quality in terms of loss to society if the service is not performed as expected.

Quality Loss Function

Taguchi doesn't agree with traditional quality thought as it relates to specification. Normally, when specifications are set, a target is specified with some allowance for variation. Taguchi doesn't agree with the notion of allowable variation. He states that any deviation from target specs results in loss to society. Alternatively, traditional thinking implies there is no loss to society if a measurement is near to being out of specification but nevertheless remains within the established specification limits. For example, if the quality standard for a restaurant is that 6 (±1) ounces of French fries be included in each order, an average of 6.90 ounces of French fries per order over long periods of time would increase costs by 15%, which could translate into hundreds or thousands of dollars in lost profit, depending on the size of the firm. The 6.90 value is closer to being out of specification than within specification, but traditional thinking asserts that no loss is incurred by the company because the variation is within specification limits (i.e., because 6.9 < 7, the process is in spec). Again, Taguchi would assert that processes should result in a fill of 6 ounces.

Robust Design

The Taguchi concept of robust design means that products and services should be designed so that they are inherently defect-free and of high quality. Taguchi devised a three-stage process

---

TABLE 2-4 The Taguchi Method

The Taguchi method provides
1. A basis for determining the functional relationship between controllable product or service design factors and the outcomes of a process.
2. A method for adjusting the mean of a process by optimizing controllable variables.
3. A procedure for examining the relationship between random noise in the process and product or service variability.

that achieves robust design through what he terms *concept design, parameter design*, and *tolerance design.*

This section has emphasized the conceptual foundation to the Taguchi method of quality improvement. Chapter 13 further explores this approach to Six Sigma quality improvement from a quantitative perspective.

LEADING CONTRIBUTORS TO QUALITY THEORY: THE REST OF THE PACK

The contributors mentioned to this point have stood the test of time, but it is important to remember that as practitioners, they suffered from the biases associated with inductive reasoning. However, as you see in this section, inductive reasoning might be preferred to the deductive development of untested theories. In the following paragraphs, several well-known quality authors are considered. Some of these individuals, such as Robert Camp and Stephen Covey, have made important contributions to our understanding of quality. Others have been proven wrong. Underlined in this section is the risk associated with following unsound quality approaches.

Robert C. Camp

Robert C. Camp is the principal pioneer of **benchmarking,** the sharing of information between companies so that both can improve. This was thought impossible just a few decades ago, but his efforts within Xerox Corporation have proved otherwise. As a result of the work of Xerox and other corporations, benchmarking is now a very important, proven practice used worldwide. Camp's best-selling book, *Benchmarking: The Search for Industry Best Practices That Lead to Superior Performance*, is an outstanding handbook. Benchmarking is discussed in greater depth in Chapter 6.

Stephen R. Covey's "8" Habits

Stephen Covey was a management consultant who led FranklinCovey, one of the most successful management consulting companies in the world. Dr. Covey is best known for his book, *The 7 Habits of Highly Effective People.* His approach to management is value-based in that he proposes that people in management live a life that balances professional with personal and spiritual growth.

According to Covey, our beliefs affect how we interact with others, which in turn affects how they interact with us. As a result, we need to focus on how we approach our lives rather than focusing on external factors that affect our lives. Implicit in many of Covey's basic teachings are quality management principles from people such as Deming. These principles are woven together with a values-based approach to life.

His seven habits include these:

1. *Be proactive.* This is the ability to control one's environment rather than have it control you, as is so often the case. Managers need to control their own environment using self-determination, and to demonstrate the power to respond to various circumstances.
2. *Begin with the end in mind.* This means that the manager needs to be able to see the desired outcome and concentrate on activities that help to achieve that end.
3. *Put first things first.* Managers need to personally manage themselves and implement activities that aim to achieve the second habit—looking to the desired outcome. Covey states that habit two is the first, or mental, creation; habit three is the second, or physical, creation.

4. *Think win-win.* This is the most important aspect of interpersonal leadership because most achievements are based on cooperative effort. Therefore, the aim needs to be win-win solutions for all.

5. *Seek first to understand and then to be understood.* By developing and maintaining positive relationships through good communications, the manager can be understood and can understand subordinates.

6. *Synergize.* This is the habit of creative cooperation—the principle that collaboration often achieves more than could be achieved by individuals working independently.

7. *Sharpen the saw.* This involves learning from previous experience and encouraging others to do the same. Covey sees development as one of the most important aspects in being able to cope with challenges and aspire to higher levels of ability.[11]

Covey also published a book with an eighth habit:

8. *Find your voice, and inspire others to find theirs.* This invites the merging of talent, passion, and conscience to achieve and to help others achieve. This is implicit in a life of service.

Covey is discussed here because wherever you work, around the world, people will be discussing Covey's habits. You should be familiar with them.

Michael Hammer and James Champy

Michael Hammer and James Champy urged a form of deductive reasoning combined with entertainment that has resulted in unfortunate consequences for many people and companies. The product of this collaboration is termed **reengineering.** The underlying precept of reengineering is sound: Firms can become inflexible and resistant to change and must be able to change in order to become competitive. The problem is in the process they promoted in the book *Reengineering the Corporation.* This process involves the CEO of the corporation developing a business case (the Harvard University B-School method) followed by a set of recommendations. He or she then charges others with rapidly implementing the recommendations without further study or analysis.

Granted that, to an extent, managers misapplied his ideas, the human and financial costs have been great. In looking for business solutions, management's objective should not be to adopt whatever tool is currently "hot." A Closer Look at Quality 2-3 looks at the available "gurus" willing to help businesses with a revolutionary idea. A firm's focus needs to be on the root causes and not the next hot concept.

By ignoring the necessity for attention to detail and analysis that has characterized many world-class firms, Hammer and Champy led many firms to make radical changes that have led to major failures. If there is a lesson to be learned from the reengineering failures, it is this: *Some quality and performance improvement approaches are brainchildren. Others have been observed to work in a number of organizations, in a variety of cultures, and in a number of economic sectors. Avoid the former until they become the latter.* This is common sense that has been validated by unfortunate experience. The risk of failure must be considered in decision making. Analysis and attention to detail cannot be overlooked. Fortunately, there are well-founded approaches to organizational redesign that can be applied and have been applied for decades. The backlash against reengineering is likely to make these efforts less positively viewed.

---

[11]Adapted from Covey, S., *The 7 Habits of Highly Effective People* (New York: Free Press, 2004).

A CLOSER LOOK AT QUALITY 2-3   Selling Quality Fads

The expansion of the management theory industry in the recent past relies on uncertainty in work and business. This uncertainty drives management to find solutions outside the organization. Management can be led to embrace the ideas of a quality management "guru." There are plenty of people willing to consult with a business and to present the latest management theory. Similar to the discussion in A Closer Look at Quality 2-1, how does a company decide which guru to endorse? Is it based on the number of books sold, charisma, consulting or speaking fee, or clientele? The list of attributes can go on and on, but none is a clear indicator of who to select.

Gurus are persuasive. With today's technology, their message can quickly go viral, thus establishing some perceived credibility. Gurus are their own brand and look to increase their influence. The ideas they propound in subsequent activities such as speech-giving and private consulting work all have to work together, building on and extending what has gone before. There will always be an element of self-interest in the advice of a guru. A company needs to be a beneficiary of the work, not another data point for the next book.

There is no clear definition of a business guru. Some successful consultants are never thought of as gurus, and some gurus have had well-known failures. Both will exist as businesses look for solutions to problems. Management must not be solely persuaded by the big new ideas or original thinking, but by results. As this textbook has pointed out, many quality leaders have good ideas. However, these ideas need to be adapted to fit the needs of the firm. Some examples of current fads include lean startups, open innovation, and business model ideation.

VIEWING QUALITY THEORY FROM A CONTINGENCY PERSPECTIVE

By now you might be asking, "With all this disagreement about how to approach quality improvement, how should I proceed?" Perhaps you have gained more empathy for CEOs and business leaders who are distrustful of quality management as a field. There is a great deal of contradictory information about how firms should improve quality.

This mass of contradictory information is not unique to quality. A similar state exists in finance, in which much divergent advice is given on how best to invest funds. In marketing, new approaches are constantly emerging. In fact, much of leadership and management has to do with being able to sort through and make sense of conflicting advice.

Because a variety of approaches can work to improve quality, it is best to focus on fundamental questions such as these: What are our strengths? Where are our competencies? In what areas do we need to improve? What are our competitors doing to improve? What is our organizational structure? These are fundamental questions that are asked during the self-assessment phase of strategic planning.

Once these questions are answered, a profound understanding of the business emerges. Based on this knowledge of the business, an understanding of the major approaches to quality improvement will provide a means for selecting those points, philosophies, concepts, and tools that will form the basis for improvement.

As already stated, Baldrige winners and other firms well known for quality do not adopt only one quality philosophy. For example, firms that are successful in quality do not adopt a blanket "Deming approach to quality." The successful firms adopt aspects of each of the various approaches that help them improve. This is called the *contingency perspective*.

The keys to the contingency approach are an understanding of quality approaches, an understanding of the business, and the creative application of these approaches to the business. Thus, the optimal strategy will apply quality philosophies and approaches to business on a contingency basis. From your own perspective, you need to make correct quality-related decisions. In doing this, consider the different quality experts in this chapter and choose those concepts and approaches that make sense for you.

RESOLVING THE DIFFERENCES IN QUALITY APPROACHES:
AN INTEGRATIVE VIEW

There are many differences among the approaches to quality management along the supply chain espoused by the experts mentioned in this chapter. However, rather than focusing on differences, it is instructional to review the literature to identify common themes and messages.

Table 2-5 provides a list of variables addressed by Deming, Juran, Crosby, Taguchi, Ishikawa, and Feigenbaum. Also included is the services approach to quality by Parasuraman, Zeithamel, and Berry (cited in Chapters 1 and 6).

By studying the common themes of the various experts, it is clear that some occur often, whereas others are more idiosyncratic. The target in Figure 2-5 shows the variables at the core of quality management and those variables that, although important, are less widely supported. The following list of variables is not intended to be all encompassing. At the same time, these are variables that firms should address when seeking to improve performance. The core variables include the following:

Leadership

The role of the leader in being the champion and major force behind quality improvement is critical. The implication is clear: Companies having weak leadership will not achieve a market advantage in quality. The task for leaders is to become conversant with quality management approaches. They must then be willing to lead by example, not just by words.

Employee Improvement

Once the leadership is enlightened and motivated to go forward in the quality effort, employees must be trained and developed. This training is a long-term undertaking that requires firms to invest in their employees. When budgeting for training, the direct training delivery costs are not the only costs that should be budgeted. There are also indirect costs associated with temporary lost productivity and time spent in training.

Quality Assurance

Quality experts agree that quality can be assured only during the design phase. Although statistical inspection is an important approach to improving quality, it is inherently reactive.

TABLE 2-5 Quality Improvement Content Variables

Variables	Deming	Juran	Crosby	Taguchi	Ishikawa	Feigenbaum	PZB
Leadership	y	y	y		y	y	
Information analysis	y	y			y	y	
Strategic planning		y	y			y	y
Employee improvement	y	y	y		y	y	y
Quality assurance of products and services	y	y		y	y	y	y
Customer role in quality	y	y				y	y
Role of quality department	y	y				y	
Environmental characteristics and constraints	y					y	
Philosophy driven	y	y	y	y	y	y	
Quality breakthrough		y					
Project/team-based improvement		y	y	y	y		

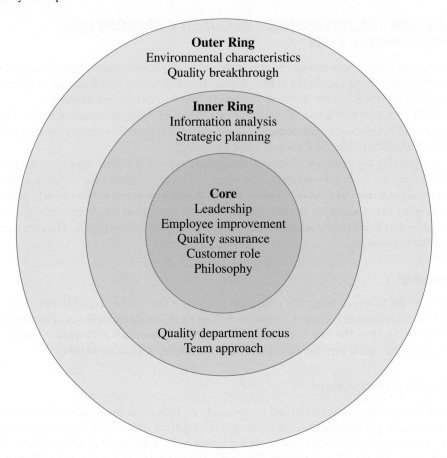

FIGURE 2-5   A Categorization of Quality Management Content Variables

Therefore, efforts must be invested in designing products, services, and processes so that they are consistently of high quality. McDonald's Corporation has built a huge competitive advantage by investing in processes and standardizing those processes so they always produce the same products regardless of location.

Customer Focus

An understanding of the customer is key to quality management efforts. Unless firms are gathering data about customers and analyzing these data, they are poorly informed about customer needs and wants. The mantra of many businesses today involves customer satisfaction. This is closely related to customer service as a central role for quality.

Quality Philosophy

Adoption of a philosophy toward quality improvement is also important. Whether it is the Deming philosophy of continual improvement, the Ishikawa philosophy of total involvement, the Juran philosophy of project-by-project improvement, or a contingency philosophy, establishing a clear message provides a company with a map to follow during its quest for improvement. It is up to each organization to determine its own philosophy.

The inner and outer rings of variables in the literature include the following:

Information Analysis

Fact-based improvement refers to an approach that favors information gathering and analysis. One of the weaknesses of the reengineering approach was that it overlooked the need for in-depth information gathering and analysis. Most of the experts discussed agree that data gathering is a key variable for the improvement of quality. Included in data gathering are statistically related quality control activities.

Strategic Planning

Juran supported the notion that quality improvement should be strategically planned. This provides a framework for a rational quality strategy that will provide alignment with key business factors relating to the company.

Environment or Infrastructure

Quality environment or infrastructure must be created that supports quality management efforts. This infrastructure must provide human resource systems and technological networks that support all the other variables mentioned here.

Team Approach

One of the contemporary approaches to quality management learned from the Japanese is teamwork. More and more, companies are forming cross-functional teams to achieve process improvement. Many firms also have formed teams to manage key processes. In some organizations, employees' jobs are defined by the teams in which they are involved. In such organizations, the firm is a collection of loosely related teams performing the work of the firm.

Two outer-ring variables are major themes emerging from several of the experts and have been adopted widely.

Focus of the Quality Department

As a result of the dispersion of responsibility for quality, the role of the quality department has changed significantly. Rather than performing the policing function, these departments are filling more of a coaching role. Also, the knowledge these quality specialists have is useful for training and in-house consulting. Many firms have now turned their quality departments into profit centers by "selling" their services, on a consulting basis, to other firms.

Breakthrough

The need to make large improvements is not precluded by continuous improvement. Firms must find ways to achieve radical improvements. The process used to achieve this often involves technology or organizational redesign. Analysis and data are necessary for successful breakthrough implementation.

THEORETICAL FRAMEWORK FOR QUALITY MANAGEMENT

As we have discussed in this chapter, many variables build the framework for a quality management theory (see Figure 2-6). Quality management begins with leadership. The organizational leaders have the authority and monetary capability to drive quality assurance, employee improvement, and the creation of a corporate philosophy.

The quality philosophy influences and guides the organizational leader to make decisions concerning quality strategy. The philosophy also helps guide decisions concerning quality assurance and employee improvement.

Leadership, quality assurance, philosophy, and employees are encompassed by a focus on the customer. From this perspective, the customer is the focus of all the activities of the firm.

The outer boxes in Figure 2-6 refer to activities and processes that help improve the core systems relating to people. The breakthrough improvement, team building, information analysis, strategic planning, and quality department role are some of the major variables forming the inter-related set of activities making up the quality system.

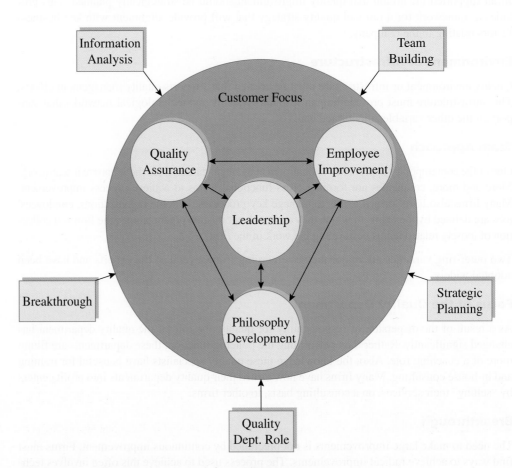

FIGURE 2-6   A Theoretical Framework for Quality Management

Summary

This chapter briefly introduced the major voices in the growth of the quality movement. Although there is no single theory that is widely adopted to explain the quality phenomenon, the basis for a theory exists. The variables proposed in Figure 2-6 form the basis of a model that is testable. We propose that the interaction of these variables forms the basis for a quality system that will result in improved quality.

We introduced a variety of models. The models discussed have been applied in many different organizations and settings all over the world. Therefore, these approaches have worked in a variety of contexts. These are not philosophies that someone just "thought up." They should be pondered and, when appropriate, implemented to achieve organizational improvement.

Key Terms

Benchmarking
Deduction
Induction
Parallel processing in focused teams

Pareto's law (the 80/20 rule)
Quality at the source
Reengineering

Sequential or departmental approach
   to design
Single source purchasing

Discussion Questions

1. Define theory. Provide an example of the use of theory in a business organization.
2. Describe the differences between induction and deduction. If you developed a theory based solely on your experiences of quality practices in business organizations, would you be basing your theory on induction or deduction? Why?
3. Do you believe that the development of a unified theory of quality management is possible? What is a unified theory?
4. Why do managers need to be cautious about purchasing material (e.g., courses, workbooks, videos, etc.) on quality management from trainers and consultants? How would you go about selecting this type of material?
5. Discuss the contributions of W. Edwards Deming to quality thinking.
6. Deming believed poor quality was not the fault of workers, but resulted from poor management of the system for quality improvement. Do you agree with Deming's stand on this issue? Why or why not?
7. Deming was not an advocate of mass inspection as a means of ensuring product quality. Explain Deming's beliefs in this area.
8. State Deming's 14 points for management.
9. Differentiate between control and breakthrough with the help of an example.
10. Is the concept of scientific management compatible with employee empowerment? Why or why not?
11. Does the phrase "quality is the responsibility of the quality department" reflect a healthy perspective of quality management? Explain your answer.
12. Briefly describe the Japanese quality revolution following World War II. What can modern-day managers learn from studying the history of this era?
13. What was Joseph Juran's primary contribution to quality thinking in America? Discuss Juran's three-step process to improving quality.
14. *Hothouse quality* refers to those quality programs that receive a lot of hoopla and no follow-through. Provide several examples of management practices that can lead to hothouse quality. How can hothouse quality be avoided?
15. Compare and contrast Deming's, Juran's, and Crosby's perspectives of quality management. What are the major similarities and differences between their perspectives?
16. Explain the Taguchi concept of robust design.
17. Why do you think reengineering programs have such a high failure rate? Can you think of ways to improve the success rate of reengineering programs?

18. Describe how the contingency perspective helps us understand why a single approach to quality management may never emerge.
19. Discuss Deming's claims that when properly adopted, a quality improvement program can create a culture of continuous improvement across a company.
20. Do you believe that CEOs and business managers should be skeptical about the quality movement, or should they embrace the quality movement and try to involve their firms in as many quality initiatives as possible? Explain your answer.

CASES

Case 2-1 Rheaco, Inc.: Making a Quality Turnabout by Asking for Advice
Rheaco Homepage: www.cpctexas.com

Rheaco, a Grand Prairie, Texas, subsidiary of Control Products Corporation that manufactures high-precision parts for the aerospace and defense industries, was in trouble. The company was behind on 50% of its deliveries, was receiving complaints from its customers about product quality, and was experiencing internal scheduling and capacity problems. To make matters worse, its customer base was shrinking as a result of cutbacks in defense spending, and many of its customers were reducing the number of suppliers that they maintained in an effort to improve their own product quality.

Rather than giving up, the top managers at Rheaco sought help. Instead of hiring a costly consultant, Rheaco asked the Automation and Robotics Research Institute (ARRI) at the University of Texas for assistance. The ARRI is a university-based institute that works with private manufacturing firms in an effort to disseminate advanced manufacturing concepts and philosophies. Initially, ARRI personnel assisted Rheaco's top management team in articulating a vision statement, examining the company's strengths and weaknesses, and pinpointing areas of concern. A number of concerns were identified that were contributing both directly and indirectly to Rheaco's problems. Surprisingly, a strength identified by ARRI's analysis was that Rheaco's employees, despite the company's difficulties, had an overall positive attitude. This attribute no doubt contributed to Rheaco's capability to eventually work through its problems and return to profitability.

A team of Rheaco and ARRI personnel tackled the company's problems, which ranged from poorly structured manufacturing processes to low cooperation among departments. Rather than telling Rheaco what to do, the ARRI team worked with Rheaco's management and frontline employees to further define problem areas and develop solutions. An Enterprise Excellence Plan was developed, which acted as a road map for Rheaco's improvement efforts. Consistent with this plan, the following initiatives were implemented, all of which were new to Rheaco:

- Cellular manufacturing
- Just-in-time inventory control
- Total quality management
- Employee empowerment

Each of these initiatives was implemented with a clear rationale and with the support of Rheaco's management and employees. For example, Rheaco had a problem in the area of product flow. Cellular manufacturing is a technique designed to improve the product flow rate by placing all the parts associated with a given product area close to one another. This technique reduces travel time, improves communication, and facilitates continuous flow of the product. The implementation of cellular manufacturing improved the efficiency of Rheaco's operations to the extent that one Rheaco employee remarked, "Material flowed like water, and people moved to the work instead of work to the people." As a result of this initiative, in one particular instance, the time required to produce a component decreased from 40 to 2 hours.

Other improvements were made, particularly in the areas of shipping and receiving, inventory control, and human resource management. After ARRI had been working with Rheaco for a period of time, the company started identifying and correcting problems on its own, which is exactly what is supposed to happen. The mission of ARRI is to transfer advanced manufacturing concepts and philosophies to a private firm and then to withdraw. ARRI also helps the firms that it works with establish relationships with other ARRI-assisted companies, which was important to Rheaco.

Rheaco got back on its feet, largely as a result of its willingness to ask for help. Its flow rate dramatically improved, its manufacturing capacity increased by 300%, and the company solidified customer relationships. The Rheaco story is a reminder that companies cannot always go it alone in terms of achieving higher

quality and improving manufacturing effectiveness. Many organizations at the federal, state, and community levels are equipped to provide assistance to business organizations at little or no cost.

Discussion Questions

1. Many companies fail in their efforts to improve quality without ever asking for advice. In your opinion, what are some of the reasons that inhibit firms from asking for timely advice? If you were a manager at Rheaco, would you have sought out an agency such as the ARRI?
2. Discuss ARRI's recommendations to Rheaco. How did these recommendations help Rheaco improve its product quality?

3. ARRI's initial evaluation of Rheaco indicated that Rheaco's employees, despite the company's difficulties, had an overall positive attitude. Do you believe this factor contributed to ARRI's capability to provide Rheaco advice? Why or why not?

Case 2-2 Has Disney Developed a Theory of Quality Guest Services Management?

Disney Homepage: disney.go.com

Walt Disney World: disneyworld.disney.go.com/

As you approach the Magic Kingdom at Walt Disney World in Orlando, Florida, the recorded voice on the monorail announces you are about to arrive at a "magical place" that appeals to both the young and the young at heart. As you enter the park, the surroundings are truly magical. The flower beds are beautiful; the grounds are clean; the buildings are spotless; and, if you're lucky, you might even catch a glimpse of Mickey, Goofy, Tigger, or Winnie the Pooh. After a while, it is easy to start believing in the myth—that this is indeed a magical place.

But what is the Magic Kingdom—really? At its essence, it is a carefully conceived, masterfully executed theatrical production. The attention to detail is remarkable. Everything that happens in the park is carefully scripted, from the way the Disney characters interact with children to the way guests are moved through the park. For instance, if you stand at the base of Cinderella's Castle and look back toward the entrance to the park, you'll notice a subtle difference between the sidewalks that lead guests either to the right or to the left as they exit Main Street and enter the attractions area. The sidewalk to the right is wider than the sidewalk to the left. Why? Because through years of experience Disney has learned that people have a natural tendency to turn to the right rather than to the left. By building bigger sidewalks on the right, Disney is better able to handle the early morning crowds. Similarly, when you stand in line waiting to go on a ride, you'll notice that the line is designed to snake back and forth rather than

extend in a straight line. Disney also has learned over the years that lines appear to be "shorter" if they snake back and forth rather than extend in a straight line. By reducing the perceived length of its lines, Disney is able to increase customer satisfaction.

Through this and similar examples, you see that what Disney has done is develop a "theory" (or theories) of how guests will behave in the Magic Kingdom and its other parks. As a result, the company can "predict" how its guests will move through its park, how they will jockey for position in line, and how they will react to a variety of circumstances. This knowledge enhances Disney's capability to deliver a high level of customer service. The lines move smoothly, the rides are easy to board, the directions are simple and clear, and the souvenir shops are right where they need to be—not by accident, but because Disney knows what works. Far from being magic, it is carefully executed guest service management based on Disney's "predictions" of how its guests will behave. At times, Disney's understanding of its guests seems almost fanatical. For instance, at the company's theme parks, most of the drinking fountains come in pairs, one high and one low, to accommodate a parent and a child. The drinking spouts are directed toward one another, so if a parent and child drink at the same time, the parent can watch the child, rather than being turned in the opposite direction. That way, the parent and the child both feel secure and can share a drink and a smile.

(continued)

In addition to anticipating how its guests will behave, Disney also enhances the quality of its guest services by "setting the stage" for good quality experiences. For instance, at the Polynesian Hotel directly across the Seven Seas Lagoon from the Magic Kingdom, you can hear Hawaiian music playing underneath the water in the hotel's main pool. At the Wilderness Lodge, you'll notice that pine needles cover the grounds. The funny thing is, there are no pine trees nearby. The pine needles are periodically brought to the property by Disney employees and spread out over the grounds. Other areas of customer service and guest relations are equally surprising.

Can a company's approach to quality be based on "theories?" At the Magic Kingdom, it appears to be so. By developing theories of their customers and other relevant activities, companies such as Disney can enhance the quality of their products and services.

Discussion Questions

1. Is Disney's level of emphasis on anticipating the behavior of its guests appropriate, or does the company expend too much effort in this area? Explain your answer.
2. Is it appropriate to think in terms of developing a "theory" of how guests will behave in a theme park or any other setting? If so, why?
3. Think about the last time you visited a theme park. Were your expectations met? Did you have a sense that the operator of the park attempted to "anticipate" the behavior of the guests? If so, provide some specific examples.

CHAPTER 3

Global Supply Chain Quality and International Quality Standards

Chapter Objectives

After completing this chapter, you should be able to:

1. Understand the importance of quality in global economics.
2. Explain the role of culture in quality approaches.
3. Compare and contrast American, European, and Japanese approaches to quality management.
4. Explain the Baldrige award process.
5. Communicate the Japanese approach to lean and total quality control.
6. Discuss ISO 9000:2015 and how it is used in firms.

International trade is not a new phenomenon. The Roman, Greek, Egyptian, Chinese, Prussian, and other great empires were built on international trade. Columbus encountered the Americas for Queen Isabella of Spain when he was trying to establish a trade route to the East Indies across the Atlantic Ocean from Europe.

Although international trade has existed for a long time, the volume of international trade exploded after World War II and has continued to reach tremendous levels. This international diversity can be seen all around us. Probably the watch you wear, the computer you use, the car you drive, or the frying pan you use to prepare breakfast are not produced in the country where you live. The nationalities of products are even obscured as companies become more internationally dispersed. The most famous electric guitar in the world is the Fender Stratocaster. If you go to your local music shop, you will find that Stratocasters vary in cost from $500 to around $3,000. Some of the variation in cost is because of different features and model names. However, closer inspection of the headstock will show that much of the price variation has to do with where the guitar is produced. Fender Stratocasters can be produced in Japan, Mexico, Korea, and the United States. You might wonder which nationality of Fender Stratocaster garners the highest price on the free market. The result might surprise you. American-made Stratocasters are the highest priced and the most coveted by guitar players. The Japanese models are judged by most guitarists to be of slightly lesser quality. The Mexican and Korean guitars generally are considered beginner's guitars—not for the serious musician. However, the perceived quality might not match the reality. Certainly, Japanese, European, or Chinese sources may be preferred for many products.

The task of managing quality is affected by this increased globalization. This chapter discusses the opportunities and obstacles created by globalization. The differences between regions of the world also include discussions of various quality approaches that have been developed in those regions and the practices that act as quality barometers within each.

MANAGING QUALITY FOR THE MULTINATIONAL FIRM (MNF)

Firms must cope with more diversity now than in the past. One of the causes of this diversity challenge has been the increased emphasis on international trade over the past half century. This growth in international trade has occurred as companies have sought new markets. Figure 3-1 shows that although the trade deficit has remained relatively constant over time, both imports and exports of products have been increasing steadily.

There are a variety of mechanisms that firms use in globalizing. The first is **licensing.** By licensing, a U.S. corporation can allow foreign firms to sell in restricted markets while using the design of the original designer. Licensing often involves the sale of the same product with another trademark in different countries. Through licensing, firms can reach international markets without having to establish international supply chains or marketing arms.

Firms also seek international markets through joint ventures, or **partnering.** This agreement is often reached when two firms have technology, products, or access to markets that each other wants.

Another approach to capturing international markets is **globalization.** The benefits of licensing and partnering are that the exporting firm does not have to globalize to make sales in international

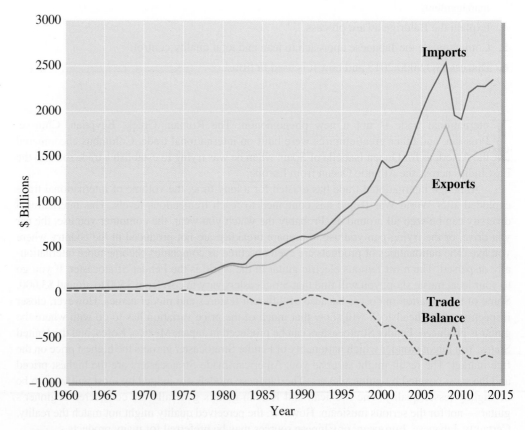

FIGURE 3-1 U.S. Trade 1960–2010 *Source:* U.S. Department of Commerce.

markets. However, they do this at the cost of sharing profits with other firms. Globalization means that a firm fundamentally changes the nature of its business by establishing production and marketing facilities in foreign countries. We refer to these firms as *multinational corporations*. With growing economies in many parts of the world, such as Mexico, India, Brazil, Eastern Europe, China, and Russia, firms need to globalize to participate in these markets. However, there are effects of globalization that firms often overlook. By globalizing, firms significantly change the physical environment, the task environment, and the social environment in which they operate. By changing their **physical environment,** firms locate near to or far away from natural resources. For example, semiconductor firms requiring large amounts of water probably will not locate in Saudi Arabia or arid parts of Mexico. However, they may locate in one of the Asian countries to be close to available supplies of water as well as expanding markets.

The advantage of saving labor costs is often overemphasized when deciding to change the physical environment. Cost savings are often offset by low levels of productivity levels and high shipping costs.

The **task environment** of the firm has to do with the operating structure that the firm encounters when globalizing. The economic structures, employee skills, compensation structure, technologies, and government agencies all vary when globalizing. The regulatory structures that firms encounter when globalizing require an understanding of international law. Although many view the U.S. government as somewhat regulatory, many times firms find themselves having to deal with very complex regulatory structures when establishing operations in countries such as Germany, Japan, or India. Technological choices vary as firms globalize. What works at home may not serve customers adequately abroad. For example, tobacco producers who globalize find that mass-production technologies used in the United States are not flexible enough for the European Economic Community, in which regulations concerning tobacco products vary a great deal from country to country.

The **social environment** facing globalizing corporations refers to cultural factors such as language, business customs, customer preferences, and patterns of communication. The cultural factors facing globalizing firms are often the most complex and difficult issues they will encounter. For example, the American businessperson who likes to have breakfast meetings will be frustrated in Spain, where people do not go to work until later in the day.

As shown in Figure 3-2, physical, task, and social environments have implications for the choices made in quality management. Differences in the physical, task, and social variables all add to the complexity and variability that firms experience. Therefore, there is significant tension between a need for standardization/high central control and loss of control because of decentralization.

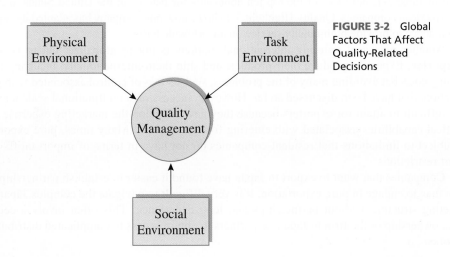

FIGURE 3-2 Global Factors That Affect Quality-Related Decisions

TABLE 3-1	U.S. Patent Applications, 2014	
Rank in 2014	Number of Patents in 2014	Organization
1	4887	International Business Machines Corporation
2	3592	Samsung Electronics Co., Ltd.
3	2901	Microsoft Corporation
4	2200	Canon Kabushiki Kaisha
5	1759	Panasonic Corporation
6	1669	Toshiba Corporation
7	1656	Sony Corporation
8	1534	Intel Corporation
9	1328	Seiko Epson Corporation
10	1269	Hewlett-Packard Development Company, L.P.
11	1188	Fujitsu Limited
12	1064	LG Electronics Inc.
13	1051	Hitachi, Ltd.
14	985	Ricoh Company, Ltd.
15	976	General Electric Company
16	966	Micron Technology, Inc.
17	913	Cisco Technology, Inc.
18	873	Fujifilm Corporation
19	725	Honda Giken Kogyo Kabushiki Kaisha (Honda Motor Co., Ltd.)
20	714	Broadcom Corporation

Market diversity drives the need for culture-specific research and development (R&D). Although this can be true within a nation that is culturally diverse, such as the United States, it is especially true on the global front. There are few products, such as Coca-Cola, that translate well across different cultural horizons. Many companies must adapt their products to the preferences of the markets they are serving. This greatly increases the complexity of international marketing and R&D. For example, in some European countries, McDonald's sells wine or beer with its meals because it is the European habit to drink wine and beer with meals.

Globalized firms also often must apply for patents in different places in the world to protect their domestic patents. Patent applications are an important indicator of R&D productivity. As shown in Table 3-1, only five of the top ten applicants for patents in the United States in 2014 were American companies. Quality Highlight 3-1 shows how one company has adapted its supply chain practice to provide high-quality service on a worldwide basis.

Another means of entering international markets is not to globalize, but to become an **exporter.** Exporters produce their products and ship them internationally, incurring high shipping costs but avoiding many of the problems, such as loss of control associated with globalization, that have been discussed so far. However, success on a multinational scale may be more difficult to attain for exporters because they never develop the marketing expertise and logistical capabilities associated with entering foreign markets. Many times, pure exporters are subject to limitations that resident companies do not have in terms of import tariffs and import restrictions.

Companies that want to export to Japan have found it easier to establish partnerships in Japan than to engage in pure exportation. It is very difficult to navigate the complex Japanese marketing structure without partnerships and long experience. This often involves ceding partial ownership of the firm to Japanese partners to obtain access to complicated distribution networks.

www.trekbikes.com

Trek Bicycle Corporation started with five employees in a barn in Waterloo, Iowa. Today the company has more than 1,700 distributors in 90 countries. In addition to having customers around the world, Trek also works with suppliers from around the world. Although managing quality with foreign suppliers can create severe headaches, Trek uses software to overcome this problem.

Beginning with suppliers in Taiwan and China, Trek has linked its quality systems via the Internet. Whereas Trek would originally find out about quality problems only after taking shipments from foreign suppliers (which takes two months from China), Trek now has a two-pronged approach to managing supplier quality: web-based statistical quality control software and localized staff in China. For bicycles, quality problems can be serious—think of a person riding on a mountain road at 50 miles per hour on a thin ribbon of rubber. As a result, Trek is driving quality up the supply chain. Using telecommunications, Trek receives quality data in real time from its major suppliers. When a quality problem occurs, Trek then contacts its quality team members in China, who can immediately visit the factory and help to resolve the quality issue.

According to Julie Wilhelm, supply chain quality manager at Trek, "It was the same cause all of the time. We hadn't reviewed what the supplier was doing thoroughly enough, and we didn't always provide them with the best specification."

Now, through the use of software, Trek's quality team members in Asia learn about quality issues as they occur. That way, they can go to the supplier on the same day to work though problems and to find solutions to the quality issues. By using this approach, the quality team at Trek was able to develop a test of the forks for their bikes, which ensured that these critical parts were defect-free when they left the factory. Still, this approach is not without problems. For example, Chinese Internet connections are much slower, which can create problems for sharing data.

[1]Reese, A., "Extending Quality into the Global Supply Chain," *Supply & Demand Chain Executive*, (2009): pp. 15–17.

Another issue with exporting is that the United States developed a negative quality image during past decades. This image improved greatly as America reached quality levels similar to Japan's in many markets. Research[2] shows that quality is a significant factor in helping U.S. exporters achieve success. Figure 3-3 shows an empirically derived model for quality-based success for exporting companies. In this model, it is shown that firms that are characteristically entrepreneurial in nature and plan their exports effectively tend to have higher quality. For exporting firms, quality leads to lower price and greater export success.

Although there are various ways to enter the global market, one thing is certain: The global market is a reality that must be addressed. Gibson Guitar in Bozeman, Montana, does not operate in a vacuum. Besides exporting guitars overseas, it must produce products that meet international standards of quality or it will not be able to sell its guitars—even in Bozeman. Through local vendors or by Internet order, Bozeman guitarists can buy many quality guitars that are made by Takamine, Yamaha, Ibanez, or other high-quality foreign companies that are competing in the local market.

Next, we continue the theme of integrative quality by exploring quality improvement within U.S., Japanese, and European contexts.

---

[2]Barringer, B., Foster, S., and Macy, G., "The Role of Quality in Determining Export Success," *Quality Management Journal* 6, 4(1999): 55–70.

FIGURE 3-3 Export
Quality Model   *Source:*
Based on B. Barringer,
S. Foster, and G. Macy,
"The Role of Quality
in Determining Export
Success," *Quality
Management Journal* 6,
4 (1999): 64.

Firm Characteristics	Product Strategy	Performance

QUALITY IMPROVEMENT: THE AMERICAN WAY

America has been home to many modern quality management leaders, such as Shewhart, Deming, Juran, and others. The U.S. military also was an early adopter of many quality techniques. Originally, the main interest in quality in the United States was in the application of statistics to solve quality problems. In recent years, the approach has become much more behavioral as teams and other approaches have been applied. We begin by discussing a very important model for quality management in the United States, the **Malcolm Baldrige award**.

THE BALDRIGE PERFORMANCE EXCELLENCE PROGRAM

At the end of Chapter 2, we discussed several operational variables that should be addressed when assessing our future directions for quality improvement. The power of these variables is that they focus management on systemic issues rather than the tactical day-to-day problems. However, management needs a means for assessing the approaches it has employed to improve operating performance. One of the most powerful self-assessment mechanisms is the Baldrige Performance Excellence Program (hereafter referred to as *Baldrige*) (Figure 3-4). The success of the Baldrige program in the United States has influenced international practice and has formed the basis for several international awards. Table 3-2 shows a listing of Baldrige winners.

The Baldrige process is open to small (fewer than 500 employees) and large firms (more than 500 employees) in the manufacturing, health care, education not-for-profit, and service sectors.

Some of the key characteristics of the quality award include the following attributes:

• The criteria focus on business results. Organizations must show outstanding results in areas such as financial performance, customer satisfaction, customer retention, product performance, service performance, productivity, supplier performance, and public citizenship. To win the award, applicants must show that they consistently have performance levels at best-in-class and best-of-the-best. Business results for the Baldrige winner must be exemplary and set the standard for the rest of the world. The importance of business results is reflected in the scoring of the Baldrige. The weight for results has ranged from 25% to 45% of the total score. The reason for the emphasis on results has to do with two related factors. It is quite embarrassing if a Baldrige winner has financial trouble, and the Baldrige winner must be able to serve as a role model to other firms.

- The Baldrige criteria are nonprescriptive and adaptable. Although the focus of the Baldrige is on results, the means for obtaining these results are not prescribed. Therefore, the criteria are not tactically prescriptive. For example, the criteria do not specify which tools, techniques, or organization a company should use to improve. However, at the strategic level, the Baldrige criteria can be viewed as prescriptive. In explanation, a company that does not gather data from its customers or a company that does not have an effective benchmarking program will not be Baldrige-qualified. Therefore, the core values and key characteristics of the Baldrige criteria can be viewed as strategically prescriptive.
- The criteria support company-wide alignment of goals and processes. Once organizational strategy is formulated, connecting and reinforcing measures are developed that support and monitor strategic outcomes. Measures aid in alignment and ensure consistency of purpose while supporting innovation. Alignment between strategic goals and operational subplans helps foster a learning-based system.
- The criteria permit goal-based diagnosis. The criteria and scoring guidelines provide assessment dimensions. These are approach, deployment, and results. The approach defines the method or system for addressing a particular performance objective. Deployment implies that the approach has been implemented in the organization. Results show the outcomes of the approach and deployment. By assessing approach, deployment, and results in several areas, firms can assess their current strengths and areas for improvement. Once areas for improvement are identified, they can be prioritized and tackled one by one.

The model for the Baldrige consists of seven interrelated categories that comprise the organizational system for performance. The seven Baldrige categories are shown in Figure 3-5,

Notice that the basis of the Baldrige model is information and analysis, which confirms the core value of management by fact. Business results are also highlighted, reinforcing the results orientation of the Baldrige framework and criteria. Each of these seven major categories

FIGURE 3-5 Baldrige
Award Framework
Source: Foundation for
the Malcolm Baldrige
Award, 2015. Criteria for
Performance Excellence,
2015.

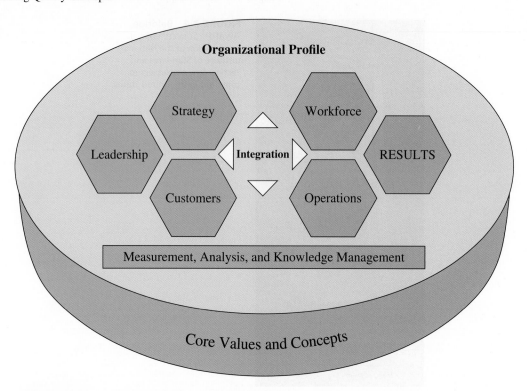

FIGURE 3-5 Baldrige Award Framework
Source: Foundation for the Malcolm Baldrige Award, 2015. Criteria for Performance Excellence, 2015.

TABLE 3-2	Baldrige Winners by Year	
	Award	**Company**
2014	Service	PricewaterhouseCoopers Public Sector
	Health Care	Hill Country Memorial
	Health Care	St. David's HealthCare
	Nonprofit	Elevations Credit Union
2013	Education	Pewaukee School District
	Health Care	Sutter Davis Hospital
2012	Manufacturing	Lockheed Martin Missiles and Fire Control
	Small Business	MESA
	Health Care	North Mississippi Health Services
	Nonprofit	City of Irving, TX
2011	Nonprofit	Concordia Publishing House
	Health Care	Henry Ford Health System
	Health Care	Schneck Medical Center
	Health Care	Southcentral Foundation
2010	Manufacturing	MEDRAD
	Manufacturing	Nestle Purina PetCare Co.
	Small Business	Freese and Nichols Inc.
	Small Business	K&N Management
	Small Business	Studer Group
	Education	Montgomery County Public Schools
	Health Care	Advocate Good Samaritan Hospital
2009	Manufacturing	Honeywell Federal Manufacturing & Technologies LLC

	Award	Company
	Small Business	MidwayUSA
	Health Care	AtlantiCare
	Health Care	Heartland Health
	Nonprofit	VA Cooperative Studies Program Clinical Research Pharmacy Coordinating Center
2008	Manufacturing	Cargill Corn Milling (CCM)
	Education	Iredell-Statesville Schools
	Health Care	Poudre Valley Health System
2007	Small Business	PRO-TEC Coating Company
	Nonprofit	City of Coral Springs
	Health Care	Mercy Health System
	Nonprofit	U.S. Army Armament Research, Development, and Engineering Center (ARDEC)
	Health Care	Sharp HealthCare
2006	Service	Premier Inc.
	Health Care	North Mississippi Medical Center
	Small Business	MESA Products Inc.
2005	Manufacturing	Sunny Fresh Foods, Inc.
	Service	DM Petroleum Operations Company
	Small Business	Park Place Lexus
	Education	Jenks Public Schools
	Education	Richland College
	Health Care	Bronson Methodist Hospital
2004	Manufacturing	The Bama Companies, Inc.
	Education	Kenneth W. Monfort College of Business
	Small Business	Texas Nameplate Company, Inc.
	Health Care	Robert Wood Johnson University Hospital Hamilton
2003	Manufacturing	Medrad, Inc.
	Service	Boeing Aerospace Support
	Service	Caterpillar Financial Services Corporation—U.S.
	Small Business	Stoner, Inc.
	Education	Community Consolidated School District 15
	Health Care	Baptist Hospital, Inc.
	Health Care	Saint Luke's Hospital of Kansas City
2002	Manufacturing	Motorola Commercial, Government & Industrial Solutions Sector
	Health Care	SSM Health Care
	Small Business	Branch-Smith Printing Division
2001	Manufacturing	Clarke American Checks, Inc.
	Education	Pearl River School District
	Small Business	Pal's Sudden Service
	Education	University of Wisconsin-Stout
	Education	Chugach School District
2000	Manufacturing	Dana Corporation—Spicer Driveshaft Division (now Torque Traction Manufacturing Inc.)
	Manufacturing	KARLEE Company, Inc.
	Service	Operations Management International, Inc.
	Small Business	Los Alamos National Bank

(continued)

Year	Award	Company
1999	Manufacturing	STMicroelectronics, Inc.—Region Americas
	Service	The Ritz-Carlton Hotel Company, L.L.C.
	Service	BI
	Small Business	Sunny Fresh Foods
1998	Manufacturing	Boeing Airlift and Tanker Programs
	Small Business	Texas Nameplate Company, Inc.
	Manufacturing	Solar Turbines Incorporated
1997	Manufacturing	3M Dental Products Division
	Manufacturing	Solectron Corporation
	Service	Merrill Lynch Credit Corporation
	Service	Xerox Business Services
1996	Manufacturing	ADAC Laboratories
	Service	Dana Commercial Credit Corporation
	Small Business	Custom Research Inc.
	Small Business	Trident Precision Manufacturing, Inc.
1995	Manufacturing	Armstrong World Industries, Inc., Building Products Operations
	Manufacturing	Corning Incorporated, Telecommunications Products Division
1994	Service	AT&T Consumer Communications Services (Now the Consumer Markets Division of AT&T)
	Small Business	Wainwright Industries, Inc.
	Service	Verizon Information Services (formerly GTE Directories Corporation)
1993	Small Business	Ames Rubber Corporation
	Manufacturing	Eastman Chemical Company
1992	Manufacturing	AT&T Network Systems Group Transmission Systems Business Unit (Now part of Alcatel-Lucent)
	Service	The Ritz-Carlton Hotel Company (Now part of Marriott International)
	Service	AT&T Universal Card Services (Now part of Citigroup)
	Manufacturing	Texas Instruments Incorporated Defense Systems & Electronics Group (Now part of Raytheon Systems Co.)
	Small Business	Graniterock Company
1991	Small Business	Marlow Industries, Inc.
	Manufacturing	Zytec Corporation (Now part of Artesyn Technologies)
	Manufacturing	Solectron Corporation
1990	Manufacturing	Cadillac Motor Car Company
	Manufacturing	IBM Rochester
	Service	Federal Express Corporation
	Small Business	Wallace Co., Inc.
1989	Manufacturing	Milliken & Company
	Manufacturing	Xerox Corporation, Business Products & Systems
1988	Small Business	Globe Metallurgical, Inc.
	Manufacturing	Westinghouse Electric Corporation Commercial Nuclear Fuel Division

Source: www.baldrige.nist.gov, 2016. The National Institute of Standards and Technology (NIST) is an agency of the U.S. Department of Commerce.

is divided into *items* and *areas to address*. The items are denoted by a decimal number, such as 1.1, 2.2, and so on. The areas are given a letter, such as 1.1.a, 2.2.b, and so forth. The number of items and areas varies from year to year because the award criteria are constantly updated by the Baldrige staff, examiners, and judges. We briefly discuss the Baldrige criteria. A complete set of the Baldrige criteria can be downloaded for free from www.nist.gov.

Category 1 provides the award criteria for leadership. This category is used to evaluate the extent to which top management is personally involved in creating and reinforcing goals, values, directions, customer involvement, and a variety of other issues. Within Category 1, the applicant outlines what the firm is doing to fulfill its responsibility as a corporate citizen. Included with corporate citizenship is a documentation of measures and facts relating to how the company fulfills its societal responsibilities.

Category 2 focuses on how the company establishes strategic directions and how it sets its tactical action plans to implement the strategic plans. In addressing *how* the company establishes strategic direction, the applicant should outline methods, measures, deployment, and evaluation/improvement factors relating to establishing strategic plans.

Category 3 addresses customer focus. To be successful in serving the customer, firms must understand the product and service attributes that are important to the customer. This is documented as well as how the firm assesses the relative importance of product or service features. The processes for listening to and learning from customers and markets also must be evaluated, improved, and kept current with changing business needs.

Category 4, measurement, analysis, and knowledge management, relates to the firm's selection, management, and use of information to support company processes and to improve firm performance. These data include both financial information, such as sales, assets, and liabilities, and nonfinancial data, such as operating measures of quality, productivity, and speed of response to customer requests. These measures are only introduced at this point; no results are provided. The applicant then describes how these measures are integrated into an information system that can be used to track and improve company performance. Once data and measures are tracked in an information system, people must deploy the data to ensure that company goals and objectives are being achieved. Robust processes for knowledge management should be described.

Category 5 deals with the workforce focus. The workforce is to be enabled to develop and use its full potential, aligned with company objectives. This involves developing an internal environment conducive to full participation and personal growth, including human resources development. This initiative is directed toward process and performance improvement. Employees must be empowered to understand and respond to changes in customer needs and requirements. To facilitate this learning, skill sharing and open communication with employees are necessary to provide a cohesive work system. The applicant outlines the systems in place that provide compensation, recognition, and workforce engagement.

Category 6 examines key aspects of operations focus. These aspects include customer focus in design, work systems, design for services and products, support processes, and processes relating to partners. Product design must be changed and upgraded to reflect changes in customer requirements and technology. Systems are outlined that measure and assess these changes in requirements. Also addressed is readiness for emergencies and supply chain management.

Category 7 documents the results of the other categories and requires a series of tables and graphs that demonstrate the operational and business results of the firm. Although all the information provided by the applicant is considered by Baldrige examiners to be highly sensitive, Category 7 is often considered the most sensitive by the applicant. For example, because reporting requirements are less exacting for privately held firms, many of the results reported are proprietary. In spite of this, if a firm wants to qualify for a site visit, the requested information must be made available to the examiners.

After this discussion of the Baldrige, you might be interested to learn about Malcolm Baldrige. A Closer Look at Quality 3-1 gives some details about his life.

A CLOSER LOOK AT QUALITY 3-1   Who Was Malcolm Baldrige?

Howard Malcolm Baldrige was the U.S. secretary of commerce from 1980 to 1987. He died while in office, doing what he loved best. He was riding his horse, practicing for the calf-roping event in a California rodeo, when the horse fell and fatally injured him. Secretary Baldrige was 64.

The competitive spirit that spurred Secretary Baldrige to win rodeo events characterized his life. A graduate of Yale University, he entered the army just prior to World War II and quickly rose through the ranks. After the war, he took a job as a supervisor in a small Connecticut foundry. His business career was marked by much success. Toward the end of his career, he led a turnaround effort at Scovill Corporation in Waterbury, Connecticut, based on a steadfast commitment to quality and customer service.

Baldrige believed in good government and was active in politics. His political activity, along with his passion for quality and reputation as a quality leader, led to his appointment as the secretary of commerce in 1980. As secretary of commerce, his top priority was strengthening American industry's capability to compete successfully in international markets. He believed that the role of the U.S. government was to establish fair trade practices, and that the role of private industry was to improve its technology and gain a global reputation for quality products and services.

The Baldrige award was a great tribute to Malcolm Baldrige. Some of the participants in the Baldrige application process have been passionate about the value of the program. Following are two quotations that illustrate this point:

In my opinion, win or lose, the greatest value in applying for the Baldrige award is the feedback report compiled by the examiners. This objective evaluation prepared by a team of well-trained, hard working experts provided the information and focus necessary for us to cause positive changes in our organization.

—HENRY A. BRADSHAW
ARMSTRONG BUILDING PRODUCTS

Participating in the Baldrige process energized improvement efforts. The energy resulted from the team motivation that occurs when pursuing a common goal. That trend has continued. We have reduced the number of in-process defects to only one-tenth what they were at the time we won the Baldrige.

—PHIL ROETHER
TEXAS INSTRUMENTS

The legacy of Malcolm Baldrige lives on in the benefits derived from the recipients and observers of the Malcolm Baldrige program competition. Much can be learned about quality by becoming a keen observer of the companies that win the coveted award.

The Baldrige Process

For the firm applying for the Baldrige award, the first step is eligibility determination. Because the Baldrige pertains only to firms chartered in the United States, eligibility must first be determined by mailing an eligibility determination form to the National Institute of Standards and Technology (NIST). Once eligibility is established, the applicant sends the completed application to NIST. The application is then subjected to first-round review by Baldrige examiners. During this review, examiners read and score the applications. Judges then review the scoring to determine which applicants will continue to *consensus*. During the consensus phase, between five and eight examiners who have scored the application participate in a conference call to determine a consensus score for each of the scoring items.

Once consensus is reached, judges receive a consensus report from the senior examiner leading the examiner team. Judges then make a site-visit determination. At this point, applicants scoring sufficiently high are granted a site visit. In the past, simply the granting of a Baldrige site visit has been cited as evidence of high-quality processes. These firms sometimes refer to themselves as "**Baldrige qualified.**"

The site visit consists of a team of four to six examiners visiting a company over a period not to exceed one week. Typically, the site visit consists of two to three days at the company site and another two days in the hotel to prepare the site-visit reports for the Baldrige judges. These reports show the results of the site visit. The purpose of the site visit is to *verify and clarify* those portions of the Baldrige application that have the greatest impact on the judges' scores. During the first round of scoring, examiners identify strengths, areas for improvement, and site-visit issues. Prior to the site visit, the site-visit team reviews and prioritizes the site-visit issues. Members of the site-visit team then assign responsibilities to team members to complete during the site-visit. After these assignments are complete, the examiners finish their reports while on the site visit. The results are transmitted for use by the judges in final determination of a winner.

One of the most important outcomes of the Baldrige process is examiner feedback to applicant companies. As shown in Figure 3-6, feedback reports are provided to the applicants as

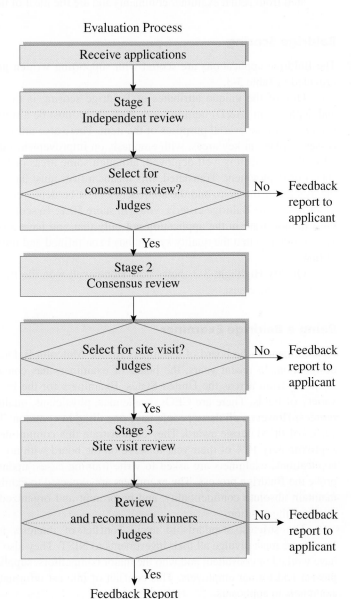

Evaluation Process

FIGURE 3-6 Baldrige Process *Source:* Foundation for the Malcolm Baldrige Award, 2015. Criteria for Performance Excellence, 2015.

part of the assessment process. Many firms have found these comments helpful for identifying gaps in deployment in their improvement processes. As the Baldrige process has matured and become more focused on overall company performance, the feedback reports have become more useful for improving overall management of processes and systems. The feedback report is one of the major benefits of the Baldrige process. The feedback report includes

- The *scoring summary*, which is a synthesis of the most important strengths and areas for improvement for each of the seven Baldrige categories.
- The *individual scoring range*, which provides a 20-point scoring range (e.g., item 2.1: 40%–60%). It gives insight concerning the relative areas of strength and areas that need improvement.
- The *scoring distribution*, which provides the percentage of applicants for a particular year that scored in each of the eight scoring bands.
- The *examiner comments*, which give feedback concerning the organization. These are created from actual examiner comments and are the meat of the feedback report.

Baldrige Scoring

The Baldrige applications are scored with supporting written guidelines. These guidelines are provided in Table 3-3.

One of the unique attributes of Baldrige scoring is the 50% anchor. For an approach and deployment (A&D) item to score 50%, there must be a sound, systematic approach that is responsive to the overall purposes of the item. There also must be fact-based improvement processes in place in key areas, with emphasis on improvement rather than reaction to problems. Also, the approach is well deployed, although some areas or work units may be in very early stages of deployment. Translated, this means a firm must have an approach that addresses all the aspects of the item, and the approaches must be deployed. So if you are doing everything according to the Baldrige criteria, you will score 50%. To score in the higher scoring bands, you must demonstrate in the application not only that you have all the major aspects of a quality system but also that the quality system has been refined and improved over an extended period of time.

Quality Highlight 3-2 shows how Honeywell won the Baldrige award by improving and refining its processes.

Being a Baldrige Examiner

Appointment to the board of examiners for the Malcolm Baldrige award is a very prestigious designation. In recent years, the board of examiners has consisted of between 200 and 300 members from across the United States. Examiners for the board of examiners come from a variety of fields. There are CEOs, academics, physicians, quality specialists, consultants, and retirees. However, all these people have one thing in common: They are committed to the core values of the Baldrige award. They demonstrate this commitment by being willing to give up approximately 10% of their year to serve on the board with no compensation. Besides scoring applications, examiners are asked to write training cases, update the criteria, and help to improve the Baldrige process. The examiners are expected to exhibit the highest professionalism, maintain absolute confidentiality, and be prompt and organized in responding to the requirements of the position.

The strictest standards to avoid conflict of interests are maintained by examiners. Examiners must divulge all their investments to NIST. They also must document for whom they have worked or consulted; and who the major competitors, suppliers, and customers are for their present and former employers. This conflict of interest information is used by NIST to assign examiners to applicants.

TABLE 3-3	Baldrige Scoring Guidelines
Score	**Process**
0% or 5%	• No SYSTEMATIC APPROACH to item requirements is evident; information is ANECDOTAL. (A) • Little or no DEPLOYMENT of any SYSTEMATIC APPROACH is evident. (D) • An improvement orientation is not evident; improvement is achieved through reacting to problems. (L) • No organizational ALIGNMENT is evident; individual areas or work units operate independently. (I)
10%, 15% 20%, or 25%	• The beginning of a SYSTEMATIC APPROACH to the BASIC REQUIREMENTS of the item is evident. (A) • The APPROACH is in the early stages of DEPLOYMENT in most areas or work units, inhibiting progress in achieving the BASIC REQUIREMENTS of the item. (D) • Early stages of a transition from reacting to problems to a general improvement orientation are evident. (L) • The APPROACH IS ALIGNED with other areas or work units largely through joint problem solving. (I)
30%, 35%, 40%, or 45%	• An EFFECTIVE, SYSTEMATIC APPROACH, responsive to the BASIC REQUIREMENTS of the item, is evident. (A) • The APPROACH is DEPLOYED, although some areas or work units are in early stages of DEPLOYMENT. (D) • The beginning of a SYSTEMATIC APPROACH to evaluation and improvement of KEY PROCESSES is evident. (L) • The APPROACH is in the early stages of ALIGNMENT with your basic organizational needs identified in response to the Organizational Profile and other process items. (I)
50%, 55%, 60%, or 65%	• An EFFECTIVE, SYSTEMATIC APPROACH, responsive to the OVERALL REQUIREMENTS of the item, is evident. (A) • The APPROACH is well DEPLOYED, although DEPLOYMENT may vary in some areas or work units. (D) • A fact-based, SYSTEMATIC evaluation and improvement PROCESS and some organizational LEARNING, including INNOVATION, are in place for improving the efficiency and EFFECTIVENESS of KEY PROCESSES. (L) • The APPROACH is ALIGNED with your overall organizational needs identified in response to the Organizational Profile and other process items. (I)
70%, 75%, 80%, or 85%	• An EFFECTIVE, SYSTEMATIC APPROACH, responsive to the MULTIPLE REQUIREMENTS of the item, is evident. (A) • The APPROACH is well DEPLOYED, with no significant gaps. (D) • Fact-based, SYSTEMATIC evaluation and improvement and organizational LEARNING, including INNOVATION, are KEY management tools; there is clear evidence of refinement as a result of organizational-level ANALYSIS and sharing. (L) • The APPROACH is INTEGRATED with your current and future organizational needs identified in response to the Organizational Profile and other process items. (I)
90%, 95%, or 100%	• An EFFECTIVE, SYSTEMATIC APPROACH, fully responsive to the MULTIPLE REQUIREMENTS of the item, is evident. (A) • The APPROACH is fully DEPLOYED without significant weaknesses or gaps in any areas or work units. (D) • Fact-based, SYSTEMATIC evaluation and improvement and organizational LEARNING through INNOVATION are KEY organization-wide tools; refinement and INNOVATION, backed by ANALYSIS and sharing, are evident throughout the organization. (L) • The APPROACH is well INTEGRATED with your current and future organizational needs identified in response to the Organizational Profile and other process items. (I)

Source: Foundation for the Malcolm Baldrige Award, 2015. Criteria for Performance Excellence, 2015.

QUALITY HIGHLIGHT 3-2   Honeywell Federal Manufacturing & Technologies

www.51.honeywell.com

Honeywell Federal Manufacturing & Technologies (FM&T), LLC, is a management and operations contractor with the National Nuclear Security Administration (NNSA) at its Kansas City, Missouri, plant and at several locations on or around Kirtland Air Force Base in New Mexico. The facilities under its management are multidisciplinary engineering and manufacturing operations specializing in electrical, mechanical, and engineered material components for national defense systems. With a reputation for being able to do the "near impossible," FM&T supports government agencies, national laboratories, universities, and U.S. industry.

Commitments to Quality

With commercial best practices such as Six Sigma and Lean (waste reduction), FM&T has built its facilities into manufacturing centers of excellence. FM&T's use of the Six Sigma Plus Continuous Improvement Model ensures integration of customer and business requirements into all design projects and has led to multiple cycles of learning and improvement for many of the organization's work processes. The result is a business culture that pays precise attention to detail and insists on delivering results—a culture FM&T describes as "Commitments Made, Commitments Kept."

Additionally, this approach has yielded impressive financial results:

- Cost savings from increased productivity and deployed innovations have been between $23.5 million and $27 million annually for the past three fiscal years.
- Energy conservation has improved by at least 20% each year from 2006 to 2009.
- Supply-chain savings have increased from approximately $2 million in 2007 to approximately $65 million in 2009.

A Culture Aligned, Checked, and Filtered for Success

FM&T's vision is to be the preferred partner with the United States government and its allies, distinguished by its trusted relationships and recognized for its capability to deliver exceptional solutions for national and homeland security. This vision goes hand in hand with the organization's mission to design and deliver products, manage operations, and provide targeted services to advance national and homeland security objectives for the United States government and its allies. To support these goals, FM&T developed a robust, systematic governing system and planning process called the Management Assurance System. By incorporating strategic planning, checks that ensure processes align with goals, and feedback scorecards, the system identifies, implements, measures, and sustains the "critical-to-quality" needs necessary for desired performance.

Throughout the Management Assurance System is an emphasis on performance measurement and management by fact. This emphasis begins with the organization's strategic plan, which annually follows eight steps to identify successes and challenges, and then uses the information obtained to improve processes. The Enterprise Alignment Process ensures that the daily accountability of the salaried and hourly workforce is aligned with the FM&T balanced scorecard and strategic plan.

The company also regularly identifies its core competencies by testing each one against a "VIRO" filter to see whether each is Valuable, hard to Imitate, Rare, and an Opportunity to exploit. Recently, FM&T underwent realignment to better focus on its strengths and improve its support to customers.

State Awards

In recent years, the number of applicants for the Malcolm Baldrige award has decreased. There are numerous explanations for this. A major reason is that applications declined in number once firms realized how difficult it would be to actually win the Baldrige award. Another reason is the existence of state awards. In recent years, more than 1,000 firms in the United States applied for state quality awards. The state awards are important because they give firms a basis to become familiar with the Baldrige process. Many recent winners of the Baldrige award have previously won state awards.

A review of the different state award programs reveals three categories of approaches to state awards. The first approach is the **full-Baldrige approach.** In these states, the Baldrige criteria have been adopted, and firms apply using the Baldrige criteria. In these cases, the criteria are used, but the scores required to win the state awards are lower than those for the national awards. This approach occurs often in more-populated states (e.g., Missouri, New York, and Florida) that have well-funded award programs.

An approach that some other states have taken is the **Baldrige-lite** approach. This approach uses the Baldrige criteria but with a simplified process and/or application. This approach occurs in states such as Massachusetts and California.

The third approach is the **multilevel approach.** Using the multilevel approach, often the top level includes the full-Baldrige criteria. At the second level, a Baldrige-lite approach is used. Then, in lower levels, recognition is provided for firms that are putting forth significant effort toward improving performance.

The state award programs are becoming important vehicles for promoting involvement in the Baldrige process. Top management might become interested in applying for a state quality award for which the competition is less demanding than the Baldrige award. State awards also provide important education for companies through conferences and the literature they provide. Examiner training given through state award programs helps to develop expertise among employees of local companies. These examiners can then disseminate this training within the firms where they work.

QUALITY IMPROVEMENT: THE JAPANESE WAY

The Japanese must be credited with raising worldwide quality to a new level of competitiveness. They created competition through quality as their automobiles and electronic products were exported to the nations of the world in huge numbers. Using quality as a competitive weapon to win orders in the marketplace, the Japanese provided an example for the rest of the world that has benefited producers and consumers all over the world.

Deming Prize

Before discussing Japanese quality approaches, we first touch on the Deming Prize. The **Deming Prize** for quality was established in 1951 by the Japanese Union of Scientists and Engineers (JUSE). The award was funded by the proceeds from Deming's book on statistical process control that resulted from his teachings in Japan. The award now commemorates the distinguished service to Japan by W. E. Deming. The Deming Prize is awarded to individuals and groups who have contributed to the field of quality control. The examination and award process is performed under the direction of the JUSE Deming Award Committee.

The Deming Prize is much more focused on processes than is the Baldrige. This is reflected in the categories and items contained in the Deming Prize. Table 3-4 compares categories of the Deming, Baldrige, and European Quality Award competitions. A review of these categories shows that the Baldrige is more general and managerial. At the same time, the Deming Prize is more prescriptive. More information about the Deming Prize can be found at http://www.juse.or.jp/english.

Other Japanese Contributions to Quality Thought

As Joseph Juran stated, the genius of the Japanese was in their ability to maintain a focus on the minutiae and detail associated with process improvement. They also set the world standard for

TABLE 3-4	Comparison of the Baldrige Award, Deming Prize, and European Quality Award	
Baldrige Award	**Deming Prize**	**European Quality Award**
Leadership	Policy management	Leadership
Customer	Daily work management	Strategy
Measurement, analysis, and knowledge management	Cross-functional activities	People
Workforce	Problem solving/task achieving activities	Partnerships and resources
Operations	QC circle activities	Processes, products, and services
Results	New product development	Customer results
	Quality assurance	People results
	Utilization of IT	Society results
	Human resource development	Business results

efficient, clean, and waste-free processes. In this section, we discuss the Japanese approach to production and service. We attempt to identify those contributions that are uniquely Japanese.

Lean Production

Two views emerge in the literature that pertain to **lean** manufacturing. The first view of lean is a philosophical view of waste reduction. This view asserts that anything in the process that does not add value for the customer should be eliminated. Given this view, quality problems cause scrap and rework and are wasteful. The second view of lean is a systems view, stating that lean is a group of techniques or systems focused on optimizing quality processes. An example of this view is the lean production system refined by the Toyota Motor Company and spread to the rest of the world. For our purposes, we combine the philosophical and systems views to define lean as *a productive system whose focus is on optimizing processes through the philosophy of continual improvement.*

LEAN AS A PHILOSOPHY As we showed in Chapter 2, philosophy is an important element in improving quality. Perhaps it is because of the difficulty associated with communicating quality that philosophies are so important. Words and definitions help us communicate on a cerebral level. Philosophies, once internalized, help individuals and organizations to communicate on a feeling-based level. For Toyota Motor Company, the focus was on the continual reduction of waste. Shigeo Shingo, the industrial engineer who was fundamental in helping Toyota to reduce waste, identified a group of seven wastes that workers could address in improvement processes (Table 3-5). Lean is a philosophy that requires discipline. As we see in Quality Highlight 3-3 problems occur when the discipline is lost.

TABLE 3-5	Seven Wastes

1. Waste of overproduction.
2. Waste of waiting.
3. Waste of transportation.
4. Waste of processing itself.
5. Waste of stocks.
6. Waste of motion.
7. Waste of making defective products.

QUALITY HIGHLIGHT 3-3   The Humbling of Toyota[3]

With a name that has been synonymous with quality, the Toyota Production System revolutionized industry and is the benchmark for many companies. No lean discussion is complete without a review of Toyota. A customer-centered focus led the company to produce quality cars at an affordable price. A trade-off between the two was not necessary. Jim Wiseman, Toyota's vice president for North American corporate communication, summed up the company's view this way: "It's not true that by reducing cost you automatically reduce quality."

This philosophy has brought great success to Toyota over the years. The company is competitive in different categories with its strong lineup: 4-Runner, Prius, Tundra, Camry, and so on. Toyota was gaining market share in the United States at a rapid pace and at one point became the world's largest automaker. Things were looking good for Toyota, while other auto companies fought to keep up.

Over the past few years, the consumer's perception of Toyota has changed as various quality issues have surfaced. The culmination was a recall of 8 million cars at the end of 2009 and the beginning of 2010. This was due to a much-publicized gas pedal malfunction. So how did a company doing so well fall so quickly? The lapse in quality did not happen overnight. A number of factors contributed to the lapse.

Reducing costs and maintaining quality require a balance. Over time, Toyota placed more emphasis on costs. Suppliers felt the pressure to cut costs at every stage. Engineers redesigned parts to reduce material, even if it meant using an untested alternative material. Along with the intense cost cutting was the rapid expansion of the company. To keep up with demand, Toyota engineers had to outsource development work. The customer-first focus had been replaced by a financial focus.

Toyota had early signals of straying from quality. The National Highway Traffic Safety Administration opened eight investigations of unintended acceleration of Toyota vehicles from 2003 to 2010. Other part failures were identified by the company as well. Top company executives were warned by other managers of slips in vehicle quality. Toyota was not staying disciplined to its quality philosophy.

The lasting effect of Toyota's quality lapse is not known. Its previous customer goodwill may have buffered some of the drop in perceived quality.

[3]Based on Chrisman, A., Green, J., and Inoue, K., "The Humbling of Toyota," *Bloomberg Businessweek* (22 March 2010): 32–36.

Japanese Total Quality Control (TQC)

Just as the Japanese lean approach requires attention to detail in every aspect of the process, so does the TQC approach. This attention to detail runs deep in the Japanese culture. About 1,200 years ago, during the eighth century A.D., Japanese swordsmiths hammered 10,000 microlayers of steel into the world's finest blades.

Of course, the Japanese philosophy of continual improvement is reflected in Deming's 14 points for management, outlined previously. However, beyond Deming's 14 points, there are several Japanese contributions to quality thought and practice that we outline here.

VISIBILITY   An important aspect of the Japanese approach to quality is visibility. When problems exist in business, the first reflex is often to hide the problems as though they don't exist. The Japanese approach does the opposite. In the Japanese approach to quality, problems must be made visible before they can be addressed. Among the approaches to improving quality is inventory reduction. Excess work-in-process inventory has the effect of hiding problems. Therefore, it is eliminated.

Another visibility technique the Japanese use is called **andon,** or warning lights. Whenever a defect occurs on the line, the line is stopped. This halts production in several workstations, not just one workstation. As a result, workers from the production line all converge on the process where the warning light went off. Teams are used to identify and eliminate the fundamental cause

ever be in is on the day you purchase the machine. By performing scheduled maintenance and improvement to equipment, machinery actually can improve with age. In the 1980s, the Toyota Kamigo Plant 9 in Japan won the Deming Prize with aged equipment. The key was that the equipment was maintained very well. With preventive maintenance, heavy unscheduled maintenance is still performed by shop engineers and maintenance specialists. However, regular cleaning, fluid changing, and light maintenance are handled on a regularly scheduled basis by the people who operate the machinery.

QUALITY IMPROVEMENT: THE EUROPEAN WAY[4]

In past decades, Europe found itself in a position similar to that of the United States. European producers of products were finding the Japanese to be formidable competitors and realized they needed to change.

It is difficult to tell where Europe now stands concerning quality management. Because of radical differences in infrastructure, politics, and business practices, it is easy to overgeneralize. **ISO 9000:2015** is the European standard for quality that has been expanded worldwide. At the same time, there has been a perception in the quality community that Europe is behind the Japanese and the United States in improving quality. For example, French and German customer service has remained low by American and Japanese standards and has not shown great improvement. However, companies such as BMW, Mercedes, and Siemens produce products that set the standard for quality.

Culture plays a greater role in European quality practices than it does in the United States. For instance, many foreigners view German service as poor. There is a historical basis for this perception. Since medieval times, shopkeepers were considered part of the land-owning, privileged class in Germanic regions. As such, they enjoyed an elevated status in society. Therefore, a patron who entered an establishment would often look up to the service provider as someone of a higher social class. This created a situation in which the patron actually would be in a position of thanking the service provider for providing service.

Servers in fine Parisian restaurants are viewed by many visitors from other countries as rude. However, in France, the culinary experience is considered high art. Much as an art expert would be aghast if someone without a trained eye belittled great art, the French server might be displeased when an untrained customer ordered the wrong wine. Those are only two examples of why, if service is to be improved, not only business practices will have to change in parts of Europe but also ingrained culture must change.

European businesses are often in a difficult dilemma. Europe is a loose federation of sovereign nations. Each country is trying to protect its own culture while, at the same time, trying to cooperate with the other countries to introduce unified standards. Two types of quality recognition are widely used in Europe: the European Quality Award (EQA) and ISO 9000:2015 certification.

European Quality Award

In 1988, a group of 14 large European companies created the European Foundation for Quality Management in reaction to increased competition from overseas, the quick success of the Baldrige award in the United States, and the recognition that changes were needed if Europe was to compete in the world market. The European Foundation for Quality Management administers the European Quality Award (EQA). The EQA has two levels: The highest level is the EQA for the most accomplished applicant in a given year, and the second level given is the European Quality Prize for other firms that meet the award criteria.

The model for the EQA is shown in Figure 3-7. Because the EQA is similar to the Baldrige in tone and process, we emphasize some of the differences between the two. The differences are found primarily in the categories of people, society results, and key results. The people category

---

[4]Based on International Standards Organization, Geneva, Switzerland, 2008.

FIGURE 3-7   European Quality Award Model   *Source:* European Foundation for Quality Management, Brussels, Belgium, 2016. Copyright © by EFQM, Brussels, Belgium, 2016. Reprinted by permission.

addresses the perceptions of employees concerning their employer. Items in this category include working environment, perception of management style, career planning and development, and job security. Whereas the Baldrige criterion of workforce and development focuses more on those things that lead to customer service and improved products, the EQA focuses more on employee satisfaction as an outcome of the quality system. From this standpoint, employee satisfaction becomes an indicator of satisfactory management.[5]

The EQA criterion of impact on society asks the applicant to document how the company is viewed by the society it affects. This includes the company's approach to quality of life, the environment, and the preservation of global resources. Therefore, charitable activities, leisure-related activities, and employment stability are all important aspects of the quality system for the Europeans.

ISO 9000:2015

On a worldwide basis, ISO 9000:2015 has had a much more significant impact than any of the quality standards or recognitions in terms of the number of companies that have implemented the approach. The focus of ISO 9000:2015 is for companies to document their quality systems in a series of manuals to facilitate trade through supplier conformance. Once the quality system is documented, ISO 9000:2015 registration states a quality system is in place and being adhered to.

ISO is the Organization for International Standards of Geneva, Switzerland (the Greek word *isos* means "equal"). The ISO standard was developed so that an international standard for documentation of quality systems could be applied in many different cultures. The ISO standards are very broad and nonspecific, so they can be adapted to many different industries.

ISO 9000:2015 BASICS   In this section we discuss ISO 9000:2015 and its requirements. ISO 9000:2015 is not a prescription for running a business or firm. However, its requirements provide a recognized international quality standard that businesses can follow. It is interesting to note that more than 1 million companies have registered using the ISO standard. To effectively use the ISO standard, you need to plan your processes, follow those processes, ensure that those processes are effective, correct deficiencies in your current processes, and continually improve your processes.

The original version of ISO 9000 was implemented internationally in 1994 after the International Organization for Standardization (ISO) Technical Committee (TC) 176 worked

---

[5]Calvo-Mora A., Navarro-Garcia, A., and Perianez-Cristobal, R., "Project to Improve Knowledge Management and Key Business Results Through the EFQM Excellence Model," *International Journal of Project Management* (2015, in press).

for eight years to develop the standard. The ISO 9000:1994 standard closely mirrored the prior British Standard 5750 in form and substance. By 1997, the ISO 9000 family of documents had become quite cumbersome, with 20 required elements and 12 standards. Three ISO 9000:2015 standards and seven clauses are listed below:

1. ISO 9000 Quality Management System: Fundamentals and vocabulary
2. ISO 9001 Specific requirements of the standard.
3. ISO 9004 Managing for the sustained success of an organization: This section provides guidance on self-assessment methods.

   ISO 9001 consists of the following seven clauses:

   Clause 4: Context of the organization

   Clause 5: Leadership

   Clause 6: Planning for the quality management system

   Clause 7: Support

   Clause 8: Operation

   Clause 9: Performance evaluation

   Clause 10: Improvement

   Source: International Standards Organization, Geneva, Switzerland, 2008.

Quality Management Principles Underlying ISO 9000:2015

The following seven principles provide the foundation for ISO 9000:2015:

1. Customer focus
2. Leadership
3. Engagement of people
4. Process approach
5. Improvement
6. Evidence-based decision making
7. Relationship management

Most of these quality management principles are self-explanatory and discussed throughout this book. TC 176 has done an excellent job of responding to the critics of the original standard by focusing on these quality management principles. Note the similarities between these principles and the Baldrige categories.

Selecting a Registrar

The ISO 9000:2015 process is very different from any of the awards processes discussed previously. To many who have implemented ISO 9000:2015, the selection of the registrar is the most important step in the ISO 9000:2015 process. It is also the messiest step of the ISO process. There is no centralized authority that qualifies ISO registrars. Although no European country requires ISO 9000:2015 registration, many firms require it. In fact, many countries officially encourage their firms to use only ISO-registered suppliers. However, certain ISO registrars have memoranda of agreement with the departments of commerce of individual countries. This means that out of the hundreds of registrars that exist in the world, only a relative few may be recognized in any particular country. Also, many registrars are not recognized officially anywhere. Therefore, when selecting a registrar, firms must be careful. They should check with customers and departments of commerce and customers within the countries to which they plan to export. This could save severe problems and a waste of money in the long run.

The ISO 9000:2015 Process

The registration process for ISO 9000:2015 typically takes several months from initial meeting to final registration audit. This time frame differs from client to client, but each process usually follows the steps outlined in Figure 3-8.

Step 1 is inquiry, where the client contacts registrars to investigate the terms for registration. The prospective client then makes a final selection of a registrar with whom he or she is comfortable.

In Step 2, the client contracts with the registrar. In this process, registration steps are determined, and a price is negotiated. A client-signed quotation or purchase order leads to the first stage of the certification process. Some clients may wish to have a preassessment or gap-analysis audit.

Step 3 often involves a phase 1 audit. At this stage, the registrar performs an onsite audit of the documented quality system against the applicable standard.

Step 4 is the certification audit. Every element of the ISO 9000:2015 standard is audited several times during the registration process. A representative sample of an organization's business processes is chosen for any audit. During each 3-year period, 100% of the organization is audited. The audit program is a valuable tool that provides a clearly and mutually defined process and snapshot of auditing—past, present, and future.

Step 5 may involve process audits (optional). The client may choose business processes for auditing to the applicable standard, allowing the client to learn and experience the registrar's auditing methods and style.

Step 6 involves the final certification audit. Once the client's documented quality system has met the applicable standard, the registrar conducts an audit to determine the system's effective implementation. This may involve interviewing the process owners and responsible personnel as designated in the documented quality system for processes chosen from the audit program.

FIGURE 3-8   An Example of the ISO Registration Process

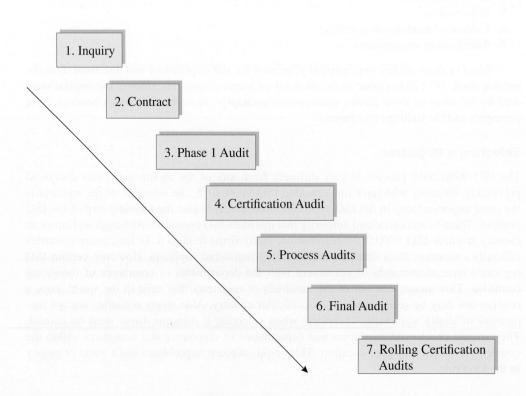

TABLE 3-6	ISO 14000 Elements
Element Number	**Title**
4.1	General requirements
4.2	Environmental policy
4.3	Planning
4.3.1	Environmental aspects
4.3.2	Legal and other requirements
4.3.3	Objectives and targets
4.3.4	Environmental management programs
4.4	Implementation and operation
4.4.1	Structure and responsibility
4.4.2	Training, awareness, and competence
4.4.3	Communication
4.4.4	Environmental management system documentation
4.4.5	Document control
4.4.6	Operational control
4.4.7	Emergency preparedness and response
4.5	Checking and corrective action
4.5.1	Monitoring and measurement
4.5.2	Nonconformance and corrective and preventive action
4.5.3	Records
4.5.4	Environmental management system audit
4.6	Management review

Source: Based on International Standards Organization, Geneva, Switzerland, 2010. http://iso14001.com.au/iso-14001-requirements.html.

After certification, Step 7 involves rolling certification audits. These are sometimes referred to as *surveillance audits*, where the registrar returns on either six-month or annual cycles.

ISO 14000

Given the success of ISO 9000, ISO developed an international standard for environmental compliance called ISO 14000. ISO 14000 is a series of standards that provide guidelines and a compliance standard.

ISO 14000 uses the same basic approach as ISO 9000:2015, with documentation control, management system auditing, operational control, records control, management policies, audits, training, statistical techniques, and corrective and preventive action. In addition to these controls, ISO 14000 includes quantified targets, established objectives, emergency and disaster preparedness, and disclosure of environmental policy. Such a system may provide the basis for developing a comprehensive environmental management system.

Table 3-6 presents the ISO 14000 elements. The process for documenting these elements and seeking registration mirrors the ISO 9000 process. Again, a key process has to do with selecting the appropriate registrar.

Outside of Europe, such as in the United States, firms have approached ISO 14000 carefully, with many firms deciding not to adopt the standard.[6] Is this because American firms are less committed to environmental quality than are European firms? The answer is probably no. ISO 14000 is very risky for U.S. firms. As a result of the self-study process incorporated in the ISO standard, firms can possibly discover violations regarding some environmental topic, such

[6]Hale, G., and Hemenway, C., "ISO 14000 Will Likely Join the Regulatory Framework," *Quality Digest* 16, 2 (1998): 29–34.

as hazardous waste. It would seem that these firms should be able to then clean up this waste. However, it is not so simple. Once these firms discover variances, they are required to report these variances to the U.S. Environmental Protection Agency (EPA). Even if the firm discovers and cleans up environmental problems, the EPA has made it clear that the firm will be subject to fines and penalties, which could include shutting down the business! As a result, firms are reticent to begin the process of self-discovery until the EPA changes its policy. Therefore, environmentally conscious firms that may want to improve their environmental management systems through ISO 14000 are potentially being dissuaded from doing so by the EPA. It will take several years for the courts to settle many of these issues. Until these issues are settled, adoption of ISO 14000 may be slow in many countries. Despite these problems, some American firms, such as Micron Technologies of Boise, Idaho, have adopted ISO 14000. It is expected that firms with little environmental exposure will adopt ISO 14000 first.

QUALITY IMPROVEMENT: THE CHINESE WAY

As you can see in Figure 3-9, total trade between the United States and China increased by 500% from 2000 to 2014. In that same time, Chinese imports to the United States increased from $100 billion to almost $300 billion. Among the important reasons for this growth in

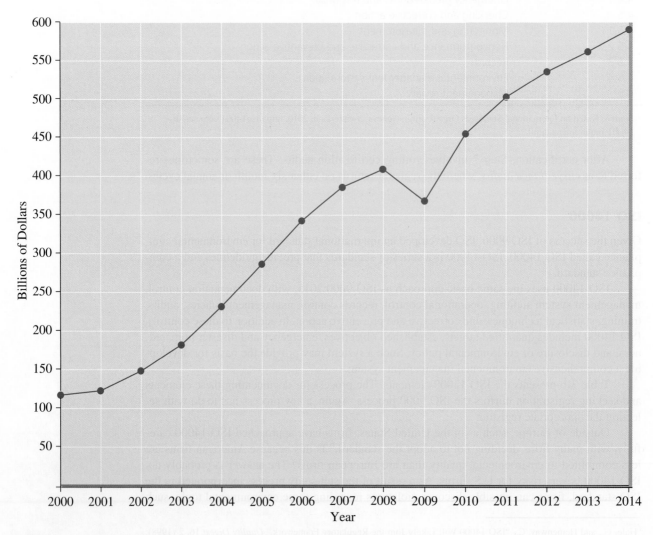

FIGURE 3-9   Total Volume of Trade between the United States and China   *Source:* U.S. Department of Commerce, 2015.

trade have been the opening of the Chinese markets to foreign trade, the constant drumbeat of U.S. and European offshoring to China, and the low cost of doing business in China. Given the growing importance of China in international trade, the question then arises about Chinese quality.

Does Chinese Quality Management Exist?

What led to this internationalization from the historically isolationist China? With the death of Chairman Mao Tse-tung in 1976, Deng Xiaoping took the reins of economic reform, leading to a so-called open-door policy for trade and economic transfer. This resulted in the creation of a socialist market economy.

Historically, China was known for fine porcelain, silks, bronze, and construction. Trade between China and the West has existed for many centuries, as is evidenced by the ancient Silk Road. Chinese products were held in such high regard that traders were willing to brave the forbidding Taklimakan desert, or "road of death," to bring Chinese products to European markets. These goods were of exceedingly high quality and value. However, it is not clear that China has continued this legacy of quality in the modern era.

Some factors have led to low quality in China.[7] Researchers state that these factors include the low level of education of some Chinese workers and lack of experience among agricultural workers who have moved into the industrial sector. These same workers are often unfamiliar with the consumer goods they are making and may not have the commitment necessary to provide long-term resources to quality improvement because they work for a short period of time and then return to their homes to farm.

Another factor omnipresent in Chinese business is *guanxi*, or "influence." *Guanxi* can range from personal relationships to bribery. Here is an example of how *guanxi* can influence perceptions of quality in China:

> We wanted to give some government officials some biscuits as presents (customary in China). The day that they came they said, "By the way, we want double." If they wanted to penalize the company they could go to the media and say that Freshbake Biscuits' products were contaminated.

In the last quarter of a century, the United States and Europe have had to improve quality as a result of international competition. As time passes, China will be subject to similar competitive pressures (see A Closer Look at Quality 3-2). Both Japan and Mexico have seen increases in salaries that have negatively impacted their cost advantages. Although it is not clear that Chinese products meet world standards for quality, over time, Chinese firms will need to meet international standards of quality if their standard of living is to increase proportionally. Foreign firms who locate in China to take advantage of low cost and forget about quality will do so at their own peril in the long term.

It is clear that Chinese manufacturers are aware of quality management practices and have made some changes to adapt certain practices.[8] What form that will take is still unclear. What is clear is that China is an economic giant. The adoption of modern quality approaches will provide it further competitive advantage in the future.

---

[7]Glover, L., and Siu, N., "The Human Resource Barriers to Managing Quality in China," *International Journal of Human Resource Management* 11, 5 (2000): 867–882.

[8]Pun, Kit-Fai, "Cultural Influences on Total Quality Management Adoption in Chinese Enterprises: An Empirical Study," *Total Quality Management* 12, 3 (2001): 323–342.

A CLOSER LOOK AT QUALITY 3-2   Outsourcing Woes

It is difficult to pick up a newspaper without finding articles showing how some firm has experienced serious quality-related problems due to outsourcing. Outsourcing to developing countries has been a trend for decades. However, recent events show that outsourcing can be a risky venture. Mattel has recalled millions of toys due to leaded paint—when in fact, it had used a long-term, trusted supplier who used leaded paint his employees had purchased over the Internet. RC2 Corp., the company that makes Thomas the Train toys, had to recall several models for leaded paint. The interesting fact with their story is that they rewarded affected customers with a free toy for their trouble and ended up having to recall the free toy for leaded paint!

Although these stories are interesting, it should be recognized that this is not just a Chinese problem. Similar things could happen to firms who outsource anywhere – across the street or across the world. It could be China, the United States, Latin America or anywhere else. It is not just in products either. Dell Corporation has now moved its customer support for business users back to the United States. The issue is not one nation. It is outsourcing. It is clear that we need to rethink outsourcing practices and implement new quality practices to mitigate the loss of control associated with outsourcing.

Changing the Focus from Cost to Quality

In point 4 of his 14 points for management, Deming stated, "End the practice of awarding business on the basis of price tag alone. Instead, minimize total cost." These words seem more prescient now than when they were first written. It appears that the primary motivation for many firms to offshore production has been to take advantage of lower labor, land, and production costs. However, many firms have also found that moving overseas is not always cheap when the entire array of life cycle costs for products and services are considered.

Firms that offshore to China and other countries place tremendous pressure for low cost on their overseas suppliers. This external pressure for low cost, when coupled with internal and external pressures to turn profits, inevitably leads to the cutting of corners. Realize that the same rules apply to suppliers overseas as domestic suppliers: These are partners. We do not want our partners to go broke. Otherwise, the partnership is not a true partnership. Negotiated costs should include room for the supplier to succeed without cutting corners. Deming was right: When there is too much focus on cost, quality concerns are lessened. Many have predicted that a day of reckoning was coming. It appears to have come for a number of companies.

Firms who win in outsourcing internationally will be those companies who understand that quality is of primary importance—coupled with price. This is what is termed a *value proposition*. Customers will not return to a company or retail chain that provides a poor value proposition. To do this properly, you must know your suppliers and enhance their performance through development and partnering. If this is not present, you will have to monitor your supplier's performance. Ultimately, this will prove much more costly because not everything can be monitored. For example, it is not clear that RC2 Corp. would have recognized the need to test for leaded paint any more than to test to make sure that their products contained cyanide. There are too many unexpected ways a rogue supplier can destroy a customer's reputation.

ARE QUALITY APPROACHES INFLUENCED BY CULTURE?

As we have seen by discussing tools, techniques, and approaches adopted within different regions of the world, a picture of diversity emerges. The U.S. approach historically has been command-and-control oriented. This might be the result of a history of political and military management as a basis for business management. Americans tend to be results oriented. The implication is that if quality does not provide bottom-line results, it is often not something to be pursued.

The Japanese approach is based on an ethic of consistency and emphasis on reduction of waste. There are cultural underpinnings for this approach. The Japanese landmass is smaller in size than California. Given that many people are contained in a small landmass, it is no surprise that a premium is placed on reducing waste. Also, consider the fact that the Japanese have almost no natural resources. For this reason, almost all raw materials must be imported at great cost. Again, this causes a cultural ethic of reduced waste. Finally, it is fairly obvious when observing Japanese business practices that they prize conformance and consistency.

The Europeans have adopted broad standards that can be adapted to the diverse nation-states in the European Union. There is also an apparent concern among the Europeans to satisfy employees, focus on work as art, and care for the environment. There are strong unions in Europe that cause the need for sensitivity toward employees. The work-as-art ethic has roots in medieval times when the artisan ethic was developed. As an example, in Germany, an aspiring shipbuilder would find employment as an apprentice with a master shipbuilder. After years as an apprentice, the student would become a journeyman shipbuilder, until one day possibly becoming a master shipbuilder. Again, the cultural roots of management and quality improvement run deep in different cultures.

Are other cultures developing quality methods that will be instructive for world competitors? The Russians have long used what is now called **group technology** to produce products and to improve production. Several Asian Tiger nations, such as Malaysia, South Korea, and Singapore, have begun to make inroads in the field of quality and will become formidable competitors in the future. Chinese quality management is a work in process. We will keep watching.

Summary

In an increasingly globalizing economy, it is important to understand the approaches that various nations use to improve quality. It is clear that the trend is toward greater participation in a global economy. As a result, the worker of the future will need to adapt to approaches having roots in other cultures.

In this chapter, we discussed the global economy and the role played by quality in that world economy. We considered different quality models from different regions such as the Malcolm Baldrige award, the Deming Prize, the European Quality award, and ISO 9000.

From an integrative perspective, it is reasonable to borrow from all these models if that will help your firm perform better. The underlying theme in this chapter is the importance of learning from other cultures to compete effectively.

Key Terms

Andon	Globalization	Licensing	Physical environment
Baldrige-lite	Group technology	Line-stop authority	Preventive maintenance
Baldrige-qualified	Horizontal deployment	Malcolm Baldrige award	Quality circles
Deming Prize	In-process inspection	Multilevel approach	Social environment
Exporter	ISO 9000:2015	$N = 2$ technique	Task environment
Full-Baldrige approach	Lean	Partnering	Vertical deployment

Discussion Questions

1. What are the advantages or disadvantages of licensing as a means of gaining access to foreign markets?
2. The World Bank ranks countries in terms of globalization. Go to the research section of the World Bank website (www.worldbank.org) and choose three countries to compare various socio-economic factors that affect quality related decisions.
3. Describe the key characteristics of the Malcolm Baldrige Award.

4. Explain the seven interrelated categories of the Baldrige Award that make up the organizational system for performance.

5. Discuss if "workforce" is a criteria in deciding quality awards in your country. Compare quality awards in your country to the Malcolm Baldrige award.

6. Do you believe the Baldrige should include a category for not-for-profit organizations? If so, what adjustments should be made in the Baldrige criteria to make it applicable for this category?

7. If you were the CEO of a manufacturing firm, would you encourage your firm to apply for the Malcolm Baldrige award? Why or why not?

8. If you were presented the opportunity to be a Baldrige examiner, would you accept it? Why or why not? Make your answer as substantive as possible.

9. Explain the concept of lean manufacturing.

10. How does visibility affect quality? Support your answer with examples.

11. Discuss the role of inventory in a production system from a Western perspective as well as from a Japanese (lean) perspective.

12. Do you think that if line employees are empowered, given authority, and required to work on quality improvement activities, their productivity will suffer?

13. Why is it a good idea for workers to inspect their own work?

14. In what ways are the Malcolm Baldrige award and the Deming Prize similar, and in what ways are they different?

15. Is it appropriate to use the criteria for quality awards as a framework for organizational improvement and change? Why or why not?

16. What are the major substantive differences between the quality awards discussed in the chapter and ISO 9000:2015? Are they intended for similar or entirely different purposes?

17. Describe the purpose and the intent of the ISO 9000:2015 program. What are the advantages of becoming an ISO 9000:2015-certified company? Are there any disadvantages?

18. What do the ISO 14000 standards entail?

19. What are the pros and cons for an American firm that is considering pursuing ISO 14000 certification? If you were the CEO of a manufacturing firm, would you pursue ISO 14000? Why or why not?

20. Do you believe quality approaches are influenced by culture? How?

CASES

Case 3-1 Denver International Airport Becomes ISO 14001 Certified[9]

Denver International Airport (DIA) aims to become a world-class airport by emphasizing service, on-time flights, and caring for the environment. Addressing environmental issues may be a new approach for an airport, but it has paid off for DIA. In 2005, it became the first international airport in the United States to be ISO 14001 (environmental management system, or EMS) registered. DIA did not set out to become certified; it simply wanted a structure to handle environmental issues. ISO 14001 provided guidelines for establishing an EMS. With the amount of effort put into complying with the standards, the next logical step was to become certified.

There are more benefits to ISO 14001 certification than the credibility and additional transparency DIA has received. DIA has a structured and EMS program that allows it to do more with less. Processes are documented, outlining employees' duties. The employees receive training and understand what is expected of them from an EMS compliance standpoint. DIA has been able to influence the environmental actions of others. Impressed by DIA's accomplishments, the city and county of Denver have established environmental programs for all their departments. DIA is working with other international airports to establish sustainability guidelines for the world's airports.

[9]Based on Maldonado, L., "Denver Airport First to Be Certified to ISO 14001," *Business and the Environment* 16, 3 (2005): 14–15.

DIA's environmental initiatives have achieved quantitative and monetary results. The goals and results are highlighted in DIA's annual reports. Following is a list of some accomplishments:

- $1.7 million in savings by recycling aircraft deicing fluid (ADF)
- $160,000 in savings from decreases in gasoline and diesel usage
- More than $2.1 million saved between 2007 and 2008
- 1,432 tons of solid waste (11.15% of total) generated in 2008 recycled
- Hazardous solid wastes reduced from 20,000 pounds to 3,760 pounds in just one year

ISO 14001 certification is not the end result for DIA. Environmental management is now incorporated into the airport's strategic planning process. The requirements and structure of ISO registration motivate DIA to be aggressive in setting new initiatives and goals. The organization wants to be proactive to stay ahead of environmental regulation. DIA's environmental impact extends beyond the company because it is involved in community outreach programs and participates as a member of various environmental organizations. In the end, ISO 14001 certification has enabled Denver International Airport to progress toward environmental accountability and sustainability.

Discussion Questions

1. What do you view as the benefits of ISO 14001 adoption and implementation?
2. Is ISO registration useful for airports? Why or why not?
3. How can the benefits of ISO registration extend outside the company?

Case 3-2 Wainwright Industries: An Entirely New Philosophy of Business Based on Customer Satisfaction and Quality

Related Web page: wainwrightindustries.com

In the early 1980s, Wainwright Industries, a manufacturer of stamped and machine parts, was facing nothing less than a crisis. Increased competition, along with intensified customer scrutiny, was forcing Wainwright to either improve quality or lose its competitive stature. In the face of this challenge, the employees of the company, led by CEO Arthur D. Wainwright, decided to make radical changes. It was clear that business as usual with a few minor improvements would not save the company. What Wainwright needed was an entire new philosophy of doing business based on quality and total customer satisfaction.

To determine how to achieve this objective, Wainwright used the criteria for the Malcolm Baldrige award as a road map. Drawing input from all levels of the company, the top management team led the process by setting goals, developing implementation strategies, and establishing key quality standards. Initially, the company emphasized three principles: employee empowerment, customer satisfaction, and continuous improvement. As a creative way of demonstrating the importance of working together, the company adopted the duck as its mascot, based on the fact that ducks fly in formation as a means of supporting one another in flight. In addition, whenever a duck falls out of formation, it suddenly feels the drag and resistance of trying to fly alone and quickly returns to the flock. Wainwright used this analogy to support the concepts of teamwork and employee empowerment, which were integral parts of the company's quality improvement efforts.

Along its journey toward improved quality, a number of specific initiatives were implemented. Lean manufacturing, statistical process control, computer-aided design, cross-training, profit sharing, and quality-minded manufacturing initiatives were put in place. Special emphasis was placed on training and benchmarking. Since it initiated its quality program, the company has spent up to 7% of its annual payroll on training. To demonstrate its resolve in this area, the company has made training an important criterion for employee advancement. Wainwright has benchmarked against a number of companies, including firms in the textiles, chemical, and electronics industries. For instance, after studying Milliken & Company, a previous Baldrige award winner, Wainwright implemented an employee suggestion program that has been very effective.

Along with the changes mentioned previously, Wainwright also has changed its culture to make it

(*continued*)

more egalitarian and quality minded. The employees at Wainwright (including the CEO) now all wear the same uniform, eat in the same cafeteria, and park in the same parking lot. Office walls have literally been torn down and replaced with glass, based on the premise that if the managers can watch the frontline employees work, the frontline employees should be able to watch the managers work, too. As a result of these changes, the managers of the company have become coaches and facilitators rather than supervisors and disciplinarians. This important change has helped facilitate the teamwork atmosphere that is supportive of high quality and total customer satisfaction.

The results of the company's continuous improvement efforts are linked to five strategic indicators: safety, internal customer satisfaction, external customer satisfaction, design quality, and business performance. The status of each of these criteria is tracked by "mission control," a room set aside to document the company's efforts. In mission control, each customer's satisfaction is documented with a plaque, a current monthly satisfaction rating, and a red or green flag that indicates the customer's status relative to objectives.

As a result of these initiatives, Wainwright has met the challenge. It has not only survived but has also emerged as an industry leader. The company has earned the status of preferred supplier to a growing number of quality-conscious customers and has received special recognition from General Motors, Ford, and IBM-Rochester. The goal of Six Sigma quality is being pursued. Perhaps most important, in the last decade, overall customer satisfaction has increased from 84% to 95%, and the company's market share, revenues, and profits are at record levels. Ironically, the company was one of the recipients of the Malcolm Baldrige award, the very award against which the company benchmarked in its early days of quality improvement.

Discussion Questions

1. In its pursuit of improved quality, Wainwright emphasized two sets of initiatives: one based on improvements in its manufacturing operations (e.g., just-in-time manufacturing, computer-aided design) and the other based on human resource management (e.g., employee empowerment, profit sharing). Why was it necessary for Wainwright to emphasize both of these sets of initiatives? How are they related?

2. What is an egalitarian culture? How does the development of an egalitarian culture help a company like Wainwright Industries become more quality minded?

3. Although quality is important for every product or service, it may be particularly important for the precision auto parts industry. Do you agree with this statement? Why or why not?

Designing and Assuring Quality

Much of the traditional approach to quality was reactive and after the fact. We have learned through experience that you can ensure quality only through the proper design of products and services. The basis for assuring quality is strategic planning that prioritizes and plans quality improvement. The question is this: "If we want to achieve our goals, how are we going to get there?"

The voice of the customer is key in designing products. We must learn how to gather information about the customer. In Chapter 5, you will learn the tools used by firms who know their customers.

By benchmarking with other firms and competitors, we learn the voice of the market. To stay ahead, a firm must know what is happening around it. This provides a logical progression from average, to market leader, to world-class firm.

We then focus on designing products and services. Once we know what the customers want, how do we design goods and processes that will satisfy these wants?

Part of designing and assuring quality is the ability to deliver products to the customer. Thus supply chain management has become a key link in providing top-quality service.

Strategic Quality Planning

Chapter Objectives

After completing this chapter, you should be able to:

1. Understand the differences between strategy content and process.
2. Discuss strategy content and strategic considerations in quality.
3. Analyze quality costs.
4. Understand the role of quality in the competitiveness of the firms.
5. Plan quality improvement using Hoshin planning.

Quality is strategic. This may seem somewhat obvious, but the actions of companies implementing quality measures often obscure this fact. This is especially true when a company is in a reactive mode and does not use effective planning. In this chapter, we discuss important aspects of strategic quality planning. Strategic planning has two important dimensions: *content* and *process*. Strategy content answers the question of what is to be contained in the strategic plan. Strategy process consists of the steps used to develop the strategy.

In this chapter, we first discuss content and then process. Finally, we look at quality results and whether quality has been shown to yield bottom-line results along the supply chain.

STRATEGY CONTENT

Why is quality planning important? As we have discussed in previous chapters, quality improvement is a planned managerial activity. As shown in this chapter, quality improvement involves identifying potential improvements, prioritizing potential areas for improvement, and planning the implementation of projects and improvements.

What are the content variables that should be included in strategic quality planning? Among the variables we discuss are time, leadership, quality costs, generic strategies (cost, differentiation, and focus), order winners, and quality as a core competency. These content variables outline key considerations when developing a strategic plan. These considerations are either explicitly or implicitly addressed in the strategic planning processes discussed later in the chapter.

THE IMPORTANCE OF TIME IN QUALITY IMPROVEMENT

Real-life experience shows that time is a key variable in improving quality. There are two aspects of time: the time it takes to achieve business goals as a result of quality and the speed at which companies improve. A major study of best quality-related practices undertaken by Ernst and Young was critical of total quality management (TQM) programs for not providing bottom-line results. At the same time, the Ernst and Young study advocated the *gradual* implementation of TQM. A comprehensive study by the U.S. General Accounting Office[1] stated that, on average, 3.5 years were required for companies to begin to see significant results from quality improvement programs. In a study of the U.S. auto industry, Narasimhan, Ghosh, and Mendez[2] found a 2.26-year lag between quality improvement and customer recognition of quality improvement. Shingo[3] stated that 25 years were required for Toyota Motor Company to achieve significant improvement and that this time could be reduced to 10 years for competitors. Deming[4] consistently stated that continuous quality improvement was a slow process that required commitment of resources and time. A review of these studies and writings suggests that time is an important variable to consider when managing successful quality improvement programs. Time is also an important component of strategy. Strategic planning implies planning for the long term. Thus strategic planning is important for continuous quality improvement.

Firms will seek and attempt to attain rapid quality improvement in order to obtain the benefits associated with improved quality, such as greater market share and increased sales. However, setting short-term goals for higher quality levels and managing toward those goals actually may prove detrimental to the firm. Managerial action that will lead to an optimal rate of quality improvement requires an understanding of the effects of rapid quality improvement. A study by Foster and Adam[5] focused on this issue of speed of quality improvement. Although their findings were preliminary, in a case study of five plants in one company, they found those plants that improved quality conformance more quickly did not see costs improve as much as plants that improved more slowly. How could this be? Let's examine this issue more closely.

We call one of the approaches that some managers use the "management by dictate" model. Using management by dictate, we set numeric goals for the coming year. For example, top management might say, "I want to see a 50% reduction in defects during the coming year." Thus a numerical goal has been put in place for lower-level managers to meet. This is analogous to what Deming (discussed in Chapter 2) referred to as creating goals and not providing systems to achieve the goals. According to Donald Wheeler, a quality expert, when goals such as these are set, one of three things will occur:

1. People will achieve the goals and positive results.
2. People will distort the data.
3. People will distort the system.

Achieving the goals is what management hopes will occur. Management truly wants to think that a goal can be attained without providing systems. Distorting the data may range from creative "cooking of the data" to finding honest data that shed the best light on the system in question. Distorting the system also can occur. For example, if we set a goal for defect reduction, we can define defects as those occurring in the final inspection. We can then implement

[1]U.S. General Accounting Office, "Management Practices: U.S. Companies Improve Performance through Quality Efforts" (Washington, DC: GAO Report to the Honorable Don Ritter, House of Representatives, 1991).
[2]Narasimhan, R., Ghosh, S., and Mendez, D., "A Dynamic Model of Product Quality and Pricing Decision on Sales Response," *Decision Sciences* 24, 5 (1993): 893–908.
[3]Shingo, S., Foreword in *Study of Toyota Production System from Industrial Engineering Viewpoint* (Tokyo: Japan Management Association, 1989).
[4]Deming, W. E., *Out of the Crisis* (Boston: MIT/CAES, 1986).
[5]Foster, S. T., and Adam, E. E., "Examining the Impact of Speed of Quality Improvement on Quality-Related Costs," *Decision Sciences* 27, 4 (1996): 623–646.

A CLOSER LOOK AT QUALITY 4-1   Bad Measurement Systems Result in Poor Outcomes[6]

When measurement systems are tied to performance ratings and money, three things can happen: The system can accurately measure good performance and all is well; people can distort the data; or people can distort the system. Sadly, the latter two are often unintended consequences of performance measurement systems.

Recently, performance measures have been implemented in education. Some of the unintended outcomes included the following:

Changing answers on standardized tests: Teachers in California, Illinois, and Michigan were caught changing student's answers.

Coaching during exams: Instructors helped students with their standard tests in Massachusetts, Nevada, and Washington.

Handing out tests in advance: This occurred in Pennsylvania and Wisconsin.

Not counting weaker students: Among the states with this dubious distinction were New York, Tennessee, and Texas.

There are other industries besides education where performance measures are resulting in unintended outcomes:

Because of ranking systems emphasizing placement rates and GMAT scores, some MBA programs have increased their rankings by decreasing the numbers of students they admit.

A fast food restaurant implemented a "chicken efficiency" ranking by measuring the amount of chicken thrown away. A manager striving to reduce this number started cooking chicken only when it was ordered. The service times were then so slow that the restaurant went out of business.

One company started measuring on-time delivery based on when products were shipped. After this change, customer complaints about late shipments increased by 50%.

An automobile plant manager declared that the only metric of importance was "meeting quotas for shipments of new autos." The problem with this approach is obvious when quality is considered.

When implementing new performance measures, management should be careful. People are smart and they will "work the system."

---

[6]Based on Grow, B., "A Spate of Cheating—by Teachers," *Bloomberg BusinessWeek* (5 July, 2004): 94–95; Anon, "When Measurement Goes Bad, *American Management Association* (5 October 2010).

---

a more rigorous in-process inspection that will eliminate defects before they arrive at final inspection. Voilà! A simultaneous reduction in defects and increase in costs. This is an example of distorting the system. A Closer Look at Quality 4-1 discusses an example of how measurement systems can be distorted.

The key, then, is for firms to put in place a process that will allow learning to occur. The plan–do–check–act cycle discussed in Chapter 1 allows for organizational learning and freezing of learning to take place. Management looking for a quick fix to long-term problems probably will not be too satisfied with this fact.

We still do not know the optimal time for learning to take place. Indeed, there are stories of companies that have had the capacity to achieve rapid improvement. However, one suspects that each of these companies also provided enormous amounts of support for employees to achieve the goals. Providing such an infrastructure is the work of management because they have the budget and authority to do it.

LEADERSHIP FOR QUALITY

Leadership is a key strategic variable for quality management. A leader organizes, plans, controls, communicates, teaches, advises, and delegates. The existence of a leader implies the existence of a follower. Therefore, the **leading** involves a power-sharing relationship between two or more individuals in which the power is distributed unevenly. For example, the leader will have more monetary and organizational authority than the follower. Thus the leader will need to share authority for the follower to complete work assignments.

Leadership is the process by which a leader influences a group to move toward the attainment of **superordinate goals.** Superordinate goals are those goals that pertain to achieving a higher end that benefits not just the individual but the group. In some organizations, leaders emerge because they are the most powerful or have the dominant voice. Some leaders are selected because they have the highest intellect. This occurs in many educational organizations in which the leaders are chosen on the basis of the number of articles written or status within an academic field. In still other organizations, leaders are appointed. This can be by popular voice, by a board of directors, or by upper management.

For followers to have power, leadership must share its power. As a result, leadership is about the sharing of power. This power takes many forms:

Power of expertise. Sometimes a leader has special knowledge (or is perceived to have special knowledge). Professors are leaders in the classroom because they have knowledge that they are sharing with the students. This type of power tends to have very narrow parameters in that the followers will follow only within the confines of the leader's expertise.

Reward power. If a leader has rewards that he or she can bestow on subordinates in return for some desirable action, the leader has reward power. This is often the case in the granting of raises, promotions, rewards, recognition, or a variety of other incentives. Prior to the fall of communism in Russia, leaders often used this mechanism to maintain their authority. Perks and privileges came to those who favored the party bosses.

Coercive power. If the leader has power to punish the follower for not following rules or guidelines, the leader has coercive power. Such power often results in unintended responses, such as the follower giving up or circumventing the leader's rule surreptitiously. Many times, the follower will rebel and attempt to even the power relationship. In the 1920s, in response to unions, managers used police powers to squash unions. This resulted in violent responses from the unions.

Referent power. If a leader is charismatic or charming, and is followed because he or she is liked, the leader has referent power. A case of referent power is the mentor who is admired by his or her protégés who want to be like the mentor. Often people will follow referent leaders on the basis of reputation alone, imbuing the referent leader with qualities the leader may or may not possess. John Kennedy was well liked by those around him. He also was viewed as charismatic and intelligent. This made people want to follow him.

Legitimate power. As a result of the positions that different people hold within an organization, the manager has the obligation to request things of subordinates, and the subordinates have the duty to comply with the request. This is the exercise of legitimate power. Legitimate power comes with the position. It has certain responsibilities and authorities. A newly appointed leader may have to rely on this positional authority in the early part of his or her tenure as a leader.

Leadership Dimensions

We have discussed leadership types. To better understand leaders, we now discuss leadership dimensions. These leadership dimensions help to define the effectiveness of leaders. One dimension of leadership is the **trait dimension.**

TABLE 4-1	Leader Skills		
Phase 1: Knowledge	**Phase 2: Communication**	**Phase 3: Planning**	**Phase 4: Vision**
Acceptance of diversity	Assertiveness	Structuring (for task accomplishment)	Assessing the climate (internal and external)
Developing competence	Conflict management	Decision making	Identifying opportunities
Health/wellness	Team building	Evaluation skills	
Learning style	Trust building	Task and time management	
Time management	Motivating others		
Ethics	Recruiting others		
Risk taking	Effective speaking		
Coping skills	Effective writing		
	Effective listening		
	Image building		

Another dimension of leadership research has to do with **leader skills.** For example, the grid in Table 4-1 shows a set of skills that effective leaders exhibit. Four important skills for leaders are knowledge, communication, planning, and vision. The different phases identify skill sets that are needed by managers.

In Phase 1, knowledge helps the leader accept risk and moderate the stress associated with the risk by using coping mechanisms or healthy outlets. In Phase 2, the leader must be able to communicate with other leaders and subordinates. In Phase 3, the leader must be able to plan and make decisions. Finally, in Phase 4, the leader must be able to formulate a coherent vision of the future toward which to plan.

Employees must trust that if they make recommendations for improvement, the recommendations will be taken seriously and considered for implementation by management. *Nothing can damage a quality improvement effort faster than management's failure to consider implementing changes that employees recommend.* Employees may begin to think "nothing will really change." Quality managers who find themselves in companies not implementing a majority of employee suggestions need to work to increase the percentage.

Another important attribute of quality managers is *commitment over the long term.* Too many leaders enter quality improvement efforts with the expectation that things will improve overnight. As we have discussed, quality management is hard, painstaking, slow work. Often, victories in quality are rare and should be celebrated—especially at first. GfK Custom Research Incorporated (CRI), the small service company that won a Malcolm Baldrige award, has weekly employee celebrations at which the employees share good news and give each other pats on the back. Management of CRI admits that sometimes reasons for the pats on the back are difficult to find. However, the positive reinforcement has been central to their improvement of business results and customer service.

Commitment to quality means that leaders provide funding, slack time, and resources for quality improvement efforts to be successful. This commitment is measured in decades, not quarters or budget cycles. One company embarked on an expensive training process, only to throw all its past efforts away by deciding to cut training in a budget cycle two years later. At last glance, this company's quality and process improvement efforts had all but disappeared.

As we see in the case of Solectron (Quality Highlight 4-1), the leadership of its CEO is key to its success. To foster a well-run workplace, leaders must be able to resolve conflict effectively.

QUALITY HIGHLIGHT 4-1   Solectron Corporation

www.flextronics.com

Solectron Corporation, a subsidiary of Flextronics is an independent producer of high-tech manufacturing services. This manufacturing includes the assembly of printed circuit boards and subsystems for computer makers and electronics product producers. In addition, Solectron provides system-level assembly services, such as PC and mainframe computer assembly. Activities performed by Solectron include design, production, assembly, consultation, and testing. Solectron has achieved outstanding results because of its strategic planning system and the personal leadership provided by its management.

By focusing on customer satisfaction, exploiting advanced manufacturing technology, and stressing continuous improvement in operations and service, the company has reached high levels of quality and efficiency, making it best-in-class and a world leader in production. Solectron is an American company that has competed successfully in international markets. Many competitors of Solectron are now customers because they found it was better to outsource to Solectron than to produce many products in-house. In addition, about 90% of all new work comes from returning satisfied customers.

Assessing Customer Needs

Solectron focused its planning processes on the customer. Solectron does not compete with its customers in designing and marketing products. Although it offers an original equipment manufacturers (OEM) design service, usually the company produces to its customers' specifications and designs. As a result of understanding its customers, the company develops strategies to meet its customers' requirements in the areas of service, quality, and cost. Solectron continually monitors customer satisfaction levels and conducts exhaustive research on competitors and markets.

Surveys of customers are conducted on a weekly basis. The results of these surveys go directly to the CEO, who reviews the information with top management in one of three weekly meetings on quality-related issues. The survey information is used to grade the performance of each of Solectron's nine divisions.

Culture of Continuous Improvement

Solectron has developed a culture that reinforces continuous improvement. Developing this culture has required arduous strategic planning. A top management team is involved in an effort to revitalize American manufacturing through quality. This team sets corporate targets and then works with teams to set supporting goals in functional areas. The company has pursued several strategies to achieve a high-energy, customer-focused workforce. These strategies include a strong family orientation, an effective communication system, and an innovative reward and recognition program. These strategies have helped the company to weather the rapid growth it has experienced. Management is participative with a focus on coaching and a high degree of autonomy for workers. The team-focused approach to employee involvement relies on training and mentorship to overcome barriers to a multilingual workforce with more than 20 ethnic backgrounds.

Each Solectron customer is served by two teams. These teams ensure quality performance and on-time delivery. A project planning team is involved in planning, scheduling, and defining customer requirements. A quality control team meets weekly to monitor and evaluate production with the aim of preventing potential problems before they occur.

The Best and Getting Better

Solectron uses a comprehensive information system, organized in a customized relational database that allows constant monitoring of internal quality performance and process control indicators. Key performance data are charted in all departments. Employees are trained and empowered to take corrective action.

Solectron works with suppliers to improve the quality and reliability of incoming components and subassemblies. Statistical process control (SPC) charts track and review results daily. These results

(continued)

are recorded on an automated SPC database. Division managers and the corporate quality director track these results on a daily basis. The company is partnering with its suppliers to improve design quality as a future strategic emphasis.

Solectron performs strategic planning in selecting its future technological choices. Investments in advanced technologies are guided by an evaluation of the customer's future requirements and top management's emphasis on enhancing manufacturing capability. All this effort is paying off for Solectron. As indicated by its chief quality measure, customer satisfaction, the company has won scores of superior performance awards in recent years. After a quality audit, a major customer rated Solectron as the "best contract manufacturer of electronic assemblies in the U.S."

QUALITY AND ETHICS

Quality appears to be good business. Quality is also good ethics. It is unethical to ship defective products knowingly to a customer. Reliable products and low defect rates reflect an ethical approach of management's care for its customers. This ethic is stated in the well-known mission statement of a New Bedford, Massachusetts, shipbuilder: "We build good ships. At a profit if we can, at a loss if we must. But we build good ships."

Companies focusing on their customers often develop a set of ethics that includes valuing employees. This is reflected in education, training, health, wellness, and compensation programs that show empathy for the employees. Increasingly, environmental friendliness is seen as an ethical concern. As a result, more companies are implementing recycling programs and making efforts to improve environmental practices.

Good quality management is good ethics. Would we want to knowingly provide poor service or ship bad product? J. R. Simplot made a promise to Ray Kroc at McDonald's that McDonald's would never run out of French fries. With a handshake, they sealed their deal, and Simplot has kept his promise.

In a study of service companies, Babbar[7] found that unethical conduct resulted in tarnished customer experiences and customer dissatisfaction, and in customer defections.

Integrity gets down to honesty. Are we honest with our customers, employees, colleagues, family members, and ourselves? This must be the basis for business. There is not a new business model that obviates the need for integrity.

QUALITY AS A STRATEGY

In Chapter 1, we raised the question of whether quality is sufficient to win orders in the marketplace. As you will recall, we stated that although quality can still win orders in some markets, in many markets quality has become an order qualifier. This means that high-quality production is an essential ingredient for participation in the market. In Chapter 3, we discussed research showing that quality is still an effective tool for successfully exporting in the international market.

We now discuss quality as a strategy from the perspective of generic strategies. These generic strategies are *cost, differentiation*, and *focus*.

Costs of Quality

One of the generic means of competing is cost. Traditionally, this meant the lowest-priced items in the industry. Many companies compete on cost (e.g., Kmart). New definitions of cost are expansive, considering the summation of costs over the life of a product. They include service, maintenance, and operating costs for the product. For example, it is recognized that ink-jet color

[7]Babbar, S., "Teaching Ethics for Quality as an Innovation in a Core Operations Management Course," *Decision Sciences Journal of Innovative Education* 8, 2 (2010): 14–19.

TABLE 4-2	Prevention Costs

The cost of setting up, planning, and maintaining a documented quality system
Quality planning: establishing production process conformance to design specification procedures, and designing of test procedures and test equipment
Quality and process engineering (including preventive maintenance)
Calibration of quality-related production equipment
Supplier quality assurance
Supplier assessment
All training
Robust design
Defect data analysis for corrective action purposes
Time spent on quality system audits

computer printers are relatively inexpensive to purchase. However, owners of these machines have found that the color cartridges dry up rapidly, and the replacement costs for the cartridges are quite high. As we discuss later, the life-cycle costs for many products may be staggering when environmental costs are considered. In this section, we discuss the cost of quality and how quality can help decrease the cost of doing business.

There are two broad categories of cost: costs due to poor quality and costs associated with improving quality. At a minimum, management must understand these costs to formulate policy concerning quality improvement. In addition, Taguchi and others have provided insights into the issue of quality costs. As an example, the title of the classic book by Crosby, *Quality Is Free*, reveals an interest in the costs of quality.

PAF Paradigm

The **PAF paradigm**[8] translates quality costs into three broad categories, which are then subdivided into other categories. The three categories are prevention, appraisal, and failure costs (hence the acronym PAF).

Prevention costs are those costs associated with preventing defects and imperfections from occurring. Prevention costs are the most subjective of the three categories of costs. Prevention costs include costs such as training, quality planning, process engineering, and other costs associated with ensuring quality beforehand (see Table 4-2).

Two caveats associated with the collection of quality-related costs include (1) there may be some debate as to whether these costs are all related to quality and (2) persons who work in prevention often do not keep accurate records of all costs.

Appraisal costs are associated with the direct costs of measuring quality. They can include a variety of activities such as lab testing, inspection, test equipment and materials, losses because of destructive tests, and costs associated with assessments for ISO 9000 or quality awards (see Table 4-3).

These costs have undergone a fundamental change as U.S. companies have progressed in quality. For example, these costs were traditionally uncomplicated to assess because appraisal was performed by a centralized quality control function. The concept of in-process inspection has made it difficult to measure appraisal costs accurately. In addition, appraisal and auditing costs have been impacted by assessment activities associated with ISO 9000 and the Malcolm Baldrige award as companies have undertaken these assessment programs.

---

[8]For a more in-depth discussion of quality-related costs, see Carson, J. K., "Quality Costing: A Practical Approach," *International Journal of Quality and Reliability Management* 3, 1 (1986): 54–65; Foster, S., "An Examination of the Relationship between Conformance and Quality Related Costs," *International Journal of Quality and Reliability Management* 13, 4 (1996): 50–63; and Williams, A., Vander Wiele, A., and Dale, B., "On Quality Costing: A Management Review," *International Journal of Management and Reviews*, 1, 4 (1999): 441–460.

TABLE 4-3	Appraisal Costs

Laboratory acceptance testing
Inspection and tests by inspectors
Inspection and tests by noninspectors
Setup for inspection and test
Inspection and test materials
Product quality audits
Review of test and inspection data
On-site performance tests
Internal test and release
Evaluation of materials and spares
Supplier monitoring
ISO 9000:2015 qualification activities
Quality award assessments

TABLE 4-4	Failure Costs	
Internal Failure Costs		**External Failure Costs**
Cost of troubleshooting		Lost production because of labor availability problems (this refers to idle time brought about by failure to plan labor efficiently)
Reinspection of stocks after defect detection		
Disruption of production schedules		Lost production caused by system problems (i.e., material or instructions not available; cost of idle time only)
Complaint handling and replacements plus extra time with customers		
Warranty (taking care not to duplicate previous item)		Concessions (design and engineering time)
Cost of holding higher levels of stock as a buffer against quality failure		Process waste (including the waste commonly regarded as unavoidable)
Cost of corrective maintenance to plant		Cost of product scrapped at product audit
Cost of corrective action to product (redesign, repair)		Cost associated with disposition of all scrap

Failure costs are roughly categorized into two areas of costs: internal failure costs and external failure costs. **Internal failure costs** are those associated with online failure, whereas **external failure costs** are associated with product failure after the production process. This includes failure after the customer takes possession of the product (see Table 4-4).

Accounting for Quality-Related Costs

One of the impediments to the collection of quality cost data has been the lack of acceptable accounting standards for these costs. For example, the standard accounting definition for quality is "meeting specifications." This narrow definition limits organizations desiring to quantify and measure customer requirements as a means of improving service to the customer. A reason for this is that accounting rules require definitions that are not open-ended or open to alternative interpretations.

EXAMPLE 4-1	Quality Costs in Action

Problem: Macaluso's manufacturing company has gathered the following quality-related costs. You are hired as a consultant to evaluate these costs and to make recommendations to management. Compute the ratios of prevention and appraisal costs to failure costs.

Annual Quality Costs		
Failure costs		
Defective products	$	5,276
Engineered scrap		17,265
Nonengineered scrap		125,274
Consumer adjustments		623,980
Downgrading products		1,430,678
Lost goodwill		Not evaluated
Customer policy changes		Not evaluated
TOTAL		2,202,473
Appraisal costs		
Receiving inspection	$	35,765
Line 1 inspection		42,234
Line 2 inspection		53,567
Spot checking		63,766
TOTAL		195,332
Prevention costs		
Quality training	$	14,500
Process engineering		
Corporate		125,678
Plant		39,124
Product redesign		16,422
TOTAL		195,724
Grand total		2,593,529

Solution: Ratio of appraisal to failure costs:

$$195,332/2,202,473 = .0887$$

Ratio of prevention to failure costs:

$$195,724/2,202,473 = .0889$$

Ratio of prevention and appraisal to failure costs:

$$(195,332 + 195,724)/2,202,473 = .1776$$

Proportion of total quality costs:

Prevention: $195,724/2,593,529 = .0755$
Appraisal: $195,332/2,593,529 = .0753$
Failure: $2,202,473/2,593,529 = .8492$

This analysis shows that failure costs are very high compared with the prevention and appraisal costs. Increasing prevention and appraisal activities (and costs) could result in a significant decrease in failure costs.

Lundvall–Juran Quality Cost Model

The PAF categorization of costs is a useful way of understanding costs. Using the law of diminishing marginal returns, quality costs can be modeled to show the trade-offs between these costs. This trade-off model, called the *Lundvall–Juran model*, is shown in Figure 4-1.

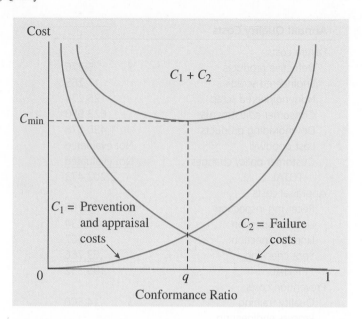

FIGURE 4-1   Lundvall–Juran Model

The Lundvall–Juran model is a simple economic model. It states that as expenditures in prevention and appraisal activities increase, quality conformance should increase. For example, the more we spend on training and developing our employees, the more benefit we should get. As conformance improves, failure costs will lessen as well. This is an interesting case because if these statements are true, there should be an economic quality level that minimizes quality-related costs, and this flies in the face of the idea of continuous improvement proposed by Deming and others.

Differentiation through Quality

Think of a product you have been desiring for some time that is priced significantly above the average market price for such a product. It might be a very expensive, brand-name cell phone or TV that you want because of its special appeal. Chances are that such a product benefits from differentiation. A Harley-Davidson motorcycle is an example of a product that is priced far above the average price for a motorcycle, yet dealers seem to have trouble keeping enough of them in stock. Differentiation is achieved by a competitor if the consumer *perceives* the product or service to be unique in an important way. Neiman-Marcus, the retailer, charges many times the prices charged by its competitors for some products. A Rolex watch or iPhone invests the owner with a certain status that other products do not. These are examples of differentiated products.

In the past, Japanese automakers differentiated their products based on mileage and quality. The quality aspect allowed Japanese automakers to gain significant market share in the United States. Eventually, U.S. automakers closed the quality gap sufficiently so that the Japanese could no longer differentiate on quality. This is the case in many markets. It is increasingly difficult to differentiate products based on quality alone. However, there is still much room to differentiate based on service to the customer in many markets.

Focus through Quality

The third generic strategy is to focus the product. For example, think of a product that is particularly regional or is marketed to a particular segment of the population. This limited customer group or segment of the market is the object of the focus strategy. As the baby-boom generation ages, many more companies are segmenting products that can be marketed to this age group.

For example, more fitness clubs for seniors are springing up around the country. Such a focus strategy can be very profitable. GfK Custom Research Incorporated reports that they reduced the number of customers they served by 40% while at the same time doubling profits. They found that by focusing on only their very large clients for advertising services, they were able to get more business with these clients and simultaneously achieve higher service ratings.

The three generic strategies of cost, differentiation, and focus have been identified as important strategic decisions. A company that emphasizes cost will use different approaches to producing quality products than will a company that emphasizes differentiation or focus.

Order Winners

Terry Hill[9] of the London Business School defined a process for setting strategy that is centered on the identification of the order-winning criterion (OWC). Although the OWC is generally associated with manufacturing strategy, the same concept can be applied to service strategy.

Table 4-5 provides an overview of the planning framework defined by Terry Hill. This framework addresses several of the problems occurring in manufacturing. At times, there is a mismatch or misalignment between corporate objectives and decisions and operational subplans. A close relationship exists between the Hill model and generic strategies that we have discussed. First, the organization determines its competitive priorities and defines how it wins orders in the marketplace. For example, if the company wins orders based on focusing on small, niche markets, marketing strategies will be developed to market a wide variety of specialized products. At the same time, this agreement on order winners allows the manufacturing people to make process choices and infrastructural decisions that support wide variety. The process choice then might be a flexible manufacturing system using short setup and change-over times.

The key to the Hill model is reaching consensus on the OWC. The process for doing this involves segmenting the business into smaller markets that can each be identified with an order-winning criterion. This provides an understanding of the markets the company is serving. Products are chosen for each market, and marketing provides sales forecasts for the identified markets. Strategic debate then occurs, resulting in the selection of an OWC. From this, manufacturing strategy is formulated.

TABLE 4-5	Hill's Strategy Framework			
Corporate Objectives	**Marketing Strategy**	**How Do Products Win Orders in the Marketplace?**	**Manufacturing Strategy**	
			Process Choice	**Infrastructure**
Growth	Product markets and segments	Price	Choice of alternative processes	Function support
Survival		Quality		Manufacturing planning and control systems
Profit	Range	Delivery speed reliability	Trade-offs embodied in the process choice	Quality assurance and control
Return on investment	Mix	Demand increases	Process positioning	
Other financial measures	Volumes	Color range	Capacity size timing location	Manufacturing systems engineering
	Standardization versus customization	Product range	Role of inventory in the process configuration	Clerical procedures
	Level of innovation	Design leadership		Payment systems
	Leader versus follower alternatives	Technical support being supplied		Work structuring
				Organizational structure

Source: Terry J. Hill (2000) *Manufacturing Strategy*, (Homewood, IL: Irwin, 2000). IBSN: 0256 230722. Copyright © 2000 by McGraw-Hill Education. Reprinted with permission.

---

[9]Hill, T. J., *Manufacturing Strategy* (Homewood, IL: Irwin, 2000).

Quality as a Core Competency

A core competency has three aspects:

1. It helps a company access markets.
2. It benefits customers.
3. It is difficult for other firms to imitate.

Using this definition of competency, quality—in and of itself—probably is not a core competency. However, for firms operating in rapidly evolving markets or industries, the capability to change can be more important than the actual changing technology of the moment. Hence organizations producing outstanding products or services with a good understanding of processes are better positioned to operate in the changing market because they can introduce new products rapidly and with fewer quality-related holdups. Therefore, core competency is built on the foundation of a long-term commitment to quality and continual process improvement.

QUALITY STRATEGY PROCESS

For the most part, we have been discussing strategy content so far in this chapter. *Content* refers to the variables, definitions, components, and concepts that are included in the strategy. With the discussion of the Hill model and core competency, we are now ready to discuss strategy process. *Process* consists of the steps for developing strategy within an organization.

There are many different processes for developing strategy. We highlight a strategic process for firms having little or no experience developing strategy, known as the *forced-choice model*. Afterward, we present a comprehensive strategy development process that has been used in companies with mature quality processes.

Forced-Choice Model

The forced-choice model of strategic planning is one of several strategic planning models that could be adapted to demonstrate integrated quality planning. The forced-choice model is selected here because of its simplicity and its usefulness for firms that are beginning strategic planning. The forced-choice model is generic and is used simply for explanation purposes. It is simple when compared with other strategic planning models that are generally more complicated. Figure 4-2 provides an outline of the forced-choice strategic planning model.

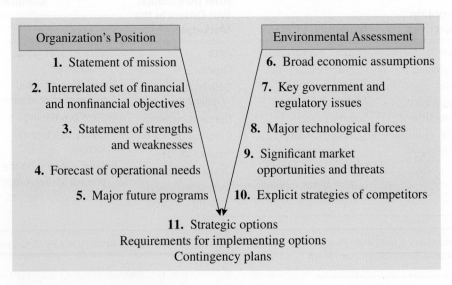

Organization's Position	Environmental Assessment
1. Statement of mission	6. Broad economic assumptions
2. Interrelated set of financial and nonfinancial objectives	7. Key government and regulatory issues
3. Statement of strengths and weaknesses	8. Major technological forces
4. Forecast of operational needs	9. Significant market opportunities and threats
5. Major future programs	10. Explicit strategies of competitors

11. Strategic options
Requirements for implementing options
Contingency plans

FIGURE 4-2 Forced-Choice Model

The forced-choice model is particularly useful for companies that are relatively inexperienced in strategic planning. The process begins by sequestering 6 to 12 members of upper management at a retreat. An organizational assessment is performed to identify strengths and weaknesses within the firm. Next, management performs an environmental assessment to evaluate the company's relative position in the marketplace. In the wrap-up session, alternative strategies are developed by executives.

DEPLOYING QUALITY (HOSHIN KANRI)

Hoshin is Japanese for a *compass*, a *course*, a *policy*, or a *plan*. This is to indicate a vision or purpose to an existence. *Kanri* refers to *management control*. In English, this is generally referred to as *policy deployment*. Hoshin has been used in Japan since the 1960s as a means of implementing policy. Implicit in the Hoshin Kanri (or Hoshin, for short) is the use of the basic seven tools of quality (discussed in Chapter 10), the new tools of quality, and quality function deployment.

In the Hoshin process, the company develops a three- to five-year plan, and senior executives develop the current year's Hoshin objectives. Then the process of catchball occurs. **Catchball** is the term used to describe the interactive nature of the **Hoshin planning process.** Catchball involves reporting from teams and feedback from management. The development of the Hoshin plan results in the cascading of action plans that are designed to achieve corporate goals (see A Closer Look at Quality 4-2).

A CLOSER LOOK AT QUALITY 4-2   A Mature Strategic Planning Process

The strategic planning process contains quality concerns at every step of the process. XYZ Corporation is a nationally known organization that has been very successful in implementing quality strategy throughout the entire organization. (The company identity is disguised because of confidentiality reasons.) The company uses an annual strategy development cycle. However, part of the annual cycle involves "roll-ups" of 5-year and 10-year planning projections. The strategic planning process for XYZ is coguided by the CFO and vice president of marketing, under direction of the corporate CEO.

As shown in Figure 4-3, the planning process begins with an annual management retreat in October to review the current year's mission statement, vision statement, values statement, and strategy. Using professional facilitators, the strategic management team reviews the current year's performance against projections and makes adjustments to the current year's plan. Once this is completed, the mission, vision, and values are reviewed and updated. Year-to-year revisions in these statements generally have been incremental and adaptive as the market has changed over the years. Another major undertaking during the management meeting is the review of key customer requirements and key business factors for the company. Once this is completed, progress against these factors is reviewed.

The second step in the process occurs during the fall strategic planning meeting and is finalized during the following months. This step involves forecasting market demand and reassessing the position of XYZ in the industry. During this step in the process, discussion of core competencies occurs, and the company develops visions and expectations for each of its product lines. Revenue projections are made by product line, and plans are made to extend core competencies.

The third step in the XYZ strategic planning process is an assessment of future markets in each of the product divisions. It occurs in January and involves an analysis of capacity needs for the coming year based on projections, changes in customer needs, technological needs assessment, profiling of major competitors, assessment of the customers of major competitors, and development of new marketing

(continued)

Prepare for next planning cycle

Step 1
Mission, vision, values,
and current strategy

Step 2
Market
assessment

Step 3
Set goals by assessing
future markets

Step 4
Develop broad goals and
plans by product line

Step 5
Review and monitor
implementation of strategic plan

FIGURE 4-3 Mature Strategic Planning
Process

plans. Based on these marketing plans, information technology and operations decisions are made concerning capital investments for the coming year.

The fourth step involves the development of broad goals and plans by product line. These plans are used to develop separate missions, visions, values, and plans by product line on a very broad basis. Key business factors and key customer requirements are reviewed and updated at this point as management has evaluated formalized input from the customers. These plans are reviewed by upper management to ensure alignment with overall corporate goals. This step generally occurs during the first quarter of the year.

The fifth step is to develop the coming year's annual strategic plan. This plan includes market and product projections, plant and equipment projections, labor projections, projections of needed competencies and capabilities, as well as the development of Hoshin plans. Hoshin plans are deployment plans for the XYZ corporate objectives.

At this point, we should mention that XYZ Corporation has many metrics, measures, and indicators in place to monitor performance as it relates to the strategic business plan. These measures and indicators, which are quality-related, financial, delivery-related, and so forth, are monitored by management on a daily basis using an enterprise resource planning (ERP) system. Indicators relating to key business factors are also monitored by the ERP. Feedback from the quarterly customer surveys is used to update key customer requirements.

Finally, the last stage of the annual strategic planning process is a review of the strategic planning process to see where potential improvement can be made. Once goals have been completed for the coming year, corporate, divisional, and departmental meetings are held to ensure that the corporate plan is distributed and discussed with employees at all levels.

Although this is a thumbnail sketch of a strategic planning process, the management of XYZ Corporation feels strongly that this process has set the stage for its global success. Financial results have been impressive for the company.

As shown in Figure 4-4, functional managers also should develop Hoshins in conjunction with upper management. This results in the development of specific plans for action and post-implementation review of Hoshins to evaluate the success of the process.

DOES QUALITY LEAD TO BETTER BUSINESS RESULTS?

One of the most common questions posed by executives seeking improvement is this: "Will this quality effort pay off?" An answer to this question was provided by W. Edwards Deming with the Deming value chain, which we consider in Chapter 1. Deming proposed a theoretical basis for concluding that quality will pay off.

The effects of quality on business results are mixed; some firms have been wildly successful with their quality efforts, and other companies have been unsuccessful in gaining bottom-line results. There are two primary reasons for this. *First, many variables affect profitability besides quality.* You might produce the highest-quality but obsolete product in the world. If you produce a high-quality product or service that no one wants to buy, quality management systems likely will not save you. Macroeconomic factors, such as the recession–boom business cycle, affect profitability. American Motors products of the early 1980s were given awards for outstanding design (e.g., the Renault Alliance). At the same time, these products were not well accepted by their customers, and the company went out of business.

Second, many companies implement quality incorrectly. That you can claim you are implementing quality does not guarantee you will be successful. Quality improvement takes a long time, and many firms desire quick returns on investment for quality training programs. When

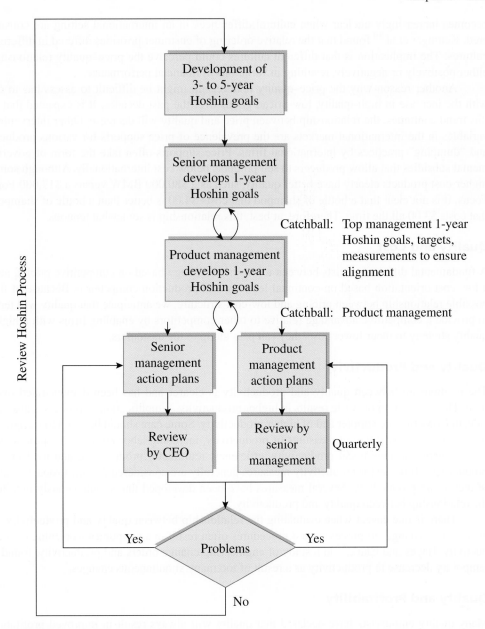

FIGURE 4-4   Hoshin Planning

these returns are slow in coming, the companies give up in midstream and wonder why their quality efforts were ineffective. At the same time, quality programs have been shown to be effective in a variety of cultures and industries when implemented correctly. Hence the mixed results. As a result, we need to understand the relationships between quality and other variables.

Quality and Price

The relationship between price and quality has long been studied. Indeed, the laws of supply and demand lead to a natural ordering of competing products on a price scale such that a superior product would be the most highly priced. Another view is that high price is a psychological enabler allowing perceptions of high quality to result. However, the price–quality relationship becomes increasingly unclear when cultural differences in an international setting are considered. Kettinger et al.[10] found that the relative ordering of customer priorities differed in different cultures. The implication is that different cultures could perceive the price–quality relationship either positively or negatively, resulting in variations in financial performance.

Another reason why the price–quality relationship might be difficult to assess has to do with the increase in high-quality, low-priced goods over the past decades. It is expected that if this trend continues, the relationship between price and quality will decrease. Other intervening variables in the international markets are the prevalence of price supports for various products and "dumping" practices by international firms. Price supports often take the form of governmental subsidies that allow producers to sell products below cost internationally. Although some higher-cost products clearly have better quality, such as a $80,000 BMW versus a $17,000 Ford Focus, it is not clear that a bottle of shampoo that costs $4.00 is better than a bottle of shampoo that costs $3.00 all the time. Therefore, at best, this relationship is somewhat tenuous.

Quality and Cost

A fundamental difference exists between a low-price strategy based on competitive pricing and a low-cost orientation based on continual learning and production competence. Because of the possible relationship between pricing and low-cost structure, we anticipate that quality will tend to provide a competitive advantage relative to other competitors by enabling firms with a high-quality strategy to incur lower costs they can pass along to the customers.

Quality and Productivity

The relationship between quality and productivity is clearer and has been demonstrated over time. The elimination of waste results in higher productivity. Simplification of processes also results in flows that are simpler and of higher productivity. Some care should be taken to recognize that there are many different measures of productivity, including labor productivity, productive use of energy, technological productivity, efficiency, multifactor productivity, and total-factor productivity. Total-factor productivity measures generally are considered the most robust means of measuring productivity. Several measures have been developed that simultaneously monitor the relationship between quality and productivity.[11]

There is one caveat when evaluating the relationship between quality and productivity. It appears that changes to processes and procedures often result in a temporary worsening of productivity. Hayes and Clark,[12] in a study of engineering change orders and productivity, found a temporary decrease in productivity as a result of too many simultaneous changes.

Quality and Profitability

Many quality enthusiasts have declared that quality will always result in improved profitability. They will further state that those cases in which quality does not lead to improved profits are the fault of the offending implementer. There are some facts to substantiate this claim. Every year, the National Institute of Standards and Technology (NIST), the administrator of the Baldrige award, touts the outstanding stock performance of Baldrige winners. In addition, the U.S. General Accounting Office[13] performed a study of 30 Baldrige award winners and found

---

[10]Kettinger, W., Lee, C., and Lee, S., "Global Measures of Information Service Quality: A Cross-National Study," *Decision Sciences* 26, 5 (1995): 569–588.

[11]See Adam, E., Hershauer, J., and Ruch, W., *Productivity and Quality: Measurement as a Basis for Improvement* (Columbia: Research Center, University of Missouri–Columbia, 1986).

[12]Hayes, R., and Clark, K., "Why Some Factories Are More Productive Than Others," *Interfaces* 64 (September–October 1986): 66–73.

[13]U.S. General Accounting Office, "Management Practices: U.S. Companies Improve Performance through Quality Efforts" (Washington, DC: GAO Report to the Honorable Don Ritter, House of Representatives, 1991).

the effects of quality improvement to include improved employee relations, lower cost, greater customer satisfaction, and improved market share. In a study of quality and profitability, Adam[14] found quality improvement in specific firms to be more long term rather than immediate. This makes some intuitive sense because quality improvement may not be recognized by the customers for some time. A study of 41 companies[15] implementing Six Sigma found somewhat mixed results. However, Six Sigma significantly affected free cash flow, earnings before interest, taxes, depreciation, and amortization (EBITDA), and asset turnover. However, it should be stated that high quality is no guarantee of success. Firms must still successfully market, manage cash, and do the many other things that ensure profitability.

Quality and Sustainability

Another strategic imperative receiving increasing attention is the effect of business on the environment. Because of regulatory pressures—both domestic and international—firms realize that they must integrate environmental concerns into their strategic plans.

Companies have to address many environmental issues. Besides the regulatory requirements, firms realize more and more that environmental friendliness is part of being a good corporate citizen. Therefore, tasks such as environmental protection, waste management, product integrity, worker health, government relations, and community relations comprise the environmentally related strategic issues that must be addressed. As a result, firms are implementing quality–based environmental management systems, sometimes referred to as *total quality environmental management* (TQEM). These systems involve a holistic "systems" view of the processes causing environmental degradation. Measurements are implemented that identify indicators of environmental performance. This involves a focus on preventive rather than reactive cleanup.

A trend in companies is to strengthen the link between quality practices and sustainability. We define **sustainability** as the ability to meet the needs of the current generation without compromising the ability of future generations to meet their needs. Most often, this relates to environmental management.

At its core, sustainability has to do with improving environmental performance and reducing waste. This seems consistent with lean and quality management philosophies relating to waste reduction and continual improvement. ISO 14000 links quality and sustainability in a unique way by applying ISO 9000 approaches to improving environmental performance. Although the literature is not clear in linking better environmental performance to enhanced financial performance, some encouraging results have come out of applying teams and continuous improvement methodologies taught in this book to environmental sustainability. For example, firms such as Hewlett Packard have reduced packaging materials in the shipment of their printers as a result of applying continuous improvement principles and methods.

SUPPLY CHAIN STRATEGY

Strategic planning is important for effective supply chain management. Figure 4-5 shows various things to consider in supply chain strategy. First, you need to understand the different classes of sourced items. Next, you need to identify your supply chain's optimal performance levels. This means you should know your objectives and metrics for performance. Third, you should understand your current levels of performance and where you can improve. Fourth, organize team projects and plans for achieving desired supply chain objectives. Fifth, implement your improvement teams and plans. Finally, monitor your results and take corrective action where needed. Notice that this process has its roots in Deming's plan-do-check-act cycle.

---

[14]Adam, E., "Alternative Quality Improvement Practices and Organization Performance," *Journal of Operations Management* 12 (1994): 27–44.
[15]Foster, S. T., "Does Six Sigma Improve Performances?" *Quality Management Journal*, 14, 4 (2007): 7–20.

FIGURE 4-5 Supply Chain Strategic Planning

Among the questions to be answered in a supply chain strategy are these:[16] How many plants are needed? Should we add new plants? Should we close plants? Should we stock inventory? For which products? In which locations? Should we outsource the task of transporting goods throughout my networks? Should we make subassemblies or purchase them? From whom?

As you can see, a good deal of planning is needed to adequately address these questions. In general, these questions fall into the following groupings:

- *Logistics* When will we ship? What mode of transportation will we use? How do we optimize our shipping practices?
- *Suppliers* Who are our preferred suppliers? What is our process for supplier selection? How do we develop suppliers? How do we link with our suppliers? Do we source globally?
- *Inventory management* Where do we optimally store inventory? How much? How long? Do we have perishable stocks? Where do we carry safety stocks? Are we maintaining good levels of services?

---

[16]Foster, S.T., Sampson, S., Wallin, C., and Webb, S., *Managing Supply Chain and Operations* (Upper Saddle River, NJ: Pearson, 2016).

The flowchart boxes read:
- Define types of sourced items
- Identify optimal state for the supply chain
- Observe current and desired levels of performance
- Organize improvement teams and projects
- Implement teams and improvement projects
- Monitor results and take corrective action where needed

- *Information flows* What kinds of enterprise resource planning systems are needed? How do we link upstream and downstream? What are data relations? What data do we need to manage our supply chain effectively?
- *Products* How many products do we stock? What product variety is necessary? How do we win orders? Where are our products in their life cycles?
- *Service* How do we define service along the supply chain? What do our customers want? Can we segment the supply chain? Who are our customers?

Summary

This chapter discussed quality from the perspective of strategy. One of the fundamental themes of this text is that quality improvement is a managed process. Although it may seem obvious now, a framework is needed to help achieve desired results. This chapter provided a strategic planning framework for this to occur. Future chapters focus on the implementation of these strategies.

We discussed various strategic issues relating to strategy content and process. Two processes were discussed: the forced-choice model and the Hoshin plan. Finally, we discussed the results associated with quality. Results are of strategic importance because they help us to determine whether we have accomplished what we wanted to.

Key Terms

Appraisal costs	Hoshin planning process	Leading	Sustainability
Catchball	Internal failure costs	PAF paradigm	Trait dimension
External failure costs	Leadership	Prevention costs	
Failure costs	Leader skills	Superordinate goals	

Discussion Questions

1. The Malcolm Baldrige award changed the name of the "Strategic Quality Planning" category to simply "Strategic Planning." Why was this change made? Do you agree or disagree with the committee's rationale?
2. Setting short-term goals for higher quality levels and managing towards these goals may prove detrimental to the firm. Explain what is meant by this statement.
3. According to the quality literature, without top management leadership, quality improvement will not occur. Why do you believe this is the case?
4. Explain the hazards of the "management by dictate" model.
5. Trust has been identified as a very important attribute for leaders who are initiating quality improvement efforts. Why do you believe trust is such an important attribute?
6. Why is commitment an important variable in quality improvement initiatives?
7. Discuss some of the ways leaders resolve conflict in organizations. Which of these ways have you found to be most effective? Why?
8. Do you agree with the statement "quality is good ethics"? Explain your answer.
9. Why do companies that focus on their customers often develop a set of ethics that includes valuing employees? Make your answer as substantive as possible.
10. Discuss the concept of prevention cost. Why is prevention cost such a pervasive consideration in quality programs?
11. Describe the difference between external and internal failure costs. Is one cost more important than the other? Explain your answer.
12. What are the quality costs incurred when your hard drive crashes?

13. Think of a product you buy that is differentiated through quality. Do you believe the manufacturer's strategy to differentiate this product through quality is sustainable, or will the manufacturer eventually have to find other ways to attract you to the product? Explain your answer.

14. Describe the concept of core competency. Can quality be considered a core competency? Why or why not?

15. Describe the difference between "strategy content" and "strategy process." Describe examples of quality-related strategy content and strategy process issues.

16. Describe the benefits of strategic planning.

17. Why is the forced-choice model particularly useful for companies that are relatively inexperienced in strategic planning? Explain your answer.

18. Should the strategic planning process consider quality concerns at every step of the process? Why or why not?

19. Describe the concept of catchball.

20. Juran argues that both incremental (continuous) improvements and stepwise (breakthrough) improvements are needed in a strategic framework. Do you agree with Juran's assessment? Why or why not?

Problems

1. Flynn Furniture Ltd., Dublin, Ireland, wishes to assess their quality performance. In order to do so they have gathered the following quality-related costs. You are hired as a consultant to evaluate these costs and to make recommendations to management.

Annual Quality Costs		
Failure costs		
Defective products	$	3,856
Engineered scrap		18,565
Nonengineered scrap		175,899
Consumer adjustments		120,563
Downgrading products		1,789,632
Lost goodwill		Not evaluated
Customer policy changes		Not evaluated
TOTAL		
Appraisal costs		
Receiving inspection	$	€20,777
Line 1 inspection		€5,439
Line 2 inspection		€6,480
Spot checking		€1,985
TOTAL		
Prevention costs		
Quality training	$	€23,500
Process engineering		
Corporate		€130,255
Plant		€40,365
Product redesign		€8,549
TOTAL		

a. Compute the ratios of prevention and appraisal costs to failure costs.

b. Compute the proportion of prevention, appraisal and failure costs to total quality costs and identify strategies for reducing the failure costs.

2. The Raven Plastics Group, Bristol, UK, has gathered the following quality-related costs data:

Annual Quality Costs		
Failure costs		
Defective products	$	5,500
Engineered scrap		24,656
Nonengineered scrap		28,675
Consumer adjustments		30,138
Downgrading products		0
Lost goodwill		Not evaluated
Customer policy changes		Not evaluated
TOTAL		
Appraisal costs		
Receiving inspection	$	€12,478
Line 1 inspection		€12,450
Line 2 inspection		€8,677
Spot checking		€13,350
TOTAL		
Prevention costs		
Quality training	$	€27,500
Process engineering		
Corporate		€145,320
Plant		€45,356
Product redesign		€12,355
TOTAL		

a. Compare the ratios of prevention and appraisal costs to failure costs.
b. What would you recommend this company do?

3. The Gorilla Manufacturing Company of Pittsburg, Kansas, recently studied its expenditures and losses relative to quality for the month of October. The company found that it had lost $300,000 in scrap and rework. It had spent $40,000 for inspection and $25,000 in prevention-related activities. Evaluate its cost ratios and suggest whether or not the expenditures are warranted.

4. Bradley, Sons and Company is a manufacturing company based in Belfast, Northern Ireland. Following an evaluation of its cost structure relating to quality costs for the previous year the company had lost $450,000 in warranty and scrap. Their rework costs were also significant. In the prior year, $90,000 was spent on training employees in quality tools and $210,000 for quality assurance personnel. Inspection costs were 3.5% of sales of $60 million. Evaluate these costs and recommend what actions should be taken by upper management. (Hint: The average company loses about 25% of sales due to poor quality.)

CASES

Case 4-1 Mallinckrodt Pharmaceuticals: Realizing Multiple Benefits through Improved Quality[17]

Mark Trudeau is the CEO of Mallinckrodt, a global specialty pharmaceutical business, established in 1840, that develops, manufactures, markets, and distributes specialty pharmaceutical products and medical imaging agents. They have approximately 5,500 employees worldwide and

commercial presence in roughly 70 countries. The company's fiscal revenue in 2013 totaled $2.2 billion.

Continuous improvement is an important part of Mallinckrodt's overall development strategy. In order to select suitable improvement projects that will have a

[17]Based on Jacobsen, J., (2014), *Clean Approach Saves Global Pharmaceutical Drug Manufacturer Time,* Money, accessed 17th March 2016 from http://rube.asq.org/2014/04/lean/clean-approach-saves-money.pdf

positive impact on the organization, they use a rigorous selection process to evaluate potential initiatives that are strongly linked with the company's strategic goals. For the purpose of this case study, the proposed project focused on procedures for cleaning equipment after one product was made and before employees could start manufacturing a different product. The process was so time consuming and ineffective that is was viewed as a low-hanging fruit. "Any improvement in the process would shorten the timeline and allow additional time for manufacture of an actual product," said lead validation engineer Cindy Duhigg, "which is profit, rather than time wasted."

An improvement team was formed with a diverse group representing multiple disciplines relevant to the project. The first step in developing an effective improvement strategy involved pinpointing issues in the current process. Some of the quality tools used to accomplish this task included process maps, waste walk, brainstorming, benchmarking, and root cause analysis. To bring greater focus to possible improvement actions, three evaluation methods were used: value stream mapping (VSM), screening experiments, and benchmarking. The maps clarified the steps needed to achieve the project's objectives. They also verified the location of the bottlenecks in the process and where non value-added waste was occurring, such as the time needed to clean out the tanks. The value stream mapping for the current process allowed the team to determine that an entirely new procedure was necessary to satisfy the project's objectives. Screen experiments for different tank-cleaning machines plotted the cleaning efficacy against time to determine whether a specific sprayball could achieve the required objectives. Finally, benchmarking activities allowed team members to learn about past successes to create a foundation for determining

the best solutions to decrease the clean-out cycle time. To gauge the effectiveness of the proposed improvements, team members collaborated with stake-holders to compare possible results of these actions against organizational goals.

The reduced changeover time helped Mallinckrodt on focusing to introduce an additional product, not originally produced in this line. This added $700,000 in increased absorption, or new product manufactured. The results had a direct impact on organizational goals as the improvements reduced the number of cleaning failures to almost zero, eliminating as many as two to three cleaning reworks per month. The project goal of promoting a zero-defect culture with a first-time right measure of 100 percent was reached, showing a 62 percent improvement. Also, nearly $2 million in back-orders were completely eliminated at this focus factory, which led to the inclusion of a new product into the schedule. In addition to the tangible financial benefits, the newly installed man-ways not only improve the facility's current good manufacturing practices, but also eliminate the potentially dangerous situation in the previous process, when 2,000-gallon tanks full of water would be heated to boiling degree and agitated, then abruptly dumped.

As a result of the success, the company is now planning improvement projects throughout the organization. The project was submitted into the ASQ (American Society for Quality) International Team Excellence Awards (ITEA) and was named a finalist in the 2012 competition. Duhigg said the project was a great match for the ITEA Process because of the value it delivered to the organization, "The benefits were so over-the-top, extravagantly obvious - $1 million a year," the only question was "Why didn't we do it sooner?"

Discussion Questions

1. Discuss the steps Mallinckrodt used to implement its quality improvement methods.
2. Identify the quality improvement tools applied in the case study and explain how they supported the identification of process improvements.
3. Discuss the benefits that Mallinckrodt achieved from it quality program. Are these benefits more encompassing than you would have expected? Why or why not?

Case 4-2 MidwayUSA[18]

www.midwayusa.com

MidwayUSA is a catalog and Internet retailer offering everything for shooters, reloaders, gunsmiths, and hunters. It is the world leader in its industry with $185

million in revenue and has the vision to be the best-run business in America. To achieve this goal, the company adopted the Baldrige Core Values and Concepts and

---

[18]Based on NIST, Profiles of Baldrige Winners, 2016.

made them an integral part of the company's culture. The values and concepts are displayed in 30 locations throughout the company.

MidwayUSA's quality efforts are customer focused. One of its core values is "customer-driven excellence." This strategy resulted in a customer retention rate of 98%. To maintain a customer focus, MidwayUSA provides customers multiple opportunities to give feedback. Customers receive help through its complaint center. The company conducts surveys. Customers can also submit reviews of items and suggest new product lines.

MidwayUSA understands the value of its employees. A component of quality customer service is employee interaction. MidwayUSA wants employees passionate about hunting, shooting, and so on. This passion can be felt when employees interact with customers. Also, the employees are able to offer personal insight and knowledge about products. MidwayUSA encourages its workforce to join the National Rifle Association and to participate in hunting and shooting events. This passion and level of interaction has contributed to a customer satisfaction rating of 93%.

MidwayUSA takes a robust approach to assess its current and future needs. Information incorporated into these projections is regularly monitored. All processes are aligned to customer needs and the company's goals. To meet production capability and capacity, the company maintains a skills inventory matrix. There are regular reviews of the company's performance and results. With this systematic approach, MidwayUSA has exceeded its nearest competitor in multiple financial categories: gross sales, net income as a percentage of net sales, earnings distribution, and inventory turns. MidwayUSA's customer focus and approach to quality position the company for continual sales growth.

Discussion Questions

1. How does MidwayUSA engage the customer in its focus on quality?
2. MidwayUSA has incorporated quality and customer focus into its culture. How does it ensure employees support the culture? Also, how do employees contribute to quality customer service?
3. MidwayUSA wants to be the best-run company in America. Is this a useful vision statement? Are there benefits to this vision instead of being the best-run company in the industry?
4. Effective quality and strategic planning are not a one-time event. In looking at MidwayUSA and other companies, what can companies do to make these a continual process?

The Voice of the Customer

Chapter Objectives

After completing this chapter, you should be able to:

1. Discuss the basics of customer relationship management.
2. Distinguish how managing quality in services is different from manufacturing.
3. Implement gap analysis in a service firm using SERVQUAL.
4. Develop a customer service survey using specific examples and critical incidents.

D ifferent customers have differing views of their service providers. We have all experienced instances of great or lousy customer service. Customer service is important for these reasons:[1]

- Customers tell twice as many people about bad experiences as good experiences.
- A dissatisfied customer tells 8 to 10 people about the bad experience.
- Seventy percent of upset customers will remain your customer if you resolve the complaint satisfactorily.
- It is easier to get customers to repeat than it is to find new business.
- Service firms rely on repeat customers for 85% to 95% of their business.
- Eighty percent of new product and service ideas come from customer ideas.
- The cost of keeping an existing customer is one-sixth of the cost of attracting a new customer.

A **customer** is the receiver of goods or services. Typically, a customer process involves an economic transaction in which something of value has changed hands.

Often, customers are defined as internal or external customers. **Internal customers** are employees receiving goods or services from within the same firm. For example, management information systems (MIS) technicians and programmers view the users within their company as internal customers. Accounting departments and finance departments often have very little interaction with the bill-paying customer. However, they have customers within the firm who use

---

[1]Kabodian, A., *The Customer Is Always Right.* (Cambridge, MA: Harvard University Press, 1996).

A CLOSER LOOK AT QUALITY 5-1   Online Review of Merchandise[2]

Consumers have multiple avenues to express their opinions about products and services they receive: Facebook, Twitter, YouTube, blogs, and so on. Online reviews can provide valuable insight about a product. In a survey by E-tailing Group, for 71% of online shoppers the most influential factor was customer reviews. Online reviews are another opportunity for retailers to gain customer feedback. Instead of scouring the Web for the information, retailers have created online reviews on their Web sites.

There are pros and cons to online reviews. Product reviews have been shown to boost loyalty and sales with customers. Retailers and designers can respond more quickly to quality issues by receiving nearly instantaneous feedback. Online customers are able to learn about products without seeing and touching them. Some retailers believe online reviews will reduce return rates and increase "conversion," the percentage of browsers who actually buy.

On the downside, there is the potential of a negative review, though reviews tend to be overwhelmingly positive. Anyone who has purchased the product can review it. As designer Carmen Marc Valvo said, "Style is a very subjective matter." In some industries, producers would prefer leaving the reviews to the experts.

As online sales increase, elite luxury stores such as Neiman Marcus and Nordstrom are changing their tune and are embracing online reviews. Nordstrom was the first in the industry to do this by adding product reviews to its Web site. Neiman Marcus has taken a modified approach by allowing only an elite group of customers to post reviews. Luxury stores are known for customer interaction and their need to realize online reviews are a new component of providing quality customer service. Customers want an objective voice and reviews give them that. In the end, elite stores may have different motivations for adding online reviews. Some may want the direct customer feedback, and others may do it in an attempt to boost sales.

[2]Based on Dodes, R., "Luxe Lowdown: Tony Sites Begin to Invite Buyer Reviews." *Wall Street Journal* (16 October 2010).

their services daily. In a sense, an economic transaction takes place in internal services in that service providers are funded as a result of the service they provide to the organization as a whole. Some have used an abstraction of the term *internal customer* to include the person at the next step in the supply chain. Therefore, the person who works at workstation 3 can be considered the customer of the worker at workstation 2.

External customers or **end users** are the bill-paying receivers of our work. The external customers are the ultimate people we are trying to satisfy with our work. If we have satisfied external customers, chances are we will continue to prosper, grow, and fulfill the objectives of the firm.

CUSTOMER-DRIVEN QUALITY

Customer-driven quality represents a proactive approach to satisfying customer needs that is based on gathering data about our customers to learn their needs and preferences and then providing products and services that satisfy the customers. Customer-driven quality is one of the core values of the Malcolm Baldrige award. A Closer Look at Quality 5-1 shows that companies have taken differing approaches to handling customer feedback.

The Pitfalls of Reactive Customer-Driven Quality

Even though it is generally understood that listening to and understanding the customer is a good thing, some companies implement customer feedback mechanisms incorrectly. As a result, these companies are placed in a reactive rather than a proactive mode with their customers.

FIGURE 5-1 Reactive Customer-Driven Quality Model *Source:* S. T. Foster, "The Ups and Downs of Customer-Driven Quality," *Quality Progress* (October 1998):70. © 1998 American Society for Quality. Reprinted with permission.

One of the difficulties of satisfying customer requirements is that in a dynamic environment, customer needs are constantly changing. Consider the example of military suppliers. For many years, cost overruns and missed schedules were allowed by the military customers. When the purchasing standards were changed by the military, many suppliers such as McDonnell Douglas were incapable of adequately responding. The results have been layoffs, corporate restructuring, and mergers. Figure 5-1 shows a model of **reactive customer-driven quality (RCDQ)**. This model shows that a firm's quality performance is increasing while customers' expectations also are increasing. Problems occur when customer requirements increase at a faster rate than quality and service improvement. This places a firm in a reactive mode that may signal the need for major process and service redesign.

The RCDQ model demonstrates conceptually and graphically the primary pitfalls and dangers of RCDQ. In a sense, manufacturers and service organizations attempting to meet customer expectations are pursuing a moving target. As the supplier's competitors improve quality, and competition increases, customers demand higher levels of quality and service. The difference between world-class and ordinary suppliers lies in whether suppliers stay ahead of the target or fall behind the target. Although a supplier to a customer might desire to provide high-quality service to the customer, the reactive posture engendered in the RCDQ approach will cause the supplier to fall farther and farther behind the moving target over time.

CUSTOMER-RELATIONSHIP MANAGEMENT

Much of the focus in marketing today is on maintaining the existing customer base that a firm has established. If it is true that 90% of the business for many service firms is in the form of repeat business, the focus of process and system design must be on developing relationships with customers rather than simply providing clean transactions at each stage of the process.

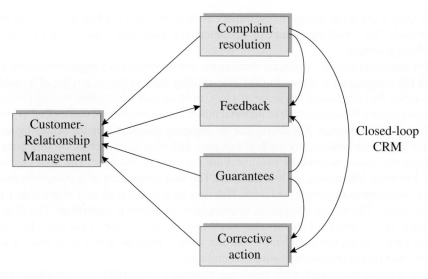

FIGURE 5-2   Four Components of Customer-Relationship Management

Process design in services has often focused on the transaction. For example, a university might focus on discrete processes for improvement in areas such as registration, financial aid, test taking, and so forth. However, some universities have learned that focusing on these internal processes does not help student retention. Therefore, new programs for student retention focus on familiarizing the student with the university and developing the skills students need to be successful in a college setting. Some of these skills might involve study skills, social skills, or managing on a limited budget. In this way, the university begins to look at the whole system relating to the student and not just internal university processes.

For many firms, the focus on process design includes the aspect of **customer-relationship management (CRM)**. This view of the customer asserts that he or she is a valued asset to be managed. This is relationship management. The tangibles (such as facilities and machinery) meet the intangibles (such as professionalism and empathy) to provide a satisfying experience for the customer. There are four important design aspects (see Figure 5-2) to customer-relationship management that we address here: complaint resolution, feedback, guarantees, and corrective action or recovery. For practical reasons, we distinguish between CRM and customer relationship management systems (CRMS). CRMS are systems used for capturing customer-related data. CRMS are discussed later in the chapter.

Complaint Resolution

As the famous saying goes, "You can please some of the people some of the time, but you can't please all of the people all of the time." As a result, complaint resolution is an important component of a quality management system. Complaints come in many forms. For our discussion, we focus on three types of complaints that need to be resolved: *regulatory complaints, employee complaints*, and *customer complaints*. Although the focus of this chapter is on the customer, it is important to recognize all three types of complaints as potential sources of information for improvement. Donald Beaver, the owner of New Pig Corporation of Tipton, Pennsylvania, has the right attitude about complaints. He states, "You should love complaints more than compliments. A complaint is someone letting you know that you haven't satisfied them yet. They have gold written all over them."[3] Complaints should be viewed as opportunities to improve.

---

[3]Whitely, R., *The Customer-Driven Company: Moving from Talk to Action* (Boston: Addison Wesley, 1991).

Because only a small percentage of customers ultimately will complain, they should be taken very seriously. This small percentage of customers may represent a much larger population of dissatisfied customers.

The complaint-resolution process involves the transformation of a negative situation into one in which the complainant is restored to the state existing prior to the occurrence of a problem. In extreme cases, the complainant has incurred a loss, as in the case of a malfunctioning product leading to injury and liability. In the case of personal injury, if the complainant was injured as a result of the malfunction of a product, it is ethical that the company should restore the person by reimbursing him or her for the product, any medical expenses, and other costs such as lost time from work.

Typically, losses incurred by customers are not quite so dramatic. The losses are smaller, such as lost time, lost money, or lost patience. The first component of a complaint-resolution process is to **compensate** people for losses. This may be as small as an easy return policy with no questions asked. The second component to complaint resolution is **contrition**. The firm should apologize to the customer for the mistakes made and invoke the Macy's mantra, "The customer is always right." Third, the complaint-resolution process must be designed to make it easy for complainants to reach resolution to simple complaints.

The process associated with resolving complaints is called the **complaint-recovery process**. Recovery design is an important activity for many firms. Complaints can come from a variety of sources, such as questionnaires (low scores on key quality indicators can be considered complaints), formal direct inquiries, or informal channels. The recovery process must be developed for documenting complaints, resolving the complaint, documenting recovery, and feedback for system improvement.

Feedback

To understand customer behavior, wants, and needs, data about the customer are necessary. Some of these data come directly from the customer. Some customer data are solicited, and other data are provided without solicitation. The following pages discuss different approaches to collecting and analyzing customer data. One way to gather data is to receive customer feedback. There are two main types of feedback: feedback to the customer and feedback to the firm as a basis for process improvements. The customer-feedback loop includes reporting the resolution of the complaint to the customer. Many times, this requires a data-gathering mechanism, such as a computerized information system, to ensure that the customer complaint has been resolved adequately. Feedback to the firm should occur on a consistent basis with a process to monitor changes resulting from the process improvement.

Guarantees

Another important aspect of customer service is the guarantee. Many firms offer service guarantees. A guarantee outlines the customer's rights. Even with high-quality companies, such as Motorola, there are product and service failures. To design a process that ignores this fact is a form of denial. The guarantee is both a design and an economic issue that must be addressed by all companies before the first sale occurs. Guarantees should be designed prior to beginning business so that employees can be trained to implement the guarantee and marketing can advertise the guarantee properly. This is an important economic issue because of the sales potential that is created by a guarantee and the costs associated with fulfillment of the guarantee.

To be effective, a guarantee should be[4]

- *Unconditional.* No "small print." Inconsistent application can make the guarantee less compelling.

---

[4]Chase, R., *Operations and Supply Chain Management* (Homewood, IL: Irwin, 2010).

- *Meaningful.* To be meaningful, customer grievances must be fully addressed. For example, any financial loss must be fully recovered by the complainant.
- *Understandable.* The customer must be able to understand easily the parameters of the guarantee and how to achieve resolution quickly.
- *Communicable.* The phrasing of a guarantee should resonate with the customer. "The best quality at the lowest prices—I guarantee it," is the famous motto at the Men's Wearhouse. Not only is this a great guarantee but it also is a great marketing line.
- *Painless to invoke.* The customer must not be inconvenienced too much. Costco has a "no questions asked" return policy that allows customers to return or exchange merchandise with a minimum of hassle. This return policy was an early service linchpin that differentiated its service from other retailers.

Corrective Action

An important aspect of customer-relationship management is corrective action. This means that when a service or product failure occurs, the failure is documented, and the problem is resolved so that it never happens again. Corporate teams or committees should be in place to regularly review complaints and to improve processes so that the problems don't recur.

Referring to Figure 5-2, the corrective action results in gathering complaint and warranty data and determining the causes of these problems. Often, teams of employees and managers study complaints, do Pareto cost analysis of the complaints, and recommend improvements to the customer service delivery system. Such systems are often referred to as a **closed-loop corrective action**. The loop is in effect *closed* because a process is in place that ensures this information is used for improvement. This is why complaint and field repair data are so golden.

THE "GAPS" APPROACH TO SERVICE DESIGN

The **gap** has been recognized in the quality literature for some time. Typically, the gap refers to the differences between desired levels of performance and actual levels of performance. This could be something like the difference between the desired conformance level versus the existing conformance level in a manufacturing environment. In services, this is the difference between the expected and the actual level of service provided. A gap is important because once it is identified, it is a candidate for corrective action and process improvement. The formal means for identifying and correcting these gaps is called **gap analysis**.

One of the differences studied by gap analysis identifies the difference between managerial and customer perceptions of what the customer wants (gap 1). When this gap is large, service providers are likely producing excellent services that no one wants. The other gaps and gap analysis are discussed in depth in Chapter 8.

In addition to the gaps model, Parasuraman, Zeithamel, and Berry contributed a number of important concepts to managing service quality. These concepts include 10 determinants of service quality (Table 5-1), service quality dimensions discussed in Chapter 1, and a questionnaire to test the hypothesized relationships in Figure 5-3. The survey instrument is called SERVQUAL.

Another approach to identifying and measuring gaps in quality service is found in the two-dimensional gaps model shown in Figure 5-4. Surveys using this approach measure customer satisfaction perceptions on the y axis and ratings of relative importance on the x axis. This approach is presented in depth in Chapter 8, but it is presented here in the context of gathering customer data to better understand the customer.

TABLE 5-1 Determinants of Service Quality

Reliability involves consistency of performance and dependability. It means that the firm performs the service right the first time. It also means that the firm honors its promises.

Responsiveness concerns the willingness or readiness of employees to provide service.

Competence means possession of the required skills and knowledge to perform the service.

Access involves approachability and ease of contact.

Courtesy involves politeness, respect, consideration, and friendliness of contact personnel (including receptionists, telephone operators, and so on).

Communication means keeping customers informed in a language they can understand and listening to them. It may mean that the company has to adjust its language for different consumers—increasing the level of sophistication with a well-educated customer and speaking simply and plainly with a novice.

Credibility involves trustworthiness, believability, and honesty. It involves having the customer's best interests at heart.

Security is freedom from danger, risk, or doubt.

Understanding/knowing the customer involves making the effort to understand the customer's needs.

Tangibles include the physical evidence of the service.

Source: Based on A. Parasuraman, V. Zeithamel, and L. Berry, "SERVQUAL: A Multiple-Item Scale for Measuring Customer Perceptions of Service Quality," *Journal of Retailing* (Spring 1988): 12–40.

FIGURE 5-3 Service Quality Model Gaps

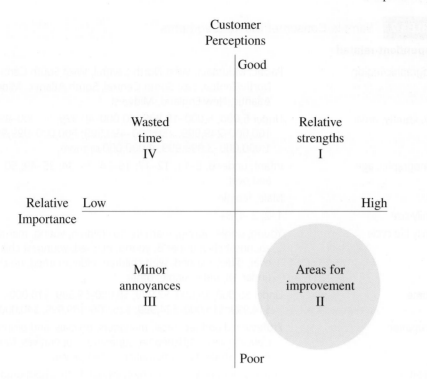

FIGURE 5-4   Gaps Model

SEGMENTING CUSTOMERS AND MARKETS

One of the preliminary steps that many analysts overlook is segmenting data. Data about customers can be gathered from a number of sources, such as industry groups, external sources, the Internet, commercially available databases, or questionnaires. The Baldrige criteria emphasize data segmentation of customers and customer markets. The segmentation is simple (e.g., consumer, commercial, or wholesalers).

To segment markets means to distinguish customers or markets according to common characteristics. Personal computer markets are segmented into home and business markets. Sometimes segmentation is more complex, involving customer characteristics and demographics, psychographics, or benefits desired. Table 5-2 shows examples of segments for consumer markets. Notice how consumer markets can be segmented. This segmentation implies that data are gathered separately for each of these segments and analyzed separately. Table 5-3 shows examples of segments for commercial markets. Therefore, you may segment your markets according to consumer markets or commercial markets. You also may segment further within these markets.

STRATEGIC SUPPLY CHAIN ALLIANCES BETWEEN CUSTOMERS AND SUPPLIERS

Traditionally, the customer–supplier relationship has been viewed as a relationship in which one party attempts to gain advantage over the other. The customer obtains advantage over the supplier by exercising the ability to change suppliers. At the same time, the supplier attempts to gain power over the customer by increasing switching costs, thereby making it difficult for customers to switch to another supplier.

The theory behind this arrangement was essentially a competitive model because competition among the suppliers drives costs lower and quality higher. However, this theory ignores the costs associated with variability created by using multiple suppliers. This variability can be seen

TABLE 5-2	Sample Consumer Market Segments

Respondent-related

Geographic region	Pacific, Mountain, West North Central, West South Central, East North Central, East South Central, South Atlantic, Middle Atlantic, New England, Midwest
City, county, area	Under 5,000; 5,000–19,999; 20,000–49,999; 50,000–99,999; 100,000–249,999; 250,000–499,999; 500,000–999,999; 1,000,000–3,999,999; 4,000,000 or more
Demographic age	Infant, under 6; 6–11; 12–17; 18–24; 25–34; 35–49; 50–64; 65 and over
Sex	Male; female
Family size	1–2; 3–4; 5+
Family life cycle	Young, single; young, married, no children; young, married, youngest child under 6; young, married, youngest child 6 or over; older, married, with children; older married, no children under 18; older, single; other.
Income	Under $5,000; $5,000–$7,999; $8,000–$9,999; $10,000–$14,999; $15,000–$24,999; $25,000–$39,999; $40,000 or over
Occupation	Professional and technical; managers, officials, and proprietors; clerical, sales; craftspeople, supervisors; operatives; farmers; retired; students; homemakers; unemployed
Education	Grade school or less; some high school; high school graduate; some college; college graduate; postgraduate
Religion	Catholic; Protestant; Jewish; Latter-Day Saint; other
Race	White; African American; Asian American; other
Nationality	American; British; French; German; other
Social class	Lower-lower; upper-lower; lower-middle; upper-middle; lower upper; upper-upper

Product-related

Benefits offered	
Need satisfiers	Motives: economic and more detailed needs
Product features	Situation specific, but to satisfy specific or general needs
Consumption/use patterns	
Rate of use	Heavy; medium; light; nonusers
Use with other products	Situation specific (e.g., gas with a traveling vacation)
Brand familiarity	Insistence; preference; recognition; nonrecognition; rejection
Buying situation	
Kind of store	Convenience; shopping; specialty
Kind of shopping	Serious versus browsing; rushed versus leisurely
Depth of assortment	Out of stock; shallow; deep
Type of product	Convenience; shopping; specialty; unsought

in process industries such as steel production, in which customers use sheet steel raw materials from suppliers. Even though the dimensions and specifications for sheet metal are the same, if different suppliers are used, there will be increased variability in the physical properties of the materials, such as tensile strength. For example, one manufacturer found that by limiting the number of suppliers of sheet steel, it reduced its defects by 40%. This demonstrated that variability in sourced materials was a major cause of defects.

TABLE 5-3	Sample Commercial Market Segments	
Type of organization	Manufacturing, institutional, government, public utility, military, farm, other	
Demographics	Size	
	Employees	
	Sales volume	
	Standard Industrial Classifications (SIC) code	
	Number of plants	
	Geographic location	
	East, Southeast, South, Midwest, Mountains, Southwest, West	
	Large city or rural area	
Type of product	Installations, accessories, components, raw materials, supplies, services	
Buying situation	Decentralized versus centralized	
	Multiple buying influence	
	Straight rebuy, modified rebuy, new buy	
Source loyalty	Weak versus strong loyalty	
	Last resort, second source, first source	
Kind of commitments	Contracts, agreements, financial aids	
Reciprocity	None versus complete	

Today, many companies use **single sourcing** as a way to reduce the number of suppliers. Single sourcing is a process for developing relationships with a few suppliers for long contract terms. Historically, this was the Japanese method of purchasing.

Increasingly, single-sourcing arrangements are developing into **strategic alliances**, in which the suppliers become de facto subsidiaries to their major customers. In these arrangements, not only are suppliers single-source providers but they also integrate information systems and quality systems that allow close interaction at all levels. Single-source suppliers to Ford are increasingly trained by Ford representatives concerning the preferred and required organizations, processes, and delivery systems. Suppliers also enter into agreements to reduce costs and improve productivity and are graded on an annual basis concerning the attainment of these targets.

Toyota employs an extensive supplier development program for each of its suppliers. As a result, variability to Toyota is reduced as the relationship between customer and supplier is enhanced over time. It is to the benefit of both parties to continue this relationship over a long period of time. In addition, some Japanese companies actually include their suppliers on their organization charts. Therefore, the task of managing suppliers is simplified over time. Variability and complexity are reduced.

Bose Company, a speaker and sound systems manufacturer, broke new ground in dealing with its suppliers. Bose actually has delegated many purchasing responsibilities to its suppliers. Using this approach, major suppliers are provided office space and are authorized to make purchases for their own accounts. Using the **vendor managed inventory (VMI)** approach, Bose suppliers provide only what is needed, when it is needed.

Process-Chain-Network (PCN) Tool for Service Design

One tool for designing processes with an eye toward better service is called a **process-chain-network diagram** (or PCN diagram). A PCN diagram is a tool managers can use when designing service delivery systems. A PCN diagram is a flowchart that evaluates the interactions between service providers and customers.

Flowcharts are graphical diagrams with boxes that represent process steps. The steps are connected by arrows that represent process dependency; an arrow between steps suggests that accomplishing one step is dependent on accomplishing another step.

FIGURE 5-5 PCN Diagram for a Pizza Maker

A PCN diagram categorizes the flowchart steps according to whether they involve interaction between entities such as providers and customers. In PCN diagrams, an **entity** is either a service provider, customer, or supplier. Entities such as supplier's suppliers or customer's customers can also be further up or down the supply chain. Figure 5-5 shows an example of a PCN diagram for a pizza restaurant. The pizza restaurant has a **process domain**, which is made of process steps that are the responsibility of the given entity (in this case, a pizza restaurant) as well as interactions with customers. A process domain has three regions:

- The **direct interaction** region includes process steps that involve the pizza restaurant's interacting with another entity, such as a local cheese supplier or a customer.
- The **surrogate interaction** region includes process steps in which the restaurant is acting on the resources coming from another entity without direct interaction. For example, the restaurant may order napkins online.
- The **independent processing** region includes process steps that the restaurant performs without interacting with other entities, such as developing recipes and turning on the ovens. PCN diagrams have been used in a variety of situations to improve customer service.

The Role of the Customer in the Supply Chain

The goal of supply chain management is customer satisfaction. But who is the customer? Figure 5-6 shows a picture of a supply chain for yogurt. Notice that the supply chain consists of several parts. In one, the farmers are providing product to a dairy. On another part of the supply chain, a chemical company provides plastic pellets to a converter who molds the cups. The label maker also provides labels to the converter. Do you suppose that the converter is primarily concerned with the final consumer who buys the yogurt? Likely not. The supply chain can be segmented. The chemical company is primarily focused on the converter. The dairy company schedules shipments to the distributors, and the distributors handle shipments to the store. The dairy works with the distributors and retailers to understand consumer preferences and to provide the flavors desired by the customers.

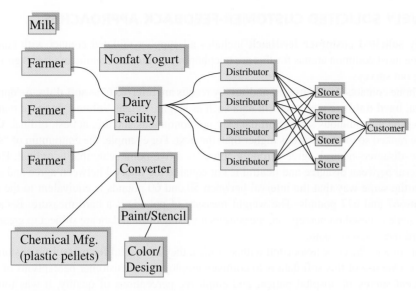

FIGURE 5-6 Segmenting the Supply Chain to Define Customers

Customer satisfaction from a supply chain perspective is made more difficult because of the realities of the market. There are more than 200 flavors of yogurt today. Forty years ago, there was only one flavor. In many industries, there are now many more high-priced premium items that must be considered. Shipping costs are also higher now. In addition, as we have discussed previously, customers are now more demanding than ever. It is clear that although much of the focus in supply chain management has been on cost reduction, supply chain managers must now focus more on service and product quality.

COMMUNICATING DOWNSTREAM

Marketing views every dollar of income equally, but operations does not. Operations views the costs and confusion associated with trying to satisfy diverse customer groups. It is less expensive to produce one item that satisfies a larger segment of the market than it is to produce several products that please several niche markets. Therefore, the operations professional does not view a dollar of income from diverse customers equally. **Customer rationalization** results from agreement between marketing and operations as to which customers add the greatest advantage and profits over time. This does not necessarily mean pursuing customers who are currently the most profitable. It could mean pursuing customers who cause the company to improve in ways necessary for continued survival. For example, consulting firms often have to turn away customers desiring services in areas outside the expertise of the company. Customer rationalization ensures that a high-quality product is provided, and the service provider stays within its field of expertise. Also, this allows firms to focus on a smaller number of key customers and to develop an **annuity relationship**, in which the customer provides a long-term, steady income stream to the provider.

As suppliers focus on satisfying their customers, these customers are recognized as primary sources of information. To better understand the customer, data about the customer must be gathered, analyzed, and used for improvement. The rest of this chapter is concerned with gathering and analyzing customer data so that the data can be used for improvement. There are a variety of means for gathering data from customers. These include **active data gathering**, such as through focus groups and surveys, and **passive data gathering**, such as through customer comment cards.

ACTIVELY SOLICITED CUSTOMER-FEEDBACK APPROACHES

Actively solicited customer feedback includes all supplier-initiated contact with customers. The three most common arenas for this are telephoning customers, conducting focus groups, and sending out surveys.

Phone contacts, focus groups, and survey results are referred to as **soft data**. As opposed to soft data, **hard data** are measurement data such as height, weight, volume, or speed that can be measured on a continuous scale. Soft data are not continuous and are, at best, ordinal. **Ordinal data** are ranked so one measure is higher than the next. For example, the continuum of "strongly disagree–disagree–neutral–agree–strongly agree" is a five-point scale that is ordinal. However, the interval between disagree and neutral is not equal to the interval between agree and strongly agree in the same way that the interval between 50 and 60 pounds is equivalent to the interval between 667 and 677 pounds. The weight measure of pounds is a hard measure. Because the ordinal scale is based on perception, measurements using ordinal data are subject to greater error than hard measurement data.

In spite of the error associated with soft data, they are useful for measuring customer perceptions. One use of this soft data is to compare employee and customer perceptions of quality. In a recent survey of hospital patient and employee perceptions of quality, it was found that patients consistently rated service quality higher than did the nurses and other employees in the survey. This can be explained in a services environment by the fact that employees have a view of the whole system, including customer contact activities and background activities that the patients do not see. Also, extremely dissatisfied hospital customers may not be able physically to respond to the survey.

Telephone Contact

Telephone surveys are often used to gather information related to customers. Most often, they are used for surveys or structured interviews. This is a type of convenience survey method. The major problem with telephone surveys is bias. Major segments of the population of interest are often not available via telephone at certain times. This makes random sampling difficult. Also, customers resent being called at inconvenient times. With recent changes in laws, service providers can be asked to remove customers from contact lists if this method is used. In addition, phone surveyors must respect state and federal do-not-call lists. However, it is often helpful to call respondents prior to sending a survey to see whether they are willing to respond to a survey.

Focus Groups

A **focus group** allows a supplier to gather feedback from a group of consumers at one time. The groups are focused in two ways. First, focus groups narrowly address a single topic or group of topics. Second, focus groups draw individuals with similar characteristics or demographics, which limits the discussion to subjects and market segments that are of particular interest to the firm. Figure 5-7 shows the steps included in performing a focus group session. After identifying the purpose of the focus group, a set of questions is developed that sequences from broad to specific. After the focus group sessions are completed with multiple groups, the notes from the sessions are reviewed to find common themes that become the basis for planning and improvement.

Focus groups are often used by business and government agencies to gauge topics or issues that elicit the strongest emotional responses from the subject. Focus groups need to be carefully facilitated so that the objectives of the research are met.

Customer Service Surveys

In Chapter 1, we said that quality ultimately is as the customer perceives it. The customer service survey is an important tool for determining customer perceptions of customer service and

FIGURE 5-7 Focus Group Steps

Identify Purpose

↓

Narrow Scope of Questions

↓

Select Target Population

↓

Develop Questions

↓

Run Multiple Groups

↓

Summarize and Develop
Common Themes

quality and is used by marketers and quality professionals to define areas of strength and areas for improvement in quality systems. It is disappointing that surveys are sometimes misused, as is shown in A Closer Look at Quality 5-2. A survey (or instrument) consists of a series of items (or questions) designed to capture perceptions. The number of items is determined by the purpose of the instrument and the willingness of respondents to spend time filling out the survey.

There are four steps to developing a useful survey: identifying customer requirements, developing and validating the instrument, implementing the survey, and analyzing the results.

1. ***Identifying customer requirements.*** Customer requirements include the dimensions of quality, service, and performance that are necessary to satisfy the customer. Identifying customer requirements initially involves reviewing the purchase orders and contracts established when the relationship with the customer begins. Second, customer needs are reviewed with marketing and production. Third, interviews are conducted with a sampling of customers to determine what to add to the list of customer requirements.

2. ***Developing and validating the instrument.*** After dimensions of customer requirements are identified, specific examples are developed to measure the particular dimensions. As shown

A CLOSER LOOK AT QUALITY 5-2   Misusing Surveys

Figure 5-8 shows a letter received by this author from a Chrysler dealer. The representative from the Chrysler dealer understands that surveys are used to evaluate dealer performance. It is unclear whether financial incentives are linked to the surveys. However, it is clear that there must be a "hammer" that comes down on the dealer when less-than-perfect responses are received by Chrysler. Therefore, this represents both a misuse of the survey data by Chrysler and a feeble attempt by the dealer to distort the process for collecting data in a way that is unhelpful to it. Remember that survey information is useful only if the data are unbiased. This is an attempt by the dealer to bias its results. This is not unusual. Hilton Corporation does the same thing with signs in the elevators encouraging guests to "check excellent" on questions on their surveys. Both Chrysler and Hilton need to reevaluate how they use survey data to improve service performance.

(continued)

July 2, 2015

Tom Foster

Dear Tom,
Thank you for your recent visit to our service department. I am following-up to ensure that you were completely satisfied with the service.

Chrysler may contact you requesting your participation in a survey. Thank you in advance for taking your time to complete their report card on Jim's performance during your last visit. Hopefully you can give him an excellent as anything less means he failed in the eyes of the manufacturer.

In our continuing effort to find new ways to improve, we value your opinion or suggestions that would allow us to better serve our customers. May we ask you, what was the one thing we could have done better on your last service visit?

If for any reason you were not completely satisfied, please feel free to rectify any concerns so you would feel comfortable giving us a perfect score. If I am not available, please leave me a message and I will be glad to get back to you. Or, you can e-mail me.

Sincerely,

Customer Care Manager.

FIGURE 5-8 Misusing Surveys

Timeliness Dimension

_____ I received my food quickly.
_____ The server responded in a timely manner.
_____ The line moved quickly.
_____ I was served rapidly.
_____ The food service at Henry's is quick.

FIGURE 5-9 Timeliness at Henry's Fast Food: Specific-Example Approach

in Figure 5-9, the dimension of timeliness is important for a fast-food restaurant. In a survey of their patrons, it had several items relating to the timeliness dimension (among others). Notice that the survey items are not questions. They are simple declarative sentences that use action verbs. Declarative statements are easy to understand and fit well with five- or seven-point scales. Each statement is a specific example of the quality dimension being measured.

An alternative means of developing survey items is the *critical-incident approach*, which involves obtaining information from customers about the process they use to receive goods and services. The critical incidents are aspects of organizational performance with which the customers come in direct contact. These are important for monitoring and measuring process performance as it relates to customer service. In your baselining system, this approach is important for determining whether your process performance is improving. Figure 5-10 shows the same dimension of timeliness for the fast-food restaurant. Notice that the items relate to specific steps in the process of purchasing product in a fast-food restaurant. As with the specific-example approach, the items relating to timeliness can be averaged to determine whether the process is performing well on that particular dimension.

3. ***Implementing the survey.*** Reliability and validity are two different but interrelated issues of survey development. We use the traditional target approach to explain this relationship. If the target in Figure 5-11 is the dimension of customer service that you are trying to measure, each arrow mark represents a single response using the survey instrument. If the measure of the dimension ascertains the dimension perfectly, the shot will be right in the center of the target.

> _____ I was greeted on entering Henry's.
> _____ There was a server available when I approached the service counter.
> _____ My line had less than three people when I arrived.
> _____ As soon as I reached the counter, the server requested what I wanted immediately.
> _____ My food was delivered within 60 seconds of entering Henry's.

FIGURE 5-10   Timeliness at Henry's Fast Food: Critical-Incident Approach

If you don't hit the center, you are not perfectly measuring the quality dimension. The more imperfect the measurement, the farther the shot will be from the center of the target.

Figure 5-11 shows four different situations. In target one, the arrows consistently hit the target in the same area but were off center. The instrument developed was reliable, but not valid. In other words, the responses were consistent, but they were not measuring the right thing. In target two, the responses were all over the target. The average responses will hit the exact center of the target; however, there is a great deal of variability in responses. In this case, the group estimate is valid, but the measurement is not reliable. This shows that reliability is directly related to variability in responses from the respondents. Target three is neither reliable nor valid because the group averages will be off center and the variability is high. Target four is both reliable and valid because the survey is both centered and there is little variability in the responses. We briefly address these two issues separately.

An instrument with low reliability is a problem; the great deal of unwanted noise or variability in the responses hides the data's message. Two approaches to testing for reliability are test/retest reliability and interjudge assessment. With test/retest, the instrument is administered to a group of respondents randomly selected from the population of interest in a pretest. The same instrument is administered to the same group of individuals at a later point after some time has passed (say two weeks). The responses are then analyzed statistically.

Sloppy or unreliable adjectives, such as *quality, outstanding,* and *acceptable* should be avoided as much as possible in designing surveys. With interjudge assessment, the survey is administered to multiple respondents and analyzed to gauge consistency of response among the respondents.

Validity is related to reliability, but a reliable instrument is not guaranteed to be valid. There are different types of validity; for example, *construct validity* refers to the use of certain terms

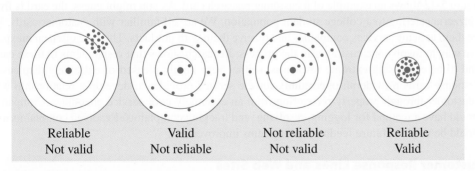

Reliable
Not valid

Valid
Not reliable

Not reliable
Not valid

Reliable
Valid

FIGURE 5-11   Reliability and Validity

and whether terms really measure what it is we want to measure. For example, self-reported measures of percentage growth in sales may not be a valid measure of success in customer satisfaction. Sales increases may instead reflect favorable market conditions. *Criterion validity* indicates that your measuring instrument has the capability to predict or agree with constructs external to that which you are measuring. *Content validity* refers to whether the item really measures what we want to measure. To help ensure (but not guarantee) content validity, it is helpful to ask some outside individuals to externally validate an instrument. Usually, this includes asking five or six "experts" to review the instrument and determine whether the instrument is valid. The experts are people who are familiar with the firm's customers or have performed previous surveying in a related area. Pretesting to externally validate the instrument can include asking managers and customers to review the instrument for understandability and completeness. Ask them what questions they would change, delete, or add. In validating a quality-related questionnaire, we found that respondents did not understand the term *conformance*. Once we replaced the term *conformance* with *meets specifications*, the survey instrument was improved.

Most of the questions will be close-ended because close-ended questions provide a better basis for data analysis. It is preferable to have at least one open-ended question in the customer service survey to allow customers to vent frustrations or make suggestions or other comments. Open-ended questions allow respondents to offer extemporaneous responses and comments.

4. *Analyzing the results.* For business purposes, data analysis generally should be kept simple. Means, histograms or numerical responses, and simple correlations are best for analyzing survey responses. Open-ended questions are analyzed with Pareto analysis using bar charts of the various categories of responses. More extensive data analysis using advanced statistical techniques—such as multiple regression, analysis of variance, or other procedures—should be performed if necessary. Explanations of these statistics can be found in introductory statistics textbooks. However, business experience has shown that simpler analysis is better because simple statistical results are easy to communicate to managers and coworkers.

PASSIVELY SOLICITED CUSTOMER-FEEDBACK APPROACHES

Customer-initiated contact, such as filling out a restaurant complaint card, calling a toll-free complaint line, or submitting an inquiry via a company's Web site, is considered **passively solicited customer feedback**.[5] According to research in the area of passive data collection, it was found that passive collections resulted in lower ratings of quality than active collections. It is not clear which approach is more biased. However, it is expected that people who fill out customer response cards based on their own initiative probably have issues they would like resolved.

Customer Research Cards

Figure 5-12 shows an example of a customer research card. As you might guess, the card is from a pizzeria catering to a college student population. We are all familiar with customer cards. We see them at many services companies and receive them with products. They are often an inexpensive way to involve the customer in the process. Research shows that respondents to these cards tend to be expressing extreme responses—either very highly pleased or extremely displeased. Response cards provide an opportunity for the service provider to develop a relationship with a customer through properly recovering from an extremely poor service encounter. Companies should have a method for logging, resolving, and tracking complaints. Resolved complaints also should be used for future feedback for systems improvement.

Customer Response Lines and Web Sites

Many companies provide Web sites and toll-free phone lines for customer complaints, questions, and inquiries. These services are offered by many third parties or can be offered in-house. For example, Heinz Frozen Food Company uses a third party to handle and resolve

---

[5]Sampson, S., "Ramifications of Monitoring Service Quality through Passively Solicited Customer Feedback," *Decision Sciences* 27, 4 (1996): 601–622.

Welcome to American Pie Pizza!

Please fill in the circle to the right with the facial expression that best reflects your experience today.

Comments:

_____

_____

_____

_____

_____

FIGURE 5-12   Pizzeria Complaint Card

complaints. If complaints are not resolved to the customer's satisfaction by the third party, the quality manager resolves complaints personally. Common problems with complaint lines occur when there are insufficient phone lines, long waits, poorly trained personnel, or unresponsive personnel.

MANAGING CUSTOMER RETENTION AND LOYALTY

An important indicator of customer satisfaction is **customer retention**, which is measured as the percentage of customers who return for more service. Such customer retention will increase by application of the service tools and concepts contained in this chapter, such as tools for data gathering and analysis. This is an important indicator that every company should track. For services in which the customers are an input to the process, variability can be reduced by maintaining a stable pool of customers who are familiar with the transaction processes.

Customer loyalty can be instilled by offering specialized service not available from competitors. It can take many forms, including high customer contact or technology advancements. If a customer and supplier are linked through electronic data interchange (EDI), it is more difficult to switch to an alternative supplier because information systems have to be upgraded to work with new suppliers. This also speeds up data transmission between supplier and customer, reducing cycle times and lead times for delivery of products and services.

There is an intangible aspect to customer loyalty. Harley-Davidson is probably the best example of brand loyalty. After all, how many products induce the kind of loyalty that causes people to tattoo the company logo on their bodies or buy garish clothing reflecting their love of the product? It is difficult to isolate the ethos that results in this type of customer loyalty. Honda, Yamaha, and Kawasaki don't elicit the same passion. Some automobile brands such as Volkswagen Beetle, Ford Mustang, Chevrolet Corvette, and Smart Car create such customer loyalty that people travel great distances to go to national expositions and jamborees that center on these products. There is a certain intrigue about these products that results in this level of excitement and loyalty.

CUSTOMER-RELATIONSHIP MANAGEMENT SYSTEMS

With business information systems—especially over the Internet and social media—companies are receiving volumes of customer-related data. These data include personal, Internet, process, and customer-preference information. As a result, systems have been created to mine these data to improve customer service and retention. These systems are called **customer-relationship management systems (CRMS)**. CRMS use data to manage the three phases of customer-relationship management: *acquisition, retention*, and *enhancement*.

CRMS technologies are used in customer data–acquisition and data-mining efforts. All firms desire profitable customers. Customer self-service and product customization are ways to acquire new customer data. Another means is to provide customer access to information technology (IT) systems for configuring orders or researching information online. Customer retention is enhanced through a variety of activities. Because it costs six times as much to acquire customers, it is cost effective to retain customers. Frequent-flier programs and grocery discount cards are examples of information-based methods for retaining customers. Enhancement involves improving service to the customer through the use of information systems. On Amazon.com, users can customize their desktops. Also, advertisements for new books in the area of interest for the customer are created based on the customer's historical purchase patterns. This is accomplished through CRMS.

In terms of functionality, CRMS allow for providing customer contact, product configuration, campaign management, dealer/distribution management, pipeline management, telemarketing, customer interaction centers, customer analysis, field service management, self-service, personalization, and supply chain management. Table 5-4 provides a more detailed listing of CRMS functions. They are listed by category.

CRMS are used to monitor customer interactions, preferences, and relationships through media such as customer transaction records, call center logs, searches, and Web site clicks. The activities monitored include **customer defections**, who are customers who do not repeat business in some fixed period of time. This involves determining who are active versus inactive customers. Personalized service to those who are in danger of becoming inactive is used to achieve **churn reduction**—that is, reduction of the loss of customers.

CRMS are used to determine which customers are profitable and those who are unprofitable. Personalized communication can take place with customers, which serves them better and helps to maintain them as customers. For companies such as Amazon.com, **clickstream** information is kept that demonstrates how a customer navigates the Web site. This allows tailoring of the Web site to the preferences of the customer.

Maintaining these types of information is referred to as **knowledge management**, which involves managing the mountain of information generated by Web site usage in a way to improve marketing to key customers. The sales activities are managed specifically to each customer's preferences. This includes **transactional analysis**, which consists of customer service policies, sales processes, service process design, and after-sales service.

Like many newer technologies such as enterprise resource planning systems, CRMS implementations often result in failure. To implement CRMS properly requires an understanding of your business, customers, competitors, culture, and processes. Many of the project management, team management, and change management techniques discussed in this book can be extremely helpful for CRMS implementation. The implementation requires strong planning and project management skills. There are many vendors of CRMS, such as Oracle, IBM, Siebel, and others.

A WORD ON EXCELLENT DESIGN

Note that not all good ideas come from customers; some excellent products also arise from advances in technology resulting from good engineering. In the early days of the computer, IBM would not have pursued the computer as a viable product if it had relied on customers to tell the company their needs. For this purpose, many high-technology companies have adopted the

TABLE 5-4

Customer-centric activities

    Consolidate customer information from multiple channels—including e-mail, call centers, mobile devices, the Internet, and in-person encounters.

    Give all departments a composite image of the customer's purchasing and service history; as well as the customer's buying, delivery, and contact preferences.

    Support coordinated interactions throughout all customer touch points, including field sales, telesales, customer service, billing, and order fulfillment.

    Analyze data to determine your most valuable customers, target services to them, and use their behavior to predict new products that will succeed in their marketplace.

Enterprise capabilities

    Marketing automation to let marketers analyze customer purchasing trends, design targeted sales and marketing campaigns, and then measure results.

    Customer service software to create customer profiles and to provide scripts to help representatives solve customers' problems and cross-sell to promote new purchases.

    Sales automation tools to help the team manage accounts and prospects, as well as check metrics and inventories.

    Partner relationship management solutions that link together vendors and other partners with your systems.

Customer acquisition

    Marketing automation

    Campaign management

    Customer analysis

    Web measurement tools

    Advertising management

Sales management

    Sales process automation

    Configuration tools

    Order management

    Sales compensation

    Channel management

    Sales planning and analysis

    Wireless device support

Customer retention and enhancement

    Customer contact center

    Web/telephone self-service

    E-mail management

    Web/interactive chat

    Workflow analysis

    Field service

Source: Microsoft Corporation, 2015.

ready–fire–aim approach as the best way to market their goods.

    Other new products are developed by identifying a need that customers do not necessarily recognize. There is much work being performed in alternative technologies to be used in developing countries that do not have the infrastructure of developed countries. One example is the Tata Nano, a low-priced ($3,000) car being sold in India.

Summary

This chapter defined the voice of the customer and presented techniques such as surveys for learning and understanding this voice. Customer focus and satisfaction are key for companies to be successful. Tools such as complaint mechanisms, feedback, guarantees, and corrective action are necessary to develop annuity relationships with customers.

There are several ways to gather data about customers, including active and passive data-gathering techniques. These activities should be a part of an ongoing process for gathering customer data, analyzing the data, and implementing improvements to processes and design.

Finally, it is through focus on the customer and ingenuity that we find better ways to serve our customers. The corporate battleground in the new century is in the area of service. Customers are demanding more, and suppliers are responding by giving better and better service.

Key Terms

Active data gathering
Actively solicited customer feedback
Annuity relationship
Churn reduction
Clickstream
Closed-loop corrective action
Compensate
Complaint-recovery process
Contrition

Customer
Customer defections
Customer-driven quality
Customer rationalization
Customer-relationship management (CRM)
Customer-relationship management systems (CRMS)
Customer retention
End user

External customers
Focus group
Gap
Gap analysis
Hard data
Internal customers
Knowledge management
Ordinal data
Passive data gathering
Passively solicited customer feedback

Process-chain-network (PCN) diagram
Reactive customer-driven quality (RCDQ)
Ready–fire–aim
Single sourcing
Soft data
Strategic alliances
Transactional analysis
Vendor managed inventory (VMI)

Discussion Questions

1. Describe the difference between the internal and the external customers of a business organization. Why is it important to distinguish between internal and external customers?
2. Describe some of the potential pitfalls of customer-driven quality. Can you think of any ways to avoid or lessen the impact of these potential pitfalls?
3. How can a supplier avoid settling into a reactive customer-driven quality (RCDQ) mode?
4. Discuss the role of customer-relationship management (CRM) for service providers in helping to maintain existing customers.
5. When was the last time you purchased a product and were asked to provide the seller or manufacturer of the merchandise information about yourself, such as your name, address, and telephone number? Did the request for information seem intrusive to you? Did you have any idea why you were being asked for the additional information?
6. Reflect on the last time that you complained to the manager of a store, restaurant, or other business about something that dissatisfied you. Was the complaint resolved to your satisfaction? Did the complaint-resolution process tell you something about the quality of the organization that you were dealing with?
7. Gap analysis is used to identify gaps between what the customer expects and what is delivered by a firm. Do you think that the use of gap analysis is a positive or negative thing for a firm? Explain your answer.
8. Describe the basic concept behind strategic alliances. In what ways can strategic alliances facilitate a firm's quest for quality?
9. Describe some great service experiences and some horror stories you have experienced. What were the variables that in your mind differentiated between the great and the horrible companies?

10. Suppose that the marketing department of a large manufacturing firm decided to adopt the motto "We will build a product to suit any buyer's needs." What type of difficulties could this philosophy impose on the operations department? Through what process could the marketing department and the operations department determine which customers add the greatest advantage and profits over time?
11. Describe the basic idea behind a focus group. Are focus groups an effective way of gathering data about customer preferences and tastes?
12. Should focus group settings be formal and highly structured? Explain the rationale for your answer.
13. How can firms gain an overall understanding of the market segments they serve? Make your answer as substantive as possible.
14. Why is it important that the facilitator of a focus group not bias the discussion in any manner? How could the results of a focus group analysis be tainted if the facilitator biased the discussion?
15. Describe a situation in which the use of an Internet customer response might be appropriate.
16. Describe the difference between actively solicited customer feedback and passively solicited customer feedback. Which type of feedback results in a lower rating of quality? Explain why.
17. Describe the difference between hard data and soft data. What are the unique advantages of each type of data in terms of obtaining information about customer perceptions?
18. Are customer surveys better suited for accessing customer perceptions in services or manufacturing? Explain your answer.
19. Explain the concepts of reliability and validity. Why is it important that survey instruments be both reliable and valid?
20. Why is it important to have open-ended questions in survey instruments?

Problems

1. One of the problems encountered by universities is developing reliable and valid course evaluation survey instruments. Choose a class you took last semester. For that class, identify two dimensions relative to course delivery. Now, develop five valid survey items for each of your two dimensions. Defend why you think these items are valid.
2. For the class you chose in Problem 1, develop five valid critical-incident survey items for each dimension. Defend why you believe your items are valid.
3. A manager for the Golden Bear publishing company found out that you are taking quality management. The manager desires to improve her supply chain performance by employing you as a consultant to provide quality improvement training to the supply chain employees. As a result, you now have to create a survey instrument to gauge the effectiveness of your training sessions. Choose four dimensions relative to your quality management training and develop five valid survey items for each dimension. Defend why you feel your survey items are valid.
4. For your performance dimensions in Problem 3, develop five critical-incident survey items for each dimension. Explain how you would demonstrate that these items are reliable.

CASES

Case 5-1 Irish Transport Provider: Continuous Quality Improvement through a Commitment to External and Internal Customers[6]

Bus Éireann was formed in 1987 to provide both long distance and city bus services throughout Ireland with the exception of Dublin City. The firm forms an integral part of Ireland's transport infrastructure. It encourages customers to make smart, green choices by leaving their cars behind and travelling on public transport. They are fully committed to meeting the needs of its customers, which is reflected in their mission statement, "To succeed by providing excellent service to our customers through a committed team." Management is very driven to deliver on this commitment through support of both their external and internal customers.

[6]Based on Business 2000, 2007, Bus Eireann, *Total Quality Management,* accessed 20th March 2016 from http://www.buseireann.ie/pdf/1360855403-Total-Quality-Management.pdf

In order to satisfy their external customers, Bus Éireann has implemented a number of customer-friendly initiatives. This includes electronic passenger information displays with up-to-the-minute information at some terminals. An online journey planner is available on the Bus Éireann website. There is a customer "e" information system at info@buseireann.ie. A customer telephone enquiry service is provided everyday between 8.30am and 7pm, and information on journeys is made available on Aertel on all days. A centrally computerized complaints-handling system is also provided to deal with customer complaints speedily and efficiently. Lastly, freepost customer comment cards are provided at a wide range of locations. Traffic congestion is a major obstacle for Bus Éireann. To keep its zero defects policy, when traffic congestion is foreseen, Bus Éireann provides additional services to maintain existing services. The firm supports the introduction of bus lanes to tackle the problem. There is continuous internal and external monitoring of bus services every six months, ensuring Bus Éireann is fully aware of the ever-increasing demands of its customers. It also enables the company not only to be reactive to changes in journey patterns and tastes, but also to be proactive. Best practice is identified by making comparisons with competing private bus companies in Ireland and Europe.

Management at Bus Éireann is also aware that their internal customers are equally important to achieving high quality. Thus, employees are given a sense of responsibility to encourage total commitment to satisfying customers. Also encouraging and respecting employees lifts their morale and creates a successful working environment. As part of the process of continually developing management skills, Bus Éireann supports a number of employees studying for a Diploma in Management Studies. This course combines practical management skills with management strategy. The activities of both drivers and garage staff are coordinated by a team of supervisors. Staff receives training in customer care courses to ensure the company has a healthy communication network. The World Wide Web is used to interact efficiently with customers. Bus Éireann implements various programs of training and development to keep employees motivated and interested in their work. Various measures have been implemented by Bus Éireann to maintain good internal relations. Ongoing driver refresher programs for regular and part-time drivers. Training for safety officers, safety representatives, manual handling and fork lift drivers is ongoing. To ensure the safety of staff, the company regularly reviews and updates its health and safety management system. Inspectors are trained in safety awareness and receive certificates from an independent body. Safety aspects of coaches are inspected all over the country. Each employee of the company is trained in the areas of honesty and integrity as part of their code of ethics.

From their commitment to both its internal and external customers, Bus Éireann has benefited in many areas, including customer satisfaction to ensure repeat business. Also new customers have come in as the organization's reputation has grown. Health and Safety is prioritized and this benefits all. Employees are empowered, making them feel motivated and loyal, which leads to increased job satisfaction. Greater efficiency has been achieved through continuous monitoring and improvement of all business procedures.

Discussion Questions

1. For a company like Bus Éireann, why is a commitment to both internal stakeholders and external customers important?
2. Discuss the initiatives Bus Éireann introduced to improve the quality of service to their external customers.

3. Discuss the benefits experienced by Bus Éireann as a result of the quality improvement project.

Case 5-2 Customer Quality Feedback at Apple Computer

Apple Computer Homepage: www.apple.com

In the fast-paced personal computer industry, it would be very tempting for a computer company to rush a new product to market without taking the time to solicit customer input and feedback during the product development cycle. To avoid this temptation and to highlight its commitment to customer satisfaction, Apple Computer has developed a program called Customer Quality Feedback (CQF). CQF is a hands-on program that enables Apple engineers to communicate with potential end users during the entire development cycle of an Apple product. The program integrates many of the features of a focus group, but is sustained on an ongoing basis. It is also a very substantive and useful tool for Apple because it keeps the company attuned to the needs, preferences, and desires of its end users.

For people interested in participating in the program, Apple has posted an application form on its Web site. The application form is fairly comprehensive and outlines the terms and conditions of participation. Although the program is open to anyone, it is clear that Apple wants well-informed participants who will stick with the program. Participants are selected based on their interest, ability to provide timely information, commitment to working with Apple personnel, and the suitability of their computing environment as it relates to Apple's current needs. Once selected, the participants become an integral part of the development process for the products they are evaluating. They are provided early prototypes of Apple products and are asked to provide feedback pertaining to the product's features, interaction with employees, ease of use, performance, compatibility with third-party software, and other topics. The participants are also asked to provide suggestions as the product development cycle matures. The information provided by the participants is fed directly to the Apple engineers who are developing and testing the products. The overriding objective of the program is to incorporate customer input into the development of Apple products before they are shipped, rather than waiting for customers to react to the company's products after they are made available for sale. Prior to a product launch, the CQF participants involved with the product are asked to write testimonials about their input into the product's final design. These testimonials are used by Apple to demonstrate to other potential end users how Apple incorporates user feedback into the design and development of its products.

Apple's CQF program is a good example of a proactive approach to satisfying customer needs. It is also evidence of the company's willingness to "listen to the voice of the customer" in its product development and design. These are important steps in the development of a customer-driven approach to quality.

Discussion Questions

1. Explain how Apple's Customer Quality Feedback program helps the firm hear the voice of the customer.
2. In your opinion, what are the most important aspects of Apple's program? Would you make any changes or modifications?
3. If you were an Apple user, would you enjoy participating in the Customer Quality Feedback program? Why or why not?

CHAPTER 6

The Voice of the Market

Chapter Objectives

After completing this chapter, you should be able to:

1. Discuss the different types of benchmarking.
2. Assess what type of benchmarking is most appropriate for a particular situation.
3. Compute single-, multi-, and total factor productivity.
4. Understand the ethical issues associated with benchmarking.

Different people have different ideas about how to perform similar work. As a result, we can benefit by exploring different perspectives in designing products and processes. In the same sense, different organizations solve problems differently and take different approaches toward their work. For this reason, it can be helpful to observe how different firms form solutions.

For example, a small computer software firm must consider many things when establishing a customer service unit. Some questions they must ask themselves include these: What type of equipment would be needed? How should customer service specialists be trained? How would customer complaints be settled? How should refunds be handled? What procedures should be established to resolve customer issues? And what is an acceptable response time for returning customer calls? One method could be for the firm to blaze forth with the new customer service department and make mistakes as it goes along. A wiser approach would be to benchmark external customer service units in other companies first.

GAINING INSIGHTS THROUGH BENCHMARKING

Strategy formation results from understanding customers and the marketplace (see Figure 6-1). The marketplace includes immediate customers as well as competitors, the customers of competitors, potential competitors, and potential customers. In every market, advances shape and reshape the markets. Each firm strives to introduce new products, develop innovative processes, and find better ways to satisfy the customer. Customers can be good sources of information about competitors. This type of data gathering should include both strengths and weaknesses of your competitors. Some customers might be reticent to share this information. However, most customers realize that it is in their best interest to improve the performance of suppliers and will

FIGURE 6-1 Strategic Quality Planning Model

eagerly help. Information from lost customers also can be extremely useful for targeting weaknesses and improving products and services.

In Chapter 5 we considered how customers shape markets and how information about customers is obtained. However, customers are not the only source of information about the market. One of the best sources of information can be other companies. By understanding our competitors, we begin to understand the marketplace better and what it takes to compete successfully there.

Suppose that you wanted to learn how to snow ski during your winter break. There are a few options available to you: You could teach yourself how to ski, you could enlist the help of your friend who learned how to ski last week, or you could take ski lessons with a certified instructor. Perhaps you could become a decent skier using any of these methods, but your odds of success in learning quickly, avoiding injury, and gaining an appropriate respect for the sport would be greatest if you opt for the lessons.

The same is true in business. For a start-up firm, a rapidly growing company, or an organization in need of some improvements, the opportunity to observe and learn from a master could be invaluable. A **benchmark** is an organization recognized for its exemplary operational performance. There are many benchmarks in the world, including Toyota for processes, Intel for design, Scandinavian Airlines for service, and Honda for rapid product development.

To be a benchmark, a company must be willing to open its doors and allow others to view its operations and tour its facilities. Thus a distinguishing feature of benchmarks is their amazing openness to other firms. Consider Toyota Motor Company. From the 1960s to the 1980s, Toyota developed the world-class production system known as just-in-time, or lean. This production system resulted in previously unseen levels of productivity, minimal cost, and a source of competitive advantage. Some companies might have put barbed wire and guard dogs around their lean facilities to keep this technology to themselves and maintain their competitive advantage. Instead, Toyota allowed employees such as Taiichi Ohno and Shigeo Shingo to write books explaining the lean concept to the rest of the world. Toyota also allowed thousands of visitors to tour its facilities and learn about the lean system. The company even entered into strategic alliances with chief competitors so that those competitors could learn about lean production.

Two rationales explain why benchmarking is good business. The first originates from Deming's thought that "the worst thing for a business is a weak competitor." Therefore, strengthening the competition forces everyone to improve in order to maintain a competitive edge. As such, *openness provides an impetus to continual improvement*. Another view is that openness can create a competitive advantage through creating *psychological barriers to competition*. A manager of a high-technology firm marketing a new product once said, "We do not mind if the others come to see how we produce our product. Once they see what we can do, they will not want to compete against us." In other words, the large amount of work it would take to establish and develop the systems that a truly outstanding competitor already has in place can be daunting and discouraging to its competitors.

TABLE 6-1	Benchmarking Types

Process benchmarking—comparing processes

Financial benchmarking—comparing business results

Performance benchmarking—comparing cost structures, speed, quality levels, etc.

Product benchmarking—comparing product attributes and functionality

Strategic benchmarking—comparing firm competitiveness along several dimensions

Functional benchmarking—comparing or learning how another firm performs a particular function

Benchmarking is the sharing of information between companies so that both can improve. The first step a benchmarking firm must take is to document current performance. This activity will allow the company to pinpoint its goals and find a company (inside or outside the industry) that already excels at what it is trying to accomplish, study what it does, and gather ideas for improvement. Benchmarking is useful for externally validating an organization's approach to its business. If the managers in a firm are unsure that they are pursuing a useful plan of action, benchmarking can help them understand how what they are doing stacks up against the masters.

There are two parties to each benchmarking relationship: an **initiator firm** and a **target firm**. The initiator firm initiates contact and studies another firm. The target firm is the firm being studied (also called a *benchmarking partner*). These are not static roles. Often the target firm enters into a reciprocal agreement to observe the initiator firm. As shown in Table 6-1, there are several types of benchmarking. Note that they are not all mutually exclusive.

Process Benchmarking

In **process benchmarking**, the initiator firm focuses its observation and investigation on business processes. This focus can involve studying process flows, operating systems, process technologies, and the operations of target firms or departments. The goal is to identify and to observe the best practices from one or more benchmark firms. By improving core processes, overall business performance is enhanced.

Financial Benchmarking

The goal of **financial benchmarking** is to perform financial analysis and to compare the results in an effort to assess your overall competitiveness. This type of benchmarking need not involve direct interaction between the initiator firm and the target firms. There is, however, interaction between the initiator and a third party that gathers this information. Usually the information can be gathered using on-line databases such as Lexis/Nexis or Compact D/SEC.

Performance Benchmarking

Performance benchmarking allows initiator firms to assess their competitive position by comparing products and services with those of target firms. Performance issues may include cost structures, various types of productivity performance, speed of concept to market, quality measures, and other performance evaluations. For example, an initiator firm may be interested in identifying other firms that have implemented effective cost accounting practices such as activity–based costing systems to observe and compare the performance of various cost drivers.

Product Benchmarking

Many firms perform **product benchmarking** when designing new products or upgrades to current products. Product benchmarking often includes **reverse engineering**, or dismantling competitors' products to understand the strengths and weaknesses of their designs. By observing the designs of others, the initiator firm can develop new ideas for product and service design. Micron Technologies maintained a cost advantage in producing DRAM computer chips because of its capability to produce chips with fewer mask levels than its competitors. To compete with Micron, competitors would have to analyze their chips and try to understand their chip-making processes.

Strategic Benchmarking

Strategic benchmarking involves observing how others compete. It often is not industry-specific because firms go outside their own industries to learn lessons from companies and organizations in different industries. Strategic benchmarking typically involves target firms that have won prestigious honors such as the Malcolm Baldrige award, the Shingo Prize, or the Deming Prize. The focus of this type of benchmarking is to identify the mix of strategies that makes these firms successful competitors. Such benchmarking can be very time-consuming and costly. When Boise Cascade Company was establishing a quality management process, the firm took a team of executives to Japan and visited several firms to get a sense of what a high-quality firm looked like. Although firms were from other industries, the executives returned with a very realistic idea of the task they faced in establishing quality processes. Pal's Sudden Service (Quality Highlight 6-1) uses strategic benchmarking.

QUALITY HIGHLIGHT 6-1   Pal's Sudden Service[1]

www.palsweb.com

A privately owned, quick-service restaurant chain, Pal's Sudden Service serves primarily drive-through customers at 27 locations, all within 60 miles of Kingsport, Tennessee, where its first restaurant opened in 1956. Carefully following its formula for standardizing high levels of product and service quality, Pal's has since grown to become a major regional competitor.

Today, Pal's employs about 900 people, 95% of whom are in direct production and service roles. The company competes directly with national fast-food chains, earning a steadily increasing—and, now, second best in its region—market share of almost 19%, doubling since 1994.

Featuring hard-to-miss exteriors festooned with larger-than-life menu items, Pal's restaurants sell hamburgers, hot dogs, chipped ham, chicken, French fries, and beverages, as well as breakfast biscuits with country ham, sausage, and gravy. The company aims to distinguish itself from fast-food competitors by offering competitively priced food of consistently high quality, delivered rapidly, cheerfully, and without error. The majority of customers live or work within three miles of Pal's locations, and nearly two-thirds are women.

Pal's is the first business in the restaurant industry to receive a Malcolm Baldrige award. For everything organizational and operational, Pal's has a process. Almost nothing—from new product introductions, to hiring decisions, to the design of support processes and work systems—is done without a thorough understanding of likely impacts on customer satisfaction.

The company's Business Excellence Process is the key integrating element used in every transaction. Carried out under the leadership of Pal's two top executives and its 21 store owner/operators, the Business Excellence Process spans all facets of the operation—from strategic planning (done annually with two-year horizons) to online quality control. Every component process, including those for continual improvement and product introduction, is interactively linked, producing data that directly or indirectly inform the others.

(continued)

[1]Based on NIST, "Profiles of Baldrige Winners, 2015."

Benchmarking underpins the entire Business Excellence Process. Managers are continually on the lookout for benchmarking candidates, and each one compiles a running list of potential subjects. For the leadership team, benchmarking yields meaningful competitive comparisons, new best practices for achieving higher performance goals, or new organizational directions. For the entire organization, benchmarking results are a constant reminder that performance always can be improved.

Pal's is exhaustive in its pursuit of useful data, the basis for sound planning and decision making. In particular, customer, employee, and supplier feedback is central to all processes, and it is gathered in numerous formal and informal ways. For example, Pal's owner/operators must devote part of every workday to "marketing by wandering around." A portion of this period is spent engaging employees and customers to hear their views on how a location is performing and to solicit ideas for improvement.

Owner/operators also go door to door within a three-mile radius of their restaurants, seeking direct input on customer requirements and satisfaction levels. Answers to predesigned questions are recorded, compiled, and later analyzed at the store and corporate levels.

Owner/operators also maintain a communications log. They record what they have learned about sales, expenses, customers, staff, products, services, equipment, and suppliers; and they list ideas for improvement. Weekly logs are sent to senior Pal's executives, who comb the entries for issues and opportunities to be addressed at formal monthly management reviews of organizational and business results.

Data are gathered systematically at all levels—process, shift, individual store, and entire business. The company's enterprise resource planning system, SysDine, is a key tool that generates store-level and company-wide data on sales, customer count, product mix, ideal food and material cost, and turnover rates. This information supports daily operational decisions. It also is used to update Pal's Balanced Scorecard of Core Performance Measures, which links directly to its key business drivers: quality, service, cleanliness, value, people, and speed.

Managers regularly review the value of the data collected, and the company employs an outside statistician to evaluate the type of information tracked, how it is used, and how it is collected.

Developed with the aid of benchmarking studies, the company's training processes support improvement in operational and business performance. Owner/operators and assistant managers have primary responsibility for staff training. They use a four-step model: show, do it, evaluate, and perform again. Employees must demonstrate 100% competence before they are certified to work at a specific work station.

In customer satisfaction, including food quality, service, and order accuracy, Pal's is outperforming its primary competitor. For example, customer scores for quality averaged 95.8%, as compared with 84.1% for its best competitor.

Functional Benchmarking

Another type of benchmarking, referred to as **functional benchmarking**, happens when a company focuses its benchmarking efforts on a single function to improve the operation of that function. An example of functional benchmarking occurs in purchasing. Often, purchasing managers use their networks to share information about the purchasing function in many different organizations. The Institute for Supply Management (ISM) provides a framework for networking purchasing professionals that facilitates the sharing of information about the purchasing function. In addition, the ISM gathers information about purchasing departments and makes this information available to members of the organization.

PURPOSES OF BENCHMARKING

There are seven primary purposes for benchmarking. These purposes require different levels of involvement in the benchmarking activities. Time consumption and costs may vary according to the purpose of benchmarking.

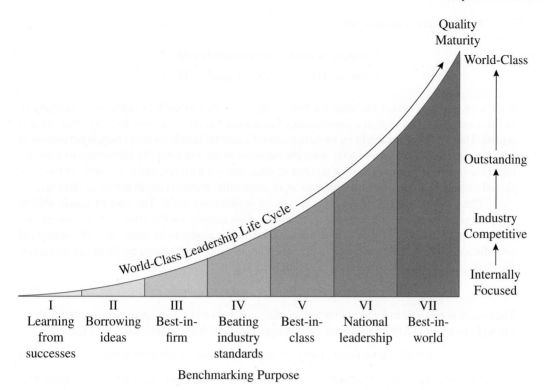

FIGURE 6-2   Benchmarking Purpose and Quality Maturity

The purposes of benchmarking range from basic learning to achieving world-class leadership. The life cycle in Figure 6-2 shows that benchmarking purposes evolve as the firm becomes more mature in its quality journey.

DIFFICULTIES IN MONITORING AND MEASURING PERFORMANCE

Firms often desire to compare financial measures between companies when benchmarking. Although this comparison can be a useful activity, there can be problems. One of the most significant problems stems from limitations of accounting systems. Often, companies have variations in the way they compute their measures that affect the results.

Consider the computation of scrap in which a company computes the ratio of cost of goods sold to scrap. The formula for this computation is

$$\text{Scrap efficiency} = \text{cost of goods sold}/\text{scrap} \qquad \textbf{(6.1)}$$

This formula normalizes the cost of scrap based on the volume of business that a firm does. The resulting ratio is the proportion of the material inputs to production that is wasted as scrap. The higher the ratio, the more efficient is the use of these materials.

Now consider two companies, A and B. Company A uses Equation 6.1 and computes scrap by weighing discarded materials at a standard cost of \$.15 per pound of scrap. However, Company B has a variation in its measures. Company B computes scrap at the industry standard of \$.15 per pound, less \$.03 per pound (the amount it receives from a recycling company that purchases its scrap). Therefore, Company B's account equation would be

$$\text{Computed ratio for Company B} = \text{cost of goods sold}/(\text{scrap} - \text{recovery}) \qquad \textbf{(6.2)}$$

The resulting equations are

$$\text{Company A ratio} = \text{cost of goods sold}/.15$$
$$\text{Company B ratio} = \text{cost of goods sold}/.12$$

If the cost of goods sold is the same for both companies, the ratio will be higher for Company B. In this case, Company A is at a disadvantage because of the differences in the ways that scrap is costed. These differences might be more apparent if a careful benchmarking study is performed in which the participants know exactly what the numbers mean and what the differences in accounting systems are. However, if a great number of data, ratios, measures, and numerical statistics are shared among the companies, the differences in accounting methods might not be as obvious.

The ratio we have focused on is a type of productivity ratio. The cost of goods sold to scrap ratio measures the efficient use of materials. One remedy for the effects of accounting differences on productivity ratios is to compute total-factor productivity measures. To understand total-factor productivity measures, we first must understand single-factor productivity measures. Single-factor productivity measures are computed as

$$\text{Single-factor productivity} = \text{output}/(\text{a single input}) \qquad \textbf{(6.3)}$$

The cost of goods sold to scrap ratio is a single factor ratio in that it focuses on scrap material alone. Multiple factor productivity measures use multiple inputs in their computation. For example,

$$\text{Multiple factor productivity} = \text{output}/(\text{the sum of multiple inputs}) \qquad \textbf{(6.4)}$$

Multiple inputs might include scrap, labor, energy, materials, equipment, and other measures of inputs. Hayes and Wheelwright[2] suggested that it is better for firms to use multiple factor productivity measures when making comparisons because these measures are more robust. The total factor productivity measure is similarly computed as

$$\text{Total factor productivity} = \text{output}/(\text{sum of all inputs to production}) \qquad \textbf{(6.5)}$$

Total factor productivity, although still subject to the "apples and oranges" problems of comparisons, is less sensitive to differences in costing conventions and accounting practices.

Notice that if you focused on plant and equipment productivity, the conclusion would be that the competitor is lagging in productivity. Also notice that labor productivity may be a small part of total productivity.[3]

EXAMPLE 6-1   **Computing Productivity**

A company has gathered the following financial information for itself and a competing firm. The company wants to compare productivity for the two firms (all the following numbers are in 000s).

	Firm A	Competition
Labor	$ 20,000	$ 15,000
Plant and equipment (P&E)	100,000	145,000
Energy	5,500	10,500
Materials	220,000	190,000
Sales	425,000	500,000

---

[2]Hayes, R., and Wheelwright, S., *Dynamic Manufacturing* (Boston: Free Press, 1988).
[3]Some firms are using a method called *data envelopment analysis* (DEA) to improve comparisons between firms. This is a linear programming approach that can potentially be used to eliminate the "apples and oranges" problem.

Labor and other productivity ratios for the two firms are computed as

Firm A labor productivity = (sales/labor) = 425,000/20,000 = 21.25

Competitor labor productivity = (sales/labor) = 500,000/15,000 = 33.33

Firm A P&E productivity = (sales/P&E) = 425,000/100,000 = 4.25

Competitor P&E productivity = (sales/P&E) = 500,000/145,000 = 3.45

Firm A energy productivity = (sales/energy) = 425,000/5,500 = 77.27

Competitor energy productivity = (sales/energy) = 500,000/10,500 = 47.62

Firm A materials productivity = (sales/materials) = 425,000/220,000 = 1.93

Competitor materials productivity = (sales/materials) = 500,000/190,000 = 2.63

Total factor productivity for Firm A = (sales/total of inputs) = 425,000/345,500 = 1.23

Total factor productivity for the competitor = (sales/total of inputs) = 500,000/360,500 = 1.39

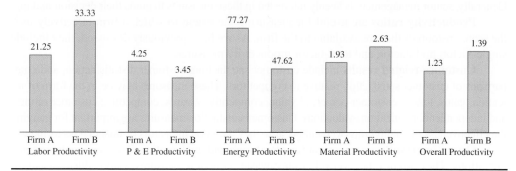

As you can see, the total factor productivity measure provides a more complete picture of firm productivity.

Another caveat for comparing measures between companies is based on the Deming arguments against such things as work measurement and management by objective. To concentrate too much on comparative measures might focus managers on results and not causes. This could result in the unfortunate development of numerical goals that ignore the necessity of improving the system of production.

Because of the possibility of serial correlation of data, even greater care should be taken when analyzing longitudinal (time-series) data. For example, company researchers might want to compare *rates of growth* for two companies in assets, sales, and other measures. If the data have serial correlation, they might reach the wrong conclusions.

Problems in comparisons are even more pronounced when comparing U.S. firms with foreign companies. The cost accounting conventions and accepted accounting principles can vary greatly between countries. For this reason, it is best not to compare accounting figures with foreign companies. However, if you must, take great care as to how the results of the comparisons are used in formulating policy.

COMMONLY BENCHMARKED PERFORMANCE MEASURES

Different firms in different industries use many different benchmarking measures. The measures that a firm chooses depend on the **key business factors (KBFs)** of each particular firm. These key business factors are factors significantly related to the business success of the firm. For example, in a given firm, customer satisfaction might be significantly related to market share. If this is the case, a company would be very interested in tracking its customer satisfaction.

Table 6-2 shows the categories of measures that are often gathered in benchmarking studies. **Financial ratios** such as return on assets (ROA) or return on investments (ROI) are probably the

TABLE 6-2	Benchmarking Data
Financial ratios	
Productivity ratios	
Customer-related results	
Operating results	
Human resources measures	
Quality measures	
Market share data	
Structural measures	

easiest to obtain and compare. For many financial ratios, all that is needed is an income statement of a firm and a balance sheet. Many of these statistics are available in annual reports and on the Internet. Generally, senior management is keenly interested in these measures to guide their decision making.

Productivity ratios are useful for measuring the extent to which a firm effectively uses the scarce resources that are available to the firm. As we have previously discussed, they include single-factor, multifactor, and total-factor productivity measures.

Customer-related results include customer satisfaction, customer dissatisfaction, and comparisons of customer satisfaction relative to competitors. These measures may be in the form of retention, gains, losses, customer-perceived value, competitive awards, competitive customer ratings, and independent organization evaluations. Customer satisfaction measures are important for gauging the effectiveness of quality improvement because they are good indicators of financial performance.

Operating results are important for monitoring and tracking the effectiveness of company operations. They might relate to cycle times, waste-reduction measures, value-added measures, lead times, time from concept to market, setup times, percent reduction in setup times, and myriad other operating results.

Often, one of the key aspects of running a business involves the people employed by the organization. Therefore, **human resources measures** provide important insights into how effectively the business is being run. Employee satisfaction is significantly related to business performance in many firms. Therefore, employee satisfaction measures, training expenditures, training hours per year, work system performance, employee effectiveness measures, turnover, safety statistics, absenteeism, and many other data might be important measures for benchmarking.

Of course, **quality measures** are often compared between firms. They can include conformance-based quality information such as reject rates, capability analysis, performance information, or other measures. These quality measures also can include scrap and rework measures, percentage of defectives, field repairs, costs of quality, and many other metrics. The quality measures also may include data concerning the performance of processes and time-related statistics. Where customer service quality is important, the types of data that are captured often include such things as percentage of customers whose phone calls are answered within seven seconds, average response time for phone inquiries, number of people a caller must contact to get a problem resolved, and many other metrics (or measures).

Market share data are an essential indicator of business success, resulting from the change in competition because of increased global competition. However, market share does not encompass only a single measure. Because markets are segmented, market share includes shares in the different markets served by the firm. Market share comparisons also are made to determine where the initiator firm ranks in the market.

Finally, with the advent of ISO standards and a move to formalized production systems, **structural measures** often are benchmarked. Structural measures include the objectives, policies, and procedures followed by a firm. They may include safety, production, accounting, financial, engineering, and other types of structural measures that are used in determining competitiveness.

Why Collect All These Measures?

Management by fact dictates that decisions are made based on the sound collection and analysis of data. The Malcolm Baldrige criteria are clear about this:

> Data and analysis support a variety of company purposes, such as planning, reviewing company performance, improving operations, and comparing company performance with competitors or with "best practices" benchmarks.[4]

A major consideration in performance improvement involves the creation and use of performance measures or indicators. Performance measures or indicators are measurable characteristics of products, services, processes, and operations that the company uses to track and improve performance. The measures or indicators should be selected to best represent the factors that lead to improved customer, operational, and financial performance. A comprehensive set of measures or indicators tied to customer and/or company performance requirements represents a clear basis for aligning all activities with the company's goals. Through the analysis of data from the tracking processes, the measures or indicators may be evaluated and changed to better support such goals.

Key Business Factors

When benchmarking, it is important to understand your target firm's key business factors (KBFs) as well as your own. Key business factors are important attributes of a business that influence its operations and decision making. Examples of KBFs include mission, vision, values, key customer segments, core capabilities, culture, governance, and other business facets. KBFs are not to be confused with **key measures** (the metrics that need to be monitored to gauge the health of the business) and **critical success factors** (factors that help to determine the success of the firm).

BUSINESS PROCESS BENCHMARKING

Many benchmarking professionals believe that the most important type of benchmarking is business process benchmarking, and with good reason. Suppose that you compare your customer service quality with a competitor's. You find out that your competitor is using a standard survey instrument to gauge customer satisfaction. You then administer the survey to your customers and find out that on a 5-point scale your company rates a 4.3 and your chief competitor rates a 4.7 (with equal dispersion). Now what do you do with this information? The fact that your score differs from your competitor's tells you nothing about how the competitor is achieving these higher scores. To understand how your competitor has achieved these scores, business process benchmarking is necessary.

Business process benchmarking is based on the concept of **5w2h** developed by Alan Robinson.[5] The 5w2h concept is labeled as such because a business process benchmarking project should result in the answers to seven questions. Five of these questions begin with the letter *w* (*w*ho, *w*hat, *w*hen, *w*here, *w*hy), and the remaining two questions begin with the letter *h* (*h*ow and *h*ow much).

The 5w2h concept is a good starting point because it focuses the participants in the benchmarking process on the nuts and bolts of what is being done. If the initiator organization can answer the 5w2h questions at the end of a benchmarking process, then information will be in place that could, for instance, help a company improve its customer satisfaction.

The 5w2h questions should be viewed in the context of a process. Figure 6-3 contains a diagram of a generic process. In a broad sense, inputs include the equipment, people, machines, materials, and design that combine to form a product or service. The inputs are combined in what is known as the **conversion process**. In the conversion process, we align the inputs together to form the product or service. Conversion processes might include turning sheet steel into chimney pipes or turning wood pulp into paper, or moving materials from point A to point B for a shipping service.

[4]*2015 Criteria for Performance Excellence* (Gaithersburg, MD: National Institute of Standards and Technology, 2015), p. 4.
[5]Aires, R., Salgado, C., and Ayres, K., "The PDCA Cycle in Practice," *International Journal of Advanced Operations* 6(4), 324–334 2014.

FIGURE 6-3 Process Model

The conversion process results in outputs that are eventually sold to customers. Notice in Figure 6-3 that there are two feedback loops in the process. The first feedback loop results from gathering data from the process. This is known as the **control process**. As we explained in Chapter 1, the control process involves gathering, analyzing, and using the data to adjust the process. This is often the result of using process control charts.

The second feedback loop in the process is the customer feedback loop and results from gathering data from the customers. Using these data, the control process is improved to give the customer greater satisfaction. A third feedback process can be added by gathering information from competitors through benchmarking.

Figure 6-4 shows what to benchmark at each stage. Again, the questions asked are similar to the 5w2h questions posed earlier.

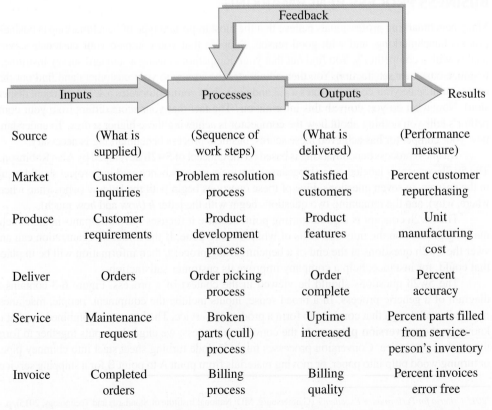

FIGURE 6-4 Process Information *Source:* R. Camp, *Business Process Benchmarking* (Milwaukee, WI: ASQ Quality Press, 1995), p. 26. Reprinted with permission from the Quality Press. © 1995 American Society for Quality.

TABLE 6-3	Benchmarking Steps at Xerox

1. Decide what to benchmark
2. Identify whom to benchmark
3. Plan and conduct the investigation
4. Determine the current performance gap
5. Project future performance levels
6. Communicate benchmarking findings and gain acceptance
7. Revise performance goals
8. Develop action plans
9. Implement specific actions and monitor progress
10. Recalibrate the benchmarks

Robert Camp's Business Process Benchmarking Process

We have already defined process benchmarking. We now discuss the benchmarking process developed by Robert Camp. Xerox was an early adopter of benchmarking and has used benchmarking effectively to improve processes. This approach includes a formal 10-step process to benchmarking, as shown in Table 6-3.

Step 1: Decide what to benchmark. There are innumerable areas for improvement in every company. Obviously, not all of these can be tackled at once. Too many simultaneous changes can result in a confused organization and actually can hurt performance. Therefore, you must prioritize those processes that offer the greatest potential for improvement. To do this, you must have identified your key processes and charted those processes for future analysis.

Step 2: Identify whom to benchmark. This involves identifying those competitors in your industry and those firms outside your industry that have outstanding results and processes for study. Those companies that have developed best practices are prime candidates for benchmarking.

Step 3: Plan and conduct the investigation. To complete this step, identify data to be collected. Next, develop a method with the target firms to determine how the data are to be collected. Once the data are selected, observe the practices of the target firm and document the best practices that are observed.

Step 4: Determine the current performance gap. Once you have collected the data about the processes, a determination is made as to which processes in the initiator company have the greatest performance gap with the target company. Brainstorming can help make this determination. This step helps to prioritize which areas are the first candidates for change and improvement.

Step 5: Project future performance levels. Predict whether the performance gap for the benchmarked processes will narrow or widen in the coming years. If the performance gaps are likely to widen in the future, project how this will affect the company.

Step 6: Communicate benchmarking findings and gain acceptance. This step begins the communication of the benchmarking findings to those who will be affected by the results. This can be done through meetings and written media. Communication keeps the process as open as possible, which minimizes uncertainty and fear.

Step 7: Revise performance goals. After best practices are identified, operational goals are revised. This process establishes measures for evaluating the results of improvements based on benchmarking.

Step 8: Develop action plans. Action plans are the specific steps and objectives for implementation. Assignments to personnel and timetables for implementation are used with a project management approach.

Step 9: Implement specific actions and monitor progress. As implementation proceeds, progress is reported to management and stakeholders.

Step 10: Recalibrate the benchmarks. Continued benchmarking with the best firms helps to identify new best practices. This process "raises the bar" for higher levels of future performance.

LEADING AND MANAGING THE BENCHMARKING EFFORT

Like other quality management efforts, benchmarking is a managed process. Therefore, management must have an understanding of the benchmarking process, the participants involved, and the objectives of the exercise.

Managing the benchmarking process involves establishing, supporting, and sustaining the benchmarking program. To begin the management process, a strategy statement outlining the goals and strategies to be used is developed (see A Closer Look at Quality 6-1).

With the strategy statement in place, management sets expectations for performance relating to the benchmarking project. At a minimum, the expectations for benchmarking are that this is an ongoing process that serves as a basis for improvement (not a one-time event) and that specific deliverables are to be identified by management that must be fulfilled.

Other activities for management include providing management awareness training, establishing a benchmarking competency center, developing guidelines for information sharing, and overseeing the development of a visit protocol. Once this benchmarking infrastructure is in place, benchmarking teams are commissioned and trained to perform the benchmarking project.

Training

Training is a key to success in all quality management approaches. This is especially true for benchmarking. Participants must have project management skills and be familiar with benchmarking approaches and protocols. Benchmarking carries with it legal liabilities that should be addressed during the training (see A Closer Look at Quality 6-2). Training should include managerial training, cross-functional benchmarking skills training, team training, and documentation training (flowcharting). Many of these training courses are available from many different consulting organizations. It is best to obtain training from organizations that are experienced with benchmarking. Many companies have established external training arms that can be hired by competing firms.

A CLOSER LOOK AT QUALITY 6-1   Benchmarking at PwC[6]

PricewaterhouseCoopers Public Sector Practice (PwC PSP) was formed in 2005 and uses several approaches to benchmarking and comparing performance to improve performance. Some of this information comes from publically available or commercial sources and some from competitors. PwC PSP employs over 2,000 people and reported a gross revenue of $265.5 million.

Customer Engagement Proves Good for Business

PwC PSP utilizes scores from the federal government's Contractor Performance Assessment Reports to improve customer satisfaction. Thanks to its Engagement Management Process (EMP), scores rating PwC PSP as "exceptional" or "very good" increased to levels at or near 100% for fiscal years 2010 through 2014. Additionally, the percentage of responders that said PwC PSP "needs improvement" decreased from 73% in fiscal year 2011 to zero in fiscal year 2014.

Among other quality tools, PwC uses net promoter scores. Net Promoter System (NPS, a tool for measuring and comparing customer engagement and loyalty) survey scores have been 50 or higher in all markets for years. These scores are equal to or better than NPS scores for some of the most respected companies in the country.

---

[6]Based on Anon, PriceWaterhouseCoopers Public Sector Practice, National Institute of Standards and Technology (Gaithersburg, MD: NIST) 2015.

A CLOSER LOOK AT QUALITY 6-2   The Legal Environment of Benchmarking

Legal issues such as antitrust, intellectual property, and trademark issues are central concerns for firms entering into benchmarking agreements. To overcome these issues, benchmark practitioners should follow a code of conduct. One such code of conduct for benchmarking has been proposed by the Strategic Planning Institute Council on Benchmarking.[7]

The Benchmarking Code of Conduct

Principles

To contribute to efficient, effective, and ethical benchmarking, individuals agree for themselves and their organization to abide by the following principles for benchmarking with other organizations:

- *Principle of legality.* Avoid discussions or actions that might lead to or imply an interest in restraint of trade: market or customer allocation schemes, price fixing, dealing arrangements, bid rigging, bribery, or misappropriation. Do not discuss costs with competitors if costs are an element of pricing.
- *Principle of exchange.* Be willing to provide the same level of information that you request in any benchmarking exchange.
- *Principle of confidentiality.* Treat benchmarking interchange as something confidential to the individual and organizations involved. Information obtained must not be communicated outside the partnering organizations without prior consent of participating benchmarking partners. An organization's participation in a study should not be communicated externally without its permission.
- *Principle of use.* Information obtained through benchmarking partnering should be used only for the purpose of improving operations within the partnering companies. External use or communication of a benchmarking partner's name with its data or observed practices requires permission of that partner. Do not, as a consultant or client, extend one company's benchmarking study findings to another without the first company's permission.
- *Principle of first-party contact.* Initiate contacts, whenever possible, through a benchmarking contact designated by the partner company. Obtain the permission of the contact before relaying any information or delegating any responsibility to other parties.
- *Principle of third-party contact.* Obtain an individual's permission before providing his or her name in response to a contact request.
- *Principle of preparation.* Demonstrate commitment to the efficiency and effectiveness of the benchmarking process with adequate preparation at each process step, especially at the initial partnering contact.
- *Principle of completion.* Keep your commitments with your benchmarking partner in a timely fashion and keep your agreements.
- *Principle of understanding and action.* Follow the golden rule with benchmarking partners. Strive to understand how your benchmarking partner wants to have information handled.

Remember:

- Keep it legal.
- Be willing to give what you get.
- Respect confidentiality.
- Keep information internal.
- Use benchmarking contacts.
- Don't refer without permission.
- Be prepared at the initial contact.

[7]Based on Productivity and Quality with Performance Measures and metrics- APQC, www.apqc.org

---

Outside consultants can be useful for providing training and coaching on benchmarking and other quality-related efforts. However, it is best for the firm that is interested in benchmarking to perform the benchmarking with its own employees rather than through consultants because a self-perpetuated approach creates the best platform for organizational learning. Although the process may take longer, it probably will be more useful to do it yourself.

BASELINING AND PROCESS IMPROVEMENT

Many firms are facing the important decision to redesign and improve business processes to enhance productivity, reduce cost, improve quality, and achieve better customer service. Process redesign is defined as a fundamental rethinking and redesign of business processes. Such change is often accompanied by the automation of business processes. Two factors are critical to achieving success through process redesign: breadth and depth. *Breadth* refers to the impact of the process redesign process to the entire organization. *Depth* refers to organizational elements such as responsibilities, measurements, information technology, and skills. These dichotomous factors imply that business process redesign will result in both localized (such as the affected work areas) and generalized (or organization-wide) performance impacts. However, these impacts are difficult to assess. Therefore, appropriate, effective methodologies are needed to assess the impacts of business process redesign.

A methodology that can be applied in assessing business process redesign impacts is baselining. **Baselining**, which has been discussed in other chapters, requires the monitoring of key internal firm performance measures over time to identify trends such as improvement (or decline) to inform managerial decision making. The baselining process involves identifying measures, establishing timeframes for future data collection, gathering data, and analyzing data on an ongoing basis to identify performance trends and changes (see Figure 6-5).

Because process redesign affects multiple levels in a firm, abrupt organizational changes are reflected in baselining results. If changes are effective in improving the organization, the data collected will reflect this improvement.

PROBLEMS WITH BENCHMARKING

Benchmarking is not a simple activity, and it can be difficult to implement any of these tools and concepts. There are four key problems with benchmarking:

1. There may be substantial difficulty obtaining cooperation from other firms in your own industry—unless you happen to be a Fortune 100 firm. Most organizations have much less clout. The thing to remember is *reciprocity*. To be effective, you must have something to offer the target firm in return for sharing information. For example, a small firm may feel that it has little to offer a larger firm. If the small firm is flexible, the Goliath firm may want to learn how to achieve that flexibility.
2. The predominance of functional benchmarking with firms in noncompeting industries makes it difficult to benchmark with these firms. It takes much ingenuity to identify benchmarks

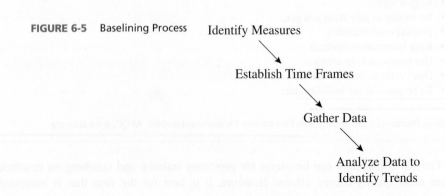

FIGURE 6-5 Baselining Process
Identify Measures
Establish Time Frames
Gather Data
Analyze Data to Identify Trends

properly from noncompeting firms. This is where the business and industry literature is very helpful in trying to identify benchmarking firms in noncompetitive industries.

3. Your efforts will be wasted unless you fully understand your own processes before you benchmark someone else. By using tools such as business process maps, you can identify the exact performance measures and metrics needed from the target firm.

4. Benchmarking is time-consuming and costly. A recent benchmarking project between two firms took nearly two years to complete and cost each of the firms more than $250,000. Of course, this was a major benchmarking project; other projects have been completed at lower costs, but some have been much more expensive. Costs of benchmarking include time for planning, travel, documentation, and implementation. By far the largest costs are associated with implementation. The investment is lost if benchmarking data are not used to drive improvement.

Summary

In this chapter, we discussed an important method for listening to the voice of the market: We discussed the purposes of benchmarking. Most often, companies benchmark processes and many performance measures such as productivity.

The goal of benchmarking is to become best in class and then best of the best. Benchmarking is more effective for firms that have been pursuing quality and process improvement over time. This is certainly not a starting point for quality improvement efforts.

Remember that the use of data and measures can result in undesired outcomes as individuals attempt to exploit the measurement system to reflect well on them. Baselines and other measures should be implemented carefully with attention to the possibility of unintended outcomes.

Key Terms

Baselining	Financial ratios	Management by fact	Quality measures
Benchmark	5w2h	Market share data	Reverse engineering
Control process	Functional benchmarking	Operating results	Strategic benchmarking
Conversion process	Human resources measures	Performance benchmarking	Structural measures
Critical success factors	Initiator firm	Process benchmarking	Target firm
Customer-related results	Key business factor (KBF)	Product benchmarking	
Financial benchmarking	Key measures	Productivity ratios	

Discussion Questions

1. Describe the concept of benchmarking. Provide an example of how a restaurant you are familiar with could use benchmarking to improve its performance.

2. What is a benchmark firm? Why is it good practice for a benchmark firm to open its doors and allow others to view its operations and tour its facilities?

3. Benchmarking is the comparing of methods/performance between companies so that both can improve. Explain the above extract from the text in the context of the steps involved in carrying out a benchmarking exercise. What is the purpose of benchmarking?

4. In the context of benchmarking, describe the distinction between an initiator firm and a target firm.

5. Describe how benchmarking can be used by a firm to validate externally the value of its present business practices.

6. Describe the concept of process benchmarking. How does process benchmarking improve a company's overall business performance?

7. Is the growing popularity of the Internet a positive development or a negative development for the future of benchmarking? Explain your answer.

8. Compare and contrast process benchmarking, product benchmarking, and strategic benchmarking.

9. When benchmarking, what is the primary hazard of comparing measures across companies to gauge performance differences?

10. When benchmarking, comparing financial performance measures such as productivity ratios can lead to difficulties due to variances in account systems applied by firms. Suggest how this difficulty may be addressed. Use an example to support your answer.

11. Is it advisable to compare U.S. firms with foreign firms as part of benchmarking? Recommend to U.S firms on how they should proceed.

12. Imagine yourself in the role of the CEO of a large furniture manufacturer wishing to expand globally. Briefly describe how you would set up a benchmarking program. Include in your description an analysis of how you would determine 'what' to benchmark and how you would determine 'whom' to benchmark against.

13. When benchmarking, a number of performance measures may be analyzed including financial productivity, customers, operating results, human resources, market share, and quality related factors. Taking the quality related performance measure, explain in detail the breakdown of how this area may be measured. How does a firm determine which of these quality measures should be included in its benchmarking program?

14. Many scholars believe that business process benchmarking is the most important type of benchmarking. Do you agree with this particular belief? Why or why not?

15. Describe the concept of 5w2h.

16. What management activities can be undertaken to support a firm's benchmarking activities? Make your answer as substantive as possible.

17. Identify and discuss the 9 principles of the benchmarking code of conduct. Use examples to support your answer.

18. Although benchmarking is a popular management technique, many firms are not engaged in the benchmarking process. Why do you think some firms avoid benchmarking? Are any of the reasons valid? Why or why not?

Problems

1. Boston Healy Consultants has gathered the following financial information for Premier Manufacturing Ltd., and Boyd Manufacturing Ltd. The consultants have been asked to compare the productivity for the two firms (all numbers in 000s).

	Premier Manufacturing Ltd.,	Boyd Manufacturing Ltd.,
Labor	$34,000	$22,000
Plant and equipment	156,000	115,000
Energy	15,700	18,500
Materials	243,000	200,000
Sales	1,500,000	1,100,000

   a. Compute partial and total factor productivity measures for Premier Manufacturing Ltd., and Boyd Manufacturing Ltd.
   b. What picture do you get of the two firms?
   c. What would you suggest to the management of Boyd Manufacturing Ltd.?

2. From the benchmarking scenario outlined in problem 1, you have been asked to write a report to accompany the performance measures calculated. Highlight any possible discrepancies that may result from the accounting practices applied. Advise the firms as to how they should proceed to deal with any discrepancies identified.

3. For the data in problem 1, suppose as a follow up to problem 2 adjustments are made by Premier Manufacturing Ltd., as to how their material costs are measured. As a result, materials costs for Premier are increased to $300,000. Recalculate the total factor productivity measures for Premier Manufacturing Ltd. Comment on the results.

4. A domestic company operating a subsidiary in a less-developed country (LDC) has shown the following financial results:

	Parent (Domestic)	Subsidiary (LDC)
Sales (units)	200,000	80,000
Labor (hours)	40,000	60,000
Materials (currency)	$40,000	FC40,000
Equipment (hours)	120,000	10,000

a. Calculate partial labor and capital productivity numbers for the parent and subsidiary. Interpret the results.
b. Compute total factor productivity figures. Does your interpretation change?
c. If $1 = 10 FC units, calculate materials productivity figures. Explain your finding.

5.

	Marketing	Manufacturing Engineering	Supply Chain
Aerospace	4.8	12.5	10.0
Automotive	8.5	5.0	6.0
Communications	11.6	11.8	20.0
Components	3.0	2.4	5.5
Computer	5.0	8.0	12.5
Electromechanical	6.3	6.0	10.0
Electronic Subsystems	4.2	4.5	8.0
Heavy Mechanical	6.0	9.0	9.0
Instrumentation	7.5	4.8	6.1
Light Assembly	2.8	2.5	3.3
Medical	3.8	4.0	13.4
Cross-Industry	4.9	6.0	8.2

The preceding table shows industry comparisons of the percentage of sales spent on salaries for marketing employees, manufacturing engineering employees, and supply chain employees for several different industries. Rank these industries by the amount spent in each of the areas and report your findings to management. What can you infer from your findings about each of the industries?

6. Using the data from Problem 5, suppose that you are a computer company that spends 9% on marketing staff, 6% on manufacturing engineering, and 8% on supply chain staff. Comparing your expenditures with the previous averages, what would you recommend to management? What more information would you want?

7. Following is an announcement from a study from The Benchmarking Network, Inc.

5th Annual Shared Services Measures

The Benchmarking Network and the Shared Services Benchmarking Association announced they will be kicking off *the fifth Annual Shared Services Measures* benchmarking study. Now is the time to join and become involved in setting the focus and direction of the study by attending the kickoff meeting. The study will review *Shared Services Measures* including research into:

• Accounting;
• Finance and Treasury;
• Human Resources;
• Information Technology;
• Procurement and Supply Chain;
• Legal;
• Regulatory;
• Auditing;
• Corporate Communications/External Affairs;
• Facilities, Real Estate, Security;
• Environmental;
• Fleet; and
• Other Shared Services Measures.

Put yourself in the place of the Benchmarking Network researchers. How would you design this study? What would you have to consider when undertaking such a study?

8. The following table shows enrollment data from several British universities.

Institution	Change in Student Numbers 2014/15 to 14/15 13/14 to 14/2015					Supporting Data 2014/15 Student Numbers	
	FT	PT	FT	PT	ALF	FT	PT
	%	%	%	%	£	FT	PT
Abingdon and Witney College	b	b	0	−7	b	b	b
Accrington and Rossendale College	−16	−1	7	−1	17.22	1246	8896
Alton College	2	34	11	10	17	1478	1522
Amersham and Wycombe College	−4	−6	5	21	17.07	1762	5064
Aylesbury College	−14	11	−5	−2	22.63	800	3117
Barking College	−6	6	2	−68	17.05	2193	8638
Barnet College	−7	−2	5	−22	17	4383	13189
Barnfield College	3	7	7	24	17	2601	15480
Barnsley College	−3	−85	−9	−24	17	3084	6029
Basildon College	−8	−43	−12	41	17	583	5695
Basingstoke College of Technology	−4	2	−6	8	17	1463	7670
Bedford College	−1	19	−3	−7	17.32	1855	8524
Beverley College of Further Education	17	6	31	4	17	851	3972

ALF = Average Level of Funding
FT = Full Time
PT = Part Time
b = Not Available

Compare the data from these schools and present them in a way that is useful for the administrators in these schools.

9. Suppose the Chancellor from Barking College asks you to infer meaning from the data in Problem 8. Put together a report for the chancellor explaining how Barking is performing relative to the other schools.

10. Choose a company in your local area. Develop a list of five companies among the best in class in their industry and the best of the best. Explain how you chose the benchmarking targets you chose. Identify a list of 20 benchmarking questions. What kind of data would you select? How would you contact the target firms?

11. Following are financial statements from American Ecology. Studying these figures, what are some possible financial benchmarks this firm might want to develop?

American Ecology Corporation Consolidated Statements of Operations: Pro Forma and Unaudited ($ in 000s except per share amounts)

	2013	2014	2015
Revenues	38,960	41,522	49,972
Operating costs	23,545	23,219	33,571
Gross profit	15,415	18,303	16,401
Selling, general, and administrative expenses	15,702	21,909	24,187
Impairment loss on long-lived assets	—	—	7,451
Loss from operations	(287)	(3,606)	(15,237)
Investment income	(618)	(1,203)	(932)
Gain (or loss) on sale of assets	(72)	(136)	(55)
Other expense	(414)	(1,723)	(1,326)
Gain (or loss) before income taxes	817	(544)	(12,924)
Income tax expense (benefit)	55	132	(1,517)
Net income (or loss)	762	(676)	(11,407)
Preferred stock dividends	417	760	465
Net income (or loss) available to common shareholders	345	(1,436)	(11,872)
Basic earnings per share	0.03	(0.17)	(1.47) actual dollars
Diluted earnings per share	0.03	(0.17)	(1.47) actual dollars

12. Baseline the data from Problem 11. Is the company's performance improving or worsening?

CASES

Case 6-1 Amgen Corporation: Using Benchmarking as a Means of Coping with Rapid Growth

Amgen: www.amgen.com
American Productivity and Quality Center: www.apqc.org

Amgen Corporation is the largest biotechnology company in the world. Founded in Thousand Oaks, California, the company produces lifesaving pharmaceutical products based on advances in cellular and molecular biology. One of the company's products, EPOGEN, is a product used for the treatment of anemia associated with chronic renal failure and is one of the top-selling pharmaceutical products in the world.

Although Amgen is very good at developing cutting-edge pharmaceutical products, the company has struggled at times with the demands of managing a rapidly growing workforce. In the past 20 years, the company has grown from a workforce of 400 employees to 18,000. In particular, Amgen has faced challenges in terms of making the transition from a single-product company to a multiproduct company and in staffing and training its growing divisions. To deal with these challenges, Amgen decided to turn to benchmarking. The first department involved with the benchmarking initiative was sales training and development because the company's employees believed that improvement was needed in that area. There also was recognition within Amgen that training and development needed to be strengthened. Commenting on the merits of the first benchmarking study, Ellen Nichols, the director of the sales training and development department, said, "We'd been clearly focused on our products and customers, but perhaps we haven't had as focused an effort on developing our people."[8]

To conduct its first benchmarking study, Amgen solicited help from the American Productivity and Quality Center (APQC) in Houston, Texas. APQC is a nonprofit organization that provides benchmarking training, maintains a best-practice database, and helps firms locate businesses to benchmark against. APQC helped Amgen develop a list of 40 potential benchmark targets, based on Amgen's criteria for selection. Amgen wanted to benchmark against companies that were high-growth, high-tech, successful, and had a geographically dispersed sales force. Eventually, Amgen narrowed the list to seven companies and benchmarked its sales training and development department against similar departments at

Dow Chemical, Lexus, Lucent Technologies, Motorola, Anheuser-Busch, Eastman Chemical, and IBM. Four of the companies invited Amgen personnel to visit their facilities, and the other three participants were interviewed over the phone. The study was successful, and Amgen redesigned its sales training and development department as a result of the benchmarking initiative.

Amgen has found other opportunities to use benchmarking to help cope with the challenges of rapid growth in a high-technology industry. For example, the company used benchmarking to study the way it moves its products from production to the end user, and it conducted a benchmarking study that examined its marketing practices. Through its experiences, Amgen has learned some of the barriers to effective benchmarking and some of the global benefits. In terms of barriers, Amgen learned that a benchmarking study is only as good as its implementation. If the implementation stage is lengthy or is not taken seriously by the people involved, the study will not be useful. Another potential barrier is finding companies that are similar enough to your company to benchmark against and that are willing to participate. Having a partner like the American Productivity and Quality Center that maintains a best-practice database to draw from helps address this concern. Amgen has learned there are also global benefits to benchmarking, beyond the specific ideas and techniques that are gleaned from a particular benchmarking study. Benchmarking helps a firm gain visibility and sends a clear message to its stakeholders that the firm is interested in continuous improvement. In addition, benchmarking helps a firm determine whether its best-in-class activities are truly best in class. Often, it is difficult for a firm to know just how good (or poor) it is at some activity until it measures its activity against a similar firm.

Amgen has been successful in its early experiences with benchmarking and serves as a model for how to initiate a benchmarking program. Although Amgen excels in the development of high-potential pharmaceutical products, it recognizes that it has a lot to learn about other management issues. Benchmarking has been a useful tool for the company in its learning efforts.

(continued)

---

[8]Based on Powers, V. J., "Amgen Succeeds with Benchmarking through Outside Facilitation, Hard-Working Teams," American Productivity and Quality Center 8 (October 1997): 1.

Discussion Questions

1. Why was benchmarking so important for Amgen at the point in the company's history when benchmarking was initiated? Do you believe that benchmarking will contribute to Amgen's long-term success?

2. Was it a good idea for Amgen to solicit the help of the American Productivity and Quality Center? Do you think that Amgen would have been successful without the APQC's involvement?

Case 6-2 AT&T Teleholdings: Making Benchmarking a Part of the Process Improvement Tool Kit

AT&T: www.att.com

AT&T Teleholdings offers local telecommunications services to people in Illinois, Indiana, Ohio, Michigan, and Wisconsin. The company has a rich history of innovation and customer service. For example, it was the first U.S. company to offer commercial cellular service. Today, the company offers a broad array of services to its customers and is an industry leader in productivity and financial performance.

AT&T Teleholdings is firmly committed to benchmarking. To maximize the potential of its benchmarking efforts, the company employs internal benchmarking experts and conducts benchmarking forums for its employees. Stories about successful benchmarking efforts in the company are always included in the forums. According to Orval Brown, the company's manager of business process architecture and benchmarking, "Other people's success stories [about benchmarking] get people interested and excited about the possibility of improvement."

The company has found three approaches helpful for attaining quality improvements:

Internal (best-of-breed) benchmarking involves a comparison of processes between different business units within the firm.

External (best-in-class) benchmarking involves finding companies to benchmark against, even if the company is in an unrelated industry.

Competitive (industry best) benchmarking against a leader in the same industry.

Each of these types of benchmarking has unique challenges and rewards. Internal benchmarking is the simplest because there is typically no problem getting access to information. External benchmarking is more challenging because of access and confidentiality issues, but the rewards can be quite good. Competitive benchmarking is the toughest because a direct competitor typically will go only so far in terms of sharing information. The rewards, however, can be substantial.

Because the company is multifaceted in its benchmarking efforts and because a lot of employees are involved, the firm uses a benchmarking code of conduct to maintain strict control of its benchmarking efforts. The benchmarking code of conduct (reflecting the guidelines from the Strategic Planning Institute Council of Benchmarking) is as follows:

- Keep it legal.
- Be willing to provide the same information you request.
- Respect confidentiality.
- Keep information internal for your use only.
- Initiate contact through benchmarking contacts.
- Don't refer possible benchmarking candidates without their permission.
- Be prepared at initial contact.
- Have a basic knowledge of benchmarking and follow the process.

This code of conduct provides a measure of continuity across the company's benchmarking efforts that is very helpful for developing a consistent set of benchmarking behaviors. It also helps ensure that benchmarking will in no way impinge on the ethical standards of the firm.

One component of the benchmarking process that the company has become very good at over the years is finding suitable firms to benchmark against. It typically looks for the following types of companies to include in benchmarking studies: companies that have received quality or business awards, companies with excellent financial results, companies with success stories published in major periodicals, and companies that are top-rated in their industries. These criteria help to select firms that have the highest potential to provide successful benchmarking results.

Management is also keenly aware of the fact that the litmus test of any management initiative is effective implementation. The company typically takes the

(continued)

following steps in implementing what it learns from a benchmarking initiative:

>   Select implementation alternatives.
>
>   Assign resources and create a schedule.
>
>   Establish goals.
>
>   Develop a monitoring plan.
>
>   Gain appropriate approval to alter current practices.

>   Implement the plan.
>
>   Communicate the benchmarking findings.

This formalized process of implementation helps ensure that a benchmarking effort translates into actual change.

As the telecommunications industry continues to become more competitive, the company's reliance on benchmarking as part of its process improvement tool kit will probably become even more pronounced.

Discussion Questions

1. Is AT&T Teleholdings' benchmarking code of conduct a good idea? What types of ethical abuses potentially could occur in benchmarking if a firm did not follow a strict code of conduct?
2. This case describes benchmarking as an important part of the company's "tools" of quality. What other tools of quality does benchmarking complement?
3. Telecommunications is a fast-paced, rapidly changing industry. Do you believe that benchmarking is particularly important in a fast-paced industry? Why or why not?

Quality and Innovation in Product and Process Design

Chapter Objectives

After completing this chapter, you should be able to:

1. Discuss the processes firms use to design products.
2. Perform "house of quality" quality function deployment (QFD) analysis.
3. Defend design concerns such as design for manufacture, maintainability, and reliability.
4. Perform rudimentary failure modes and effects analysis.
5. Discuss green design.

Have you ever needed a copy quickly but the copy machine was jammed? Have you ever worked against an impending deadline only to have a computer or a printer fail? Have you ever gotten into your car on a cold day to find it would not start? These annoyances are relatively minor. However, other examples of product failures can be catastrophic. If a lumberjack uses a defective chainsaw, he or she might lose an arm. If a heart pacemaker malfunctions, the results might be fatal to a patient. A race car driver's tire blows out at 210 miles per hour, and a spinout results. A faulty fire alarm fails to alert the home's occupants until it is too late. These are major product failures that can result in severe injury or death.

In this chapter we focus on quality assurance. You have already learned that quality cannot be ensured at the final stages of inspection. After all, assurance is best achieved at the design stage.

DESIGNING PRODUCTS FOR QUALITY

When designing products, we must first answer many questions. For example, what are the functions the customer wants? What are the capabilities of current products? What are the limitations of the materials we have selected for the product? Are there better materials available? How much will the product cost to make? How much must the product cost to make it successful in the marketplace?

What does it mean to design products for quality? As we have already said, quality has many different dimensions. David Garvin's dimensions of quality from Chapter 1 make it clear that each dimension poses different design problems. Take the first dimension of performance. What are the critical measurements of performance? How much performance does the customer want? How much performance is overkill? How do we balance competing dimensions

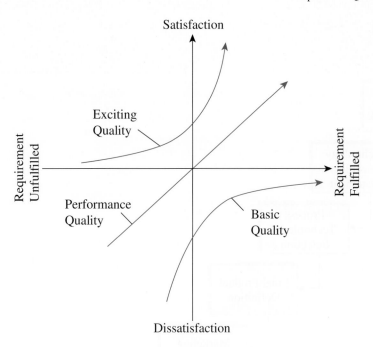

FIGURE 7-1 The Kano Model

of performance (e.g., audio output versus distortion)? Similar questions could be constructed concerning any of Garvin's product quality dimensions. All these questions must be answered early in the design process. For example, if durability is an important quality dimension for the producer of a cell phone, the design team might actively investigate new polymers to find a durable housing for the internal electronics.

It might seem that materials choices are technical and should be made by engineers. However, engineers need input from marketing and operations to understand customer needs, marketing requirements, and the realities of production. Supply chain functions provide inputs on needs such as sourcing, logistics, and collaborations. Given free rein, engineers would design many products to the nth degree. If you don't believe this, look at a remote control for a DVD player or a television set. You will never use many of the buttons on the remote. A study was performed by Sony Corporation to determine which buttons were actually used by the customer. Based on the results of the study, the remotes for Sony televisions were simplified.

Professor Noriaki Kano of the Science University of Tokyo illuminates the relationship between quality and design with the **Kano Quality/Design Model** in Figure 7-1. The Kano model shows that quality is a function of fulfilling customer requirements and achieving high levels of satisfaction. He then distinguishes between basic quality, performance quality, and exciting quality. The goal should be exciting quality. As you contemplate the Kano model, you should realize that as time passes, customer demands will increase, and what was once exciting will become a basic expectation.

THE DESIGN PROCESS

There are many different approaches to designing products. Even within the same industries, the approaches vary in some important ways. Yet there are some similarities across the board. For example, design projects often involve a project team rather than a single designer working independently. Preferably, these teams will work closely with customers to ensure that customer needs are met.

Figure 7-2 shows a generic approach to designing products. The design process includes nine phases that are interrelated. These stages begin with product idea generation and end with

FIGURE 7-2 Product
Development Process
Source: LiPo Ching/MCT/
Newscom.

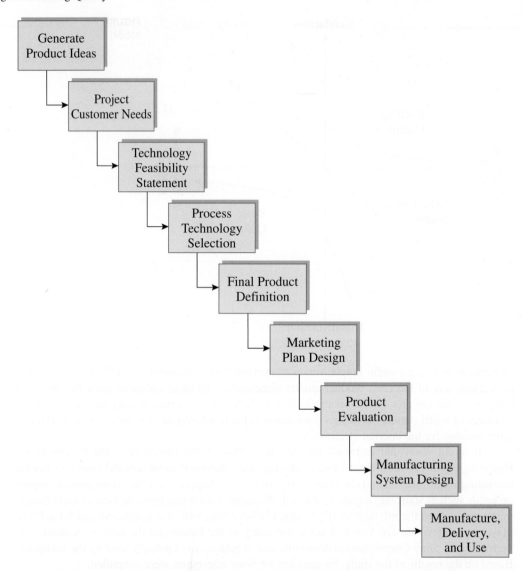

manufacture, delivery, and use. Project managers monitor design projects at each stage for cost and adherence to schedules.

Product idea generation is the first step. During this stage, external and internal sources brainstorm new concepts. Internal sources include marketing, management, research and development (R&D), and employee suggestions. The primary source for external product ideas is the customer. Original equipment manufacturers (OEMs) and contract manufacturers work closely with customers to develop new products. In other circumstances, customer needs are identified to generate product ideas. Other external sources for product ideas can be market-related sources such as industry experts, consultants, competitors, suppliers, and inventors. There are fundamental differences between R&D-generated ideas (known as *R&D push*) and marketing-generated ideas (known as *marketing pull*). R&D-generated ideas tend to be groundbreaking, risky, and technologically innovative. An example of R&D-based development was the Altair microcomputer. In the mid-1970s, the Micro Instrumentation and Telemetry Systems (MITS) Altair 8800 appeared on the cover of *Popular Electronics*. At the time, there was a very small market for this product. However, the article inspired two computer whizzes named Paul Allen and Bill Gates to develop a BASIC Interpreter for the Altair. The rest is history. Although there was not a large established market for personal computers, they have radically affected business and home life since their introduction.

Source: LiPo Ching/San Jose Mercury News/MCT/Newscom

Marketing-generated ideas tend to be more incremental—that is, they build on existing designs—and are better aligned with customer needs. For example, at the product idea-generation stage, a gap in the market or a customer need should be identified. Preliminary assessment of the marketability of the product is performed and funding provided for beginning development of a prototype of the product. Recent developments in computers have included technological developments such as improved multimedia capabilities and faster speeds as well as cosmetic changes in casings such as tablet designs and the use of clear plastics. These are marketing-oriented changes. As shown in Quality Highlight 7-1, new product ideas need to be clearly communicated to design partners.

Stage 2 is **customer future needs projection**, which uses data to predict future customer needs. Designers for Intel, the maker of the microprocessors for personal computers, have been masters at this. They have been able to project and introduce new products that are well timed to fit with changes in the technology requiring them. With the explosion of graphics in programs and on the Internet, Intel developed new chips to fit these needs. The

QUALITY HIGHLIGHT 7-1   Apple's Watch: A Philosophy of Design

www.apple.com/watch/

At the time of development of the new edition of this book, the news is full of hype about the new Apple Watch. Because this product has not yet been launched, it is too soon to evaluate its success. However, Apple has done an excellent job of communicating with app developers relative to design attributes for the new watch. We will discuss some highlights here.

Apps for the new watch are to be personal. According to Apple, the watch interface is attuned to the user's presence. Included with the design are digital touch, heartbeat monitoring, and sketch features.

The watch design should be holistic. Terms such as "force touch" and "nuanced software application" are used to describe the watch's usage. App designers are instructed to make the experience between software and hardware indistinguishable.

If you go to developer.app.com, you can see more detailed instructions for developers. The bottom line is that Apple understands that the watch needs to have killer apps to be successful. Apple does a good job of taking technical requirements and translating them into a philosophy of design.

company also has introduced these microprocessors at a rate that has not outstripped the capability of the market to absorb the new technology. At the same time, the company has been able to outpace competing microprocessor developers by staying slightly ahead of the technological curve.

The task of the product designer is to offer products with value that exceed customer needs at any point in time by careful planning and thought as to what future customer needs will be. There is no single approach to gathering information about future customer needs. Surveys might give insights, but they are usually insufficient to uncover emerging customer needs.

During **technology selection for product development**, designers choose the materials and technologies that will provide the best performance for the customer at an acceptable cost. A **technology feasibility statement** is used in the design process to assess a variety of issues such as necessary parameters for performance, manufacturing imperatives, limitations in the physical characteristics of materials, special considerations, changes in manufacturing technologies, and conditions for quality-testing the product. At this stage, preliminary work can be performed to identify key quality characteristics and potential for variability with each of the different materials.

Technology development for process selection means choosing those processes used to transform the materials picked in the prior step into final products. Careful technology selection of both automated and manual processes is key from a quality perspective because machinery, processes, and flows need to be developed that will result in a process insensitive to variations in ambient and material-related conditions.

Final product definition results in final drawings and specifications for the product with product families by identifying base product and derivative products.

Product marketing and supply chain preparation are marketing-related activities such as developing a marketing plan. The marketing plan should define customers and distribution streams. The production-related activities are identifying supply chain activities and defining distribution networks. Nowadays, this step often requires the design of after-sales processes such as maintenance, warranties, and repair processes that occur after the customer owns the product.

Product design and evaluation require definition of the product architecture; design, production, testing of subassemblies; and testing of the system for production. A product design specification (PDS) demonstrates the design to be implemented with its major features, uses, and conditions for use of the product. The PDS contains product characteristics, the expected life of the product, intended customer use, product development special needs, production infrastructure, packaging, and marketing plans.

Manufacturing system design is the selection of the process technologies that will result in a low-cost, high-quality product. The selection of process technology is a result of projected demand and the firm's finances. Processes must be stable and capable of producing products that meet specification. One of the major developments in this area is that firms now want to be able to change over to new products with a minimum of cost associated with defects. In the past, it was considered standard operating procedure to produce a certain amount of bad product to prove that the system works. For example, a producer of stove pipe would process a small batch of pipe, inspect the pipe and then adjust the line, produce another small batch and reinspect, and so forth until they *proved* the process. This is no longer considered a cost-effective means of introducing new products.

Finally, **product manufacture, delivery, and use** finish this process. The consumer then enjoys the result of the design process.

QUALITY FUNCTION DEPLOYMENT (QFD)

When you have determined customer needs, those needs must be translated into functional product design. **Quality function deployment (QFD)** describes a method for translating customer requirements into functional design. Sometimes, this process of translation is referred to as the *voice of the customer*. The quality function deployment approach was developed by Dr. S. Mizuno,[1] a former professor of the Tokyo Institute of Technology. Since then, this approach has been used extensively throughout the world. In the United States, Hauser and Clausing,[2] two MIT professors, were central in researching and publishing articles describing this approach.[3]

Designers need a means for implementing customer requirements into designs. The house of quality illustrated in Figure 7-3 shows how QFD is used to accomplish this. The left wall on the **house of quality** contains a listing of customer requirements. The roof on the house of quality lists technical requirements. We introduce QFD step by step so that you can see how a house of quality is developed and analyzed. Following are the steps to perform a QFD:

1. *Develop a list of customer requirements.* The list of customer requirements includes the major customer needs as they relate to a particular aspect of a process. In Figure 7-4, a part of a QFD house of quality is shown with customer requirements for a restaurant. Customers want to have a clean restaurant, a comfortable seating arrangement, delicious food, and responsive servers.

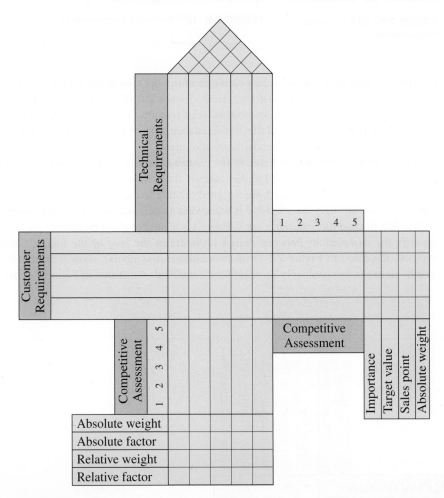

FIGURE 7-3   QFD Layout: The House of Quality

[1]Mizuno, S., and Akao, Y., QFD: *The Customer-Driven Approach to Quality Planning and Development* (Tokyo: Asian Productivity Organization, 1994).
[2]Hauser, J., and Clausing, D., "The House of Quality," *Harvard Business Review* (May–June 1988): 63–73.
[3]Ibid.

	Clean facilities
Customer Requirements	Comfortable seating
	Delicious food
	Responsive servers

FIGURE 7-4 QFD Customer Requirements

FIGURE 7-5 QFD Technical Requirements

2. *Develop a listing of technical design elements along the roof of the house.* These are the design elements that relate to customer needs. Figure 7-5 shows the design elements for the restaurant that may affect the customers' requirements. These design elements include building materials such as type of tile, dirt resistance of floor tiles, material used in making seats, training for servers, and standardization of menu.

3. *Demonstrate the relationships between the customer requirements and technical design elements.* A diagram can be used to demonstrate these relationships. The symbols shown in Figure 7-6 are used, and scores are assigned relating to these symbols (i.e., 1, 3, and 9), where 9 means strongly associated, 3 is somewhat associated, and 1 is weakly associated. Notice that tile and dirt resistance are strongly associated to clean facilities.

4. *Identify the correlations between design elements in the roof of the house.* Using the symbols identified in Figure 7-6 (with two additional symbols), show whether different design elements are positively or negatively correlated. As shown in Figure 7-7, positive

FIGURE 7-6 QFD Technical Requirements and Customer Requirements Relationships

		Type of tile	Dirt resistance of floor tiles	Seat material	Server training	Menu standardization
Customer Requirements	Clean facilities	●	●	○	△	
	Comfortable seating			●		
	Delicious food				△	●
	Responsive servers				●	○

Symbols
● = 9 (Strong association)
○ = 3 (Somewhat associated)
△ = 1 (Weak association)

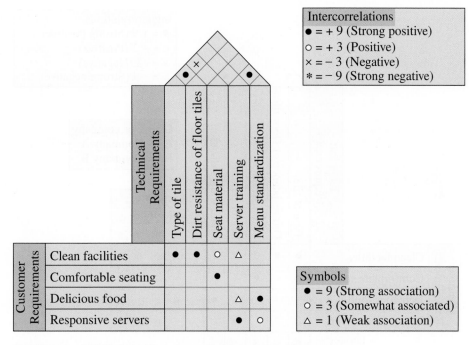

FIGURE 7-7   QFD Technical Requirements Interrelationships

and negative scores are assigned to each symbol as shown. Notice that seat material and type of tile are negatively related, whereas type of tile is strongly positively related to dirt resistance. Server training and menu standardization are also strongly positively related.

5. *Perform a competitive assessment of the customer requirements.* On both the right side and in the lower middle portion of Figure 7-8, there is an assessment of how your product compares with those of your key competitors. These comparisons are on a 5-point scale, with 5 as the highest. A stands for competitor A, B means competitor B, and Us stands for the company in question. Note that there are two assessments, one for customer requirements and another for technical requirements.

6. *Prioritize customer requirements.* On the far-right side of Figure 7-9 are customer requirements priorities. These priorities include importance to customer, target value, sales point, and absolute weight. A focus group of customers assigns ratings for importance. This is a subjective assessment of how critical a particular customer requirement is on a 10-point scale, with 10 being most important. Customer requirements with low competitive assessments and high importance are candidates for improvement. Target values are set on a 5-point scale (where 1 is no change, 3 is improve the product, and 5 is make the product better than the competition). With the target value, the design team decides whether to change the product.

   The sales point is established by the QFD team members on a scale of 1 or 2, with 2 meaning high sales effect and 1 being low effect on sales. The absolute weight is then found by multiplying the customer importance, target factor, and sales point. This is expressed in the following equation:

$$\text{Absolute weight} = \text{customer importance} \times \text{target value} \times \text{sales point} \qquad (7.1)$$

7. *Prioritize technical requirements.* As shown in Figure 7-10, technical requirements are prioritized by determining degree of difficulty, target value, absolute weight, and relative weight. The degree of difficulty is assigned by design engineers on a scale of 1 to 10, with 1

FIGURE 7-8 Competitive Assessment

being least difficult and 10 being most difficult. The target value for the technical requirements is defined the same way the target values for the customer requirements were assigned.

The values for absolute and relative weights are now established. The value for the absolute weight is the sum of the products of the relationship between customer and technical requirements and the importance to the customer columns (fourth column from the right). The value for relative weight is the sum of the products of the relationship between customer requirements and technical requirements, and the customer requirements absolute weights (the farthest right column).

8. *Final evaluation.* The relative and absolute weights for technical requirements are evaluated to determine what engineering decisions need to be made to improve the design based on customer input. This evaluation is performed by computing a percentage weight factor for each of the absolute weight and relative weight numbers (see Figure 7-11).

As you can see in this example, the standardized menu has a very high relative importance. It gives the restaurant a focus for the coming period.

Finally, the house of quality we have shown is only the first level. As shown in Figure 7-12, a similar process is followed when rolling out a new design. The first stage we have discussed is the *technical requirement stage.* During the second stage, a house of quality is completed for *component attributes* to prioritize components and subsystems. At the third level, *process operations,* process engineers use QFD to prioritize process points that can lead to better customer

FIGURE 7-9 Competitive Assessment Requirement Priorities

satisfaction. At the fourth stage, the *quality control plan* is put in place to ensure that customer needs are given proper priority.

TECHNOLOGY IN DESIGN

No longer are the tools of the designer a square, a pencil, and a drafting table. Today, a designer is much more likely to use a **computer-aided design (CAD) system**. These systems are used for designing anything from an ultralight airplane, to a hamburger, to a home, or to a new intersection that can handle higher volumes of traffic. Computer-aided tools greatly improve the ability of designers to generate new and varied designs. In addition, they simplify the design process. For example, auto designers once had to place mock-ups of automobiles into wind tunnels to test the aerodynamics of a design. However, now the wind resistance coefficients for automobiles can be simulated on computers, cutting costs and design times and allowing for quick adjustments to the design. CAD systems help to develop more reliable and robust designs.

FIGURE 7-10   QFD Example

An important advance in CAD systems has been the advent of **multiuser CAD systems**. Using a common database in a network, multiple designers in locations worldwide can work on a design simultaneously around the clock. Consider a multinational corporation developing a new product. When the U.S. designers sleep, Asian and European designers work. When the U.S. designers return to work, they can see the progress that has been made overnight. For example, when developing a new airplane, Boeing used hundreds of designers on the project simultaneously. These designers used their CAD systems to ensure there were no inconsistencies in design that would render the airplane unusable.

CAD systems are used in geometric design, engineering analysis, design review and automation, and automated drafting. **Geometric modeling** is used to develop a computer-compatible mathematical description of a part.[4] The image developed is typically a wire-frame drawing of a component. This part may appear in two dimensions, as a two-dimensional drawing of a three-dimensional object, or in a full three-dimensional view with complex geometry.

---

[4] Stroud, I., and Nagy, H., *Solid Modelling and CAD Systems* (New York: Springer, 2011).

FIGURE 7-11   QFD Example

   Engineering analysis may involve many different engineering tests such as heat-transfer calculations, stress calculations, or differential equations to determine the dynamic behavior of the system being designed. Analysis-of-mass-properties features in CAD systems automatically identify properties of a designed object such as weight, area, volume, center of gravity, and moment of inertia. CAD systems allow for the automatic calculation of these properties.

   Designs are checked for accuracy during **design review**. Using CAD, the designer can zoom in on any part of design detail for close inspection of a part. Layering also is performed during design review by overlaying the geometric images of the final shape of a part over an image of a rough casting. This layering validates the design by ensuring that enough material is available on the casting to accomplish the final machined dimensions of the part.

   Examining a design to see whether different components in a product occupy the same space is called **interference checking**. Interference checking is of major importance in airplane design. Hundreds of pipes and thousands of wires occupy the walls of the aircraft. Interference checking in design review ensures that designs are feasible. This is especially important for airplane makers because so many engineers are participating in the design. Automated drafting results in the creation of a final drawing of the designed product and its components. Some of the features of an

FIGURE 7-12 The Houses of Quality

engineered drawing include automated dimensioning, generation of cross-hatched areas, scaling of the drawing, development of sectional views, and enlarged views of particular part areas.

CAD systems can be stand-alone or tied into computer-assisted manufacturing (CAM) systems that are used in automated production systems. Another important component of a CAD system is the **group technology** component that allows for the cataloging and standardization of parts and components for complex products. Standard parts can result in fewer suppliers, simpler inventory, and less variability in processes.

CAD/CAM systems are often tied together in a closed-loop system with **computer-aided inspection (CAI)** and **computer-aided testing (CAT)** quality control systems. CAI and CAT allow for 100% inspection of products at a relatively low cost. Inspection is performed by 3-D laser scanning and noncontact sensors that enable parts to be inspected without handling, thereby reducing the chance of damage to products.

OTHER DESIGN METHODOLOGIES

Organizing the Design Team

If the design process steps discussed previously are performed sequentially, the design process will be very time-consuming. Therefore, the steps are performed simultaneously as often as possible. This approach, which is called **concurrent engineering**, has been very helpful for speeding up the design life cycle. Products such as John Deere tractors and all-new automobiles have been designed using this strategy. Teams are a primary component of concurrent engineering and include program management teams, technical teams, and design-build teams.

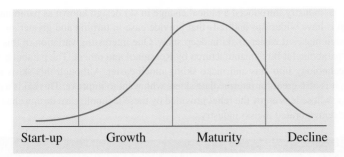

FIGURE 7-13 Phases of the Product Life Cycle

The benefits of concurrent engineering primarily include communication among group members and speed. By working on products and processes simultaneously, the group makes fewer mistakes, and the time to get the concept to market is reduced drastically. The team concept joins people from various disciplines, which enhances communication and the cross-fertilization of ideas.

Another benefit of concurrent engineering is increased interaction with the customer. Often, customers are included in concurrent engineering teams to give immediate feedback on product designs. This requires contractual agreements between suppliers and customers because the customer representatives may work for the design team on a contract basis. However, the immediate feedback is very helpful.

The Product Life Cycle

As is shown by the ski industry (see A Closer Look at Quality 7-1), product development is not a static process. Once new products are developed, work may already be under way to introduce the next generation of products. The product life-cycle concept demonstrates the need for developing new products by showing product design, redesign, and complementary product development on a continuum. Figure 7-13 shows a product life cycle for a typical product. As soon as a product is developed, it is on its way to decline.

A CLOSER LOOK AT QUALITY 7-1   Ski Design

www.rossignol.com

During the 1930s and 1940s, skiing in the United States was a sport for the very wealthy, who could afford to take a train to Sun Valley, Idaho, or a resort in Colorado. By the 1950s and 1960s, middle-class people had taken up skiing. By the 1970s, skiing was at the peak of its popularity. People in the 1960s and 1970s began spending more time outside and were living a less sedentary lifestyle. However, by the 1980s, skiing had begun to decline. Other winter sports were becoming popular. The baby boomers were aging, and many downhill skiers were turning to cross-country skiing. This resulted in a decline of sales for ski makers such as K2 and Rossignol. These companies responded by pouring more money into research and development. One development was the introduction of snowboards. Snowboards appealed to skate boarders and young people. This market grew steadily, and now almost all ski areas in the United States have snowboard parks with half-pipes (a snowboarding area) and other amenities for snowboarders. In the early 1990s, ski sales were still flat, and "capped" skis were introduced. The theory behind ski capping was that shock was more evenly dispersed throughout the skis. However, it was suspected that the real appeal of the capped ski was that it could hold 30% more graphics than the traditional models. In the mid-1990s, "fat boy" skis were introduced. These were skis that were much shorter and wider than traditional skis, which made it much easier to ski in deep-powder snow and frozen, chunky, icy snow.

(continued)

Later, the industry introduced a radical change in ski design known as parabolic, or shaped, skis. The shaped skis have wider tips and tails that provide ease in turning and greater stability in the snow. "Rocker" design makes it easier to ski in deep snow. One interesting variation of this growth in ski designs is the "parabolic fat boy" manufactured by Rossignol and others. The parabolic skis have adapted snowboard technology into skis and make skiing much easier. Although this ski is recommended for expert skiers, it is also great for intermediate skiers who want to improve. This ski is a pleasure for aging baby boomers, whose legs enjoy the relief provided by these technological design changes. These design changes have reinvigorated the ski industry.

Source: Rossignol S3 Freeride Ski. Copyright © 2015 by Rossignol. Reprinted by permission

Product Families and the Product Life Cycle

Two imperatives have come to the forefront in the study of product life cycles. The first is that product life cycles are becoming shorter. This means that obsolescence is a greater problem for designers and that the speed at which new product concepts are delivered to market is becoming much more important for companies around the world. The second imperative is that as product life cycles shorten, product variety and change become much more important to the successful competitor because complementary products are needed to consume productive capacity. Complementary products are needed for two reasons. First, as discussed, product obsolescence requires that products be updated. Second, some products have seasonal demand, which necessitates counterseasonal products. **Variety** refers to the differences in products that are produced and marketed by a single firm at any given time. **Change** is the magnitude of the differences in a product when measured at two different times.[5] Using the framework for variety and change developed by Sanderson and Uzumeri,[6] variety is the range of different items produced by a firm. Variety is related to a specific family of products. Change can occur as a result of either evolutionary small changes or drastic big changes to a product.

Complementary Products

What do we mean by managing product life cycles? Don't they just occur naturally? Well, yes, they do occur naturally. There probably isn't a lot you can do to control the rate at which the life cycle occurs. However, we can plan to introduce new and **complementary products**, which are new products using similar technologies that can coexist in a family of products. These products extend the life of the product line by offering new features or improvements to prior versions of the product. Sometimes, these improvements are cosmetic; at other times, they are substantive. One example of a complementary product is a product that has a counterseasonal demand when compared with a base product such as a motorcycle or a snowmobile. Arctic Cat produces ATVs for summer use and snowmobiles for winter use, allowing for level production rates throughout the year.

When we study issues such as variety and change, it becomes clear that at a strategic level, the problem of the product life cycle is not that a single product is becoming obsolete. Rather, if a variety of products are produced by a given company, management must be aware that several product life cycles must be managed simultaneously.

Designing Products That Work

As A Closer Look at Quality 7-2 shows, there are many things to consider when designing products. One of the biggest considerations is **design for manufacture (DFM)**—"Now that we have

---

[5]Ashby, W. R., *An Introduction to Cybernetics* (New York: Methuen, 1956).
[6]Sanderson, S. W., and Uzumeri, M., *Managing Product Families* (Chicago: Irwin, 1997).

designed it, can we make it?" Loosely speaking, design for manufacture means to design products so that they are cost-effective and simple to build. However, there are many other considerations in a design. One consideration is how we design the product so it is easy to maintain. After all, maintenance, if required, can be very expensive. Another aspect is designing for reliability. It makes little sense to design a product that is capable and stable, but not reliable. Another issue relating to design is *speed,* the time it takes for a concept to reach the market. If it takes a long time for products to reach the market, competitiveness may be hampered. Product designs must be simple. Designing for simplicity means standardizing parts, modularizing, and using as few components as possible in a design. Environmental issues also have become key considerations for companies designing products. With changes in regulations around the world, products must be designed for reuse, disassembly, and remanufacture.

Design engineers, operations managers, supply chain managers, marketing managers, and others involved in the design process must consider each of these topics simultaneously. Although it might seem complicated, in fact, design's cycle times have improved for many companies.

A CLOSER LOOK AT QUALITY 7-2   It Takes a Scientist to Design a Winter Coat[7]

You might think that it is easy to design products such as clothing, but it's not just about style and fit. There is also a lot of technology that goes into keeping skiers warm. First, there is a need. For example, Vermont's Jay Peak is known as one of the coldest ski areas in the United States. Where else can you find a lift nicknamed "The Freezer"? Temperatures can hit minus 30°F with 50-mph winds. Last winter, a group of frigid skiers had to be rescued by the ski patrol. "They were so cold," says patrol director Peg Doheny, "that their brains were freezing up."

Cold and skiing go together like noses and sniffles. Now, thanks to advances in the science and technology of skiwear, modern skiers can stay warmer longer. "If your clothing performs at a higher level, you can accomplish more and enjoy skiing more," says Tom Duguid, brand-marketing director for Arc'teryx. Battling the cold is big business. Consumers spent more than $1.1 billion on cold-weather apparel last winter. "We want to keep people warm, dry, and protected," says Woody Blackford, vice president of innovation at Columbia Sportswear.

Modern ski clothing is an amalgam of synthetics, insulations, and chemical treatments that make the best down jackets of only a few years ago seem like wool knickers. Take Patagonia's Nano Storm jacket. It has a breathable waterproof H2No barrier bonded to a 2.6-ounce, 50-denier nylon shell. Beneath is a layer of 60-gram PrimaLoft One polyester insulation. To shed moisture, the shell and 22-denier polyester lining are treated with Deluge DWR water-repellent finish. You almost need a PhD to buy cold-weather apparel these days.

Not surprisingly, textile companies such as GoreTex have chemists devising new fabrics, insulations, membranes, and coatings. Polartec works with military researchers. PrimaLoft uses technology from the aerospace industry. Others turn to physiologists to understand how the body reacts to temperature changes. Columbia Sportswear has hired electrical engineers to develop heated garments. On the materials front, the company's Omni Heat jackets and gloves have metallic-dot linings to reflect and preserve warmth.

Sewing machines? Ha. Manufacturing modern ski garments requires machines that spray, heat, inflate, and laminate the layers together. Columbia Sportswear uses high-pressure compressors to adhere the interior membranes and baniers of its gloves to the outer fabric layers. The gloves are then baked to activate adhesives.

"Body mapping"—structuring a garment to provide heat retention in some zones and breathability in others—is a recent development. Body-mapped jackets often have waterproof fabric on the

(continued)

---

[7]Based on Tolme, P., "The Cold War," *Ski* (January 2011): 24–26.

shoulders and breathable fabric on the core and sides, mimicking the body's own natural heat-retention systems. Wet skin loses heat 30 times faster than dry skin. "Staying dry is paramount to staying warm," says Dr. Gregory Haggquist, founder and chief scientist of Cocona, a fabric technology company.

Insulation is where the big advances are taking place. Powderhorn weaves ceramic yarn into its goose down to better disperse heat. To mimic down, synthetic insulation makers combine a variety of fiber and filament sizes. Electronic apparel is the new frontier. Until now, electrically heated apparel suffered from short battery life and electronics that were too bulky, not durable, or had burn risks. But modern materials are making heated garments, or "wearable technology," more viable.

Columbia Sportswear's Circuit Breaker Softshell uses lithium polymer batteries and carbon fiber instead of metal wire to conduct heat. Carbon fiber is stronger, lighter, and corrosion resistant. "In 10 years, heated products will be commonplace," Columbia Sportswear's Blackford predicts.

"Today's ski apparel is light-years better," says John Seifert, an associate professor at Montana State University, who has done research for The North Face in the school's Subzero Lab, a 2,700-square-foot meat locker. The facility has cold rooms, environmental chambers, CT scanners, a treadmill, and medical devices to measure cold's impact on performance.

Although modern lab research is vital, nothing can replace fieldwork. That's why garment makers have teams of product testers. Columbia has 300 worldwide. Greg Hill is Arc'teryx's star tester. He's attempting to ski 2 million vertical feet in one winter, providing product feedback and marketing buzz.

Companies use a range of tests to quantify a garment's performance. The hydrostatic resistance test, for instance, measures how hard it is to force water through fabric at high pressure. Other tests include the dynamic moisture permeation cell, which changes humidity and air pressure levels to mimic weather conditions. The moisture-vapor transmission-rate test involves heating water beneath a piece of fabric and measuring how much vapor moves through the material in 24 hours.

But are the marketing hype and performance pledges just hot air? Sometimes. Many companies, for instance, cite their garments' wicking capabilities. "A paper towel wicks," says Polartec's Simmons, "but you're not going to wear paper-towel underwear." What matters most is a garment's capability to transport moisture away from the body after it's been wicked.

There isn't government oversight of marketing claims for ski apparel. "This is where consumers get left out in the cold," Cocona's Haggquist says. Testing standards organizations such as ASTM ensure that everyone uses the same protocols.

But not everyone agrees on the best tests. Sometimes tests developed for other industries are used by apparel makers. One example is the ASTM E96 test, which was developed to measure vapor transmission in building materials. With a combination of proper design and testing, we will see better options for winter wear in the future.

Design for Manufacture Method

The overriding concept to consider when discussing DFM is to *make it easy to build*. Although this concept may seem intuitive, it is sometimes difficult to be intuitive when you are too close to a process (for example, the people who design products). The reason for this difficulty may be more behavioral or organizational than technical. In the old world of designing products, there existed a hierarchy of engineers. At the top of this hierarchy was the product design engineer. Lower down the hierarchy were the process design engineers. Often, these different engineers worked in totally different departments. The fact that they were in different departments often impeded communication.

This organizational problem has been referred to as the **over-the-wall syndrome**, which is demonstrated by looking at the design process sequentially. First, the product design engineers would develop a design. This product design would then be approved by the manager or the vice president of product design. The design would then go to the manager or vice president of process design. Process design engineers would then develop the processes to make the product. If at any point a problem with the product design were found by the process engineers, a request for redesign would be sent to the manager of product design. Product design engineers would solve the problem and send the new product design back to the process designers. The process designers would then continue their work of developing the process. When other problems occurred, they would have to be referred to the product design engineers. Many times, it took years to develop a new product, and the results were processes that built poorly functioning products. DFM methods are designed to eliminate the over-the-wall syndrome and radically reduce design cycle times.

Many firms use **enterprise resource planning (ERP) systems** to integrate financial, planning, and control systems into a single architecture. As a result, there is an effort in the business world to include computerized design systems in these ERP systems. An important component of such design software is the **product data management (PDM)** tool. PDM is a general extension of techniques commonly known as *engineering data management, document management*, and other similar names. PDM helps manage both product data and the product development process by tracking the masses of data needed to design, manufacture, support, and maintain products. It does this in part using a bill of materials that is later transferred to manufacturing, planning, and control systems after the design phase of the product life cycle.[8]

Design for Maintainability

One of the major concerns with new products is ease of maintainability. It often seems cheaper to replace a product than to repair it. This certainly is true for inexpensive products such as electric can openers, toasters, and other small appliances. However, the cost of repairing relatively expensive products such as personal computers, automobiles, and large appliances is also becoming prohibitive. Consider a broken video camcorder. A new, relatively inexpensive camcorder may cost $250. If the camcorder breaks, a repair may cost half to two-thirds of that number. The decision to repair is essentially an economic decision involving costs, benefits, and trade-offs. This decision becomes particularly difficult when the product life cycle is short. Suppose that you owned a personal computer for the past few years. You purchased the computer for $1,000, and it satisfied your needs at the time. Now you realize that you need more memory, your sound card is inadequate, and you need a larger hard drive. If you go to a discount store, you can purchase the upgrades you need for about $500. At the same time, for a little more money you can purchase a new computer that has all the desired features as well as many others. For example, the new computer will be faster than your old computer. Should you spend $1,000 on a new computer or $500 to upgrade your old computer? One solution to this problem is to design for maintainability. Design for maintainability concepts include

> Components that are easily replaced
>
> Components that are easily removed with standard tools
>
> Adequate space to perform the maintenance function
>
> Nondestructive disassembly
>
> Safe maintenance
>
> Available adequate owners' manuals and documentation (e.g., wiring diagrams, help facilities, and videos showing how to perform minor repairs)

Many personal computer manufacturers include how-to videos in their memory that demonstrate maintenance functions such as adding memory, connecting interfaces, and other simple maintenance functions. Craftsman tractors sold by Sears include videos that demonstrate how to change oil, operate the tractor, and perform other service functions. The bottom line is that customers should be provided with the necessary information and ease of access to the product that allow for simple or preventive maintenance.

---

[8]Bourke, R. "PDM and ERP Continuing to Converge," *APICS: The Performance Advantage* (August 1997): 66–67.

An important issue is the ease of delivery of more serious maintenance. Many repairs can be performed only by trained professionals. Many personal computer companies offer at-home maintenance for their personal computers. It is common for auto repair facilities to offer rides and loaner cars for customer use. Car rental companies typically offer on-the-road repair and towing service when their cars break down. It is important to recognize that service is also a design issue. At the design phase, after-sale processes must be designed so that maintenance is received simply, rapidly, and cost effectively. Experience has shown that consumers are willing to pay more for products that are supported by outstanding service.

A recent trend in service is remote monitoring of products that diagnoses problems and dispatches repair people before breakdowns occur. BMW has experimented with this approach. One of the leaders in this area is Otis Elevator, with its Remote Elevator Monitoring system (REM). REM tracks system functions on elevators. The system diagnoses an emerging problem in an elevator and automatically makes a service call to a repair person. Often, problems are fixed before elevator owners know that a problem has occurred.

DESIGNING FOR RELIABILITY

Reliable products are always available when you need them, and you can depend on them to work properly. Reliability, as it relates to products, results from the interaction of multiple components in a system. Quality Highlight 7-2 shows how a luxury product is designed to be reliable at Vuitton. Reliability has two dimensions, *failure rate* and *time,* both of which can be applied to components and to systems. **Component reliability** is defined as the propensity for a part to fail over a given time. **System reliability** refers to the probability that a system of components will perform the intended function over a specified product life. It is important to recognize the difference between component reliability and system reliability. The levels of measurement are different for system and component reliability. When we talk of component reliability, we refer to a finite aspect of the overall product. System reliability is computed from the aggregation of multiple components. Reliability models are discussed in Chapter 13.

QUALITY HIGHLIGHT 7-2   **Designing Reliable Luxury at Vuitton**[9]

www.louisvuitton.com

Behind a locked door in the basement of Louis Vuitton's elegant Paris headquarters, a mechanical arm hoists a brown and tan handbag a half meter off the floor and then drops it. The bag, loaded with an eight-pound weight, will be lifted and dropped, over and over again, for four days. This is a type of rapid-life-testing usually reserved for designing reliability into machinery and vehicles. Here it is being used on elegant handbags.

Vuitton has designed a high-tech torture chamber for testing its products. A piece of lab equipment bombards handbags with ultraviolet rays to test resistance to fading. Still another machine tests zippers by tugging them open and closing them 5,000 times. There's even a mechanized mannequin hand, with a Vuitton charm bracelet on its wrist, being shaken vigorously to make sure that none of the charms falls off.

If you think about Louis Vuitton, you likely don't think about robots beating up on bags. You probably think of waiflike supermodels or lithe Hollywood celebs toting Vuitton luggage to Dubai. However, to understand what makes Vuitton tick, you have to look behind the glittery façade and look closely at the world's most profitable luxury moniker.

---

[9]Adapted from Matlack, C., "The Vuitton Machine," *BusinessWeek*, (22 March, 2004): 98–102. Used with permission.

Vuitton focuses relentlessly on quality in design and performance. Remember that the robot makes sure that Vuitton rarely has to make good on its lifetime repair guarantee. The supply chain is rigorously controlled, and no bag is ever discounted. Above all, there's the efficiency of a finely tuned machine, fueled by ever-increasing productivity in design and manufacturing—and, as Vuitton grows bigger, the capability to step up advertising and global expansion without denting the bottom line.

Following are some examples of how attention to design detail sets the Vuitton bag apart:

- Zipper: Laboratory equipment randomly tests zippers by opening and closing them 5,000 times.
- Production: Manufacturing methods adopted from automakers and other industries are boosting productivity by 5% per year.
- Handle Metal Ring: To cut costs, Vuitton pressured the metal rings supplier to improve production efficiency.
- Leather Trim: Vuitton uses hides from northern European cattle, which have fewer blemishes from insect bites.
- Price Tag: Forget bargains: Vuitton never holds sales, and price increases are common.

Reliability Analysis Tools

There are many ways to make designs more reliable. These methodologies include failure modes and effects analysis; fault-tree analysis; and failure modes, effects, and criticality analysis.

Failure Modes and Effects Analysis

Failure modes and effects analysis (FMEA) systematically considers each component of a system—identifying, analyzing, and documenting the possible failure modes within that system and the effects of each failure on the system. It is a bottom-up analysis beginning at the lowest level of detail to which the system is designed and works upward. The FMEA process results in a detailed description of how failures influence system performance and personnel safety. FMEA answers the question, "How do the systems or components fail?"

Failure modes and effects analysis was created by the aerospace industry in the 1960s and is used extensively in Six Sigma (see Chapter 14). An early application of FMEA occurred when Ford Motor Co. used it to analyze engineering design. Ever since, Ford has tried to refine FMEA through continued use in its operations, as many software applications have evolved recently that aid in the use of FMEA. Some benefits that can be derived through the use of FMEA include

1. Improvement of the safety, quality, and reliability of products
2. Improvement of a company's image and its competitiveness
3. Increased satisfaction from a user standpoint
4. Reduction in product development cost
5. Record of actions taken to reduce a product risk

There are five basic areas in which FMEA can be applied: concept, process, design, service, and equipment.

Concept. FMEA is used to analyze a system or its subsystems in the conception of the design.

Process. FMEA is applied to analyze the assembly and manufacturing processes.

Design. FMEA is used for analysis of products before mass production of the product starts.

Service. With respect to services, FMEA is used to test industry processes for failure prior to their release to customers.

Equipment. A company also can use FMEA to analyze equipment before the final purchase.

FIGURE 7-14   FMEA Steps

9. Eliminate or reduce highest risks.

8. Identify highest risks.

7. Estimate failure detection.

6. Estimate likelihood of failure.

5. Determine hazard likelihood and categorize.

4. Describe effects of each failure mode.

3. List one or two failure modes for each function.

2. List functions for each part.

1. Assign each component an identifier.

How FMEA Works

As is shown in Figure 7-14, failure modes and effects analysis uses a nine-step process:

1. The first FMEA step is to give each component in the system a unique identifier so that none of the parts will be overlooked in the analysis.
2. In the second step, list all the functions each part of the system performs. This step requires you to develop a block diagram for the design description.
3. List one or two failure modes for each function from the second step. The best description of a failure mode is a short statement of how a function may fail to perform. What a product does or does not do when it fails describes the failure mode.
4. The fourth step describes what effects each failure mode of the component will have, especially the effects perceived by the user or operator. Analysis of the effects should follow a hierarchical order because any effect should be fairly detailed so that the severity of each effect can be judged. Some of these effects measure the consequence of failures on a component or part of a device, the whole system, the user, and/or the public.
5. Determine whether the failure will result in a potential hazard to personnel or the system. Then categorize how severe each hazard will be. There are four basic categories of hazards: catastrophic, critical, marginal, and negligible.
6. Estimate the relative likelihood of occurrence for each failure. The likelihood of occurrences is estimated using a 10-point scale and described in steps 4 and 5, ranging from highly unlikely (1) to very likely (10).
7. Estimate the ease with which the failure may be detected. If the failure takes so long to be detected that it becomes too late to replace or repair, the magnitude of the problem is likely to be much greater than if the failure can be easily detected.
8. Use the estimates from steps 5, 6, and 7 to identify the highest risks related to the system.
9. Decide what action will be taken to eliminate or reduce the highest risks in the system. The most common decision is to alter the design to reduce the likelihood of occurrence and failure severity or simply to bring about easy failure detection. Figure 7-15 shows an example of an FMEA form.

Function	Failure Modes	Severity Score	Causes	Occurrence Score	Current Controls	Detection Score	Risk Priority Number Score	Corrective Actions
Manual application of protective coating material on windows.	Bubbles	8	Faulty sprayer head	5	Visual inspection	5	200	Hourly inspection of sprayer head
	Scratches	8	Mishandling during production	2	Visual inspection	4	64	Recycle glass

FIGURE 7-15   FMEA Form

Fault-Tree Analysis

Fault-tree analysis (FTA) is an analytical tool that graphically renders the combinations of faults that lead to system failure. This technique is useful for describing and assessing the events within a system. Such events can be either normal or abnormal, but it is their sequence and combination that are important. FTA shows the probabilities of systems failure caused by any event and is widely used in the aerospace, electronics, and nuclear industries. A fault tree is a qualitative model that also can be evaluated quantitatively. FTA, which is used for reliability, maintainability, and safety analysis, was used originally in 1961 at Bell Labs to evaluate Minuteman Launch Control Systems to avoid inadvertent missile launches.

Failure Modes, Effects, and Criticality Analysis

Failure modes, effects, and criticality analysis (FMECA) is an extensive but simple method for identifying ways in which an engineered system could fail. As with FMEA, failures, effects, and causes are identified. FMECA rates failure modes by ranking each possible mode according to both the probabilities of its occurrence and the severity of its effects. The primary goal of FMECA is to develop priorities for corrective action based on estimated risk. FMECA is used to analyze a probable cause of a product failure, to determine how the problem affects a customer, to identify the probable manufacturing or assembly processes responsible, to identify which process control variable to focus on for prevention detection, and to quantify the effects on the customer.

Criticality in FMECA is important because it prioritizes how the design team should be spending its resources. In general, criticality refers to how often a failure will occur, how easy it is to diagnose, and whether it can be fixed. Criticality assessment is somewhat subjective because it depends on the viewpoint of a service or field engineer. This view is markedly different from the designer or marketing manager. All members of an interdisciplinary team should participate in ranking criticality so that their concerns are factored into rankings. As a design team considers the various failure modes in the ramifications, one or more of the team members fills out a structured FMECA form that summarizes all that is involved in what can go wrong. In general, a design FMECA includes

1. A description of the product's function
2. Listings of the potential failure modes
3. Potential effects each failure mode could have on the end user
4. Potential causes of each failure mode with the likelihood ranking for each
5. Preventive measures in place for firmly scheduling by the time production starts
6. Ranking of the effectiveness of each preventive measure
7. A ranking of the difficulty of detection
8. An estimate of the probability that the cause of a potential failure will be detected and corrected before the product reaches the end user

Product Traceability and Recall Procedures

Although FMEA and FTA help predict where defects will occur and what their effects will be, unforeseen defects occur from time to time that can result in dangerous and costly results that can subject the firm to liability.

For example, on one cool summer morning, a young pilot was asked to fly some hunters over extremely remote wilderness territory. The pilot was rather inexperienced at flying in these types of conditions; after all, backcountry flying is dangerous, and experience is hard to obtain. However, the temperature and weather conditions were perfect. The adventure proceeded without incident until the final leg of the trip over some of the most extreme country. The wind began to pick up and gusted to more than 100 miles per hour. The light aircraft had never experienced these types of winds before. The young pilot pulled out of the mountainous canyon to get well above the mountaintops, which caused the aircraft to pitch and roll, and the wind shear coming over the mountaintops stressed the plane. The plane's vertical stabilizer was rendered useless by the powerful winds, but the team returned to the airport safely.

Subsequent investigation showed that an alloy structural support had been stressed to the breaking point in the plane's vertical stabilizer. The plane's manufacturer issued a recall of 1,200 planes fitted with the same special alloy in the vertical stabilizer. The problem occurred in one piece used in the manufacturing process that was produced by another vendor. An identification number allowed the plane manufacturer to track the purchase of this part back to its supplier. All aircraft built with the weak structural piece were recalled to replace the defective vertical stabilizer. Without proper identification techniques and sufficient tracking systems, potentially hazardous products could remain in use without any way of recalling or repairing them.

This characteristic is called **product traceability**. Product traceability and **recall procedures** are important aspects of product design. Because companies are liable for the products they create, it is important to be able to identify the origins of defective products or components through product traceability procedures.

In 1972, Congress created the **Consumer Product Safety Commission (CPSC)** to protect citizens from unreasonable risks of injury and death. To avoid being listed on the CPSC list of hazardous products, a company must have a system in place for tracing components. When a recall is demanded by the CPSC, a company needs to narrow its recall to a particular identification (ID) number or product line. Therefore, a good ID system can help isolate where the breakdown in the product occurred.

A major goal of product traceability and recall procedures is to be able to trace products with a minimum of cost. Product traceability also helps limit product liability relating to safety hazards.

ENVIRONMENTAL CONSIDERATIONS IN DESIGN

Currently, society demands much more from product designers than just high-quality products. Many manufacturers have turned to a more environmental form of manufacturing that offers positive returns on investment. Many companies, such as Siemens, Caterpillar, Xerox, Hewlett Packard, and others, are using environmentally friendly forms of manufacturing.

The move to **green manufacturing** began in Germany with requirements for importers to remove packaging materials. Using a life-cycle approach to product design causes designers to focus not only on incoming materials, manufacturing processes, and customer use but also on the eventual disposal of the product. This life-cycle approach has led to practices known as **design for reuse**, **design for disassembly**, and **design for remanufacture**.

Table 7-1 lists several concepts for green design. These principles are encapsulated in Ford Motor's green design. In addition to other green breakthroughs, it uses soy-based foam in seats and has created a policy that engineers must use sustainable materials in auto production.

There is great potential for reuse of products. Consider that currently two computers are discarded for every three computers purchased. The method for designing for reuse involves analyzing existing products for materials, identifying other uses for these materials, and developing a disassembly process to sort out these materials. This is good business for the producers of personal computers because if chemicals used in making PCs were to find their way into groundwater, the manufacturers could be held liable. The resulting costs could be in the billions of dollars.

The principles for design for disassembly include using fewer parts and fewer materials, using snap-fits instead of screws, making assembly efficient and improving disposal, using design for disassembly experts in concurrent design teams, and avoiding waste through better design.

TABLE 7-1   Green Design Concepts
Use nonhazardous materials if possible.
Avoid waste.
Include air and water purification in process design.
Product components should operate efficiently.
Accept costs associated with reuse, recycling, and disposal.
Make products durable.
Don't over-engineer products to do too much.
Design products so they can be used, recycled, and reused.
Use reusable energy when possible.

Summary

As life cycles for products become shorter, a focus on quality in the product design process is necessary to remain competitive. Many of the dimensions of quality we discussed in Chapters 1 and 2 are addressed in the design phase of the product life. By focusing on issues such as maintainability, assembly, reliability, and product traceability, we can continually improve our ability to make things.

We have said that you should design products so they are easy to build. By simplifying design processes (through concurrent design teams, by standardizing, and through the use of modular designs), we make products that are more reliable.

Companies have implemented these processes with great results that have facilitated huge increases in production capacity, coupled with a reduction in cost. These cost savings do not always result in higher profits. As you have seen, the costs of computer chips dropped consistently. However, a company that does not become better at design will simply not be competitive in the future.

Key Terms

Change	Design for manufacture	Green manufacturing	Product marketing
Complementary products	(DFM)	Group technology	and supply chain
Component reliability	Design for remanufacture	House of quality	preparation
Computer-aided design	Design for reuse	Interference checking	Product traceability
(CAD) system	Design review	Kano Quality/Design Model	Quality function
Computer-aided inspection	Engineering analysis	Manufacturing system	deployment (QFD)
(CAI)	Enterprise resource	design	Recall procedures
Computer-aided testing	planning (ERP) systems	Multiuser CAD systems	System reliability
(CAT)	Failure modes and effects	Over-the-wall syndrome	Technology development
Concurrent engineering	analysis (FMEA)	Product data management	for process selection
Consumer Product Safety	Failure modes, effects,	(PDM)	Technology feasibility
Commission (CPSC)	and criticality analysis	Product design and	statement
Criticality	(FMECA)	evaluation	Technology selection for
Customer future needs	Fault-tree analysis (FTA)	Product idea generation	product development
projection	Final product definition	Product manufacture,	Variety
Design for disassembly	Geometric modeling	delivery, and use	

Discussion Questions

1. Product idea generation initiates the process of designing a product by generating ideas from external and internal sources. What are some examples of external and internal sources that are used in this process?
2. Discuss the concept of consumer future needs projection. Does a firm that excels in this area have a competitive advantage? Explain your answer.
3. What is a technology feasibility statement? Why is it important?
4. Briefly describe the role of computer-aided design (CAD) in the product design process. How has CAD changed the way that product designers do their jobs?
5. Describe the concept of concurrent engineering. How does concurrent engineering improve the product design process?
6. The product life cycle for many products is getting shorter. In what ways does this trend complicate the product design process? Can you think of any advantages to shorter product life cycles for firms that have exemplary product design processes?
7. Product variety and change are two approaches employed by firms to deal with shortened product life cycles. Explain the difference between these two approaches using examples to illustrate your answer. How do these approaches help deal with shortened product life cycles?
8. What is meant by design for manufacture?
9. The design for maintainability concept states that a product should be designed to make it easy for a consumer to maintain it. What product attributes make it easy for a product to be serviced or maintained?
10. What is the over-the-wall syndrome? How can the over-the-wall syndrome be avoided?
11. Product reliability is measured via failure rate and time. Explain what product reliability is, and how these two dimensions can assure product reliability.
12. Describe the concept of failure modes and effects analysis (FMEA). What is the end result of an FMEA analysis? What are some of the ancillary benefits that can be derived through engaging in FMEA?

13. What is the primary purpose of conducting a fault-tree analysis?
14. Describe a method for identifying ways in which an engineered system could fail. What is the primary goal of this method of analysis?
15. Discuss the importance of product traceability and recall procedures. Why is product traceability considered an important consumer safety issue?
16. The Waste Electrical & Electronic Equipment (WEEE) directive is a European wide measure to address environmental concerns in the life cycle of electrical and electronic goods. Investigate this directive (using the link http://ec.europa.eu/environment/waste/weee/index_en.htm) and report on how it works. How does it assist in environmentally conscious product design processes?
17. Compare the job of a product designer 20 years ago with the job of today's product designer. In your opinion, what has been the single most significant technological advancement that has changed the job of a product designer?

Problems

1. Flowchart the design and production processes for writing a book such as *Managing Quality: Integrating the Supply Chain.* Use the standard process for designing products in the chapter.
2. Define key customer requirements for a chair. Next, define key technical requirements. Create a matrix showing the relationship between technical and customer requirements using the QFD format.
3. Define key customer requirements for a fridge. Next, define key technical requirements. Create a matrix showing the relationship between technical and customer requirements using the QFD format.
4. For the QFD Problem 4 Matrix, compute the
   a. Customer requirements absolute weight.
   b. Technical requirements absolute weight and factor.
   c. Technical requirements relative weight and factor.
   d. Which design and technical factors should be emphasized? Why?

Problem 4 Matrix

5. For the QFD Problem 5 Matrix, compute the
   a. Customer requirements absolute weight.
   b. Technical requirements absolute weight and factor.
   c. Technical requirements relative weight and factor.
   d. Which design and technical factors should be emphasized? Why?

Customer Requirements	Technical Requirements 1	2	3	4	5	Competitive Assessment 1 2 3 4 5	Importance	Target	Sales point	Absolute weight
A	△	●	△		●		2	1	2	
B	△	○		○			8	1	1	
C	●	△	●		●		5	5	2	
D			●	○	△		3	4	2	
E	○	△		△	△		2	3	1	
Difficulty										
Target										
Absolute weight										
Absolute factor										
Relative weight										
Relative factor										

Problem 5 Matrix

6. For the QFD Problem 6 Matrix, compute the
   a. Customer requirements absolute weight.
   b. Technical requirements absolute weight and factor.
   c. Technical requirements relative weight and factor.
   d. Which design and technical factors should be emphasized? Why?

Customer Requirements	Technical Requirements 1	2	3	4	5	Competitive Assessment 1 2 3 4 5	Importance	Target	Sales point	Absolute weight
A	●	△	●		△		6	4	1	
B		○	●	○			9	5	2	
C	△	●		○	●		9	3	2	
D	○	△	△	○			4	4	1	
E	●				●		2	2	2	
Difficulty										
Target										
Absolute weight										
Absolute factor										
Relative weight										
Relative factor										

Problem 6 Matrix

7. What are important design elements for a pair of pants?
   a. Define the customer requirements.
   b. Define technical requirements.
   c. Using the QFD format, show the relationships with strengths (i.e., 1, 3, or 9) between a and b.

8. Using the format in Figure 7-15, develop an FMEA for a pair of women's panty hose.

CASES

Case 7-1 Keeping Apple's iPhone Competitive[10]
www.apple.com

The past several years have seen an increase in smartphone ownership by cellphone users. In its infancy, the smartphone was produced by only a few companies, such as RIM's Blackberry and Motorola. However, the market is now crowded. Still, Apple's introduction of the iPhone changed the industry. The purpose of a smartphone has shifted from e-mail and business to apps and functionality.

The cellphone industry must be in tune with the customer. Apple attempts to incorporate popular features in its designs. The iPhone includes the Apple staples of app capability and interfacing with other Apple products. The iPhone is operated using a touchscreen and plays music and video. Like other smartphones, the iPhone can manage e-mail accounts and thousands of apps.

With a new generation introduction, customers expect improvements to the features, including front and back cameras for video conferences. Including dual cameras in the design required Apple to create new software for video conferencing. Camera quality in phones is improving as people rely on them more than handhelds. Knowing that quality is important to some customers, a reviewer of the iPhone commented, "It isn't

the best cellphone camera I've tested, but it is a big improvement." This is an example of the trade-offs that may occur in product design. With so many features to incorporate, it may not be possible for a company to have the best for each. A company must decide which areas to focus on in the design.

The iPhone has addressed other areas of cellphone design. Apple claims that the iPhone is the world's thinnest smartphone and sports the world's highest-resolution smartphone screen. The high-resolution screen helps compensate for its smallish screen.

Battery life is a concern for all cellphone designs, and Apple has increased talk-time battery life. New multitasking software manages apps to reduce battery drain.

The iPhone incorporates some features over which Apple has limited control. Facebook, Twitter, and Pandora are popular apps among customers. Incorporating these features requires limiting battery consumption, but allows for frequent updates. Some users want to be constantly connected to their social networks. Apple's multitasking feature addresses some of these issues but may still disappoint some users.

Discussion Questions

1. The case discusses the issues of trade-offs in design. What are some smartphone trade-offs? Why are these important to consider in design.
2. Choose another product besides a smartphone. What are some important trade-offs for that product design?
3. How should Apple evaluate the "quality" of its iPhone?
4. How could Apple improve its design processes for the iPhone?

Case 7-2 Food Processing Plant: Creating a Quality Product using Blending Improvement Methods[11]

This case is based on a food processing plant that went beyond traditional lean approaches and an effective training program to improve quality. The plant was highly automated and fairly lean with respect to its headcount and overhead. Its goal was to minimize waste and increase production by 25%, or 2.5 million pounds a shift. The project team comprised several consultants

from various backgrounds, each with their own style and approach. The team analyzed and assessed the plant's operational processes and the various waste points, identifying various process maps and improvement opportunities. To better understand the problems and get to the root causes, cause and effect diagrams and the "five whys" technique was used along with two new

[10] Mossber, W., "Thinner, Faster, Smarter iPhone Raises the Stakes," *Wall Street Journal* (20 June 2010).
[11] Based on Hernandez Jr., F.A., (2013), *No Silver Bullet,* accessed 17th March 2016 from http://rube.asq.org/six-sigma/2013/08/six-sigma/case-study-no-silver-bullet.pdf

assessment tools. The two new tools included a holistic analysis of the plant's management operating system (MOS) and an assessment of personnel behaviors of the frontline management and staff.

MOS is defined as a compilation of activity, communication, controls, and tools used to achieve organizational goals and objectives. Its five key functions are forecasting, planning, scheduling, monitoring, and reporting. The MOS assessment consisted of a gap analysis of the availability of tools that fall into key functions, and the use and effectiveness of the tools. The team conducted a separate assessment of personnel behaviors to engage them in productive and value-added work, and help facilitate their job function. With respect to management behaviors, team leads were assessed on their ability to manage and direct their teams, such as their ability to provide clear directions and follow-up on assignments—key management traits that are often taken for granted. They were also assessed on their problem solving skills. The assessment identified many improvement opportunities, including monitoring tools, the implementation of problem resolution processes, and the elimination of waste. The production leads and operating team members were trained in the process improvements made, the tools developed, and the pending changes to be installed. While the installation led to production gains, after a few weeks, it was noted that the production performance was inconsistent across the lines and, although overall productivity was up, the team was falling short of its target goals. The organization had processes and the tools, but were missing the right behaviors. In response, the team decided to pull together a team of installation specialists (IS) to leverage the ISs to support, educate, and instill the behaviors and best practices needed to achieve the targets.

The organization initially sought the support of various plant leaders, but eventually decided against it as they needed people who not only understood the importance of change, but also treated employees as human beings. The ISs were primarily selected due to their ability to influence and coach production leads and frontline associates in adopting behavioral practices to support the improvement changes. Ultimately, the intent of the implemented MOS and required behaviors was to course-correct production before falling behind in achieving production targets. The repetitive coaching created a habit of practice and instilled a practical understanding of the tools implemented, leading to a more effective adoption of change. After about four weeks, a behavioral shift was noticed on the production floor, with teams taking full ownership of the tools and processes implemented. The production leads had established the practice of the short-interval reviews and production was consistently hitting 2.5 million pounds.

After the success in the first plant, the IS and the project teams were given approval to expand the project efforts across other plants. The team has since debated what truly drove the savings; whether the key was the changes to the MOS, modified behaviors, or process improvements. One thing, however, is certain: without the blending of methods, the right tools, and the right people, the company would have never been able to deploy a genuinely holistic solution.

Discussion Questions

1. Describe how the current state analysis was conducted management operating system (MOS) was assessed by the food processing plant.
2. Discuss the obstacles the food processing plant met post initial success of process or behavioral improvements. How did they overcome these obstacles?
3. What role did the installation specialists play in ensuring process and behavioral improvements became part of everyday activities rather than a short term initiative?

CHAPTER 8

Designing Quality Services

Chapter Objectives

After completing this chapter, you should be able to:

1. Discuss how services are categorized and what implications those categorizations have for quality.

2. Discuss the dimensions of service quality to better define customer needs.

3. Perform SERVQUAL analysis, including two-dimensional differencing.

4. Perform services blueprinting.

5. Brainstorm ways to failsafe service processes.

6. Define a services benefits package for a firm.

7. Perform service transaction analysis.

High-quality service is essential for competitiveness and can even improve employee satisfaction. However, service, like quality, is a multidimensional term. To provide high-quality service, we need a profound understanding of the needs, wants, and desires of the customer and an understanding of who the customer is.

Quality service is not only an imperative for competitiveness but also a sign of quality maturity. As we have discussed previously, even manufacturing firms—after reliability, conformance, design, and other requirements have been met—eventually focus on service throughout the supply chain. In today's economy, service still is a major differentiator that allows firms to beat competitors in the marketplace. If customers are satisfied, they will be loyal. Revenue streams will increase—as will as profits. If a credit card customer leaves after one year, the credit card firm will lose money. For example, for every dollar lost in year one of card membership, 60 cents is made in year two, and the profits grow as time passes. Profit per customer for the laundry industry increases steadily year after year as well. This principle is the same for other service industries.

In this chapter, we first discuss services in general and then services from a quality perspective. Tools such as the SERVQUAL, gap analysis, and services blueprinting will be developed. The central theme of this chapter is to understand customers' needs and to use that understanding to design services that will satisfy customers.

DIFFERENCES BETWEEN SERVICES AND MANUFACTURING

In Chapter 1 we talked about the multidimensional nature of quality. If quality is multidimensional for manufactured products, it will be more so for services. Understanding some of the differences between manufacturing and services helps to design useful approaches to quality improvement in services. Using a contingency perspective, we understand that the nature of services causes us to approach service quality improvement from a different direction than manufacturing.

Services are distinguished from manufacturing on several dimensions. First, many service attributes are **intangible**, which means that they cannot be inventoried or carried in stock over long periods of time. However, all services have some tangible aspects as well. The outputs of services are also **heterogeneous**, which means that for many companies, no two services are exactly the same. Consider, for instance, an advertising firm. No two advertising campaigns are alike. Customer requirements are different, and campaigns are launched for different customers according to their needs. A third factor is that production and consumption of services often *occur simultaneously*. If you hire someone to mow your grass, you'll receive the service exactly at the same time it is produced.

The term *service* is very broad and covers many diverse industries, such as hotels, hospitals, financial services, and even prisons. Are financial services distinctly different from transportation, health care, or law firms? Certainly, there are similarities among the problems faced by these different categories of firms. However, there are also many dissimilarities.

One useful distinction between services and manufacturing centers on the aspect of **customer contact**. Customers tend to be more involved in the production of services than they are in production of goods. For instance, you probably have never seen anything you own during its manufacturing stage. In fact, many of the products you own were manufactured overseas. However, you probably are actively involved in the production of services you receive. If you work for a firm that hires a consultant, you will work closely with the consultant as he or she provides the services you purchased. When you receive a haircut, you are actively involved in the service by providing information and sitting still. In many restaurants, it is not uncommon for the customers to fill their own drinks. This is called **customer coproduction**.

Because customers are actively involved in producing the services they consume, they create problems for service providers. For example, the time required to serve different customers can vary widely, making it difficult to plan capacity. The varying demands of customers also contribute to process variability that makes quality production of services difficult. Therefore, even though customers are the reason for the existence of services firms, they also make providing good service difficult.

The good news for customers is that by being actively involved in the production of the service, they can exert control over the service provider and achieve customization. This control can be manifested in a variety of different ways. For instance, if you have never visited the producer of a food product you purchase, you may not be aware of many issues concerning the products, such as sanitation or environmental pollution. However, you are not likely to remain a customer of a restaurant that is unclean or creating environmental problems. As a result of this greater customer control, service facilities, processes, and interactions must be designed in a way that promotes a positive encounter with the customer.

Internal versus External Services

An aspect of services that affects the definition of quality is whether a service is internal or external. **External services** are those whose customers pay the bills. **Internal services** are in-house services such as data processing, printing, and mail. Typically, these services are separate from the external customer. However, customer service to internal customers is very important to internal service because their services often can be outsourced. There is a trend in companies to outsource internal services. In a sense, this presents a competitive pressure on internal services.

Although internal and external services may be very different, they do have many similarities. In both cases, competitive pressures can result in the possible loss of customers.

Voluntary versus Involuntary Services

Another way services differ is by being voluntary or involuntary. **Voluntary services** are services that we actively seek out and employ of our own accord. Generally, we research a voluntary service, such as a gas station, a restaurant, or a hotel, and have certain expectations when we engage its services. Even doctors often provide many voluntary services because patients can choose among different doctors to some extent.

The quintessential example of an **involuntary service** is a prison. Other involuntary services include hospitals, the IRS, the police department, the fire department, and other services that you do not choose. If you have the chance to engage this type of service at some point, you likely will have vague expectations about the experience. It is generally more difficult to achieve high levels of customer satisfaction in involuntary services. For example, does anyone really enjoy visiting a hospital or a dental clinic? A customer service survey would be laughable for a county jail. Yet employees of these organizations often desire to provide better service to the patrons. For example, many IRS agents are involved in quality improvement activities. Certainly, our perceptions and expectations of service quality can be affected by whether the service is voluntary or involuntary.

How Are Service Quality Issues Different from Those of Manufacturing?

We've identified three major realities in services that affect the approaches to quality adopted by service providers: intangibility, simultaneous production and consumption, and customer contact. Not surprisingly, these lead us to the major differences between services and manufacturing when it comes to quality.

Because services' attributes can be intangible, it is sometimes difficult to obtain hard data relating to services. In manufacturing, dimensions such as height, weight, and width are available for measurement. Conformance to these measurements implies a certain dimension of quality. However, in services, such measurable dimensions are often unavailable. For this reason, many services organizations that use quality control charts encounter difficulty in using them, or they use them incorrectly. This is not to say that control charts cannot be used in services. However, compared with manufacturing, their use in services is quite low. Generally speaking, time (such as cycle time or response time) is a primary measurement available in service environments.

Simultaneous production and consumption of services means that you have to do it right the first time. You can't easily inspect and rework defects in a hair salon the way you can in manufacturing.

Customer contact leads to an increase in variability in the process. This leads to a high degree of customization in services as well as great variability in the time required to perform services. In manufacturing, repetitive tasks are easily measured, and cycle times are generally consistent. When customers are intimately involved in processes, there is much more customization and much more variability than in manufacturing.

Services design, as is discussed in this chapter, is also very different from design in manufacturing. Because services involve intangibles, warranty or repair processes are not as important as recovery or reimbursement processes (see A Closer Look at Quality 8-1). Also, the design of the services must take into account such variables as customer moods and feelings because these affect customer perceptions of service quality.

Product liability issues in services are very different from manufacturing. Whereas in manufacturing liability issues center around safety concerns, in services liability issues often relate to **malpractice**, which refers to the professionalism of the service provider and whether reasonable measures were taken to ensure the customer's well-being. However, services also may have liability issues. In the Rocky Mountains, ski areas are sued regularly by customers who are injured. In many states, laws protect ski areas from such lawsuits by limiting liability for injuries.

A CLOSER LOOK AT QUALITY 8-1   Service Warranties: Profitable or a Rip-off—You Decide[1]

Here's a secret that one of the nation's largest consumer electronics retailers doesn't want you to know: Many times, they make more money off service contracts than they do selling products. Best Buy Co. isn't banking on sales of TVs, computers, and DVD players to make profits. It is counting on the service contracts to make them profitable.

Just look at the numbers. At Best Buy, service contracts are 4% of sales, but provide 45% of profits. Before bankruptcy at Circuit City, the numbers were 3.3% and 100%! The profit margins on these contracts are between 50% and 60%. If you spend $400 on a service contract, Best Buy keeps $240 and gives $160 to the insurer. As profitable as these contracts are, it is interesting that Walmart has been slow to jump aboard. However, unlike Best Buy, it doesn't have as many salespeople to pitch these contracts.

As service contracts have become more profitable, Best Buy has cut back on disclosure. The company no longer reports its warranty profits separately. Best Buy's spokesperson says the products and contracts should be seen as inseparable.

At Amazon.com, extended warranties for electronics are as high as 40% of the purchase price. These policies offered through Allianz Cornhill are a good deal for Amazon profits[2].

So as a consumer, when do service contracts make sense? Most often, the correct answer is "Never!" Typically, only 20% goes to repair or replacement of products. That's why consumer organizations generally counsel against service contracts. According to one consumer advocate, "The worst rip-off is on appliances because they have gotten so reliable."

Consumer Reports cites four products for which contracts *might* make sense: treadmills, elliptical trainers, plasma TVs, and laptop computers. Remember that most products come with manufacturer warranties, and extended warranties can often be purchased more cheaply directly from the manufacturer.

[1]Adapted from Symonds, W. "The Warranty Windfall," *BusinessWeek* (20 December, 2004): 84–89.
[2]Anon. "Extended Warranties? In Our View, It's a Rip-off," *The Telegraph* (April 15, 2015): D-1.

Services do not have as long a history of quality practice as does manufacturing. Although many quality techniques such as control charts have been adopted by services companies, this trend is still new. Certainly, as time passes, more quality techniques are being developed specifically for services. For example, a new tool is emerging for service supply chains known as process chain network (PCN) diagrams.

How Are Service Quality Issues Similar to Manufacturing?

For both manufacturing and service firms, the customer is the core of the business, and customer needs provide *the* major input to design. By focusing on the customer, many manufacturers and services firms have come to view themselves as service providers. Companies from Harley-Davidson to Hewlett Packard have spent extraordinary amounts of time designing services for their customers.

WHAT DO SERVICES CUSTOMERS WANT?

In Chapter 1, we considered the different quality dimensions relating to services, as follows:

Tangibles

Reliability

Responsiveness

Assurance

Empathy

Parasuraman, Zeithamel, and Berry[3] provided this list of dimensions of service quality after extensive research in a number of services sectors, and they have become widely accepted. However, this does not mean that your particular services industry does not include other dimensions. Therefore, the adoption of these dimensions in your service should include a careful consideration of the applicability of these and other dimensions.

As in any industry, the concept of leadership is one that Parasuraman, Zeithamel, and Berry believe is the key to success. However, they define this leadership role in a way that is quite interesting. The key aspects of a leader in services are given in Table 8-1.

First, a leader has a *service vision*. Such leaders really view service quality as the force underlying profitability and business success. When selecting strategies for improvement, leaders see quality as the winning strategy. Such a vision can be translated into action and excitement for others in the company. To win in services, a firm must develop a passion for service quality within the entire workforce. When there is intense interaction between customers and service providers, the attitude of employees is the key element for achieving service success. Active and involved leadership is very important for attaining this important organizational attribute.

Services leaders have *high standards*. In services, you will notice that some firms are better equipped and maintained than others. Sometimes this is evident in the small details. Some doctors' offices have a better selection of magazines than others; some restaurants are more comfortable than competitors' restaurants; some grocers have a better selection of products; the list goes on and on. Those things don't happen by magic. They are the result of a leader with high standards and a focus on details. Have you noticed that some professors come to class impeccably prepared, and others appear somewhat disorganized? This is so because the student/customer-oriented professor has higher standards for preparation and presentation than other professors. Think about yourself in a work situation. Do you provide a high level of service that reflects a high standard?

Outstanding services leaders have an *in-the-field style of leadership*. Because there is so much contact with the customer in a service system, the field is where the action is. Sam Skaggs, the founder of American Stores Corporation in Salt Lake City, Utah, was famous for stopping by his stores to make sure that things were in order. He viewed this as an important way of keeping the management on its toes. If Skaggs showed up at a single store in Kansas City, Missouri, for example, the manager immediately contacted all the other managers in town to give them a "heads up" that Skaggs was in town. Too often, owners can become isolated from their businesses. By being in the field, they gain a better understanding of the business and how to serve the customer.

Quality Highlight 8-1 shows how Ritz-Carlton uses a gold standard to keep its managers in touch with its customers.

TABLE 8-1   Attributes of Services Leaders
Service vision
High standards
In-the-field leadership style

---

[3]Zeithamel, V., Parasuraman, A., and Berry, L., *Delivering Quality Service* (New York: Free Press, 1990).

QUALITY HIGHLIGHT 8-1   Ritz-Carlton Hotels[4]

www.ritzcarlton.com

The Ritz-Carlton hotel company is a success in one of the economy's most logistically complex service businesses. Targeting primarily industry executives, meeting and corporate travel planners, and affluent business travelers, the Atlanta-based company manages more than 60 luxury hotels that pursue the goal of being the very best in each market. Ritz-Carlton does so on the strength of a comprehensive service quality program that is integrated into marketing and business objectives.

Hallmarks of the program include participatory executive leadership, thorough information gathering, coordinated planning execution, and a trained workforce that is empowered to satisfy customers. Quality planning begins with the president, the CEO, and the 13 senior executives who make up the corporate steering committee. This group, which doubles as the senior quality management team, meets weekly to review the quality of products and services, satisfaction, market growth and development, organizational indicators, profits, and competitive status. Each year executives devote about one-quarter of their time to quality-related matters.

The company's business plan demonstrates the value placed on goals for quality products and services. Quality goals draw heavily on consumer requirements derived from extensive research by the travel industry and the company's customer reaction data, focus groups, and surveys. The plan relies on a management system designed to avoid the variability of service delivery traditionally associated with hotels. Processes are well defined and documented at all levels of the company.

Key products and service requirements of the travel consumer have been translated into Ritz-Carlton *gold standards,* which include a credo, 3 steps of service, and 20 "Ritz-Carlton basics." Each employee is expected to understand and adhere to the standards with defined processes for solving guests' problems as well as detailed grooming, housekeeping, safety, and efficiency standards. Company studies prove that this emphasis is on the mark, paying dividends to customers and ultimately to Ritz-Carlton.

The corporate motto is "Ladies and gentlemen serving ladies and gentlemen." To provide superior service, Ritz-Carlton trains employees with a thorough orientation, followed by on-the-job training and then job certification. Ritz-Carlton values are reinforced continuously by daily "line-ups," frequent recognition for extraordinary achievement, and a performance appraisal based on expectations explained during the orientation, training, and certification processes.

To ensure that problems are resolved quickly, workers are required to act at first notice regardless of the type of problem or customer complaint. All employees are empowered to do whatever it takes to provide "instant pacification." No matter what their normal duties are, other employees must assist if aid is requested by a co-worker who is responding to a guest's complaint or wish.

Much of the responsibility for ensuring high-quality guest services and accommodations rests with the employees. Surveyed annually to ascertain their levels of satisfaction and understanding of quality standards, workers are keenly aware that excellence in guest services is a top hotel and personal priority. At each level in the company—from corporate leaders to managers and employees in individual work areas—teams are charged with setting objectives and devising action plans, which are reviewed by the corporate steering committee. In addition, each hotel has a "quality leader" who serves as a resource and advocate as teams and workers develop and implement their quality plans.

Teams and other mechanisms cultivate employee commitment. For example, each work area is covered by three teams responsible for setting quality-certification standards for each position, solving problems, and planning strategy.

---

[4]NIST, Profiles of Baldrige Winners, 2015.

SERVQUAL

An important tool developed by Parasuraman, Zeithamel, and Berry for assessing services quality is **SERVQUAL**. The SERVQUAL survey has been used by many firms and is an off-the-shelf approach that can be used in many services situations. The SERVQUAL instrument, a survey, has many advantages. Among these are the following:

- It is accepted as a *standard* for assessing different dimensions of services quality.
- It has been shown to be *valid* for a number of service situations.
- It has been demonstrated to be *reliable*, meaning that different readers interpret the questions similarly.
- Each instrument is *parsimonious* in that it has only 22 items. This means that it can be filled out quickly by customers and employees.
- Finally, it has a standardized analysis procedure to aid both interpretation and results.

One of the benefits of statistical quality control (SQC) is that it is an accepted procedure for assessing process variability. One of the comforts of implementing SQC is knowing that many other firms have used this approach and benefited from it. Although the SERVQUAL survey is not as widely used as SQC, it is a standardized approach to gathering information about customer perceptions of service quality. As such, it provides a base, or a means, to get started in assessing customer perceptions of quality.

Expectations

The SERVQUAL survey has two parts: **customer expectations** and **customer perceptions**. Before discussing SERVQUAL expectations, we should first discuss the reasons for assessing both expectations and perceptions.

Let's say that you want to improve service quality along some dimension—either tangibles or reliability. The natural question is this: "Which will create the *greater* improvement to the system for service?" If we understand both customer expectations and perceptions, we can assess the **gap** in these areas. For example, if customers have higher expectations for tangibles than for reliability, and customers perceive tangibles as poor, a large gap or disconnect exists between the expected and delivered performance on tangibility. Given that this gap is larger, the greater potential for increasing customer satisfaction lies in addressing tangibles first. This type of analysis provides a good way to understand how best to improve customer satisfaction.

Figure 8-1 shows the 22 survey items for expectations. The wording of the statements in the expectations survey relates to a generic firm in an industry that interests you. For example, if you were assessing customer service for a given grocery store, you might first administer the expectations survey to customers concerning a grocery store in general. Later, the perceptions survey might be administered to the customers of the particular grocery store.

Table 8-2 shows the items that address specific service quality dimensions. The averaged scores for these dimensions provide SERVQUAL difference scores (demonstrated later).

TABLE 8-2	SERVQUAL Items and Dimensions
Dimension	**Items**
Tangibles	1–4
Reliability	5–9
Responsiveness	10–13
Assurance	14–17
Empathy	18–22

	Strongly Disagree						Strongly Agree
1. Excellent _____ companies will have modern-looking equipment.	1	2	3	4	5	6	7
2. The physical facilities at excellent _____ companies will be visually appealing.	1	2	3	4	5	6	7
3. Employees at excellent _____ companies will be neat-appearing.	1	2	3	4	5	6	7
4. Materials associated with the service (such as pamphlets or statements) will be visually appealing in an excellent _____ company.	1	2	3	4	5	6	7
5. When excellent _____ companies promise to do something by a certain time, they will do so.	1	2	3	4	5	6	7
6. When a customer has a problem, excellent _____ companies will show a sincere interest in solving it.	1	2	3	4	5	6	7
7. Excellent _____ companies will perform the service right the first time.	1	2	3	4	5	6	7
8. Excellent _____ companies will provide their services at the time they promise to do so.	1	2	3	4	5	6	7
9. Excellent _____ companies will insist on error-free records.	1	2	3	4	5	6	7
10. Employees in excellent _____ companies will tell customers exactly when services will be performed.	1	2	3	4	5	6	7
11. Employees in excellent _____ companies will give prompt service to customers.	1	2	3	4	5	6	7
12. Employees in excellent _____ companies will always be willing to help customers.	1	2	3	4	5	6	7
13. Employees in excellent _____ companies will never be too busy to respond to customers' requests.	1	2	3	4	5	6	7
14. The behavior of employees in excellent _____ companies will instill confidence in customers.	1	2	3	4	5	6	7
15. Customers of excellent _____ companies will feel safe in their transactions.	1	2	3	4	5	6	7
16. Employees in excellent _____ companies will be consistently courteous with customers.	1	2	3	4	5	6	7
17. Employees in excellent _____ companies will have the knowledge to answer customers' questions.	1	2	3	4	5	6	7
18. Excellent _____ companies will give customers individual attention.	1	2	3	4	5	6	7
19. Excellent _____ companies will have operating hours convenient to all their customers.	1	2	3	4	5	6	7
20. Excellent _____ companies will have employees who give customers personal attention.	1	2	3	4	5	6	7
21. Excellent _____ companies will have the customer's best interests at heart.	1	2	3	4	5	6	7
22. The employees of excellent _____ companies will understand the specific needs of their customers.	1	2	3	4	5	6	7

FIGURE 8-1 SERVQUAL Expectations Survey *Source:* Based on V. Zeithamel, A. Parasuraman, and L. Berry, "SERVQUAL: A Multiple-Item Scale for Measuring Customer Perceptions of Service Quality," *Journal of Retailing* (Spring 1988): 12–40. Copyright Elsevier.

Perceptions

The SERVQUAL perceptions survey shown in Figure 8-2 is administered to customers in the same way that the expectations survey was administered. Notice that the perceptions survey also contains 22 items that are matched with the same 5 service quality dimensions as the expectations survey (the dimensions are listed in Table 8-2).

Gap Analysis

The SERVQUAL instrument is useful for performing what is called **gap analysis**. Because services are often intangible, gaps in communication and understanding between employees and customers have a serious negative effect on the perceptions of services quality. The model in Figure 8-3 shows the gaps that commonly occur and can affect the perceptions of services quality.

Each of the gaps in the model demonstrates differences in perceptions that can have a detrimental effect on quality perceptions in services. The SERVQUAL survey instrument can be administered in a variety of ways that examine each of these gaps. For example, SERVQUAL can

	Strongly Disagree						Strongly Agree
1. XYZ Co. has modern-looking equipment.	1	2	3	4	5	6	7
2. XYZ Co.'s physical facilities are visually appealing.	1	2	3	4	5	6	7
3. XYZ Co.'s employees are neat-appearing.	1	2	3	4	5	6	7
4. Materials associated with the service (such as pamphlets or statements) are visually appealing at XYZ Co.	1	2	3	4	5	6	7
5. When XYZ Co. promises to do something by a certain time, it does so.	1	2	3	4	5	6	7
6. When you have a problem, XYZ Co. shows a sincere interest in solving it.	1	2	3	4	5	6	7
7. XYZ Co. performs the service right the first time.	1	2	3	4	5	6	7
8. XYZ Co. provides its services at the time it promises to do so.	1	2	3	4	5	6	7
9. XYZ Co. insists on error-free records.	1	2	3	4	5	6	7
10. Employees in XYZ Co. tell you exactly when services will be performed.	1	2	3	4	5	6	7
11. Employees in XYZ Co. give you prompt service.	1	2	3	4	5	6	7
12. Employees in XYZ Co. are always willing to help you.	1	2	3	4	5	6	7
13. Employees in XYZ Co. are never too busy to respond to your requests.	1	2	3	4	5	6	7
14. The behavior of employees in XYZ Co. instills confidence in you.	1	2	3	4	5	6	7
15. You feel safe in your transactions with XYZ Co.	1	2	3	4	5	6	7
16. Employees in XYZ Co. are consistently courteous with you.	1	2	3	4	5	6	7
17. Employees in XYZ Co. have the knowledge to answer your questions.	1	2	3	4	5	6	7
18. XYZ Co. gives you individual attention.	1	2	3	4	5	6	7
19. XYZ Co. has operating hours convenient to all its customers.	1	2	3	4	5	6	7
20. XYZ Co. has employees who give you personal attention.	1	2	3	4	5	6	7
21. XYZ Co. has your best interests at heart.	1	2	3	4	5	6	7
22. Employees of XYZ Co. understand your specific needs.	1	2	3	4	5	6	7

FIGURE 8-2   SERVQUAL Perceptions Survey   *Source:* Based on V. Zeithamel, A. Parasuraman, and L. Berry, "SERVQUAL: A Multiple-Item Scale for Measuring Customer Perceptions of Service Quality," *Journal of Retailing* (Spring 1988): 12–40. Copyright Elsevier.

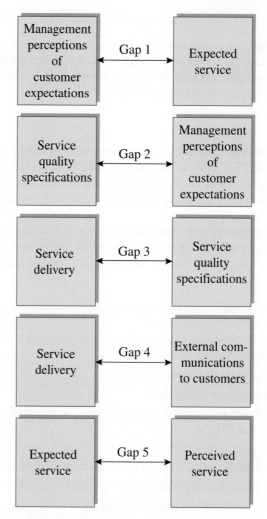

FIGURE 8-3 Gaps 1–5

be used to explore differences in perceptions between customers, between managers, between managers and customers, and between employees. We briefly examine each of the different gaps in the next paragraphs.

Gap 1 shows that there can be a difference between *actual* customer expectations and *management's idea* or perception of customer expectations. As a customer, have you ever wanted to tell a service provider, "I don't want you to do that; I want you to do something else!" It is very difficult for managers or employees to break out of the internal, process-oriented view of the business. Many times, improving processes does not equal improving customer service. To truly improve customer service, we must understand what the customer wants. The SERVQUAL instrument can be used to help in this understanding (see Figure 8-3).

Managers' expectations of service quality may not match service quality specifications. This mismatch is demonstrated in *gap 2*. Once managers truly understand what the customer wants, a system can be developed to help provide exactly what the customer wants. Because firms do not specify customer requirements according to a well-defined process, there is often no way to know whether customer specifications and management expectations are aligned.

After services specifications have been established, the delivery of perfect services quality is still not guaranteed. Inadequate training, communication, and preparation of employees who interact with the customer, referred to as **contact personnel**, can lower the quality of service delivered. This mismatch is *gap 3*.

Gap 4 shows the differences between services delivery and external communications with the customer. Companies influence customer expectations of services through word of mouth and through other media such as advertising. As a result, there could be a difference between what customers hear you say you are going to deliver as a service provider and what you actually deliver. Have you ever heard someone say, "They promised me one thing and gave me another"? This gap can lead to seriously negative customer perceptions of service quality.

Gap 5 is the difference between perceived and expected services, which we considered briefly when we introduced the SERVQUAL instrument. Think of the first time you dealt with your university admissions office or financial aid office. In many universities and colleges, these offices are well run and provide great service. However, in other colleges, their service is not so good. The difference between your expectations and your perceptions is directly related to your perception of service quality.

The key to closing gap 5 is to first close gaps 1 through 4 through thoughtful systems design, careful communication with the customer, and a workforce trained to provide consistently outstanding customer service. As long as these gaps exist, there will be lowered perceptions of customer service.

Assessing Differences in Expectations and Perceptions by Using the Differencing Technique

Let's suppose that you have administered both the expectations and the perceptions SERVQUAL instruments to your customers. Typically, you need a sample size of between 50 and 100 for each of the surveys (i.e., $50 < n < 100$, where n is the sample size). The difference score for SERVQUAL is computed by the following steps. Separate the SERVQUAL dimensions as follows:

Dimension	Items
Tangibles	1–4
Reliability	5–9
Responsiveness	10–13
Assurance	14–17
Empathy	18–22

For each respondent, sum the SERVQUAL scores for each set of items relating to a given dimension. Sum across the n respondents and divide the total by n.

EXAMPLE 8-1   **SERVQUAL Differencing**

Recently, a hospital administered the SERVQUAL survey to its customers as a way to determine where it should focus the training of its employees to best improve customer service. Fifty surveys were administered to customers before and after they were treated. In cases where the patients were in too much pain to fill out the perceptions survey after a procedure, they were asked to fill out the survey at the follow-up visit. On the basis of the 50 responses, the following averages were computed for each item:

Item Number	Average Perception	Average Expectation
1	6.5	6.3
2	6.4	6.4
3	6.9	6.2
4	6.8	6.8
5	3.2	5.2
6	3.4	6.1
7	3.3	6.3
8	3.5	5.9
9	3.6	6.6
10	5.2	2.4
11	5.5	2.2
12	5.6	2.4
13	5.8	2.6
14	4.1	3.2
15	5.5	3.3
16	4.3	3.4
17	4.1	3.2
18	4.2	3.5
19	2.6	6.5
20	2.8	6.6
21	2.5	6.4
22	2.4	6.3

On the basis of these means, the following overall averages were computed for the different dimensions:

Perception Averages		Average Perception	Average Expectation	Expectation Averages	
Tangibles:	6.650	6.5	6.3	Tangibles:	6.425
(Avg. items 1–4)		6.4	6.4	(Avg. items 1–4)	
		6.9	6.2		
		6.8	6.8		
Reliability:	3.400	3.2	5.2	Reliability:	6.020
(Avg. items 5–9)		3.4	6.1	(Avg. items 5–9)	
		3.3	6.3		
		3.5	5.9		
		3.6	6.6		
Responsiveness:	5.525	5.2	2.4	Responsiveness:	2.400
(Avg. items 10–13)		5.5	2.2	(Avg. items 10–13)	
		5.6	2.4		
		5.8	2.6		

(continued)

Perception Averages		Average Perception	Average Expectation	Expectation Averages	
Assurance:	4.500	4.1	3.2	Assurance:	3.275
(Avg. items 14–17)		5.5	3.3	(Avg. items 14–17)	
		4.3	3.4		
		4.1	3.2		
Empathy:	2.900	4.2	3.5	Empathy:	5.860
(Avg. items 18–22)		2.6	6.5	(Avg. items 18–22)	
		2.8	6.6		
		2.5	6.4		
		2.4	6.3		

The averages for each of the dimensions of service quality were computed by averaging the items pertaining to each dimension. Finally, differences for the dimensions were computed as follows:

	Perception		Expected		
Tangible difference =	6.65	less	6.425	equals	0.225
Reliability difference =	3.4	less	6.02	equals	–2.62
Responsiveness difference =	5.525	less	2.4	equals	3.125
Assurance difference =	4.5	less	3.275	equals	1.225
Empathy difference =	2.9	less	5.86	equals	–2.96

The differences show that the greatest negative mismatch exists in the dimension of empathy, with reliability as a close second. Therefore, the training program should focus on teaching employees to be empathetic. Also, the process improvement efforts should focus on improving reliability. These changes will lead to the greatest improvements in customer service.

EXAMPLE 8-2   SERVQUAL Two-Dimensional Differencing

If there is enough variation in the responses given to different dimensions, the two-dimensional differencing technique is very useful for evaluating SERVQUAL responses. Note that this technique is also used for specific questionnaires relating to specific services offered by companies. For example, St. John's Hospital administers surveys to patients asking about several specific services such as food, laundry, nursing, and many other services. The two-dimensional differencing technique allows the hospital to determine which services it should emphasize to improve customer perceptions and those that make little difference.

Using the information from Example 8.1, it is fairly simple to develop a two-dimensional services plane. The vertical axis reflects the expectations score and the horizontal axis relates to the perceptions score (Figure 8-4), using 4 (the neutral response) as the origin. The hospital analyst learns that emphasis is needed in the areas of reliability and empathy because these are areas for which expectations are high and perceptions are relatively low.

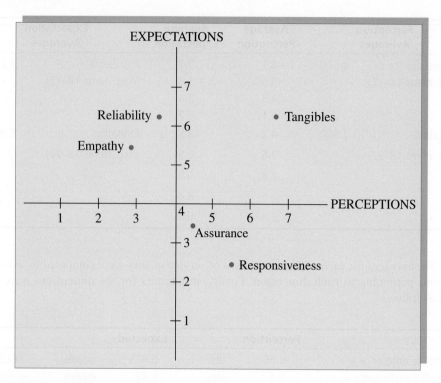

FIGURE 8-4   Two-Dimensional Differencing Plane

DESIGNING AND IMPROVING THE SERVICES TRANSACTION

So far in this chapter, we have discussed customer perceptions of quality. One of the ways to improve customers' perceptions of quality is to improve the process of delivery of the service. Just as teams can succeed in manufacturing, teams in services can develop ways to improve processes and customer satisfaction.

Other concepts and tools include services blueprinting, moments-of-truth concept, and the Japanese method known as poka-yoke. Each of these is discussed in the following paragraphs.

Services Blueprinting

Lynn Shostack, CEO of Joyce International, Inc., is known for the statement, "The process is the service." Shostack also developed the process known as **services blueprinting**.[5] A services blueprint is a flowchart that isolates potential fail points in a process. She recommends that blueprints be kept on every process in a service and that a "keeper of the blueprint" make the blueprints available for others in the firm. If possible, the blueprint also should be available on a computer network for all to view. There are four steps to developing a services blueprint:

1. *Identify processes.* In this step, processes are flowcharted so that the bounds of the process are identified. Figure 8-5 shows a simple process used by Shostack to demonstrate services blueprinting, in this case for a hair salon's processes.
2. *Isolate fail points.* Notice in Figure 8-5 that the hair coloring stage is a possible fail point. What can happen here? The wrong color could be applied, and the hair style will be ruined. This would be a very expensive mistake.

---

[5]Shostack, G. L., "Designing Services That Deliver," *Harvard Business Review* 62, 1 (1984): 135.

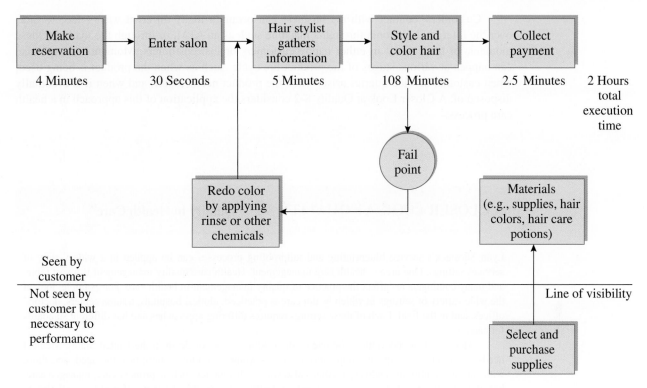

FIGURE 8-5 Services Blueprinting Example in a Hair Salon

3. ***Establish a time frame.*** In a hair salon operation, time is a major determinant of profitability. As a result, those steps that waste time result in lost income. The analyst observing this process should establish a standard time for each step in the process.
4. ***Analyze profits.*** The customer spends about two hours in the process. As errors occur in the process, the salon owner becomes liable, and other business is lost.

Notice also that Figure 8-5 includes a line of visibility. The activities below the line of visibility are not seen by the customer, but they influence performance. This is true in many organizations. The area above the line of visibility is often referred to as the *front office*, and the area below the line of visibility is referred to as the *back office*. Many times process improvements focus on back-office activities, whereas front-office activities that involve high customer interaction are ignored. Services process blueprinting places the focus on front-office activities.

To understand how you could apply services blueprinting, think about a restaurant. Typically, when you first enter a restaurant, you expect to be greeted at the door. Can you remember a time when you weren't? This has happened to all of us at some point. A restaurant can install sensors or provide backups for the greeter so that this breakdown never occurs. Services blueprinting is a tool to help with brainstorming activities that lead to customer service improvement.

Moments of Truth

The fail points in the services blueprints are often referred to as **moments of truth**. These are the times at which the customer expects something to happen. Remember the SERVQUAL items? Expectations are a major determinant of customer perceptions of service quality. Therefore, when the customer expects something to happen, it has to happen. It is that simple! Some companies list these moments of truth and define fail-safes and procedures to see that they result in satisfied customers.

Customers' contact with the business can occur in many different ways—face to face, over the Internet, by phone, through a machine such as an ATM, or through the mail. All these moments of truth result in either happy customers or lost customers. Moments of truth also can happen at various stages of the product life cycle, such as when the product is being used, when customer service queries arise, when the product needs repair, and when it is eventually disposed of. A Closer Look at Quality 8-2 considers the application of this approach in a health care process.

A CLOSER LOOK AT QUALITY 8-2   Quality in Health Care[6]

Lynn Shostack's service blueprinting and failproofing processes can be applied in a wide variety of services settings. One area is health care management. Health care quality management is a vast topic, and many contingencies affect the practice of quality management in health care. For example, look at the wide variety of settings in which health care is practiced: clinics, hospitals, trauma centers, doctors' offices, and in the field. Each of these settings requires differing approaches and has different standards for care.

Medical errors continue to be one of the leading causes of death in the United States. Medical needs are different for specific populations such as women, children, minorities, the aged, and those with chronic conditions. Delivery methods also vary with vehicles such as primary care, managed care, hospitals, health maintenance organizations, and others. Given this diversity of problems relative to health care quality management, much work is needed in this area.

Following is a list of 20 steps to improve health care from the U.S. Agency for Healthcare Research and Quality. Note how these steps appear to walk the patient through the entire health care process to isolate possible fail points.

1. Be an active member of your health provider team.
2. Make sure your doctor knows all medicines you are taking.
3. Let your doctor know about any allergies you have to medications.
4. Read the doctor's prescriptions.
5. Understand your medications.
6. Make sure you get the right medicine from your pharmacy. An estimated 88% of medicine errors involve the wrong drug or dosage.
7. Ask pharmacists about your medicines.
8. Ask how best to measure liquid medicines.
9. Understand your medicine's side effects so you are aware if they occur.
10. If possible, go to a hospital where they often perform the procedures or surgeries you need.
11. Ask your health care personnel if they have washed their hands before they touch you.
12. Understand your treatment plan when you are discharged from a hospital.
13. Understand any surgical procedures you will experience.
14. Speak up if you have questions or concerns.
15. Make sure your personal doctor is in charge of your care.
16. Make sure all of your health care providers know your health history.
17. Get others involved in your health care, such as family members in case you are incapacitated.
18. Know that "more is not better." You may not need some care.
19. If you have a test, don't assume that no news is good news. They may have failed to contact you.
20. Learn more about your condition and treatments by asking your doctor and nurse and other reliable sources.

[6]Adapted from "20 Tips to Prevent Medical Errors—Patient Fact Sheet," Agency for Healthcare Research and Quality, 2008.

Poka-yoke

Dr. Richard Chase and Dr. John Grout have been influential in promoting the use of **poka-yokes** (fail-safes) in services.[7] The idea behind fail-safing is to ensure that certain errors will never occur. Just as many processes seem to be designed to fail, they also can be designed *not* to fail. In services, Chase defines different classifications for fail-safe devices. These are

Warning methods

Physical contact methods

Visual contact methods

Fail-safe methods can also be defined by the "**three Ts**" (see Figure 8-6):

Task to be performed

Treatment provided to the customer

Tangibles provided to the customer

These poka-yoke classifications and Ts occur in many different forms. Some examples include[8] beepers in ATM machines that warn you to remove your card, toilets and sinks that automatically flush and shut off, the mechanism that stops you from inserting a USB drive upside-down in a computer, surgical trays that have indentations for different instruments, needle removers that prevent accidental needle pokes, requirements that bank tellers enter a customer's eye color before beginning a transaction so that identity is confirmed, or a file cabinet that locks the other drawers when any one drawer is opened so the cabinet doesn't fall over.

Poka-yokes such as these represent a good amount of creativity and are very often used by Japanese and American companies to help ensure quality service. In a nutshell, you should isolate fail points in a process and then fail-safe the process to make sure that errors don't occur.

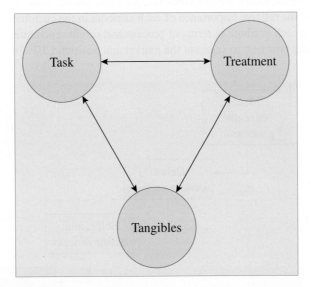

FIGURE 8-6   The Three Ts

---

[7]Chase, R., and Stewart, D., "Make Your Service Fail-Safe," *Sloan Management Review* 35, 3 (1994): 35–44.

[8]For an extensive literature review and interesting information about poka-yoke, check out Dr. John Grout's homepage on the Internet (facultyweb.berry.edu/jgrout/pokayoke.html). He has devoted a great deal of time to developing this resource, and it is the most concise one on poka-yoke available. Grout is currently Dean of the Campbell School of Business at Berry College in Mount Berry, Georgia.

Thinking back to Lynn Shostack's hair salon process, how would you fail-safe the process so that the wrong color would never be applied?

THE CUSTOMER BENEFITS PACKAGE

Just as many organizations have employee benefits packages, services firms can develop **customer benefits packages (CBPs)**. A customer benefits package consists of both tangibles that define the service and intangibles that make up the service. The tangibles are known as *goods-content*. Intangibles are referred to as *service-content*. The only difference between an employee benefits package and a services benefits package is the ultimate recipient of the benefits package.

CBPs are important not only in that they help define what it is that your service firm *will* provide to the customer but also in helping to define what *will not* be provided to the customer. More and more, firms are focusing on better defining the niches that they serve. As a result, the question of what they *will not* provide to the customer is often as important as what they *will* provide. By helping to answer this question, CBPs provide a foundation for developing a service strategy. The four stages of the service benefit package design process are as follows (see Figure 8-7):

1. Idea/concept generation
2. The definition of a services package
3. Process definition and selection
4. Facilities requirement definition

As defined by David Collier,[9] a professor at Florida Gulf Coast University, the objectives of customer benefits package design are to

- Make sure the final CBP attributes you are using are the correct ones.
- Evaluate the relative importance of each attribute in the customer's mind.
- Evaluate each attribute in terms of process and service encounter capability.
- Figure out how best to segment the market and position CBPs in each market.

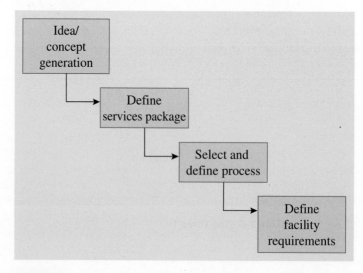

FIGURE 8-7 CBP Design Process

---

[9]Collier, D., *The Service/Quality Solution* (Milwaukee, WI: Irwin/ASQC, 1994).

Services Process Structure	Services Package Structure			
	Unique services packages	Selective services packages	Restricted services packages	Generic services packages
Expert service	Doctor's office			
Service shop	Mass entertainment			
Service factory				Home repair

FIGURE 8-8   Service Process/Service Benefits Package Matrix   *Source:* Based on D. Kellogg and W. Nie, "A Framework for Strategic Service Management," *Journal of Operations Management* 13, 4 (1995): 323–327.

- Avoid CBP duplication and proliferation.
- Bring each CBP, and associated process and service encounters, to market as quickly as possible. Use the CBP framework and final attributes to design facilities, processes, equipment, jobs, and service encounters.
- Maximize customer satisfaction and profits.

The CBP is defined largely by the degree of freedom allowed by the firm in the customization of the services package. Deborah Kellogg and Winter Nie[10] provided a services process/services package matrix. As shown in Figure 8-8, firms will offer **unique services packages**, **selective services packages**, **restricted services packages**, or **generic services packages**. Generic services packages are of the one-size-fits-all variety. Unique services packages are especially tailored for each customer. Your firm's capability to custom-tailor a benefits package depends on the amount of flexibility you have as a service provider. Strategic issues such as organizational flexibility, top-management skill, employee motivation, training, hiring practices, culture of the service customer, nature of the service, and technological choice affect your ability to provide unique services packages.

Table 8-3 shows a customer benefits package from the Slide-Master firm. Notice that Slide-Master has taken great care in defining tangibles and intangibles for its CBP. Slide-Master evaluates its CBP performance using monthly surveys of employees and customers.

SERVICE TRANSACTION ANALYSIS

Because we have discussed the design of services processes and improving services processes, we can now present **service transaction analysis (STA)**.[11] This is a service improvement technique that allows managers to analyze their service processes at a very detailed level. As we stated, Crosby views service encounters as a series of transactions (or moments of truth). STA is a method for identifying these transactions and evaluating them from the customer's perspective to determine whether there is a gap between service design and what the customer perceives as the service.

---

[10]Kellogg, D., and Nie, W., "A Framework for Strategic Service Management," *Journal of Operations Management* 13, 9 (1995): 323–337.

[11]Johnston, R., "Towards a Better Understanding of Service Excellence," *Managing Service Quality* 14, 2/3 (2004): 129–134.

TABLE 8-3	Final CBP Attributes for Slide-Master

Tangible (Goods-Content)	Intangible (Service-Content)
Slides	*Convenience and Timeliness*
Quality, durable, clean, new film, and cardboard	Facility close to downtown
High-resolution pictures and slides	Pickup and delivery service
Multiple color combinations (6 million)	Telephone/fax order capability
Slide properly centered and focused	Standard 3-day service
	Rush 1-day service
Equipment/Technology	Really try to handle last-minute customer changes
Latest computer hardware	Accurate, itemized billing by fifth working day of each month
State-of-the-art software	
High-quality camera	*Professionalism*
Superior maintenance of all equipment	Absolutely confidential services
Well-maintained delivery vehicles with ads on the sides	Emphasis on telephone courtesy
Flexible for custom designs	Refer to client by name
	Client order documentation correctly filled out
People	and processed
Clean and very well groomed	Flexible to customer needs
Attractive uniforms	
	Consulting Services
Packaging	Artistic expertise
Heavy, clear, high-quality sleeves	History of previous jobs
Sequenced and numbered properly	Technical knowledge
Loaded in attractive boxes or slide carousels	Nonbusiness hours on-call professional
Facilities	*Service Attitude*
Ample parking spaces	User-friendliness
Secure parking lot	Polite, responsive attitude
Attractive signs	Do exactly what we promise
Clean, attractive building—outside	Script dialogues for order taking and postpurchase callbacks
Upscale indoor wall pictures and decor	Confident but relaxing behavior
Reception area and service counter—clean and professional appearance	
Soft, relaxing background music	
Plush furniture	
Bright lighting	
Complimentary coffee and soft drinks	
Restrooms, soap, etc.—clean	

Source: Adapted from David Collier, *The Service/Quality Solution* (Milwaukee, WI: Irwin/ASQC, 1994). Used with permission of David Collier.

Figure 8-9 shows a service transaction analysis sheet. This sheet is a tool in STA. After you have specified the service process to be studied, "mystery shoppers," or independent consultant-customers, walk through the entire process. After receiving the service, they then rate each transaction in the process with either a "+" (delighting), "0" (satisfactory), or "−" (unsatisfactory). The rationales for these scores are entered into the right side of the sheet, and an overall evaluation is provided in the bottom of the sheet. Using these sheets, service designers, managers, and staff can attempt to understand why the customer did not like certain aspects of the service and use this as an input into improving the process.

SERVICE TRANSACTION ANALYSIS SHEET

Legal Firm:	Lawyer	Service concept:
Process:	Reception	General legal services for personal customers in a user-friendly, sympathetic, and nonintimidating way
Customer type:	Personal client	

Transaction	Score: +	0	−	Message
Imposing oak entrance door, firmly shut.				"Trustworthy, professional but a little formidable."
Second door with advertisement for a lending company.				"They like constructing barriers." "They may not be impartial."
Carpeted corridor but no sign of receptionist.				"Homey but is this the right place?" "Unhelpful."
Receptionist behind desk ignores customer and continues typing.				"They don't seem to care about me." "They don't think I am important."
She says, "Yes?"				"Not very welcoming." "I feel like I am intruding on her work."
Phone rings, which receptionist answers.				"I am not important." "Other people have priority on her time."

Overall evaluation
Poor service design. Little thought or concern for clients. Unfriendly and intimidating service.

FIGURE 8-9 STA Sheet

EXAMPLE 8-3 Service Transaction Analysis in Action

In the transaction analysis sheet in Figure 8-9, the large oak door, although professional, looks forbidding. When going to this lawyer's office, the client is probably nervous about approaching the attorney and can find the décor daunting and scary. The message on the second door made it appear that the attorneys may not provide impartial advice due to their relationships with a lending company. The not-so-subtle message sent by the rude receptionist demonstrated a mismatch between the service design and execution … and so forth. The application of this technique alerted the partners to what was really going on in their own office. Changes were made to address these problems.

IMPROVING CUSTOMER SERVICE IN GOVERNMENT

If customer service is the battlefield for business in the twenty-first century, then government is probably the last frontier. There are some evidences of improvement in several aspects of government. Some federal government agencies have adopted quality management (see A Closer Look at Quality 8-3). Quality professionals know that the military has long been an early adopter of statistical quality techniques. Many standards have been established. The government has developed a searchable list of 4,000 customer service standards for 570 federal departments and agencies. This effort started with an executive order for a "customer-driven government that matches or exceeds the best service available in the private sector." In the first year, only three agencies responded with agreements to commit to service standards. These early adopters were the Social Security Administration, the IRS, and the Postal Service.

States are also jumping on the bandwagon. By 2011, 32 states had established quality award programs. Many state agencies around the country have adopted quality techniques. However, many of these implementations appear to be in the early stages. Overall, government is lagging

---

A CLOSER LOOK AT QUALITY 8-3   **Government Service Quality: A Stop-and-Go Process**

Ever since the 1980s, quality in government has been a hot topic. A mess-up such as the botched rollout of the Obamacare website or poor management of the U.S. Postal Service can create unflattering front page headlines. Here is a short history of how different administrations have handled improvement in government. For the most part, there has been a lot of hoopla in the initial launching of these programs, but very little real success. It should be noted that some of the best successes have occurred at lower levels in government as employees have caught the vision of improvement.

- During the Reagan administration, Deming concepts were used to implement improvement in government, and the Baldrige Award was created.
- George Bush continued the legacy of the Reagan administration, but provided very little momentum for quality improvement.
- Bill Clinton was a big supporter of the Baldrige program because he had promoted the program as Arkansas governor. Al Gore was put in charge of reinventing government with a lot of fanfare. However, the effort fizzled and ended up being perceived as window dressing.
- George W. Bush used executive orders to drive improvement and little else.
- The Obama administration created the Chief Performance Officer under the Office of Management and Budget. Although some savings have been created as a result of process improvements, the federal budget has exploded under Obama.

These efforts demonstrate the difficulties associated with managing quality in the federal government. Some fear that the government has become too large and unwieldy to drive long lasting improvement. We shall see. The good sign is that there is much potential for improvement as new quality professionals enter government. Some prescriptions for improvement in government include these:

- Use statutes instead of executive orders. The laws stay around longer.
- Look closely at the structure of government. There are many departments and offices that overlap and are redundant; there is much opportunity for pruning.
- Any improvements need to be bipartisan, which provides an opportunity for real change.

behind the private sector in quality adoption. Although the results are mixed, it is clear that private-sector quality management practices are being adopted in government. Why is this progress occurring? Many used to question whether the government had the inclination to adopt quality techniques, given the lack of profit motive. However, several factors seem to be driving this change:

- People want and desire to do good quality work.
- Because quality management is associated with improved employee satisfaction, there is a major impetus to improve.
- Government leaders are mandating standards, strategic plans, and new levels of performance at all levels of government. These standards are being adopted in government agencies because of the mandates.
- Demand for government services is growing at a faster rate than funding for them. The natural reaction is to simplify processes that have become bloated.
- Finally, the threat of privatization in government has led to an improvement in service in many areas.

QUALITY IN HEALTH CARE

Another area of services that is receiving much attention is health care. Several factors have contributed to this phenomenon:

- Health care is facing the same "cost squeeze" that government is facing.
- The Affordable Care Act has mandated improvements to the delivery of health care—coupled with more regulations.
- A move toward health maintenance organizations (HMOs) is causing hospitals to streamline operations.
- There is increasing diversity in health care.

In some cases, insurers such as Blue Cross are encouraging the use of quality management approaches. Health care workers are becoming increasingly knowledgeable about quality management practices and concepts. In fact, the very nature of health care requires careful and well-planned procedures.

Many health care customers, however, are uncomfortable with these changes to government and health care. If quality approaches are applied, it is probably best that efforts not focus entirely on efficiency. Reliability and empathy are dimensions that can only be good for health care.

SUPPLY CHAIN QUALITY IN SERVICES

As we have talked about before, one of the major differences between services and manufacturing is the involvement of the customer in the process. As shown in Figure 8-10, service supply chains are bidirectional. This means that service customers actually provide inputs to the supply chain. Many times, these inputs can be information or, in some cases, labor—as in the case of a

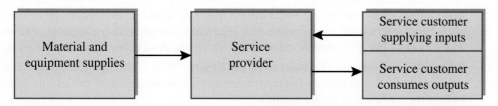

FIGURE 8-10 Bidirectional Services Supply Chain   *Source:* S. E. Sampson, "A Customer-Supplier Paradigm for Service Science," in (refereed) *Proceedings of the DSI Services Science Miniconference,* Pittsburgh, PA, May 2007. Copyright © 2007 by Scott E. Sampson. Reprinted by permission.

self-service gas station. Therefore, effective communication is necessary between customers and suppliers to prevent inadequate fulfillment of customer expectations. The concept of garbage in, garbage out implies that the quality of a service supply chain will be limited by the quality of the supplied inputs. Even if customers provide poor inputs (inaccurate information), they may still expect accurate outputs. This expectation has implications for service design. In an integrated supply chain, the service provider still has greater responsibility for verifying customer inputs to ensure that they are accurate. In some cases, the service provider may be able to initiate communication of customer-input delivery expectations, such as through reservation systems. This may be complicated by the fact that service delivery systems are often inherently just-in-time. Of course, in services, there are other suppliers besides the customers. They are often managed in a more traditional supply-chain manner. However, the customer-supplier linkage makes services unique.

A THEORY FOR SERVICE QUALITY MANAGEMENT

As we studied in Chapter 2, theory development in the area of quality is an important work that continues. Dr. Scott Sampson of Brigham Young University is a researcher who is developing theory in services management. His **unified theory for services management** provides interesting insights for quality management.[12] This theory consists of several propositions, which are based on the definitions of services that were introduced early in this chapter. Some of the propositions are as follows:

> *Proposition 1: The Unified Services Theory.* "With services, the customer provides significant inputs into the production process. With manufacturing, groups of customers may contribute ideas to the design of the product; however, individual customers' only part in the actual process is to select and consume the output. Nearly all other managerial themes unique to services are founded in this distinction."

> *Proposition 2: The Unreliable Supplier Dilemma.* "With services, the customer-suppliers often provide unreliable inputs."

> "The Unreliable Supplier Dilemma" occurs because service customers provide themselves, their belongings, and/or their information as process inputs (by the Unified Services Theory). This simultaneous relationship as supplier and customer makes it difficult for the service provider to control the supplied inputs.

> *Proposition 3: Capricious Labor.* "With services, customer-labor may ignore, avoid, or reject technologies or process improvements which are intended to increase quality and productivity. As a result, customer buy-in to process changes must be carefully addressed."

> Capricious labor occurs because many services customers provide themselves as labor inputs into the production process. In manufacturing organizations, labor is expected to conform to corporate policy. If the manufacturer mandates that a quality initiative be implemented, labor is generally expected to conform, even when labor thinks the initiative is a bad idea.

> Imagine a manufacturer that invests in technology that will improve quality of production. Then imagine that some of the employees reject the technology, stating, "I am more comfortable doing it the old way," even though the old way is inefficient and results in poor quality. How would management respond to those self-willed employees? Unless those employees were children of the owner, one might suspect their jobs would be in jeopardy. In services, much labor is performed by customers who coproduce. Therefore, they can adopt or reject what they don't like. For example, customers don't have to stand in line if they don't want to.

> *Proposition 4: Everyone Presumes to Be an Expert.* "With services, the customer often provides product specifications (what to make) and process design (how to make it), often without the invitation of the service provider."

---

[12]Sampson, S., "Understanding Service Supply Chains," *Proceedings of the 3rd International Conference on Operations and Supply Chain Management,* Wuhan, China, 2009, p. 54. Copyright © 2009 by Scott Sampson. Reprinted by permission.

"Everyone thinks they're an expert" occurs because the necessity for customer inputs in service processes means that most customers have extensive experience with the service process. This experience breeds process knowledge and ideas for improvement. The words of Richard Chase capture this idea well: "Everyone is an expert on services. We all think we know what we want from a service organization and, by the very process of living, we have a good deal of experience with the service creation process."[13]

Summary

In this chapter, we have studied quality in services. Because services involve intangibles, they are different from manufacturing. Because of the lack of hard measures, statistical quality control techniques are not always as successful in services as they are in manufacturing. This doesn't mean that statistical thinking is not extremely useful in services.

Services definitions and classifications were presented that help us better understand services. We have provided tools for services such as SERVQUAL, services blueprinting, moments of truth, poka-yokes, and customer benefits packages.

The bottom line is a satisfied customer. Customers pay the bills. They are the object of our efforts. At times, all the customer wants is a caring ear to bend. In our race for profits, efficiencies, and better processes, let's not forget the human touch.

Key Terms

Contact personnel	Gap	Moments of truth	SERVQUAL
Customer benefits packages (CBPs)	Gap analysis	Poka-yoke	Three Ts
Customer contact	Generic services packages	Product liability	Unified theory for services management
Customer coproduction	Heterogeneous	Restricted services packages	Unique services packages
Customer expectations	Intangible	Selective services packages	Voluntary services
Customer perceptions	Internal services	Service transaction analysis (STA)	
External services	Involuntary service	Services blueprinting	
	Malpractice		

Discussion Questions

1. Discuss the ways in which services are unique in comparison with manufactured goods. How do these differences affect the management of service quality?
2. Provide an example of customer coproduction other than the example provided in the text. What are the advantages and disadvantages of customer coproduction for service providers?
3. Are quality techniques in the service industry well developed or still fairly immature? If you believe that they are immature, why do you think this is the case?
4. Why do you believe that quality techniques in the service industry are less mature than quality techniques for manufactured products? What can be done to bring quality techniques for the services industry up to a higher level?
5. Discuss the distinction between voluntary services and involuntary services. Why is this distinction important in our understanding of service quality?
6. Are the Baldrige criteria applicable to service situations? If so, how?
7. List Zeithamel, Parasuraman, and Berry's five dimensions of service quality. Is the list identical for every service provider or does it vary from company to company? Explain your answer.

---

[13]Jacobs, H., and Chase, R., *Operations and Supply Chain Management* (Homewood, IL: Irwin, 2010), p. 56

8. Discuss some of the qualities of an effective leader in a service context.
9. What is SERVQUAL? How does SERVQUAL help a firm assess its service quality?
10. What are the advantages of the SERVQUAL instrument?
11. Discuss the concept of gap analysis in the context of a SERVQUAL assessment.
12. What is a services blueprint? How is a services blueprint developed?
13. Describe the concept of moment of truth in a service context. Describe a moment of truth that you recently experienced as a consumer. Was your service experience satisfactory or unsatisfactory? Explain your answer.
14. How can the moment-of-truth concept be used as a training tool in a service setting?
15. What is a customer benefits package? What is the purpose of developing customer benefits packages in a service context?
16. In what ways will the globalization of services alter the way that businesses manage their service quality?
17. Discuss the initiatives that a government within Europe has taken to increase its emphasis on service quality. Are they effective?
18. Discuss several of the factors that have contributed to an increase in attention directed toward quality in health care.
19. Discuss the unified theory for services management developed by Dr. Scott Sampson. Do you agree or disagree with the principles underlying Sampson's theory? Explain your answer.
20. In your judgment, will the management of "service quality" ever progress as far as the management of "manufactured goods quality"? Make your answer as substantive as possible.

Problems

1. A national electronics retail chain charges $350 for a service contract. Of this, the company sends $120 to an insurer. Calculate the profit margin for the service contract.
2. Using the example of the service transaction analysis (STA) worksheet in Figure 8-10, chart and evaluate the transactions for your university or college advising office. Report your findings and overall evaluation.
3. Develop a consumer benefits package for a service business in your community. Be exhaustive and explicit in your package identification.
4. Develop a services blueprint for a local car wash. Identify possible fail points, back-office processes, and fail-safes.
5. Recently, a medical office administered the SERVQUAL survey to its customers as a way to determine where it should focus the process improvement. Forty surveys were administered to customers before and after they were treated. On the basis of the 40 responses, averages were computed for each item. Using the averages in the table that follows, compute dimension averages. Based on your findings, which dimensions should be emphasized?

Item	Perception Average	Expectation Average	Differences
1	5.5	2.3	3.2
2	5.4	2.4	3.0
3	5.9	2.2	3.7
4	5.8	2.8	3.0
5	3.2	3.2	0
6	4.4	4.1	0.3
7	4.3	5.3	−1.0
8	2.5	4.9	−2.4
9	4.6	5.6	−1.0
10	6.2	3.4	2.8
11	6.5	3.2	3.3
12	6.6	3.4	3.2
13	6.8	3.6	3.2
14	3.1	3.2	−0.1
15	4.5	3.3	1.2

Item	Perception Average	Expectation Average	Differences
16	3.3	3.4	−0.1
17	3.1	3.2	−0.1
18	3.2	3.5	−0.3
19	1.6	6.5	−4.9
20	1.8	6.6	−4.8
21	1.5	6.4	−4.9
22	1.4	6.3	−4.9

6. For the data in Problem 5, perform a two-dimensional differencing analysis. Do your results differ from your answer in Problem 5?

7. The averages for different dimensions of service quality were computed by averaging the items pertaining to the dimension. Use the following data to determine which dimensions to emphasize.

	Perceptions	Expectations
Tangibles =	5.40	1.42
Reliability =	3.20	6.40
Responsiveness =	2.45	2.30
Assurance =	5.60	3.30
Empathy =	1.90	6.40

a. Using simple differencing, determine which dimensions should be emphasized.
b. Use two-dimensional differencing to determine which dimensions should be emphasized.
c. Based on your findings, choose the most important dimension and describe how you would develop a process improvement program to address the dimension that needs to be improved.

8. A state university wants to perform a gap analysis to determine what student traits corporate CEOs find most important. The exercise is to be administered to CEOs and involves two surveys: an expectations survey and a perceptions survey. All questions are answered on a 10-point scale. The attributes the CEOs are asked to rate are propensity for lifelong learning, ability to work in teams, innate ability, and cognitive ability. The results of nine surveys are synopsized in the following table:

	Lifelong Learning		Teamwork		Innate Abilities		Cognitive Abilities	
Respondent	Expectations	Perceptions	Expectations	Perceptions	Expectations	Perceptions	Expectations	Perceptions
1	8	0	8	10	2	5	3	9
2	7	4	9	9	6	5	4	8
3	9	2	9	10	4	5	2	7
4	10	5	10	9	7	4	3	8
5	5	1	8	7	5	6	4	9
6	9	1	7	9	2	7	2	10
7	9	3	9	10	2	5	3	10
8	8	2	10	10	3	6	2	10
9	7	0	9	10	2	5	4	9
Average	8.00	2	8.78	9.33	3.67	5.33	3.00	8.89

Perform a gap analysis by developing a two-dimensional differencing plane, and evaluate the results.

9. Following is a transaction analysis for a movie theater. Please answer the following questions:
a. Based on the service transaction analysis, what is your assessment of the movie theater?
b. In what areas can the movie theater improve?
c. Are there any additional customer touch points you can think of in this process? What could the company do to make them a positive experience?

SERVICE TRANSACTION ANALYSIS SHEET FOR PROBLEM 9

Organization:	Movie Theater	Service Concept:
Process:	Buying Ticket	Provide comfortable experience in viewing today's
Customer Type:	Movie Goer	current releases.

Transaction	+	0	−	Message
		Score:		
Exterior façade with movie posters.				"See what is playing or coming soon." "We are showing the movies you want to watch."
A single, winding ticket line with multiple tellers at the end.				"Everyone is herded together." "Ticket booth was crammed in the corner of theater." "They just wanted my money."
Ticket collectors near ticket booth tell where the theater is.				"Employees very knowledgeable and care that I get to the correct theater." "They want me to enjoy the movie/experience right away."
Concession stand in the middle of open area and brightly lit.				"They want me to spend more money." "The movie won't be the same without snacks and drinks."
Large displays of coming attractions posted at theater entrance. Some movies have offensive words and pictures.				"I feel like this is the movie I'm supposed to see next. The company doesn't care if it is good, as long as I come and see it." "The movie display was offensive and not appropriate for all ages."
Movie theater has food on floor and is sticky.				"Only the big items are worth our time to pick up." "Cleanliness isn't as important in the movie-going experience." "Once I start watching the movie, they don't care as much about the experience."

Overall Evaluation:
The movie theater is about selling tickets. They are helpful until I am done spending my money. More consideration is needed to keep me coming back to this theater.

10. Following is a service transaction analysis for a lube shop. Answer the following questions:
   a. Based on the service transaction analysis, what is your assessment of the lube shop?
   b. In what areas can the lube shop improve?
   a. Are there any additional customer touch points you can think of in this process? What could the company do to make them a positive experience?

SERVICE TRANSACTION ANALYSIS SHEET FOR PROBLEM 10

Organization:	Auto Service	Service Concept:
Process:	Oil Change	Provide speedy service that keeps cars running properly. Inform customer of potential issues.
Customer Type:	Average Driver	

Transaction	+	0	−	Message
Open bay door.				"I can get in quickly." "They want me to see what is happening so I can decide if now is the right time to enter."
Mechanic guides me in and walks me to waiting room.				"They are concerned about my safety." "My comfort is more important than starting the job and getting me out the door."
Mechanic confirms oil change and asks about additional work.				"Explaining the different oil options makes sure I am making the best choice for the vehicle." "The upselling is annoying. They ask to do the same thing every time I come in."
Waiting room is plain, but has a TV, magazines, and drinks.				"We want you to enjoy your stay." "This is a time to relax while we do all the work."
Reviewed work done on the car: oil change, tire pressure, and fluid check.				"Our service extends beyond the oil change." "Your overall safety is the most important to us." "We want to see you again."
Presented coupon for free car wash.				"We appreciate your business." "Your car is important to us, too."
Walked to car and guided out of bay.				"Safety is a priority." "Our service to you doesn't have an end point."

Overall Evaluation:
The service was very quick and professional. The focus is on the clients and having them come back—not because they have to, but because they want to.

CASES

Case 8-1 Google Designs Quality Services with Customers in Mind
Google: www.google.com

Millions of people from all over the world log on to the Internet every day and use the services of Google, the world's most popular search engine. Over the course of the past decades, Google has evolved into a firm that provides comprehensive Internet services to a global clientele. Google has come a very long way since its inception in 1997 and has now evolved into a premiere thought leader in a progressive technology world. The story of how Google started and how it has attracted such a loyal clientele in an extremely competitive industry is quite amazing.

The domain name *Google.com* was registered on September 15, 1997 by creators Larry Page and Sergey Brin. The two cofounders met at Stanford University when Sergey, 21, was assigned to show Larry, 22, around the campus. Larry was a recent University of Michigan graduate and was considering attending Stanford University for graduate school. Within a year of meeting, Larry and Sergey created their first search engine called BackRub and gained enough users at Stanford alone to eventually take up too much of the university's bandwidth. They spent the entire year of 1996 working toward their new idea, Google, until finally launching it in 1997.

The search engine Google is free to its users and generates revenue from selling advertising spaces within the search engine. What is particularly remarkable about Google is the customer base that the company has established in only a few short years. Billions of users access Google every day.

How does Google succeed in obtaining and maintaining such a large customer base? Important contributors are Google's efforts to determine what its customers want and then design quality services to meet its customers' needs. For example, Google gives its users the option of creating their own personal profiles, in which they can list demographic information about themselves including their age, where they are from, where they attend school, and so on. Google also tracks specific search trends both on a worldwide level and on an individual level to ensure that search results within the search engine reflect the interests and desires of its customers.

A few years after launching, the engineers at Google noticed that many users were constantly searching for pictures, news articles, and directions to reach specific destinations. Thus, driven by its customers' desires, Google integrated three new search filters to more accurately help its customers find what they need. The three search filters are now known as Google Images, Google Maps, and Google News. Google's customers can now use these filters to find up-to-date news articles on virtually any subject they can think of, find both high- and low-resolution images to use in their presentations at work, and download a map with perfect directions to assist them on the road to their destinations of choice. There now are many more specific filters that can be applied to anyone's searches on the search engine and their overall ease of use keep Google's customers happy and most importantly, loyal.

Another particularly intriguing way that Google has enhanced its search engine to appeal to its customers is its overall customizability for each user. For example, Google search is offered in 40 different languages in over 150 different countries. The search engine may also be customized to give you specific search results based on the location of the search. For example, if you are from Seattle, the search engine can be set to give you specific results based on Seattle locations, political topics, and so on. There are also filters that can be set by adults to monitor their children's searches to prevent them from searching for unsafe material.

One challenge that Google and its competitors face is keeping up with customers' preferences and demands. For this reason, the company launched a campaign site called Google Feedback where customers can go to let their opinions and preferences be heard by Google employees. Everyone can log on to Google Feedback and offer their voices to help Google better assist its valued customers to reach their desired outcomes. Another thing that Google does well is to make sure that all its products reach a high standard of quality, ensuring that those who are loyal to Google stay that way.

Although Google has displayed an incredible amount of market dominance over the past decade, competitors Yahoo! and Bing continue to strategically sharpen their competitive angles to attract more customers. Google will have to continue on its path as a thought leader within the industry to maintain its reputation as the Internet's most–used search engine. What other companies can learn from Google is that a thorough understanding of customer needs is the first step toward designing high-quality service products. Also, a strong follow-through and a willingness to listen to customer suggestions and complaints are key attributes to a service company's success.

Discussion Questions

1. Think about the Internet search engine you use most often. If it is Google, what is it about Google that attracts you as a user? If it is not Google, what could Google learn from the search engine you use that could help make it better?
2. What parallels do you see between developing a high–quality service product and a high–quality manufactured product? Make your answer as substantive as possible.
3. Is Google a company that was simply at the right place at the right time, or are many of its service innovations truly unique? Explain your answer.

Case 8-2 UPS: Delivering the Total Package in Customer Service
UPS: www.ups.com

In 1907 there was a great need in the United States for private messenger and delivery services. The U.S. Postal Service was not yet offering parcel delivery, and few offices and private homes had telephones, so messages had to be delivered by hand and packages by courier. To help meet customers' communication needs, an energetic 19-year-old, James (Jim) E. Casey, started the American Messenger Company in Seattle. Although the company began with a small staff and faced stiff competition, it did fairly well, primarily because of Casey's strict policies. He built his business on four principles: customer courtesy, reliability, around-the-clock service, and low rates.

Casey's company eventually became United Parcel Service, or UPS. The name United Parcel Service was chosen to draw attention to the words *United*, to emphasize the fact that shipments were consolidated to increase efficiency, and *Service*, because the company recognized that service was all it had to sell. UPS grew quickly through the years and became well known for its chocolate-colored delivery vans and courteous drivers. The public also liked the UPS business concept. It was convenient to send packages by UPS, and people trusted UPS to deliver packages safely to their destinations. All kinds of people and businesses used UPS services, from pharmaceutical companies that shipped life-saving drugs across the country to grandparents who sent their grandchildren birthday presents and boxes of candy at Christmas.

Although UPS has always been a friendly company, until the mid-1980s it relied primarily on technology to maintain efficiency, keep prices low, and provide new services. A major internal change took place at UPS in the mid-1980s when the company decided to shift its emphasis from technology to satisfying customer needs. This shift represented a recognition that UPS customers were becoming more sophisticated and had a variety of needs that the company was uniquely equipped to satisfy. Paramount among these were an increased need for information, a desire to move packages even more quickly and efficiently, tremendous competitive pressure from Federal Express, and a demand for customized prices and services.

UPS moved quickly to satisfy its customers' needs by developing new service products. For example, TotalTrack, which is available at the UPS Web site, can instantly provide customers with tracking information on all bar-coded UPS packages. This service helps vendors know when their buyers have received their shipments. Inventory Express is a contract logistics management service in which UPS stores a customer's merchandise and then ships it when it is needed, often on a just-in-time basis.

UPS also has improved its basic package pickup and delivery services. Customers with urgent shipments can telephone UPS to take advantage of On-Call Air Pick Up, which provides fast pickup at the customer's home and overnight delivery of packages. To accommodate customers who ship to sparsely populated areas in the United States and abroad, UPS has improved its geographic reach to every address in the United States and locations in more than 185 countries and territories.

Discussion Questions

1. Based on the description of UPS, what do you believe are its strengths and weaknesses?
2. How has UPS used technology in its design of quality services? Make your answer as substantive as possible.
3. Describe a positive or negative experience that you have had with UPS (or one of its competitors, such as FedEx or the U.S. Postal Service). If the experience was positive, reflect on whether the experience is consistent with UPS's new emphasis on customer needs. If the experience was negative, what could UPS have done to better satisfy your needs?

CHAPTER 9

Managing Supplier Quality in the Supply Chain

Chapter Objectives

After completing this chapter, you should be able to:

1. Explain why the concept of the value chain is important for quality management.
2. Discuss how quality approaches are used to manage supplier alliances.
3. Explain how ISO/TS 16949 is used to improve supplier performance in the auto industry.

A great deal of thought has gone into managing the supply function at firms such as Hewlett Packard Corporation (HP). HP uses analytical, accounting, and managerial tools to improve its performance. HP is known for its commitment to its customers and for understanding that quality performance is closely related to supply chain activities. HP therefore focuses a lot of attention on those supply chain activities.

In this chapter, we discuss the roles of purchasing, supplier development, logistics, and other supply chain functions. In the appendix to Chapter 9, we also introduce some statistical quality control tools that are used to evaluate the inputs provided from suppliers. Remember that the performance of your suppliers directly affects your reliability and your ability to satisfy customers. As a result, the supplier is key. This connective relationship between suppliers, producers, and consumers is both important and timely as firms are attempting to improve quality along with on-time performance. This is a major theme of this chapter.

THE VALUE CHAIN

To understand the **supply chain**, we first discuss the economic concept of the value chain. Michael Porter,[1] the noted economist and author, identified a systematic means for examining all the activities a firm performs and how those activities interact. The **value chain** is a tool that disaggregates a firm into its core activities to help reduce costs and identify sources of competitiveness. It is part of the **value system** that consists of a network of value chains. The value chain and core activities that are performed by any company include inbound logistics, operations, outbound logistics, marketing and sales, and service.

---

[1]Porter, M., *On Competition* (Cambridge, MA: Harvard School Press, 2008).

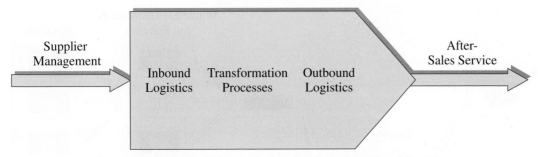

Support activities include accounting, legal, design, advertising, etc.

FIGURE 9-1 Value Chain Activities *Source:* Based on M. Porter, *Competitive Advantage: Creating and Sustaining Superior Performance* (New York: Free Press, 1995).

Figure 9-1 shows Porter's value chain. Notice that it is a chain for a single firm; however, the firm's suppliers also have value chains. The core activities shown in the figure are termed **value-chain activities** because they are the tasks that add value for the customer. If a firm performs these core functions well, the result is high customer satisfaction. Non-value-chain activities typically have costs but no effect on the customer and are referred to as the **hidden factory**. The hidden factory contains all the bureaucratic processes that are not part of the core activities in Figure 9-1.

The Chain of Customers

From a quality perspective, an interesting variation of the value chain is the concept of the **chain of customers**.[2] Looking at the activities along the value chain sequentially, we see that the links in the value chain are really people performing different functions. The chain of customers is revealed when you view the step in the chain after you as your own customer. This means that if you work at workstation 4 in a process at the core of the value chain, you will make sure that the work you do is absolutely impeccable before you release it to your "customer" in workstation 5. This chain extends from raw materials through supplier firms to the producing firm, with the final link in the chain being the ultimate consumer of the product. The notion is that if each of us along a chain works to satisfy our own customer, the final customer will be very satisfied, and our products and services will be free of defects and mistakes.

Managing the Supply Chain

The concept of supply-chain management extends the economic concept of the value chain. Figure 9-2 shows a rendering of a supply chain. Notice that it includes several suppliers, plants, distribution centers, and customer groups. This is a useful extension of the value chain because it provides a more realistic picture of the value chain. Notice that the value chain focuses on activities such as inbound and outbound logistics, which are supply-chain activities. One of the most significant aspects of the value chain is the *linkage* between a series of suppliers and consumers. This linkage is especially tenuous because it involves the complex interaction of logistics, systems, and human behavior. These linkages and relationships between suppliers and customers have undergone radical changes in the past decade. Much of this chapter focuses on this linkage.

SUPPLIER ALLIANCES

Managing inbound logistics in the supply chain involves working with suppliers who provide parts, raw materials, components, and services. As we have already discussed, there has been a trend toward developing closer working relationships with fewer suppliers. Given this new

---

[2]Schonberger, R., *Building a Chain of Customers* (New York: Free Press, 2007).

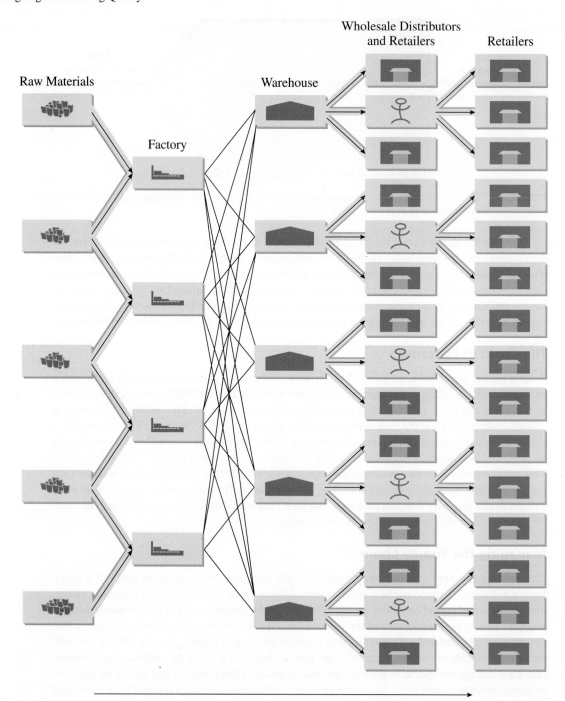

FIGURE 9-2 A Supply Chain

approach to suppliers, a big part of quality improvement requires developing and assisting suppliers so they can provide needed products with low levels of defects, in a reliable manner, while conforming to requirements. Several approaches to improving suppliers result in what are called **supplier alliances**. Inspired by lean purchasing approaches learned from Japanese industry, supplier–alliance relationships have emerged that treat suppliers as de facto subsidiaries of the

TABLE 9-1	Supplier Development Approaches

Single sourcing
Dual sourcing
Supplier evaluation
Sole-source filters
    ISO 9000
    Baldrige Award
Supplier certification or qualification programs
Supplier development programs
Supplier audits
Alliances

customer organization. We say de facto subsidiaries because as information is shared and communications are improved, the relationship begins to resemble a parent/subsidiary instead of separate firms.

As shown in Table 9-1, a number of systems are used to help develop suppliers. **Single sourcing** refers to narrowing down the list of approved suppliers for a single component to just one supplier. Companies that are uncomfortable with using a single supplier may use **dual sourcing**, in which the number of approved suppliers is reduced to just a few. Dual sourcing reduces the exposures of having a single supplier.

Supplier evaluation is a tool used by many firms to differentiate and discriminate between suppliers. Supplier evaluations are often recorded on *report cards* in which potential suppliers are rated based on criteria such as quality, technical capability, and ability to meet schedule demands.

Sole-source filters that are used in many companies rely on external validation of quality programs. The external validation comes from outside examiners and registrars that are used in these processes. This gives customers the comfort that outside authorities have given your company a sort of seal of approval. Two of the most commonly used filters are the Baldrige criteria and ISO 9000 (Chapter 3). In these cases, companies must show either that they are using the Baldrige criteria to improve or that they have become ISO 9000 registered. The ISO 9000 filter is used commonly in the international community.

Many companies perform lengthy inspections of their suppliers that involve long-term visits and evaluations. These programs are often called **supplier certification** or **qualification programs** if the focus is entirely on evaluation. If the focus is on helping the supplier to improve by training the supplier over long periods of time, they are termed **supplier development programs**.

Another tool used often is the **supplier audit**. It is similar to supplier certification except that a team of auditors visits the supplier and then provides results of the audit to the customer. The audits are performed to ensure that product quality and procedural objectives are being met. Supplier audits tend not to have the developmental component that is found in supplier development programs.

We should mention that there are drawbacks to single sourcing. When there are few suppliers, there is more exposure to supply interruption. For example, General Motors experienced a major shutdown as a result of single sourcing from a single supplier named Delphi. If labor relations are not solid, single sourcing can have the effect of shifting negotiating power to unions in supplier plants. Other problems include possible interruptions because of transportation problems, quality problems, disagreements concerning pricing, or global security problems (see A Closer Look at Quality 9-1).

A CLOSER LOOK AT QUALITY 9-1	Supply Chains Disruption and Risk Mitigation

An important quality concern is supply chain risk and disruption. In a typical year, 80% of companies experience some kind of supply chain disruption, making it a big deal. As companies are interacting with so many suppliers around the world, political, logistical, and natural risks have come to the forefront. We will present some common supply chain risks and then suggest ways to mitigate these risks. Among the risks are the following:

Lean: As supply chains have become leaner, there is less room for variation and poor performance.

Single Suppliers: Related to lean is the reduction in numbers of suppliers. If you have fewer suppliers, you can be without important parts and components if one is disrupted.

Speed: Supply chain disruptions seem to be coming with greater frequency and speed because of better communications and more complex supply chains.

Physical Damage to Supplies: Sometimes when parts are shipped internationally, parts and components can be damaged. Surprisingly, this is not a top five cause for supply chain disruption. It is a real concern, however.

Terrorism: With groups such as ISYL and others around the world, supply chains have become a target for terrorism, including nuclear materials in containers and disruptions in waterways.

People: Related to the terrorism threat is the exposure related to employees who are planted to either spy or disrupt operations. One oil company dealt with this recently when it found out that an employee was a Syrian mole.

Natural Disasters: There have been many, including the Japanese tsunami, Icelandic volcano, earthquakes in Chengdu Province in China, and many others.

Cyber Attack: These attacks include malware and cyberterrorism.

Civil Unrest/Armed Conflict: The 9/11 incident halted all air traffic in the United States for a week. There were also disruptions in trucking and shipping as America became very cautious.

Strikes and Port Closures: Recently, the ports in Los Angeles and Long Beach went on slowdown, causing serious supply chain disruptions.

Telecomm/IT Outages: In a recent year, almost 2/3 of companies reported a supply chain disruption relating to outages in telecommunications or information technology.

Quality Issues: Bad parts and components in a lean environment can cause big disruptions.

With all these problems, how do firms respond to supply chain disruptions or mitigate supply chain risk? Although there is obviously no single panacea, some suggestions include the following:

Prepare for the worst and hope for the best. These are good words to live by. Contingency plans are useful. Try to brainstorm possible failures and do "fire drills" to act out what you will do to respond.

Use reputable supply chain brokers, 3PLs, and freight forwarders.

Develop an understanding of your company's exposures and mitigate these risks through planning.

Have transparent and highly visible supply chains. Map your supply chains and know where all the possible broken links may potentially exist.

Implement quick "sense and response": Part of the problem with supply chain disruption is slow response. Be poised to respond quickly and accurately to supply chain problems.

Insurance: Some firms now offer supply chain disruption insurance that can provide a sense of safety.

Single-Sourcing Examples

In the 1980s, a defective rate of 5% for a supplier was acceptable. In this new century, parts-per-million levels of quality are expected from suppliers. In addition, many companies such as Mercedes-Benz are moving to single-source suppliers. However, outsourcing is not without its difficulties (see Quality Highlight 9-1). Other changes have occurred as well. Purchasing groups

QUALITY HIGHLIGHT 9-1   A Bumpy Ride at Boeing[3]

While we have discussed the advantages of alliances and partnering with suppliers, if they are not managed correctly, problems may occur. Consider the case of the Boeing 787 Dreamliner. What was initially viewed as a smooth journey to the Valhalla of energy efficiency and high-tech wizardry, the trip for Boeing has been turbulent, indeed. One of the contributors to Boeing's poor performance in this project may be poorly managed outsourcing.

The culture of Boeing is deeply ingrained in engineering and design, and has been centrally located in Seattle. With the 787, much of its engineering and production were outsourced to a complex supply chain of about 50 suppliers.

According to Tom McCarty, president of the Society of Professional Engineering Employees in Aerospace, "Plane-making is best done by a group of engineers and builders working in close proximity without the distractions of language barriers, cultural differences, and bureaucracy." Although this is the expected view of labor unions, international outsourcing is very much a political as well as an operational necessity because more than 80% of Boeing's sales are outside of the United States. However, Boeing may have been overly aggressive in outsourcing two-thirds of its production. According to McCarty, "Now with the 787, management felt they knew how to outsource the design jobs. Turns out they didn't."

Figure 9-3 shows a picture of Boeing 787 subsystems and suppliers. As you can see, this is a large number of suppliers to manage. There is often no playbook that shows the best way to manage such large networks of suppliers. Boeing has acknowledged these problems and the criticism it has received. Boeing CEO Jim McNerney stated, "In retrospect, our 787 game plan may have been overly ambitious, incorporating too many firsts all at once—in the application of new technologies, in revolutionary design-and-build processes, and in increased global sourcing of engineering and manufacturing content."

FIGURE 9-3   Boeing 787 Suppliers   *Source:* Based on www.seattlepi.com/.

---

[3]Based on Peterson, K., "A Wing and a Prayer: Outsourcing at Boeing," *Reuters* (January 2011).

were viewed in the past as in-house experts who expedited orders and solved materials supply problems. The dollars spent on supply were not critical as long as parts were available for manufacture. Strategies are different now. The way to develop a supplier is to have adequate communications, linear production schedules, and time to make necessary changes. Supplier contacts are one way to ensure adequate communication. Assigning one person or a team to each supplier can reduce the potential for miscommunication. Another way to communicate is through supplier programs where the product or service producer ensures supplier access to information. This provides open communication on mutually critical issues between the customer and the supplier. Another issue of communication between suppliers and customers is that production schedules must match. Suppliers constantly must be updated as to when the customers need products with lead times becoming shorter.

Electronic data interchange (EDI) is a system that aids customer and supplier communication by linking together supplier and customer information systems. Customers now are helping suppliers to isolate bottlenecks in the operation, balance production systems, and reduce setup times in an effort to reduce lead times. For example, suppliers of seats to Chrysler Motor Corporation must be able to meet the schedule changes within 36 hours. Schedules are communicated through an electronic data interchange link on a real-time basis.

Single sourcing has changed the landscape of purchasing. Prior to single sourcing, Xerox used 5,000 suppliers. Since implementing single sourcing, Xerox uses only 300 suppliers. Suppliers were chosen for their current quality practices and their willingness to work with Xerox to implement a quality improvement program. In Britain, dual sourcing, or multisourcing, has been chosen by many major customers, predominantly to avoid unfair pricing and the possibility of the customer's production being disrupted by suppliers' labor disputes. Having a limited set of suppliers also reduces shopping around for the best price.

The Dell Computer Company's goal was to work with suppliers to figure out how to minimize the supply chain and hold the least amount of inventory. Personal computer production is characterized by a tremendous inventory control problem. Suppliers who win in this industry are suppliers who can help the personal computer producers to overcome this inventory control problem. Dell is responding by bringing in suppliers who understand the personal computer production business. If suppliers don't understand your business, you end up creating buffers that translate into inventory.

Lockheed-Martin was a defense contractor (now merged with Boeing) that worked closely with its suppliers. At its Aeronautics Materials Management Center, a special program for suppliers was developed. This program was called the Star Supplier Program. Lockheed-Martin developed criteria that each supplier had to meet. Quality was a top requirement. Each Star Supplier was required to use statistical process control, have a 0% rejection rate at the point of inspection for six months, and achieve zero nonconformance—documented at the Aeronautics Materials Management Center. The next requirement was to meet scheduled delivery dates. A supplier had to maintain a 98% concurrency to contract delivery schedules. Finally, cost criteria were used, which showed favorably improving price trends and favorable purchase order administration.

Perhaps the most extreme example of supplier partnering comes from the Bose Corporation. Bose has implemented what it terms JIT II. In this effort, Bose eliminated a large part of its purchasing department and empowered suppliers to write their own purchase orders. In effect, this made the suppliers responsible for managing inventories and keeping inventory costs low. It is now called **vendor-managed inventory (VMI)**.

SUPPLIER DEVELOPMENT

Supplier development has to do with the activities a buyer undertakes to improve the performance of its suppliers. Some of these activities may include supplier evaluation, supplier training, consultation, data sharing, and processes sharing. Although companies such as Toyota and Honeywell have become very good at developing suppliers, recent data suggests that many companies do not have adequate supplier development programs. There is much work left to be done in this area.

There are seven steps for supplier development. First, *identify critical products and services*. This involves identifying strategic products and components (those that are difficult to obtain, have high costs, or are high volume). Second, *identify critical suppliers*. They may be suppliers who provide strategic components but do not meet quality or reliability objectives, or suppliers who do not meet schedules. Third, *form cross-functional teams*. The buyer forms a cross-functional team to work with the supplier. Fourth, *meet with supplier top management*. This meeting is held to discuss details of strategic alignment, performance expectations and measurement, and processes for improving. Fifth, *identify key projects*. These occur when there is agreement about how the supplier needs to improve and where. Projects are selected in the same way Six Sigma projects are selected, by criteria such as impact, ROI, feasibility, and required investments. Sixth, *define details of agreement*. This definition involves cost (and benefit sharing), commitments of resources, metrics for improvement, project charters, accountability, and deliverables. Finally, *monitor status and modify strategies*. To ensure success, management must actively monitor progress and revise strategies as needed.

There are some dimensions of supplier development that have emerged in the literature, including providing resources for development programs, trying to determine the right numbers of suppliers to use, and finding ways to measure procurement efficacy.[4]

Note that many companies confuse *supplier evaluation* with *supplier development*. They are not synonyms. Implicit to supplier development is the expenditure of resources designed to improve supplier performance, which may occur over a long period of time—sometimes months or years. Many companies couple this with expectations for shared cost reductions. For example, Toyota sets goals for cost reductions with its suppliers. If the target is 10%, Toyota may ask for a cost reduction of 5% and provide the other 5% benefit to the supplier. Suppliers who successfully complete development activities are often designated as preferred suppliers due to their alignment with customer needs. Quality Highlight 9-2 shows how 3M evaluates its suppliers.

QUALITY HIGHLIGHT 9-2   Integrating Forward along the Supply Chain: 3M Dental Products Division[5]

A customer satisfaction rating of "good" is no longer good enough for 3M Dental Products Division (DPD), a Minnesota-based supplier of products used around the world. The 700-employee division of 3M has determined that only by striving to earn grades of "excellent" in all product and service areas can it set clear goals for performance improvement, continue to increase sales, and boost productivity at industry-leading rates.

Pursuit of excellence explains why 3M DPD's customer surveys no longer combine "good" and "excellent" responses in a single category, why it has developed a comprehensive network of customer "listening posts," and why it has built an information system that tracks the purchasing decisions of dentists. It also accounts for how 3M DPD sets its priorities—by concentrating people and resources on opportunities most likely to improve products and services beyond customer expectations.

The division's careful reading of customer requirements drives a finely tuned innovation process that delivers a steady stream of new or improved products. Products introduced within the last 5 years now account for 45% of total annual sales, up from 12% in 1992.

3M DPD manufactures and markets more than 1,300 dental products, including restorative materials, crown and bridge materials, dental adhesives, and infection-control products. Most of its 700 employees are based at its St. Paul, Minnesota, headquarters and at its manufacturing and distribution facility in Irvine, California.

---

[4]Foster, S. T., "Furthering the Study of Global Supply Chain Quality Management," Volume 18, Number 2 *Quality Management Journal* 18(2) (2011): 7–10.

[5]Adapted with permission from the Malcolm Baldrige Award Profiles of Winners, 2015. Retrieved from http://patapsco .nist.gov/Award_Recipients/PDF_files/1997_3M_Dental_Products_Division.pdf

In the United States, in which it has a leading share of the market, 3M DPD competes with more than 100 manufacturers of dental products. Sales and distribution to U.S. dentists are carried out through a network of independent distributors. In foreign markets, the division uses 3M subsidiaries for sales, marketing, and customer support. Sales of 3M DPD products outside the United States account for 65% of the division's total sales.

3M DPD aims "to become THE supplier of choice" of dental professionals worldwide. Setting a clear course to achieve this aim is the objective of the division's systematic strategic planning process, cited as an industry best practice by *Fortune* magazine. Led by a steering committee of top executives and senior managers, the process is designed to build consensus on what needs to be improved and how it will be accomplished. More than 20% of employees participate. The result is a 10-year vision, a detailed 5-year strategic plan, and a 1-year operating plan.

For each priority improvement, the steering committee negotiates with the appropriate department or functional unit to establish the anticipated business impact, determine resource allocations, and set metrics and target values for assessing progress.

The Employee Contribution and Development Plan is the division's chief personnel appraisal tool. It sets individual goals in the areas of business results, team effectiveness, and employee development; and is used to determine performance ratings and to guide promotion decisions.

3M DPD's measurement system—the Business Performance Management Matrix—provides an easy-to-grasp framework for aggregating performance measures and for directly linking these measures to key business drivers and goals.

Most dentists in the United States and Europe—the division's largest markets—already use 3M DPD products. Future growth will depend largely on expanding existing customers' options—and spending—for 3M dental products. To do this, the division must have a thorough knowledge of customer requirements.

The division has graded the dentist market, resulting in five groups that reflect differences in satisfaction, purchasing behavior, referrals, repurchases, and number of 3M DPD products used. In-house and third-party surveys, focus groups, and hands-on evaluations are among the wide variety of methods that the division uses to listen to and learn from dentists in each segment. In addition, virtually all customer contacts—from visits by field representatives to calls to the technical hotline—provide additional information that also is entered into the division's customer information system. This extensive database provides the information necessary to determine whether specific products and services are meeting key customer satisfaction goals and to spot opportunities for new products.

Insights into changing customer requirements—combined with knowledge of technological, societal, and environmental trends—are the starting point for product and process innovations. Dentists, distributors, and major suppliers are involved in the division's systematic approach to translating key customer requirements into design requirements, prototypes, and—ultimately—reliable, quality products.

Continually raising the bar for performance improvement, 3M DPD is realizing benefits in nearly all facets of its business. Over the last 10 years, the division has doubled global sales and market share.

Supplier Awards

Many times, companies will provide awards to outstanding suppliers. This provides an opportunity to celebrate supplier performance that is best of the best. Some of these awards are based on the Baldrige criteria or are decided by a committee within the buyer's company. An example of a supplier award is the Ford World Excellence Award. Its program includes Gold, Silver, and Recognition level awards.

Supplier Relationship Management System (SRMS)

Elsewhere in this text, we discuss customer relationship management systems (CRMS). For upstream activities, there are similar systems called **supplier relationship management systems (SRMS)**. These systems include spend analytics, sourcing execution, procurement execution, payment, supplier scorecarding, and performance monitoring. In SAP ERP systems, the SRMS have the following capabilities:

- Create complete spend transparency.
- Develop a comprehensive, accurate profile of the supplier base.
- Identify opportunities for optimal sourcing of materials, equipment, and services.
- Consolidate and prioritize suppliers based on quality, performance, and on-time delivery.
- Ensure contract compliance and reduce maverick spending.
- Ensure the quality of purchased items.
- Ensure appropriate levels of supply.

APPLYING THE CONTINGENCY PERSPECTIVE TO SUPPLIER PARTNERING

Different firms take different approaches to supplier development. Remembering the contingency perspective discussed in Chapter 1, you should not be surprised. Apparently, one variable that affects what customers want from their suppliers is the customer's position in the supply chain.

A SUPPLIER DEVELOPMENT PROGRAM: ISO/TS 16949

Now that we have discussed supplier development conceptually, let's look at a specific example of a supplier development program: ISO/TS 16949. The goal of developing your suppliers is based on the need to provide high quality to the customer. Because variability is anathema to quality, the supplier's processes must be consistent with those of the customer. In the late 1980s, U.S. automakers developed certification programs for suppliers. The General Motors program was called "Targets for Excellence," and Ford used a program called "Q1." With the increase in popularity of ISO 9000, suppliers asked auto companies to adopt a single standard for certifying suppliers. The result, called **QS 9000**, provided a common standard for DaimlerChrysler, General Motors, and Ford. This standard has gone through an update and was supplanted by ISO/TS 16949.

ISO/TS 16949

The **ISO/TS 16949** standard applies only to automotive companies. ISO/TS 16949 is an International Standards Organization (ISO) Technical Specification that aligns existing automotive quality system requirements within the global automotive industry. ISO/TS 16949 specifies the quality system requirements for the design/development, production, and, where relevant, installation and servicing of automotive-related products.

ISO/TS 16949 was written by the International Automotive Task Force (IATF). The IATF consists of an international group of vehicle makers, including Ford, General Motors, and Chrysler, as well as several automotive trade associations. Representatives and subcommittees of TC 176 also helped to prepare ISO/TS 16949. We discuss ISO/TS 16949 in more depth later.

ISO/TS 16949 is based on the model in Figure 9-4. This model shows that ISO/TS 16949 is closely aligned with ISO 9000 in that it is founded on a systems view of automotive production. This system for continual improvement involves management responsibility; resource management; product realization; and measurement, analysis, and improvement.

The sections of ISO/TS 16949[6] are shown in Table 9-2. We discuss sections 4 through 8 in more detail.

Quality Management System

For the quality management system, suppliers must recognize key processes and document these processes. They must establish sequences and linkages for these processes. The organization

---

[6]The facts for this section are drawn from Technical Specification ISO/TS 16949, International Standards Organization, 2006.

FIGURE 9-4   Model of a Process-Based Quality Management System

TABLE 9-2	ISO/TS 16949 Sections
0. Introduction	6. Resource management
1. Scope	7. Product realization
2. Normative reference	8. Measurement, analysis, and improvement
3. Terms and definitions	Annex—Control plan
4. Quality management system	Bibliography
5. Management responsibility	

must determine how effective their operations are; make resources and information available in sufficient quality and quantity to run the business; monitor, measure, and analyze the business to ensure effective operations; and take actions to ensure that the planned results are attained and continual improvements are being made.

Management Responsibility

For this section of ISO/TS 16949, the extent to which management is committed to the development and implementation of quality management and continuous improvement is documented. Management is responsible for developing policy, communicating with the organization relative to customer service, establishing quality objectives, conducting managerial reviews, and providing resources. For example, managers with responsibility and authority for corrective actions will need to be informed when products do not meet specifications and see that corrective action is taken to ameliorate the problems.

Resource Management

For management to fulfill its responsibility, it must provide resources. These resources are used to maintain the quality management system and meet customer requirements, including training and development for human resources. Management is required to provide infrastructure such as bricks and mortar, equipment, and support systems. They must be planned and implemented properly; a safe, clean, and adequate work environment is established for worker satisfaction.

Product Realization

Products and processes should be adequately planned, including quality objectives for the products. Customer-related processes should be designed so that customer needs are fully considered and regulatory requirements are met. This section considers all aspects of product and process design as well as purchasing, suppliers, control plans, setups, preventive maintenance, traceability, and many other aspects of designing and producing products.

Measurement, Analysis, and Improvement

For this requirement, the company needs to provide documentation that it can demonstrate product conformity, quality management system conformity, and continual improvement of the quality management system. This requirement includes aspects such as statistical tools, measurement systems, customer satisfaction measurement, internal audits, and other considerations.

BUILDING AN UNDERSTANDING OF SUPPLY CHAIN QUALITY MANAGEMENT

Recent work has been performed in the area of supply chain quality management that is helping us better understand this field. A question remains: As business and engineering schools place more emphasis on supply chain management, what impact will it have on how we approach and teach quality management? Although our understanding is still preliminary, we are beginning to create a body of knowledge in this area. **Supply chain quality management (SCQM)** is defined as a systems-based approach to performance improvement that leverages opportunities created by upstream and downstream linkages with suppliers and customers.[7]

In a recent study of supply chain quality practices, we asked supply chain managers to rank the quality tools they used. The ranking is shown in Table 9-3. Note that all of these approaches and topics are addressed in this book.

TABLE 9-3	Rankings of Tools for Supply Chain Professionals
Variable	**Ranking**
Training	1
Data management	2
Supply chain management	3
Customer relationship management	4
Leadership	5
Benchmarking	6
Project management	7
Surveys	8
Complaint resolution	9
Supplier development	10

---

[7]For a review of recent research in supply chain quality, see *Journal of Operations Management* 26, 4(2008) [special issue on supply chain quality], edited by S. Thomas Foster, Jr.

Summary

In this chapter, we focused on the front end of the supply chain. Supplier development holds the greatest quality-related benefit for manufacturing and services firms that want to improve quality. After all, if you purchase components or supplies from another firm, to ensure high quality you need a process for making sure you can believe in the products and services you are receiving.

The ISO standard TS 16949 was presented here as a good example of how automakers are developing and evaluating their suppliers. Supplier development efforts have resulted in greatly improved product quality for many firms. Although ISO standard TS 16949 is just one representative example, several firms are using approaches that are extensions of ISO 9000. For newer suppliers or where the situation dictates, acceptance sampling may be needed. This topic is discussed further in the appendix to this chapter.

As firms learn more about developing suppliers, new practices will emerge. The eventual goal of supplier development is that the supplier resembles a de facto subsidiary of your company. This closer relationship between supplier and customer holds great potential for improved quality in products and services.

Key Terms

Acceptance sampling
Chain of customers
Dual sourcing
Electronic data interchange (EDI)
Hidden factory
ISO/TS 16949
QS 9000

Single sourcing
Sole-source filters
Supplier alliances
Supplier audit
Supplier certification or qualification programs
Supplier development

Supplier development programs
Supplier evaluation
Supplier relationship management systems (SRMS)
Supply chain

Supply chain quality management (SCQM)
Value chain
Value-chain activities
Value system
Vendor-managed inventory (VMI)

Discussion Questions

1. What is the supply value chain? How does the supply value chain help organizations manage their supply chains?
2. Describe the concept of the hidden factory. How can a realization that the hidden factory exists help managers?
3. Think about a job you have had or an organization for which you volunteered. Did this organization have a hidden factory? If so, describe at least two activities that you would associate with the organization's hidden factory.
4. Describe the concept of chain of customers. How does this concept benefit the ultimate consumer of a product or service?
5. What is the purpose of single sourcing? How can single sourcing help firms meet their quality objectives?
6. What are two of the most commonly used single-source filters? Do you believe these sources are appropriate? Explain your answer.
7. What is the purpose of a supplier certification or qualification program? What is the difference between a supplier certification program and a supplier development program?
8. How does electronic data interchange facilitate the supply chain process?
9. How does the contingency perspective apply to supplier partnering?
10. What is a supplier audit? How does a supplier audit differ from a supplier certification program?
11. Describe the concept referred to as *supplier alliances*. How does this concept differ from the traditional form of the supplier–customer relationship?

12. ISO/TS 16949 is a concept developed by Chrysler, Ford, and General Motors. Explain what ISO/TS 16949 is and how it has helped its developers.
13. Is ISO/TS 16949 a good thing for auto suppliers as well as auto manufacturers? Explain your answer.
14. How does ISO/TS 16949 differ from ISO 9000? Is the distinction between the two quality concepts important for the adopters of ISO/TS 16949?
15. What is acceptance sampling? Is acceptance sampling needed?

CASES

Case 9-1 AT&T: Setting High Standards for Suppliers and Rewarding Supplier Performance
AT&T: www.att.com

If you live in California or frequently call someone in the California area, you have invariably done business with AT&T (formerly SBC). AT&T provides telephone service to the majority of California's residents. Along with telephone service, the company also provides a full array of wireless communications products for individuals and businesses.

In an effort to increase quality and decrease costs, AT&T has been working hard to find new ways to manage its supply chain. The result has been the development of a comprehensive program that sets high standards for suppliers and rewards exemplary supplier performance. The program begins with training. All of AT&T's procurement managers are required to participate in an Applied Total Quality program. The program consists of six 30-hour courses that teach TQM and supplier management. Suppliers also are encouraged to participate in the program at no cost.

The requirements that AT&T places on its suppliers are demanding, but they are communicated clearly to the suppliers in advance. For its top suppliers, a contract is negotiated on a yearly basis that defines the objectives of the relationship between AT&T and the supplier for the next year. Senior managers from AT&T and the supplier meet twice per year to discuss the performance of the relationship and iron out any problems that have occurred. AT&T's minor suppliers receive a one-page Supplier Quality Report every month. AT&T and the supplier agree on criteria for performance in advance (e.g., on-time delivery, invoicing accuracy), and the supplier receives a score each month from AT&T based on its record. Both the company and its suppliers take these reports very seriously. If a supplier receives a poor score, it typically calls AT&T to provide an explanation or ask for suggestions for improvement.

Although the company's approach to supply management sounds rigid, the company works hard to develop lasting positive relationships with its suppliers. The company maintains a steady flow of communications with its suppliers to work through any problem that might arise. For example, the company has a toll-free 800 number that suppliers and potential suppliers can use to familiarize themselves with company requirements. AT&T also asks its suppliers to tell it how it is doing, although this program has been only partially successful. According to the former executive director of contracting and supplier management at AT&T, "Suppliers are always leery of telling customers about their problems."[8] As a result of supplier reluctance in this area, they are thinking about making the supplier feedback reports a requirement for certification.

To its credit, AT&T goes to great lengths to reward supplier performance. The following goals are in place:

1. To communicate to suppliers that their internal quality processes and performance results are critical.
2. To demonstrate that quality pervades all aspects of the business relationship.
3. To share expectations and information to build partnerships toward world-class performance.
4. To recognize a supplier's overall level of quality. There are three levels of recognition: the Gold Award, the Silver Award, and the Bronze Award. The Gold Award is awarded to the company's top suppliers. To win this award, a supplier must "delight" the company by providing superior products/services and customer service for more than a year.

(continued)

[8]George, S., and Weimerskirch, A., *Total Quality Management* (New York: Wiley, 1994), p. 190.

As the telecommunications industry continues to become more competitive, AT&T's efforts to maximize the performance of its supply chain will undoubtedly intensify. Setting high standards for suppliers and rewarding performance are the essence of this philosophy of supply chain management.

Discussion Questions

1. Do you believe that AT&T's standards for its suppliers are too rigid? Why or why not?
2. Is the "Supplier Quality Report" a good idea, or are monthly reports too frequent and intrusive? Explain your answer.
3. Do you believe suppliers should receive awards and designations of merit from the companies that purchase their products? Explain your answer.

Case 9-2 Managing the Supply Chain at Honeywell

Honeywell: www.honeywell.com

If you own a home, work in an office building, or travel by air, the chances are excellent that a Honeywell product has affected your life. The Honeywell Corporation is the world's leading maker of control systems and related components for buildings, homes, industry, space, and aviation. The most recognizable Honeywell product is the automatic thermostat control for home heating that can be found in millions of U.S. homes. Less-recognizable Honeywell products are used in commercial and military aircraft, industrial applications, home security systems, and the U.S. space program.

Like many companies, Honeywell is in a competitive environment that demands high-quality products at affordable prices. To meet these challenges, Honeywell has worked hard on its supply chain management. In an effort to maximize the value that suppliers make to its business units, Honeywell has developed a distinctive approach to supplier management. The distinctive approach contains the following key components:

The company is shifting from a focus on price to a focus on total cost. As a result, the company does not always buy from the lowest price suppliers. Instead, it buys from the supplier that it believes will provide it the lowest cost in the "long term."

The company is shifting toward longer-term relationships with its suppliers and is treating its suppliers as if they are extensions of its own businesses rather than vendors.

The company is asking its suppliers to provide business solutions instead of simply dropping products off at the loading dock.

Rather than treating suppliers in an adversarial manner, Honeywell is treating its suppliers like business partners and is looking for opportunities to partner with suppliers in a wide variety of areas.

The motivation for these criteria is not grounded in better public relations or altruism, but in the belief that prudent supply chain management saves money and creates a competitive advantage. The company's willingness to focus on issues other than price is central to the success of this philosophy. Commenting on this issue, a supply chain manager at Honeywell remarked, "We have to reengineer our mindset to focus on improving the benefits we can receive from the suppliers versus just concentrating on prices. Many business organizations hold price so sacred that they miss the free things that suppliers will do for you."[9] Good suppliers want to be closely scrutinized by their buyers because the suppliers get a chance to showcase their on-time performance and other positive attributes.

The consistent theme that is reflected in all aspects of Honeywell's approach to supply chain management is an effort to maximize the value of its supplier relationships. The company asks a lot of its suppliers, from on-time deliveries to providing input on the design of Honeywell products. In exchange, Honeywell gives its preferred suppliers millions of dollars per year in business and conducts itself in a responsible manner by making payments on time and treating its suppliers with respect. This overall approach to supplier management creates what Honeywell believes is a win-win partnership

(continued)

---

[9]"How Honeywell Works to Gain Greater Value from Their Suppliers," *Supplier Selection & Management Report,* The Institute of Management and Administration, www.ioma.com (2000).

between itself and its suppliers. The more Honeywell's suppliers contribute to the profitability of its businesses, the more business Honeywell will give to its suppliers.

Although Honeywell is fully vested in its distinctive approach to supply chain management, the company is also firmly committed to cost containment. Fortunately, supply chain management and cost containment are not at odds at Honeywell. The firm is very careful about the suppliers it chooses and works hard to find the right mix of price and performance. Honeywell involves its suppliers in every aspect of improving the efficiency of the supply chain. This creates a healthy working relationship between Honeywell and its channel partners.

Honeywell is firmly committed to prudent supply chain management. The company has quantified the results of its initiatives in several areas. For example, in terms of treating suppliers like business partners rather than arm's-length vendors, the company has learned that "partners" rather than "vendors" produce more cost savings, have better on-time delivery, supply better-quality products, and provide more suggestions for supply chain improvements. These results, along with positive results in other areas of the company's approach to supply chain management, have affirmed to the company the value of its approach to supply chain management.

Discussion Questions

1. Why does Honeywell spend so much time dealing with supply chain management issues? Wouldn't the company be better off focusing on its own manufacturing operations? Explain your answer.
2. What aspect or aspects of Honeywell's approach to supply chain management appear to be particularly prudent? Can you suggest any additions to Honeywell's supply chain management program?
3. Do you believe that Honeywell's approach to supply chain management creates a win-win situation between the company and its suppliers? Why or why not?

Acceptance Sampling

Chapter Objectives

After completing this chapter, you should be able to:

1. Discuss when to use acceptance sampling.
2. Use OC curves to evaluate single-sampling plans.
3. Develop OC curves.
4. Develop double-sampling plans.

In Chapter 9, we focused on managing supply chain quality. Now we turn our attention toward managing incoming materials and components from suppliers that may or may not be perfect. Sometimes incoming quality is monitored using acceptance sampling. **Acceptance sampling** is a technique used to verify that incoming goods from a supplier comply with quality standards. Acceptance sampling inspection can range from 100% of incoming materials to a relatively few items inspected based on computed sample sizes.

IS ACCEPTANCE SAMPLING NECESSARY?

Acceptance sampling is controversial. Some critics of the technique believe that the assumption that a percentage of parts or components will be defective or less than perfect (called *acceptable quality level* or *AQL*) is counter to Deming's concept of continual improvement. However, there is still a need for acceptance sampling in many different situations. Here are some cases in which the acceptance sampling techniques discussed here might be needed:

   When dealing with unproven suppliers

   During start-ups and when making new products

   When components can be damaged in shipping

   When dealing with extremely sensitive products that can be damaged easily

   When products can spoil during shipment

   When a supplier has had quality problems in the past

ACCEPTANCE SAMPLING FUNDAMENTALS

When compared with statistical quality control, acceptance sampling is defined by its occurrence after production has been completed. Acceptance sampling inspection can occur at the beginning of the process when receiving components, parts, or raw materials from a supplier or at the end of production, as in the case of final inspection. Again, we focus here on inspection of incoming materials.

One interesting application of acceptance sampling occurs with agricultural seed producers. Because of the organic nature of seed, a supplier can place the seed on a truck in perfect condition and the seed can arrive at its destination in an unsuitable state. Therefore, large bulk purchasers of seed and other agricultural products are avid users of acceptance sampling techniques.

PRODUCER'S AND CONSUMER'S RISK

Producer's risk is the risk associated with rejecting a lot of materials that have good quality. Think of it this way. You are the producer of a product that has high quality, but your customer has concluded that your product has poor quality and returns the product to you. In this case, you have been judged inaccurately. **Consumer's risk** is the exact opposite. As a consumer, you receive a shipment of poor-quality product, but you believe that it is a good-quality product. Therefore, you pay for the product, use it in your production process, and suffer the consequences.

Producer's risk is denoted by *alpha* (α) and is called a Type I error. Consumer's risk is denoted by *beta* (β) and is referred to as a Type II error. Table 9A-1 contrasts alpha and beta risk. The goal of acceptance sampling is to reduce producer's risk at acceptable levels.

ACCEPTABLE QUALITY LEVEL

The **acceptable quality level (AQL)** is the maximum percentage or proportion of nonconforming items or number of nonconformities in a lot or batch that can be considered satisfactory as a process average. To statisticians, AQL denotes an economic decision that is associated with producer's risk.

LOT TOLERANCE PERCENT DEFECTIVE (LTPD)

Lot tolerance percent defective (LTPD) is the level of poor quality that has historically been experienced from a particular component and supplier. The difference between AQL and LTPD is sometimes confusing to students. Lots of incoming materials should usually have a 5% (or some other specified percentage) designated as alpha (α), or less chance of rejection. AQL relates to Type I error or producer's risk, which is the probability that good products will be rejected by the consumer. For example, if a consumer concludes that a product is defective even though it is flawless, a Type I error has occurred.

TABLE 9A-1	Alpha and Beta Risk		
		State of Nature	
		Product Is Good	**Product Is Defective**
Outcome	Consumer accepts project	OK	Consumer's risk (β) (TYPE II)
	Consumer rejects project	Producer's risk (α) (TYPE I)	OK

Lots of LTPD or worse should have a designated beta risk; for example, a 10% or less chance of acceptance. LTPD relates to Type II error or consumer's risk. Conversely, a consumer's risk is the chance that a product that seems perfect is really defective. Theoretically, there is only one combination of sample size *(n)* and acceptance number *(c)* that meets both conditions simultaneously. In practice, we cannot meet both conditions precisely, so we must choose a combination of *n* and *c* that approximates both conditions simultaneously.

n AND *c*

For the most part, the assignment of AQL, LTPD, alpha (α), and beta (β) is a management decision. Once these values have been determined, *n* and *c* can be determined; these values in turn define the **sampling plan**. The bottom line in acceptance sampling is that acceptance sampling plans are designed to give us two things: *n* and *c*, where:

n = the sample size of a particular sampling plan

c = a number that, if exceeded by the number of defectives in the sample, causes rejection of the lot (also known as the acceptance number)

The average sampling plan can be stated in simple terms: *n* = 20 and *c* = 5, which clearly communicates the bounds of the sampling plan. That is, take a sample of 20 items and if more than 5 are defective, reject the lot of materials. Remember to always randomize when selecting products from a supplier to be inspected.

OC CURVES

The **operating characteristic (OC) curve** provides an assessment of the probabilities of acceptance for a shipment, given the existing quality of the shipment. An OC curve is constructed to show the probability of accepting individual lots when the percent defective of the various individual lots is known or assumed to be at a given level. These curves also can be used to develop sampling plans.

Figure 9A-1 shows an OC curve for an optimal sampling plan. The *ideal* sampling plan shows that given a probability of acceptance of 98%, this sampling plan should be used. In this example, the probability of accepting a lot of goods with less than 2% defective is 100%. This means that the customer has considered the trade-offs and has determined that a lot of materials with only 3% defective is acceptable given the circumstances.

However, OC curves never appear like the *ideal* case. Figure 9A-2 shows OC curves for a sample size of *n* = 100 and *c* = [0, 1, 2, 3]. Notice that as *c* gets smaller, the OC curve gets

FIGURE 9A-1

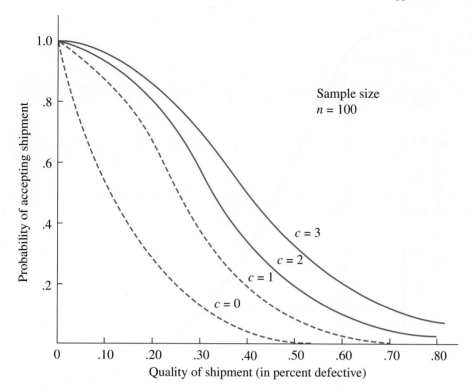

steeper. Generally speaking, this means that higher values of c lead to higher probabilities of accepting bad shipments (consumer's risk). Also, higher values of n affect the OC curves so that we have greater confidence that we have accepted a good shipment.

Figure 9A-3 shows an OC curve for $n = 5$ and $c = 2$ (for a lot of size 200; N = 200). This curve shows that the probability of accepting a lot with 2% defective product is 92%. Also, the chance of accepting a lot of 12% defective product is 6%. This means that if a lot has 2% defective, and this sampling plan is used (i.e., $n = 5$, $c = 2$), the producer's risk is 8%. Notice that if the lot really has much poorer quality, say 8% defective, the chance of acceptance is quite low, about 24%. So there is a consumer's risk of 24% with the poor quality lot.

EXAMPLE 9A-1   OC Curves

Problem: Let's suppose that we use a sampling plan with N = 200, $n = 5$, and $c = 2$. In the past, good-quality shipments from suppliers had about 1% defective, and poor quality shipments had about 6% defective. We want to know producer's and consumer's risk. Using Figure 9A-3, estimate these probabilities.

Solution: Using Figure 9A-3, it appears that the probability of acceptance of a good lot is 98%, which translates to a producer's risk of 2%. Using the same figure, it appears that the probability of accepting a poor lot is 42%, which is consumer's risk.

BUILDING AN OC CURVE

There are various ways to construct OC curves: The first uses the binomial distribution; the second uses the Poisson distribution. Using a sample size n and average percent defective p, we can develop an OC curve using a Poisson approximation of a binomial distribution.

FIGURE 9A-3

Rather than computing the distributions from formulas, we rely on tables that have been developed for ease in computing single-sampling plans. Single sampling means that we use only one value of c to make a decision. Multiple sampling plans are discussed later. Table 9A-2 shows values used to simplify such calculations. While holding c and n constant, we can vary the percent defective p to calculate various points on the OC curve.

EXAMPLE 9A-2   **Developing Single-sampling Plans Using OC Curves and Table 9A-2**

Problem: We want to develop an OC curve for a good single-sampling plan using Table 9A-2. The sample size n is 50, and the maximum acceptance number (c) is 2.

Solution: Note that an OC curve has two values: proportion nonconforming (p) and probability of acceptance ($P(a)$). Using Table 9A-2, we know that the np (where the sample size is $n = 50$ in this case) and p is proportion nonconforming. The acceptance number (c) is in the second column and the probability of acceptance is given in the third column. The proportion nonconforming is computed by dividing np (from the table) by n (the sample size). These computations are as follows for each np value in Table 9A-2:

$$n = 50; c = 2$$
$$P_{.5} = .5/50 = .01; P(a)_{.5} = .98$$
$$P_1 = 1/50 = .02; P(a)_1 = .92$$

TABLE 9A-2	Values for Creating OC Curves ($n = 50$)	
np	*c*	*P(a)*
.5	1	.93
	2	.98
	3	.99
1	1	.75
	2	.92
	3	.98
2	1	.48
	2	.70
	3	.88
3	1	.20
	2	.48
	3	.76
4	1	.10
	2	.30
	3	.48
5	1	.09
	2	.18
	3	.35

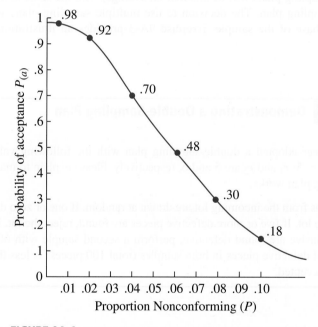

FIGURE 9A-4

$P_2 = 2/50 = .04; P(a)_2 = .70$
$P_3 = 3/50 = .06; P(a)_3 = .48$
$P_4 = 4/50 = .08; P(a)_4 = .30$
$P_5 = 5/50 = .10; P(a)_5 = .18$

The results are shown in Figure 9A-4.

MORE-COMPLEX SAMPLING PLANS

So far, we have focused on sampling plans for single samples, but they are not the limit of sampling plans. More-complex sampling plans are referred to as *multiple sampling plans* or *sequential sampling plans*. With these sampling plans, the acceptance sampling rules might occur as follows:

$$n_1 = \text{Sample size for sample 1}$$

$$n_2 = \text{Sample size for sample 2}$$

$$n_n = \text{Sample size for sample } n$$

$$c_1 = \text{Acceptance number for sample 1}$$

$$c_2 = \text{Acceptance number for sample 2}$$

$$c_n = \text{Acceptance number for sample } n$$

$$r_1 = \text{Rejection number for sample 1}$$

$$r_2 = \text{Rejection number for sample 2}$$

$$r_n = \text{Rejection number for sample } n$$

Multiple sampling plans have advantages over single-sampling plans. The sample size used in multiple sampling plans will be smaller, on average, with the same amount of protection as a single-sampling plan. The decision to use multiple sampling plans will usually be made in the first phase of the sample. Exercise 9A-3 provides an illustration of a double-sampling plan.

EXERCISE 9A-3   **Demonstrating a Double-Sampling Plan**

Problem: An engineer adopted a double-sampling plan with the following values: $n_1 = 40$; $c_1 = 1$; $n_2 = 60$; $c_2 = 5$; r_1 and r_2 are 5 and 6, respectively. Please explain to management how this double-sampling plan works.

Solution: Forty items from the incoming lot are drawn at random. If one or zero defective pieces are found, accept the lot. If five or more defective pieces are found, reject the lot. If between two and four pieces inclusive are found defective, perform a second sample with 60 pieces. If the combined number of defective pieces in both samples (total 100 pieces) is less than or equal to five, the lot can be accepted.

DEVELOPING DOUBLE-SAMPLING PLANS

Although OC curves can be used to develop double-sampling plans, the calculations to develop the OC curves are much more complex than for single-sample plans. For this reason, we will use a standard approach that is used by many practitioners. The main limitation of this plan is that sample sizes must be specified, as well as AQL, LTPD, producer's risk, and consumer's risk.

The double-sampling plan we will develop has the following parameters:

$$AQL = 0.020$$
$$LTPD = 0.040$$
$$\text{Producer's risk} = 0.05$$
$$\text{Consumer's risk} = 0.10$$
$$n_1 = .5n_2$$

First, we compute the ratio of LTPD to AQL:

$$LTPD/AQL = 0.040/0.020 = 2$$

The parameters for the appropriate double-sampling plan are found in Tables 9A-3 and 9A-4. Table 9A-3 is used when $n_1 = n_2$, and Table 9A-4 is used when $n_1 = .5n_2$. For this example, we will use Table 9A-4 because n_2 is twice the size of n_1.

Because LTPD/AQL was 2, in Table 9A-4, we will use double-sampling plan number 15 (because 1.97 is closest to our value of 2). We see immediately that c_1 and c_2 are 4 and 20, respectively. Next, we compute the sample size by using column 5 from the table. If we want to use a probability of acceptance of .95, we use column 5. For sample plan 15, the value of $p'n_1$ is 4.75. Then we compute n_1 as follows:

$$n_1 = p'n_{.95}/AQL = 4.75/0.020 = 237.5 \approx 238$$

As shown, $n_1 = 238$ and $n_2 = 475$ (remember that n_2 is twice the size of n_1). These are rather large sample plans, so we may want to reconsider our parameters to reduce these sample sizes.

The process for developing sampling plans where $n_1 = n_2$ is the same as the previous process. Just use Table 9A-3.

TABLE 9A-3	Values for Constructing a Double-Sampling Plan Having a Specified p'_1 and p'_2 ($n_1 = n_2$, $\alpha = 0.05$, $\beta = 0.10$)			
		Acceptance Numbers		Approximate Values of $p'n_1$
Plan Number	$R = p'_2/p'_1$	c_1	c_2	$P = 0.95$
1	11.90	0	1	0.21
2	7.54	1	2	0.52
3	6.79	0	2	0.43
4	5.39	1	3	0.76
5	4.65	2	4	1.16
6	4.25	1	4	1.04
7	3.88	2	5	1.43
8	3.63	3	6	1.87
9	3.38	2	6	1.72
10	3.21	3	7	2.15
11	3.09	4	8	2.62
12	2.85	4	9	2.90
13	2.60	5	11	3.68
14	2.44	5	12	4.00
15	2.32	5	13	4.35
16	2.22	5	14	4.70
17	2.12	5	16	5.39

| TABLE 9A-4 | Values for Constructing a Double-Sampling Plan Having a Specified p'_1 and p'_2 ($n_2 = 2n_1$, $\alpha = 0.05$, $\beta = 0.10$) |

		Acceptance Numbers		Approximate Values of $p'n_1$
Plan Number	$R = p'_2/p'_1$	c_1	c_2	$P = 0.95$
1	14.50	0	1	0.16
2	8.07	0	2	0.30
3	6.48	1	3	0.60
4	5.39	0	3	0.49
5	5.09	1	4	0.77
6	4.31	0	4	0.68
7	4.19	1	5	0.96
8	3.60	1	6	1.16
9	3.26	2	8	1.68
10	2.96	3	10	2.27
11	2.77	3	11	2.46
12	2.62	4	13	3.07
13	2.46	4	14	3.29
14	2.21	3	15	3.41
15	1.97	4	20	4.75
16	1.74	6	30	7.45

Summary

The single- and double-sampling plans we have discussed are called *lot-by-lot sampling plans*. As we perform separate samples, we receive additional lots of materials. Sometimes it is not feasible to collect products into lots because they are produced in a continuous manner. In these cases, acceptance sampling procedures for continuous production are used. These procedures typically involve alternating between 100% inspection and sampling inspection. Although we did not develop a methodology for continuous acceptance sampling here, MIL STD 1235C (1988), named "Single and Multiple-Level Continuous Sampling Procedures and Table for Inspection by Attributes," is available from the Department of Defense. Any of the military standards mentioned in this appendix can be ordered from the Department of Defense directly by accessing the DOD SSP on the Internet (Department of Defense Single Stock Point for Specifications and Standards).

Key Terms

Acceptable quality level (AQL)	Lot tolerance percent defective (LTPD)	Producer's risk
Acceptance sampling		Sampling plan
Consumer's risk	Operating characteristic (OC) curve	

Discussion Questions

1. Define producer's risk and consumer's risk.
2. Define the concept of acceptable quality level. Why has this concept been troublesome to many people?
3. What is the term used to designate the level of poor quality included in a lot of goods? Describe the role of this term in the quality management process.
4. What is an operating characteristic curve? What is the function of this curve in the quality management process?

Problems

1. Using Figure 9A-2 with a sample size of $n = 100$ and an acceptance number $c = 1$, if a good shipment has no more than 0.05 defective, what is the probability of acceptance? What type of risk is this?
2. Using Figure 9A-2 with a sample size of $n = 100$ and an acceptance number of $c = 2$, if a bad shipment has 40% defective, what is the probability of acceptance? What type of risk is this?
3. Using Figure 9A-2 with a sample size of $n = 100$ and an acceptance number of $c = 3$, if a good shipment has no more than .02 defective, what is the probability of acceptance? What type of risk is this?
4. Using Figure 9A-2 with a sample size of $n = 100$ and an acceptance number of $c = 1$, if a good shipment has no more than .30 defective, what is the probability of acceptance? What type of risk is this?
5. Develop an OC curve using Table 9A-2, a sample size of 50, and the following np values: 0.5, 1, 2, 3, 4, 5. The maximum acceptance number is $c = 1$.
6. From the OC curve developed in Problem 5, if a good shipment is 0.02 defective, what is the probability of a Type I (producer's) error?
7. From the OC curve developed in Problem 5, if a bad shipment is defined as having at least 10% defective, what is your estimate of Type II (consumer's) risk?
8. Develop an OC curve using Table 9A-2, a sample size of 50, and the following np values: 0.5, 1, 2, 3, 4, 5. The maximum acceptance number is $c = 3$.
9. From the OC curve developed in Problem 8, if a good shipment is .04 defective, what is the probability of a Type I (producer's) error?
10. From the OC curve developed in Problem 8, if a bad shipment is defined as having at least 15% defective, what is your estimate of a Type II (consumer's risk) error?
11. Please explain the following sampling plan in easily understood terms:

$n_1 = 50$
$c_1 = 2$
$n_2 = 100$
$c_2 = 5$
$r_1 = 4$
$r_2 = 6$

12. Please explain the following sampling plan in easily understood terms:

$n_1 = 125$
$c_1 = 3$
$n_2 = 150$
$c_2 = 6$
$n_3 = 200$
$c_3 = 12$

13. We want to develop a double-sampling plan where $n_1 = n_2$ (see Table 9A-3). Here are the needed parameters:

AQL = .010
LTPD = .030
Producer's risk = .05
Consumer's risk = .10

14. Rework Problem 13 where n_2 is twice the size of n_1 (see Table 9A-4).

15. We want to develop a double-sampling plan where $n_1 = n_2$ (Table 9A-3). Here are the necessary parameters:

    AQL = .020
    LTPD = .080
    Producer's risk = .05
    Consumer's risk = .10

16. Rework Problem 15 where n_2 is twice the size of n_1 (Table 9A-4).

17. Your boss wants you to develop a double-sampling plan where $n_1 = n_2$ (using Table 9A-3). Here are some parameters for your use:

    AQL = .015
    LTPD = .040
    Producer's risk = .05
    Consumer's risk = .10

18. Rework Problem 17 where n_2 is twice the size of n_1 (Table 9A-4).

Implementing Quality

Everyone will tell you that the conceptual stuff is nice, but how do you actually implement quality throughout your supply chain? Once you understand and have planned and designed where you want to go, the tools of quality provide an important basis for improvement. More than 90% of successful quality implementations involve the basic tools of quality, which should be used and commonly practiced in most companies. Chapter 10 introduces the seven managerial tools for quality improvement. These tools are behavioral and help managers to optimize the use of team processes.

In Chapters 11 and 12, you will learn about an efficient and effective method for teaching statistical quality and $\bar{x}$, R, p, np, u, and c charts (among others). Many of the behavioral implications of statistical process control are also discussed.

Chapter 13 introduces Lean-Six Sigma, which is a widely adopted method for improving the designs of products and processes to ensure quality.

CHAPTER 10

The Tools of Quality

Chapter Objectives

After completing this chapter, you should be able to:

1. Use process maps to improve a process.
2. Use extended value stream maps to improve supply chain performance.
3. Implement Ishikawa's seven basic quality tools for improvement.
4. Use the new seven tools to improve managerial decision making.
5. Discuss other tools such as balanced scorecards, spider charts, and dashboards.

To be effective, quality improvement in manufacturing or services should address the needs of the system as a whole. In this book we have addressed quality management from an integrative perspective. This perspective has encompassed the many functional areas of business, including supply chain management, marketing, accounting, human resources, operations, engineering, and strategy. None of these fields of endeavor operates in a vacuum. They are all interrelated and interdependent.

IMPROVING THE SYSTEM

To be successful, a business or organization must balance the needs of these different functional areas around a coherent business vision and strategy. The objective of the system is to satisfy the customer. Customer satisfaction means higher customer retention, which leads to improved profitability.

A quality system (Figure 10-1) uses the business model with a focus on the customer and includes the dynamics of continual improvement, change, planning, and renewal. Continual improvement is necessary for a company to learn to grow. Companies that cannot adapt find themselves with stagnant cultures and labor forces. Many managers, on discovering that their organization has reached this point, believe they must resort to draconian measures such as layoffs and organizational reengineering to achieve change. If they had pursued continual improvement and learning in the first place, they might not have reached this juncture.

This quality system (which is discussed in greater depth in Chapter 15) is not just a series of variables and relationships. It is an interconnected, interdisciplinary network of people, technology, procedures, markets, customers, facilities, legal requirements, reporting requirements,

FIGURE 10-1   Quality System Model

and assets that interact to achieve an end. The most important aspect of the system is the people. People are the engine of creativity and innovation. Technology is very good at performing rote tasks; however, technology in and of itself cannot innovate. Therefore, how we manage people may be the most important key in this system to unlock an organization's potential. W. Edwards Deming was always adamant that we should continually and forever improve the system of production. The system includes people.

In this chapter, we introduce the **basic seven (B7) tools of quality** and the new seven (N7) tools (also referred to as the *managerial tools*). The seven basic tools are simple to use in continuous improvement efforts. The tools often are used by individuals and in teams, are useful at all levels of the organization, and can be applied by people of different educational levels. As you learn and apply the tools of quality, you will also appreciate their wide application and usefulness.

ISHIKAWA'S BASIC SEVEN TOOLS OF QUALITY

The basic seven tools of quality may be used in a logical order. Note that this is only a "typical" order of use for these tools; they can be used in almost any order. Figure 10-2 shows this order. The flowchart gives the team the big picture of the process to be improved. Process data are collected using a check sheet. The data are analyzed using either histograms, scatter plots, or control charts. The root causes of the problems associated with the process are identified using a cause-and-effect diagram. Finally, causes are prioritized using Pareto analysis. These tools are discussed in more depth on the following pages.

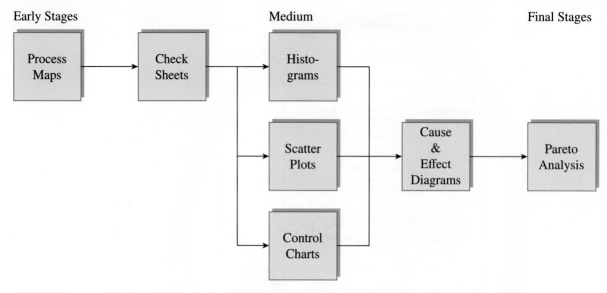

FIGURE 10-2   Logical Map of the Order for the Basic Seven (B7) Tools   *Source:* Based on M. Brassard, *The Memory Jogger II,*
published by GOAL/QPC, 2 Manor Parkway, Salem, New Hampshire, 2004. Reprinted with permission of GOAL/QPC.

Process Maps

A **process map** is a picture of a process. The first step in many process improvement projects
is to create a map of the process as it exists. This useful step also determines the parameters for process improvement. The concept is that we must know the process before we can
improve it.

The language of process maps can vary from the simple to the complex. A simple set of
symbols is provided in Figure 10-3. The diamond indicates there is a decision to be made, and
they often identify different paths of sequences in the process map. The parallelogram appears
whenever materials, forms, or tools enter or leave the process. The rectangle is the processing
symbol—the work that is actually performed. The start/stop symbol and the page connector are
used for the convenience of the people using the process map. A few simple rules for process
maps follow:

- Use these simple symbols to chart the process from the beginning, with all arcs in the process map leaving and entering a symbol. The arcs represent the progression from one step
  to the next. (See A Closer Look at Quality 10-1.)
- Develop a general process map and then fill it out by adding more detail or a subflowchart
  to each of the elements.

FIGURE 10-3   Basic Mapping Symbols

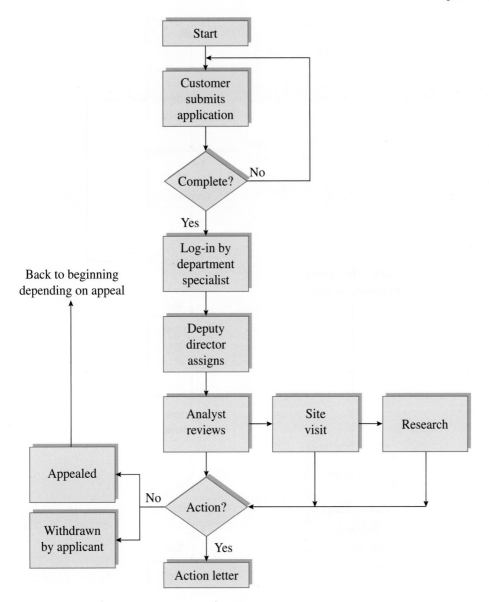

FIGURE 10-4   Process Mapping: Home Occupation Process— Current

- Step through the process by interviewing those who perform it—as they do the work.
- Determine which steps add value and which don't in an effort to simplify the work.
- Before simplifying work, determine whether the work really needs to be done in the first place.

The process map in Figure 10-4 shows a simple process used in a city planning department to issue permits allowing applicants to take possession of newly built homes. Figure 10-4 shows the current process. In Figure 10-5, the process is simplified because the front desk is given more authority and training to process the forms without assigning them for analyst review. The analyst review does not add value for the organization or the customer, so it can be eliminated. The steps of process mapping include

1. Settling on a standard set of process mapping symbols to be used.
2. Clearly communicating the purpose of the process map to all the individuals involved in the exercise.

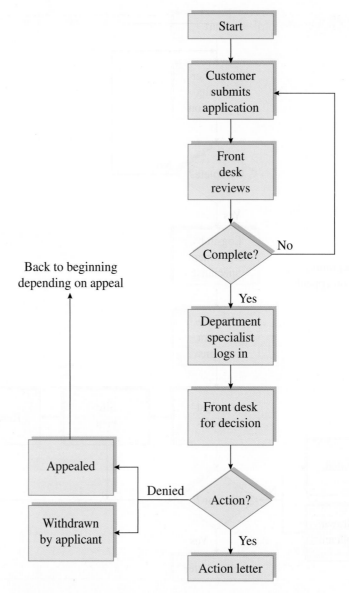

FIGURE 10-5   Process Mapping: Home Occupation Process—
Proposed

3. Observing the work being performed by shadowing the workers performing the work.
4. Developing a map of the process.
5. Reviewing the process map with the employees to make needed changes and adjustments to the process map. (Note that it is often helpful to chart processes from the customer's point of view in addition to the worker's point of view.)
6. Developing a map of the improved process.

A special type of process map is called a SIPOC diagram. **SIPOC** is an acronym for suppliers, inputs, processes, outputs, and customers. This type of diagram is useful when it is not clear who your customers are, where specifications for inputs exist, and when clarifying customer requirements. SIPOC diagrams are often used in Six Sigma projects.

EXAMPLE 10-1 Process Maps

Problem: The well construction unit of a state department of water resources entered into a multiyear project to update its database management system. As part of the process, the well construction staff was asked to document its current process flows.

Solution: The resulting process map is shown in Figure 10-6. Through a brainstorming process, the well construction team was asked to rethink its processes to simplify the workflow and to take advantage of new technology. The team worked together to develop the new process, which resulted in a streamlined flow that required less time for drillers to receive permits.

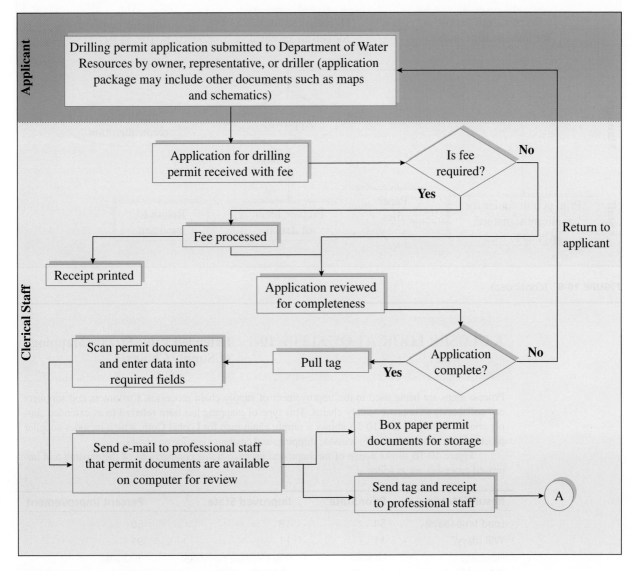

FIGURE 10-6 Process Map with Responsibility of Existing Process

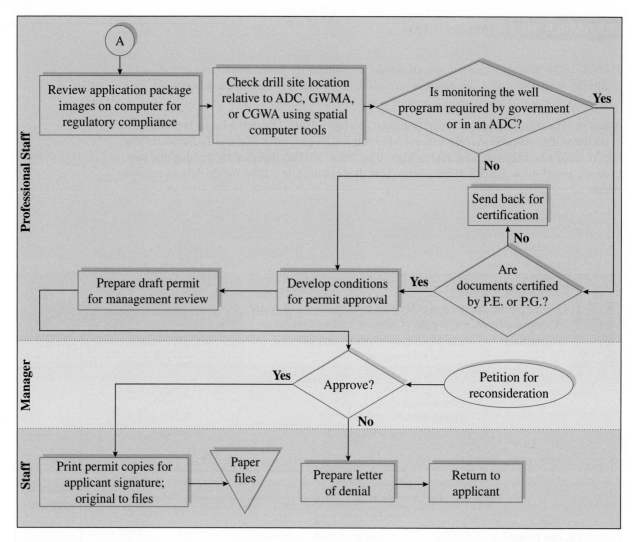

FIGURE 10-6 (*Continued*)

A CLOSER LOOK AT QUALITY 10-1   **Extended Value Stream Mapping of Supply Chains**

Process maps are being used in the improvement of supply chain processes. Customers and suppliers can collaborate to improve supply chains. This type of mapping has been referred to as extended supply chain mapping. Figure 10-7A shows a supply chain map for Global Corp, which includes supplier processes, receiving, internal processes, shipping, and customer service processes.

Figure 10-7B shows a map of the improved process. Some comparisons of the existing and improved processes are as follows:

Results Metrics	Prior State	Improved State	Percent Improvement
Lead time (days)	54	18	60
WIP (days)	11	1	91
Flexibility	Limited	9% increase per week	300/year
Unit price	$12,000	$10,000	16

FIGURE 10-7A Global Corp. Prior-State Extended Value Stream Map

FIGURE 10-7B Global Corp. Ideal-State Extended Value Stream Map

FIGURE 10-8 Copier
Problem Check Sheet

Problem Type	Monday	Tuesday	Wednesday	Thursday	Friday	Total
Setup routines not standardized						
Missing equipment for setup						
Failure to separate internal and external tasks						
Extensive machine resetting and paper change						
Other						

Check Sheets

Check sheets are data-gathering tools that can be used to provide data for histograms; they can be either tabular, computer based, or schematic. An example of a tabular check sheet for a Pareto chart is shown in Figure 10-8. It provides a chart for copier operators to mark each time a delay occurs in setting up new jobs.

Setting up a check sheet involves the following steps:

1. Identify common defects occurring in the process.
2. Draw a table with common defects in the left column and time period across the tops of the columns (see Figure 10-8) to track the defects.
3. The user of the check sheet then places check marks on the sheet whenever the defect is encountered.

EXAMPLE 10-2 Check Sheets

Problem: A copying company wants to set up a check sheet so that it can keep track of error sources. Following are the major error types with frequencies.

Solution: Figure 10-8 showed a check sheet for these data. The check sheet will be kept to monitor how well workers are adhering to the new procedures.

Type of Problem	Frequency	Percentage
Setup routines are not standardized	315	52.1%
Equipment needed for setup is missing	124	20.5
Internal and external setup tasks are not separated	87	14.4
Extensive machine resetting and paper change are needed	56	9.2
Other	23	3.8
Total	605	100%

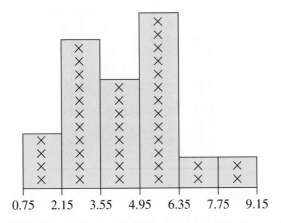

FIGURE 10-9   Histogram from Example 10-3

Histograms

As shown in Figure 10-9, **histograms** are simply graphical representations of data in a bar format. (Note that a frequency chart is used for categorical data, whereas histograms are used for continuous numerical data.) Histograms are also used to observe the shape of data (see Figure 10-9). For example, how are the data in an interval scale distributed? There are several rules for developing histograms:

- The width of the histogram bars must be consistent (i.e., class widths are the same where each bar contains a single class).
- The classes must be *mutually exclusive* and *all-inclusive* (or *collective exhaustive*).
- A good rule of thumb for the number of classes is given by the model

$$2^k \geq n \tag{10.1}$$

where n is the number of raw data values and k is the number of classes. Solving this equation for k, we obtain

$$k \geq \log n / \log 2 \tag{10.2}$$

Using this formula, we find

Number of Observations	Number of Classes
9 to 16	4
17 to 32	5
33 to 64	6
65 to 128	7
129 to 256	8

EXAMPLE 10-3   Histograms

Problem: The Big City Cafeteria wants to determine the distribution of its sales during lunchtime. On a given day, the manager randomly selects 40 sales from the sales register receipt. The following table shows the sales (in dollars):

4.51	0.79	4.19	2.29
5.96	3.49	2.25	3.45
2.24	5.25	5.36	1.15
7.28	5.25	4.29	5.25
3.96	6.79	4.66	3.56
8.22	2.56	5.25	3.33
5.55	2.24	8.95	2.49
5.25	2.26	0.79	5.25
4.11	6.11	5.25	4.56
1.15	5.25	2.21	5.25

Develop a histogram of the sales.

Solution: It is helpful to compute the mean, standard deviation, maximum value, and minimum value when developing a histogram because the histogram is often used to determine whether the data are normally distributed. Following are these statistics from the previously given data:

Mean = 4.20
Maximum value = 8.95
Minimum value = .79
Difference = 8.16
Sum = 168
Using Formula (10.2)

$$k \geq \log 40/\log 2$$
$$k \geq 5.32$$

The number of classes is 6. Therefore,
Classes = 6
Class width = 8.16/6 = 1.36 $\sim$ 1.40
Classes = 0.76–2.15; 2.16–3.55; 3.56–4.95; 4.96–6.35; 6.36–7.75; 7.76–9.15

The histogram is displayed in Figure 10-9. Thus, the manager finds that sales occur in a skewed distribution with a mean of $4.20.

Scatter Diagrams

The **scatter diagram or scatter plot** is used to examine the relationships between variables. These relationships are sometimes used to identify indicator variables in organizations. For example, in a hospital, the postoperative infection rate has been found to be associated with many different factors, such as the sterile procedures used by the doctors and nurses, cleanliness of the operating rooms, and sterile procedures for handling the utensils used in surgery. Therefore, the postoperative infection rate is an important variable for hospital quality measurement.

It is quite easy to develop scatter plots using the charting facilities in spreadsheet packages such as Excel. Figure 10-10 shows a scatter plot of the relationship between conformance data and prevention and appraisal quality-related costs in a real firm. Note that the figure shows the unexpected outcome of higher-quality costs with higher levels of conformance. Later analysis showed that this firm was trying to "inspect in" quality, meaning that it was throwing a lot of in-process work away as a result of more rigorous inspection. Use the following steps when setting up a scatter plot:

1. Determine your *x* (independent) and *y* (dependent) variables.
2. Gather process data relating to the variables identified in step 1.

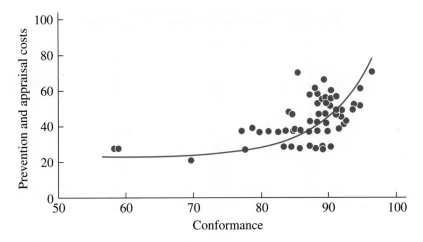

FIGURE 10-10   Prevention Costs and Conformance

3. Plot the data on a two-dimensional plane.
4. Observe the plotted data to see whether there is a relationship between the variables. (Note that it is helpful to plot the data in Excel or another spreadsheet and to perform a correlation test to determine whether the variables have a statistically significant relationship.)

EXAMPLE 10-4   Scatter Diagrams

Problem: Healthy People, Inc., a company specializing in home health care solutions for U.S. consumers, was a growing company. The company wanted to study the relationship between absenteeism and the number of overtime hours worked by employees. Thirty employees were randomly selected, and numbers of overtime hours were graphed against numbers of days absent for the previous year (see Figure 10-11).

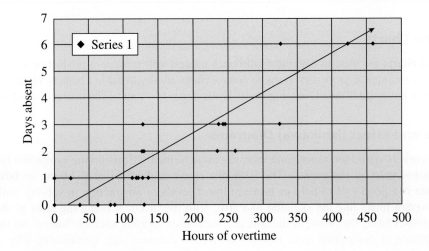

FIGURE 10-11   Scatter Plot of Overtime Hours versus Days Absent

Employee	Hours of Overtime	Days Absent
1	243	3
2	126	2
3	86	0
4	424	6
5	236	3
6	128	0
7	0	0
8	126	2
9	324	3
10	118	0
11	62	0
12	128	3
13	460	6
14	135	1
15	118	1
16	260	2
17	0	1
18	126	1
19	234	2
20	246	3
21	120	1
22	80	0
23	112	1
24	237	3
25	129	2
26	24	1
27	36	0
28	128	2
29	246	3
30	326	6

This analysis showed that there appeared to be a positive relationship between the number of days absent and hours of overtime. Subsequent analysis showed that, in fact, these variables were significantly related. It led management to recalculate the actual cost of overtime.

Control Charts

Control charts are used to determine whether a process will produce a product or service with consistent measurable properties. Because control charts are discussed in Chapters 11 and 12, they will not be presented in detail here. Figure 10-12 illustrates two control charts usually used together.

Cause-and-Effect (Ishikawa) Diagrams

Often workers spend too much time focusing improvement efforts on the symptoms of problems rather than on the causes. The Ishikawa **cause-and-effect** or **fishbone** or **Ishikawa diagram** is a good tool to help us move to lower levels of abstraction in solving problems. The diagram looks like the skeleton of a fish, with the problem being the head of the fish, major causes being the "ribs" of the fish, and subcauses forming smaller "bones" off the ribs. A facilitator or designated team member draws the diagram after questioning why certain

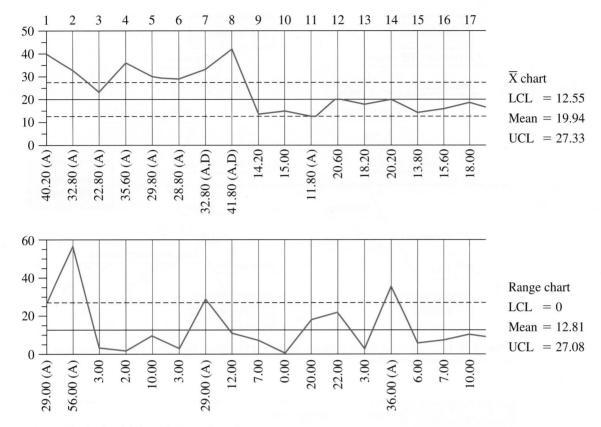

X̄ chart
LCL = 12.55
Mean = 19.94
UCL = 27.33

Range chart
LCL = 0
Mean = 12.81
UCL = 27.08

FIGURE 10-12   Partial *x̄* and *R* Charts for a Process

situations occur. It has been said that for each circumstance, the facilitator should ask "Why?" up to five times. This is sometimes referred to as the "five whys." Fishbone (cause-and-effect) diagrams are created during brainstorming sessions with a facilitator by following these steps:

1. State the problem clearly in the head of the fish.
2. Draw the backbone and ribs. Ask the participants in the brainstorming session to identify major causes of the problem labeled in the head of the diagram. If participants have trouble identifying major problem categories, it may be helpful to use materials, machines, people, and methods as possible bones.
3. Continue to fill out the fishbone diagram, asking "Why?" about each problem or cause of a problem until the fish is filled out. Usually it takes no more than five levels of questioning to get to root causes—hence the "five whys."
4. View the diagram and identify core causes.
5. Set goals to address the core causes.

Figure 10-13 shows an Ishikawa diagram prepared for a wood mill that was experiencing problems with wobbling blades in its saws. The symptom of the problem was the wobbly blades. The major causes were associated with machines, materials, people, and methods. Concerning people, it was found that workers were not properly trained. For machines, it was found that the blades were being incorrectly set up off-center.

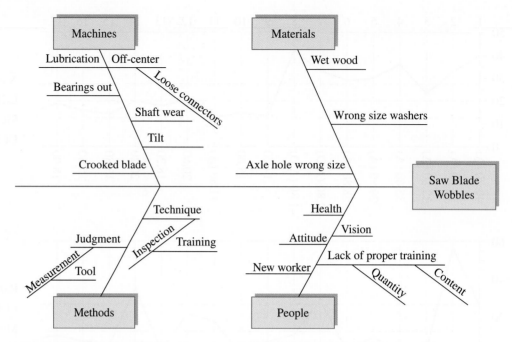

FIGURE 10-13 Cause-and-Effect Diagram: Wobbling Saw Blade Example   *Source:* Reprinted by permission from Patrick Shannon.

EXAMPLE 10-5 Ishikawa Diagrams

Problem: A team of employees from the adjudication team at a department of water resources was assigned to improve its process. Adjudication is a process of going through the courts to settle legal disputes, in this case concerning water rights. Prior to brainstorming improvements for the process, the employees were asked to brainstorm some of the causes of problems with the existing system. A fishbone (Ishikawa) diagram was used to help identify causes of problems they were experiencing.

Solution: Figure 10-14 shows the resulting fishbone diagram. The fishbone diagram shows that three major areas of concern are contractors, region office–state office communication, and database management. The facilitator used the "five whys" to get team members to reach lower levels of abstraction. After reaching these lower levels of abstraction, participants were asked to identify what they felt were major causes of the problems. This fishbone diagram was later complemented with further brainstorming for issues relating to the adjudication process.

Pareto Charts

Pareto charts are used to identify and prioritize problems to be solved. They are actually frequency charts that are aided by the 80/20 rule adapted by Joseph Juran from Vilfredo Pareto, the Italian economist. As you may remember, the 80/20 rule states that roughly 80% of the problems are created by roughly 20% of the causes, which means that there are a *vital few* causes that create most of the problems. This rule can be applied in many ways, and 80% and 20% are only estimates; the actual percentages may vary.

In a positive sense, a store manager could understand that 20% of the stock in a store holds 80% of the value of the store inventory; 20% of the customers might provide 80% of the revenue. In a grocery store, a small number of quality problems created 80% of the complaints. The good

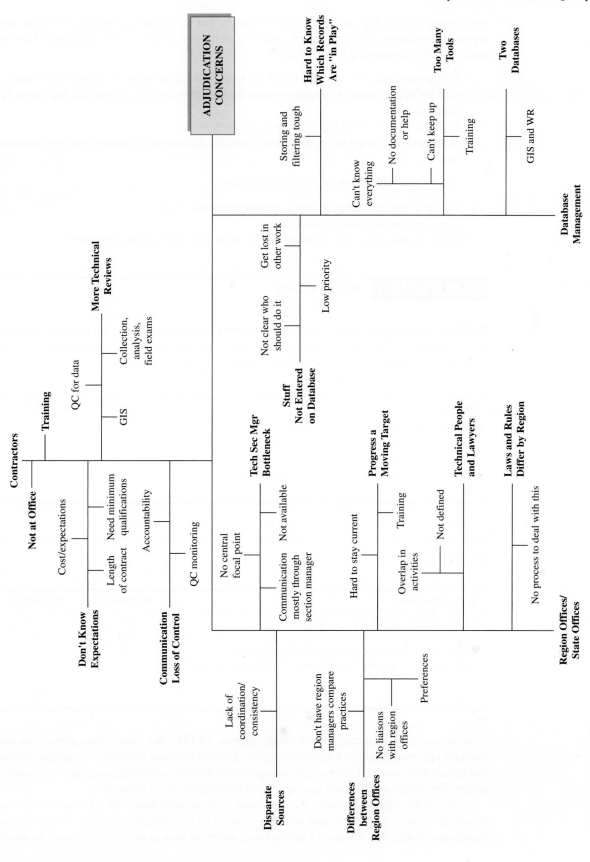

FIGURE 10-14   Adjudication Fishbone Diagram [Example 10-7]

news is that by focusing on the *vital few,* inventory can be controlled, satisfaction of the most important customers can be increased, and 80% of the complaints can be eliminated. Here are some rules for constructing Pareto charts:

- Information must be selected based on types or classifications of defects that occur as a result of a process. An example might be the different types of defects that occur in a semiconductor.
- Data must be collected and classified into categories.
- A frequency chart must be constructed, showing the number of occurrences in descending order.

The steps used in Pareto analysis include these:

1. Gather categorical data relating to quality problems.
2. Draw a frequency chart of the data.
3. Focus on the tallest bars in the frequency chart first when solving the problem.

EXAMPLE 10-6   **Pareto Charts**

Problem: A copying company is concerned because it is taking too long for operators to set up new printing jobs. They decide to use Pareto analysis to find out why setup times are taking so long. The data gathered reflect the following major causes:

Type of Problem	Frequency (Number of Times)
Equipment needed for setup is missing	124
Internal and external setup tasks are not separated	87
Setup routines are not standardized	315
Extensive machine resetting and paper change are needed	56
Other	23

Solution: First, order the problems by frequency and compute the percentage of problems related to each cause:

Type of Problem	Frequency	Percentage
Setup routines are not standardized	315	52.1%
Equipment needed for setup is missing	124	20.5
Internal and external setup tasks are not separated	87	14.4
Extensive machine resetting and paper change are needed	56	9.2
Other	23	3.8
Total	605	100%

Next, draw a frequency chart of the results (Figure 10-15). This Pareto chart shows that non-standardized procedures for setting up copying jobs are the most frequently occurring problem that causes slow setups. Therefore, the company can institute a training program to routinize its setups. This program will result in a significant reduction in setup slowdowns.

Two points should be made. We also could analyze these data from a number of different perspectives, such as average time per type of delay or cost per type of delay. Also, this chart shows graphically that the law of diminishing marginal returns does have a place in quality

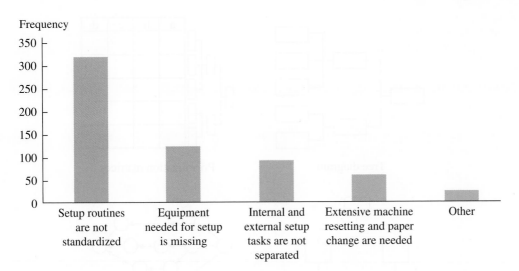

FIGURE 10-15 Pareto Analysis

thinking. As the group addresses each problem, the savings from correcting the problems decrease. There is no guarantee, however, that addressing the fourth problem will take any less effort than the first.

THE SEVEN NEW TOOLS FOR IMPROVEMENT

In addition to the basic seven tools of quality, there is another set of tools that focuses on group processes and decision making: the new tools for management. The **new seven (N7) tools** were developed as a result of a research effort by a committee of the Japanese Society for QC Technique Development. They are shown in Figure 10-16 and are discussed in the following pages.

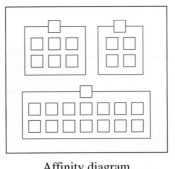

FIGURE 10-16 Seven New Tools for Management *Source:* From M. Brassard, "The Memory Jogger™ Plus+." Boston: GOAL/QPC, 2004. Reprinted with permission of GOAL/QPC.

Affinity diagram   Interrelationship digraph

	a	b	c	d	e	f	g	h
1								
2								
3								
4								
5								
6								

Matrix diagram

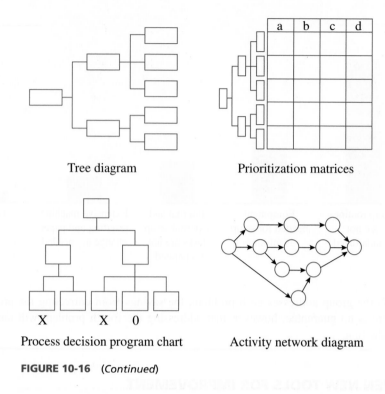

Tree diagram   Prioritization matrices

Process decision program chart   Activity network diagram

FIGURE 10-16   (*Continued*)

GOAL/QPC, the consulting firm, is a major force for disseminating information about the N7 tools. GOAL/QPC recommends that the N7 tools be used in a "cycle of activity,"[1] in which one tool provides inputs to another tool. One possible cycle is shown in Figure 10-17, in which the affinity diagram or interrelation digraph is being used as inputs to the tree diagram, and so forth. Let us discuss each of these tools and the purposes they serve.

FIGURE 10-17   Seven Management and Planning Tools: Typical Flow   *Source:* From M. Brassard, "The Memory Jogger™ Plus+," Boston: GOAL/QPC, 2004. Reprinted with permission of GOAL/QPC.

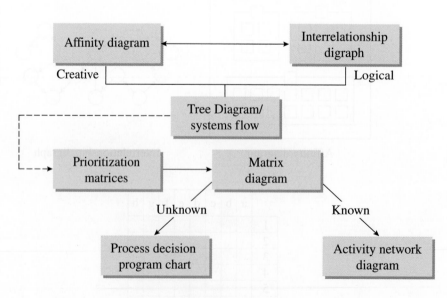

[1]Brassard, M. "The Memory Jogger II." Boston: GOAL/QPC, 2004. Reprinted from "The Memory Jogger Plus+" with permission of GOAL/QPC, 12B Manor Parkway, Salem, NH 03079, www.goalqpc.com.

The Affinity Diagram

When we are solving a problem, it is often useful to first surface all the issues associated with the problem. A tool to do this is the **affinity diagram**, which helps a group converge on a set number of themes or ideas that can be addressed later. An affinity diagram creates a hierarchy of ideas on a large surface, as shown in Figure 10-18. The steps used in establishing an affinity diagram are as follows:

1. Identify the problem to be stated. Create a clear, concise statement of the issue that is understood by everyone.
2. Give the team members a supply of note cards and a pen. Ask them to write down issues that relate to the problem. There should only be one idea per card. Ask them to use at least four or five words to clearly explain their thinking.
3. Allow only about 10 minutes for this writing activity.
4. Place the written cards on a flat surface.
5. Lay out the finished cards so all participants can see and have access to all the cards.
6. Let everyone on the team move the cards into groups with a similar theme. Do this work silently because it does not help to discuss your thinking. Work and move quickly.
7. If you disagree with someone else's placement of a note card, say nothing, but move it.
8. You reach consensus when all the cards are in groups, and the team members have stopped moving the cards. Once consensus has been reached concerning placement of the cards, you can create header cards.
9. Draw a finished affinity diagram and provide a working copy for all participants.

As illustrated in Figure 10-18, you should have a table with an issue statement, subissue header cards, and note cards with ideas. It will provide the basis for further discussion and brainstorming.

Zoo personnel at a zoological park used an affinity diagram to help develop a mission statement. The problem was stated as "Issues surrounding the mission of the Metropolitan City Zoo." The managers and zoo workers filled about 80 sticky notes with issues concerning the zoo's mission. Next, the team members placed the sticky notes into groups and ultimately defined a mission with six major elements, which provided a foundation for a final mission statement.

FIGURE 10-18 Affinity Diagram

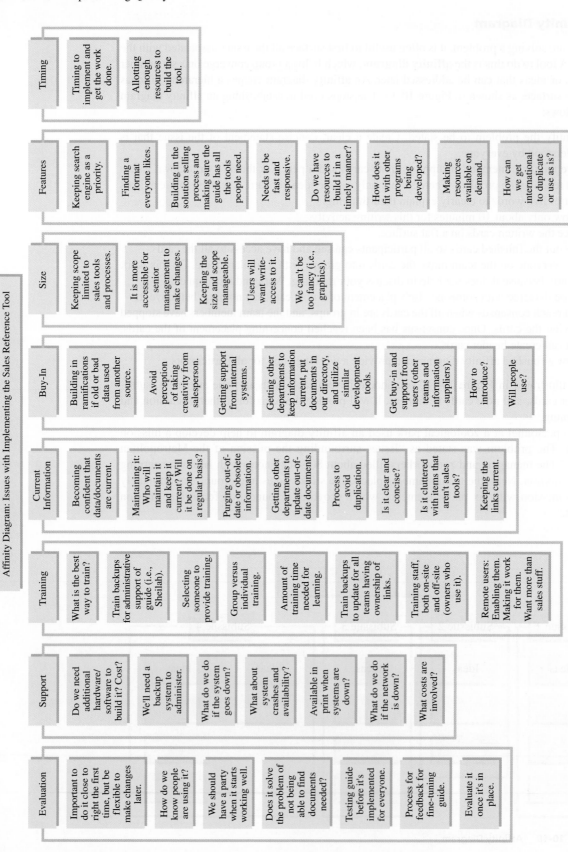

FIGURE 10-19   Affinity Diagram: Issues with Implementing the Sales Reference Tool

| **EXAMPLE 10-7** | **Affinity Diagrams** |

Problem: The sales team at HealthWise Corporation, a supplier of medical information, decided to develop a sales reference tool (SRT) as a means of improving its training processes for new salespeople in the field. It was decided that this SRT would be available on the company intranet. A team of experienced salespeople was assembled who cataloged all the current sales material in many different locations. These materials were then reviewed by the team. Prior to performing preliminary design work for the SRT, the team members had to identify issues relating to the implementation of the SRT. The results are shown in Figure 10-19.

Solution: This analysis helped team members identify key issues in the design and implementation of the SRT. It was discovered that they needed to focus on eight issues in implementation: evaluation, support, training, current information, buy-in, size, features, and timing. The notes underneath the headers present some of the issues identified by the participants.

The Interrelationship Digraph

After completing the affinity diagram, it might be useful to understand the causal relationships between the different issues that surfaced. Also, it is helpful to identify the most important issues to be focused on when pursuing the solution to a problem. A finished **interrelationship digraph** is shown in Figure 10-20. This interrelationship digraph shows the relationships between different issues. We will address how to develop this digraph, but note that the shaded boxes are major

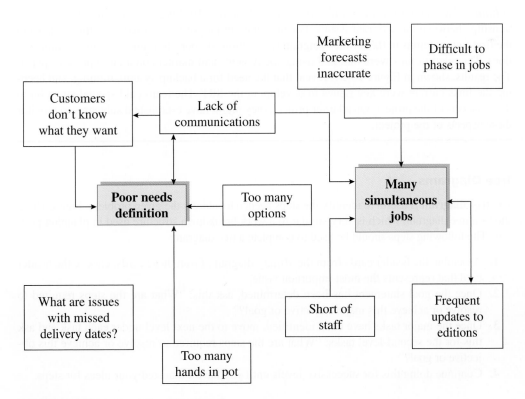

FIGURE 10-20   Interrelationship Digraph

issues that need to be addressed when developing improvement strategies. The steps to complete the interrelationship digraph are as follows:

1. Construct an affinity diagram to identify the issues relating to a problem. After you have done this, place the cards with related issues in columns with gaps between the cards. It is helpful to use sticky notes on a large piece of flipchart paper.
2. Create the digraph by examining the cards one by one, asking, "What other issues on this digraph are caused or influenced by this issue?" As team members identify issues that are related, draw a one-way arrow from the first issue (the cause) to the second issue (the one influenced by the cause). Do this until all the issues have been discussed.
3. After reviewing the arrows and making needed revisions, count the numbers of arrows pointing to each note, and write the numbers on the notes.
4. Identify the cards with the most arrows as the "key factors." Experience has shown that there should not be more than 5 to 10 key factors, depending on the issue being discussed. Some cards may have several arrows, but for one reason or another they are not really key factors; these cards can be dropped from consideration at this point. Boxes with the most outgoing arrows tend to be root causes; those with incoming arrows tend to be performance indicators.
5. Draw a *double* box around the key factors and brainstorm ways to address these issues.

EXAMPLE 10-8 | **Interrelationship Digraphs**

Problem: For the issues relating to sales reference tools in Figure 10-19, team members were interested in knowing what issues had the greatest effects on other issues. This would help them to know where to focus their efforts in coming weeks.

Solution: The cards from the affinity diagram in Example 10-7 were used to identify the relationships between the different issues. For presentation purposes, we used only the cards from the first four columns in the affinity diagram (evaluation, support, training, and current information). The relationships were outlined using sticky notes and markers on a large piece of paper. The results, shown in Figure 10-21, reveal that the need for a backup system, training, and keeping the links current were key issues in developing the SRT. The team paid special attention to these aspects of the project. On a larger project, they might have established subteams to monitor these aspects of the project.

Tree Diagrams

The **tree diagram** is useful to identify the steps needed to address the given problem. Figure 10-22 shows a tree diagram, which is very similar to a work breakdown structure used in planning projects. The following steps should be used to complete a tree diagram:

1. Assemble the header cards from the affinity diagram. From these cards, choose the header card that represents the most important issue.
2. Once the goal statement has been determined, ask this: "What are the steps required to resolve or achieve this major objective or goal?"
3. Once the major tasks have been identified, move to the next level under each task and ask this for the second-level tasks: "What are the steps required to resolve or achieve this objective or goal?"
4. Continue doing this for successive levels until you have exhausted your ideas for steps.

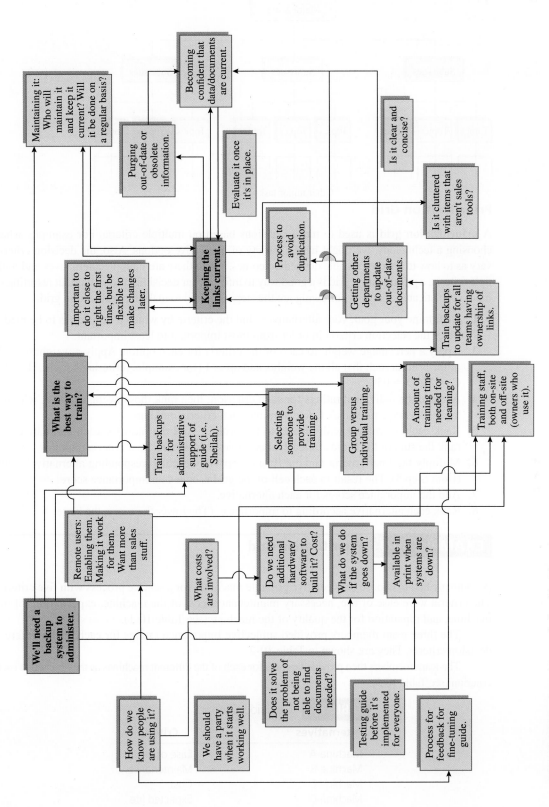

FIGURE 10-21   Actual Interrelationship Digraph

FIGURE 10-22 Tree Diagram

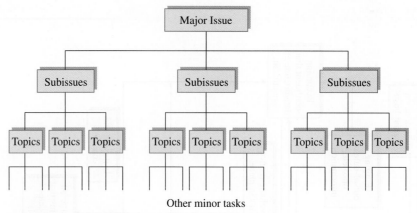

Other minor tasks

Prioritization Grid

A **prioritization grid** is used to make decisions based on multiple criteria. For example, when choosing a technology, we might have a variety of alternative options. Also, the decision criteria vary as to how to choose possible desired outcomes. When there are multiple alternatives and multiple criteria, a prioritization grid is a good way to inform your decision making without resorting to more sophisticated analysis. Following are the steps required to make a prioritization grid:

1. Determine your goal, your alternatives, and the criteria by which a decision is to be made.
2. Place the selection criteria in order from most important to least important.
3. Apply a percentage weight to each of the criteria for each option. Apply a weight to each of the criteria such that all the weights add up to 1 (for example, [criteria] A = .40, B = .30, C = .25, D = .05).
4. Average the individual ratings for each criterion; then rank those average scores, with the highest average ranked as 1, to determine final criteria rankings.
5. Rank each alternative with respect to the criteria. Add the rates for each alternative and rank the sum of the scores for each alternative to determine final criteria rankings.
6. Multiply the final criteria ranking (from Step 4) by each corresponding alternative's rank (from Step 5). The result in each cell of the grid is called an importance score.
7. Add the importance scores for each alternative.
8. Rank each alternative according to importance. (The lower the score, the better.)

EXAMPLE 10-9 Prioritization Grid

A company had to choose between five possible machines for a service process with five criteria. The criteria were ease of use, necessary maintenance, cost of the machine, expected life of the machine, and reputation for the quality of the machine (see Table 10-1).

The three team members provided subjective importance ratings for each of the different decision criteria. They are shown in Table 10-2.

The team members then provided ratings for each of the different machines as they related to each criterion (see Table 10-3).

TABLE 10-1 Decision Criteria

Alternatives	Criteria
Machine A	Ease of use
Machine B	Maintenance
Machine C	Cost
Machine D	Expected life
Machine E	Reputation

TABLE 10-2 Importance Ratings					
Criteria	Person 1	Person 2	Person 3	Average Score	Final Criteria Ranking
Ease of use	0.4	0.2	0.5	0.366	1
Maintenance	0.3	0.3	0.3	0.300	2
Cost	0.2	0.2	0.1	0.166	3
Expected life	0.05	0.1	0.05	0.066	5
Reputation	0.05	0.2	0.05	0.100	4
	1	1	1		

TABLE 10-3 Final Rankings					
	Ease of Use				
Alternatives	Person 1	Person 2	Person 3	Sum of Scores	Final Ease of Use Ranking
Machine A	1	1	1	3	1
Machine B	2	3	2	7	2
Machine C	4	4	4	12	4
Machine D	5	5	5	15	5
Machine E	3	2	3	8	3
	Maintenance				
Alternatives	Person 1	Person 2	Person 3	Sum of Scores	Final Maintenance Ranking
Machine A	2	2	1	5	1
Machine B	1	3	2	6	2
Machine C	5	5	4	14	5
Machine D	4	4	5	13	4
Machine E	3	1	3	7	3
	Cost				
Alternatives	Person 1	Person 2	Person 3	Sum of Scores	Final Cost Ranking
Machine A	4	4	5	13	5
Machine B	5	3	4	12	4
Machine C	1	1	2	4	1
Machine D	2	2	1	5	2
Machine E	3	5	3	11	3
	Expected Life				
Alternatives	Person 1	Person 2	Person 3	Sum of Scores	Final Expected Life Ranking
Machine A	1	2	1	4	1
Machine B	2	3	2	7	2
Machine C	3	4	5	12	4
Machine D	4	5	4	13	5
Machine E	5	1	3	9	3
	Reputation				
Alternatives	Person 1	Person 2	Person 3	Sum of Scores	Final Reputation Ranking
Machine A	4	4	5	13	5
Machine B	5	3	4	12	4
Machine C	1	1	2	4	1
Machine D	2	2	1	5	2
Machine E	3	5	3	11	3

TABLE 10-4 Combining Rankings

Final Criteria Ranking	Final Ease of Use Ranking	Final Maintenance Ranking	Final Cost Ranking
1	1	1	5
2	2	2	4
3	4	5	1
5	5	4	2
4	3	3	3

Final Expected Life Ranking	Final Reputation Ranking
1	5
2	4
4	1
3	2
5	3

Scores

Machine A: 1(1) + 2(1) + 3(5) + 5(1) + 4(5) = 43
Machine B: 1(2) + 2(2) + 3(4) + 5(2) + 4(4) = 44
Machine C: 1(4) + 2(5) + 3(1) + 5(4) + 4(1) = 41
Machine D: 1(5) + 2(4) + 3(2) + 5(5) + 4(2) = 52
Machine E: 1(3) + 2(3) + 3(3) + 5(3) + 4(3) = 45

Final Rankings

1	C
2	A
3	B
4	E
5	D

Machine C is the best choice.

The final rankings were computed by multiplying the various rankings by their importance. It looks like alternative C is the best choice. Note that the lowest score is the best (see Table 10-4).

Matrix Diagram

The **matrix diagram** is similar in concept to quality function deployment in its use of symbols, its layout, and its application. Because the matrix diagram is one of the N7 tools, we mention it here. However, the prior presentation of QFD is much more complete, so we will keep it short. Like the other N7 tools, the matrix diagram is a brainstorming tool that can be used in a group to show the relationships between ideas or issues. Matrix diagrams are simple to use and can be used in two, three, or four dimensions. The steps are as follows:

1. Determine the number of issues or dimensions to be used in the matrix.
2. Choose the appropriate matrix.
3. Place the appropriate symbols in the matrix.

Figure 10-23 shows a *responsibility* matrix diagram. The legend at the bottom of the figure shows the extent of responsibility among the different people. No example is provided here because we discussed QFD earlier in Chapter 7. This grid in Figure 10-23 gives a simplified version of a QFD matrix.

Reducing the Number of Billing Errors

People needed	Improve database	Improve definition	Specify costs	Lessen options	Revise pricing	Simplify process	Total
Layout engineers		◎				◎	18
Software designers			○	◎	◎	△	22
Engineers	◎	○		○		◎	24
Human resources			○			△	4
Systems	○				○		6
Options	Improve database	Improve definition	Specify costs	Lessen options	Revise pricing	Simplify process	

◎ High (9) [Prime responsibility]

○ Medium (3) [Secondary responsibility]

△ Low (1) [Kept informed]

FIGURE 10-23 Responsibility Matrix Diagram

Process Decision Program Chart

A **process decision program chart** is a tool to help brainstorm possible contingencies or problems associated with the implementation of some program or improvement. Figure 10-24 shows such a chart in tree form (the outline form is not presented here). The steps are as follows:

1. When developing the tree diagram, place the first-level boxes in sequential order. (These are the boxes in the first column in Figure 10-24.)
2. Moving to the second level, list implementation details at a fairly high level. Try to be all-inclusive at a macro level.
3. At the third level, ask this: "What unexpected things could happen in this implementation?" or this: "What could go awry at this stage?"
4. At the fourth level, brainstorm possible countermeasures to the problems identified at the third level.
5. Evaluate the countermeasures for feasibility, and mark those that are feasible with an O and those that are not feasible with an X.

Activity Network Diagram

The **activity network diagram**, also known as a *program evaluation and review technique* (PERT) *diagram* or a *critical-path* (longest path in time from beginning to end) *diagram*, is used for controlling projects. Figure 10-25 shows an activity network PERT diagram with its nodes and times. The nodes are circles, and the times are given in days. Activity network diagrams are discussed in depth in Chapter 14.

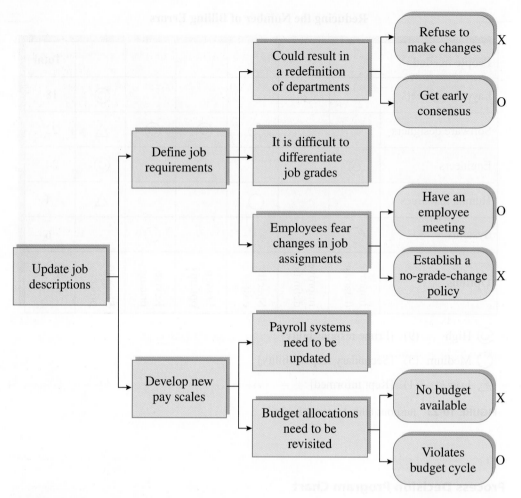

FIGURE 10-24   Process Decision Program Chart

A process decision program chart is a tool to help identify what might go wrong in a plan under development. This tool started with the implementation of value engineering in Japan. Figure 10-24 shows a process decision program chart from a billing process improvement. The steps are as follows:

1. When developing the tree diagram, place the first-level events in sequential order. The se are the steps in the first column in Figure 10-24.
2. Moving to the second level, list implementation details at a fairly high level. Try to be all-inclusive at a macro level.
3. At the third level, ask the questions, "What could happen that could happen in this implementation?" or that "What could go wrong at this step?"
4. At the fourth level, brainstorm possible countermeasures to the problems identified at the third level.
5. Evaluate the countermeasures for feasibility, and mark those that are feasible with an O and those that are infeasible with an X.

Activity Network Diagram

The **activity network diagram**, also known as the **arrow diagram** and better yet as unique (PERT) Program Evaluation and Review Technique diagram or the traditional (CPM) Critical Path for completing projects. Figure 10-25 shows an activity network, PERT diagram with its nodes and times. The nodes are circles, and the times are given in days. Activity network diagrams are discussed in depth in Chapter 1

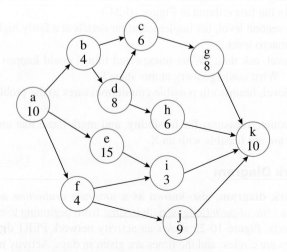

FIGURE 10-25   Activity Network Diagram

Reflections on the Managerial N7 Tools

As you can see, the N7 tools are useful for managing long projects that involve teams. With the B7 and N7 tools, you have a reasonably good set of skills that will help manage many projects. They have been used successfully in many different settings and for many different purposes.

The power of these tools is that with the **Plan–do–check–act (PDCA) cycle**, they give companies a simple and easy-to-understand methodology for solving unstructured problems. They are especially useful when used in teams. Many of these tools are also fun to use. By using them effectively, managers can reduce unproductive meeting time to a minimum and make good, fact-based decisions.

OTHER TOOLS FOR PERFORMANCE MEASUREMENT

There are other tools used in communicating performance to employees. The justification for these tools is to present data in an economical and understandable way. We present three such tools.

Spider Charts

Spider charts are graphs that present multiple metrics simultaneously in a two-dimensional plane. Figure 10-26 shows a spider chart. In this case, we show six different metrics (A–F), and report goals and results. A quick review of the figure shows that the firm has not met performance goals on metrics A, B, D, and E. The firm has met the goal relative to metric C and has exceeded the goal on metric F.

Other values that might be included on spider charts besides current performance and results are baseline performance measures and benchmark values. At times, this information can be found in QFD matrices.

Balanced Scorecards

A very important tool for measuring performance is a **balanced scorecard**. Balanced scorecards are usually spreadsheets that are communicated to management on a regular basis—weekly, monthly, quarterly, and annually. The usefulness of the balanced scorecard comes from integrating financial measures of business success, such as key metrics, along with nonfinancial, operational information about the business, such as customer satisfaction and process performance measures.

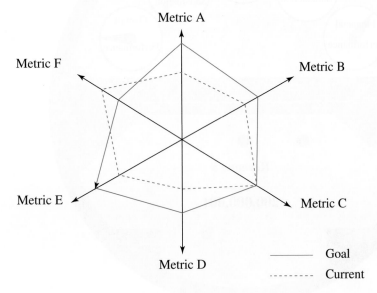

FIGURE 10-26   Spider Chart Example

Strategic Theme	Objectives	Measurement	Target	Initiative
Financial Performance	Profitability More Customers Less Investment	Market Value Truckload Rev. EVA Charge	Increase Market Share by 5% Increase Truck Revenue by 10%	Promote Delivery Service
Customer Satisfaction	Orders Delivered on Time Lowest Prices	Number of Orders Delivered on Date Promised	Exceed Customer Expectations 95%	Establish Specific Delivery Routes by Customer
Process Improvement	Efficient Staging and Loading of Customer Orders	Number of Orders Prestaged on Time for Loading	85% by June 20XX	Optimize Order Prestaging Process
Employee Satisfaction	Improved Communication Channels	Percent of Staff Trained in Teamwork	90% by June 20XX	Teamwork and Communication Skills Training

FIGURE 10-27 Balanced Scorecard Example

Figure 10-27 shows a very simplified layout for a balanced scorecard. Notice that this balanced scorecard combines financial, customer, process, and employee information into a single form. Often, these forms are color-coded to show whether goals are being met or performance is unsatisfactory. Scorecards, if used effectively, can be used to monitor and drive improvements in performance.

FIGURE 10-28
Dashboard Example

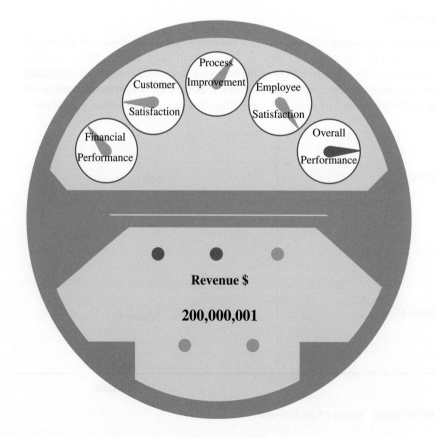

Dashboards

Dashboards look like electric meters or car dashboards. Figure 10-28 shows a dashboard that looks like an electric meter. Each of the "gauges" on the dashboard shows a different metric.

Notice in this case that the gauges in Figure 10-28 match the metrics reported in our balanced scoreboard discussed in Figure 10-27. This dashboard quickly communicates performance levels. Again, the focus is on easy, clear communication.

Summary

In this chapter we have briefly introduced the basic tools of quality. These tools should be adapted to the specific needs of your company. You also do not need to always use all the tools in a single project.

The B7 and N7 are useful in their simplicity and power. It is an easy undertaking to train employees to use these tools. However, many companies provide the training and then wonder why the employees don't use them. The reason is that along with the tools, cultural change is needed to ensure that implementation can be successful. Also, if management doesn't support the use of the tools in all possible situations, they do not become inculcated in the organization. In the following chapters, we discuss the context within which these tools can be successful.

Key Terms

Activity network diagram

Affinity diagram

Balanced scorecard

Basic seven (B7) tools of quality

Cause-and-effect (or fishbone or Ishikawa) diagram

Check sheets

Control charts

Dashboards

Histogram

Interrelationship digraph

Matrix diagram

New seven (N7) tools

Pareto charts

Plan–do–check–act (PDCA) cycle

Prioritization grid

Process decision program chart

Process map

Scatter diagram or scatter plot

SIPOC

Spider charts

Tree diagram

Discussion Questions

1. Why is it important to pursue quality management from a systems perspective?
2. Why is continual improvement necessary for a business organization?
3. The statement has been made that "A quality system is not just a series of boxes and arrows. It is an interconnected, interdisciplinary network of people, technology, procedures, markets, customers, facilities, legal requirements, reporting requirements, and assets that interact to achieve an end." What does this statement mean to you?
4. How do the basic tools work within W. E. Deming's plan–do–check–act (PDCA) cycle as a process for continual improvement?
5. What are the seven basic tools of quality? Who developed these tools?
6. Describe the purpose of a histogram.
7. Describe the purpose of a Pareto chart. Describe an instance (other than the one in the book) in which a Pareto chart could be effectively used.
8. List the steps in Pareto Analysis and indicate the source where data can be collected.
9. What is the purpose of a cause-and-effect (Ishikawa) diagram?
10. Describe the purpose of a check sheet. Describe an instance (other than the ones in the book) in which a check sheet could be effectively used.
11. Describe the purpose of a scatter diagram.
12. Describe the purpose of a flowchart. What are three of the rules for designing and using flowcharts?
13. What is the purpose of a control chart?
14. Which of the seven (Ishikawa) tools of quality described in the chapter have been the most helpful to you in your experiences? Make your answer as substantive as possible.

15. Describe the purpose of an affinity diagram.
16. Describe the purpose of an interrelationship digraph.
17. Describe the purpose of tree diagrams. Describe an instance in which a tree diagram could be used.
18. Describe the purpose of a prioritization grid.
19. Describe the purpose of a matrix diagram. In what ways is the matrix diagram a brainstorming tool?
20. What is the purpose of a process decision program chart?

Problems

1. Develop a process map of washing a car. Include a high level of detail in your map. Make six recommendations for improvements to your process.
2. Take the process map from Problem 1 and develop it into an extended process map. Make five recommendations for simplifying the extended process as it exists.
3. Develop a process map for making chocolate chip cookies. Include a high level of detail if you need to. You may need to consult a cookbook. Make three recommendations for improvements to your process. Discuss these with the class.
4. Take the process map from Problem 3 and develop an extended value stream process map. Make recommendations for three improvements to the extended process. Be sure to include all suppliers and logistics associated with the customers.
5. Develop a check sheet for defects in a flat-screen computer monitor.
6. Develop a check sheet for defects in a quality management class exam. Identify how you would use the check sheet to improve performance on future exams.
7. Develop a histogram for the following data:

Employee	Hours of Overtime	Days Absent
1	243	3
2	126	2
3	86	0
4	424	6
5	236	3
6	128	0
7	0	0
8	126	2
9	324	3
10	118	0
11	62	0
12	128	3
13	460	6
14	135	1
15	118	1
16	260	2
17	0	1
18	126	1
19	234	2
20	246	3
21	120	1
22	80	0
23	112	1
24	237	3
25	129	2
26	24	1
27	36	0
28	128	2
29	246	3
30	326	6

Develop two separate histograms for hours of overtime and days absent. How do the data appear to be distributed?

8. Using the data in Problem 7, develop a scatter plot of hours of overtime versus days absent. Do the data overtime hours and days absent appear to be correlated?

9. Develop a histogram using the following data:

    4.7, 4.7, 5.0, 5.6, 5.6, 5.6, 5.9, 5.9, 5.9, 5.9, 6.2, 6.2, 6.2, 6.2, 6.2, 6.2, 6.5, 6.5, 6.5, 6.5, 6.5, 6.5, 6.8, 6.8, 9.8, 9.8, 9.8, 9.8, 6.8, 6.8, 6.8, 6.8, 6.8, 6.8, 6.8, 6.8, 6.8, 6.8, 6.8, 7.1, 7.1, 7.1, 7.1, 7.1, 7.1, 7.1, 7.1, 7.1, 7.1, 7.1, 7.1, 7.1, 7.4, 7.4, 7.4, 7.4, 7.4, 7.4, 7.4, 7.4, 7.7, 7.7, 7.7, 7.7, 7.7, 7.7, 7.7, 7.7, 7.7, 7.7, 7.7, 7.7, 7.7, 7.7, 7.7, 7.7, 7.7, 8.0, 8.0, 8.0, 8.0, 8.0, 8.0, 8.3, 8.3, 8.3, 8.3, 8.3, 8.3, 8.6, 8.6, 8.6, 8.6, 8.6, 8.6, 8.9, 8.9, 8.9, 9.2, 9.2, 9.8.

    Do the data appear to be normally distributed?

10. If you have 60 data points, use the log formula to determine how many classes you should use in your histogram.

11. Use the logarithmic formula in the chapter to determine how many classes you should use for the following numbers of data:
    a. 35 b. 200 c. 600

12. Think about the following questions, and develop fishbone diagrams for each of them:
    a. What is the major service problem in your university?
    b. What is the major thing that interferes with your study?
    c. What is the major problem with your school newspaper?
    d. What is the major social problem in society?

13. For the following data, develop a Pareto analysis. The letters A, B, C, D, E, and F are problems that occur in a process. Which cause should you focus on first?

A	B
B	C
A	A
C	A
D	A
A	C
B	A
D	C
B	B
A	A
A	C
B	D
D	B
C	E
A	F
B	E
C	A
D	B
A	A
A	C
A	D
B	B
C	B
B	A
C	A
A	A
B	D
A	C
C	B
A	E

14. For the following data, develop a Pareto chart. The letters V, X, Y, and Z are problems that occur in a process. Which cause should you address first if the fixes for the problems are $1.00, $1.20, $.90, and $2.00, respectively?

    VXZZZYYXXYVVYYXXZZYZZYXXVYVYVYVYXXXYVYZVYXXXYVYVYVXXXXV-
    VVVYYYYVYVYVYXYXYXVXVZZZXYXYXYVYYXZZZ

15. Either alone or as a team, draw a fishbone diagram about the following topics:
    a. What are the causes of poor grades?
    b. Why do college students drink too much?
    c. Why do I not have enough money?
    d. What are the causes of poor response times on the Internet?

16. *Quality Is Personal* by Roberts and Sergesketter is a popular book. In it, the authors recommend using the basic tools of quality in our personal lives. Develop a check sheet to keep track of personal defects you have in your life (such as sleeping too late, being too grumpy, and so on). Use this check sheet for two weeks to track these personal defects. After two weeks, perform a Pareto analysis to determine where you have the greatest need for improvement. Next, use the fishbone diagram to identify the underlying causes of the personal defects. After making changes, use a control chart to track your defects.

17. For the following data, draw a scatter diagram to see if time lost because of injuries and overtime hours are related. What do you conclude?

Plant	Lost Time Days	Overtime Hours
A	5	254
B	3	114
C	6	350
D	4	219
E	10	496
F	5	218
G	7	279

18. Develop a process map for the registration process at your university. Analyze the number of value-added and non-value-added steps.

19. Develop a process map for receiving financial aid at your university. Analyze the process and develop a proposal for improvement.

20. With a team of students, develop an affinity diagram relating to the following problem statement: "What are issues relating to finding a job in the current economy?" What did you find?

21. Form a team and develop an affinity diagram for the following problem statement: "What are issues associated with completing a university or college degree in a reasonable amount of time?"

22. Using the affinity diagram from Problem 21, develop an interrelationship digraph. What do you generalize from the interrelationship digraph?

23. Develop a tree diagram for building a home.

24. Develop a tree diagram for writing a major research paper. Now take the steps you identified for this project and develop an activity network diagram.

25. Complete the analysis for the following prioritization grid information by finding the final ranking:

Decision Alternatives
Machine 1
Machine 2
Machine 3
Machine 4

Decision Criteria	Importance
A	.3
B	.2
C	.5

Final Rankings

Criterion A	Ranking
Machine 1	1
Machine 2	2
Machine 3	3
Machine 4	4

Criterion B	Ranking
Machine 1	3
Machine 2	2
Machine 3	4
Machine 4	1

Criterion C	Ranking
Machine 1	4
Machine 2	2
Machine 3	1
Machine 4	3

26. Develop a process decision chart for completing your college degree.

CASES

Case 10-1 Corporate Universities: Teaching the Tools of Quality

Motorola Solutions Learning: learning.motorolasolutions.com
Sears University: www.searsholdings.com

Although most of us are familiar with major public universities such as Penn State, Colorado–Boulder, Georgia, and Ohio State, we are typically unfamiliar with corporate universities such as Motorola Solutions Learning, Intel University, and the AT&T Learning Center. This is because corporate universities are a fairly new concept, and they are created to serve the needs of a particular company's employees and other stakeholders.

The term *corporate university* has been adopted by firms that have significantly upgraded their training and development activities by creating learning centers within their corporations. These learning centers are typically designed to prioritize a firm's training initiatives, and to quickly share with a firm's employees the skills, techniques, and best practices that are necessary to remain competitive. For example, when a new quality tool or technique is developed, it is often the responsibility of a firm's corporate university to develop a plan to equip the firm's employees with the skills necessary to quickly incorporate the new tool or techniques into their work areas.

Following are brief descriptions of two corporate universities. After reading these descriptions, ask yourself the following rhetorical question: "Are these corporations well equipped to teach their employees the tools of quality?"

Motorola Solutions Learning (MSL)

Motorola Solutions Learning (MSL) began as the Motorola Training and Education Center. Initially, the purpose of MSL was to help Motorola strengthen its training efforts and build a quality-focused corporate culture. Through the years, MSL has grown in both size and stature and now has a staff of more than 400 employees and seven facilities across the world. The stated objectives of MSL are as follows:

- To provide training and education to all Motorola employees
- To prepare Motorola employees to be best-in-class in their industries
- To serve as a catalyst for change and continuous improvement to position Motorola Corporation for the future
- To provide added value to Motorola in the marketing and distribution of products throughout the world

To accomplish these objectives, MSL does many things. For example, each of the company's employees is required to take a minimum of 40 hours per year of job-relevant training and education. MSL also provides consulting services in a number of areas to its employees, including benchmarking, cycle time reduction, quality improvement processes, and statistical tools and problem-solving techniques.

One unique aspect of MSL is that it reaches beyond the Motorola Corporation. MSL provides training and certification programs for Motorola suppliers and also provides consulting services and training for other corporations on a fee basis.

Sears University

Sears University was established with the ambitious goal of becoming an integral part of the company's turnaround efforts. The university was opened with the idea of offering a wide selection of formal training and self-study courses for Sears's employees. In its first year of operation, approximately 10,000 of the company's employees participated in formal programs that ranged from one day to one week in duration. Another 4,000 employees completed self-study courses each month.

In addition to offering training programs in areas such as merchandising, operations, customer service, and human resources management, Sears University also provides programs designed to help company employees function as change agents and strategic leaders within the corporation. For example, participants in financial management training programs use computer-based simulations to model the impact of various financial strategies on business unit performance. Particular attention is paid to trying to help employees see the company's operations from the customer's perspective. The courses are taught by seasoned line managers along with professional facilitators and Sears University personnel.

Discussion Questions

1. Are corporate universities a good idea? If so, why?
2. How can a corporate university do a better job of teaching a firm's employees the "tools of quality" than traditional training programs?
3. Select a corporate university and visit its Web site. How does the company's corporate university facilitate the company's overall quality-related goals and initiatives?

Case 10-2 Zurich: Creating Quality Customer Care
Zurich: www.zurich.com

Zurich Insurance Group delivers insurance products and services in more than 170 countries. The group has been in operation since 1872 and has more than 60,000 employees. The purpose of Zurich's product is to provide people and businesses with financial protection in the event of something going wrong. Zurich emphasizes that customers' needs are at the core of its business strategy.[2]

Zurich realizes that successful quality improvement requires commitment. They continuously listen to customers' needs and expectations and put in place processes and people to meet them. Zurich's approach to managing quality uses a combination of methods. The iQuality system was developed to help employees deliver quality consistently to customers. The acronym defines what quality looks like at Zurich.

[2]Case Study Adapted from *Creating Quality Customer Care: A Zurich Case Study.*

i – You, Me, Everyone
Q – Question
U – Understand
A – Act
L – Lead
I – Inspire
T – Teamwork
Y – You

Zurich carries out regular quality sampling of the customer care it provides and the outputs it produces. The amount of quality sampling it carries out differs depending on factors such employee experience and trend of errors. Should a Zurich employee produce a high rate of errors, the sampling will be increased to monitor the process more closely. When errors are found, the "five whys" method is used to identify the source (a technique used in six sigma DMAIC methodology). When the root cause has been identified, a solution is implemented and the process is monitored to ensure the solution is addressing the error.

Zurich's commitment to customer centricity aims to go beyond standards set by regulatory bodies. As a global organization, Zurich aims to be the best insurer as measured by all its main stakeholder groups: its customers, its shareholders and its employees. For a customer focused organization, high levels of customer satisfaction is a key indicator of successful quality management. Market research involving large numbers of Zurich's customer's helps in hearing the voice of the customer (VOC). Additionally, as part of Zurich's customer impact scheme, customers were asked to rate the company's performance. Results showed that most customers gave a rating of good, very good and excellent.

In the financial services industry, products and prices can appear very similar to customers, so customer care is the differentiating factor between providers. Customers that have a positive experience are much more likely to renew their policies, buy other products and services, and recommend the company to others. Not managing quality could lead to unsatisfied customers, who could easily choose to take their business elsewhere. Zurich's customer care sets it apart from others in the industry while maximizing retention of its customers.

A measure of the success of Zurich's quality management methods are the numerous awards the company has received from within its own industry. Recent awards for Zurich include two Five Star Service Awards at the FT Financial Adviser Awards. This followed an intensive voting process involving 25,000 questionnaires - the biggest poll in the financial services industry. Zurich also received an Outstanding Achievement Award at the FT Adviser Online Service Awards in recognition of the way that it has maintained a level of excellence since the awards began.

Any organization that is serious about quality, not only strives to fulfill customer requirements and expectations, it inspires to exceed them. Zurich places quality as a core element of their business strategy. It actively manages and measures the quality of the service it provides to make sure its customers receive the best possible level of customer care.

Discussion Questions

1. Identify some of the ways in which Zurich ensures quality is a core value throughout the organization.
2. Discuss the quality tools used by Zurich to identify the source of errors and how the organization is ensuring that errors do not occur repeatedly.
3. Do you believe Zurich is a pioneer of quality management in the financial services industry? Why or why not?

Statistically Based Quality Improvement for Variables

Chapter Objectives

After completing this chapter, you should be able to:

1. Discuss the basics of process variation and applied statistical methods.
2. Demonstrate the differences between random and non-random variation.
3. Implement $\bar{x}$, R, X, MR, median, and s charts.
4. Develop control charts using Excel.
5. Interpret control charts.

As we view the world about us, statistics are everywhere. We hear statistics about politics, health, inflation, and the economy on digital or social media on a daily basis. Yet many people view the topic of statistics with fear, loathing, and trembling. The purpose of statistics is clear. Statistics is a group of tools that allows us to analyze data, make summaries, draw inferences, and generalize from data.

Statistics are very important in the field of quality. In fact, during the first half century of the quality movement, nearly all the work done in the field of quality related to statistics. This work resulted in a body of tools that are used worldwide in thousands of organizations.

This chapter focuses on the use of statistical tools—not as control mechanisms, but as the foundation for continual improvement. We present many statistical techniques and different types of control charts. These tools represent powerful techniques for monitoring and improving processes. We also discuss the behavioral aspects of statistical process improvement. It is important to recognize that it is not enough to learn the different charts and statistical techniques. We also must know how to apply these techniques in a way that will document and motivate continual improvement in organizations.

These techniques can be enjoyable to use, and we present them in a way that is intuitive and easy to understand. Where possible, we develop shortcuts and simple statistical techniques instead of more complex models. The primary goal is that these tools be used.

STATISTICAL FUNDAMENTALS

What Is Statistical Thinking?

Statistical thinking is a decision-making skill demonstrated by the ability to draw conclusions based on data. We make a lot of decisions based on intuition and gut feelings. Often we choose friends, homes, and even spouses based on feelings. Therefore, intuition and feelings are very important in making good decisions in certain circumstances.

However, intuitive decisions are sometimes biased and wrong-headed. Consider the case of government. Many times it is the most vocal groups that seem to control political agendas. It is difficult for mayors, governors, or presidents to determine exactly what the voting public wants on any issue. As a result, decisions are sometimes made that satisfy the few but irritate the many. Statistical thinking is based on these three concepts:

- All work occurs in a system of interconnected processes.
- All processes have variation (the amount of variation tends to be underestimated).
- Understanding variation and reducing variation are important keys to success.

In business, decisions need to be made based on data. If you want to know how to satisfy your customers, you need to gather data about the customers to understand their preferences. It is one thing to watch a production process humming along. It is a completely different thing to gather data about the process and make adjustments to the process based on data. Statistical thinking guides us to make decisions based on the analysis of data (see Quality Highlight 11-1).

QUALITY HIGHLIGHT 11-1   Statistical Tools in Action

Statistical tools have long been staples of the quality professional. Around the world, many firms have adopted statistical tools with good results. One of the appealing features of statistical tools is that they can be adapted and used in a wide variety of situations. For example, Ore-Ida Corporation, a subsidiary of Heinz Corporation and a nationally known producer of consumer food products, uses statistics to ensure that its food meets weight and measure requirements. One of the products that Ore-Ida produces is called a Pita Pocket sandwich. The problem with the Pita sandwich was that if the sandwiches were too large, they would not fit into the formed plastic Pita-holding package, and excess costs would be incurred. If the sandwiches were too small, customers would perceive them as having less value. As a result, Ore-Ida used statistical process control, experimental design, and process capability studies to ensure that the sandwiches met requirements.

Statistical process control is not always immediately successful. Simplot Corporation, a competitor of Ore-Ida's, attempted statistical process control and other tools of quality in its Caldwell, Idaho, facility. According to Bob Romero, manager of total quality management services, the company had to do an educational assessment of its employees, which resulted in a picture that was anything but flattering. Many of Simplot's employees had marginal literacy skills. As a result, the company undertook a lengthy program of training and education in literacy, after which new standards were created for employees that included overall standards for literacy and the ability to use word-processing software and spreadsheets. After completing this program, management again implemented statistical process control and other quality management tools. This time they were successful in improving processes and reducing costs.

Jaco Manufacturing Company, a producer of industrial components, tube fittings, and injection-molding machines, implemented statistical process control, process capability studies, and quality management tools as a means for improving customer service. G. K. Products, Inc., of Ann Arbor, Michigan—a Jaco customer—asked Jaco to reduce its costs by improving its inspection of plastic float bodies. These float bodies are used in gas tanks so that the flow of fuel to the car's engine will shut off in case of rollover. Benefits that were achieved through this program included a 14% reduction in cycle time, a decrease in scrap, thousands of dollars in cost savings, improved morale, and improved customer satisfaction.

(continued)

As we learn from these examples and countless others, companies around the world either now have implemented statistical quality tools or are in the process of adopting these tools. All processes exhibit variability. This fact alone makes statistical process tools invaluable to manufacturing and services companies alike.

Why Do Statistics Sometimes Fail in the Workplace?

Video Clip:
Behavioral Aspects of SPC

Before beginning a discussion of statistical quality improvement, we must remember that many times statistical tools do not achieve the desired results. Why is this so? Many firms fail to implement quality control in a substantive way. That is, they prefer form over substance. We provide several reasons as a guide, which you can use to assess whether your organization will be successful in using statistics to improve. Reasons for failure of statistical tools include the following:

- Lack of knowledge about the tools; therefore, tools are misapplied.
- General disdain for all things mathematical creates a natural barrier to the use of statistics. When was the last time you heard someone proclaim a love for statistics?
- Cultural barriers in a company make the use of statistics for continual improvement difficult.
- Statistical specialists have trouble communicating with managerial generalists.
- Statistics generally are poorly taught, emphasizing mathematical development rather than application.
- People have a poor understanding of the scientific method.
- Organizations lack patience in collecting data. All decisions have to be made "yesterday."
- Statistics are viewed as something to buttress an already-held opinion rather than a method for informing and improving decision making.
- People fear using statistics because they fear they may violate critical statistical assumptions. Time-ordered data are messy and require advanced statistical techniques to be used effectively.
- Most people don't understand random variation, resulting in too much process tampering.
- Statistical tools often are reactive and focus on *effects* rather than *causes*.
- Another reason why people make mistakes with statistics is founded in the notions of type I and type II errors. In the study of quality, we call a type I error **producer's risk** and a type II error **consumer's risk.** In this context, producer's risk is the probability that a good product will be rejected. Consumer's risk is the probability that a nonconforming product will be available for sale. Consumer's risk happens when statistical quality analysis fails to result in the scrapping or reworking of a defective product. When either type I or type II errors occur, erroneous decisions are made relative to products that can result in high costs or lost future sales. Given these problems, we adopt the approach that statistics should be used, they should be used correctly, and they should be taught correctly.

Understanding Process Variation

All processes exhibit variation. There is some variation that we can manage and other variation that we cannot manage. If there is too much variation, parts will not fit correctly, products will not function properly, and a firm will gain a reputation for poor quality.

Two types of process variation commonly occur: random and nonrandom variation. Random variation is uncontrollable, and nonrandom variation has a cause that can be identified. The statistical tools discussed later in this chapter are useful for determining whether variation is random.

Random variation is centered around a mean and occurs with a somewhat consistent amount of dispersion. This type of variation cannot be controlled, so we refer to it as "uncontrolled variation." The amount of random variation in a process may be either large or small. When the variation is large, processes may not meet specifications on a consistent basis.

The statistical tools discussed in this chapter are *not* designed to detect random variation. Figure 11-1 shows normal distributions resulting from a variety of samples taken from the same population over time. We find a consistency in the amount of dispersion and the mean of the

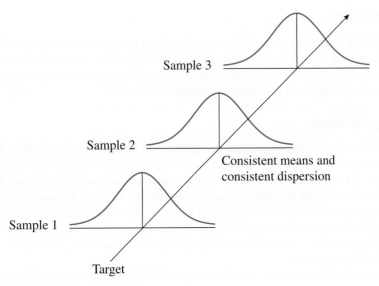

FIGURE 11-1   Random Variation

process. The fact that not all observations within the distributions fall exactly on the target line shows that there is variation. However, the consistency of the variation shows that only random causes of variation are present within the process. This means that in the future, when we gather samples from the process, we can expect that the distributions associated with such samples also will take the same form.

Nonrandom (or "special cause") **variation** results from some event. The event may be a shift in a process mean or some unexpected occurrence. For example, we might receive flawed materials from a supplier. There might be a change in work shift. An employee might come to work under the influence of drugs and make errors. The machine may break or not function properly. Figure 11-2 shows distributions resulting from a number of samples taken from the same population over time where nonrandom variation is exhibited. Notice that from one sample to the next, the dispersion and average of the process are changing. When we compare this figure to random variation, it is clear that nonrandom variation results in a process that is not repeatable.

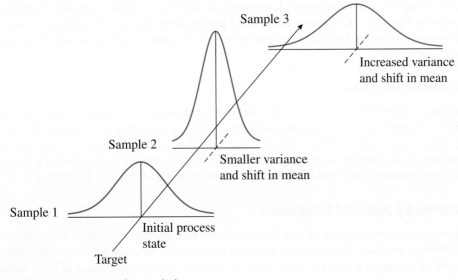

FIGURE 11-2   Nonrandom Variation

Process Stability

Process **stability** means that the variation we observe in the process is random variation (common cause) and not nonrandom variation (special or assignable causes). To determine process stability, we use process charts. **Process charts** are graphs designed to signal process workers when nonrandom variation is occurring in a process.

Sampling Methods

To ensure that processes are stable, data are gathered in samples. Process control requires that data be gathered in samples. For the most part, sampling methods have been preferred to the alternative of 100% inspection. The reasons for sampling are well established. Samples are cheaper, take less time, are less intrusive, and allow the user to frame the sample. In cases where quality testing is destructive, 100% inspection would be impossible and would literally drive the company out of business. In some processes, chemicals are used in testing, or destructive pull tests are applied to cables. These destructive tests ruin the sample, but are useful to show that a good product is being made.

However, recent experience has shown that 100% inspection can be effective in certain instances. One hundred percent samples are also known as *screening samples*, *sorting samples*, *rectifying samples*, or *detailing samples*. They have been most common in acceptance sampling (refer to Chapter 9 Appendix), where a lot of material has been rejected in the past and materials must be sorted to keep good materials and return defective materials for a refund.

Another example of 100% inspection is used when performing in-process inspection. Many companies have asked their employees to inspect their own work as the work is being performed, which can result in 100% inspection at every stage of the process! We should clarify that in-process inspection also can be performed on a sampling basis. Because sampling is so important, let's look at some different types of samples.

Random Samples

Randomization is useful because it ensures independence among observations. To *randomize* means to sample in such a way that every piece of product has an equal chance of being selected for inspection. This means that if 1,000 products are produced in a single day, each product has a 1/1,000 chance of being selected for inspection on that day. Random samples are often the preferred form of sampling and are yet often the most difficult to achieve. This is especially true in process industries, in which multiple products are made by the same machines, workers, and processes in sequence. In this case, there is not independence among observations because the process results in ordered products that can be subject to machine drift (going out of adjustment slowly over time).

Systematic Samples

Systematic samples have some of the benefits of random samples without the difficulty of randomizing. Samples can be systematic according to *time* or according to *sequence*. If a sample is systematic according to time, a product is inspected at regular intervals of time, say, every 15 minutes. If a systematic sample is performed according to sequence, one product is inspected every tenth iteration. For example, every tenth product coming off the line is sampled.

Sampling by Rational Subgroups

A *rational subgroup* is a group of data that is logically homogeneous; variation within these data can provide a yardstick for computing limits on the standard variation between subgroups. For example, in a hospital it may not make sense to combine measurements such as body temperature or medication levels taken in the morning with measurements taken in the evening. Morning measurements occur before medications are given and before the first meal of the day and constitute a rational subgroup. Evening measurements, another such subgroup, are taken after treatment has been provided during the day, medications have been administered, and patients have been nourished. If data are gathered that combine these two subgroups (e.g., the night and day measurements), differences between morning results and evening results will not be detected. If variation among different subgroups is not accounted for, an unwanted source of nonrandom variation is being introduced.

Planning for Inspection

As you can see, much planning must be performed in developing sampling plans. Questions must be answered about what type of sampling plan will be used, who will perform the inspection, who will use in-process inspection, sample size, what the critical attributes to be inspected are, and where the inspection should be performed. There are rules for inspection that help to prioritize where the inspection should be performed. Many firms compute the *ratio between the cost of inspection and the cost of failure* resulting from a particular step in the process, in order to prioritize where inspection should occur first.

Control Plans

Control plans are an important part of a quality control system and are a required part of an ISO 9000 **quality management system (QMS)**. After performing process failure modes and effects analysis (PFMEA), inspection is put in place at critical points in a process. **Control plans** provide a documented, proactive approach to defining how to respond when process control charts show that a process is out of control.

Figure 11-3 shows a sample control plan. In the production of a sprinkler head, four machines are used. The control plan outlines critical product characteristics that can be observed or measured at each stage of the process. It shows how the inspection is to be performed and prescribes reactions when a problem is detected.

The far-right column is referred to as the **reaction plan.** Control plans are usually kept by the quality assurance people involved with ISO 9000 and are made available to line workers who are responsible for executing process controls.

PROCESS CONTROL CHARTS

Now that we have discussed variation, it is time to learn about the tools used to understand random and nonrandom variation. Statistical process control charts (also referred to as process charts or control charts) are tools for monitoring process variation. Figure 11-4 shows a **control chart** that has an upper limit, a center line, and a lower limit. Several different types of control charts are discussed later. In this chapter, we introduce different statistical charts one by one. However, you should know there is a generalized process for implementing all types of process charts that we introduce first. This is a useful approach to learning control charts because the process for establishing different types of control charts is the same. Although the process for establishing different control charts is the same, the formulas used to compute the upper limit, center line, and lower limit are different. You will learn the formulas later.

Variables and Attributes Control Charts

To select the proper process chart, we must differentiate between variables and attributes. As we already stated, a **variable** is a continuous measurement such as weight, height, or volume. An **attribute** is an either-or situation. Here are examples of attributes: The motor is either starting or not starting, or the lens is scratched or it is not. We discuss measurements in this chapter and attributes in Chapter 12. While discussing attributes, we will also introduce reliability theory.

Part Number:	Part Name Description: Sprinkler Head			Plant:					
		Characteristics		**Methods**					
Process Name/Operation	**Machine/Tools Fixture**	**Product**	**Process**	**Specifications/Tolerance**	**Measurement Technique**	**Sample Size**	**Sample Freq.**	**Control Method**	**Reaction Plan**
Plastic Injection Molding	Machine 1	Appearance		Free of Blemishes	Visual Inspection	100%	Continuous	100% Inspection	Notify Supervisor
				Flow Marks	1st Piece Inspection			Check Sheet	Adjust Machine
				Pot Holes	1st Piece Inspection			Check Sheet	Adjust Machine
	Machine 2	Mounting Hole Location		Nozzle Diameter	Vernier Caliper		Rectifying Sample	Check Sheet	Adjust Machine
				15 ± 1 mm			Every 1/2 Hour	$\bar{x}$ & R Chart	Quarantine and Cause-and-Effect Analysis
	Machine 3	Dimensional		6 ± 1 mm	Fixture 2		Sample	Check Sheet	Adjust/Recheck
	Fixture #1	Perimeter		6 ± 1 mm	Check Gap to Fixture and Datum		Every 1/2 Hour	$\bar{x}$ & R Chart	Quarantine and Cause-and-Effect Analysis

FIGURE 11-3 Control Plan

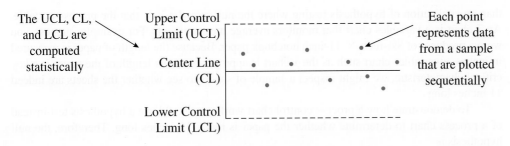

The UCL, CL, and LCL are computed statistically

Upper Control Limit (UCL)

Center Line (CL)

Lower Control Limit (LCL)

Each point represents data from a sample that are plotted sequentially

FIGURE 11-4 Control Chart

Table 11-1 shows the most common types of variable and attribute charts. The variables charts are X, x-bar ($\bar{x}$), R, MR, and s charts. The attributes charts are the p, np, c, and u charts. In the following pages, we introduce and develop these basic charts. We begin by introducing the generic process for developing all charts and then discuss the charts individually. There are four central requirements for properly using process charts:

1. You must understand this generic process for implementing process charts.
2. You must know how to interpret process charts.
3. You need to know when different process charts are used.
4. You need to know how to compute limits for the different types of process charts.
5. We treat each of these topics separately.

A Generalized Procedure for Developing Process Charts

The process for developing a process chart is the same for almost all charts. The only differences are in the actual statistical computations. Following are the steps used in developing process control charts:

1. Identify *critical operations* in the process where inspection might be needed. These are operations in which the product will be negatively affected if the operation is performed improperly.
2. Identify *critical product characteristics*. These are the aspects of the product that will result in either good or poor functioning of the product.
3. Determine whether the critical product characteristic is a variable or an attribute.
4. Select the appropriate *process control chart* from among the many types of control charts. This decision process and the types of charts available are discussed later.
5. Establish the *control limits* and use the chart to *continually monitor and improve*.
6. *Update the limits* when changes have been made to the process.

Understanding Process Charts

Before showing how to establish process charts, you need to understand what process charts are and how they work. We use the chart to illustrate the fact that the process chart is nothing more

TABLE 11-1	Variables and Attributes
Variables	**Attributes**
X (process population average)	p (proportion defective)
$\bar{x}$ (mean or average)	np (number defective or number nonconforming)
R (range)	c (number nonconforming in a consistent sample space)
MR (moving range)	
s (standard deviation)	u (number defects per unit)

than an application of hypothesis testing where the null hypothesis is that the process is stable. An $\bar{x}$ chart is a variables chart that monitors average measurements. For example, suppose you were a producer of 8½-inch × 11-inch notebook paper. Because the length of paper is measured in inches, a variables chart such as the $\bar{x}$ chart is appropriate. If the length of the paper is a key critical characteristic, we might inspect a sample of sheets to see whether the sheets are indeed 11 inches long.

To demonstrate how a process control chart works, we could use a hypothesis test instead of a process chart to determine whether the paper is really 11 inches long. Therefore, the null hypothesis is

$$H_0 : \mu = 11 \text{ inches}$$

The alternative hypothesis is

$$H_1 : \mu \neq 11 \text{ inches}$$

To perform the hypothesis test, we establish a distribution with the following 95% ($Z = 1.96$) rejection limits. If the standard error of the sample distribution ($n = 10$) is .001 inch, the rejection limits are $11 \pm 1.96(.001) = \{11.00196, 10.99804\}$. Figure 11-5 shows the distribution with its rejection regions.

Next, to test this hypothesis, we draw a sample of $n = 10$ sheets of paper and measure the sheets. The measurements are shown in the following table:

Sheet Number	Measurement
1	11.0001
2	10.9999
3	10.9998
4	11.0002
5	11.0004
6	11.0020
7	10.9980
8	10.9999
9	10.9870
10	11.0004
Sum	109.9877
Sample mean	10.99877

FIGURE 11-5
Hypothesis Testing

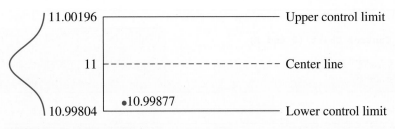

FIGURE 11-6 Process Chart

Because 10.99877 does not fall within either of the rejection regions shown in Figure 11-5, we fail to reject the null hypothesis and conclude that the sheets do not differ significantly from an average of 11 inches.

This is a basic hypothesis test. Now we use a process control chart to monitor this paper production process. With process charts, we place the distribution on its side, as shown in Figure 11-6. We draw a center line and upper and lower rejection lines, which we call *control limits*. We then plot the sample average (10.99877) on the control chart. Because the point falls between the control limits, we conclude that the process is in control. This means that the variation in the process is random (common).

Notice that the preceding example was based on a sample of $n = 10$. This means that the distribution we drew was a sampling distribution (not a population distribution). Therefore, we can invoke the *central limit theorem*. The central limit theorem states that when we plot the sample means, the sampling distribution approximates a normal distribution.

$\bar{x}$ and R Charts

Now that we have developed a process chart, you need to understand the different types of charts. First, we discuss two charts that go hand in hand: $\bar{x}$ and R charts. We developed an $\bar{x}$ chart in the prior example. When we are interested in monitoring a measurement for a particular product in a process, there are two primary variables of interest: the mean of the process and the dispersion of the process. The $\bar{x}$ chart aids us in monitoring the process mean or average. The R chart is used in monitoring process dispersion.

The $\bar{x}$ **chart** is a process chart used to monitor the average of the characteristic being measured. To set up an $\bar{x}$ chart, select samples from the process for the characteristic being measured and then form the samples into rational subgroups. Next, find the average value of each sample by dividing the sums of the measurements by the sample size and plot the value on the process control $\bar{x}$ chart.

The R **chart** is used to monitor the dispersion of the process. It is used in conjunction with the $\bar{x}$ chart when the process characteristic is a variable. To develop an R chart, collect samples from the process and organize them into subgroups, usually of three to six items. Next, compute the range R by taking the difference of the high value in the subgroup minus the low value. Then plot the R values on the R charts.

A standard process chart form is shown in Figure 11-7. This form has spaces for measurements and totals. In the example in Figure 11-8, our control chart form is filled out with measurements from a process. Notice that there are $k = 25$ samples of size $n = 4$. For each of the samples, totals, ranges, and averages are computed. The range is the difference between the largest measurement and the smallest measurement in a particular sample.

Now that we have measurements, we need to compute a center line and control limits for our $\bar{x}$ and R charts. The center line is the process average. The upper and lower control limits are usually located three standard deviations from the center line. The formulas for computing these lines are given in Figure 11-9. Figure 11-10 shows the completed formulas for the example in Figure 11-8. Notice that the A_2 and D_4 table values come from the Factor for Control Limits

FIGURE 11-7 $\bar{x}$ and R Chart

table in the lower-right corner of Figure 11-10. These table values provide estimates for the three standard deviation limits for the $\bar{x}$ and R charts (when combined with R-bar [the mean of the R values]). You also may notice that no formula is given for the lower limit of the R chart. This is because the lower limit of R is zero for sample sizes less than or equal to six. For sample sizes greater than six, D_3 values must be used from Table A-1 in the appendix (the formula for the lower control limit is shown in Table A-1). Notice that we have superimposed the control limits computed in Figure 11-10 on the charts in Figure 11-8.

Interpreting Control Charts

Before introducing other types of process charts, we discuss the interpretation of the charts. Figure 11-11 shows several different signals for concern that are sent by a control chart, as shown in the second and third boxes. When a point is found to be outside of the control limits, we call this an "out-of-control situation." When a process is out of control, variation is probably no longer random. If there are three standard deviation limits, the chance of a sample average or range being out of control when the process is stable is less than 1%. Because this

FIGURE 11-8 Completed $\bar{x}$ and R Chart

probability is so small, we conclude that this was a nonrandom event and search for an assignable cause of variability.

Figure 11-11 presents examples of where nonrandom situations occur. You need not only have an out-of-control situation to signal that a process is no longer random. Two points in succession farther than two standard deviations from the mean likely will be a nonrandom event because the chances of it happening at random are very low. Five points in succession (either all above or below the center line) are called a *process run*, which means that the process has shifted. Seven points that are all either increasing or decreasing result in *process drift*. Process drift usually means that either materials or machines are drifting out of alignment. An example might be a saw blade that is wearing out rapidly in a furniture factory. Large jumps of more than three or four standard deviations result in *erratic behavior*. In all these cases, process charts help us to understand when the process is or is not in control.

If a process loses control and becomes nonrandom, the process should be stopped immediately. In many modern process industries where lean is used, this will result in the stoppage of several workstations. The team of workers who are to address the problem should use a control planning structured problem-solving process using brainstorming and cause-and-effect tools

Control Limits
Subgroups included _____   _____

$\bar{R} = \dfrac{\Sigma R}{k} =$ ——————— = ———

$\bar{\bar{X}} = \dfrac{\Sigma \bar{x}}{k} =$ ——————— = ———

or

$\bar{x}$ (Midspec or std) =

$A_2\bar{R} =$ ×   = ———

$UCL_{\bar{x}} = \bar{\bar{X}} + A_2\bar{R}$ =

$LCL_{\bar{x}} = \bar{\bar{X}} - A_2\bar{R}$ =

$UCL_{\bar{R}} = D_4\bar{R} =$ ×   =

Limits for Individuals
Compare with specification or tolerance limits

$\bar{\bar{X}}$ =

$\dfrac{3}{d_2}\bar{R} =$ ×   = ———

$UL_x = \bar{x} + \dfrac{3}{d_2}\bar{R}$ =

$LL_x = \bar{x} - \dfrac{3}{d_2}\bar{R}$ =

US   =

LS   = ———

US − LS   =

$6\sigma = \dfrac{6}{d_2}\bar{R}$ =

Modified Control Limits for Averages
Based on specification limits and process capability
Applicable only if   US − LS > 6σ

US   =   LS   =

$A_m\bar{R} =$ ×   = ——— $A_m\bar{R}$ = ———

$URL_{\bar{x}} = US - A_m\bar{R}$ = $LRL_{\bar{x}} = LS + A_m\bar{R}$ =

Factors for Control Limits

n	A_2	D_4	d_2	$\frac{3}{d_2}$	A_m
2	1.880	3.268	1.128	2.659	0.779
3	1.023	2.574	1.693	1.722	0.749
4	0.729	2.282	2.059	1.457	0.728
5	0.577	2.114	2.326	1.290	0.713
6	0.483	2.004	2.534	1.184	0.701

FIGURE 11-9 $\bar{x}$ and R Chart Calculation Work Sheet

Control Limits
Subgroups included _____   _____

$\bar{R} = \dfrac{\Sigma R}{k} = \dfrac{217}{25} = 8.68$ ———

$\bar{\bar{X}} = \dfrac{\Sigma \bar{x}}{k} = \dfrac{731.25}{25} = 29.25$ ———

or

$\bar{x}$ (Midspec or std) =

$A_2\bar{R} = .729 \times 8.68 = \underline{6.328}$

$UCL_{\bar{x}} = \bar{\bar{X}} + A_2\bar{R}$ 29.25+6.328 = 35.578

$LCL_{\bar{x}} = \bar{\bar{X}} - A_2\bar{R}$ 29.25-6.328 = 22.922

$UCL_{\bar{R}} = D_4\bar{R} = 2.282 \times 8.68 = 19.808$

Limits for Individuals
Compare with specification or tolerance limits

$\bar{\bar{X}}$ =

$\dfrac{3}{d_2}\bar{R} =$ ×   = ———

$UL_x = \bar{x} + \dfrac{3}{d_2}\bar{R}$ =

$LL_x = \bar{x} - \dfrac{3}{d_2}\bar{R}$ =

US   =

LS   = ———

US − LS   =

$6\sigma = \dfrac{6}{d_2}\bar{R}$ =

Modified Control Limits for Averages
Based on specification limits and process capability
Applicable only if   US − LS > 6σ

US   =   LS   =

$A_m\bar{R} =$ ×   = ——— $A_m\bar{R}$ = ———

$URL_{\bar{x}} = US - A_m\bar{R}$ = $LRL_{\bar{x}} = LS + A_m\bar{R}$ =

Factors for Control Limits

n	A_2	D_4	d_2	$\frac{3}{d_2}$	A_m
2	1.880	3.268	1.128	2.659	0.779
3	1.023	2.574	1.693	1.722	0.749
4	(0.729)	(2.282)	2.059	1.457	0.728
5	0.577	2.114	2.326	1.290	0.713
6	0.483	2.004	2.534	1.184	0.701

FIGURE 11-10 Calculation Work Sheet for Figure 11-8 Data

Normal behavior.

One data point out, above. Investigate for cause of poor performance.

One data point out, below. Investigate for cause of improvement.

Two data points near upper limit (beyond 2 standard deviations from the mean). Investigate for cause of poor performance.

Two data points near lower limit (beyond 2 standard deviations from the mean). Investigate for cause of improvement.

Five successive data points above central line. Investigate for cause of sustained poor performance.

Five successive data points below central line. Investigate for cause of sustained below-mean performance.

Seven successive data points on increasing or decreasing line. Investigate for cause of progressive change.

Erratic behavior. Investigate.

Sudden change in level. Investigate.

UCL = Upper control limit
CL = Center line
LCL = Lower control limit

FIGURE 11-11 Control Chart Evidence for Investigation *Source:* Hansen, Bertrand L. *Quality Control: Theory and Applications.* Upper Saddle River, NJ: Pearson Education (1964). ISBN: 013745208X. ©1964, p.65. Reprinted and Electronically reproduced by permission of Pearson Education, Inc., New York, NY.

such as those discussed in Chapter 10 to identify the root cause of the out-of-control situation. Typically, the cause is somewhere in the interaction among processes, materials, machinery, or labor. Once the assignable cause of variation has been discovered, corrective action can be taken to eliminate the cause. The process is then restarted, and people return to work.

The cause of the problem should be documented and discussed later during the weekly departmental meeting. All workers should know why a problem in the process occurred. They should understand the causes and the corrective actions that were taken to solve the problem.

Production companies that embark on this level of delegation of authority and development of employees find the transition difficult because the process is often stopped, and work is interrupted. However, as time passes, the processes become more stable as causes of errors are detected and eliminated. One manufacturer regularly produced poor-quality material that needed to be scrapped. As a result, it had increased its master production schedules by 20% to cover up this problem. The company decided instead to embark on a lot-size reduction program coupled with giving the workers line-stop authority. During the first shift, the company reduced the number of scrapped pieces from an average of more than 1,000 to 6! At first, production suffered. However, within two weeks of implementation, output volume had increased by more than 30%. This was the result of less rework, scrap, and other problems because of poor quality. It is interesting to note that staff and machinery were not changed during this period. At first, management thought its workers were unmotivated, resulting in the poor work. It wasn't the people; it was the process and the management.

Excel File: Example 11-1

Day	x				Means	Ranges
1	6	6	5	7	6	2
2	8	6	6	7	6.75	2
3	7	6	6	6	6.25	1
4	6	7	5	4	5.5	3

Control Limits

Subgroups included _____ _____

$\bar{R} = \dfrac{\Sigma R}{k} = \dfrac{8}{4} = 2$ ___

$\bar{\bar{X}} = \dfrac{\Sigma \bar{x}}{k} = \dfrac{24.5}{4} = 6.125$ ___

or

$\bar{x}$ (Midspec or std) =

$A_2\bar{R} = .729 \times 2 = \underline{1.458}$

$UCL_{\bar{x}} = \bar{\bar{X}} + A_2\bar{R} = 7.583$

$LCL_{\bar{x}} = \bar{\bar{X}} - A_2\bar{R} = 4.667$

$UCL_{\bar{R}} = D_4\bar{R} = 2.282 \times 2 = 4.564$

Limits for Individuals

Compare with specification or tolerance limits

$\bar{\bar{X}}$ =

$\dfrac{3}{d_2}\bar{R} = \quad \times \quad =$ ___

$UL_x = \bar{x} + \dfrac{3}{d_2}\bar{R} =$

$LL_x = \bar{x} - \dfrac{3}{d_2}\bar{R} =$

US =

LS = ___

US − LS =

$6\sigma = \dfrac{6}{d_2}\bar{R} =$

Modified Control Limits for Averages

Based on specification limits and process capability

Applicable only if   US − LS > 6σ

US = ___   LS = ___

$A_m\bar{R} = \quad \times \quad = \underline{\quad}$ $A_m\bar{R} = \underline{\quad}$

$URL_{\bar{x}} = US - A_m\bar{R} =$ $LRL_{\bar{x}} = LS + A_m\bar{R} =$

Factors for Control Limits

n	A_2	D_4	d_2	$\dfrac{3}{d_2}$	A_m
2	1.880	3.268	1.128	2.659	0.779
3	1.023	2.574	1.693	1.722	0.749
4	0.729	2.282	2.059	1.457	0.728
5	0.577	2.114	2.326	1.290	0.713
6	0.483	2.004	2.534	1.184	0.701

FIGURE 11-12 Calculation Work Sheet and $\bar{x}$ Chart

EXAMPLE 11-1 Using $\bar{x}$ and R Charts

Active Model: Example 11-1

Problem: The Sampson Company produces high-tech radar that is used in top-secret weapons by the Secret Service and the Green Berets. It has had trouble with a particular round component with a target of 6 centimeters. Samples of size 4 were taken during four successive days. The results are in the following table.

Solution: The grand mean is 6.125. $\bar{R}$ is 2.

Develop a process chart to determine whether the process is stable. Because these are measurements, use $\bar{x}$ and R charts. Using the calculation work sheet, Figure 11-12 shows the values for the process control limits.

The $\bar{x}$ control chart for this problem is shown with the appropriate limits. The R chart is also in control. The sample averages were placed on the control chart, and the process was found to be historically in control. Because the averages and ranges fall within the control limits, and no other signals of nonrandom activity are present, we conclude that the process variation is random. Note that this example is very simple. Generally, you use 15 to 20 subgroups to establish control charts.

Using Excel to Draw $\bar{x}$ and R Charts

The problem in EXAMPLE 11-1 can be solved easily using Excel. Although there are more elegant ways to develop control charts in Excel,[1] we will demonstrate a simple "brute force" method for creating $\bar{x}$ and R charts in Excel.

As you can see in Figure 11-13, we place the data in rows. From this we compute averages ($\bar{x}$s), Rs, and $\bar{R}$. Using these data, the center line (CL), upper limits (UCL), and lower limits (LCL) are computed. Figure 11-13 provides all the needed equations. Try doing this for yourself.

FIGURE 11-13 Example 11-1 Using Excel.
Source: Microsoft Excel, Microsoft Corporation. Used by permission.

---

[1] There are several software packages and Excel add-ins that create control charts. A good place to find free Excel control chart templates is www.freequality.org or on www.pearsonglobaleditions.com/foster.

X and Moving Range (*MR*) Charts for Population Data

At times it may not be possible to draw samples because a process is so slow that only one or two units per day are produced. If you have a variable measurement that you want to monitor, the *X* and *MR* charts might just be the thing for you.

Important caveats are associated with the *X* and *MR* charts. Because you will not be sampling, the central limit theorem does not apply, which may result in the data being non-normally distributed and an increase in the likelihood that you will draw an erroneous conclusion using a process chart. Therefore, it is best to first make sure that the data are normally distributed.

If data are not normally distributed, other charts are available. A *g* chart is used when data are geometrically distributed, and *h* charts are useful when data are hypergeometrically distributed. In statistics, an *X* is an individual observation from a population. Therefore, the **X chart** reflects a population distribution. We call the three standard deviation limits in an *X* chart the *natural variation* in a process. This natural variation can be compared with specification limits. So, strictly speaking, *X chart limits are not control limits; they are natural limits.*

The formula for the center line and the natural limits for an *X* chart is as follows:

$$\bar{x} \pm E_2(\overline{MR}) \tag{11.1}$$

where

$$\bar{x} = \frac{\Sigma X}{k}$$

and

X = a population value

k = the number of values used to compute $\bar{x}$

$E_2 = 2.66$ ($n = 2$) (see Table A-1 in the Appendix)

The formula for the *MR* chart is similar to that for the *R* chart (where $n = 2$), except that the ranges are computed as the differences from one sample to the next [$n = 2$; UCL $= D_4(\overline{MR})$; LCL $= 0$].

EXAMPLE 11-2   *X* and *MR* Charts in Action

Active Model:
Example 11-2

Excel File:
Example 11-2

Problem: The EA Trucking Company of Columbia, Missouri, hauls corn from local fields to the SL Processing Plant in Lincoln, Nebraska. Although the trucks generally take 6.5 hours to make the daily trip, recently there seems to be more variability in the arrival times. Mr. Everett, the owner, suspects that one of his drivers, Paul, may be visiting his girlfriend Janice en route in Kansas City. The driver claims that this is not the case and that the increase is simply random variation because of variability in traffic flows. The drivers keep written logs of departure and arrival times. Mr. Everett has listed these times in the following table. You are chosen as the analyst to investigate this situation. What do you think?

Date	Travel Times (Hrs.)	Moving Range
1	6.4	—
2	6.2	0.2
3	5.8	0.4
4	7.3	1.5
5	8.6	1.3
6	6.0	2.6
7	6.5	0.5

Date	Travel Times (Hrs.)	Moving Range
8	6.3	0.2
9	7.2	0.9
10	7.3	0.1
11	7.5	0.2
12	7.2	0.3
13	8.0	0.8
14	7.8	0.2
15	8.2	0.4
16	7.0	1.2
17	7.8	0.8
	$\bar{x} = 7.1235$	$\overline{MR} = .725$

Solution: You decide to develop an X and MR process chart to test the hypothesis concerning the change. You conclude that, in fact, a run (from point 9 to point 15) indicates that trip times may be increasing. However, this does not imply that the girlfriend is the cause. Further investigation may be needed. (Note that $E_2 = 2.66$ and $D_4 = 3.268$.)

Using Excel to Draw X and MR Charts

The problem in Example 11-2 is now solved using Excel. Again, we use the "brute force" method for creating X and MR charts in Excel. The process is very similar to what we did before. Notice that E_2 and D_4 are both constants.

Interpreting the charts, there is a run on the X chart and an out-of-control point on the sixth (fifth observation in the graph because there was no moving range for the first). This was because of the jump from 8.6 hours down to 6 hours. It might be that our hero thought he should be on better behavior after the long day on the fifth (see Figure 11-14).

FIGURE 11-14   Example 11-2 Using Excel.   *Source:* Microsoft Excel, Microsoft Corporation. Used by permission.

TABLE 11-2	Median Chart Values	
n	$\tilde{A}_2$	D_4
3	1.187	2.575
5	0.691	2.115
7	0.508	1.924
9	0.412	1.816

Median Charts

Although $\bar{x}$ charts generally are preferred for variables data, sometimes it is too time consuming or inconvenient to compute subgroup averages. Also, there may be concerns about the accuracy of computed means. In these cases, a **median chart** may be used (aka an $\tilde{x}$ chart). The main limitation is that you will use an odd sample size to avoid calculating the median. Generally, sample sizes are 3, 5, or 7. Like the $\bar{x}$ chart, small sample sizes generally are used, although the larger the sample size, the better is the sensitivity of the chart as a tool to detect nonrandom (special cause) events (this is also true for $\bar{x}$ charts).

To prepare median charts, determine your subgroup size and how often you will sample. The rule of thumb to establish a median control chart is to use 20 to 25 subgroups and a total of at least 100 individual measurements.

Equations for computing the control limits are

$$\text{Mean of medians} = \text{sum of the medians/number of medians} = \overline{\overline{x}} \qquad (11.2)$$

$$\text{LCL}_{\tilde{x}} = \overline{\overline{x}} + \tilde{A}_2 \overline{R} \qquad (11.3)$$

$$\text{UCL}_{\tilde{x}} = \overline{\overline{x}} - \tilde{A}_2 \overline{R} \qquad (11.4)$$

$\tilde{A}_2$ values are found in Table 11-2. Median charts are usually used with R charts.

EXAMPLE 11-3   **Median Charts in Action**

Active Model:
Example 11-3

Excel File:
Example 11-3

Problem: The Luftig food company has gathered the following data with weights of its new health food product. Because the published weight on the package is 6 ounces, Mr. Luftig wants to know if the company is complying with weight requirements. Twenty samples of size 5 were drawn.

Solution: The data are given here. Twenty samples of size 5 were drawn. Results show that the process is not in control, with an average median of 6.23. The median process chart (see Figure 11-15) does show that some product is being made that is below 6 ounces. It also shows that points 4, 7, and 10 are out of control.

Sample	Observation 1	Observation 2	Observation 3	Observation 4	Observation 5
1	6.2	6.1	6.3	6.5	6.4
2	6.2	6.2	6.2	6.3	6.4
3	6.3	5.9	6.2	6.4	6.3
4	5.3	5.1	5.3	5.1	5.3
5	6.1	6.6	6.3	6.2	6.4
6	6.2	6.2	6.2	6.2	6.2
7	5.8	5.7	5.9	7.2	5.2

Sample	Observation 1	Observation 2	Observation 3	Observation 4	Observation 5
8	6.3	5.9	6.2	6.4	6.3
9	6.3	5.9	6.2	6.4	6.3
10	7.4	7.4	7.1	7.3	7.1
11	6.2	6.3	6.2	6.3	6.2
12	6.4	6.3	6.2	6.1	6.1
13	6.3	6.4	6.2	6.3	6.1
14	6.1	6.1	6.1	6.1	6.1
15	6.3	6.4	6.1	6.3	6.1
16	6.4	6.2	6.4	6.2	6.2
17	6.2	6.4	6.3	6.4	6.2
18	6.1	6.2	6.3	6.4	6.5
19	6.2	6.1	6.1	6.1	6.1
20	6.4	6.3	6.2	6.5	6.3

FIGURE 11-15 Example 11-3 Using Excel. *Source:* Microsoft Excel, Microsoft Corporation. Used by permission.

Using Excel to Draw Median Charts

Figure 11-15 shows the results for Example 11-3. Again, the columns are ordered such that the data can be grouped properly and drawn using Excel. Excel makes creation of the chart quick and easy. You will have the best results if you start with Example 11-1 and work all the Excel examples. By now, you should have the hang of it. A good shortcut is to highlight the data in columns B through F prior to invoking the Chart function.

x̄ and s Charts

When you are particularly concerned about the dispersion of the process, it might be that the R chart is not sufficiently precise. In this case, the $\bar{x}$ chart is recommended in concert with the s **chart or standard deviation chart**. The standard deviation chart is often used where variation in a process is small. For example, s charts are often used in monitoring the production of silicon chips for computers.

Unfortunately, when using the s chart, because we do not compute ranges, new formulas are used to compute the $\bar{x}$ limits. We introduce the formulas for the $\bar{x}$ and s charts because of their importance for high-tech production.

The control limits for the s chart are computed using these formulas:

$$\text{UCL}_s = B_4 \times \bar{s} \tag{11.5}$$

$$\text{LCL}_s = B_3 \times \bar{s} \tag{11.6}$$

where

B_3 and B_4 come from Table 11-3;

and

$$\bar{s} = \Sigma s_i / k \tag{11.7}$$

where

s_i is the standard deviation for sample i

k is the number of samples.

Note that it is easy to find the sample standard deviation in Excel. If you don't have Excel, use the usual formulas for computing the sample standard deviations. We will show you how to do this in Excel in Example 11-4.

After computing the limits, plot your sample means to see if the process is in control. If the s chart is not in control, determine the cause for the out-of-control point, eliminate the cause, and then recompute your control limits by throwing out the out-of-control data point(s). Do not eliminate samples with out-of-control points if a cause cannot be identified.

When your s chart is in statistical control, use the following formula to estimate the process standard deviation:

$$\sigma_{\text{est}} = \bar{s} \times \sqrt{(1 - C_4^2)/C_4} \tag{11.8}$$

where

C_4 can be found in Table 11-3.

Formulas for the $\bar{x}$ chart can now be created using the following formulas:

$$\text{UCL}_{\bar{\bar{x}}} = \bar{x} + A_3(\bar{s}) \tag{11.9}$$

$$\text{LCL}_{\bar{\bar{x}}} = \bar{x} - A_3(\bar{s}) \tag{11.10}$$

where

A_3 can be found in Table 11-3 and $\bar{\bar{x}}$ is the grand mean.

TABLE 11-3 Values for $\bar{x}$ and s Charts

n	B₃	B₄	C₄	A₃
2	0	3.267	0.7979	2.659
3	0	2.568	0.8862	1.954
4	0	2.266	0.9213	1.628
5	0	2.089	0.9400	1.427
6	0.030	1.970	0.9515	1.287
7	0.118	1.882	0.9594	1.182
8	0.185	1.815	0.9650	1.099
9	0.239	1.761	0.9693	1.032

EXAMPLE 11-4 $\bar{x}$ and s Charts in Action

Problem: Twenty samples were taken for a milled rod. The diameters are needed to determine whether the process is in control. Because these milled rods must be measured within 1/10,000 of an inch, it is determined that the process dispersion is important. Therefore, you need to use an s and $\bar{x}$ chart to monitor the process. The data are found in Figure 11-16. We have 20 samples with $n = 3$.

Active Model:
Example 11-4

FIGURE 11-16
Example 11-4 Using Excel. *Source:* Microsoft Excel, Microsoft Corporation. Used by permission.

Solution: The control charts in Figure 11-16 show that the process is in control. There is no need for corrective action. The solution method is demonstrated in the next section.

Excel File:
Example 11-4

Using Excel to Draw $\bar{x}$ and s Charts

Figure 11-16 shows the solution method for Example 11-4. Using the preceding formulas, we computed the CL, UCL, and LCL for each chart. Notice that the LCL for the s chart is zero. Also, notice that we have taken some shortcuts (What short cuts?) here compared with some of the other charts we have drawn.

Other Control Charts

Table 11-4 shows all the formulas for the process charts we have discussed in this chapter. These are the major charts that are used the vast majority of times. Some other charts that are used more rarely should be mentioned.

Moving Average Chart

The moving average chart is an interesting chart used for monitoring variables and measurement on a continuous scale. This chart uses past information to predict what the next process outcome will be. Using this chart, we can adjust a process in anticipation of its going out of control.

Chart	LCL	CL	UCL	Constant Values
$\bar{x}$	$\bar{\bar{x}} - A_2\bar{R}$	$\bar{\bar{x}}$	$\bar{\bar{x}} + A_2\bar{R}$	(Appendix Table A-1)
R	$D_3\bar{R}$	$\bar{R}$	$D_4\bar{R}$	(Appendix Table A-1)
X	$\bar{\bar{x}} - E_2(\overline{MR})$	$\bar{\bar{x}}$	$\bar{\bar{x}} + E_2(\overline{MR})$	(Appendix Table A-1)
Median	$\bar{\bar{\tilde{x}}} - \tilde{A}_2\bar{R}$	$\bar{\tilde{x}}$	$\bar{\bar{\tilde{x}}} + \tilde{A}_2\bar{R}$	(Appendix Table A-4)
$\bar{x}$ (with s)	$\bar{\bar{x}} - A_3\bar{s}$	$\bar{\bar{x}}$	$\bar{\bar{x}} + A_3\bar{s}$	(Appendix Table A-3)
s	$B_3\bar{s}$	$\bar{s}$	$B_4\bar{s}$	(Appendix Table A-3)

TABLE 11-4 Summary of Variables Chart Formulas

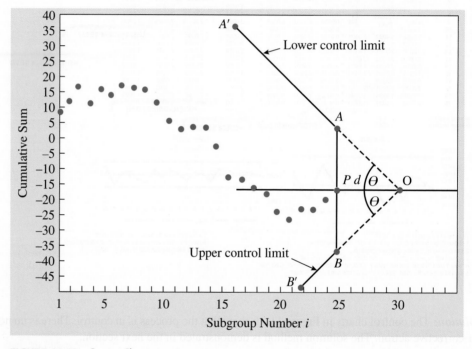

FIGURE 11-17 Cusum Chart

Cusum Chart

The cumulative sum, or cusum, chart is used to identify slight but sustained shifts in a universe in which there is no independence between observations. A cusum chart looks very different from a Shewhart process chart, as shown in Figure 11-17.

SOME CONTROL CHART CONCEPTS FOR VARIABLES

Choosing the Correct Variables Control Chart

Now that we have developed control charts, we are in a position to discuss briefly some important control chart concepts before moving to process capability. The first concept has to do with choosing the correct chart. Obviously, it is key to choose the correct control chart. Figure 11-18 shows a decision tree for the basic control charts. This flowchart helps to show when certain charts should be selected for use.

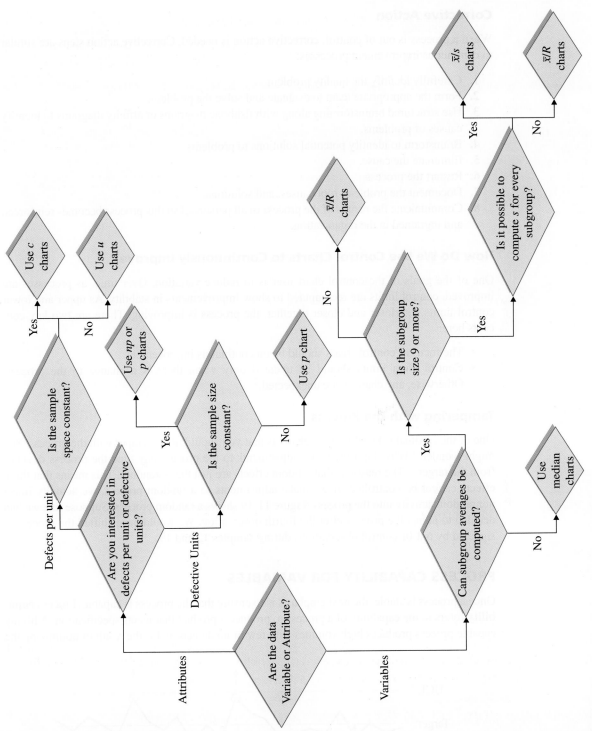

FIGURE 11-18 Process for Selecting the Right Chart

Corrective Action

When a process is out of control, corrective action is needed. Corrective action steps are similar to continuous improvement processes:

1. Carefully identify the quality problem.
2. Form the appropriate team to evaluate and solve the problem.
3. Use structured brainstorming along with fishbone diagrams or affinity diagrams to identify causes of problems.
4. Brainstorm to identify potential solutions to problems.
5. Eliminate the cause.
6. Restart the process.
7. Document the problem, root causes, and solutions.
8. Communicate the results of the process to all personnel so this process becomes reinforced and ingrained in the organization.

How Do We Use Control Charts to Continuously Improve?

One of the goals of the control chart user is to reduce variation. Over time, as processes are improved, control limits are recomputed to show improvements in stability. As upper and lower control limits get closer and closer together, the process is improving. There are two key concepts here:

- The focus of control charts should be on continuous improvement.
- Control chart limits should be updated only when there is a change to the process. Otherwise, any changes are unexpected.[2]

Tampering with the Process

One of the cardinal rules of process charts is that you should never tamper with the process. You might wonder, "Why don't we make adjustments to the process any time the process deviates from the target?" The reason is that random effects are just that—random. This means that these effects cannot be controlled. If we make adjustments to a random process, we actually inject nonrandom activity into the process. Figure 11-19 shows a random process. Suppose that we had decided to adjust the process after the fourth observation. We would have shifted the process—signaled by out-of-control observations during samples 12 and 19.

PROCESS CAPABILITY FOR VARIABLES

Once a process is stable, the next emphasis is to ensure that the process is capable. Process **capability** refers to the capability of a process to produce a product that meets specification. A highly capable process produces high volumes with few or no defects and is the result of optimizing the

FIGURE 11-19 The Effects of Tampering

---

[2] Wheeler, D., "When Do I Recalculate My Limits?" *Quality Progress* (May 1996): 79–80.

interactions between people, machines, raw materials, procedures, and measurement systems. World-class levels of process capability are measured by parts per million (ppm) defect levels, which means that for every million pieces produced, only a small number (fewer than 100) are defective. A Closer Look at Quality 11-1 looks at the need for capability in software.

Video Clip:
Process Capability

A CLOSER LOOK AT QUALITY 11-1   A Justification for Meeting Standards in Software Quality[3]

In this chapter, we discuss the importance of meeting standards and having controlled processes. We see all around us the results of poor quality and defects. Among the areas where this is important is software quality. Consider the following examples.

Poor software design in a radiation machine, known as Therac-25, contributed to the deaths of three cancer patients. The Therac-25 was built by Atomic Energy of Canada Ltd., which is a Crown corporation of the government of Canada. In 1988, the company incorporated and sold its radiation-systems assets under the Theratronics brand. According to Nancy Leveson, now a professor at MIT, the design flaws included the incapability of the software to handle some of the data it was given and the delivery of hard-to-decipher user messages.

During Operation Desert Storm, an Iraqi Scud missile hit a U.S. Army barracks in Saudi Arabia, killing 28 Americans. The approach of the Scud should have been noticed by a Patriot missile battery. A subsequent government investigation found a flaw in the Patriot's weapons-control software that prevented the system from properly tracking the incoming missile.

During Operation Iraqi Freedom, the Patriot missile system mistakenly downed a British Tornado fighter and (according to the *Los Angeles Times* an American F/A-18c Hornet). Reports show that investigators were looking at a glitch in the missile's radar system that made it incapable of properly distinguishing between a friendly aircraft and an enemy missile.

In 2002, the Food and Drug Administration (FDA), which oversees medical-device software, said that of 3,140 medical-device recalls, 242 were attributed to software failures. The FDA also says that the number of software-related recalls may be underreported because it is often hard to determine the exact cause of a problem in the immediate aftermath of an accident.

It is expected that these types of losses are likely to mount as complex software programs are tied across networks. Imagine all the various pieces of corporate data that come together in systems for CRMSs, SCMs, or ERPs. "Software is the most complicated thing that the human mind can come up with and build," says Gary McGraw, the chief technology officer at Citigal, a consulting firm specializing in improving software quality. Tools introduced in this chapter will be key for detecting whether future software is functioning properly.

---

[3] Gage, D., and J. McCormick, "Why Software Quality Matters," *Baseline* 28 (March 2004): 34–59.

Six Sigma programs, such as those pioneered by Motorola Corporation, result in highly capable processes. Six Sigma is a design program that emphasizes engineering parts so that they are highly capable. As shown in Figure 11-20, these processes are characterized by specifications that are ±6 standard deviations from the process mean. This means that even large shifts in the process mean and dispersion will not result in defective products being built. If a process average is on the center line, a Six Sigma process will result in an average of only 3.4 opportunities for defects per million units produced. The Taguchi method is a valuable tool for achieving Six Sigma quality by helping to develop robust designs that are insensitive to variation.

Population versus Sampling Distributions

To understand process capability, we must first understand the differences between population and sampling distributions. *Population distributions* are distributions with all individual

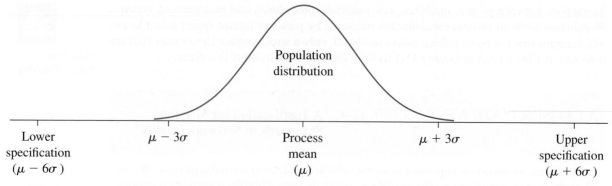

| Lower specification $(\mu - 6\sigma)$ | $\mu - 3\sigma$ | Process mean (μ) | $\mu + 3\sigma$ | Upper specification $(\mu + 6\sigma)$ |

FIGURE 11-20 Six Sigma Quality

responses from an entire population. A *population* is defined as a collection of all the items or observations of interest to a decision maker. A **sample** is a subset of the population. *Sampling distributions* are distributions that reflect the distribution of sample means. We can demonstrate the difference between a sample and a population. Suppose that you want to understand whether a product conforms to specifications. Over a month's time, a firm produces 10,000 units of product to stock. Because the product is fragile, it is not feasible to inspect all 10,000 units and risk damaging some of the product in the inspection process. Therefore, 500 units are randomly selected from the 10,000 to inspect. In this example, the population size N is 10,000 and the sample size n is 500.

We now demonstrate the difference between a sampling distribution and a population distribution. Understanding the differences between sampling and population distributions is important: Population distributions have much more dispersion than sampling distributions. Consider a class of 40 students, in which the tallest student is 6 feet 4 inches, and the shortest is 5 feet in height. As shown in Figure 11-21, student height for this population is normally distributed, with a mean of 5 feet 8 inches and a distribution ranging from 5 feet to 6 feet 4 inches.

Now suppose that you draw samples of size five from the population (with replacement). Notice in Figure 11-21 that the mean of the sample is still 5 feet 8 inches, but the distribution ranges only from 5 feet 4 inches to 6 feet. This is so because it is difficult to randomly obtain a sample average that is more than 6 feet or less than 5 feet 4 inches. As a result, we see that sampling distributions have much less dispersion than population distributions.

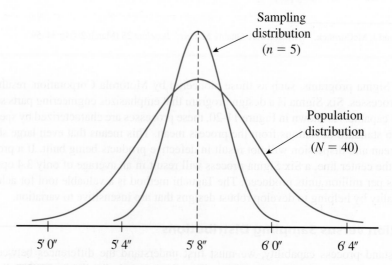

| 5' 0" | 5' 4" | 5' 8" | 6' 0" | 6' 4" |

FIGURE 11-21 Population and Sampling Distributions for Class Heights

In the context of quality, specifications and capability are associated with population distributions. However, sample-based process charts and stability are computed statistically and reflect sampling distributions. Therefore, *quality practitioners should not compare process chart limits with product specifications.* To compare process charts limits with specification limits is not so much like comparing apples to oranges as it is comparing apples to watermelons. We later show that process chart limits are statistically computed from sample data. Specification (or tolerance) limits are set by design engineers who establish limits based on the design requirements for a product. These design requirements might have to do with making parts fit together properly or with the properties of certain materials used in making products.

Capability Studies

Now that we have defined process capability, we can discuss how to determine whether a process is capable. That is, we want to know if individual products meet specifications. There are two purposes for performing process capability studies:

1. To determine whether a process consistently results in products that meet specifications.
2. To determine whether a process is in need of monitoring through the use of permanent process charts.

Process capability studies help process managers understand whether the range over which natural variation of a process occurs is the result of the system of common (or random) causes. There are five steps to perform process capability studies:

1. Select a critical operation. These may be bottlenecks, costly steps of the process, or places in the process in which problems have occurred in the past.
2. Take k samples of size n, where x is an individual observation.
   - Where $19 < k < 26$
   - If x is an attribute, $n > 50$ (as in the case of a binomial)
   - Or if x is a measurement, $1 < n < 11$
   (*Note*: Small sample sizes can lead to erroneous conclusions.)
3. Use a trial control chart to see whether the process is stable.
4. Compare process natural tolerance limits with specification limits. Note that natural tolerance limits are three standard deviation limits for the population distribution. This can be compared with the specification limits.
5. Compute capability indexes: To compute capability indexes, you compute an upper capability index (Cpu), a lower capability index (Cpl), and a capability index (**Cpk**). The formulas used to compute these are

$$\text{Cpu} = (\text{USL} - \mu)/3\hat{\sigma} \qquad (11.11)$$

$$\text{Cpl} = (\mu - \text{LSL})/3\hat{\sigma} \qquad (11.12)$$

$$\text{Cpk} = \min\{\text{Cpu, Cpl}\} \qquad (11.13)$$

where

USL = upper specification limit

LSL = lower specification limit

μ = computed population process mean

$\hat{\sigma}$ = Estimated process standard deviation = $\hat{\sigma} = R/d_2$ $\qquad (11.14)$

Make a decision concerning whether the process is capable. Although different firms use different benchmarks, the generally accepted benchmarks for process capability are 1.25, 1.33, and 2.0. *We will say that processes that achieve capability indexes (Cpk) of 1.25 are capable, 1.33 are highly capable, and 2.0 are world-class capable (Six Sigma).*

EXAMPLE 11-5 | Process Capability

Problem: For an overhead projector, the thickness of a component is specified to be between 30 and 40 millimeters. Thirty samples of components yielded a grand mean $(\bar{x})$ of 34 millimeters with a standard deviation $(\hat{\sigma})$ of 3.5. Calculate the process capability index by following the steps previously outlined. If the process is not highly capable, what proportion of product will not conform?

Solution:

$$Cpu = (40 - 34)/(3)(3.5) = .57$$

$$Cpl = (34 - 30)/(3)(3.5) = .38$$

$$Cpk = .38$$

The process capability in this case is poor. To compute the proportion of nonconforming product being produced, we use a Z table (Appendix A-2) with a standardized distribution. The formula is

$$Z = (x - \mu)/\hat{\sigma} \qquad (11.15)$$

Thus, for the lower end of the distribution:

$$Z = (30 - 34)/3.5 = -1.14$$

For the upper end of the distribution:

$$Z = (40 - 34)/3.5 = 1.71$$

Using a Z table (Table A-2 from the Appendix), the probability of producing bad product is $.1271 + .0436 = .1707$. This means that, on average, more than 17% of the product produced does not meet specification. This is unacceptable in almost any circumstance.

$.5 - .3729 = .1271$
$p = .3729$
$p = .4564$
$.5 - .4564 = .0436$

$\mu - 3\sigma = 23.5$ LSL = 30 $\mu = 34$ USL = 40 $\mu + 3\sigma = 44.5$
$(\mu - 1.140\sigma)$ $(\mu + 1.710\sigma)$

FIGURE 11-22 Proportion of Product Nonconforming for Example 11-5

Ppk

If your data are not arranged in subgroups, and you have only population data to compute your capability, use Ppk to compute your capability. **Ppk** stands for *population capability index*. Rather than using the within-groups variation to estimate the sigma that you used in Cpk, use the population standard deviation to compute your capability. Otherwise, the computations are the same as Cpk. Here are the formulas:

$$\text{Ppk} = \min\left\{\text{Ppu, Ppl}\right\} \qquad (11.16)$$

$$\text{Ppu} = (\text{USL} - \mu)/3\sigma \qquad (11.17)$$

$$\text{Ppl} = (\mu - \text{LSL})/3\sigma \qquad (11.18)$$

$$\sigma = \sqrt{\Sigma(x_i - \bar{x})^2/(n-1)} \qquad (11.19)$$

where

USL = upper specification limit

LSL = lower specification limit

μ = population mean

σ = population process standard deviation

Interpretation for Ppk is the same as for Cpk. The only difference is the use of population parameters when computing the indexes.

EXAMPLE 11-6   **Population Process Capability**

Problem: The upper and lower specification limits (tolerances) for a metal plate are 3 millimeters ±0.002 millimeters. A sample of 100 plates yielded a mean $\bar{x}$ of 3.001 millimeters. We know that the population standard deviation is .0002. Compute the Ppk for this product.
Solution:

$$\text{Ppu} = (3.002 - 3.001)/(.0002 \times 3) = 1.67$$

$$\text{Ppl} = (3.001 - 2.998)/(.0002 \times 3) = 5$$

$$\text{Ppk} = 1.67$$

Therefore, the process is highly capable.

The Difference between Capability and Stability

Once again, *a process is capable if individual products consistently meet specification. A process is stable if only common variation is present in the process.* This is an important distinction. It is possible to have a process that is stable but not capable. This would happen where random variation was very high. It is probably not so common that an incapable process would be stable.

OTHER STATISTICAL TECHNIQUES IN QUALITY MANAGEMENT

Throughout this chapter, we have focused on hypothesis testing and process charts. In Chapter 13 we discuss experimental design and off-line experimentation. Correlation and regression also can be useful tools for improving quality, particularly in services.

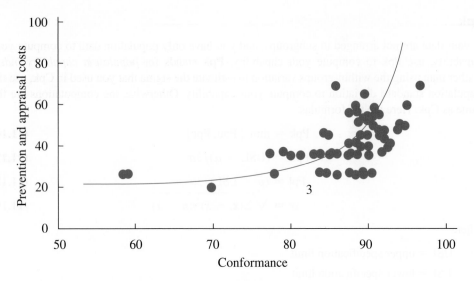

FIGURE 11-23 Plot of Prevention and Appraisal Costs with Conformance *Source:* Based on S. T. Foster, Quality Costs Working Paper.

TABLE 11-5	Relationship between Conformance and PA Costs	
Model	R^2	**p**
First order	0.4002	0.0001
Quadratic	0.4675	0.0001

Source: Based on S. T. Foster, "Quality Costs Working Paper."

Although it is almost never appropriate to use regression on process data used in developing control charts, other types of data can be correlated and regressed to understand the customer. For example, Figure 11-23 shows where conformance rates and quality costs were correlated in one company. As conformance increased, costs increased as well. Table 11-5 shows that these variables were significantly and positively related. The R^2 values show the strength of the relationships between the variables for linear and nonlinear (quadratic) models.[4]

Such correlation is called *interlinking*.[5] Interlinking is useful in helping to identify causal relationships between variables.

Summary

In this chapter we have introduced the basic process charts and the fundamentals of statistical quality improvement. The process for developing process charts is the same regardless of chart. Therefore, the things that are required are:

You need to know the generic process for developing charts.

You need to be able to interpret charts.

[4] To learn more about this, see Foster, S. T., "An Examination of the Relationship between Conformance and Quality-Related Costs." *International Journal of Quality and Reliability Management* 13, 4 (1996): 50–63.

[5] Collier, D., *The Service/Quality Solution* (Homewood, IL: Irwin, 1994).

You need to be able to choose which chart to use.

You need the formulas to derive the charts.

You need to understand the purposes and assumptions underlying the charts.

We have given you all these things for variables in this short chapter. You have everything you need to get started. Have fun and enjoy yourself. Remember that the purpose of process charts is to help you continually improve.

Key Terms

Attribute	Nonrandom variation	Random variation	Variable
Capability	Ppk	Reaction plan	X chart
Consumer's risk	Process charts	s chart or standard	$\bar{x}$ chart
Control chart	Producer's risk	deviation chart	
Control plan	Quality management	Sample	
Cpk	system (QMS)	Stability	
Median chart	R chart	Statistical thinking	

Discussion Questions

1. Discuss the concept of control. Is control helpful? Isn't being controlling a negative?
2. The concept of statistical thinking is an important theme in this chapter. What are some examples of statistical thinking?
3. Sometimes you do well on exams. Sometimes you have bad days. What are the assignable causes when you do poorly?
4. What is the relationship between statistical quality improvement and Deming's 14 points?
5. What are some applications of process charts in services? Could demerits (points off for mistakes) be charted? How?
6. What is random variation? Is it always uncontrollable?
7. When would you choose an *np* chart over a *p* chart? An *X* chart over an *x̄* chart? An *s* chart over an *R* chart?
8. Design a control chart to monitor the gas mileage in your car. Collect the data over time. What did you find?
9. What does "out-of-control" mean? Is it the same as a "bad hair day"?
10. Design a control chart to monitor the amounts of the most recently charged 50 debits from your debit card. What did you find?

Problems

1. Return to the chart in Figure 11-8. Is this process stable? Explain.
2. Return to the data in Figure 11-8. Is this process capable? Compute both Cpk and Ppk.
3. For the following product characteristics, choose where to inspect first:

Characteristic	Cost of Inspection	Cost of Failure
A	$2.50	$20
B	$2.00	$19
C	$4.00	$37
D	$3.00	$38

4. For the following product characteristics, choose where to inspect first:

Characteristic	Cost of Inspection	Cost of Failure
A	$75	$475
B	$90	$550
C	$60	$320
D	$65	$395

5. Interpret the following charts to determine whether the processes are stable.

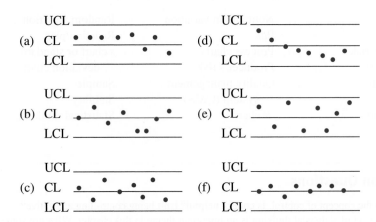

6. Interpret the following charts to determine whether the processes are stable.

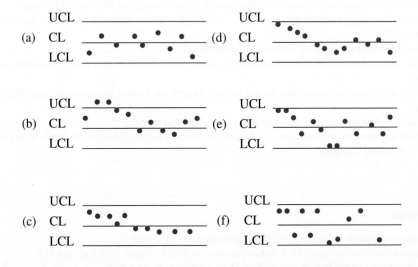

7. Tolerances for the inside diameter of an injection molded bottle cap are 20mm ± 0.5mm. When cooled, the bottle caps have an inside diameter mean of 20.31mm with a population standard deviation of 0.38mm. The process population is normally distributed.
   a. Is the process capable?
   b. If not, what proportion will meet specifications?
   c. Within what values will 99.5% of sample means of this process fall if the sample size is constant at 10 and the process is stable?

8. Specifications for a part are 62″ +/− .01.″ The part is constructed from a process with a mean of 62.01″ and a population standard deviation of .033. The process is normally distributed.
   a. Is the process capable?
   b. What proportion will meet specifications?
   c. Within what values will 95% of sample means of the process fall if the sample size is constant at 5 and the process is stable?

9. Tolerances for a bicycle derailleur are 6 cm +/− .001 cm. The current process produces derailleurs with a mean of 6.0001 with a population standard deviation of .0004. The process population is normally distributed.
   a. Is the process capable?
   b. If not, what proportion will meet specs?
   c. Within what values will 75% of sample means of this process fall if the sample size is 6 and the process is stable?

10. A services process is monitored using $\bar{x}$ and R charts. Eight samples of $n = 10$ observations have been gathered with the following results:

Sample	Mean	Range
1	4.2	.43
2	4.4	.52
3	3.6	.53
4	3.8	.20
5	4.9	.36
6	3.0	.42
7	4.2	.35
8	3.2	.42

   a. Using the data in the table, compute the center line, the upper control limit, and the lower control limit for the $\bar{x}$ and R charts.
   b. Is the process in control? Interpret the charts.
   c. If the next sample results in the following values (2.5, 5.5, 4.6, 3.2, 4.6, 3.2, 4.0, 4.0, 3.6, 4.2), will the process be in control?

11. A production process for the JMF Semicon is monitored using $\bar{x}$ and R charts. Ten samples of $n = 15$ observations have been gathered with the following results:

Sample	Mean	Range
1	251	29
2	258	45
3	233	36
4	275	25
5	234	35
6	289	20
7	256	3
8	265	19
9	246	14
10	323	46

   a. Develop a control chart and plot the means.
   b. Is the process in control? Explain.

12. *Experiment*: Randomly select the heights of at least 15 of the students in your class.
   a. Develop a control chart and plot the heights on the chart.
   b. Which chart should you use?
   c. Is this process in control?

13. A finishing process packages assemblies into boxes. You have noticed variability in the boxes and desire to improve the process to fix the problem because some products fit too tightly into the boxes and others fit too loosely. Following are width measurements for the boxes.

				Sample			
1	**2**	**3**	**4**	**5**	**6**	**7**	**8**
68.51	68.94	68.66	68.49	68.64	68.34	68.99	68.92
68.46	68.20	68.44	68.94	68.63	68.42	68.94	68.91
68.54	68.54	68.55	68.56	68.62	68.99	68.95	68.97
68.34	68.56	68.77	68.62	68.32	68.02	68.95	68.93
68.46	68.70	68.70	68.69	68.34	68.03	68.94	68.96
68.46	68.70	68.64	68.56	68.24	68.47	68.97	68.95

Using $\bar{x}$ and R charts, plot and interpret the process.

14. For the data in Problem 13, if the mean specification is $68.5 \pm .25$ and the estimated process standard deviation is .10, is the process capable? Compute Cpu, Cpl, and Cpk.

15. For the data in Problem 13, treat the data as if they were population data and find the limits for an X chart. Is the process in control? Compare your answer with the answers to Problem 14. *Hint*: Use the formula $CL_x = \bar{x} \pm (3/d_2)\bar{R}$ (Figure 11-9).

16. A sheet glass manufacturer produces standard 6mm thickness panes for double glazing windows. Following are thickness dimensions taken from samples during the production process.

Sample	x1	x2	x3	x4	x5
1	6.45	6.12	6.03	5.89	5.92
2	5.76	6.23	6.05	6.32	5.89
3	6.11	6.15	5.93	6.21	5.96
4	5.74	6.03	6.02	6.2	6.04
5	6.35	6.07	5.88	5.93	6.06

Use $\bar{x}$ and R charts to determine if the process is in control.

17. Using the data from Problem 13, compute the limits for $\bar{x}$ and s charts. Is the process still in control?

18. Using the data from Problem 16, compute the limits for $\bar{x}$ and s charts. Is the process still in control?

19. Use a median chart to determine whether the process for the following data is centered.

Sample	Observation 1	Observation 2	Observation 3	Observation 4	Observation 5
1	8.06	7.93	8.19	8.45	8.32
2	8.06	8.06	8.06	8.19	8.32
3	8.19	7.67	8.06	8.32	8.19
4	6.89	6.63	6.89	6.63	6.89
5	7.93	8.58	8.19	8.06	8.32
6	8.06	8.06	8.06	8.06	8.06
7	7.54	7.41	7.67	9.36	6.76
8	8.19	7.67	8.06	8.32	8.19
9	8.19	7.67	8.06	8.32	8.19
10	9.62	9.62	9.23	9.49	9.23
11	8.06	8.19	8.06	8.19	8.06
12	8.32	8.19	8.06	7.93	7.93
13	8.19	8.32	8.06	8.19	7.93
14	7.93	7.93	7.93	7.93	7.93
15	8.19	8.32	7.93	8.19	7.93
16	8.32	8.06	8.32	8.06	8.06
17	8.06	8.32	8.19	8.32	8.06
18	7.93	8.06	8.19	8.32	8.45
19	8.06	7.93	7.93	7.93	7.93
20	8.32	8.19	8.06	8.45	8.19

20. Use an $\bar{x}$ chart to determine whether the data in Problem 19 are in control. Do you get the same answer?

21. The following data are for a component used in the space shuttle. Because the process dispersion is closely monitored, use an $\bar{x}$ and s chart to see whether the process is in control.

Sample	Observation 1	Observation 2	Observation 3
1	4.8000	4.7995	4.8005
2	4.7995	4.8007	4.8005
3	4.7995	4.8002	4.8012
4	4.7993	4.8000	4.8010
5	4.8007	4.8007	4.8005
6	4.8010	4.8007	4.8000
7	4.7995	4.7995	4.7995
8	4.8000	4.8002	4.8002
9	4.8012	4.8000	4.7998
10	4.7988	4.7995	4.8002
11	4.8005	4.7998	4.8002
12	4.8005	4.7995	4.8012
13	4.8000	4.8002	4.7995
14	4.8000	4.8005	4.8010
15	4.7986	4.8002	4.7990
16	4.7998	4.8007	4.7983
17	4.8005	4.7995	4.8010
18	4.8000	4.8002	4.8002
19	4.7993	4.7986	4.7995
20	4.8007	4.8017	4.7998

22. Develop an R chart for the data in Problem 21. Do you get the same answer?

23. Using the data from Problem 21, compute limits for a median chart. Is the process in control?

24. Design a control plan for your daily budget. Estimate your daily expenditure over a period of time to create your data. What type of chart would best describe if your expenditure is in or out of control? Discuss the results of your analysis and recommend remedial action to be taken if an out-of-control situation were to occur.

25. For the sampling plan from Problem 24, how would you measure process capability?

26. For the data in Problem 16, if the process target is 6mm with specification limits of ± 0.1mm, describe statistically the problems that would occur if you used your specification limits on a control chart where $n = 5$. Discuss whether type I or type II error is occurring.

CASES

Case 11-1 Ore-Ida Fries

www.heinz.com

An innovation in the frozen french fry industry was the upright bag. When new equipment was introduced to produce the bags, the Heinz Frozen Food Corporation facility in Ontario, Oregon, was selected to produce the new bag type.

When the new bags were produced, there were problems with consistency. It was unclear whether the problem was with the machinery or the "film" (the material used in the bags). One of the key measurements was the distance from the universal product code (UPC) and a black mark on the bag. A number of rolls of film were randomly selected, and this measurement was taken. The result of this actual study was the data that follow.

We need to know whether the film is consistent. Take the data that follow and use control charts to determine whether the measurements are consistent. Report your results to management.

(continued)

Sample	Millimeters from Code to UPC Box					Sample	Millimeters from Code to UPC Box				
1	7	7	8	6	7	41	10	10	10	11	10
2	6	5	6	5	7	42	11	11	11	10	10
3	7	7	8	6	8	43	10	10	10	10	10
4	6	8	8	7	7	44	11	10	10	10	10
5	6	7	6	6	7	45	10	10	10	10	10
6	6	6	5	6	5	46	10	10	10	10	10
7	5	6	4	4	4	47	10	10	10	10	10
8	4	5	5	5	6	48	10	10	10	11	12
9	5	6	5	5	5	49	10	11	10	11	11
10	5	5	5	5	5	50	12	12	11	11	11
11	6	6	7	7	7	51	12	11	11	10	10
12	7	7	6	7	7	52	12	12	11	11	10
13	6	7	7	7	7	53	10	11	11	11	11
14	6	7	7	7	7	54	11	10	11	12	11
15	6	6	6	6	6	55	11	10	12	11	11
16	6	6	6	6	6	56	11	11	12	11	11
17	6	7	7	6	7	57	10	10	12	12	11
18	6	7	6	7	7	58	10	11	11	11	11
19	6	6	6	6	6	59	11	11	16	16	17
20	5	6	5	6	6	60	18	17	17	16	16
21	9	12	10	10	10	61	18	17	16	16	16
22	10	10	9	10	10	62	17	17	17	17	16
23	10	10	10	9	10	63	16	16	16	15	16
24	10	10	10	10	10	64	16	17	18	16	16
25	10	10	10	10	10	65	16	17	17	17	16
26	10	10	10	11	10	66	16	17	17	17	17
27	11	12	10	11	11	67	15	15	17	16	17
28	11	12	10	11	12	68	16	15	16	17	17
29	10	11	11	11	11	69	16	16	16	18	16
30	10	11	12	10	10	70	16	15	17	16	16
31	10	11	11	11	11	71	16	15	16	15	16
32	11	11	11	12	12	72	16	16	16	16	16
33	11	11	0	0	5	73	15	15	15	16	16
34	6	4	4	5	7	74	16	15	16	16	16
35	7	6	6	0	1	75	16	16	16	16	15
36	6	7	6	7	6	76	16	16	15	16	17
37	6	6	5	6	7	77	16	16	16	16	16
38	10	9	10	10	9	78	17	16	15	16	16
39	10	9	8	8	11	79	17	17	17	16	16
40	10	10	10	10	10	80	16	16	16	16	16

CHAPTER 12

Statistically Based Quality Improvement for Attributes

Chapter Objectives

After completing this chapter, you should be able to:

1. Discuss the differences between attributes and variables.
2. Implement the process for creating attributes control charts.
3. Interpret attributes control charts.
4. Develop p, np, u, and c charts.
5. Develop control charts in Excel.
6. Perform reliability analysis.

In supply chain quality, we usually ask these questions: "Is it a defect or not?" and "Is the piece defective, or is it not?" Defined by Webster, an *attribute* is a "peculiar and essential characteristic." It is something that either does or does not exist.

As shown in Table 12-1, there are five types of attributes. **Structural attributes** have to do with physical characteristics of a particular product or service. For example, an automobile might have electric windows. Services have structural attributes as well, such as a balcony in a hotel room.

Sensory attributes relate to senses of touch, smell, taste, vision, and sound. For products, these attributes relate to form design or packaging design to create products that are pleasing to customers. In services such as restaurants and hotels, atmosphere is very important to the customer experience.

TABLE 12-1 Types of Attributes

Structural attributes
Sensory attributes
Performance attributes
Temporal attributes
Ethical attributes

Performance attributes relate to whether a particular product or service performs as it is supposed to. For example, does the lawn mower engine start? Does the sound system meet a certain threshold for low distortion?

Temporal attributes relate to time. Were delivery schedules met? This often has to do with the reliability of delivery.

More and more, **ethical attributes** are important to firms. Do they report properly? Is their accounting transparent? Is the service provider empathetic? Is the teacher kind?

As you can see, all these types of attributes have to do with some state of being. These are often binary in nature. Either the flaw exists or it does not. From a quality management point of view, we understand there is a difference between attributes that are desired by customers and attributes that are monitored in the production processes. *Customer-based attributes* are more associated with customer satisfaction. *Production-related attributes* are more internal and engineering-oriented. Both types of attributes are important. In this chapter, we focus more on process-oriented attributes.

First, we introduce quality control for attributes, including four types of control charts. After introducing these control charts, we then present reliability models. We do this because reliability has to do with whether or not products fail—where failure is an attribute.

GENERIC PROCESS FOR DEVELOPING ATTRIBUTES CHARTS

In Chapter 11, we discussed the use of control charts, so we will not repeat control chart basics here. Attribute charts are developed and interpreted the same way as variables charts. The only difference is the statistic of interest. Previously, we dealt with measurements; in this chapter, we deal with states of being.

To reiterate, the generic process for developing process charts consists of the following six steps:

1. Identify *critical operations* in the process where inspection might be needed. These are operations that will have a negative effect on the product if performed improperly.
2. Identify *critical product characteristics*. These are the attributes of the product that will result in either good or poor form, fit, or function for the product.
3. Determine whether the critical product characteristic is a variable or an attribute.
4. Select the appropriate *process chart* from the many types of charts. The decision process and the types of charts are defined and discussed in Chapter 11 and Chapter 12.
5. Establish the control limits and use the chart to continually monitor and improve.
6. Update the limits when changes have been made to the process.

UNDERSTANDING ATTRIBUTES CHARTS

Attributes charts use binomial and Poisson processes that are not measurements. We will now think in terms of defects and defectives rather than diameters and widths. A *defect* is an irregularity or problem with a larger unit. The larger unit may contain many defects. For example, a piece of glass may contain several bubbles or scratches. Some of these defects may be detectable only with a magnifying glass. Defects are countable, such as six flaws within a particular glass pane. A *defective* is a unit that, as a whole, is not acceptable or does not meet performance requirements. For example, a letter with a wrong address is defective. Also, a letter could have several defects, but the entire unit is labeled defective if there is a single defect. Defectives are monitored using *p* and *np* charts. Defects are monitored using *c* and *u* charts.

p Charts for Proportion Defective

The *p* **chart** is a process chart used to graph the proportion of items in a sample that are defective (nonconforming to specification). *p* charts are effectively used to determine when there has been a shift in the proportion defective for a particular product or service. Typical applications of the *p* chart include late deliveries, incomplete orders, calls not getting dial tones, accounting transaction errors, clerical errors on written forms, parts that do not mate properly, and so on.

The subgroup size on a *p* chart is typically between 50 and 100 units. The subgroups may be of different sizes for a *p* chart. However, it is best to hold subgroup sizes constant. Usually at least 25 subgroups are used to establish a *p* chart. The formulas for the *p* chart are as follows:

$$\text{Control limits for } p = \bar{p} \pm 3\sqrt{[(\bar{p})(1-\bar{p})/n]} \qquad (12.1)$$

where

p = the proportion defective
$\bar{p}$ = the average proportion defective
n = the sample size

EXAMPLE 12-1 | *p* Charts in Action

Problem: A city police department was concerned that the number of convictions was decreasing relative to the number of arrests. The suggestion was raised that the district attorney's office was becoming less effective in prosecuting criminals. You are asked to perform an analysis of the situation. The data for the previous 27 weeks are provided in the following table:

Active Model:
Example 12-1

Excel File:
Example 12-1

Sample	Number of Cases Reviewed	Number of Convictions	Proportion
1	100	60	.60
2	95	65	.68
3	110	68	.62
4	142	62	.44
5	100	56	.56
6	98	58	.59
7	76	30	.39
8	125	68	.54
9	100	54	.54
10	125	62	.50
11	111	70	.63
12	116	58	.50
13	92	30	.33
14	98	68	.69
15	162	54	.33
16	87	62	.71
17	105	70	.67
18	110	58	.53
19	98	30	.31
20	96	68	.71
21	100	54	.54
22	100	62	.62
23	97	70	.72
24	122	58	.48
25	125	30	.24
26	110	68	.62
27	100	54	.54
	$\bar{p} = 14.63/27 = .54$		Sum = 14.63

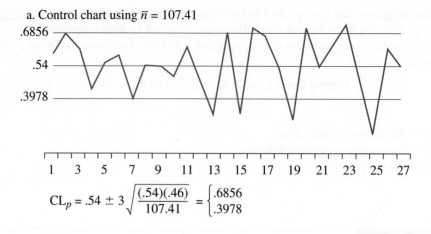

a. Control chart using $\bar{n} = 107.41$

$$CL_p = .54 \pm 3\sqrt{\frac{(.54)(.46)}{107.41}} = \begin{cases} .6856 \\ .3978 \end{cases}$$

b. Control chart using different sample sizes.

$$CL_p = .54 \pm 3\sqrt{\frac{(.54)(.46)}{n_k}}, \text{ where } n_k = \text{size of sample } k$$

FIGURE 12-1 *p* Charts for Example 12-1

Solution: Notice that in this problem, the sample size is not constant. When this happens, you have at least two options:

1. Compute the control limits using an average sample size (this is easier to understand).
2. Compute the control limits using the different sample sizes (this is statistically more correct).

Based on this analysis, *p* charts for this process were established. As seen in Figure 12-1, the *p* charts computed by using the two methods show that although it is not clear that the number of prosecutions is declining consistently, the process is becoming much more erratic, resulting in 2 months of particularly poor performance (periods 19 and 25). Investigations should be undertaken to identify assignable causes of variation.

Using Excel to Draw *p* Charts

Figure 12-2 shows the Excel® solution for Example 12-1. As in Chapter 11, we generated this graph using the "brute force" method. Review Example 11-1 (Figure 11-13) for an in-depth

FIGURE 12-2   Example 12-1 Using Excel   *Source:* Microsoft Excel, Microsoft Corporation. Used by permission.

discussion of how to generate the charts. Again, the chart shows that the process is erratic and out of control. This chart was drawn using the average sample size to compute the limits.

np Charts

The **np chart** is a graph of the number of defectives (or nonconforming units) in a subgroup. The *np* chart requires the sample size of each subgroup to be the same each time a sample is drawn. When subgroup sizes are equal, either the *p* or *np* chart can be used. They are essentially the same chart. Some people find the *np* chart easier to use because it reflects integer numbers rather than proportions. The uses for the *np* chart are essentially the same as the uses for the *p* chart.

Subgroup sizes for the *np* chart are normally between 50 and 100. Usually, at least 25 subgroups are used in developing the *np* chart. Again, *subgroup sizes must be equal*. To compute the control limits on an *np* chart, the following formula is used:

$$CL_{np} = n(\bar{p}) \pm 3s_{np} \qquad (12.2)$$

where

n = the sample size

$\bar{p}$ = the average proportion defective

s_{np} = standard error of $\sqrt{n\bar{p}(1 - \bar{p})}$

Active Model:
Example 12-2

Excel File:
Example 12-2

EXAMPLE 12-2 *np* **Charts in Action**

Problem: Within the J. Kim Insurance Company of Boston, Massachusetts, management found that too many of its policies were rated incorrectly. Management directed that policy applications be reviewed for the past 24 months on a sampling basis. One hundred policies from each month were selected for review. As an analyst, you are asked to review the policies for correct rating. If any problem is found with the rating of a policy, it is said to be defective.

Month	Number of Policies Reviewed	Number of Policies with Rating Errors	p
1	100	11	.11
2	100	10	.10
3	100	12	.12
4	100	6	.06
5	100	14	.14
6	100	8	.08
7	100	10	.10
8	100	9	.09
9	100	12	.12
10	100	2	.02
11	100	14	.14
12	100	18	.18
13	100	7	.07
14	100	13	.13
15	100	14	.14
16	100	12	.12
17	100	11	.11
18	100	8	.08
19	100	9	.09
20	100	17	.17
21	100	18	.18
22	100	20	.20
23	100	25	.25
24	100	28	.28
		Mean = .13	

Solution: The results of the control chart are shown in Figure 12-3. The chart shows that rating errors are increasing. Assignable causes should be identified through investigation.

FIGURE 12-3 *np* Chart for Example 12-2

$$\text{Control Limits } np = 100(.13) \pm 3\sqrt{100(.13)(.87)} = \begin{cases} 22.88 \\ 2.80 \end{cases}$$

	A	B	C	D	E	F
1	Month	Policies	Defects	CL	UCL	LCL
2	1	100	11	12.83333	22.86833	2.798333
3	2	100	10	12.83333	22.86833	2.798333
4	3	100	12	12.83333	22.86833	2.798333
5	4	100	6	12.83333	22.86833	2.798333
6	5	100	14	12.83333	22.86833	2.798333
7	6	100	8	12.83333	22.86833	2.79833
8	7	100	10	12.83333	22.86833	2.79833
9	8	100	9	12.83333	22.86833	2.798
10	9	100	12	12.83333	22.86833	2.79835
11	10	100	2	12.83333	22.86833	2.798333
12	11	100	14	12.83333	22.86833	2.798333
13	12	100	18	12.83333	22.86833	2.798333
14	13	100	7	12.83333	22.86	
15	14	100	13	12.83333	22.86	
16	15	100	14	12.83333	22.86833	2.798333
17	16	100	12	12.83333	22.86833	2.798333
18	17	100	11	12.83333	22.86833	2.798333
19	18	100	8	12.83333	22.86833	2.798333
20	19	100	9	12.83333	22.86833	2.798333
21	20	100	17	12.83333	22.86833	2.798333
22	21	100	18	12.83333	22.86833	2.798333
23	22	100	20	12.83333	22.86833	2.798333
24	23	100	25	12.83		2.798333
25	24	100	28	12.83		2.798333
26		Mean	12.83333			
27		Sample Size	100			
28		p-bar	0.128333			
29		1-p-bar	0.871667			
30		Std err of np	3.345			

Callouts in figure: =$C$26-3*$C$30 (pointing to LCL), =$C$26+3*$C$30 (pointing to UCL), =$C$26 (pointing to CL).

Chart title: np chart. Legend: Defects, CL, UCL, LCL. Annotation: OOC Points.

FIGURE 12-4 Example 12-2 Using Excel *Source:* Microsoft Excel, Microsoft Corporation. Used by permission.

Using Excel to Draw *np* Charts

Figure 12-4 contains the Excel spreadsheet for Example 12-2. As you can see, the process has drifted out of control.

c and *u* Charts

The ***c* chart** is a graph of the number of defects (nonconformities) per unit. The units must be of the same metric such as size, height, length, volume, and so on. This means that the "area of opportunity" for finding defects must be the same for each unit. Several individual units can comprise the sample, but they will be grouped as if they are one unit of a larger size. If multiple units are used, the same number of units must be in each subgroup. The control limits for the *c* chart are computed based on the Poisson distribution.

Like other process charts, the *c* chart is used to detect nonrandom events in the life of a production process. Typical applications of the *c* chart include number of flaws in an auto finish (for a particular model), number of flaws in a standard typed letter, number of data errors in a standard form, and number of incorrect responses on a standardized test.

Again, the *c* chart is used when you are always inspecting the same size sample space. When the sample space is varied, such as in the inspection for flaws of different models of cars within a model family, a *u* chart is used.

The ***u* chart** is a graph of the *average number* of defects per unit. Contrast this with the *c* chart, which shows the *actual number* of defects per standardized unit. The *u* chart allows for the units sampled to be different sizes, areas, heights and so on; and allows for different numbers of units in each sample space. The uses for the *u* chart are the same as the *c* chart.

The formulas for the *c* and *u* charts are the following:

$$CL_c = \bar{c} \pm 3\sqrt{\bar{c}} \qquad (12.3)$$

$$CL_u = \bar{u} \pm 3\sqrt{\frac{\bar{u}}{n}} \qquad (12.4)$$

where

n = average sample size
$\bar{c}$ = process average number of nonconformities
$\bar{u}$ = process average number of nonconformities per unit

As Example 12-3 shows, the limits for the *u* chart are more conservative than are the limits for the *c* chart.

Active Model:
Example 12-3

Excel File:
Example 12-3

EXAMPLE 12-3   *c* and *u* Charts in Action

Problem: The J. Grout Window Company makes colored-glass objects for home decoration. J. Grout, the owner, has been concerned about scratches in the finish of recently made product. The company makes two products: Demi-Glass, which comes in one standard configuration; and Streakless-Glass, which comes in three similar models. Using high-power magnifying glasses, the company examined 25 each of the Demi (one style only) and the Streakless (randomly selected in all three styles). As an analyst, you are asked to evaluate the process by determining whether the processes are stable. Assume that, on average, the Streakless are 1.5 times the size of the Demis.

Item Number	Demi Defects	Streakless Defects
1	5	6
2	4	4
3	6	7
4	3	9
5	9	5
6	4	8
7	5	7
8	4	4
9	3	5
10	7	4
11	9	5
12	12	4
13	3	5
14	6	6
15	2	4
16	8	8
17	5	5
18	7	7
19	12	10
20	4	5

(Continued)

Item Number	Demi Defects	Streakless Defects
21	6	4
22	8	7
23	5	5
24	7	6
	Sum c = 144	Sum u = 140
	$\bar{c}$ = 6	$\bar{u}$ = 5.83

Solution: As shown in Figure 12-5 and Figure 12-6, the process for Demis appears to be in control. However, the process for Streakless shows a run of five points below the mean. An assignable cause should be sought.

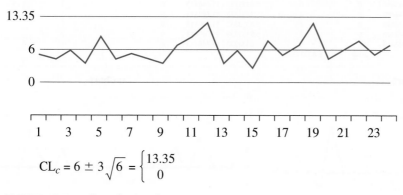

$$CL_c = 6 \pm 3\sqrt{6} = \begin{cases} 13.35 \\ 0 \end{cases}$$

FIGURE 12-5   *c* Chart for Demis

$$CL_u = 5.83 \pm 3\sqrt{\frac{5.83}{1.5}} = \begin{cases} 11.74 \\ 0 \end{cases}$$

FIGURE 12-6   *u* Chart for Streakless

Using Excel to Draw *c* and *u* Charts

Figure 12-7 shows the Excel *c* and *u* charts from Example 12-3. As you can see, these charts are drawn using the typical method. Formulas are provided in the figure. Note that because the lower control limits were computed to be negative numbers, zero is used as the lower limit for both charts.

FIGURE 12-7 Example 12-3 Using Excel   *Source:* Microsoft Excel, Microsoft Corporation. Used by permission.

ATTRIBUTES CHARTS SUMMARY

Table 12-2 shows all the formulas for the process charts we have discussed in this chapter. These are the major attributes charts used the vast majority of the time.

CHOOSING THE RIGHT ATTRIBUTES CHART

When choosing the right process chart, the key questions are whether you are interested in defects or defectives, and whether your sample sizes are constant. As we said before, for c and u charts, we are more interested in whether the sample space is constant. This is the standardized chart used by auto companies such as Ford when selecting charts.

TABLE 12-2   Summary of Chart Formulas

Chart	LCL	CL	UCL
p	$\bar{p} - 3\sqrt{\bar{p}(1-\bar{p})/n}$	$\bar{p}$	$\bar{p} + 3\sqrt{\bar{p}(1-\bar{p})/n}$
np	$n\bar{p} - 3\sqrt{n\bar{p}(1-\bar{p})}$	$n\bar{p}$	$n\bar{p} + 3\sqrt{n\bar{p}(1-\bar{p})}$
c	$\bar{c} - 3\sqrt{\bar{c}}$	$\bar{c}$	$\bar{c} + 3\sqrt{\bar{c}}$
u	$\bar{u} - 3\sqrt{\bar{u}/n}$	$\bar{u}$	$\bar{u} + 3\sqrt{\bar{u}/n}$

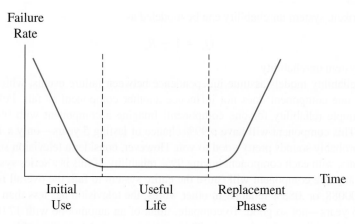

FIGURE 12-8 Bathtub-shaped Hazard Curve

RELIABILITY MODELS

Although there are several reliability models, we discuss only some of the simpler ones. The first model is graphic (see Figure 12-8) and is called the **bathtub-shaped hazard function**. The vertical axis on the bathtub function is the failure rate. The horizontal axis is time. This model shows that products are more likely to fail either very early in their life or late in their useful life. Consider this function when you purchase major appliances. It is now very common for appliance vendors to offer service contracts at an additional cost. However, notice from the bathtub function that products likely will fail either very early in their life or after their expected useful life. Because most major appliances include a one-year warranty that covers all the labor and parts needed to repair the appliance, and most appliances are made to last several years, you are really insuring the product during the part of its life when it is least likely to fail by purchasing a service contract. This appears to be a very good deal for the appliance vendor.

Series Reliability

Components in a system are in a series if the performance of the entire system depends on all the components functioning properly. The components need not be physically wired sequentially for the system to be in series. However, all parts must function for the system to function. Figure 12-9 shows n components in a series. System reliability for the series is expressed as[1]

$$R_s = P(x_1 x_2 \cdots x_n) \tag{12.5}$$

$$= P(x_1)P(x_2|x_1)P(x_3|x_1 x_2) \cdots P(x_n|x_1 x_2 \ldots x_{n-1}) \tag{12.6}$$

where

R_s = system reliability
$P(x) = 1 -$ probability of failure for component x_i

FIGURE 12-9 n Components in Series

---

[1]Ramakumar, R., *Engineering Reliability* (Englewood Cliffs, NJ: Prentice Hall, 1996).

By the same token, system unreliability can be modeled as

$$Q_s = 1 - R_s \qquad (12.7)$$

where Q_s = system unreliability

These reliability models assume independence between failure events, which means that the failure of one component does not influence another component to fail. Following is an example of simple reliability for one component: Imagine a component with 99% reliability over 5 years. This component will have a 99% chance of lasting 5 years—only a 1% chance of failure. This probably sounds pretty good to you. However, consider a television set made up of 700 components, with each component having 99% reliability. If this is a series system in which the failure of any one component will cause the entire system to fail, the overall reliability will be $.99^{700} = .00088$, or .088% reliable. In other words, the television has less than a 1% chance of surviving 5 years—not so good. To compare, think of an automobile with 17,000 parts or a space shuttle with millions of components. This gives you an understanding of how difficult it is to make a product that will last.

Now let's suppose that we want this television with 700 components to have 90% overall reliability. If we want $0.90 = R^{700}$, we find that $R = (0.90)^{1/700} = .99985$, which is the required component reliability.

Parallel Reliability

As discussed, a high-reliability system often requires extremely high component reliability. At times when such high reliability is an impossibility, an alternative is to use a backup system. (Other words for a backup system are *redundant* or *parallel systems*.) If a set of components is in parallel, as opposed to being in series, the system can function if a given component in the system fails. System reliability is then expressed as

$$R_P = P(x_1 + x_2 + \cdots + x_n) = 1 - P(\bar{x}_1 \bar{x}_2 \cdots \bar{x}_n) \qquad (12.8)$$

Given that component failures are independent of one another, redundant reliability is modeled as

$$R_p = 1 - P(\bar{x}_1)P(\bar{x}_2|\bar{x}_1)P(\bar{x}_3|\bar{x}_1\bar{x}_2) \cdots P(\bar{x}_n|\bar{x}_1\bar{x}_2 \cdots \bar{x}_{n-1}) \qquad (12.9)$$

Therefore, system unreliability is modeled as

$$Q_p = \prod_{i=1}^{n} Q_i \qquad (12.10)$$

EXAMPLE 12-4　**Parallel and Series Reliability**

At times, systems have some components in series and some components in parallel (or redundancy). Figure 12-10 has one such system.

Overall reliability for this system is

$$R = .98 \times .99 \times (1 - (.1 \times .1)) \times .97 = .932$$

To continue the example, it is interesting to compare the overall reliability of this system without component C_2. It equals

$$R = .98 \times .99 \times .90 \times .97 = .847$$

Thus the overall improvement in system reliability by adding the additional component is

$$D = .932 - .847 = .085$$

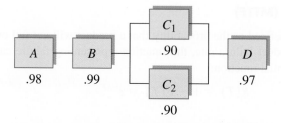

FIGURE 12-10 Series and Redundant Reliability

This is an 8.5% improvement in system reliability resulting from the additional component.

A space shuttle would be unreliable using a series system, given the millions of components contained in the shuttle. Therefore, many redundant systems are used in the shuttle. This choice improves the likelihood that the shuttle will function properly, but it is not a guarantee. For example, the O-rings that exploded on the space shuttle *Challenger* included a second set of redundant O-rings. It has been suggested that the engineers working for NASA made the mistake of concluding that failure of the redundant O-rings would be independent of the failure of the original O-rings. However, they were not independent, and both sets of O-rings failed, which demonstrates the importance of the independence assumption. These formulas assume that the failure of one component is independent of another component. Independence is modeled using conditional probability notation as

$$\text{If } P(x_1|x_2) = P(x_1), \text{then events } x_1 \text{ and } x_2 \text{ are independent} \qquad \textbf{(12.11)}$$

where $P(x)$ is the probability of some event (x)

Measuring Reliability

Let's discuss some basic reliability functions. Failure rate is measured using the following equation:

$$\text{Failure rate} = \lambda = \text{number of failures}/(\text{units tested} \times \text{number of hours tested}) \qquad \textbf{(12.12)}$$

Note that some care should be exercised in using this function because there is no distinction as to whether the hours of testing are continuous or performed at separate times. For example, there is no difference in testing hours if five units are tested for 100 hours each or if one unit is tested for 500 hours.

EXAMPLE 12-5 Reliability Measurement—Failure Rates

Problem: Suppose that we tested 25 ski exercise machines under strenuous conditions for 100 hours per machine. Of the machines tested, three experienced malfunctions during the test. What is the failure rate for the exercise machines?

Solution: Failure Rate $= 3/(25 \times 100) = .0012$ failures per operating hour

Mean Time to Failure (MTTF)

Because reliability can be defined as the probability that a product will not fail over its defined product life, if λ is the product failure rate, the function representing failure can be modeled using the following exponential function:

$$R(T) = 1 - F(T) = e^{-\lambda T} \tag{12.13}$$

where

$R(T)$ = reliability of the product
$F(T)$ = unreliability of a product
λ = failure rate
T = product's useful life expressed as a function of time

Using another useful function, $1/\lambda$ is called the **mean time to failure (MTTF)**. This is the average time before the product will fail.

EXAMPLE 12-6 — MTTF

Problem: Suppose that a product is designed to operate for 100 hours continuously with a 1% chance of failure. Find the number of failures per hour incurred by this product and the MTTF.

Solution:

$$0.99 = e^{-\lambda(100)}$$
$$\ln 0.99 = -100\lambda$$
$$\lambda = -(\ln 0.99)/100$$
$$= .01005/100$$
$$= .0001005$$
$$\text{MTTF} = 1/.0001005 = 9950.25 = 1/\lambda \tag{12.14}$$

This means that the failure rate for this product is .0001005, and the average time before failing is 9950.25 hours.

Another function of interest is the **mean time between failures (MTBF)**. This tells us the average time from one failure to the next when a product can be repaired. The formula is

$$\text{MTBF} = \text{total operating hours}/\text{number of failures}$$

This formula is important for scheduling service calls. Consider the plight of the Otis Elevator Company, which is trying to determine the number of service representatives needed in New York City. If it knows its MTBF, the number of elevators in service, and the hours those elevators are in use, it can calculate how many service reps are needed. A Closer Look at Quality 12-1 looks at quality control for a major supplement retailer and producer.

A CLOSER LOOK AT QUALITY 12-1 — Quality Control at GNC[2]

Although you might think that all this talk of statistics is somewhat esoteric, it isn't. GNC, the nation's largest dietary supplement retailer, recently was confronted with an accusation from the attorney general of New York that its supplements contained hazardous substances and impurities.

---

[2]O'Connor, A., "GNC to Strengthen Supplement Quality Controls." *The New York Times* (March 30, 2015): 3A.

GNC has responded by being the first supplement maker in the industry to implement additional quality controls and testing.

With more than 6,500 stores and revenues over $2.5 billion, GNC stands to lose revenue if it is shown that its quality tests are insufficient. In addition to statistical tests, GNC has stated that it will use DNA testing to authenticate the ingredients in its products. Now that GNC has agreed to such testing, the New York attorney general's office is turning to other retailers such as Walgreens and Walmart to follow suit.

These products are regulated by the federal government, but the testing proposed by GNC goes well beyond what the government has required. Many firms around the world have implemented the tools from Chapter 11 and Chapter 12 to ensure that products will satisfy customers.

EXAMPLE 12-7   MTBF

Problem: A product has been operated for 10,000 hours and has experienced four failures. What is the MTBF?

Solution:

$$\text{MTBF} = 10{,}000/4 = 2{,}500 \text{ hours between failures}$$

The failure rate is then calculated as $\lambda = 1/2{,}500 = .0004$ failures per hour.

System Availability

Remember that mean time between failures is a useful measure for many products. In Example 12-7, 2,500 hours between failures may not make sense because many products are never used that many hours. To clarify, MTBF is generally used as an average over several products.

A useful measure for maintainability of a product is system availability, which considers both MTBF and a new statistic: **mean time to repair (MTTR)**. **System availability (SA)** gives the "uptime" of a product or system. Here is the formula:

$$\text{SA} = \text{MTBF}/(\text{MTBF} + \text{MTTR}) \qquad \textbf{(12.15)}$$

EXAMPLE 12-8   System Availability

Problem: Jami Kovach has to decide between three suppliers for a network server. Other factors being equal, she will base her decision on system availability. Given the following data, which supplier should she choose?

Supplier	MTBF (h)	MTTR (h)
A	67	4
B	45	2
C	36	1

Solution: Formula 12.15 has the following solutions:

$$\text{SA}_\text{A} = 67/(67 + 4) = .944$$
$$\text{SA}_\text{B} = 45/(45 + 2) = .957$$
$$\text{SA}_\text{C} = 36/(36 + 1) = .973$$

Choose supplier C. As you can see, service does matter.

Summary

In Chapter 11 and in this chapter, we introduced the basics of quality control. Remember that the object of using process charts is to continually improve your processes. Monitoring processes is not enough. As we make changes and improvements to the processes, our attributes charts will improve—there will be fewer defects and defectives. As this improvement takes place, the control limits constrict and draw closer to zero (for attributes charts). This is the goal. If you are not seeing this type of improvement in your processes, you should work harder to improve them.

We also introduced a number of reliability models, which included series reliability, parallel reliability, and reliability functions. Reliable processes are both cost effective and productive.

In the last few chapters we introduced several quality tools and models. In the next chapter, we apply them in a Six Sigma setting.

Key Terms

Bathtub-shaped hazard function	Mean time to failure (MTTF)	np chart	Structural attributes
c chart	Mean time to repair (MTTR)	p chart	System availability (SA)
Ethical attributes		Performance attributes	Temporal attributes
Mean time between failures (MTBF)		Sensory attributes	u chart

Discussion Questions

1. What are key attributes for a high-quality university?
2. What are some attributes you can identify for an automobile tire?
3. What are some attributes for a university financial aid process?
4. What are some personal attributes you could monitor using control charts? Which control chart would you use?
5. What are some examples of structural attributes?
6. What are some examples of sensory attributes?
7. What are some examples of performance attributes?
8. What are some examples of temporal attributes?
9. What are some examples of ethical attributes?
10. What ethical attributes might you use to determine where to work after graduation?

Problems

1. Suppose that you want to inspect a lot of 10,000 products to see whether or not they meet requirements. Design a sampling plan used to test these products.
2. Suppose that a product is made of 100 components, each with a 97% reliability. What is the overall reliability for the product?
3. Suppose that a product is made of 1,000 components, each with .999 reliability. What is the unreliability of this product? Is this acceptable? Why or why not?
4. An old set of Christmas tree lights are wired in series; if one bulb fails, all will go out. The set contains 80 bulbs; each bulb has an average reliability of 98%. What is the overall reliability for the product?
5. A radio is made up of 125 components. What would have to be the average reliability for each component for the radio to have a reliability of 98% over its useful life?

6. List five products with low reliability. List five that have high reliability. What are the elemental design differences between these products? In other words, what are the factors that make some products reliable and others unreliable?

7. A medical device consists of 128 critical components; failure of any of these components will result in product failure. To achieve an overall reliability 99.5%, what must the average reliability factor be for each component?

8. An electronic circuit board has six resistors wired in series. The average reliability for each resistor is R1 = 99%, R2 = 95%, R3 = 98%, R4 = 98%, R5 = 99%, and R6 = 97%. What is the overall reliability for this circuit?

9. Suppose that redundant components are introduced for each of two components in Problem 8 with the lowest reliability. What is now the overall reliability for this product?

10. Suppose that redundant components are introduced for all the components in Problem 8. What is now the overall reliability for the product?

11. A product is made up of components A, B, C and D. These components are wired in series. Their reliability factors are 0.97, 0.998, 0.999 and 0.992 respectively. What is the overall reliability for this product?

12. A product is made up of components A, B, C, D, E, F, G, H, I, and J. Components A, B, C, and F have a 1/10,000 chance of failure during useful life. D, E, G, and H have a 3/10,000 chance of failure. Components I and J have a 5/10,000 chance of failure. What is the overall reliability for this product?

13. For the product in Problem 12, if parallel components are provided for components I and J, what is the overall reliability for the product?

14. A product is made up of 20 components in a series. Ten of the components have a 1/10,000 chance of failure. Five have a 3/10,000 chance of failure. Four have a 4/10,000 chance of failure. One component has a 1/100 chance of failure. What is the overall reliability for this product?

15. For the product in Problem 14, if parallel components are used for any component with worse than a 1/1,000 chance of failure, what is the overall reliability? How many components will the new design have? What will be the average component reliability for the redesigned product?

16. A Quality Manager at an Auto Body Shop visually inspects 25 re-sprayed vehicles each week for aesthetics. The Quality Manager will reject any car if the finish is blemished. Following are results from 10 weeks of inspections.

Week	1	2	3	4	5	6	7	8	9	10
Defective	3	6	2	6	5	4	3	9	14	2

a. Given these results, using a p chart, determine if the process is stable.
b. What would need to be done to improve the process?

17. Use the data in Problem 16 to compute the limits for an np chart.

18. Suppose that a company makes the following product with the following numbers of defects. Construct a p chart to see whether the process is in control ($n = 100$).

Sample	Defectives
1	67
2	28
3	45
4	32
5	30
6	48
7	32
8	24
9	25
10	27
11	28
12	29
13	65
14	66
15	69

Sample	Defectives
16	70
17	26
18	13
19	45
20	46
21	47
22	48
23	28
24	29
25	75

19. Using the data from Example 12-3, evaluate the Demis using a u chart and evaluate the Streakless using a c chart. Assume that the Demis are twice the size of the Streakless on average.

20. Politicians closely monitor their popularity based on approval ratings. For the previous 16 weeks, Governor Johnny's approval ratings have been (in percentages):

Week	1	2	3	4	5	6	7	8	9	10	11	12	13	14	15	16
Approval %	65	62	59	64	61	60	58	52	51	53	54	52	62	65	66	67

    a. Prepare a report for the governor outlining the results of your analysis. Use control charts to analyze the data ($n = 200$).

    b. What action would you propose to the governor based on your analysis?

21. Construct and interpret a c chart using the following data:

Sample	Defects
1	6
2	5
3	7
4	6
5	8
6	5
7	6
8	7
9	6
10	8
11	7
12	6
13	7
14	8
15	7
16	6
17	5
18	2
19	1
20	0
21	12
22	4
23	6
24	7
25	8

(Continued)

Sample	Defects
26	3
27	2
28	3
29	2
30	3

22. Construct and interpret a u chart using the following data. Assume that the average size is two times the original product.

Sample	Defects
1	4
2	7
3	6
4	7
5	4
6	5
7	7
8	4
9	5
10	7
11	5
12	3
13	5
14	6
15	3
16	7
17	6
18	8
19	4
20	5
21	6
22	7
23	3
24	2
25	3
26	2
27	3

23. The Hydrus Power company tested 400 hydraulic valves for 1000 hours each. During the testing 12 failures were reported. Compute the number of failures per hour. What is the mean time between failures?
24. Collier Company tested 200 products for 100 hours each. During this time, it experienced 12 break-downs. Compute the number of failures per hour. What is the MTBF?
25. The Auto Belt Company tested 175 products for 1500 hours each. During the test 68 products failed. Compute the number of failures per hour and the mean time between failures.
26. Suppose that a product is designed to function for 10,000 hours with a 3% chance of failure. Find the average number of failures per hour and the MTTF.
27. Suppose that a product is designed to function for 100,000 hours with a 1% chance of failure and sup-pose that six of them are in use at a facility. Find the average number of failures per hour and the MTTF.

28. Suppose that there are 42 pumps used in a refinery that are continuously being used with a 2% chance of failure over 50,000 hours. If the repair time is 10 hours to install a new rebuilt pump, how many pumps should be kept on hand to keep the chance of a plant shutdown to less than 1%É (*Hint*: Treat this problem as a traditional safety stock problem and use a z table.)

29. A product is designed to work for 5,000 hours with a 1% chance of failure. Find the average number of failures per hour and the MTTF.

30. A product has been used for 5,000 hours with 1 failure. Find the mean time between failures (MTBF) and λ.

31. You have to decide between three potential suppliers for an assembly for a product you are designing. After performing life testing on several assemblies, you find the following:

Supplier	MTBF (hr)	MTTR (hr)
A	45	2
B	100	6
C	150	9

Based on system availability, which supplier should you choose?

32. You want to choose a copier supplier on reliability and service. After gathering data about the alternatives, here is what you found. What do you recommend?

Supplier	MTBF (hr)	MTTR (hr)
1	45	2
2	90	2
3	120	6
4	200	6

CASE

Case 12-1 Decision Sciences Institute National Conference
www.decisionsciences.org

During a recent Decisions Sciences Institute National Conference, I served as a track chair for the Manufacturing Track. One hundred and seventy-four authors submitted papers to this track of the conference, hoping that their papers would be accepted and they would be given the opportunity to present their research to colleagues from around the world at the conference in Las Vegas.

The 174 papers were sent to reviewers with the results shown in Table 12-3. Following is a key to understanding the codes:

r = reject

t = table topic (a lower level of acceptance)

f = full session presentation

fy = full session and recommended for best paper contest

One of the difficulties of statistical analysis is to figure out how to analyze, interpret, and present the results of your analysis. Take these raw data and develop research questions. Next, using the statistical tools from this chapter, analyze the data. Finally, put the data into a form that will be useful for decision makers. Good luck.

TABLE 12-3 DSI Review Results

Paper Number	Reviewer 1	Reviewer 2	Reviewer 3	Paper Number	Reviewer 1	Reviewer 2	Reviewer 3
1	r	f	t	49	f	t	f
2				50	fy		f
3	f	f	f	51	f	f	f
4				52	f	f	f
5	f	f	f	53	t	f	f
6	r		r	54	f	t	f
7	t		t	55	f		f
8	f		f	56	f		f
9	t	t	t	57	f		f
10	fy		f	58	t	f	f
11	fy	fy	f	59	t	f	f
12	f	f	f	60	fy	f	f
13	f		f	61	f	f	f
14	f		f	62	fy	fy	f
15	r		r	63	f		f
16	f		f	64	t	f	t
17	r	f	t	65	f	r	f
18	t	f	f	66	fy	f	t
19	f		f	67	r	f	t
20	t		t	68	f	f	f
21	f		f	69	f		f
22	r		r	70	f		f
23	t		t	71		t	Workshop
24	f	t	f	72	t	t	t
25	fy		f	73	f		t
26	t		t	74	t	f	t
27	f	f	f	75	t		f
28				76	f		f
29				77		r	
30	fy	fy	f	78	r	f	r
31	fy	fy	f	79	f	f	f
32	t		t	80	f		f
33	f		f	81	fy		f
34	f	f	f	82	f		f
35	f	f	f	83			
36	f	f	f	84	t		t
37	fy	fy	f	85	f	f	f
38	fy		f	86	f		f
39	f	fy	f	87	fy	f	f
40	f	t	f	88	fy		f
41	f	fy	f	89	fy	fy	f
42				90	f	f	f
43	f		f	91	r		r
44	f		f	92	t		t
45	f	f	f	93	f	f	f
46	r	f	t	94	t	t	t
47				95	t		t
48	r		r	96	f	f	f

(Continued)

Paper Number	Reviewer 1	Reviewer 2	Reviewer 3	Paper Number	Reviewer 1	Reviewer 2	Reviewer 3
97	f		f	136	f		f
98	f	f	f	137	f	f	f
99	t	f	f	138	f		f
100	r	t	t	139	t		t
101	t	f	f	140	t	f	f
102	f	f	f	141	r		r
103	f		f	142	fy	f	f
104	f	r	t	143	f		f
105	f	t	f	144	r	f	t
106	t	t	t	145	f	t	f
107	f	t	f	146	f	t	f
108	f		f	147	f		f
109	f		f	148			
110	fy	f	f	149	fy	f	f
111	f	f	f	150	fy	f	f
112	t	f	f	151	f	f	f
113	r	f	t	152	t		t
114	f	f	f	153	f		f
115	t	t	t	154	t	f	f
116	t	f	f	155	t	r	t
117	t	f	f	156	t	f	f
118	t	f	f	157			
119	t		t	158	f	f	f
120				159			
121	f		f	160	fy	f	f
122	t		t	161	t	f	f
123	f	f	f	162	f	f	f
124				163			
125	f	t	f	164	f	f	f
126				165	f	f	f
127	f		f	166	f		f
128				167	r	f	t
129	f	f	f	168	f	f	f
130	fy		f	169	f		f
131	f	r	t	170	r	t	t
132	t	t	t	171	f	f	f
133	fy		f	172	t		t
134	f	fy	f	173	f		f
135	r	r	r	174	f		f

Note: If a space is blank, the reviewer failed to return a review. Consider it a missing value.

CHAPTER 13

Lean-Six Sigma Management and Tools

Chapter Objectives

After completing this chapter, you should be able to:

1. Explain how to organize Six Sigma in a firm.
2. Distinguish the different steps in the DMAIC process.
3. Use a Six Sigma project risk and return analysis to evaluate possible Six Sigma projects.
4. Implement an XY matrix to identify important inputs and outputs to a process.
5. Perform gauge R&R.
6. Design a Taguchi experiment.

As evidenced by a quick Internet search, **Six Sigma** is a very popular approach to improving quality. Several distinctions about Six Sigma differentiate it from traditional continuous improvement. First, Six Sigma represents a well-thought-out packaging of quality tools and philosophies in an honest effort to provide rigor and repeatability to quality improvement efforts.

Second, Six Sigma is much more cost-reduction-oriented than traditional continuous improvement. It is this second aspect of Six Sigma that has made it so popular with CEOs. In fact, many quality practitioners are uncomfortable with the focus on results, stating that this approach violates several of Deming's points, especially in setting targets and goals for cost reduction. But proponents of Six Sigma state that this focus on profits is one of the strengths of a Six Sigma approach.

The third fundamental nuance of Six Sigma is the way it is organized. Six Sigma is a bonanza for consultants and providers of training because it is organized around creating champions, black belts, green belts, and, in some situations, yellow belts. Later in the chapter, we discuss how Six Sigma efforts are normally organized.

Fourth, Six Sigma and lean production have been combined into an approach termed *Lean-Six Sigma*. It is Six Sigma with an increased emphasis on reducing waste.

For this text, we approach Six Sigma from a contingency perspective. This is simply one of the more popular current approaches to quality improvement. If after studying this chapter you feel the Six Sigma approach will be helpful to your company, you can strongly support implementation.

WHAT IS SIX SIGMA?

Video Clip: Six Sigma at
Kurt Manufacturing

The *sigma* in Six Sigma refers to the Greek symbol σ, which designates a standard deviation in statistics. The *six* refers to the number of standard deviations from a specification limit to the mean of a highly capable process.

There are two key versions of Six Sigma. From one perspective, Six Sigma is a program that began at Motorola in 1982. That year, Motorola's CEO requested that costs be cut in half. He then repeated the same request the following year. These efforts pointed out that Motorola needed to improve its product designs and analytical techniques to achieve these goals. Motorola emphasized designing products to achieve Six Sigma. Figure 13-1 shows what this means. In the figure, distribution *a* shows a typical product design with 3-standard-deviation specifications (or tolerances). If this is the case, about 0.5% of products will not meet specification. As shown in part *b* of the figure, if the tolerances are 6 standard deviations, the probability of producing a bad part is very low. Notice that in part *b* the mean or dispersion of the process could change significantly, and the product still would meet specs. Table 13-1 shows the number of defective parts per million (ppm) that are produced between one and Six Sigma levels. Using this definition, Six Sigma translates into more robust designs, radically lower defect levels, and lowered costs of poor quality (COPQ).

From the early days of improving the robustness of design at Motorola, Six Sigma has morphed into an organization-wide program for improvement involving hierarchical training, organizational learning, and pay for learning. As you will see in this chapter, none of the analytical tools used in Six Sigma efforts is new. What is new is how they are packaged and deployed within a company.

Some argue that Six Sigma is an advanced quality improvement approach designed to help tackle the most difficult quality problems. As you can see in the pyramid in Figure 13-2, the basic tools of quality can be used to handle 90% of quality problems. Most of the next 10% requires

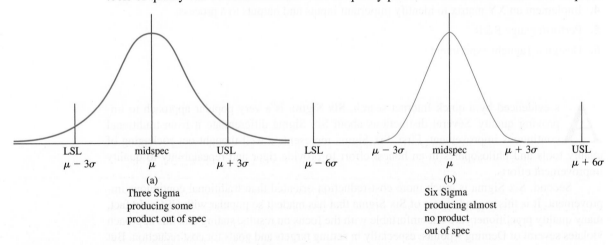

(a)
Three Sigma
producing some
product out of spec

(b)
Six Sigma
producing almost
no product
out of spec

FIGURE 13-1   Six Sigma Variation

TABLE 13-1	Sigma Levels and ppm Defects
Sigma Level	**Long-Term ppm* Defects**
1	691,462
2	308,538
3	66,807
4	6,210
5	233
6	3.4

*ppm = parts per million.

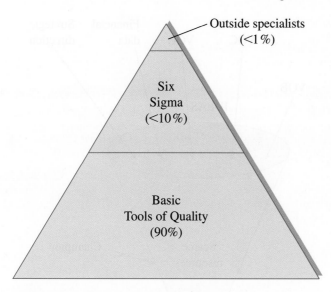

FIGURE 13-2 Six Sigma Effectiveness

advanced training and analytical techniques. Beyond that, there are a few problems that require expertise that may not be found within the company. Thus you can see that care should be taken when determining what projects should be undertaken by Six Sigma specialists.

At the core of Six Sigma is the following equation:

$$Y = f(X) \qquad \qquad (13.1)$$

Strictly speaking, it means that Y (the dependent variable) is a function of X (an independent variable). To Six Sigma practitioners, it means that an output is a function of inputs and processes, where

Y = output (key business objectives and measures)

f = function (interrelationships to be controlled and managed)

X = controllable and noncontrollable variables that affect Y

For example, the profitability of a company (Y) is affected by several variables (Xs), including customer retention, inventory turnovers, rolled throughput yield, production costs, and many others. If our objective is to improve profits, we focus on these variables on a project-by-project basis and improve our performance. In this scenario, the job of management is to identify and prioritize projects to achieve the goal of lowered costs and higher profits. The job of employees is to obtain the training and expertise required to meet these objectives.

As you can see, Six Sigma started as a single firm's approach to reducing costs and improving quality. Currently, it is much more. It involves planning, organization, training, human resources planning, and pay for knowledge. This requires both organizational and individual cooperation to achieve a goal. At GE, management made it clear that participation in Six Sigma was a prerequisite for advancement within the company.

ORGANIZING LEAN-SIX SIGMA

Probably you have heard about lean-Six Sigma black belts. This is the designation for a person who has completed rigorous (and costly) black-belt training and has completed one or more lean-Six Sigma projects (depending on the company providing the training and the certificate) with demonstrated results. The cost of training generally runs between $10,000 and $20,000 for a single black belt. Expected returns from Six Sigma projects can run into the hundreds of

FIGURE 13-3 Champion Decision Making

thousand dollars. Although these payoffs are attractive to management, they do provide quite a bit of pressure for the organization to achieve outstanding results from their Six Sigma efforts.

The following list shows some of the key players in Six Sigma efforts:

Champion. The job of the **champion** is to work with black belts and potential black belts to identify possible projects. They get information from a variety of sources such as the *voice of the business* (VOB), the *voice of the customer* (VOC), and the *voice of the employee* (VOE) for potential project ideas. As shown in Figure 13-3, they act as a funnel for project ideas and use Pareto analysis (Chapter 10) to analyze the ideas to determine where the best return on investment lies. It can involve COPQ analysis and regression studies to determine the main causes of quality-related losses. From the champion's perspective, Six Sigma is not so much about tools; it is about managing the process for improvement. The champion provides continuing support for the project and validates the results at the end of the project. In a small company, the champion might be the CEO. In larger companies, champions may be senior executives.

Master black belts. In some firms, experienced black belts are designated **master black belts.** In these cases, master black belts serve as mentors and trainers for new black belts. This brings the training in-house and can reduce costs.

Black belt. The **black belt** is the key to lean-Six Sigma. Black belts are specially trained individuals who train for about four months. After completing training, these individuals are committed full time to completing cost-reduction projects. At GE, black belts were expected to complete two more projects after their certification. Each project lasts from two months to a year, depending on the project scope. The black belt is a specialist. It has been suggested that small to mid-sized companies may need only between one and five black belts at one time. Individuals usually spend about 2 years as a black belt and are then moved into management jobs. The black-belt designation is also very valuable for finding new jobs.

Green belts. **Green belts** are trained in basic quality tools and work in teams to improve quality. Green belts are assigned part-time to work on process and design improvement. In some cases, the results of green-belt activities are the same as black belts; in other organizations, green belts are involved in less-critical projects. In a small company of 100 employees, there might be 1 black belt and 60 green belts. Some companies also have **yellow belts**, who are employees familiar with improvement processes.

Packaging Lean with Six Sigma

When firms undertook implementing Six Sigma, many saw that it had a lot of things in common with lean manufacturing. Rather than having two competing models for improvement, many have combined Six Sigma with lean. This is often referred to as **lean-Six Sigma**. In this section, we elaborate on the concepts relating to lean production. Companies who implement lean-Six Sigma still generally follow the DMAIC process described in the next section. However, with lean, the focus of Six Sigma becomes more oriented toward reducing wastefulness in organizations. In lean-Six Sigma, the Japanese term **muda** is often used to describe process waste.

Lean focuses on continually pursuing the reduction of waste with an emphasis on just-in-time practices such as **pull production**. This recognizes that all processes are inherently wasteful and include the possibility of improvement. As a starting point, Shingo's seven wastes of overproduction, defects, inventory, motion, overprocessing, conveyance, and waiting are targeted as opportunities for improvement.

Although lean and Six Sigma approaches have been combined, lean especially uses value stream and SIPOC diagrams to identify and isolate steps in key processes that do not add value for customers. By isolating and identifying these non-value-added activities, Lean can result in lower costs, lower defects, and improved customer value. Figure 13-4 shows a simplified value-stream map for a typical process that shows information flows, process steps, and average times relating to different steps in the value stream. Often, value stream maps show cycle times for particular tasks, costs, and work-in-process (WIP) inventory at each stage of the process. This provides a basis for studying the value stream and identifying its costs and inefficiencies. A Closer Look at Quality 13-1 discusses lean/Six Sigma at Textron.

A CLOSER LOOK AT QUALITY 13-1   Lean/Six Sigma at Textron[1]

Textron, an international company with more than 40,000 customers, makes everything from helicopters to golf carts. At Textron, quality improvement efforts are called Textron Six Sigma (TSS).

Although TSS has been successful, Textron found that it had to do some things to fine-tune its efforts after using Six Sigma for a number of years. It saw a difference between newly adopted Six Sigma and more mature Six Sigma efforts. First, although Six Sigma is focused on cost savings in many companies, Textron chose to emphasize customer impact. Even with this change of focus, recent TSS efforts saved nearly $10 million. In addition, they developed a rapid problem-solving green belt track to help shop floor workers work on immediate problems.

Although black belts were originally managed at the VP level, Textron found that it could better create improvement by moving the ownership further down the organization, including the plant manager and operational levels such as operations, supply chain, and engineering. Quality leadership also implemented a Six Sigma health metric to monitor Six Sigma success. These changes caused the perception of Six Sigma to increase from 4.5 (on a 7-point scale) to 5.8.

---

[1]Kelley, L., "Taking the Reins." *Quality Progress* (September 2010): 18–23.

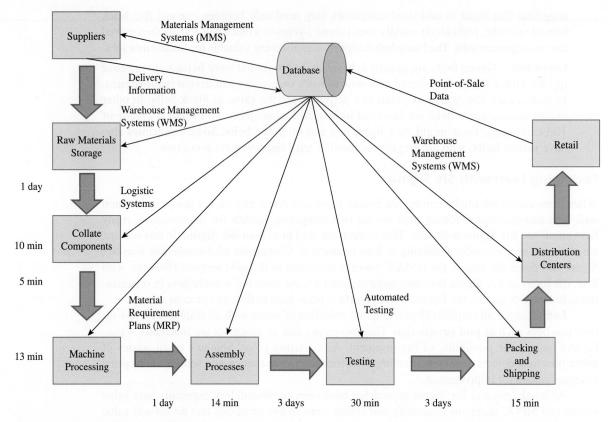

FIGURE 13-4 Simple Value-Stream Map

DMAIC OVERVIEW

Table 13-2 shows the steps in the **DMAIC process.** DMAIC stands for *define*, *measure*, *analyze*, *improve*, and *control*. It is very similar to the PDCA cycle proposed by Shewhart and Deming. We discuss each of these steps in two parts. Here, we define each of the steps and then we fit quality tools to each of these steps. Figure 13-5 shows an overview of the tools used at each stage of the DMAIC process. We discuss them in much more depth over the next several pages. In some cases, where we have already presented a tool such as the basic seven (B7) tools, we mention the tool. However, it is up to you to refer to the other chapter where the tool is defined and explained. A Closer Look at Quality 13-2 shows some results of DMAIC processes in different companies.

TABLE 13-2		The Six Sigma Process—DMAIC
DMAIC	**Define**	Define the project goals and customer (internal and external) deliverables
	Measure	Measure the process to determine current performance
	Analyze	Analyze and determine the root cause(s) of the defects
	Improve	Improve the process by eliminating defects
	Control	Control future process performance

Source: www.freequality.org (2009).

A CLOSER LOOK AT QUALITY 13-2   DMAIC in Action

While Kevin Colby was working on a Six Sigma project at the Truck Components Automated Products Division of Eaton Corporation, the company was examining cost-savings opportunities. The division produced transmissions that included speed sensors, which measure shaft speeds and work in conjunction with the gears produced by the Cleveland, Ohio-based company. The gears with holes caused signal fluctuations that affected the sensors. Two electronic control units (ECUs) with different circuit speeds were manufactured to allow the sensor to work with both types of gears.

Engineers within the division's design group who were involved with the gear project realized that they could simultaneously have an impact on two divisions. Jerry Ganski, principal engineer who led the effort to eliminate the second ECU, said, "We realized that removal of the holes in the gears would allow the Automated Products Division to eliminate the special ECU we had to manufacture to deal with the holes. We now use a common ECU for all our platforms and thus save the money it took to build, stock, and handle two ECU styles where the only difference between them was the speed sensor circuit. The savings is estimated at approximately 12 percent." Based on the improvements realized from these three projects, Eaton is investigating other gear-related projects for potential improvement opportunities.

DEFINE PHASE

In the **define phase**, projects are identified and selected. Project selection is performed under the direction and with the participation of the champion. Also involved in selection are master black belts and black or green belts. We discuss this in four phases:

1. Developing the business case
2. Project evaluation

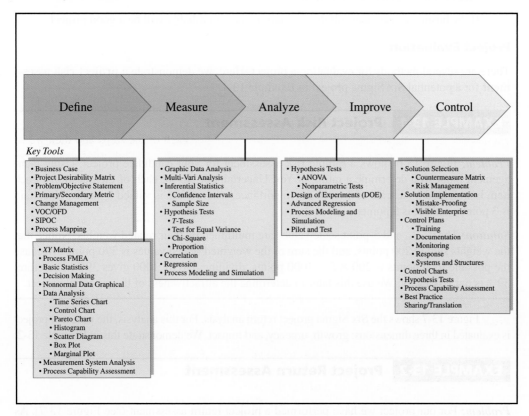

FIGURE 13-5 Overview of the Six Sigma Process

3. Pareto analysis
4. Project definition

Developing the Business Case

Business case development involves

- Identifying a group of possible projects
- Writing the business case
- Stratifying the business case into problem statement and objective statements

Following is a sample business case. As you can see, the **business case** is a short statement outlining the objectives, measurables, and justification for the project.

Business Case: During the four-week period from January 1, 2016, to February 1, 2016, the throughput yield for plant number 3 in region 4 was at 57% of capacity, resulting in an annualized COPQ of $5.6 million. This gap of rolled throughput yield mandates a business objective to improve throughput by 50%, from 57% of design capacity to 85% by February 1, 2017, representing $3 million in savings. This project will increase the throughput for plant 3 in region 4 to meet the year 2017 corporate goal of increasing sales in region 4 by $10 million.

The mnemonic device **RUMBA** is used to check the efficacy of a business case. Evaluating your business case, is it

- *R*ealistic?—Are the goals attainable; is the timeline feasible?
- *U*nderstandable?—Do I understand the case?
- *M*easurable?—Do we show the measures?
- *B*elievable?—That is a lot of money. Can it be done?
- *A*ctionable?—Can it be implemented?

If the business case meets all these requirements, it probably will be a good project.

Project Evaluation

There are several methods for evaluating a project. Here, we demonstrate a **project risk assessment** for a potential Six Sigma project in Example 13-1.

EXAMPLE 13-1   Project Risk Assessment

Problem: Figure 13-6 shows a sample risk assessment for your candidate project. Using management input, you determine a rating of Yes, Uncertain, or No for each of the questions. Each item is weighted on a scale of 1 to 10 for importance, where a Yes is valued 0 points, Uncertain is 3 points, and No is 5 points.

Solution: The 0-, 3-, and 5-point scale values are multiplied by their related weights. Notice that the weights sum to 200 points, and the sum of the weighted scaled values is 390 points. Because the possible total points is $200 \times 5 = 1000$ points, dividing 390 by 1000 gives 39%. Therefore, 39% is our risk factor. We use this later to determine the attractiveness of the potential project.

Figure 13-7 shows the Six Sigma project return analysis. For this analysis, the potential project is evaluated in three dimensions: growth, urgency, and impact. We demonstrate this in Example 13-2.

EXAMPLE 13-2   Project Return Assessment

Problem: For our project we have performed a project return assessment (see Figure 13-7). As is shown, using the return scales for growth, urgency, and impact each time the project rates a 2.

Six Sigma Project Risk Worksheet

Before worksheet can be completed, the following questions must be answered

1. *Is the defect/key characteristic known?*
2. *Is the defect/key characteristic measurable?*
3. *Is the solution to the problem unknown?*

Project Name: Plant 3 Throughput

Belt: Foster

Sponsor(s): Shannon

Mentor(s): _____

Date: Sept. 12, 2016

Risk Value: 39%

For questions 1 through 3...
  If you answered Yes, proceed with answering each criteria question below.
  If you answered No, see your mentor. Your project may be better completed by means other than Six Sigma.

Category	Criteria	Rating		Weight	Total
Define Opportunity	(Six Sigma Risk Rating Scale: Yes = 0; Uncertain = 3; No = 5)	Scale values			
	1 Are we currently measuring the defect(s)/key characteristic(s)?	Yes	0 ▼	10	0
	2 Is historical data currently available?	Yes	0 ▼	10	0
	3 Is it easy to acquire additional data?	Uncertain 3 ▼		10	30
	4 Are the specifications for the process or product defined?	No	5 ▼	5	25
	5 Do you know how the specifications were defined?	No	5 ▼	5	25
	6 Is the defect measured where it occurs in the process?	No	5 ▼	10	50
	7 Is the defect frequency continuous? ("No" for sporadic or cyclical)	No	5 ▼	5	25
Customer Focus					
	8 Has/have the customer(s) been identified?	Yes	0 ▼	5	0
	9 Have you verified what is important to the customer?	Yes	0 ▼	10	0
	10 Is this defect/key characteristic important to the customer?	Yes	0 ▼	10	0
	11 Will the customer see the result of eliminating/reducing the defect?	Uncertain 3 ▼		10	30
Company Benefit/ Leveraging					
	12 Does the defect relate to the mission, a business driver, or a reliability measure?	Yes	0 ▼	10	0
	13 Does the defect impact operations?	Yes	0 ▼	10	0
	14 Can the results of the project be applied to other processes or products?	Yes	0 ▼	5	0
	15 Can the impact be quantified in dollars?	Uncertain 3 ▼		10	30
Project Leadership/ Global Bounding					
	16 Are all managers, at all levels, in agreement that your project is important?	No	5 ▼	5	25
	17 Is your team the only effort currently pursuing this defect?	Yes	0 ▼	10	0
	18 Can adequate visibility for the problem and solution be created?	Uncertain 3 ▼		10	30
	19 Is the team comprised of representatives from only one location/business function?	Uncertain 3 ▼		10	30
	20 Are appropriate resources available to participate on the team?	Uncertain 3 ▼		10	30
	21 Can the project be bounded to an effective size?	Yes	0 ▼	10	0
	22 Can the project be completed on schedule within 4–6 months?	Uncertain 3 ▼		5	15
	23 Do we know the boundaries of the process(es)?	Uncertain 3 ▼		5	15
	24 Can process changes be implemented within the project schedule?	Uncertain 3 ▼		10	30
	Totals			200	390
	$390/(200 \times 5) = 39\%$				

FIGURE 13-6   Risk Assessment

Solution: Totaling the score, 6 out of a possible 15 points yields a return factor score of 40%. Combining our scores for both risk and return into a project risk and return matrix (Figure 13-8), we see that this project is classified as low-hanging fruit. This means that this project is worthwhile if it can be completed quickly.

Six Sigma Project Return

Before this worksheet can be completed, the following questions must be answered: *Does the defect / key characteristic for this project relate to one of the company's business drivers, or a reliability or service measure?*

If you answered *Yes,* proceed with the worksheet.
If you answered *No,* see your sponsor or mentor. This project may not provide appropriate returns.

Project:	Plant 3 Throughput	Growth Score:	2/5
Belt:	Foster	Urgency Score:	2/5
Sponsor(s):	Shannon	Impact Score:	2/5
Date:	Sept. 12, 2016	Return Value:	6/15 = 40%

Growth = Competitive Advantage
Choose the single best answer

Return Scale		
0	☐	The project does not result in incremental sales with paying customer(s).
1	☐	The project does not create incremental sales with paying customer(s), but does improve the competitive position of the company by improving operating efficiencies that bear on competitive performance.
2	☑	The project does not create incremental sales with paying customer(s), but does improve the competitive position of the company by improving operating efficiencies in a key strategic area.
3	☐	The project provides some degree of incremental sales with paying customer(s) and moderately improves the competitive position of the company.
4	☐	The project provides a moderate degree of incremental sales with paying customer(s) and substantially improves the competitive position of the company by providing a higher level of service.
5	☐	The project provides a high degree of incremental sales with paying customer(s) and greatly improves the competitive position of the company by providing a level of service unmatched by competitors.

Urgency = Competitive Response
Choose the single best answer

Return Scale		
0	☐	The project can be postponed for at least 12 months without affecting competitive position, or existing processes or procedures can produce substantially the same result and will not affect competitive position.
1	☐	The postponement of the project does not affect competitive position, and minimal incremental operating costs are expected to be incurred to produce substantially the same result.
2	☑	The postponement of the project does not affect competitive position; however, operating costs may escalate to produce substantially the same result.
3	☐	If the project is postponed for now, the company remains capable of responding to the needed change without affecting its competitive position. However, it is expected the company will be substantially hindered in responding rapidly and effectively to future changes in the competitive environment.
4	☐	The postponement of the project may result in further competitive disadvantage to the company, or in a loss of competitive opportunity; or existing successful activities in the company may be curtailed because of the lack of the proposed system.
5	☐	The postponement of the project will result in further competitive disadvantage to the company, or in a loss of competitive opportunity; or existing successful activities in the company must be curtailed because of the lack of having a solution to this problem.

Impact = Annual Expected Financial Savings
Choose the single best answer

Return Scale	
0	☐ Less than $20,000*
1	☐ $20,000–$99,999*
2	☑ $100,000–$200,000
3	☐ $200,001–$300,000
4	☐ $300,001–$400,000
5	☐ Over $400,000

(*Projects are expected to have, on average, an annual expected savings of $100,000 or more. If the project does not meet this criteria, it should have significantly high scores in the Growth and Urgency categories)

FIGURE 13-7 Project Return Analysis

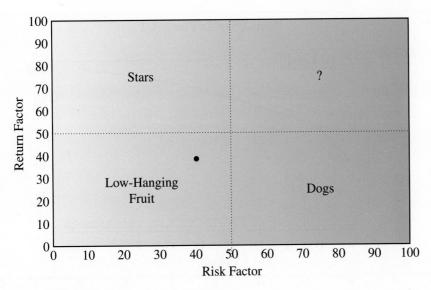

FIGURE 13-8   Project Risk and Return Matrix

Pareto Analysis

Part of the responsibility of the champion is to perform a cost of poor quality (COPQ) analysis. This is based on the PAF categorization of costs (see Chapter 4). Performing a study of internal and external failure costs will help determine where the most benefit can be found. Figure 13-9 shows a two-level Pareto analysis of COPQ. The first-level analysis shows $5.6-million quality costs in plant A, which is the plant with the highest losses. When we study causes of poor quality in plant A, it becomes clear that operation P accounts for about 62% of the $5.6 million loss (in the second-level analysis). For this reason, this project holds great promise for breakthrough improvement.

Problem Definition

Once the risk analysis and Pareto analysis have been completed for the project, a project definition consists of a problem statement, project goals/objectives, primary metrics, secondary metrics, and team member identification. Figure 13-10 shows an example of problem definition.

MEASURE PHASE

The **measure phase** involves two major steps:

1. Selecting process outcomes
2. Verifying measurements
   We discuss these separately.

Selecting Process Outcomes

Table 13-3 shows the tools often used in the measure phase. To define process outcomes, you first need to understand the process, which involves process mapping. The process map uses the same approach defined in Chapter 10. A *process map* is a flowchart with responsibility.

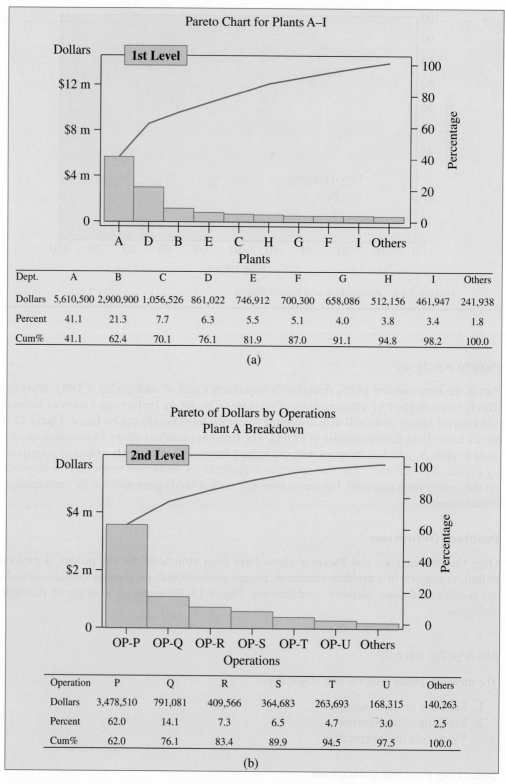

FIGURE 13-9 Pareto Analysis

Problem Statement:	In 2016, plant A lost $5.6 million on COPQ. Of this, almost $3.5 million occurred in operation P (see Figure 13-9). This has resulted in a loss of profitability for the firm.			
Project Goals/Objective:	Reduce COPQ for operation P by 30% by year end.			
Primary Metrics:	COPQ	Secondary Metrics:	Downtime for process	
	Rework (% of sales)		Plant sales	
	Scrap (% of sales)		Labor productivity	
Team Members:	Bill S.	John G.	Scott W.	
	Cynthia W.	Scott S.		

FIGURE 13-10 Problem Definition

In Figure 13-11 there is a high-level process map showing champion responsibilities in the Six Sigma process. Notice that any of the individual steps could be broken out into lower-level process maps. The goal with a process map is to identify non-value-added activities. Two important measures that are monitored are **defects per unit (DPU)** and **defects per million opportunities (DPMO).**

The **XY matrix** is used to identify inputs (Xs) and outputs (Ys) from a project you have mapped and are desiring to pursue. Figure 13-12 shows an XY matrix for a potential project. The inputs include dimensions, standard operating procedures (SOPs), and other inputs along the left-hand column. Output variables include key dimensions, sizes, flashing, and the presence of all needed welds. Each of the outputs is provided an importance weight (1–10). The relationship between each of the Xs and Ys is placed in the matrix (1–10 scale). These are multiplied horizontally, with ranks and scores computed by multiplying each matrix cell by its weight and summing the products horizontally. As you can see, the most important aspects of the process are SOPs, weld schedules, and daily tip dressing.

TABLE 13-3 Measure-Phase Tools

Process map
XY matrix
FMEA
Gauge R&R
Capability assessment

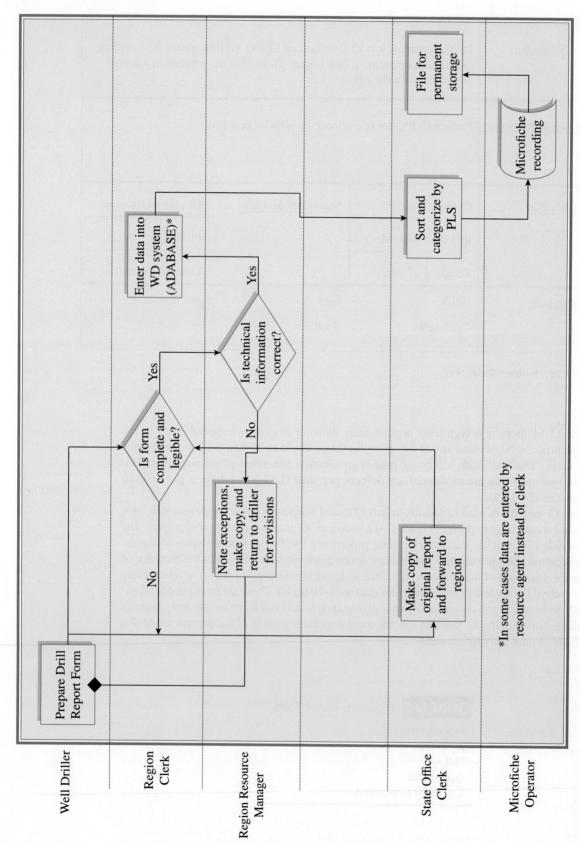

Well Driller	Prepare Drill Report Form ◆
Region Clerk	Is form complete and legible? — Is technical information correct? — Enter data into WD system (ADABASE)*
Region Resource Manager	Note exceptions, make copy, and return to driller for revisions
State Office Clerk	Make copy of original report and forward to region — Sort and categorize by PLS
Microfiche Operator	Microfiche recording — File for permanent storage

*In some cases data are entered by resource agent instead of clerk

FIGURE 13-11   High-Level Process Map

Inputs	Width Dimension	Length Dimension	Assembly Size	Flash Free	All Welds Present	Product	Rank
Rank	5	7	9	8	10		
1 Width Grommet 1	10					50	8
2 Length Grommet 1		7				49	10
3 Subassembly Width	7					35	12
4 Subassembly Length		10				70	1
5 All SOPs	9	9		9	6	240	1*
6 Weld Schedule			10		10	190	2*
7 Air Pressure			5	5	5	135	4
8 Line Voltage			5	5	5	135	4
9 H$_2$O Circulation			5	5	5	135	4
10 Width Bracket 2	10					50	8
11 Length Bracket 2		7				49	10
12 Daily Tip Dressing			10	8		154	3*
13							
14							
15							

XY Matrix — Project: Welding Operation — Date: Oct. 14, 2016

Importance weights

$(9\times5)+(9\times7)+(9\times8)+(6\times10)=240$

Relationship weights

FIGURE 13-12 *XY* Matrix

EXAMPLE 13-3 **XY Matrix in Action**

Problem: Figure 13-13 shows a matrix for a services process. On the left, inputs *A* through *G* are listed with their associated correlations with five different outputs.

Solution: Figure 13-14 shows the solution for Example 13-3. As you can see, inputs *F* and *D* should be studied especially closely.

FMEA

FMEA is used to identify ways in which a process or product can fail to meet critical customer requirements.

Verifying Measurements

When measuring critical characteristics of processes, it is necessary to use gauges, calipers, and other tools. Although these tools are often very accurate, there can be problems with variation in measurements. As a result, **measurement system analysis (MSA)** is used to determine whether

Project: Service Process

Date: Oct. 14, 2016

	Output Variables	Vendor Selection	Component Selection	Internal Lead Time	Cost	Ship to Location					
	Rank	7	10	8	9	5					
	Inputs										
1	A		10	4	5						
2	B	9		7	2						
3	C	8	4		10						
4	D	10	9	8							
5	E	4		3		10					
6	F	4	7	8	5	10					
7	G	3	7		10						
8											
9											

FIGURE 13-13 *XY* Matrix for Example 13-3

measurements are consistent. Another approach for verifying measurements is to perform product and process capability analysis.

Gauge R&R

The most commonly used MSA is **gauge repeatability and reproducibility analysis (gauge R&R, sometimes referred to as gage R&R)**. Gauge R&R is used to determine the accuracy

Project: Service Process

Date: Oct. 14, 2016

	Output Variables	Vendor Selection	Component Selection	Internal Lead Time	Cost	Shift to Location			Total	Rank	
	Rank	7	10	8	9	5					
	Inputs										
1	A		10	4	5				177	5	
2	B	9		7	2				137	6	
3	C	8	4		10				186	3	
4	D	10	9	8					224	2	*
5	E	4		3		10			102	7	
6	F	4	7	8	5	10			257	1	*
7	G	3	7		10				181	4	
8											
9											

FIGURE 13-14 Solution to Example 13-3

and precision of your measurements. If your measurements are imprecise, there will be a large amount of variation as a result of measurement error. Obviously, you do not want to draw incorrect conclusions as a result of measurement error. Problems in measurement can result for a variety of reasons:

- The measurement gauges are faulty.
- Operators are using gauges improperly.
- Training in measurement procedures is lacking.
- The gauge is calibrated incorrectly.

Statistical experiments using analysis of variance (ANOVA) are useful when performing gauge R&R. Two-way ANOVA is used to determine whether variation comes from the part being measured, differences in operator measurements, or the measurement instrument.

EXAMPLE 13-4 Gauge R&R in Action

Problem: Table 13-4 contains measurement data for a particular operation with three operators taking two measurements per part.[2] In other words, there are three operators and 20 parts. Each operator measures each part twice using a gauge and logs these measurements. For example, operator 1 measures part 1 twice, with resulting measurements of 21 and 20 millimeters. The same operator measures part 2 and gets the results of 24 and 23 millimeters. As you can see, there is measurement variation. However, we do not know whether the variation comes from the gauge, the part, or the operators.

TABLE 13-4 Gauge R&R Data

Part Number	Operator 1	Operator 2	Operator 3
1	21	20	19
	20	20	21
2	24	24	23
	23	24	24
3	20	19	20
	21	21	22
4	27	28	27
	27	26	28
5	19	19	18
	18	18	21
6	23	24	23
	21	21	22
7	22	22	22
	21	24	20
8	19	18	19
	17	20	18
9	24	25	24
	23	23	24
10	25	26	24
	23	25	25
11	21	20	21
	20	20	20

[2]Montgomery, D., *Design and Analysis of Experiments* (New York: Wiley, 1997), p. 473.

Part Number	Operator 1	Operator 2	Operator 3
12	18	17	18
	19	19	19
13	23	25	25
	25	25	25
14	24	23	24
	24	25	25
15	29	30	31
	30	28	30
16	26	25	25
	26	26	27
17	20	19	20
	20	20	20
18	19	19	21
	21	19	23
19	25	25	25
	26	24	25
20	19	18	19
	19	17	17

FIGURE 13-15 Gauge R&R in Excel *Source:* Microsoft Excel, Microsoft Corporation. Used by permission.

Solution: Figure 13-15 shows the ANOVA table for these data. From the ANOVA table, you can see that parts contribute most of the variation (sample row in the ANOVA table, $p = .000$), operator effect is insignificant (columns row in the ANOVA table, $p = .275$), and part–operator interactions are insignificant ($p = .881$). As a result, we conclude that the gauge measurement is repeatable and reproducible.

Using Excel to Perform Gauge R&R Analysis

The data need to be entered into an Excel spreadsheet exactly as shown in Figure 13-15. The labels for the operators are inserted in row 1. The part numbers are listed only once in column A as shown. And the data are entered as shown. This problem is set up for only two measurements per part. Follow the steps outlined in the figure. *Note*: Use two-factor analysis of variance with replication.

     The results for Example 13-4 are shown in Figure 13-15. The *P*-value column in the ANOVA table shows what variables significantly contribute to variation.

ANALYZE PHASE

The **analyze phase** involves gathering and analyzing data relative to a particular black-belt project. Following are the analyze-phase steps:

1. Define your performance objectives.
2. Identify independent variables (*X*s).
3. Analyze sources of variability.

     We discuss each of these steps separately. Because the tools used in this analysis were already discussed in Chapter 10, Chapter 11, and Chapter 12, we refer only to these tools. You may need to refer to the other chapters to refresh your memory about these tools.

Defining Objectives

When defining performance objectives, you are attempting to determine what characteristics of the process need to be changed to achieve improvement. First, capability analysis is reviewed to determine where the processes are incapable. These areas are prioritized in order of importance. As shown in Figure 13-16, capability analysis demonstrates whether certain quantitative parameters or discrete events are meeting specification. It helps to determine whether these parameters or events are centered on the mean and whether they meet specification. If they are not centered on the desired mean, the process mean needs to be adjusted. If there is too much variability, the variability is reduced. We discuss means for reducing variation in the improve phase.

Identifying *X*s

This step involves identifying the independent variables in which data will be gathered. They are variables that contribute significantly to process or product variation. Process maps, *XY* matrices, brainstorming, and FMEAs are the primary tools used in identifying *X*s.

Analyzing Sources of Variation

The goal of this step is to use visual and statistical tools to better understand the relationships between dependent and independent variables (*X*s and *Y*s) for use in future experimentation. A number of tools are used in this analysis. They include histograms, box plots, scatter plots, regression analysis, and hypothesis tests.

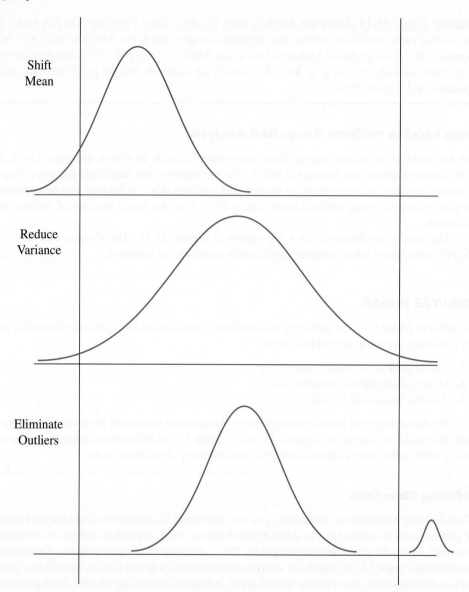

Shift
Mean

Reduce
Variance

Eliminate
Outliers

FIGURE 13-16 Capability Results

IMPROVE PHASE

The **improve phase** of the DMAIC process involves offline experimentation. Offline experimentation involves studying the variables we have identified and using ANOVA to determine whether these independent variables significantly affect variation in our dependent variables. We introduce an important method for performing offline experiments: the *Taguchi method*.

CONTROL PHASE

The **control phase** involves managing the improved processes using process charts and implementing control plans. These topics were covered in Chapter 11 and Chapter 12.

TAGUCHI DESIGN OF EXPERIMENTS

Many different factors, inputs, or variables need to be considered when making a product. For example, suppose that you wanted to bake a cake. How much flour should you use? How many eggs? How long should it bake? At what temperature should you set the oven? Probably you would find a recipe to follow. What if there were no recipes, and you were the pioneer trying to invent the best combinations of inputs to bake a cake? You would probably have to resort to trial and error. However, there is a better way to design an experiment to find out the best combination of variables to make your product (cake).

The **Taguchi method** is a standardized approach for determining the best combination of inputs to produce a product or service. This is accomplished through **design of experiments (DOE)** for determining parameters. DOE is an important tool in the arsenal of tools available to the design and process engineer. It provides a method for quantitatively identifying just the right ingredients that go together to make a high-quality product or service. In this section, we discuss first the Taguchi definitions, stages, and behavioral issues that form Taguchi's approach to design of experiments. The purpose here is to introduce concepts and processes relating to the Taguchi method from a managerial perspective. The more technical engineering explanation is available in a variety of engineering books. Taguchi approaches design from four perspectives: robust design, concept design, parameter design, and tolerance design. These perspectives are defined in the following paragraphs.

Robust Design

The Taguchi concept of **robust design** states that products and services should be designed so that they are inherently defect-free and insensitive to random variation. The concept is not necessarily new. The notion that products and services should be designed to be of high quality or that processes should be defect-free is as old as mass assembly. However, Taguchi has provided new approaches for creating robust designs through a three-step method of concept design, parameter design, and tolerance design.

Concept design is the process of examining competing technologies to produce a product. Concept design includes process technology choices and process design choices. Appropriate choices in these areas can reduce production costs and result in higher-quality products. In a *copying* store, concept design includes layout choices and choices of technology. Each candidate copying machine is tested separately to determine its suitability for the job. In financial services companies, this step likely will involve user groups, MIS staff, and systems analysts in defining processes and choices of equipment and technology.

Parameter design refers to the selection of **control factors** and the determination of **optimal levels** for each of the factors. Control factors are those variables in a process that management can manipulate. For example, the type and amount of training provided to customer service representatives is controlled by management. If it is determined that the amount of training received by customer service representatives determines the quality of service provided to the customer, training is identified as a control factor. Control factors do not affect production costs. Optimal levels are the targets or measurements for performance. For example, a sheet of paper is 8.5 inches wide; it would be the target. The goal is to find the most efficient process and service design. Parameter design involves selecting the best level for performance. For example, when baking cookies, what is the best temperature and time for baking? These parameters can be determined through experimentation.

Tolerance design deals with developing specification limits. Tolerance design occurs after parameter design has been used to reduce variation and the resulting improvement has been insufficient. This often results in an increase in production costs. For example, in tolerance design, engineers selectively tighten specified tolerances and require the use of higher-grade materials in production.

Of these four design considerations, the Taguchi method focuses primarily on parameter design. Getting back to our cake-baking example, by using the Taguchi method, we could identify the best amounts of heat, baking time, flour, eggs, and other ingredients to make the best-tasting cake. These ingredients are called *parameters*, and their best amounts are referred to as *levels* or *settings*.

BACKGROUND OF THE TAGUCHI METHOD

The Taguchi method was first introduced by Dr. Genichi Taguchi to AT&T Bell Laboratories in 1980. Thanks to its wide acceptance and utilization, the Taguchi method for improving quality is now commonly viewed as comparable in importance to statistical process control (SPC), the Deming approach, and the Japanese concept of total quality control. From a historical perspective, Taguchi's method is a continuation of the work in quality improvement that began with Shewhart's work in statistical quality control (SQC) and Deming's work in improving Japanese quality. The Taguchi method provides

1. A basis for determining the functional relationship between controllable product or service design factors and the outcomes of a process.
2. A method for adjusting the mean of a process by optimizing controllable variables.
3. A procedure for examining the relationship between random noise in the process and product or service variability.

Among the unique aspects of the Taguchi method are the Taguchi definition of quality, the quality loss function (QLF), and the concept of robust design. These are discussed briefly in the following paragraphs.

Taguchi Definition of Quality

The traditional definition of quality was conformance to specification. However, Taguchi diverges from the traditional view of conformance quality. In Taguchi terms, **ideal quality** refers to a reference point or target value for determining the quality level of a product or service. This reference point is expressed as a target value. Ideal quality is delivered if a product or a tangible service performs its intended function throughout its projected life under reasonable operating conditions without harmful side effects. In services, because production and consumption of the service often occur simultaneously, ideal quality is a function of customer perceptions and satisfaction. Taguchi measures service quality in terms of loss to society if the service is not performed as expected.

Quality Loss Function

In Figure 13-17 a measurement is taken of the critical product characteristic. This is shown in the figure as *A*. If *A* is within the specification limits, the traditional conclusion was that it wasn't a problem. However, point *A* is closer to being out of specification than to being at the target measurement. This means that over time it might cause a problem. Taguchi calls this potential for

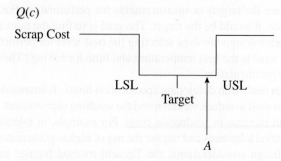

FIGURE 13-17 Classical QC-Step Function

FIGURE 13-18 Taguchi Quadratic Loss Function

problem a potential **loss to society**. In a "hard-core" manufacturing operation, Taguchi identifies these losses to society not only in terms of rejection, scrap, or rework but also in terms of pollution that is added to the environment, products that wear out too quickly, or other negative effects that occur. Loss to society is the cost of a deviation from a target value.

To quantify loss to society, Taguchi used the concept of a *quadratic loss function.* Figure 13-18 shows that any variation from the target of six (where *Target* = 6) results in some loss to the company. The **quality loss function (QLF)** focuses on the economic and societal penalties incurred as a result of purchasing a nonconforming product. Losses may include maintenance costs, failure costs, ill effects to the environment such as pollution, or excessive costs of operating the product. The QLF is determined by first computing the constant

$$K = C/T^2 \tag{13.2}$$

where

    K = a constant

    C = the unit repair cost

    T = a tolerance interval (the allowable variation in a parameter)

After computing the constant, next compute

$$L = K * V^2 (\$/\text{unit})$$

where

    L = the economic penalty incurred by the customer as a result of the product quality deviation

    V^2 = the mean squared deviation from the desired target value

The application of this concept is demonstrated in the followed example.

EXAMPLE 13-5 **Application of the QLF**

Problem: Suppose the cost to repair an automobile radiator is $200. Compute the QLF for losses incurred as a result of a deviation from a target setting where a tolerance of 6 ± 0.5 mm is required, and the mean squared deviation from the target is $(1/6)^2$.

Solution:

$$K = 200/.5^2 = 800, \text{ and}$$

$$L = K * V^2 = 800 * (1/6)^2 = \$22.22/\text{unit}$$

Therefore, the loss caused by deviation from the target standard is $22.22 per unit. When we can compare the costs of other defectives, we can establish priorities for implementing product design improvement.

The QLF deviated from the historical concept of statistical-based control charting and the establishment of specification limits in that any deviation from the target or mean specification is expressed in terms of an economic loss to the customer.

THE TAGUCHI PROCESS

An outline is presented here of the steps in the Taguchi process. Although the Taguchi process is viewed as fairly technical and statistical, a major component involves behavioral steps such as teamwork and brainstorming. We now examine the steps in the Taguchi process. As shown in Figure 13-19, a series of six steps is followed in the initial phase of the Taguchi experiment. These steps are described in the following paragraphs.

   1. *Problem identification.* First, the production problem must be identified. The problem may have to do with the production process or the service itself.

   2. *Brainstorming session.* Second, a brainstorming session to identify variables that have a critical effect on service or product quality takes place. At a minimum, the brainstorming session is attended by the project facilitator/leader and workers taking part in the process to be changed. Managers attending the brainstorming session should be careful that their attendance does not stifle frank discussion among the session participants. In services and manufacturing environments, managerial practices are often critical variables impeding ideal quality results. When appropriate, technical staff members such as computer programmers or systems analysts also attend. The role of the facilitator is to initiate the brainstorming session, to maintain a non-judgmental environment conducive to discussion, and to document the discussion for future use.

   The critical variables identified in this session are referred to by Taguchi as *factors.* They may be identified as either *control factors* (variables that are under the control of management) or **noise factors** (uncontrollable variation). Examples of control factors within a production process can be procedures, amount of lighting, or ambient temperature setting. Noise-factor examples include uncontrollable variation in temperature, variations in human performance, or environmental variables that cannot be controlled.

   Once these factors have been identified, different levels or settings of the control factors are defined. For example, three or four possible levels of ambient temperature settings may be identified for the production of silicon wafers. At least three levels should be used for each factor in order to identify functional forms (such as interactions) of the effects more clearly. Possible

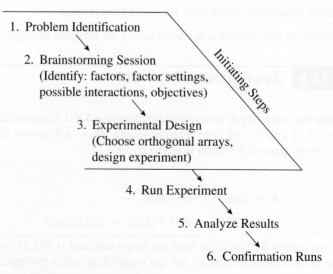

FIGURE 13-19 Taguchi Process

interactions between factors should be identified during the brainstorming session. Noise factors can be measured at the time of the experiment and included in the analysis.

Once the decision variables are established, *objectives of the experiments should be defined.* Examples of objectives are the less the better, nominal is best, or the more the better. These objectives are defined as follows:

- *The less the better.* This desired level of defectives or errors is as close to zero as possible. For example, in a cake-baking process, we may want zero "fallen" cakes. In an egg-packaging process, we desire the lowest number possible of broken eggs.
- *Nominal is best.* This desired outcome usually relates to a measurement. For example, we may desire to have all boards exactly 0.75 inches thick or all sheets of paper 8.5 inches wide.
- *The more the better.* This desired outcome is the opposite of the less the better. We may desire the maximum number of computer chips per lot without defects. We may want maximum weight gain from a nutrient we give to a farm animal.

3. *Experimental design.* Using the factors, factor levels, and objectives from the brainstorming session, the experiment is designed. The Taguchi method uses **offline experimentation** as a means of improving quality. This contrasts with traditional online (in-process) quality measurement. For this reason, the experimental design is a key consideration in conducting a Taguchi experiment. As with any experiment, care should be taken when selecting an appropriate number of trials and with the conditions for each trial, such as means of performing measurements, maintaining continuity with objectives, and reducing random noise by providing sufficient controls. The number of **replications** to be used in the experiment should be established beforehand.

4. *Experimentation.* Different Taguchi analysis approaches use quantitatively rigorous techniques, such as ANOVA, signal-to-noise (S/N) ratios, and response charts. These approaches, although not always theoretically sound,[3] are useful for engineering-related projects involving engineered specifications, torques, and tolerances.

For services, the approach advocated by Ross[4] may be the most useful. This methodology is more intuitively understandable for management and provides essentially the same results as ANOVA and S/N ratios. What is compromised with the Ross methodology is the additional information provided by the more quantitative results of ANOVA and S/N ratios. Here are the experimental steps used in this methodology:

- **a.** Choose the appropriate orthogonal array for the experiment. (**Orthogonal arrays** are tools to maintain independence between the successive trials of a Taguchi experiment.) The appropriate orthogonal array is determined by the number of factors and levels chosen from the brainstorming session. A number of standard orthogonal arrays can be found in the books mentioned in the footnotes.
- **b.** Run the experiment for the appropriate number of replications and record the results.
- **c.** Compute average performance levels for each of the factors and levels.
- **d.** Plot the average responses on a response chart showing the best outcomes in accordance with the objective of the experiment.

5. *Analysis.* Experimentation is used to identify the factors that result in closest-to-target performance. In essence, the best levels for all factors are determined. If interactions between factors are evident, two alternatives are possible. Either ignore the interactions (there is inherent risk to this approach) or, provided the cost is not prohibitive, run a full factorial experiment to detect interactions. The full factorial experiment tests all possible interactions among variables.

---

[3]Box, G. E. P., and Bisgaard, S., "The Scientific Context of Quality Improvement," *Quality Progress* 20, 6 (June 1987): 54–61.
[4]Ross, P., *Taguchi Techniques for Quality Engineering* (New York: McGraw-Hill, 1988).

6. *Confirming experiment.* Once the optimal levels for each of the factors have been determined, a confirming experiment with factors set at the optimal levels should be conducted to validate the earlier results. If earlier results are not validated, the experiment may have somehow been significantly flawed. If results vary from those expected, interactions also may be present, and the experiment should therefore be repeated.

EXAMPLE 13-6 Taguchi Method in Action

Problem: Here is a standard Taguchi problem. In this experiment, it was determined that there were three important factors (Xs) in producing a wood product. These factors were

- *A*: Pressure applied in treatment
- *B*: Drying temperature
- *C*: Process time

For each of these factors, two levels were established for each setting:

- *A*: 250 psi, 300 psi
- *B*: 150 degrees, 180 degrees
- *C*: 3 hours, 4 hours

We need to determine the best levels for each of the settings. The objective is the more the better.

Solution: When performing a Taguchi experiment, you need to use an orthogonal array. Because we have three levels with two factors, a full-factorial experiment would require $2^3 = 8$ trials. The Taguchi method is much more economical, so the L_4 (2^3) orthogonal array (the right array for the job) is used to perform this experiment. The array looks like this:

	Factors			
Trials	A	B	C	Responses
1	1	1	1	25
2	1	2	2	30
3	2	1	2	28
4	2	2	1	36

Interpreting the orthogonal array, you see there are three factors, and only four trials are needed to run the experiment. Following the first line, this means that for the first trial we use settings A_1, B_1, and C_1. This means we use pressure applied at 250 psi, drying temperature at 150 degrees, and a process time of 3 hours. We then measure the outcome, and the responsiveness of the wood product is rated at 25. Similarly, for trial 2, we set the pressure at 250 psi, the temperature at 180, and the time at 4 hours. As you can now see, the 1s and 2s in the orthogonal array correspond to levels for each of the factors to be used during each trial of the experiment. Remember that a trial is an iteration or "run" of the experiment.

Determining the best levels for each factor requires computing averages and analysis of variance. We demonstrate this in Excel.

Using Excel to Solve Taguchi Experiments

Figure 13-20 shows the results of our Taguchi experiment. To compute our mean scores, we averaged the responses for each factor and level. That is, in trials 1 and 2, factor *A* was set at level 1.

	A	B	C	D	E
1	**Trial**	**Factor A**	**Factor B**	**Factor C**	**Responses**
2	1	1	1	1	25
3	2	1	2	2	30
4	3	2	1	2	28
5	4	2	2	1	36
6					
7					
8	**Var & Level**	**Mean Scores**			
9	A1	27.5	(E2+E3)/2		
10	A2	32	(E4+E5)/2		
11	B1	26.5	(E2+E4)/2		
12	B2	33	(E3+E5)/2		
13	C1	30.5	(E2+E5)/2		
14	C2	29	(E3+E4)/2		
15					

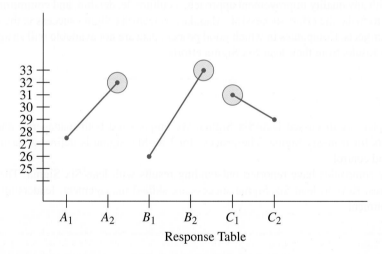

Response Table

FIGURE 13-20   Example 13-6 Results   *Source:* Microsoft Excel, Microsoft Corporation.
Used by permission.

Therefore, the average response when factor A was at level 1 was $(25 + 30)/2 = 27.5$. However, when factor A was set at level 2, the mean response was 32. Because our objective is the more the better, the higher response is preferred. Similarly, B_2 and C_1 are preferred settings. This means that the best settings are as follows:

- Pressure applied in treatment = 300 psi
- Drying temperature = 180 degrees
- Process time = 3 hours.

DESIGN FOR SIX SIGMA

Design for Six Sigma (DFSS) is used for designing new products and services with high performance, as measured by customer-based, critical-to-quality metrics. Instead of the DMAIC methodology, DFSS requires the **DMADV process** (design, measure, analyze, design, verify). Another method for DFSS is **IDOV** (identify, design, optimize, verify). IDOV is focused on final engineering design optimization. These methods are customer-focused, encompass the entire business-to-market process, and pertain to both services and products. Whereas DMAIC pertains to improving existing processes and products, DMADV pertains to developing new processes and products.

LEAN-SIX SIGMA FROM A CONTINGENCY PERSPECTIVE

As we stated early in the chapter, lean-Six Sigma is a very popular approach for improving the robustness of designs and processes. As you have seen, this approach is very technical and requires special expertise in the form of black-belt specialists. This method can be very useful for companies that need to improve their cost and efficiency through quality efforts.

As with any quality improvement approach, when people implement lean-Six Sigma without thoroughly understanding their processes, sometimes processes fail. Some reasons for lean-Six Sigma failures include

- Lack of leadership by champions.
- Misunderstood roles and responsibilities.
- Lack of appropriate culture for improvement.
- Resistance to change and the Six Sigma structure.
- Faulty strategies for deployment.
- Lack of data.

As with any quality improvement approach, a culture, leadership, and commitment need to be in place to make the effort successful. Also, key to lean-Six Sigma success is the availability of data for projects. Companies in which good process data are not available will struggle getting outstanding results from their lean-Six Sigma efforts.

Summary

In this chapter, we discussed lean-Six Sigma. We emphasized both managerial and technical requirements for lean-Six Sigma. The process for lean-Six Sigma is define, measure, analyze, improve, and control.

Many companies have reported outstanding results with lean-Six Sigma. There are also many failures. Keys to lean-Six Sigma success are skilled management, leadership, and long-term commitment.

Key Terms

Analyze phase
Black belt
Business case
Champion
Concept design
Control factors
Control phase
Defects per million opportunities (DPMO)
Defects per unit (DPU)
Define phase
Design for Six Sigma (DFSS)
Design of experiments (DOE)

DMADV (design, measure, analyze, design, verify) process
DMAIC (define, measure, analyze, improve, control) process
Gauge repeatability and reproducibility analysis (gauge R&R)
Green belts
Ideal quality
IDOV (identify, design, optimize, verify)
Improve phase

Lean
Lean-Six Sigma
Loss to society
Master black belts
Measure phase
Measurement system analysis (MSA)
Muda
Noise factors
Offline experimentation
Optimal levels
Orthogonal arrays
Parameter design
Project risk assessment

Pull production
Quality loss function (QLF)
Replications
Robust design
RUMBA (realistic, understandable, measurable, believable, actionable)
Six Sigma
Taguchi method
Tolerance design
XY matrix
Yellow belts

Discussion Questions

1. Where do you think that lean-Six Sigma can be used effectively?
2. How will risk assessments vary from industry to industry?
3. What industries would be the best candidates for the lean-Six Sigma approach? Why?
4. In the Taguchi method, critical variables are referred to as factors. Identify the two types of groups and discuss the means for detecting factors.
5. Can you think of an example for which the Taguchi quality loss function (QLF) would work in real life? Discuss how it might work.
6. How does the Taguchi concept of ideal quality compare to other definitions of quality discussed in Chapter 1?
7. How could the Taguchi method be used to design a course in quality management? Identify all the variables, measures, and objectives.
8. Why are behavioral processes such as brainstorming important for the Taguchi method?
9. How would you cost-benefit a Taguchi experiment? What might be some of the quantifiable parameters you would use in evaluating the worth of a Taguchi experiment?
10. The chapter cites different services implementations of the Taguchi method. Do you think the Taguchi method is useful for services? Why or why not? Why do you think the technique has not been widely adopted in services?

Problems

1. Part of a Six Sigma project is to identify Xs and Ys. What are the Xs you can identify for student satisfaction with a quality management course? Use the Y (dependent variable) of student satisfaction with a quality management class.
2. Part of a Six Sigma project is to identify Xs and Ys. Identify Xs and Ys for an athletic director of a major university (insert the name of your university here) who is interested in increasing attendance at football games.
3. Part of a Six Sigma project is to identify Xs and Ys. Identify these variables for the owner of a copy shop who is interested in reducing mistakes in orders.
4. Develop a problem definition (see Figure 13-10) for the project in Problem 3.
5. Complete the XY matrix for the following data:

XY						
Matrix						
	Outputs					
	A	**B**	**C**	**D**	**Total**	**Rank**
Ranks:	4	6	5	9		
Inputs						
1	10					
2			5			
3		7				
4				8		
5		3	5			

Which inputs are the most important?

6. Complete the *XY* matrix for the following data:

XY							
Matrix							
	Output						
	A	**B**	**C**	**D**	**E**	**Total**	**Rank**
Ranks:	3	8	9	6	7		
Inputs							
1	4	3	5	1	2		
2	5	3	6		2		
3		7	9		2		
4	3	5	4	8	2		
5	1	3	5	1	2		

Which inputs are the most important?

7. Find the QLF for the following information:

   $C = 575$

   $T = 0.50$

   $V = 1/7$

8. Find the QLF for the following information:

   $C = 750$

   $T = 0.75$

   $V = 1/8$

9. It costs $150 to replace a lighting component in a computer monitor. Compute the QLF for losses incurred as a result of a deviation from a target setting with a nominal tolerance of 1700 ± 50 Lumens. The mean squared deviation is 30.

10. It costs $350 to repair a refrigerator compressor. Compute the QLF for losses incurred as a result of a deviation from a target setting with a nominal tolerance of 60 amps, where a 2-amp variation is acceptable. The mean squared deviation is 1/5.

11. For a component, the following measurements were taken:

50.05	49.95	49.98	50.01
49.92	50.09	50.01	49.98
50.06	50.04	50.04	49.96
50.04	50.06	49.97	49.93
50.03	49.93	50.02	49.97

If the nominal target value is 50 ± 0.5, compute the QLF for this component where the repair cost is $350.

12. Here are answers to the worksheets in Figure 13-6 and Figure 13-7. Using these responses, develop a risk assessment for this project. Produce a risk and return matrix to determine if this project is worth pursuing. Use the weights in Figure 13-6.

    1. Yes
    2. No

3. No
4. Uncertain
5. Yes
6. No
7. No
8. No
9. Uncertain
10. Yes
11. No
12. Uncertain
13. Yes
14. Yes
15. Yes
16. No
17. No
18. No
19. Yes
20. Yes
21–24. All Uncertain

Return scale A: 1 (growth)
Return scale B: 4 (urgency)
Return scale C: 3 (impact)

13. Here are answers to the worksheets in Figure 13-6 and Figure13-7. Using these responses, develop a risk assessment for this project. Produce a risk and return matrix to determine whether this project is worth pursuing. Use the weights in Figure 13-6.

1. No
2. Yes
3. No
4. Yes
5. Uncertain
6. Yes
7. No
8. No
9. Uncertain
10. No
11. Yes
12. Yes
13. Yes
14. Yes
15. Yes
16. Yes
17. Uncertain
18. Yes
19. Yes
20. Yes
21–24. All Uncertain

Return scale A: 3 (growth)
Return scale B: 4 (urgency)
Return scale C: 5 (impact)

14. Using the following data, perform a gauge R&R analysis where there are two replications for each part number.

Part Number	Operator 1	Operator 2	Operator 3
1	28.35	27.20	26.03
	27.00	27.20	28.77
2	32.40	32.64	31.51
	31.05	32.64	32.88
3	27.00	25.84	27.40
	28.35	28.56	30.14
4	36.45	38.08	36.99
	36.45	35.36	38.36
5	25.65	25.84	24.66
	24.30	24.48	28.77
6	31.05	32.64	31.51
	28.35	28.56	30.14
7	29.70	29.92	30.14
	28.35	32.64	27.40
8	25.65	24.48	26.03
	22.95	27.20	24.66
9	32.40	34.00	32.88
	31.05	31.28	32.88
10	33.75	35.36	32.88
	31.05	34.00	34.25
11	28.35	27.20	28.77
	27.00	27.20	27.40
12	24.30	23.12	24.66
	25.65	25.84	26.03
13	31.05	34.00	34.25
	33.75	34.00	34.25
14	32.40	31.28	32.88
	32.40	34.00	34.25
15	39.15	40.80	42.47
	40.50	38.08	41.10
16	35.10	34.00	34.25
	35.10	35.36	36.99
17	27.00	25.84	27.40
	27.00	27.20	27.40
18	25.65	25.84	28.77
	28.35	25.84	31.51
19	33.75	34.00	34.25
	35.10	32.64	34.25
20	25.65	24.48	26.03
	25.65	23.12	23.29

15. Perform a gauge R&R analysis for the following data where there are three replications. What are your findings?

Part Number	Operator 1	Operator 2	Operator 3
1	21	20	19
	20	20	21
	21	20	21
2	24	24	23
	23	24	24
	22	23	24

Part Number	Operator 1	Operator 2	Operator 3
3	20	19	20
	21	21	22
	22	22	22
4	27	28	27
	27	26	28
	26	25	26
5	19	19	18
	18	18	21
	19	18	16
6	23	24	23
	21	21	21
	22	22	22
7	22	22	22
	21	24	20
	24	24	23
8	19	18	19
	17	20	18
	18	18	19
9	24	25	24
	23	23	24
	24	25	24
10	25	26	24
	23	25	25
	25	24	26
11	21	20	21
	20	20	20
	26	26	25
12	18	17	18
	19	19	19
	18	19	20
13	23	25	25
	25	25	25
	24	24	24
14	24	23	24
	24	25	25
	24	23	24
15	29	30	31
	30	28	30
	25	26	31
16	26	25	25
	26	26	27
	26	25	28
17	20	19	20
	20	20	20
	20	20	20
18	19	19	21
	21	19	23
	22	22	22
19	27	26	25
	25	25	25
	26	24	25
20	19	18	19
	19	17	17
	18	19	18

CASE

Case 13-1 The Neiman-Marcus Cookie

One of the fun urban legends to pop up on the Internet has been the Neiman-Marcus Cookie. This work is in the public domain and you might have seen it before. We present the legend here and propose that you develop a Taguchi experiment based on this recipe. It is written in the first person by an anonymous author:

My daughter and I had just finished a salad at Neiman-Marcus in Dallas and decided to have a small dessert. Because our family are such cookie lovers, we decided to try the "Neiman-Marcus Cookie." It was so excellent that I asked if they would give me the recipe, and the server said with a small frown, "I'm afraid not." Well, I said, would you let me buy the recipe? With a cute smile she said, "Yes." I asked how much, and she responded, "Two-fifty." I said with approval, just add it to my tab.

Thirty days later, I received my Visa statement from Neiman-Marcus, and it was $285. I looked again and I remembered I had only spent $9.95 for two salads and about $20 for a scarf. As I glanced at the bottom of the statement, it said, "Cookie Recipe—$250." Boy, was I upset!! I called Neiman's accounting department and told them the waitress said it was "two-fifty," and I did not realize she meant $250 for a cookie recipe.

I asked them to take back the recipe and reduce my bill, and they said they were sorry, but because all the recipes were this expensive so that not just anyone could duplicate any of the bakery recipes, the bill would stand.

I waited, thinking of how I could get even or even try and get any of my money back.

I just said, "Okay, you folks got my $250, and now I'm going to have $250 worth of fun." I told her that I was going to see to it that every cookie lover will have a $250 cookie recipe from Neiman-Marcus for nothing. She replied, "I wish you wouldn't do this."

I told her I was sorry, but this is the only way I feel I can get even, and I will.

So here it is, and please pass it to someone else or run a few copies. I paid for it; now you can have it for free.

The Neiman-Marcus Cookie (recipe may be halved)

5 cups blended oatmeal

2 cups brown sugar

2 cups sugar

2 cups butter

2 tsp. soda

1 8-oz. Hershey bar, grated

2 tsp. baking powder

2 tsp. vanilla

4 cups flour

24 oz. chocolate chips

1 tsp. salt

4 eggs

3 cups chopped nuts

Measure oatmeal and blend in a blender to a fine powder. In a separate bowl, cream the butter and both sugars. Add eggs and vanilla, mix together with oatmeal, flour, salt, baking powder, and baking soda. Add chocolate chips, Hershey bar, and nuts. Roll into balls and place two inches apart on a cookie sheet. Bake for 10 minutes at 375 degrees. Makes 112 cookies.

Using this recipe and these production procedures, develop a Taguchi experiment to find the optimal process for making chocolate chip cookies. Be careful when identifying control factors, noise factors, and objectives, and design the whole experiment.

PART FOUR

Forever Improving the Quality System

This section is for the organizations that have gone through the hard work outlined in the first 13 chapters of this book and are trying to get to the next level—managing the growth of the individuals within the organization.

Chapter 14 takes a hard look at team facilitation and organizational improvement. As a manager, the future will demand that you can effectively assess, develop, and train your employees. This certainly is a key aspect of quality management. Many of the quality concepts you have learned in this text need to be taught to your fellow employees. Managing organizational learning is key to your success as a manager—regardless of whether you specialize in quality. It is interesting that this concept is largely overlooked in the quality literature. Yet everyone in quality is involved in training.

Finally, Chapter 15 provides a means for outstanding companies to assess themselves and to determine where they need to improve. If you are the benchmark or standard, you often have to look within to see where to improve. Here you will find a method for accomplishing this important task.

Managing Quality Improvement Teams and Projects

Chapter Objectives

After completing this chapter, you should be able to:

1. Discuss how to organize teams for maximum performance.

2. Discuss the stages of team development and activity.

3. Develop team ground rules to improve team performance.

4. Practice resolving conflicts between team members using constructive conflict resolution.

5. Develop a project charter.

6. Implement an activity network diagram.

Employee participation is a key element for managing changing organizations in an increasingly complex world. W. Edwards Deming, among others, argued for employee participation and teamwork.

Why do you suppose so many influential voices call for participation and teamwork to manage businesses today? There are several reasons. One of the biggest is *complexity* in the workplace. Given the large volumes of data available to managers, is it any surprise that unilateral decision making is a thing of the past? Also, business is transforming itself from a "command and control" environment to one of *collaboration*. Such collaboration is needed as complexity drives workers from routine work to **knowledge work**, or work that involves the development and transmission of knowledge and information. Knowledge work implies a greater amount of ambiguity, searching, researching, and learning in the job environment.

Knowledge work is effective when workers are given a certain amount of autonomy and decision-making authority. Companies such as 3M encourage their employees to become more entrepreneurial in their approach to work, which regularly results in new products and markets for the company.

As more collaborative practices are being adopted in business, teamwork is the natural result. For our purposes, a **team** is defined as a finite number of individuals who are united in a common purpose. This chapter discusses an approach to improving quality that uses teams and collaboration as a means for improvement. Often these team approaches are used in conjunction with the tools of quality, as discussed in Chapter 10.

Joseph Juran long emphasized the importance of teams and projects in the improvement of quality. He stated that the improvement of quality should be approached on a "project-by-project basis, and in no other way." Teams are a fundamental part of projects. Philip Crosby also supported the use of teams in improving quality. Although there are notable failures of teams, on the whole it is such a widely practiced approach to quality improvement that we discuss teams in some depth.

This chapter focuses on two interrelated topics: *leading teams* and *managing projects*. The first half of the chapter focuses on the behavioral aspects of making teams work. The second half of the chapter is about managing and controlling projects. We treat these topics together in the same chapter because they are interrelated.

WHY EMPLOYEES ENJOY TEAMS

We should note that well-led teams often lead to improved employee morale. Employees like teams for many reasons. In a study of project managers who were involved in project teams, five motivators emerged:[1]

Mutuality. The need for mutual support and encouragement between line management and project managers as well as personal loyalty of project managers to their teams and organizations.

Recognition for personal achievement. The opportunity for personal development as well as recognition for personal achievement through rewards, incentives, or status.

Belonging. The individual's need for supportive, cohesive, and friendly team relations. This implies clear communications both within the team and within the larger organization, as well as clear information and project goals.

Bounded power. The need for authority and control over project resources and people, personal accountability and challenge, individuals' abilities to influence decisions that affect the project, and opportunities for personal growth and development.

Creative autonomy. The need for individuals to have opportunities to use their creativity and potential during the course of a project and to enjoy good working conditions.

These motivators provide strong reasons for individuals to be involved in teams and show why teamwork is often correlated with positive attitudes.

LEADING TEAMS FOR QUALITY IMPROVEMENT

Employee Empowerment and Involvement

When we begin to use teams, decision-making authority is given to team members. **Empowerment** means giving power to team members who perhaps had little control over their jobs. When such power is given, management must follow through and give up a reasonable amount of control.

Implicit in empowerment is a series of promises to employees. These implicit promises include the following:

You will have greater control over your own work.

You will not be penalized for making painful changes.

Video Clip:
Teams at the Ritz

---

[1]Tampoe, M., and Thurloway, L., "Project Management: The Use and Abuse of Techniques and Teams," *International Journal of Project Management* 11, 4 (1993): 245–250.

Management is changing and becoming more contemporary.

Management is committed to quality improvement over the long haul.

Management will concede more control over company systems to you.

Management values your ideas and opinions and will give them serious consideration.

Management trusts you and is worthy of trust in return.

You will be rewarded for making decisions that benefit the company.

Labor is capable of decision making concerning its own jobs and company processes.

This approach to managing labor is an important factor in improving employee morale. It means a lot to employees to be told that their thoughts and ideas are valued. The Baldrige criteria encourage employee participation, adding that

> A company's success depends increasingly on the knowledge, skills, and motivation of its workforce. Employee success depends increasingly on having opportunities to learn and to practice new skills. Companies need to invest in the development of the workforce through education, training, and opportunities for continuing growth. Opportunities might include classroom and on-the-job training, job rotation, and pay for demonstrated knowledge in skills. On-the-job training offers a cost-effective way to train and to better link training to work processes. Workforce education and training programs may need to utilize advanced technologies, such as computer-based learning and satellite broadcasts. Increasingly, training, development, and work units need to be tailored to a diverse workforce and to more flexible, high-performance work practices.
>
> Major challenges in the area of workforce development include: … integration of human resources practices—selection, performance, recognition, training, career advancement, and the alignment of human resource management with strategic change processes. Addressing these challenges requires use of employee-related data on knowledge, skills, satisfaction, motivation, safety, and well-being. Such data need to be tied to indicators of company or unit performance such as customer satisfaction, customer retention, and productivity. Through this approach, human resource management may be better integrated and aligned with business directions.[2]

A number of preconditions are necessary for empowerment:

- *Clear authority and accountability.* Employees must know what is expected of them and be given authority over their own work.
- *Participation in planning at all levels.* Employees should be involved in planning related to their jobs. They should be provided with planning tools.
- *Adequate communication and information for decision making.* If employees are to make decisions related to their jobs, they need the right managerial information.
- *Responsibility with authority.* Employees should be given a definition of power that focuses on getting things done rather than exerting influence over people.[3]

Of course, granting authority to employees doesn't guarantee that people will work well together or necessarily achieve all the lofty goals that are espoused in this approach. Many issues surround empowerment and teamwork that must be addressed (see A Closer Look at Quality 14-1). These issues range from operations and behavior to organizational design. For example, if the existing culture does not reward this type of activity, it is doubtful that participatory approaches will work until the cultural issues are resolved. However, using teams can lead to cultural changes that facilitate improvement. This chapter focuses on the issues related to managing projects and teams to help make the transition succeed.

---

[2]2012 Criteria for Performance Excellence, Malcolm Baldrige National Quality Award (Gaithersburg, MD: NIST, 2012).
[3]Adapted from class notes from Dr. Catherine Beise (Kennesaw, GA: Kennesaw State College, 2016).

A CLOSER LOOK AT QUALITY 14-1   Empowerment in Action[4]

www.srcreman.com

Empowerment has been used in a number of companies very successfully, including Springfield ReManufacturing Corporation of Springfield, Missouri. This company, founded by Jack Stack, has successfully applied empowerment principles among its employees. Stack uses surprising candor with his employees, sharing all financial information with them each month. Stack tells how a janitor persuaded him to expand into a new product line. The company experienced difficult times. In order to avoid bankruptcy, Stack persuaded his employees to invest in the company. Since that time, monthly bank reports that include cash flow projections have been distributed to all employees. During this period, the company experienced 15% annual growth. The company uses the following credo:

> As employees of SRC, we are more than just operators—we're owners. This gives us the incentive to be disciplined and determined to make SRC the best remanufacturer of engines and components. Each department has a healthy competitive spirit, but we're all in the game together. Our sole objective is to produce the best remanufactured engines and components that money can buy. As an employee-owned corporation, we at Springfield ReManufacturing Corporation can account our success to the commitment of each SRC employee. Our philosophy is simply "providing the customer with the highest quality product possible at a competitive price."

From a behavioral perspective, empowerment is a way to enhance organizational learning. **Organizational learning** leads to change in organizational behavior in a way that improves performance.[5] This type of learning takes place through a network of interrelated components that include teamwork, strategies, structures, cultures, systems, and their interactions. Corporate learning relies on an open culture in which no one feels threatened to expose opinions or beliefs—a culture where individuals can engage in learning, questioning, and not remain constrained by "taboos" or existing norms. This strategy includes continuous improvement projects as a governing principle for all team members.[6]

Flattening Hierarchies for Improved Effectiveness

Along with the emphasis on teamwork and empowerment, there has been a move toward flattening hierarchies in organizations. Led by consultants such as Tom Peters and others, top managers have eliminated layers of bureaucratic managers to improve communication and simplify work. Having many layers of management can have the effect of increasing the time required to perform work. For example, it has been reported that in the past, one of the largest automobile manufacturers in the United States required 6 months to determine its standard colors for office phones. Probably this decision required many, many meetings and proper authorization. However, such decisions are minor when compared with competitive decisions that had to be made. The time required to make this decision was excessive.

Too many layers of management also can impede creativity, stifle initiative, and make empowerment impossible. With fewer layers of management, companies tend to rely more on teams.

---

[4]Burlingham, B., *Small Giants: Companies That Choose to Be Great Instead of Big* (New York: Portfolio Hardcover, 2005).

[5]Lichtenthaler, U., "Absorptive Capacity, Environmental Turbulence, and the Complementarity of Organizational Learning Processes," *Academy of Management Journal* 52, 4(2009): 822–846.

[6]Deiser, R., *Designing the Smart Organization* (Hoboken, NJ: Pfeiffer, 2009).

Team Leader Roles and Responsibilities

Quality professionals are unanimous—to be successful in achieving teamwork and participation, strong leadership both at the company level and within the team is essential. However, what is not always clear is what it means to be an effective team leader. We know that leaders are responsible for setting team direction and seeking future opportunities for the team. Leaders reinforce values and provide a system for achieving desired goals. Leaders establish expectations for high levels of performance, customer focus, and continuous learning. Leaders are responsible for communicating effectively, evaluating organizational performance, and providing feedback concerning such performance.

An important aspect of leadership is the organization's preparedness to follow the leadership. The best general is probably not going to be successful if the troops are not well trained or prepared. Hersey, Blanchard, and Johnson[7] propose a theory called a **situational leadership model** that clarifies the interrelation between employee preparedness and effectiveness of leadership. According to Hersey, Blanchard, and Johnson, situational leadership is based on interplay among the following:

The amount of guidance and direction a leader gives (task behavior)

The amount of socioeconomic support a leader provides (relationship behavior)

The readiness level that followers exhibit in performing a specific task, function, or objective

Therefore, if team members are trained and prepared so that they are *task ready*, leadership will be more effective. **Readiness**, in this context, is the extent to which a follower has the ability and willingness to accomplish a specific task. Readiness is a function of two variables: ability and technical skills (job maturity) and self-confidence in one's abilities (psychological maturity). Therefore, effective leadership helps employees become competent and instills confidence in employees that they can do the job.

Figure 14-1 shows the Hersey, Blanchard, and Johnson model of situational leadership with four different styles of leadership. As the model shows, different contingencies drive different approaches to leading. According to Hersey, Blanchard, and Johnson, the best approach to leading (i.e., telling, selling, participating, or delegating) depends on the readiness of employees to perform tasks and functions or accomplish objectives.

	Guidance (Structure)	
	Low	High
High	Participating	Selling
Emotional Support (Consideration)		
Low	Delegating	Telling

FIGURE 14-1 Hersey, Blanchard, and Johnson's Situational Leadership Model

---

[7]Hersey, P., Blanchard, K., and Johnson, D., *Management of Organizational Behavior* (Englewood Cliffs, NJ: Prentice Hall, 2007).

| TABLE 14-1 | Belbin's Team Roles |

Key Stages of Team Activity	Team Roles Relevant to Particular Stages
1. Identifying needs	Key figures at this stage are individuals with a strong goal awareness. Shapers and coordinators make their mark here.
2. Finding ideas	Once an objective is set, the means of achieving it are required. Here plant and resource investigators play a crucial role.
3. Formulating plans	Two activities help ideas turn into plans. One is weighing up the options; the second, making good use of all relevant experience and knowledge to ensure a good decision.
4. Making contacts	People must be persuaded that an improvement is possible. Champions of the plans and cheerleaders must be found. This is an activity where resource investigators are in their element.
5. Establishing the organization	Plans must turn into procedures, methods, and working practices to become routines. Implementers are the people required here. Identify people to fit the system.
6. Following through	Too many assumptions are made that all will work out well in the end. Good follow-through benefits from the attentions of completers. Implementers, too, pull their weight in this area because they pride themselves on being efficient in anything they undertake.

Source: Based on R. M. Belbin, *Team Roles at Work* (Boston: Butterworth-Heinemann, 2010).

As it relates to quality management, leadership is especially difficult. Leaders are told that they should empower employees. To many leaders, this implies a laissez-faire or hands-off approach to management. In other words, many leaders feel they are to provide resources, but should not be involved in overly controlling employee behavior. Although the literature contains examples of companies that have been successful in delegating authority to this extent, quality management is not a vehicle by which leaders abdicate their responsibility.

Team Roles and Responsibilities

Besides team leaders, there are a variety of roles that individuals occupy in teams. Meredith Belbin provides a widely adopted typology of team roles. Table 14-1 contains names and profiles for each of these roles. Belbin notes that each of these roles may be more relevant at different stages during a project. Also, these roles are not mutually exclusive: one person can fulfill different roles on a team.

Also, team roles can be defined functionally. Often teams require different functional talents such as management, human resources, engineering, operations, accounting, marketing, management information systems, and others. In these cases, the managers overseeing the project help to identify the talents needed and then search for the team members to provide these talents.

Team Formation and Evolution

The way a team is formed depends—to an extent—on the objectives or goals of the team. Regardless of the type of team your firm employs, teams experience different stages of development (see Figure 14-2). These stages include the following: **Forming**, during which the team is composed, and the objective for the team is set; **storming**, during which the team members begin to get to know each other, and agreements have not yet been made that facilitate smooth interaction between team members; **norming**, during which the team becomes a cohesive unit, and interdependence, trust, and cooperation develop; and **performing**, during

FIGURE 14-2 Stages of a Team's Development

which a mutually supportive, steady state is achieved. And in successful projects, the final stage is **mourning**, during which team members regret the ending of the project and the breaking up of the team.

Team Rules

During the norming stage, teams develop ground rules. Such ground rules can forestall conflict. Common ground rules for teams in projects are shown in Table 14-2. It is often useful to establish ground rules first in order for a team to be functional. If a team is functional, individual participation enhances the group's effectiveness. If the team is dysfunctional, such participation reduces the effectiveness of the group. Acts of commission include talking behind the backs of other team members or otherwise acting out one's feelings. There are also acts of omission in such passive-aggressive behavior such as forgetting to attend meetings or withholding information. Counteractive behavior improves the group's effectiveness by negating dysfunctional

TABLE 14-2 Ground Rules for Effective Teams
1. Test assumptions and inferences.
2. Share all relevant information.
3. Focus on interests, not positions.
4. Be specific—use examples.
5. Agree on what important words mean.
6. Explain the reasons behind one's statements, questions, and actions.
7. Disagree openly with any member of the group.
8. Make statements; then invite questions and comments.
9. Jointly design ways to test disagreements and solutions.
10. Discuss undiscussable issues.
11. Keep the discussion focused.
12. Do not take cheap shots or otherwise distract the group.
13. All members are expected to participate in all phases of the process.
14. Exchange relevant information with nongroup members.
15. Make decisions by consensus.
16. Do self-critiques.

Source: R. Schwarz, "Ground Rules for Effective Groups," *Popular Government* 54, 4 (1989): 25–30. Reprinted by permission of the Institute of Government, the University of North Carolina at Chapel Hill. Reprinted with permission of the School of Government, copyright 1989 by the Institute of Government. This copyrighted material may not be reproduced in whole or in part without the express written permission of the School of Government, CB# 3330 UNC Chapel Hill, Chapel Hill, North Carolina 27599-3330; Telephone: 910-966-4119; Fax: 919-962-2707; web address: www.sog.unc.edu.

TABLE 14-3	Types of Teams
Team Type	**Scope**
Process improvement team	Local or single department
Cross-functional team	Multiple departments
Tiger team	Organization-wide
Natural work group	Customer- or region-centered
Self-directed work team	Narrow or broad
Virtual team	Narrow or broad

behavior. Counteractive behavior can be enacted either by the team, the facilitator, the team manager, or even the offending individual.

TYPES OF TEAMS

At this point, we pause to define the various types of teams used to improve quality. Continuous process improvement often requires small teams that are segmented by work areas. Projects with multiple departments in a company require cross-functional teams. Large projects require teams with large budgets and multiple members. Smaller projects, such as "formulating a preventive maintenance plan for oiling the metal lathes," probably will require a much smaller team. The literature is full of different types of teams and approaches to teamwork. Table 14-3 contains a list of a few of the major types of teams found in the literature. In the following sections we list and define a number of team types.

Process Improvement Teams

Process improvement teams work to improve processes and customer service. These teams may work under the direction of management or may be self-directed. In either case, process improvement teams are involved in some or all of the following activities: identifying opportunities for improvement, prioritizing opportunities, selecting projects, gathering data, analyzing data, making recommendations, implementing change, and conducting postimplementation reviews. Many process improvement teams are an outgrowth of quality-related training. These teams use the basic tools and the plan–do–check–act cycle to effect change relating to processes.

Cross-Functional Teams

Cross-functional teams enlist people from a variety of functional groups within the firm. In the real world, problems often cut across functional borders. As a result, problem-solving teams are needed that include people from a variety of functions. These cross-functional teams often work on higher-level strategic issues that involve multiple functions. Such teams often work on macro-level, quality-related problems such as communication or redesigning company-wide processes.

Tiger Teams

A **tiger team** is a high-powered team assigned to work on a specific problem for a limited amount of time. These teams are often used in reengineering efforts or in projects where a specific problem needs to be solved in a very short period of time. The work is very intense and has only a limited duration.

Natural Work Groups

Natural work groups are teams organized around a common product, customer, or service. Many times these teams are cross-functional and include marketers, researchers, engineers, and producers. The objective of natural work groups includes tasks such as increasing responsiveness to customers and market demand. In order to implement natural work groups, a great deal of effort is typically expended relating to organizational redesign and systems redesign. Commonly cited outcomes of natural work groups are improved job design and improved work life for employees. The key elemental impact of natural work groups is to improve service by focusing work units in an organization on the customer. A positive byproduct is improved communication with customers. Often a natural work group is established for a specific customer.

Self-Directed Work Teams

A **self-directed work team** is chartered to work on projects identified by team members. There is little managerial oversight except to establish the teams and fund their activities.

Self-directed teams are identified as either *little s* or *big S* teams. Little *s* self-directed work teams are made up of employees empowered to identify opportunities for improvement, select improvement projects, and complete implementation. Big *S* self-directed teams are involved in managing the different functions of the company without a traditional management structure. These types of teams contain totally self-directed employees who make decisions concerning benefits, finances, pay, processes, customers, and all the other aspects of running the business. Often big *S* self-directed work teams hold partial ownership of the companies they work for so that they participate in the benefits of their teamwork.

Virtual Teams

The term **virtual teams** is emerging as more companies become "virtual organizations": loosely knit consortia that produce products and services. Virtual teams rarely or never physically meet, except in electronic meetings using group decision software. Among virtual organizations, projects often cross organizational boundaries. Today, Internet and intranet-based applications called **teamware** such as Google Docs allow us to access the Web and build a team, share ideas, hold virtual meetings, brainstorm, keep schedules, and archive past results with people in far-flung locations around the world. Hectic schedules and the difficulty in finding convenient times to meet to solve problems will make teams of this type more important in the future (see A Closer Look at Quality 14-2).

A CLOSER LOOK AT QUALITY 14-2   **Lessons from Effective Teams Outside the Business World[8]**

Many teams outside business can serve as examples to business. In this Closer Look at Quality we consider several outstanding teams that display many of the attributes needed in quality improvement teams.

Navy SEALs

Navy SEALs are an elite team of individuals who perform very dangerous missions for the Navy. Even though the first four weeks of Navy SEAL training are grueling, they pale in comparison with the fifth week, known as hell week. During hell week, recruits swim many, many miles in cold water in the Pacific Ocean, row rubber boats for hours on end, run obstacle courses over and over, perform grueling calisthenics using 300-pound logs, and sustain personal insults from trainers. During the entire hell week, recruits sleep for perhaps 4 hours.

[8]Based on Labich, K., "Elite Teams Get the Job Done," *Fortune* 133, 3 (1996): 90.

About 30% of the recruits drop out during the five-day hell week experience. Commitment is needed because hell week is followed by months of rigorous underwater training, weapons training, explosives training, parachute training, and a six-month probationary period. The ultimate success rate for recruits is about 30%.

Teamwork is essential because SEALs never operate on their own, and team members identify totally with the group. Navy SEALs will never leave the battlefield if a fallen SEAL remains. The SEALs teach us about the necessity of training and cohesion among team members.

Massachusetts General Hospital Emergency Room

Every day about 200 patients arrive in the emergency room at Massachusetts General Hospital—one of the finest hospitals in the world. Working as a team in an emergency-trauma unit, doctors, nurses, and aides have to deal with great amounts of stress, fatigue, and emotional baggage.

Seamless role playing is important as gurneys are rolled into the trauma center. The triage nurse determines the severity of an injury. Next, the team of doctors, nurses, and aides leaps into action, performing the tasks it has performed many times before. Each person performs his or her task—assessing the patient, starting an IV, scoping the wounds, or hooking up heart monitors. At Mass General, "nobody bosses anybody around; if someone has a thought that's useful, we are open to suggestions." As with any effective team, the members understand and flawlessly execute their roles under stressful conditions.

Childress NASCAR Team

Former racer Richard Childress has taken part in several Winston Cup championships for the top prize in NASCAR racing since founding his Childress Racing maintenance teams. How did he do it?

Childress has a keen eye for young mechanical talent that fits into the team concept he has built. "I'd rather train them our way than try to break old habits," says Childress.

Almost everyone starts at the bottom—cleaning up after the other mechanics and running for parts and coffee. On the road, they fill water bottles and stack tires. During this time, they are judged less for their actual performance than for their ability to work with the team. Says one team member, "Attitude is more important than expertise—you've got to be able to have people who won't let you down." The proof of this message is in the results. A team of 17 people, 7 working on the car and 10 behind the wall, can change 4 tires, pump 21 gallons of gas, clean the windshield, and give the driver a drink in less than 18 seconds. The Childress team excels because of its focus on detail and maintenance of team member roles.

IMPLEMENTING TEAMS

The teams in our examples have something in common. The performance of the team is essential for individual successes, and sometimes even lives hang in the balance. If the NASCAR team performs ineffectively, the driver loses. If the Massachusetts General hospital team is ineffective, people die. If the SEALs don't function properly, lives are lost, and the mission fails. How do we engender this sense of urgency in quality improvement teams? How do we create a momentum or team ethic that will help us beat the odds and be successful? Accomplishing it often requires facilitation and team building. **Facilitation** is helping or aiding teams by maintaining a process orientation and focusing the group. **Team building** is accomplished by following a process that identifies roles for team members and then helps them to become competent in achieving those roles.

The role of the facilitator is very important for managing teams, particularly when team members have little experience with teamwork. The role of the **facilitator** is to make it easy for the group to know where it is going, why it wants to get there, how to get there, and what it will do next.

A facilitator focuses the group on the process it must follow. Successful facilitation does not mean that the group always achieves its desired results. The facilitator is responsible for ensuring that the team follows a meaningful and effective process to achieve its objectives.

How is this accomplished? The facilitator should plan how the group will work through a task, help the group stay on track and be productive, draw out quiet members, discourage monopolizers, help develop clear and shared understanding, watch body language and verbal cues, and help the group achieve closure. Again, facilitators must remain neutral on content; they cannot take sides or positions on important areas of disagreement. However, facilitators should help key members reach points of agreement.

Meeting Management

Effective **meeting management** is an important skill for a facilitator of quality improvement teams. Quality improvement often involves a series of meetings of team members who meet to brainstorm, perform root-cause analysis, and carry out other activities. Tools for successful meeting management include an agenda, predetermined objectives for the meeting, a process for running the meeting, processes for voting, and development of an action plan. Using these tools requires outstanding communication skills as well as human relations skills. These are the steps required for planning a meeting:

1. Define an agenda.
2. Develop meeting objectives.
3. Design the agenda activity outline.
4. Use process techniques.

Structured processes, a set of rules for managing meetings, work well for conducting meetings. It is paradoxical that structured processes are inhibiting, time-consuming, and unnatural—which is why they work. Why do we use processes in meetings? The answers are clear. We want meetings to stay focused, to involve deeper exploration, to separate creative from evaluative activities, to provide equal opportunity for contribution, to encourage reflection, to provide objective ground rules to reduce defensiveness, and to separate the person from the idea.

Table 14-4 identifies some meeting structured process techniques. Tools such as flipcharts, sticky dots, whiteboards, and sticky notes are used commonly in structured process activities. The focus of team meetings moves from clarifying to generating ideas, to evaluating ideas, and

TABLE 14-4 Structured Process Activities		
By Activity Type	**Approaches**	**Tools**
• Clarify techniques 　—Lasso • Generate techniques 　—Structured brainstorming 　—Round-robin contribution 　—Silent writing 　—Sticky notes recording 　—Brain writing • Evaluate techniques 　—Reduce list 　—Pros and cons 　—Force fields 　—Silent voting 　—Sticky dots 　—Idea writing • Action planning	• Individual • Subgroups 　("buzz groups") • Full group	• Verbal • Flipcharts • Whiteboard • Paper pads • Sticky notes • Sticky dots • Computer

Source: Based on Anson, R., "Facilitation Skills for Focussed Meetings," Working Paper (Boise, ID: Boise State University, 2012).

FIGURE 14-3 Parking Lot

to action planning. Some of the techniques, such as silent voting and idea writing, help team members reach consensus rapidly.

Another useful meeting management tool pioneered by Hewlett Packard is the "**parking lot**." The parking lot (see Figure 14-3) is a flipchart or whiteboard on which topics that are off the subject are *parked* with the agreement that these topics will be candidates for the next meeting's agenda. At the end of the meeting, the group agrees on the agenda for the following meeting, and the parking lot is erased.

Conflict Resolution in Teams

As people work closely together in teams, conflicts arise, so conflict resolution is a hugely important topic for team leaders and members. Conflicts are endemic to all kinds of team projects. Using team processes, assumptions are questioned, change is brainstormed, and cultures are challenged. This type of creative activity results in possible conflict. It is claimed that team leaders and project managers spend more than 20% of their time resolving conflict. If this is true, conflict resolution resounds as one of the very important underdiscussed topics in team building.

There are many sources of conflict. Some conflicts are internal, such as personality conflicts or rivalries; some are external, such as disagreements over reward systems, scarce resources, lines of authority, or functional differentiation (see Figure 14-4). Teams bring together individuals from a variety of cultures, backgrounds, and functional areas of expertise. Being on a team can create confusion for individuals and insecurity as members are taken out of their comfort zones. It is interesting to note that these are also some of the reasons teams are successful. Some organizational causes of differences are more insidious: faulty attribution, faulty communication, or grudges and prejudice.

Four recognizable stages occur in the conflict resolution process:[9]

Frustration. People are at odds, and competition or aggression ensues.

Conceptualization and orientation. Opponents identify the issues that need to be resolved.

[9] Behfar, K., Peterson, R., Mannix, E., and Trochim, W., "The Critical Role of Conflict Resolution in Teams: A Close Look at the Links between Conflict Type, Conflict Management Strategies, and Team Outcomes," *Journal of Applied Psychology* 93, 1 (2008): 170–188.

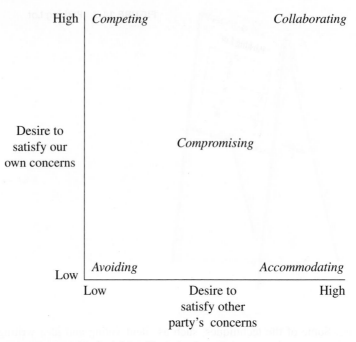

FIGURE 14-4 Modes of Conflict Behavior *Source:* Based on T. L. Ruble and K. W. Thomas, "Support for a Two-Dimensional Model of Conflict Behavior," *Organizational Behavior and Human Decision Processes* 16 (1976): 221–237, with permission of Elsevier Science.

Interaction. Team members discuss and air the problems.

Outcome. The problem is resolved.

One of the things a leader must be able to do is manage conflict in the organization. To foster a well-run workplace, leaders must be able to resolve conflict effectively in organizations. Leaders resolve conflict in a variety of ways:

Passive conflict resolution. Some managers and leaders ignore conflict. This is probably the most common approach to working out conflict. There may be positive reasons for this approach. The leader may prefer that subordinates work things out themselves, or the conflict may be minor and will take care of itself over time. Leaders may feel that some issues are small enough not to merit micromanagement.

Win–win. Leaders might seek solutions to problems that satisfy both sides of a conflict by providing win-win scenarios. One form of this is called *balancing demands* for the participants, which happens when the manager determines what each person in the conflict wants as an outcome and looks for solutions that can satisfy the needs of both parties.

Structured problem solving. Conflicts can be resolved in a fact-based manner by gathering data regarding the problem and having the data analyzed by a disinterested observer to add weight to the claims of one of the conflicting parties.

Confronting conflict. At times, it is best to confront the conflict and use active listening techniques to help subordinates resolve conflicts. This provides a means for coming to a solution of the conflict.

Choosing a winner. In some cases, if the differences between the parties in the conflict are great, the leader may choose a winner of the conflict and develop a plan of action for conflict resolution between the parties.

TABLE 14-5	Constructive Conflict Resolution Components

1. *Goal structure*—Goals should be well-defined and operational, and should reflect each unit's contribution to the total organization. Managers, in turn, should convey to their subordinates as precisely as possible the feeling that their own unit is dependent on the work of other units.

2. *Reward systems*—Each unit's contribution to the effectiveness of the total organization should be assessed carefully and rewarded accordingly. Where high levels of interdependence exist, reward systems should be designed specifically to reflect interdependence. Such a reward system will encourage cooperation among organization units.

3. *Contact and communication*—Frequent contact and communication between organization units needs to be encouraged. Individuals should be rotated through related organization units in order to have them gain experience, understanding, and empathy for the work done and the problems encountered in other units.

4. *Coordination*—Liaison roles should be established when potential communication and coordination problems exist (e.g., between R&D and manufacturing at the point where a new product moves from advanced development into the pilot stage of production). The liaison role can be used to facilitate necessary interaction, thus reducing the time and information content lost when using formal channels. In addition, the liaison becomes better acquainted with the work of the different units and can provide continuous updating to each of the other units.

5. *Competitive systems*—Competition, where it does exist, should be examined carefully. Although competition can facilitate productivity, it can also produce conflict whenever organization units are interdependent. In such situations, competition need not be eliminated, but its benefits should be evaluated against its potential for causing conflict. Clearly, organization units should not be forced into win-lose situations.

Source: Based on Ronald J. Ebert, Charles N. Greene, and Everett E. Adam Jr., *Management for Effective Performance*, 1st ed. (Upper Saddle River, NJ: Pearson Education, 1985), p. 454. ISBN: 0135485045.

Selecting a better alternative. Sometimes there is an alternative that neither of the parties to the conflict has considered. The leader then asks the conflicting parties to pursue an alternative plan of action.

Preventing conflict. Skilled leaders use different techniques to create an environment that is relatively free of conflict. These approaches are more strategic in nature and involve organizational design fundamentals. As shown in Table 14-5, these organizational design fundamentals are useful for reducing conflict in organizations. By carefully defining goals, rewards, communication systems, coordination, and the nature of competition in a firm, conflict can be reduced or eliminated. Conflicts often are the result of the reward systems in the firm. A systems approach will focus attention on organizational design rather than individual interactions.

Generally speaking, these conflict-resolution approaches involve three alternatives: *avoidance*, *defusion*, or *confrontation*. Avoidance involves letting things work themselves out without involving a leader. Defusion means smoothing ruffled feelings while getting the team project back on track. Confrontation involves injecting the leader into the conflict to find a solution.

Saving Quality Teams from Failure: Diagnosing Problems and Intervening Before it Is Too Late

In the prior section, we talked about handling conflict. Sometimes quality improvement teams embark on improvement projects and, for whatever reason, things begin to fall apart, and the team risks failure. It is usually easy to see when a quality improvement team project is going awry. There are cost overruns. Deadlines and schedules are not met. Frustration abounds. People are trying to deflect responsibility or bailing out. At such times, it is critical to be able to diagnose and intervene to save the project.

The diagnosis-intervention cycle must be undertaken by the facilitator, team leader, or team members. The cycle is followed to diagnose team failure and to intervene before the team fails. This requires observing the behavior of team members—you may see team members exhibiting nonverbal body language during team meetings. As a facilitator, you may have team members contacting you outside of team meetings to let you know what is "really happening." Drawing inferences about the meaning of the behavior means that, as a facilitator or team leader, you need to determine and understand the root causes of the behavior you are observing. Is fear present? Are people feeling external pressure? Do certain team members behave in a way that is dysfunctional?

Next, you need to decide whether to intervene to improve the behavior. This is an important decision that requires insight. Is it better to intervene, or will the problems solve themselves over time? Describing your observations to the team is a means of "putting the issues on the table" so that they can be discussed. When you test inferences about observations, you open up a group discussion to let others understand why they are exhibiting difficult behavior. Helping the group decide whether and how to change the problematic behavior is the remedial step in which the leader or facilitator helps to resolve the problem.[10]

Recognition and action are keys to saving teams that are troubled. Eliyahu Goldratt,[11] in his book *Critical Chain,* a thought-provoking text on project management, demonstrates that people usually blame others when projects fail, or they blame uncertainty. The problem is that uncertainty is common in all projects. Skilled facilitators and team leaders recognize this fact and use effective communication to keep projects on track.

MANAGING AND CONTROLLING PROJECTS

Up to this point, we have discussed team building from an organizational behavior perspective. Our discussion has focused on topics such as leadership, team roles, forming teams, facilitating teams, resolving conflict, and intervening to save teams. At this point, we shift our discussion to the activities associated with controlling projects.

Too often, companies attempt to implement teams and projects in a poorly planned manner. The ultimate result is a number of operating teams with no clear methodology for coordinating the different activities of the teams. In the following pages, we discuss how to coordinate and manage projects. From this perspective, we adopt an organizational theory–based approach to project management. The question is this: How can we manage quality improvement projects so that they will be coherent, thoughtful, and in alignment with organizational objectives?

We introduce the tools used in controlling projects in order of sequence. Because some of these tools were introduced in Chapter 10, we now consider them in the context of their implementation.

Qualifying Projects

As we discussed in more detail in Chapter 13, an important function of management is to select and qualify projects. To qualify a project means to determine the worthiness of a project on different dimensions. Commonly used methods for qualifying projects are **cost-benefits analysis (CBA)** using **payback period** calculation. Both of these methods involve identifying direct and indirect project costs and expected returns for projects. These analyses are often used for comparing and selecting projects. For these calculations, use the following formulas:

$$C_t = \sum(C_d + C_i) \tag{14.1}$$

where:

C_t = total project costs

C_d = direct project costs

C_i = indirect project costs

$$PP = C_t/B_a \tag{14.2}$$

[10]Schwarz, R., *The Skilled Facilitator* (San Francisco: Jossey-Bass, 1994).
[11]Goldratt, E., *Critical Chain* (Great Barrington, MA: North River Press, 1997).

where:

PP = payback period

C_t = total project costs

B_a = annualized benefits

When evaluating projects, you need to understand the differences between **soft costs** and **hard costs**. Soft costs are costs not easily recovered in project savings, usually because the benefits of the project add to organizational slack without resulting in actual dollar savings. An example of soft cost savings is the reduction of task time in a noncritical process task. This means that the process will have more slack. However, it does not mean that cycle time is reduced for production of a particular product—thereby resulting in no actual increase in productive capacity. Hard costs are just that—the reduction of rent, equipment costs, or labor direct costs—hard savings. It is best to justify savings based on hard costs that accrue to the bottom line.

EXAMPLE 14-1   **Cost-Benefit Analysis in Action**

A Six Sigma master black belt has asked you to help analyze a possible project. This project involves implementing a computer-based sales system to improve supply chain performance. Some of the direct and indirect costs are as follows:

Direct Costs

- Twenty networkable PCs—$1,500/each
- A server—$2,000
- Peripherals—$2,000
- Network installation—$5,000
- Sales system software—$10,000

Indirect Costs

- Training—$10,000
- Lost time—30 days × $120/day
- Sales-related losses during implementation—$25,000

Annualized Benefits

- Increased sales capacity—$200,000
- Improved customer retention—$500,000
- Improved follow-up sales opportunities—$100,000

Total costs = $49,000 + $38,600 = $87,600
Benefits = $800,000 per year
Payback period = $87,600/$800,000 = .11 years

Project Charters

Project charters are simple tools to help teams identify objectives, participants, and expected benefits from projects. The charter includes spaces for signatures to identify reporting relationships for planning purposes. In some firms, these signatures are for approvals; in other firms, they are for information only.

Date: June 9, 2012

Project Charter for the Document Checklist Team

Team members: Jody, Hollie, Elaine

_____

Objective(s): Create document checklists to accompany texts, covers, and fulfillment.

_____

Projected benefits: Help the Roles and Responsibilities team; clarify status of jobs; enable backup people to take over when needed; reduce time to complete a project; reduce stress; reduce errors, omissions, and rework.

Approvals:

_____*F. Andren*_____ *Responsible Manager*
_____*Jim*_____ *Department Head*
_____*ST*_____ *Leadership Council*
Completion Date: 9/14/17

FIGURE 14-5   An Actual Project Charter

Figure 14-5 shows a charter for an actual project. Notice that the prior identification of benefits helps team members and management identify measures for a postimplementation review to see whether the project reaped the expected benefits.

FORCE-FIELD ANALYSIS

A useful tool for planning projects is **force-field analysis**. This tool is designed to identify and quantify all the forces for or against organizational change. It allows you to identify possible project assassins and to fortify support for a project. To perform force-field analysis, perform the following steps:

1. List all forces for change in the first column and all forces against change in the third column.
2. Assign a score for each force, where 1 = weak and 5 = very strong.
3. Sum the forces for and against the change and draw a diagram showing the forces.

EXAMPLE 14-2   **Force Fields in Action**

A project was performed to determine the feasibility of implementing a new customer relationship management system (CRMS). A group of experts within the firm identified major forces for and against implementing the new CRMS. These forces and scores are shown in Figure 14-6.

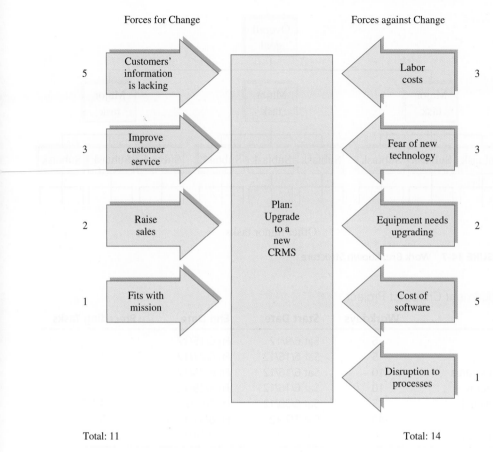

FIGURE 14-6   Force-Field Analysis

Solution: The scores show that there are significant forces that militate against change. Work is needed to develop more forces in favor of change.

Work Breakdown Structure (WBS)

After chartering the project, the next step is to begin planning the project. The work break-down structure (WBS) introduced in Chapter 10 is an excellent tool for determining the tasks to complete a project. Figure 14-7 shows an outline of a WBS for a project. Team members identify the major tasks required to perform the project. The tasks for an actual project—the Document Checklist Project—are listed in Table 14-6 with their appropriate start times, number of workdays, and predecessor tasks. After the tasks were identified, the question was asked, "What subtasks will be needed to complete the identified major tasks?" Next, the same questions were asked for the subtasks until we had a complete tree of major tasks, subtasks, and minor tasks.

Note that with large projects, it is often best to develop a separate WBS for each of the major tasks because separate individuals or groups may be involved in different tasks. Therefore, the marketing department can develop a WBS for the marketing portion of the project, and operations can develop a WBS for the operations portion. In the end, these WBSs must be combined into an overall WBS for the project.

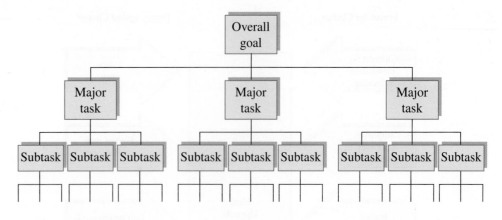

FIGURE 14-7 Work Breakdown Structure

TABLE 14-6 Tasks for the Document Checklist Project

Tasks	Workdays	Start Date	End Date	Preceding Tasks
1. Use flowcharts to list steps	5	Sat 6/9/12	Fri 6/15/12	
2. Preliminary design of form	5	Sat 6/16/12	Fri 6/22/12	1
3. Check against Roles team and Andrea	10	Sat 6/16/12	Fri 6/29/12	
4. Develop procedures for using form	10	Sat 6/16/12	Fri 6/29/12	
5. Preliminary draft of form completed	5	Sat 6/30/12	Fri 7/6/12	4,2,3
6. Test-run form and procedures	40	Sat 7/7/12	Fri 8/31/12	5
7. Revise and finalize form and procedures	10	Sat 9/1/12	Fri 9/14/12	6

Identifying Precedence Relationships

The WBS tasks are placed on individual note cards, and precedence relationships are identified for all the tasks. The note cards are placed in order on a large sheet of paper, and arrows are drawn between the tasks.

Identifying Outcome Measures

During the planning stage of the project, the team should refer to the project charter and identify measures against which team performance can be judged. This oft-overlooked step in planning is useful because some needed measures may not exist in current cost accounting systems. It is important to have preliminary and post hoc data so that baselining or intervention analysis can be performed effectively. This involves gathering preliminary data and postimplementation data. Then statistical tests are used to test for improvement.[12]

Identifying Task Times

Now we identify completion times for all the tasks. To do this, identify three time estimates for each task:

a = the optimistic completion time

m = the most likely completion time

---

[12]For a good example of project-based intervention analysis, see Foster, S. T., Jr., and Franz, C. R., "Assessing Process Reengineering Impacts through Baselining," *Benchmarking for Quality Management and Technology* 2, 3 (1995): 4–19.

b = the pessimistic completion time

t = task time

T = project completion time

Next, the expected task time (t_e) is calculated using the following formula:

$$\text{Expected time} = (a_t + 4m_t + b_t)/6 \tag{14-3}$$

The task variance is computed as

$$\sigma_t^2 = [(b_t - a_t)/6]^2 \tag{14-4}$$

The project variance is computed as the sum of task variances

$$\sigma_T^2 = \sum_{t=1}^{n} \sigma_t^2 \tag{14-5}$$

Finally, the project standard deviation is

$$\sigma_T = \sqrt{\sigma_T^2} \tag{14-6}$$

EXAMPLE 14-3   Calculating Task Times

The following tasks were identified for a major project using a WBS. Team members also identified optimistic, most likely, and pessimistic task completion times for each task. They have asked you to compute *task times* and *task variances* for this project (solution in italics).

Task	a	m	b	Expected Times	Variances		Predecessors
A	1	3	5	*3 ((1 + (4)3 + 5)/6) = 3*	*.444*	*((5 – 1)/6)² = .444*	—
B	5	6	7	*6*	*.111*		—
C	6	9	12	*9*	*1.000*		—
D	3	4	5	*4*	*.111*		A
E	3	4	23	*7*	*11.111*		A
F	8	10	12	*10*	*.444*		A
G	12	17	22	*17*	*2.778*		A
H	5	9	13	*9*	*1.778*		B, D
I	13	15	17	*15*	*.444*		B, D
J	10	11	12	*11*	*.111*		B, D
K	1	8	15	*8*	*5.444*		C, E
L	2	3	16	*5*	*5.444*		F, H, K
M	8	10	12	*10*	*.444*		F, H, K
N	4	7	11	*7.17*	*1.361*		G, I, L
O	3	10	11	*9*	*1.778*		J
P	3	4	5	*4*	*.111*		M, N, O

Activity Network Diagrams

The following steps are used to develop an activity network diagram (PERT chart):

1. Using the inputs from a tree diagram listing tasks to be performed in the project, list all the tasks.
2. Determine task times.

3. Determine the precedence relationships between the tasks; that is, indicate which tasks depend on the completion of other tasks in the process.
4. Draw the network diagram.
5. Compute early start and early finish times by working from left to right in the network. These are the earliest times that individual tasks can be started and finished.
6. Compute late start and late finish times by moving from right to left in the network. These times are the latest times that tasks can possibly be started or finished.
7. Compute slack times and determine the critical path. The critical path links activities with zero slack.

$$\text{Slack time} = \text{late start} - \text{early start} \qquad (14\text{-}7)$$

EXAMPLE 14-4 | **Activity Network Diagram**

A company developing a new advertising brochure identified the steps in the project. These were placed in the tree diagram shown in Figure 14-8. Table 14-7 lists all the tasks with their brainstormed times and predecessors. Figure 14-9 shows the network with tasks. This also shows times and precedence relationships using activity-on-node (AON).

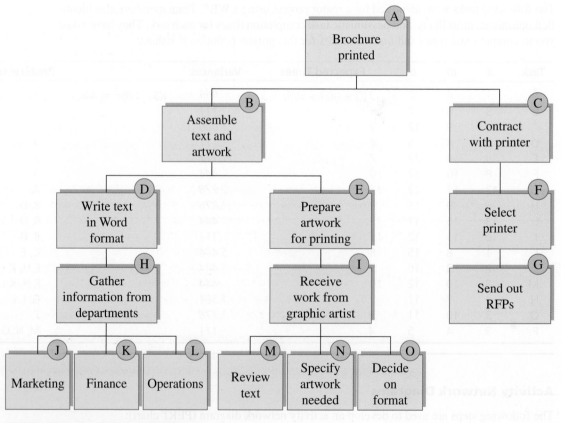

FIGURE 14-8 Tree Diagram of Tasks

TABLE 14-7	Tasks		
Task	**Task IDs**	**Predecessors**	**Expected Time (Weeks)**
Brochure printed	A	B, C	4
Assemble text and artwork	B	E, D	1
Contract with printer	C	F	2
Write text in Word format	D	H	2
Prepare artwork for printing	E	I	4
Select printer	F	G	2
Send out RFPs	G	—	3
Gather information from departments	H	J, K, L	1
Receive work from graphic artist	I	M, N, O	4
Marketing	J	—	1
Finance	K	—	1
Operations	L	—	1
Review text	M	—	1
Specify artwork needed	N	—	1
Decide on format	O	—	1

In the next step, we compute the early start and early finish times. This shows that the project is expected to be completed in 14 weeks (see Figure 14-10). Next, we compute the late start and late finish times by working from right to left. Notice that the late finish time for task A is 14 and the late start is 10 (see Figure 14-11). Task B then has a late finish of week 10 and an early start of week 9.

FIGURE 14-9 AON Network

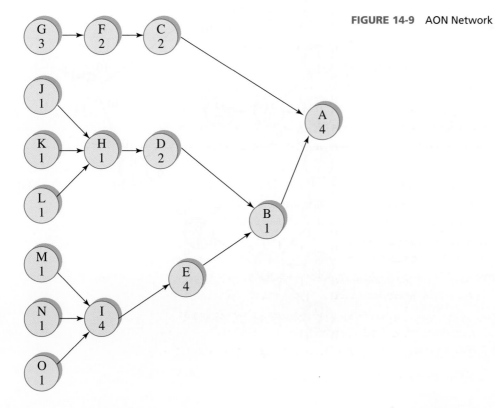

FIGURE 14-10 AON with Early Times

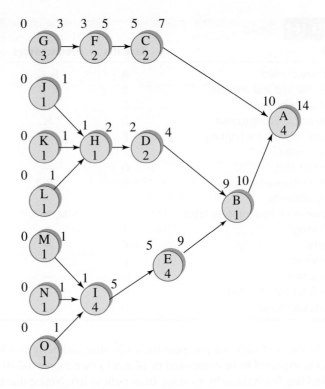

FIGURE 14-11 AON with Late Times

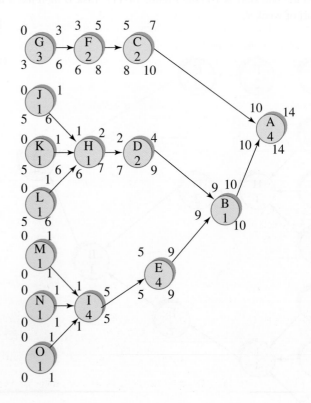

The slack times for this project are computed by taking the late start times minus the late finish times. From this diagram it appears that initially there is no slack for activities M, N, O, I, E, B, and A; and a lot of slack for all other activities. The critical path is the longest path in time from beginning to end (the path of activities with no slack).

Arrow Gantt Charts

Most college texts covering project management treat PERT (program evaluation and review technique) charts separately from Gantt charts. However, with many current software packages, these differences are becoming inconsequential. In this chapter we demonstrate both methods. Software packages vary, so it is best that you understand both methods.

Continuing our Document Checklist Project example from Table 14-6, the already-identified tasks have been entered in a planning software package called Microsoft Project. This is a commonly used and inexpensive project control software package that requires little expertise to run.

Using the data given in Table 14-6, the PERT chart for the document checklist project is as shown in Figure 14-12. The start time was June 9, and the expected completion date was September 14.

Managing Multiple Projects

At times, several projects occur simultaneously in a firm, and coordination can be difficult. Implementations have to be coordinated. Also, individuals within the company should not be involved in too many teams so they remain effective. The multiple-project control form[13] in Figure 14-13 is a management tool to aid company-wide coordination of multiple projects. By using this form, management can keep track of multiple projects and which employees are involved in those projects. Notice that the form identifies participants with varying levels of responsibility as well as the project managers. Also, management's duty is to ensure that employees have ample time to work on projects so their successful completion is facilitated.

FIGURE 14-12 Project PERT Chart Showing Tasks Needed to Perform the Document Checklist Project

[13]Van Der Merwe, A. P., "Multi-project Management Organizational Structure and Control," *International Journal of Project Management* 15, 4 (1997): 223–233.

FIGURE 14-13
Multiple-Project
Control Form

	Chris	Reba	Garth	Barney	Aunt B	Andy	Hawkeye	Hot Lips	Klinger
Project 1	T	C	S			T		☆	
Project 2		T	S		C			☆	
Project 3			T			S		C	☆
.									
.									
.									

T: Team member

S: Sponsor

C: Champion

☆: Project manager

Summary

In this chapter, we explored the use of teams and collaboration as a means of improvement. We focused on the behavioral aspects of building and leading effective teams. As companies focus on knowledge work and flatten their hierarchies, we have seen a movement toward more teamwork.

Team leaders are responsible for providing leadership and training so that team members have the skills to perform required tasks. Leaders also need to be sensitive to the amount of social support team members need to be effective. Part of this is to identify and assign team roles and to establish team norms and rules.

Once the teams are established, they evolve through the stages of forming, storming, norming, performing, and (with successful projects) mourning. Team members should be aware of these stages so that they can successfully complete each stage.

The type of team should be considered as teams are formed. Teams might be process improvement teams, cross-functional teams, tiger teams, natural work groups, self-directed teams, or virtual teams. The type of team chosen depends on the team objective.

Team leaders may use facilitators and meeting management techniques to help the team achieve success. When teams struggle, conflict resolution might be needed to overcome problems. Before problems threaten the success of a team, the process-intervention cycle provides a basis for recognizing and remediating problems in time.

Finally, we presented some project planning fundamentals that can be combined with the new seven tools discussed in Chapter 10. These planning tools, such as charters, work breakdown structures, models for determining task times, and PERT/CPM (critical path methods), are useful for controlling team projects for quality improvement. Note that many projects are controlled using software such as Oracle's Primavera or MS Project. Figure 14-14 shows an example of a simple project in MS Project.

FIGURE 14-14 MS Project Gantt Chart *Source:* Microsoft Project, Microsoft Corporation. Used by permission.

Teams can either be a drag on an organization's resources or they can provide the basis for improved competitiveness. There is some ambiguity in the quality literature as to whether managers should aggressively manage these teams. In truth, a balance needs to be established between control that is too tight and too loose. Achieving that balance requires insight and skill. The concepts and tools given here will help you to achieve this balance. Remember that many firms cannot absorb too much change. Therefore, the rate of change needs to be managed and planned.

Key Terms

Cost-benefits analysis (CBA)
Cross-functional teams
Empowerment
Facilitation
Facilitator
Force-field analysis
Forming

Hard costs
Knowledge work
Meeting management
Mourning
Natural work groups
Norming
Organizational learning
Parking lot

Payback period
Performing
Process improvement teams
Project charters
Readiness
Self-directed work team
Situational leadership model

Soft costs
Storming
Team
Team building
Teamware
Tiger team
Virtual teams

Discussion Questions

1. Why has increased complexity in the workplace resulted in an increased emphasis on employee participation and teamwork?
2. What is the difference between routine work and knowledge work? Provide examples of each type of work.
3. What is meant by employee empowerment? What is the relationship between employee empowerment and teamwork?
4. In what ways can employee empowerment facilitate and contribute to organizational learning?
5. What are the major disadvantages of multiple layers of management in a business organization? Is teamwork typically implemented in organizations that have multiple layers of management or organizations that have fairly flat hierarchies? Explain your answer.
6. Describe the principal attributes of Hersey, Blanchard, and Johnson's situational leadership model. Is this model of leadership appropriate for a quality-minded company?

7. What does "readiness" refer to in a leadership context? What are the two variables that an employee's level of readiness is a function of?
8. In general, do employees enjoy working in teams? Why or why not?
9. Briefly describe the five stages of the life cycle of a team. Is it important for a team to pass through each of these stages? Why or why not?
10. What is the purpose of a process improvement team? Provide an example of a process improvement team for a business organization.
11. What is meant by a self-directed work team? In your judgment, are self-directed work teams a good idea? Explain your answer.
12. Describe the role of the facilitator of a team. Is the role of the facilitator important or is it primarily ceremonial?
13. What is meant by *team building?* Is team building a concept from which all teams can benefit?
14. In a meeting management context, to what does *parking lot* refer?
15. What are the primary sources of conflict in work teams? What are some of the methods for resolving team conflict?
16. Describe what is meant by *virtual teams*. Provide an example of a virtual team in a business organization.
17. How does a project charter help a team identify issues relevant to team success?
18. Describe the critical path method for organizing work projects. When is the use of this method appropriate?
19. Describe the difference between critical tasks and a critical path.
20. Describe an experience you have had working in a team (in a work setting or in a college class). Describe how your experience either confirms or refutes one of the principles of teamwork described in this chapter.

Problems

1. Perform a Cost-Benefit Analysis with payback period for a project where indirect costs are $125,000, direct costs are $150,000, and annualized benefits are $550,000.
2. Perform a cost-benefit analysis using the following data:

   Direct Costs
   - Ten laptops—$2,000/each
   - A server—$2,000
   - Network installation—$15,000
   - Software—$20,000

   Indirect Costs
   - Training—$15,000

   Annualized Benefits
   - Increased capacity—$100,000
3. Following are activities, precedence relationships, and task times for a number of tasks.

Task	Task Time (days)	Preceding Task
A	5	None
B	2	A
C	4	A
D	5	B
E	6	C
F	7	D
G	4	E
H	5	D
I	1	C
J	4	I, F
K	3	G, J
L	7	H, K
M	4	L

   a. Construct a precedence diagram.
   b. Compute early and late times.
   c. Compute the slack for each task.

d. Which tasks could the project manager delegate?
e. Find the critical path.
f. Which tasks would you shorten first to shorten the project completion time?
g. What is the expected project completion time?
h. What is the probability of completing the project in the time identified in g?

4. Following are activities, precedence relationships, and task times for a number of tasks.

Task	Task Time (days)	Preceding Task
A	70	None
B	25	A, C
C	89	None
D	50	A
E	46	B, D
F	72	C
G	46	E
H	25	G
I	30	F
J	14	I
K	36	H, J
L	77	J

a. Construct a precedence diagram.
b. Compute early and late times.
c. Compute the slack for each task.
d. Which tasks could the project manager delegate?
e. Find the critical path.
f. Which tasks would you shorten first to shorten the project completion time?
g. What is the expected project completion time?

5. For the following data:

Task	Predecessor	Time Estimates (days)		
		t_a	t_m	t_b
A	—	3	5	13
B	A	2	5	8
C	A	1	4	6
D	A	4	6	10
E	B	2	8	11
F	B	5	9	16
G	C	4	12	20
H	C	6	9	13
I	D	3	7	14
J	D	8	14	22
K	F, G	9	12	20
L	H, I	6	11	15
M	E	4	7	12
N	J	3	8	16
O	M, K, L, N	5	8	10

a. Draw an AON diagram.
b. Compute the expected completion time for each task.
c. Compute slack for all tasks.
d. Identify the critical path and the expected completion time.
e. Your project manager wants you to compute a completion time (in days) that gives you a 95% chance of success. He will use this time estimate when negotiating a completion date for the project.

6. For the following data:

Task	Predecessor	T_o	T_m	T_p
A	—	5	7	10
B	—	1	2	4
C	—	10	15	22
D	E	5	8	12
E	A, B	4	10	18
F	D, G	1	2	4
G	E	2	5	7
H	G	4	8	14
I	C, F	2	4	7
J	I	3	6	10
K	J, H	1	3	7

   a. Draw a pert Diagram.
   b. Compute expected completion times for all tasks.
   c. Find the critical path and expected project completion time.
   d. What is the completion time that gives you 75% chance of success?

7. (Team project) Develop a project plan for buying a house. Use the following steps:
   a. Use a work breakdown structure (tree diagram—Chapter 10) to identify tasks for completing the project. Be complete (at least 50 tasks) and use sticky notes.
   b. Laying out your sticky notes, identify the precedence relationships for each task.
   c. Brainstorm optimistic time, most likely time, and pessimistic time for each task.
   d. Compute expected completion time for each task.
   e. Draw your network diagram, compute early and late times, and find the critical path.
   f. Compute the 90% completion time for your project.

8. (Team project) Complete the steps in Problem 7 for the following project: completing a university degree program (choose any major).

9. (Team project) Develop a Gantt chart for welcoming a new baby into the world (conception has already occurred). Remember that you have only nine months to complete the project.

10. Complete a Cost-Benefit Analysis for investing in an automobile. Be sure to include all direct and indirect costs. Take into account all financial benefits associated with the investment.

11. Complete a cost-benefit analysis for a marriage. Be sure to include both the benefits and costs in your model. Model the marriage given two scenarios: a strong marriage and a poor marriage. (Hint: You should find that the benefits for a strong marriage approach infinity, and the benefits of a poor marriage approach zero.)

12. Meet with a favorite professor to perform a force-field analysis relating to adding a new course to your major in your university. Would you recommend this project?

CASE

Case 14-1 General Motors: Technical Problem Solving Group Drives Excellence

Founded in 1908, General Motors (GM) is an American multinational automotive corporation. The corporation employs 212,000 people and operates in more than 120 countries. General Motors led the global vehicle sales for 77 consecutive years between 1931 to 2007, longer than any other automobile manufacturer, and is currently among the world's largest automakers by vehicle sales units. In 2009, GM undertook operational restructuring to address past failures and improve its overall cost structure.

Before 2009, GM employed 150 full time Red X Masters working in its technical problem solving group, which was dedicated to vehicle performance investigation and improvement. Red X strategies are based on the philosophies developed by Dorian Shanin. GM has been using the Red X strategy as a technical problem solving tool for twenty years. It is used primarily to understand vehicle performance issues. Red X emphasizes that most problems can be corrected by identifying the root cause and controlling it.

After the restructuring of GM in 2009, the strength of the Red X team was reduced to 32. Following this, the team became determined to increase its output of completed projects and strengthen its role in making every GM vehicle better than the last. The General Motors Global Manufacturing System (GM-GMS) is rooted in lean methodology and structured around five principles: people involvement, built in quality, standardization, short lead time, and continuous improvement. The Red X team recognized an opportunity to align the group's goals with those of the GM-GMS and expand its role within the GM quality organization.

Initially the team was unable to determine where to focus its improvement efforts. Using Value Stream Mapping, the team was able to highlight areas where improvements were needed. It discovered an accessible and readily available system, known internally as the Problem Resolution Tracking System (PRTS), which is used throughout the company to document all issues that arise during a vehicle's life cycle. The team worked with the PRTS to develop an application to track and generate data needed to complete its vehicle performance analysis. It was also able to track problem resolution time and with the data, focused its improvement efforts on reducing the time to complete the process steps involved in repairing a vehicle fault while on warranty.

When a fault was identified, different repair teams had their own ways of resolving the issues and informing the design team, so that the fault could be eliminated at the source. The team found that some could identify the source of the problem and complete the project in 25 days, while, others would take up to 200 days as different processes were used by different problem solvers to resolve an issue. This variation led to some issues being resolved more efficiently in certain aspects of the process than others. Based on the value stream map, standard operating procedures were created to define each step of the problem solving process. This eliminated confusion and defined responsibilities for all stakeholders.

Internal stakeholders were involved through all phases of the project and were asked to complete surveys and audits to ensure any changes that were implemented would be beneficial to all team members. The team felt that increasing the speed of the problem identification process would improve the customer experience and better their ability to service and repair customers' vehicles. In order to validate the effectiveness of the team's improvements to standardized work activities, the iterative steps of the PDCA framework were used. This approach facilitated continuous improvement as the team quickly reacted when refinements to documents supporting standardized work were required.

Initially the team had feared that standardized work would stifle creative strategic thinking. In the end, however, the team discovered that standardizing the inputs to the problem solver actually increased the creative process and allowed them to do what they do best: provide every customer with a vehicle built from the latest knowledge. As a result of the Red X team's efforts, a 50% reduction in warranty incidents was achieved between 2009 and 2012 and they ended up as finalists of the 2012 ASQ International Team Excellence Awards Competition.

Discussion Questions

1. Discuss if the reduction of the Red X team staff numbers in 2009 had a significant impact on motivation?
2. Discuss the differences between the Red X strategy and Six Sigma. How would the Team have improved process and project times if Six Sigma methods were employed?
3. What do you think are the advantages and disadvantages of working in a team at GM?

Implementing and Validating the Quality System

Chapter Objectives

After completing this chapter, you should be able to:

Explain the building blocks for a system of quality improvement.

1. Discuss the three spheres of quality.

2. Implement a quality system assessment tool.

3. Explain a process for validating a quality management system.

A firm that skillfully implements the tools, philosophies, and techniques in this book will improve its quality management system, which should result in better performance. When you reach best-in-class or best-in-the-world status, how do you get beyond that point? If you have reached the limit of your knowledge and yet feel that more improvement can be made, how do you determine the next step? Answering these questions is the goal of this chapter—that is, to discuss how to discover the next step that will form the foundation for continually improving once you have reached quality maturity.

Remember that world-class competitors did not achieve that status by merely adopting tools or techniques. They got there because they were very good at performing the fundamentals. They understand their customers, products, employees, competitors, markets, and technologies. World-class performers have a good understanding of where they are and where they want to be. They are excellent at being creative and devising processes for achieving goals.

This type of progression is like life. Successful people are good at progressing from one plateau to another in a relatively short period of time. Rarely do people become successful overnight; it is more a process of continual growth and improvement. The same holds true for firms. They have to grasp, feel, make mistakes, and stumble on the way to the next level.

In this final chapter, we present processes for assessing where you are and identifying how your firm can move to the next level. These include defining, understanding, and assessing the quality system in your organization.

BUILDING BLOCKS FOR THE SYSTEM OF QUALITY IMPROVEMENT

A quality system depends on the interactions of many different variables, as evidenced in the quality system model shown in Figure 15-1. As we have demonstrated throughout this book, quality improvement is not a stand-alone discipline. Quality improvement requires the interactions, on a contingency basis, of many different disciplines to create products, services, processes, and systems that effectively serve customers. Another factor driving the integrative approach is the increasing complexity of work. Complexity requires people from different disciplines to settle on standardized methods for serving customers that result in work simplification. In the following section, we discuss the parts that go together to create a quality system.

People

The model in Figure 15-1 is built on a base of people. People represent the core of a firm's capabilities because they provide the intellect, empathy, and ability that is required to provide outstanding customer service. Therefore, systems must be in place to develop, train, care for, and motivate people to serve the customer properly. The management of a small metal fabrication plant was concerned that a particular production line was exhibiting particularly bad quality. The managers discussed all they had tried to do to improve quality on this line. They stated that they had even fired all the employees who previously worked on the line and replaced them with new employees. However, they were disconcerted that the quality

FIGURE 15-1   Quality System Model

problems persisted. The managers were then told that they were primarily responsible for the poor quality of the production. The employees had changed; however, the management had remained constant. To their credit, they peacefully responded, "We suspected we were the problem." At this point, they began to change the culture they had created to include improved input from employees.

For a quality system to function effectively, employees must understand that they are integral to that system. They must be made to feel important and necessary for the continued survival and growth of the company. This does not mean that management is unnecessary. Remember that employee empowerment does not mean abdicating authority. Rather, it means to share in decision making in areas that affect employees.

Another people-related issue involves organizational restructuring and redesign. Often, these efforts result in mass layoffs and much turmoil among employees. Although companies must sometimes necessarily take these measures to respond to economic realities such as downturns in sales or the national economy, layoffs should never be associated with quality improvement efforts.

Also, layoffs should occur only as a last resort. Quality improvement efforts, when performed properly, are associated with improved morale and confidence among employees that the company is becoming more competitive and the employees' personal security is improving. Many managers forget that human beings desire security. At the same time, some managers believe that insecurity results in better job performance. However, the opposite is most likely true. At times of high insecurity, the best employees leave, and the unmarketable employees remain. As a result, the capability for organizational learning to take place decreases, and even the capability of the firm to attract top talent in the future is impaired.

Recently, a major military contractor announced the layoffs of several hundred engineers in a large metropolitan city. At the same time, the company was recruiting engineers from a nearby engineering school at a major university. Needless to say, the best engineering graduates were not interested in interviewing with this firm. They knew the obvious: This firm did not care about employees' personal needs over the long term. Therefore, they would not interview nor accept employment with such a firm.

Evidence indicates that some employees will forgo higher wages to achieve higher job security. A good example is the tenured professor who turns down employment that would pay much better in the private sector to enjoy the benefits of tenure. Without tenure, there would be upward pressure on faculty salaries.

Organizational Learning and Knowledge

The second building block of a quality system is organizational learning and knowledge. Knowledge is the capital that fuels outstanding quality results. Business leaders report that lifelong learning is a key attribute for employees. These same CEOs and presidents of companies should also carefully consider the organizational and cultural aspects of their companies that inhibit and fail to reward lifelong learning.

A visitor to a manufacturer of components for automobiles heard from the employees that they felt as if they were hired from the "neck down" to do a job and did not feel that management valued their knowledge or opinions. One of the byproducts of a quality improvement effort is the realization by managers that rank-and-file employees are primary sources for in-depth knowledge relating to processes and that organizational learning is the sum of the learning of individual employees.

Learning needs assessment, training design, and delivery of training are important for competitiveness. Outstanding customer service results from providing employees with outstanding knowledge and training. Organizational learning is required for consistency in operations, approaches, and customer contact. After developing a new database system to tie together customer information with production planning, financial planning, and other functions, a service firm recently found that the database system was not yielding the expected integration and the desired results. On studying the problem, management found that employees were inputting customer-related information on the system using inconsistent methods. Therefore, customer information was found in inconsistent places in the system. A cause-and-effect study revealed that employees had received minimal and ineffective training on the new system during implementation. Such costly lack of attention to employee needs resulted in greater cost and poor use of information resources.

Culture

Culture refers to the norms and beliefs that lead to decision-making patterns and actions in an organization. Experienced quality practitioners and consultants claim that some organizations have cultures conducive to quality improvement, and others make quality improvement very difficult. Some of the key aspects of culture include attitudes toward change; presence or absence of fear; degree of openness, fairness, and trust; and employee behavior at all levels. Companies that play the so-called blame game end up with cultures in which trust is absent, and employees act in ways that appear self-defensive. Companies that work in an environment of fear find that distrust takes root between labor and management, between midmanagers and vice presidents, and between departments. Such distrust is the opposite of the open and trusting culture that is required for a company to be able to respond rapidly to changing customer needs. When distrust is present, control systems are put into place that result in lost time, capacity, and flexibility. (Traditional cost accounting systems have been criticized for these reasons.)

Companies that respond quickly to customers' needs have cultures in which decision making is open, information is available to everyone, and risks are rewarded. Some companies have cultures that are very control-oriented; and a large number of younger companies foster quite different environments, including "granola cultures" in which managers and employees view the company as a means of achieving happiness for all employees.

Closeness to Customers

Closeness to customers describes the firm's understanding of the customers, their needs, and their wants. Notice that the building block of "closeness to customers" is built on people, organizational learning and knowledge, and culture. All these things result in a supportive environment in which employees can be close to customers. Companies that value knowledge will gather data about customers and will study and understand changing customer needs. Companies that are close to their customers retain those customers. And, as we have seen, customer retention is closely related to profitability.

As we discussed in Chapter 6, for customer closeness to be achieved, systems must be put in place for gathering data about customers, analyzing the data, and implementing change systems based on the analysis. Not only is an understanding of customers required but also an understanding of competitors' customers. When you understand the customers of your competitors, you'll be able to put into place marketing methods that will attract those customers away from your competitors.

Customer closeness engenders loyalty. People who drive Harley-Davidsons and Mercedes automobiles identify with those products. As a result, these customers return to buy new products, replacement components, and accessories; and to get service. Brand loyalty may become less important as time passes and consumers move to an ethos in which product choices are valued over brands. This is particularly true with e-commerce. In this environment, personal relationships between vendors, suppliers, and customers become important differentiators. Consider the example of a doctor. Once patients find a doctor they believe is competent and trustworthy, they will remain with that doctor for many years. How does one achieve such loyalty?

The answers are different for different markets. However, close, empathic service appears to be one way to achieve closeness to customers.

Customer closeness is especially key in services. The level of customer contact achieved in services requires an understanding not only of customers' current wants but also of their emerging wants. Sensitivity to changing needs, moods, stages in life, and environmental conditions are possible only when supported by knowledgeable employees and a culture that values people. This means that a company should be focused on whom it chooses to serve. An understanding of the types of customers that a firm will serve and a focus on key capabilities are important for determining which customers a firm should become close to.

Information and Finance

Information systems provide the core of the support system for satisfying the customer. Well-designed information systems, such as those we've described at Ritz-Carlton Hotels, become the institutional memory for customer needs. If information systems are not well-designed, and information is difficult or slow to obtain, customers will go elsewhere. Banks that do not provide ready account information over the Internet or by phone will find that customers go elsewhere for their banking.

Electronic data interchange (EDI) is of increasing importance for satisfying customer needs. These systems allow customers and suppliers to tie their systems together to enhance planning, purchasing, and coordination. The objective of a quality information system is to gather information relating to the key variables that affect customer services and product quality. The scope of the information system includes the entire organization, linkages to customers, and linkages to suppliers. Better information leads to better customer service. The actions required to make the information system effective are problem identification, analysis, and corrective action.

Finances are listed in the building block in Figure 15-1 with information because financial resources are needed to provide the infrastructure and services that customers want. It takes money for doctors to decorate their offices in a way that is pleasing to patients, to have state-of-the-art technology that will result in state-of-the-art care, and to provide the equipment needed to achieve customer satisfaction. It is interesting to note that most firms that are world-class examples of quality are also financially successful. Research has shown that high quality can improve bottom-line results and enhance financial stability. Therefore, finance is a two-way street. Companies that are financially successful are able to invest in systems that will satisfy customers; and high-quality processes, products, and services lead to financial success.

The Three Spheres of Quality

The building blocks we have discussed provide the foundation to the quality system that supports the three key spheres of quality: quality planning and management, quality assurance, and quality control. These spheres were discussed in Chapter 1. Notice that they are closely related to enterprise capabilities and customer service. **Enterprise capabilities** are those capabilities firms have that make them unique and attractive to customers. Steven Appleton, the CEO of Micron Corporation, the worldwide cost leader in D-RAM computer chip production, was asked what his firm's core competency was. Appleton answered, "Micron's ability to improve productivity at a rate of 14% to 20% per year, year after year." Such capability is possible only if quality assurance, quality control, and quality management systems are effective. All Micron's systems and culture are focused on achieving this goal. *Customer service* is both a goal and an outcome of systems. Processes, procedures, training, and enterprise capabilities must be focused on providing good customer service.

The Integrative Approach

The integrative approach outlined in this book provides the glue that binds together the systems that result in high-quality products and services. Because quality is not under the purview of any specific functional group and is the responsibility of everyone, cross-functional approaches are required to achieve the desired results. The integrative systems view recognizes that all the building blocks must be in place in all the functional areas and throughout all levels of the organization for quality improvement to be both horizontally and vertically deployed in world-class companies.

Successful companies that provide high-quality products and services are increasingly able to take the focus away from narrow functional orientations and turn it to broad, customer-centered systems. In such organizations, all the foundation blocks we have identified in Figure 15-1 are in place to support the customer-focused environment.

Alignment between the Quality System and Strategy

The design of the quality system must have focus. A strategic framework is necessary to achieve this focus, which means that the design of the quality system must be in alignment with the strategic objectives and plans of the organization.

Hoshin planning or policy deployment, discussed in Chapter 4, provides a framework for achieving alignment through the catchball process. Through this process, strategic objectives are translated into specific projects and plans. Project teams are empowered to carry out the strategic objectives. Strategic objectives could be to develop and design a quality management system, a quality assurance system, or a quality control system. See Quality Highlight 15-1, which discusses how Ford is linking quality and strategy.

QUALITY HIGHLIGHT 15-1   Back to Basics at Ford[1]

It was an interesting day when Nick Scheele, COO of Ford Motor Company, announced that the company would move forward by "going back to the basics." What did that mean? Table 15-1 shows the different phases Ford has gone through—from mass production to the new era. By making the decision to focus more on the basics of running the company, Ford saw a 27% decrease in warranty spending and saved more than $2 billion with Six Sigma.

According to Scheele, "Going back to basics means building quality products on time and at the right price—with a value proposition that is absolutely compelling." It blends a driving vision with a mission and guiding principles that lead to quality by valuing people, teams, and processes.

According to Ford's CEO, Jim Padilla, the following are vital priorities:

- Improve quality
- Deliver exciting products
- Achieve competitive cost and revenue
- Build relationships.

Only time will tell if Ford can execute this plan. This focus does show that it is not all about new efforts and programs. It is about understanding your business and establishing a strategy that works for competitiveness.

INTERNAL VALIDATION: DOCUMENTING AND ASSESSING THE QUALITY SYSTEM

Once a quality system has been established, the system must be allowed to operate effectively over time. Of course, the system is in constant change as continuous improvement efforts occur throughout the organization. At times, managers in firms have difficulty finding new ideas for

[1]Smith, L., "Back to the Future at Ford," *Quality Progress* 38, 3 (2005): 50–56.

TABLE 15-1 Ford's Timeline

	1977 to 1980: Mass Production	1981 to 1993: Competitive Quality	1994 to 1998: Global Economy	1999 to 2004: Niche Markets/ Acquisitions	2005–Present
Management	• Mass production in a captured market, with Big Three competition. • Reduce short-term cost.	Emphasis on: • People (employee involvement). • Teamwork. • Processes. • Systems thinking. • Cost.	• Cycle plan. • Worldwide centers of excellence. • Common world vehicles and processes. • Customer satisfaction emphasis via added vehicle features.	• Emphasis on developing markets and acquisitions. • Push for youth and diversity in management (outside hires). • A, B, C ranking of people. • Bias for actions that provide rapid returns.	Emphasis on: • People and niche knowledge. • Teamwork. • Processes. • Systems thinking • Cost/profit. • Eco-effective design.
Manufacturing	• Reliance on manufacturing experience. • Inspection department to find and contain defective product.	• Quality is job number one. • Q1: basic quality system. • Variability reduction using statistical process control (SPC) and design of experiments (DOE). • Process improvement. • Regular senior management quality meetings.	• Plant vehicle teams established for find-and-fix problem solving. • Focus on top 25 issues. • Advanced product quality planning. ISO 9000 and lean emphasis.	• Strategy of "seek contain repair" for product issues and improvement. • Implementation of lean and flexible manufacturing systems. • Short-term cost (not profit) focus. • Six Sigma used for find and fix.	• Q1: basic quality system. • Variability reduction SPC and DOE. • Process improvement. • Lean/flexible manufacturing. • Six Sigma problem solving. • Regular senior management quality meetings.
Engineering	• Reliance on engineers with great experience. • Find and fix warranty. • Push on failure mode and effects analysis (FMEA) and basic reliability tools. • Design standards and verification manuals.	• Increased emphasis on "prevent." • Training and books available on statistics, learning organization, SPC, quality function deployment (QFD), DOE, and Taguchi from world experts. • Increased interaction with customers, manufacturing, and suppliers.	• Reorganized into platform teams; engineers rapidly rotate jobs. • Quality training centralized, but no longer taught by subject matter experts. • QFD replaced with marketing reports activity.	• Program content costly and complex. • Emphasis on analytical models. • Heavy cost reduction focus and program cutting. • Quality training available on the Web. • Push on FMEA and basic reliability disciplines.	• Q1 program for engineering. • A disciplined system to implement "prevent" quality methods tied to reward and recognition (design for Six Sigma). • Training and software on powerful, cutting-edge methods of TRIZ and axiomatic design.
Suppliers	• Multiple suppliers for each part. • Most business sourced to the lowest bidder.	• Strive to reduce supply base and establish collaborative partnerships. • Increased interaction with Ford engineers in design, quality, and cost. • Transfer of engineering competence to full-service suppliers (FSSs) begins.	• Supplier technical assistance reorganized under purchasing. • Supplier technical assistance staff greatly reduced; suppliers self-certify. • Cost reduction emphasis.	• Visteon becomes a supplier. • Further reductions in supply base emphasize lowest bidder. • Increased STA staff to deal with program issues.	• Longer-term collaborative partnerships operating in a lean value stream.

Source: Adapted from L. Smith, "Back to the Future at Ford," *Quality Progress* 38, 3 (2005): 50–56. Reprinted with permission from Quality Progress © 2005 ASQ, http://asq.org

Stage 1: Surveying	Stage 2: Categorizing	Stage 3: Investigating	Stage 4: Evaluating
Generate list of strengths and weaknesses from primary and support activities of the firm's value chain.	Reconceptualize list in terms of resources and capabilities and complete deeper inspection with the application of key questions.	Determine where, along the firm's value chain, potential competitive advantage lies. Look at each competitively relevant resource and capability relative to its potential as a cost or uniqueness driver.	Choose the appropriate generic strategy for the firm—cost leadership or differentiation.

FIGURE 15-2 Internal Environmental Analysis Process *Source:* Based on W. J. Duncan, P. Ginter, and L. Swayne, "A Competitive Advantage and Internal Organization Assessment," *Academy of Management Executive* 12, 3 (1998): 6–16.

improvement. The firm is operating well, is competitive, and is profitable. Benchmarking can be used to observe the practices of others and achieve even higher levels of performance.

Once this higher performance has been achieved, however, what happens? What is next when your firm is the benchmark or at the top of its industry? Where do you go from there? This is a nice problem to have.

When you have achieved benchmark or role model status, the ideas and initiatives for improvement must come from within. In this case, self-assessment is a good tool to spur improvement. The goal of self-assessment is to observe current practices, to assess those practices, and to identify gaps in deployment. Once gaps have been identified, new levels of performance can be achieved by filling gaps. It is interesting that Flextronics, a California company, is the first two-time Baldrige award winner as of this writing. Flextronics management has stated that the Baldrige self-assessment process has resulted in continual improvement over several years.

Figure 15-2 shows a generic process for performing self-assessment in a four-stage process of surveying, categorizing, investigating, and evaluating. In the following pages, we discuss various types of audits. The generic process is reflected in each of the audit types. **Surveying** is the means of generating lists of strengths and weaknesses for the organization. Some attempt should be made to prioritize these strengths and weaknesses because many bear no relationship to company competitiveness.

Stage 2 is **categorizing** the strengths and weaknesses. Strengths can be categorized as strategic resources or strategic capabilities that help define the path for improvement the firm should undertake. The next stage (3) is **investigating** the sources of competitive advantage. This investigation should answer questions concerning how the firm markets itself, differentiates itself from competitors, wins orders in the marketplace, and achieves competitive advantage over competitors. Companies that are at the later stages of competitive advantage in manufacturing or services should identify internal operational efficiencies that result in competitive advantages. These sources of competitive advantage then are related to the resources and capabilities defined in stage 2. This is done to determine how the competitive factors actually add value for the customers. If they are not found to add value, adjustments should be made to improve operational focus or become more customer oriented.

Stage 4 relates to **evaluation** of competitive advantage to assess how relevant resources and capabilities are in terms of generic strategies. Remember from Chapter 3 that the generic strategies are cost leadership, differentiation, and focus. Again, the primary question is the extent to which there is alignment between resource allocation in the firm and primary marketing and operational objectives. A Closer Look at Quality 15-1 shows a simple self-assessment tool.

A CLOSER LOOK AT QUALITY 15-1   A Simple Self-Assessment Tool

The Malcolm Baldrige office at NIST released the following self-assessment tool for use in companies (see Figure 15-3). This is one example of a tool that can be used in improving quality. A good class exercise involves teams performing this assessment and reporting their results to the company.

ARE WE MAKING PROGRESS?

Your opinion is important to us. There are 40 statements below. For each statement, check the box that best matches how you feel (strongly disagree, disagree, neither agree nor disagree, agree, strongly agree). How you feel will help us decide where we most need to improve. We will not be looking at individual responses but will use the information from our whole group to make decisions. It should take you about 10 to 15 minutes to complete this questionnaire.

Senior leaders, please fill in the following information:

_____

Name of organization or unit being discussed

CATEGORY 1: LEADERSHIP

		Strongly Disagree	Disagree	Neither Agree nor Disagree	Agree	Strongly Agree
1a	I know my organization's mission (what it is trying to accomplish).	❑	❑	❑	❑	❑
1b	My senior (top) leaders use our organization's values to guide us.	❑	❑	❑	❑	❑
1c	My senior leaders create a work environment that helps me do my job.	❑	❑	❑	❑	❑
1d	My organization's leaders share information about the organization.	❑	❑	❑	❑	❑
1e	My senior leaders encourage learning that will help me advance in my career.	❑	❑	❑	❑	❑
1f	My organization lets me know what it thinks is most important.	❑	❑	❑	❑	❑
1g	My organization asks what I think.	❑	❑	❑	❑	❑

CATEGORY 2: STRATEGIC PLANNING

2a	As it plans for the future, my organization asks for my ideas.	❑	❑	❑	❑	❑
2b	I know the parts of my organization's plans that will affect me and my work.	❑	❑	❑	❑	❑
2c	I know how to tell if we are making progress on my work group's part of the plan.	❑	❑	❑	❑	❑

(continued)

FIGURE 15-3 A Simple Self-Assessment Tool *Source:* NIST, Gaithersburg, MD, 2015, US Department of Commerce.

CATEGORY 3:
CUSTOMER AND MARKET FOCUS

Note: Your customers are the people who use the products of your work.

		Strongly Disagree	Disagree	Neither Agree nor Disagree	Agree	Strongly Agree
3a	I know who my most important customers are.	❏	❏	❏	❏	❏
3b	I keep in touch with my customers.	❏	❏	❏	❏	❏
3c	My customers tell me what they need and want.	❏	❏	❏	❏	❏
3d	I ask if my customers are satisfied or dissatisfied with my work.	❏	❏	❏	❏	❏
3e	I am allowed to make decisions to solve problems for my customers.	❏	❏	❏	❏	❏

CATEGORY 4: MEASUREMENT, ANALYSIS, AND KNOWLEDGE MANAGEMENT

4a	I know how to measure the quality of my work.	❏	❏	❏	❏	❏
4b	I know how to analyze (review) the quality of my work to see if changes are needed.	❏	❏	❏	❏	❏
4c	I use these analyses for making decisions about my work.	❏	❏	❏	❏	❏
4d	I know how the measures I use in my work fit into the organization's overall measures of improvement.	❏	❏	❏	❏	❏
4e	I get all the important information I need to do my work.	❏	❏	❏	❏	❏
4f	I get the information I need to know about how my organization is doing.	❏	❏	❏	❏	❏

CATEGORY 5: HUMAN RESOURCE FOCUS

5a	I can make changes that will improve my work.	❏	❏	❏	❏	❏
5b	The people I work with cooperate and work as a team.	❏	❏	❏	❏	❏
5c	My boss encourages me to develop my job skills so I can advance in my career.	❏	❏	❏	❏	❏
5d	I am recognized for my work.	❏	❏	❏	❏	❏
5e	I have a safe workplace.	❏	❏	❏	❏	❏
5f	My boss and my organization care about me.	❏	❏	❏	❏	❏

FIGURE 15-3 A Simple Self-Assessment Tool (*Continued*)

CATEGORY 6: PROCESS MANAGEMENT	Strongly Disagree	Disagree	Neither Agree nor Disagree	Agree	Strongly Agree
6a I can get everything I need to do my job.	❑	❑	❑	❑	❑
6b I collect information (data) about the quality of my work.	❑	❑	❑	❑	❑
6c We have good processes for doing our work.	❑	❑	❑	❑	❑
6d I have control over my work processes.	❑	❑	❑	❑	❑

CATEGORY 7: BUSINESS RESULTS					
7a My customers are satisfied with my work.	❑	❑	❑	❑	❑
7b My work products meet all requirements.	❑	❑	❑	❑	❑
7c I know how well my organization is doing financially.	❑	❑	❑	❑	❑
7d My organization uses my time and talents well.	❑	❑	❑	❑	❑
7e My organization removes things that get in the way of progress.	❑	❑	❑	❑	❑
7f My organization obeys laws and regulations.	❑	❑	❑	❑	❑
7g My organization has high standards and ethics.	❑	❑	❑	❑	❑
7h My organization helps me help my community.	❑	❑	❑	❑	❑
7i I am satisfied with my job.	❑	❑	❑	❑	❑

Would you like to give more information about any of your responses? Please include the number of the statement (for example, 2a or 7d) you are discussing.

_____
_____
_____
_____
_____
_____
_____
_____
_____
_____
_____

FIGURE 15-3 A Simple Self-Assessment Tool (*Continued*)

QUALITY AUDITS

The model in Figure 15-2 is a generic internal assessment model that can be used in many firms. We now discuss specific internal assessment models such as the Baldrige criteria and presidential audits. Note that ISO 9000 also uses repetitive audits to ensure compliance and to maintain registration. The approaches discussed here involve helping competitive organizations to become even more competitive. There are other ways to improve that we will discuss. In the abstract, these techniques involve audit processes. We start with internal assessment models based on auditing.

There are a number of different approaches to auditing company systems. We should first define what we mean by audits. These are not the compliance audits that internal auditing departments perform to ensure that generally accepted accounting principles are being followed. These are not audits to ensure that companies and employees are acting honestly. These are audits that can be defined as *an internal assessment tool to identify areas for improvement.*

Quality audits study ways to improve customer service and ascertain whether current customer service processes are being performed. The audit process is based on a framework of standards, concepts, procedures, and reporting practices. Steps for auditing include familiarization, verification, evaluation, and recommendation (see Figure 15-4). This disciplined process relies heavily on evidence, analysis, convention, and informed professional judgment.

Although intuition from past experience has an important role in auditing, intuition alone does not constitute a sufficient conceptual basis for a proper audit. In-depth knowledge of auditing standards, proper establishment of audit objectives, carefully planned audit procedures, controlled execution of audit steps, and disciplined adherence to proper auditing methods in arriving at conclusions are all requisite for accurate audits. An audit must be both planned and executed in a highly objective and unbiased manner.

Investigations designed to select only the "right" evidence and ignore the "other" cannot be termed audits. An audit must be designed and conducted to gather all the facts relevant to the matter in question, weighing the "good" against the "bad." Once these objectives are achieved, the auditor then renders professional judgment.

The three main ingredients to an audit are auditing principles, auditing standards, and auditing procedures. An *auditing principle* is a fundamental truth, primary law, or doctrine. Although an auditing principle is not a primary truth or law in the philosophical sense, it

FIGURE 15-4 Generic Auditing Steps

does constitute a rule that is derived from reasoning and experience. Auditing principles guide the auditor. Therefore, auditing principles are basic truths and doctrines that indicate the objective of auditing. They also suggest the manner in which the objectives are achieved. In other words, auditing principles constitute the basis for the application of audit procedures in a logical manner, which in turn will fulfill the objectives of the audit. A principle may result from accepted practice or it may develop as a result of general acceptance of a consistently applied procedure.

An *auditing standard* is a measurement of performance or a criterion establishing professional authority and consent. Therefore, a principle is a primary law, whereas a standard is a performance-measuring device. Some examples of general standards include the following:

- The audit must be performed by a person having adequate technical training and proficiency as an auditor.
- In all matters relating to the assignment, independence in mental attitude is to be maintained by the auditor so as to establish the "third-party viewpoint."
- Professional care is to be exercised in the performance of the examination and in the preparation of the report.

The *auditing procedure* establishes the courses of action available to the auditor to judge the adherence to the standards and the validity of the application of the principles. Although auditing concepts and methods are not as rigid as methods in the physical sciences, there is a similarity. For example, in auditing there is evidential support for every conclusion; otherwise, there could not be an audit opinion. For auditing purposes, an "audit-scientific" method should be developed and followed because any scientific method is concerned with searching for the truth based on evidence. In a scientific method, unsupported ideas and prejudices must be excluded from consideration because of lack of evidential support.

Quality Audit Process

Although there are many types of quality-related audit approaches, the basic quality audit follows these steps:

Preparation: Develop lists of questions, gather materials, form a list of candidates for the audit team, establish schedules, and perform the other activities required for beginning an audit.

Audit team selection: Select the right members for the team. Technical and managerial expertise is very important.

Develop checklists: The checklists contain the questions to be studied in the audit. Checklists also identify who will perform audits in various departments.

The opening meeting: A meeting between the auditing team and the management of the area being audited is called in which ground rules for the audit are established. An especially important agreement is that all pertinent information will be made available to the auditing team.

Implementing the audit: The audit is conducted and pertinent information gathered.

Analysis: The data are analyzed and preliminary results are developed.

The exit meeting: Preliminary results are shared with management at the exit meeting.

Reporting and corrective action: The final report is provided to management and plans are made for taking corrective action. Management implements the corrective action.

Follow-up: A postimplementation review is performed to ensure that the corrective actions were taken and the desired results obtained.

Closure: The audit is closed for the current audit cycle.

Types of Audits

In the following pages we discuss the different approaches to quality auditing that are used most often. Remember the focus is on studying current systems to understand how they can be improved.

OPERATIONAL AUDITS   Quality audits are based on the practice of operational auditing. **Operational auditing** is the term that was first used by nontraditional internal auditors many years ago to describe the work they were doing. This work includes a specific objective of improving the operations that are being audited. Much of the application of operational auditing has been in industrial companies. However, operational auditing is being used now frequently for services and government.

In a broad sense, the approach and the state of mind of the auditor characterize operational auditing—not the methods. Operational studies are seldom made as special and distinct audits. Instead, operational audits represent the application of the talents, background, and techniques of the auditors to the operating controls that exist in the business.

The general objective of the operational audit is to assist all members of management in the effective discharge of their responsibilities by furnishing them with objective analyses, appraisals, recommendations, and pertinent comments concerning the activities reviewed. Operational audits may follow organizational or functional lines, but the majority are organization-wide because such an audit presents a complete appraisal of the internal operations of an organizational unit. However, the auditor must always have in mind the division of functional responsibilities among organizational units.

PERFORMANCE AUDITS   As shown in Table 15-2, there are several major types of performance audits. **Supplier audits** are conducted by purchasers of their suppliers. In the automotive industry, for example, these audits are conducted using the ISO/TS 16949 standards. Toyota Motor Company in the United States spends months developing its suppliers using its own framework. Periodic audits are then performed to ensure that the supplier is maintaining standards and to improve the performance of suppliers. This approach is referred to as *supplier development.*

Certification audits are used to maintain a certification such as ISO 9000, ISO 14000, or other standards. These audits focus on the documentation of systems and adherence to those standards.

Award audits such as the Baldrige, state quality awards, customer awards, and other prizes involve site visits to externally validate the claims made by applicants in their applications. These visits exist to clarify and verify the information that has been provided by the applicant.

Consultant audits are studies performed by consultants to determine the maturity of a company in the quality pursuit and to help identify areas to be addressed in future quality plans. These are sometimes called *quality maturity studies.*

TABLE 15-2   Types of Performance Audits
Supplier audits
Certification audits
Award audits
Consultant audits
Presidential audits
Qualitative audits

Presidential audits are audits performed by a team led by the president of the company. These audits are usually operational and quality-related in focus. This gets the president of the firm actively involved in the quality audits and design of the quality system. Question-and-answer sessions are held in the morning with the people who work in the areas being audited. Visits are conducted in the afternoon to areas such as research and development, design, purchasing, manufacturing, quality control, marketing, training, and administrative services. In these audits, an overall assessment of the organization is performed, and this information is inserted into the following year's strategic plans.

Qualitative and Quantitative Elements in Audits

Some audits have more of a quantitative flavor when focusing on issues such as conformance and quality control. These audits may involve reviewing quality control check sheets to model trends in defect rates. Cost-of-quality audits may be conducted to determine whether quality costs are lessening and the programs are working.

Qualitative audits compare current practice against structural measures. *Structural measures* are the documents relating to processes. These include standards, contracts, procedures, regulatory requirements, and hierarchical standards. In qualitative audits, studies are performed to see that procedures are being followed. For example, as quality improvement becomes more behavioral and emphasizes decision making, it will be important to know whether employees are using structured processes for decision making. Hence qualitative audits should become more important as time passes.

VALIDATING THE QUALITY SYSTEM

In the following paragraphs, we outline a process for reenergizing quality efforts in organizations. This is a process I have used in actual companies to assess the status of their improvement efforts.

1. *Assemble the right team.* The reenergizing quality team should be made up of quality managers, people involved in the data analysis, a facilitator, and appropriate operating force participants. This is quite variable. If your analysis shows that you need to focus on improving design, you may need to include some design engineers. As project leader, you should use your judgment in assembling the team. This is a balancing act between too much involvement and not enough involvement. Make sure that you professionally facilitate all meetings using structured meeting approaches to get the most out of each meeting.

2. *Go over your results.* This usually takes about half a day. Present your evaluation of the current state of your improvement efforts to the team. This evaluation involves identifying quality-related practices in your organization for relevance and efficacy. Bring everyone up to speed. Use your best judgment as to what level of detail you will provide. You may decide to provide a report to the team and give them a few days to read and internalize the report. *This is not an evaluation of the quality management manager and should not be used as such.* This is an effort to reenergize your quality approaches.

3. *Identify those approaches that are working well.* Using your data, gain consensus from the team as to what quality improvement approaches are getting results. Remember that most managers' eyes glaze over when you discuss p-values and other statistical jargon. Keep your presentations focused and simple.

4. *Identify what is not working well.* Using your findings, gain consensus among team members as to what approaches should be eliminated. Identify promising approaches that are unsuccessful but hold promise due to high relevance ratings. There may be timing or implementation issues that, if addressed, could turn these results around.

5. *Identify additional areas in quality deployment that are not being addressed.* Conducting an in-depth study of this type will naturally result in an understanding of areas that need to be addressed that current quality approaches do not address. This is one of the major benefits of validating quality systems. It will help you close the gaps in your quality deployment.

6. *Develop your signature strategy.* Your signature (or specially tailored) strategy contains the bundle of quality improvement approaches that will help you to achieve the outcomes you desire. It links your current states (givens) to your desired states (shoulds) and clearly identifies your methods for achieving those results (hows). This is a statement that clearly identifies who you are, where you want to go, and how you are going to get there for the entire organization. Your signature strategy is a focused strategy that outlines a lean, well-defined, and well-understood approach to improvement of quality in services and processes. The signature strategy is a living document that will change as products and business realities change.

7. *Develop a plan for implementation with time frames and costs.* One of the important mantras for any quality effort is to maintain the highest professionalism. Using a modern project management approach, you should develop a project plan that includes estimating tasks, precedence relationships, timeframes, and costs. Remember that expenditures for projects of this type are nonlinear, so you should develop a budget on a monthly basis.

8. *Implement the project plan.* Get to work and implement your focused signature strategy. This is where the fun begins. Remember the fundamentals of change management and political change management when pursuing the project.

9. *Repeat this on an annual basis.* By performing this analysis annually, you will be able to baseline your results and establish trends.

Summary

In this chapter we identified ways for outstanding firms to get better. Once your firm has achieved role model status, it is difficult to find ways to improve. However, the recognition that there are endless ways to improve should lead firms to audit and self-assess.

The audit processes and Baldrige self-assessment discussed here provide a means for top management to improve its leadership in the area of quality management. These models reinforce the importance of the role of top management leadership in enhancing the system for improvement.

Although the firm that is looking to improve on already-high standards need not be large or world-class, it should be moderately mature in its quality journey. It is unlikely that you would want to perform a full-blown Baldrige assessment if you are a novice to quality improvement. However, once you are at the point at which you have measurable results, self-assessment can help to prioritize where to go next.

Companies also should recognize that these approaches are not short-term fixes. They require long-term commitment and support that are probably going to be more obvious in firms that have established quality programs.

Key Terms

Award audits	Consultant audits	Investigating	Qualitative audits
Categorizing	Enterprise capabilities	Operational auditing	Supplier audits
Certification audits	Evaluation	Presidential audits	Surveying

Discussion Questions

1. The model in Figure 15-1 shows people as the basis of the quality system. Do you agree with this assertion? Why or why not?
2. There are regions in which the three spheres of quality overlap. What are some of the overlaps between management, assurance, and control? Why are they important?
3. Review the concept of enterprise capabilities. Pick a firm and determine what you think is the enterprise capability for that firm.
4. What are the organizational benefits of conducting quality audits?
5. What can go wrong if the implementation of quality audit findings is delayed?
6. At what stage does a company become ready for Baldrige–based internal assessment?
7. Define the different types of audits. Pick a company and define which type would be best for it. Support your answer.
8. How can the education and healthcare sectors benefit from adopting the Baldrige Performance Excellence Program?
9. What are the *enablers* for quality improvement in a school? What are they in a firm in which you have worked? (See Figure 15-4.)

Problems

1. Administer the survey instrument in A Closer Look at Quality 15-1 to a local business owner and report your findings.
2. Using an organization where you have past or current experience as an employee, complete the survey instrument in *A Closer Look at Quality 15-1*. Do the results reflect an organization with good or poor organizational quality?

CASE

Case 15-1 Setting Priorities Using the Baldrige Criteria[2]
www.nist.gov

On the following pages are examiner evaluation notes for category 2 for a fictional company (the entire report is not provided because of length consideration).

Given this feedback, develop a plan for improvement for NuGrain. Include prioritization of the different new projects.

Discussion Questions

1. How did you select particular projects from the feedback report?
2. What are some of the weaknesses of this approach?
3. Why would it be good to use a mix of internal and external examiners as is recommended in the chapter?
4. How did you prioritize projects for improvement?
5. Was all of the feedback meaningful? What are some of the attributes of useful feedback?

2.1   Strategy Development

STRENGTHS

- NuGrain conducts planning annually through a 12-step strategic process plan (SPP). Participants include senior leaders (SLs), the North Florida University (NFU) chancellor, industry partners, collaborating universities, program managers, and agricultural community members. Blind spots are identified through data analysis; the environmental scan; the strengths, weaknesses, opportunities, and threats (SWOT) analysis; and input from stakeholders. SWOT results are used to identify strategic challenges and advantages. The short-term planning horizon is set to allow for rapid changes in the political, economic, or regulatory environment, and the long-term planning horizon is set to align with research timelines and to stretch beyond the U.S. Department of Agriculture (USDA) contract timeline. The SPP is evaluated annually, and improvements include revision of planning horizons, the introduction of the Strategic Alignment Document, and the formation of the Metrics Infrastructure Group (MIG), which is responsible for providing data to leaders for performance review.
- To help ensure that the SPP addresses various key factors, the MIG collects data and information for analysis by SLs one month before the planning retreat. Data are collected on customer needs, industry trends, the competitive environment, technology shifts, human resource needs and capabilities, organizational capabilities, financial capabilities and needs, partner/supplier directions and capabilities, and regulatory issues. These inputs allow NuGrain to perform the SWOT analysis in step 5 of the SPP. To ensure NuGrain's capability to execute the Strategic Plan, the budget, human resources, and information technology (IT) plans are aligned with the Strategic Plan; and progress is closely monitored throughout the year through NuGrain's performance review process so that action plans can be modified or added as needed.
- NuGrain uses the Strategic Alignment Document to outline the strategic objectives that are determined during the SPP. Each objective is aligned to NuGrain's core competencies, strategic challenges, and strategic advantages. Each objective has associated key measures with short-term action plans, as well as both short-term and longer-term projections. In many cases, best-in-class or competitors' projections also are included. NuGrain considers input from all stakeholder groups during step 1 of the SPP, and it includes representatives from industry and the agricultural community in the strategic planning retreat.

OPPORTUNITIES FOR IMPROVEMENT

- Although NuGrain identifies short- and longer-term projections, no goals are presented. Setting goals may serve to focus NuGrain more clearly on achieving its vision to be the premier government-owned laboratory system.
- It is not evident how NuGrain's strategic objectives balance short- and longer-term challenges and opportunities, or address future core competencies. Additionally, although NuGrain uses key stakeholder input in the SPP, it is unclear whether this approach ensures that the strategic objectives balance the needs of all key stakeholders, such as NFU, collaborating universities, and students. This lack of balance may make it difficult to ensure organizational sustainability in light of NuGrain's key strategic challenges of uncertain funding, changing contract performance requirements, and competition with other contractors.

2.2 Strategy Deployment

STRENGTHS

- Short- and long-term action plans are outlined. Key planned changes identified by NuGrain include improving key work processes to address stagnant or declining financial and human resources. SLs lead teams that include staff members, suppliers, and partners in developing short-term action plans and measures using the Work System Design Process. A standardized template is used to record and track action-plan progress, which the senior leadership team (SLT) reviews monthly as part of an organizational performance review. Action plans are deployed to the entire workforce through interactive Web-based sessions and meetings at each location. Workforce members' accountability for completion of action plans is incorporated into the performance plans that are part of the Workforce Performance Management (WPM) Process, and employee incentives are based on completion of action plans. Key supplier and partner responsibilities are reviewed monthly at supplier meetings.

---

[2]NuGrain Feedback Report (Gaithersburg, MD: NIST, 2012). Retrieved from http://www.nist.gov/baldrige/publications/upload/2010_NuGrain_Feedback_Report.pdf

(Continued)

- Human resource allocation occurs in step 8 of the SPP. A 10-year workforce Capability and Capacity Plan is developed and linked to NuGrain's strategic short- and long-term action plans. For example, key elements of the plan that are aligned with NuGrain's strategic challenge of a declining number of agricultural graduates include recruitment, a development plan for new hires, scholarship support, and incentives.
- To identify the potential need to modify or revise action plans, the SLT conducts a monthly review of action plan templates and the SLT Scorecard as part of the organization's performance review process. Strategic objective teams routinely review their metrics; progress is communicated and needed changes are identified through regular meetings with the workforce, suppliers, and partners. Changing customer requirements, including changes related to policy and emergencies, also may necessitate modification of action plans. When changes are implemented, they are deployed through discussions and meetings.

OPPORTUNITIES FOR IMPROVEMENT

- Although NuGrain notes a few improvements (e.g., the introduction of a standardized template for action plan design and tracking and its later revision to include budget information), there is no evidence that the approaches used to develop and deploy action plans are evaluated in a fact-based, systematic way to identify opportunities for improvement. A systematic approach in this area may support NuGrain's principal success factor of strong business practices that provide systematic, repeatable results.
- Although strategic objective teams identify the performance projections for the organization and for competitors and best-in-class organizations and many reported results, the approach the teams use to determine NuGrain's performance projections and those of its key comparisons is not evident. For example, although NuGrain notes that it analyzes its competitive environment and considers prior performance against goals, it is unclear what steps are in place to estimate the organization's rate of improvement and change. Determining an effective approach may help NuGrain more accurately estimate future performance and its progress on achieving its vision.
- It is not evident that NuGrain has a systematic approach for assessing and managing financial and other risks associated with action plans. Although NuGrain has a small contingency fund for unanticipated circumstances, it is not clear how this fund is set up, evaluated to mitigate potential risks, or deployed in times of need. A systematic approach to address these risks may be particularly important because upcoming changes may require NuGrain to do more with stagnant or declining resources, and it has identified the uncertain funding environment as a strategic challenge.

APPENDIX

TABLE A-1 Factors for Determining Control Limits for $\bar{x}$ and R Charts

Number of Observations in Subgroup n	Factor for $\bar{x}$ Chart A_2	Factor for X Chart E_2	Factors for R Chart	
			Lower Control Limit D_3	Upper Control Limit D_4
2	1.88	2.66	0	3.27
3	1.02	1.77	0	2.57
4	0.73	1.46	0	2.28
5	0.58	1.29	0	2.11
6	0.48	1.18	0	2.00
7	0.42	1.11	0.08	1.92
8	0.37	1.05	0.14	1.86
9	0.34	1.01	0.18	1.82
10	0.31	0.98	0.22	1.78
11	0.29		0.26	1.74
12	0.27		0.28	1.72
13	0.25		0.31	1.69
14	0.24		0.33	1.67
15	0.22		0.35	1.65
16	0.21		0.36	1.64
17	0.20		0.38	1.62
18	0.19		0.39	1.61
19	0.19		0.40	1.60
20	0.18		0.41	1.59

$$\text{Upper control limit for } \bar{x} = UCL_{\bar{x}} = \bar{\bar{x}} + A_2\bar{R}$$
$$\text{Lower control limit for } \bar{x} = UCL_{\bar{x}} = \bar{\bar{x}} - A_2\bar{R}$$

(If aimed-at or standard value $\bar{x}'$ is used rather than $\bar{\bar{x}}$ as the central line on the control chart, $\bar{x}'$ should be substituted for $\bar{\bar{x}}$ in the preceding formulas.)

$$\text{Upper control limit for } R = UCL_R = D_4\bar{R}$$
$$\text{Lower control limit for } R = LCL_R = D_3\bar{R}$$

All factors in Table A-1 are based on the normal distribution.

$$\text{Upper control limit for } X = UCL_X = \bar{\bar{x}} + E_2\overline{MR}$$
$$\text{Lower control limit for } X = LCL_X = \bar{\bar{x}} - E_2\overline{MR}$$
$$\text{Upper control limit for } MR = UCL_{MR} = D_4\overline{MR}$$
$$\text{Lower control limit for } MR = LCL_{MR} = D_3\overline{MR}$$
$$\text{Upper control limit for } \bar{x} = UCL_{\bar{x}} = \bar{\bar{x}} + A_3\sigma$$
$$\text{Lower control limit for } \bar{x} = LCL_{\bar{x}} = \bar{\bar{x}} - A_3\sigma$$

(If aimed-at or standard value $\bar{x}'$ is used rather than $\bar{\bar{x}}$ as the central line on the control chart, $\bar{x}'$ should be substituted for $\bar{\bar{x}}$ in the preceding formulas.)

$$\text{Upper control limit for } s = UCL_s = B_4 \bar{s}$$
$$\text{Lower control limit for } s = LCL_s = B_3 \bar{s}$$

All factors in this table are based on the normal distribution.
Median chart formulas:

$$CL_{\tilde{x}} = \bar{\bar{x}} \pm \tilde{\tilde{A}}\,\bar{R}$$

$$\text{Average} = \frac{\text{sum of medians}}{\text{number of medians}} = \bar{\tilde{x}}$$

The numbers represent the proportion of the total area away from the mean, μ, to one side. For example, the area between the mean and a point that is 1.55 standard deviations to its right is .43943.

TABLE A-2 Normal z Curve Areas

z	.00	.01	.02	.03	.04	.05	.06	.07	.08	.09
0.0	.00000	.00399	.00798	.01197	.01595	.01994	.02392	.02790	.03188	.03586
0.1	.03983	.04380	.04776	.05172	.05567	.05962	.06356	.06749	.07142	.07535
0.2	.07926	.08317	.08706	.09095	.09483	.09871	.10257	.10642	.11026	.11409
0.3	.11791	.12172	.12552	.12930	.13307	.13683	.14058	.14431	.14803	.15173
0.4	.15542	.15910	.16276	.16640	.17003	.17364	.17724	.18082	.18439	.18793
0.5	.19146	.19497	.19847	.20194	.20540	.20884	.21226	.21566	.21904	.22240
0.6	.22575	.22907	.23237	.23565	.23891	.24215	.24537	.24857	.25175	.25490
0.7	.25804	.26115	.26424	.26730	.27035	.27337	.27637	.27935	.28230	.28524
0.8	.28814	.29103	.29389	.29673	.29955	.30234	.30511	.30785	.31057	.31327
0.9	.31594	.31859	.32121	.32381	.32639	.32894	.33147	.33398	.33646	.33891
1.0	.34134	.34375	.34614	.34850	.35083	.35314	.35543	.35769	.35993	.36214
1.1	.36433	.36650	.36864	.37076	.37286	.37493	.37698	.37900	.38100	.38298
1.2	.38493	.38686	.38877	.39065	.39251	.39435	.39617	.39796	.39973	.40147
1.3	.40320	.40490	.40658	.40824	.40988	.41149	.41309	.41466	.41621	.41174
1.4	.41924	.42073	.42220	.42364	.42507	.42647	.42786	.42922	.43056	.43189
1.5	.43319	.43448	.43574	.43699	.43822	.43943	.44062	.44179	.44295	.44408
1.6	.44520	.44630	.44738	.44845	.44950	.45053	.45154	.45254	.45352	.45449
1.7	.45543	.45637	.45728	.45818	.45907	.45994	.46080	.46164	.46246	.46327
1.8	.46407	.46485	.46562	.46638	.46712	.46784	.46856	.46926	.46995	.47062
1.9	.47128	.47193	.47257	.47320	.47381	.47441	.47500	.47558	.47615	.47670
2.0	.47725	.47778	.47831	.47882	.47932	.47982	.48030	.48077	.48124	.48169
2.1	.48214	.48257	.48300	.48341	.48382	.48422	.48461	.48500	.48537	.48574
2.2	.48610	.48645	.48679	.48713	.48745	.48778	.48809	.48840	.48870	.48899
2.3	.48928	.48956	.48983	.49010	.49036	.49061	.49086	.49111	.49134	.49158
2.4	.49180	.49202	.49224	.49245	.49266	.49286	.49305	.49324	.49343	.49361
2.5	.49379	.49396	.49413	.49430	.49446	.49461	.49477	.49492	.49506	.49520
2.6	.49534	.49547	.49560	.49573	.49585	.49598	.49609	.49621	.49632	.49643
2.7	.49653	.49664	.49674	.49683	.49693	.49702	.49711	.49720	.49728	.49736
2.8	.49744	.49752	.49760	.49767	.49774	.49781	.49788	.49795	.49801	.49807
2.9	.49813	.49819	.49825	.49831	.49836	.49841	.49846	.49851	.49856	.49861
3.0	.49865	.49869	.49874	.49878	.49882	.49886	.49889	.49893	.49897	.49000
3.1	.49903	.49906	.49910	.49913	.49916	.49918	.49921	.49924	.49926	.49929

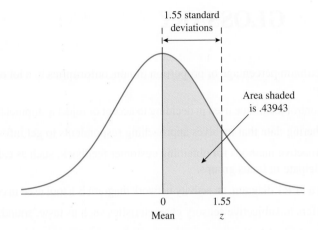

| 1.55 standard deviations |
| Area shaded is .43943 |
| 0 Mean | 1.55 z |

TABLE A-3 Factors for Determining the 3-Sigma Control Limits for $\bar{x}$ and s Charts

Number of Observations in Subgroup n	Factor for $\bar{x}$ Chart A_3	Factors for s Chart		
		Lower Control Limit B_3	Upper Control Limit B_4	Divisiors for Estimate of σ C_4
2	2.659	0	3.27	0.7979
3	1.954	0	2.57	0.8862
4	1.628	0	2.27	0.9213
5	1.427	0	2.09	0.9400
6	1.287	0.03	1.97	0.9515
7	1.182	0.12	1.88	0.9594
8	1.099	0.19	1.81	0.9650
9	1.032	0.24	1.76	0.9693
10	0.975	0.28	1.72	0.9727
11	0.927	0.32	1.68	0.9754
12	0.886	0.35	1.65	0.9776
13	0.850	0.38	1.62	0.9794
14	0.817	0.41	1.59	0.9810
15	0.789	0.43	1.57	0.9823
16	0.763	0.45	1.55	0.9835
17	0.739	0.47	1.53	0.9845
18	0.718	0.48	1.52	0.9854
19	0.698	0.50	1.50	0.9862
20	0.680	0.51	1.49	0.9869
21	0.663	0.52	1.48	0.9876
22	0.647	0.53	1.47	0.9882
23	0.633	0.54	1.46	0.9887
24	0.619	0.55	1.45	0.9892
25	0.606	0.56	1.44	0.9896

TABLE A-4 Factors for Median Charts

n	$\tilde{A}_2$	D_4
3	1.187	2.575
5	0.691	2.115
7	0.508	1.924
9	0.412	1.816

GLOSSARY

acceptable quality level (AQL)   The maximum percentage or proportion of nonconformities in a lot or batch that can be considered satisfactory as a process average.

acceptance sampling   Statistical quality control technique used in deciding to accept or reject a shipment of input or output.

active data gathering   A method for gathering data that involves approaching respondents to get information.

actively solicited customer feedback   Proactive methods for obtaining customer feedback, such as calling customers on the telephone or inviting customers to participate in focus groups.

activity network diagram   Also known as a PERT diagram, an activity network diagram is a tool used in controlling projects.

aesthetics   A dimension of quality that refers to subjective sensory characteristics such as taste, sound, look, and smell.

affinity diagram   A tool used to help groups identify the common themes that are associated with a particular problem.

after-sale service   Any service provided to the customer after the customer has purchased a product or service.

alignment   Consistency between strategy and operational plans.

analyze phase   Six Sigma phase in which the collected data are analyzed.

andon   A Japanese term that refers to the warning lights on an assembly line that light up when a defect occurs. When the lights go on, the assembly line is usually stopped until the problem is diagnosed and corrected.

annuity relationship   Relationship that occurs when a business receives many repeat purchases from a customer. The income is received steadily over time from a single customer.

appraisal costs   Expenses associated with the direct costs of measuring quality.

assurance   A dimension of service quality that refers to the knowledge and courtesy of employees and their ability to inspire trust and confidence.

attribute   A binomial state of being.

attrition   Reducing headcount by not hiring replacements when people quit.

award audits   Site visits relating to award programs.

balanced scorecard   A tool for monitoring both financial and operational metrics in one document.

Baldrige-lite   Term used to depict states' quality award programs using the same criteria as the Malcolm Baldrige Award, but with a simplified process or application.

Baldrige-qualified   Term used by firms that have been granted a site visit by the judges in the Malcolm Baldrige Award competition.

baselining   The process of monitoring internal metrics over time.

basic seven (B7) tools of quality   The fundamental methods for gathering and analyzing quality-related data. They include fishbone diagrams, histograms, Pareto analyses, flowcharts, scatter plots, run charts, and control charts.

bathtub-shaped hazard function   Reliability model that shows that products are more likely to fail either very early in their useful life or very late in their useful life.

benchmark   An organization that is recognized for its exemplary operational performance in one or more areas and is willing to allow others to view its operations and tour its facilities.

benchmarking   The process of finding a company that is superior in a particular area, studying what it does, and gathering ideas for improving one's own operation in that area.

best in class   Benchmarks who exhibit performance that is better than competitors.

best of the best   Benchmarks who exhibit best in the world performance levels.

black belt   A designation given to someone who has completed intensive quality training and has demonstrated results from one or more major projects.

business case   A mechanism used in Six Sigma and reengineering to outline a basis for improvement.

c **chart**   A chart used to monitor the number of defects in a production process.

capability   Likelihood that a product will meet specification.

catchball   Term used to describe the iterative nature of the Hoshin planning process.

categorizing   The act of placing strengths and weaknesses into categories in generic internal assessment.

cause-and-effect (or fishbone or Ishikawa) diagram   A diagram designed to help workers focus on the causes of a problem rather than the symptoms.

certification audits   Audits relating to registration (e.g., ISO 9000 audits).

chain of customers   A philosophy that espouses the idea that each worker's "customer" is the next worker in the chain of people that produces a finished product or service.

champion   Sponsor of a Six Sigma project.

change   In the context of quality management, change means to move from one state of operation to another state of operation.

check sheets   Data-gathering tools that can be used in forming histograms. The check sheets can be either tabular or schematic.

churn reduction   A process for reducing customer defections.

clickstream   The path customers use to navigate Web sites.

closed-loop corrective action   The process of ensuring that data and customer feedback are used to improve processes and service.

common cause variation   Random variation

compensate   (1) To pay or remunerate for some work; (2) to make up for some lack of ability or acuity.

complaint-recovery process   Process associated with resolving complaints.

complementary products   Products that use similar technologies and can coexist in a family of products.

component reliability   The propensity for a part to fail over a given time.

computer-aided design (CAD) system   A system for digitally developing product designs.

computer-aided inspection (CAI)   A system for performing inspection through the use of technology. For example, some systems use infrared to detect defects.

computer-aided testing (CAT)   Technology for conducting tests or examinations.

computer-based training   Training classes that are usually online.

concept design   The process of determining which technologies and processes will be used to produce a product.

concurrent engineering   The simultaneous performance of product design and process design. Typically, concurrent engineering involves the formation of cross-functional teams that enable engineers and managers of different disciplines to work together simultaneously when developing product and process designs.

conformance   A dimension of quality that refers to the extent to which a product lies within an allowable range of deviation from its specification.

consultant audits   Inspections that are performed by consultants to determine how an organization should be changed for improvement.

Consumer Product Safety Commission (CPSC)   An independent federal regulatory agency that helps keep American families safe by reducing the risk of injury or death from consumer products.

consumer's risk   The risk of receiving a shipment of poor quality product and believing that it is good quality.

contact personnel   The people at the "front lines" who interact with the public in a service setting.

contingency theory   A theory that presupposes there is no theory or method for operating a business that can be applied in all instances.

contrition   Remorse for error or mistake.

control charts   Tools for monitoring process variation.

control factors   Variables in a Taguchi experiment that are under the control of the operator, including temperature or type of ingredient.

control phase   Six Sigma phase in which improved process performance is monitored.

control plan   The part of the quality management system that outlines how quality control activities will be performed. This is a requirement for ISO 9000.

control process   A process that involves gathering process data, analyzing process data, and using this information to make adjustments to the process.

control vs. breakthrough   Juran's method for distinguishing between large-scale change and continuous improvement.

conversion process   Aligning the inputs of a process together to form a product or service.

core processes   Self-identified processes that are central to the organization and its customers.

core values   Beliefs central to a company's identity such that they can provide a basis for decision making.

cost-benefits analysis (CBA)   An analysis to determine the efficacy of a proposed improvement.

cpk   Capability index.

critical success factors   Metrics that companies monitor to determine whether their improvement efforts are having positive effects.

criticality   A term that refers to how often a failure will occur, how easy it is to diagnose, and whether it can be fixed.

cross-functional teams   Teams with members from differing departments and vocations.

cross-training   Teaching a person how to perform tasks in more than one job.

customer   The receiver of the goods or services that are produced.

customer benefits package (CBP)   The package of tangibles and intangibles that make up a service.

customer contact   A characteristic of services that notes that customers tend to be more involved in the production of services than they are in manufactured goods.

customer coproduction   The participation of a customer in the delivery of a service product. For example, in many restaurants it is not uncommon for customers to fill their own drinks.

customer defections   The number of customers who do not repeat with a particular firm.

customer-driven quality   Term that refers to a proactive approach to satisfying customer needs.

customer expectations   (1) What customers expect from a service provider; (2) a part of the SERVQUAL questionnaire.

customer future needs projection   Predicting the future needs of customers and designing products that satisfy those needs.

customer perceptions   (1) How customers view products or services; (2) the second part of the SERVQUAL survey.

customer rationalization   The process of reaching an agreement between marketing and operations as to which customers add the greatest advantage and profits over time.

customer-related ratios   Performance measures that have to do with customer satisfaction.

customer-related results   Outcomes that indicate customer satisfaction with a product or service.

customer-relationship management   A view of the customer that asserts the customer is a valued asset that should be managed.

customer-relationship management systems (CRMSs)   Computerized systems for managing customer-related information.

customer retention The percentage of customers who return to a service provider or continue to purchase a manufactured product.

dashboards Tools for easily tracking metrics.

deduction An approach to theory development based on modeling.

defects per million opportunities (DPMO) Six Sigma measure of the goodness of a product.

defects per unit (DPU) An overall average of number of defects occurring in a particular product.

define phase The first phase of the Six Sigma process in which a Six Sigma project is chartered.

Deming Prize A Japanese quality award for individuals and groups that have contributed to the field of quality control.

design for disassembly (DFD) A method for developing products so that they can easily be taken apart.

design for manufacture (DFM) The principle of designing products so that they are cost effective and easy to make.

design for remanufacture (DFREM) A method for developing products so that the parts can be used in other products. Associated with green manufacturing.

design for reuse Designing products so that components can be used in later generations of products.

design for Six Sigma (DFSS) A process for designing products that results in robust designs.

design of experiments (DOE) An approach to product design that involves identifying and testing alternative inputs to the production of a product to identify the best mix of inputs.

design review The process of checking designs for accuracy.

development plan Plans intended to improve employee knowledge.

distance learning Classes provided through technology to people in differing locations.

DMADV process Design for Six Sigma process with the define, measure, analyze, design, and verify stages.

DMAIC process Six Sigma improvement process with define, measure, analyze, improve, and control.

downstream Processes that are closer to the end customer.

dual sourcing Using only a few suppliers for a single component.

durability A dimension of quality that refers to a product's capability to withstand stress or trauma.

electronic data interchange (EDI) Using computers to share data between customers and suppliers.

empathy A dimension of service quality that refers to the amount of caring and individualized attention exhibited by the service firm.

employee empowerment The act of moving decision-making authority to lower levels in an organization.

empowerment A management initiative designed to move decision making to the lowest level in the organization.

end user The ultimate user of a product or service.

engineering analysis The process of applying engineering concepts to the design of a product, including tests such as heat transfer analysis, stress analysis, or analysis of the dynamic behavior of the system being designed.

enterprise capabilities Capabilities that make firms unique and attractive to customers.

enterprise resource planning (ERP) system A system that integrates financial, planning, and control systems into a single architecture. Examples include the SAP system and Oracle.

ethical attributes Attributes having to do with the honesty and goodness of people in a firm.

evaluation Assessment of how relevant resources and capabilities are to generic strategies in generic internal assessment.

experiential training techniques Learning by doing.

exporter A firm that ships its product in another country for sale.

extended value stream mapping Flowcharts used to map an entire supply chain.

external customers   The ultimate consumers of the goods that an organization produces.

external events   Happenings that affect a firm from the outside.

external failure costs   Monetary losses associated with product failures after the customer has possession of the product. They may include warranty or field repair costs.

external services   Services that are provided by companies other than yours.

external validation   Operational studies performed by outside entities to improve performance.

facilitation   Helping a team or individual achieve a goal. Often used in meetings or with teams to help the teams achieve their objectives.

facilitator   The person who performs facilitation. This person may be trained in group dynamics, teamwork, and meeting management methods.

failure costs   Two sets of costs: internal failure costs and external failure costs. Internal failure costs include those costs associated with failure during production, whereas external failure costs are associated with product failure after the production process.

failure modes and effects analysis (FMEA)   Method for systematically considering each component of a system by identifying, analyzing, and documenting the possible failure modes within a system and the effects of each failure on the system.

failure modes, effects, and criticality analysis (FMECA)   FMECA is an extensive but simple method for identifying ways in which an engineered system could fail. The primary goal of FMECA is to develop priorities for corrective action based on estimated risk.

fault-tree analysis (FTA)   An analytical tool that graphically renders the combination of faults that lead to the failure of a system.

features   A dimension of quality that refers to those attributes of a product that supplement the item's basic performance.

final product definition   The process of articulating the final drawings and specifications for a product.

financial benchmarking   A type of benchmarking that typically involves using CD-ROM databases such as Lexis/Nexis or Compact Disclosure to gather information about competing firms to perform financial analyses and compare results.

financial ratios   Numerical ratios of firm performance such as return on equity, return on assets, and earnings per share.

5 Ss   Techniques designed to improve orderliness in the workplace.

5w2h   Who, what, when, where, why, how, and how much.

flowcharts   Pictures of a process using a set of icons.

focus group   A group of people who are brought together to share their opinions about a particular product or service.

force-field analysis   A tool for evaluating forces for or against change.

forming   The first stage of team development, in which the team is formed and the objectives for the team are set.

full-Baldrige approach   Term used to depict states' quality award programs using the same criteria as the Malcolm Baldrige award.

functional benchmarking   A type of benchmarking that involves the sharing of information among firms that are interested in the same functional issues.

gage R&R (also gauge R&R)   A process for determining whether measurements from gauges are repeatable and reproducible. Used during the measurement stage of Six Sigma projects.

gap   The difference between desired levels of performance and actual levels of performance.

gap analysis   A term associated with the SERVQUAL survey instrument, gap analysis is a technique designed to assess the gap that can exist between a service that is offered and customer expectations.

generic services packages   Services packages that can be applied in many circumstances.

geometric modeling   A technique used to develop a computer-based mathematical description of a part.

global sourcing Purchasing from foreign suppliers.

globalization An approach to international markets that requires a firm to make fundamental changes in the nature of its business by establishing production and marketing facilities in foreign markets.

green belt Someone who has completed green-belt Six Sigma training.

green manufacturing A method for manufacturing that minimizes waste and pollution. These goals are often achieved through product and process design.

group decision support systems Software designed to enhance group decision making.

group technology A component of CAD that allows for the cataloging and standardization of parts and components for complex products.

hard costs Costs that actually reduce company expenditures. Usually associated with cost-reduction efforts.

hard data Measurements data such as height, weight, volume, or speed that can be measured on a continuous scale.

hardware mock-ups Prototypes designed to look like a final product.

heterogeneous A characteristic of services that means that for many companies, no two services are exactly the same. For example, an advertising company would not develop the same advertising campaign for two different clients.

hidden factory A term introduced by Wickham Skinner that refers to firm activities that have no effect on the customer.

histogram A representation of data in a bar chart format.

horizontal deployment A term that denotes that all of the departments of a firm are involved in the firm's quality efforts.

Hoshin planning process A policy deployment approach to strategic planning originated by Japanese firms.

house of quality Another name for quality function deployment.

human resource measures Ratios that are used to measure the effectiveness of a firm's human resource practices.

ideal quality A reference point identified by Taguchi for determining the quality level of a product or service.

IDOV A design for the Six Sigma process with identify, design, optimize, and validate stages.

improve phase Six Sigma phase in which improvements to products and processes are implemented.

inbound logistics Associated with the movement of purchased products.

induction An approach to theory development based on observation and description. Although the process of induction is useful, it is subject to observer bias and misperception.

initiator firm The firm that is interested in benchmarking and initiates contact with benchmark firms.

in-process inspection The practice of inspecting work, by the workers themselves, at each stage of the production process.

intangible A characteristic of services that means that services (unlike manufactured goods) cannot be inventoried or carried in stock over a long period of time.

interference checking A feasibility test for product designs to make sure that wires, cabling, and tubing in products such as airplanes do not conflict with each other.

internal customers Individuals within the organization who receive the work that other individuals within the same organization do.

internal failure costs Losses that occur while the product is in possession of the producer, including rework and scrap costs.

internal services Services that are provided by internal company personnel. For example, data processing personnel are often considered providers of internal services.

interrelationship digraph A tool designed to help identify the causal relationships between the issues affecting a particular problem.

investigation Ability to find sources of competitive advantage in generic internal assessment.

involuntary services A classification for services that are not sought by customers. They include hospitals, prisons, and the Internal Revenue Service.

ISO 9000   The registration standard from the International Organization for Standardization.

ISO/TS 16949   A standard for evaluating and improving automotive suppliers.

job analysis   The process of collecting detailed information about a particular job. This information includes tasks, skills, abilities, and knowledge requirements that relate to certain jobs.

just-in-time (JIT)   (1) A method for optimizing processes that involves continual reduction of waste; (2) the Toyota Motor Company production system; (3) an umbrella term that encompasses several Japanese management techniques.

Kano Quality/Design Model   A method for categorizing customer preferences during the design of a product.

key business factors (KBF)   Those measures or indicators that are significantly related to the business success of a particular firm.

key measures   Important metrics and structural measures that are monitored. They are often associated with the Baldrige process.

knowledge-growth systems   A compensation system that increases an employee's pay as he or she establishes competencies at different levels relating to job knowledge in a single job classification.

knowledge management   The process of maintaining and using company information.

knowledge work   Jobs that consist primarily of working with information.

law of diminishing marginal returns   A law that stipulates there is a point at which investment in quality improvement will become uneconomical.

leader behavior   A view of leadership stating that leadership potential is related to the behaviors an individual exhibits.

leader skills   A view of leadership stating that leadership potential is related to the skills possessed by an individual.

leadership   The process by which a leader influences a group to move toward the attainment of a group of superordinate goals.

leading   The act of guiding or directing the activities of others.

lean   A waste-free approach to process management.

lean production   An approach for reducing waste in production processes using just-in-time concepts.

Lean-Six Sigma   Combining the philosophies of lean management with Six Sigma improvement processes.

learning curve effect   A theoretical concept that suggests the more you do something, the better you become at doing it.

licensing   A method of reaching international markets that does not require the establishment of international supply chains or marketing arms.

life testing   A facet of reliability engineering concerned with determining whether a product will fail under controlled conditions during a specified life.

line-stop authority   The authority to stop a production line whenever a problem is detected.

loss to society   According to Taguchi, this loss occurs every time a dimension in a product varies from its target dimension. It is associated with Taguchi's "ideal quality."

lot tolerance percent defective (LTPD)   The maximum level of percent defective acceptable in production lots.

Malcolm Baldrige award   A U.S. national quality award sponsored by the U.S. Department of Commerce and private industry. The award is named after former Secretary of Commerce Malcolm Baldrige.

malpractice   The result of mistakes made by a professional service provider.

management by fact   A core value of the Baldrige award that focuses on data-based decision making.

manufacturing-based   Dimensions of quality that are production related.

manufacturing system design   The process of designing a manufacturing system.

market-share data   A comparative measure that determines relative positions of firms in the marketplace.

master black belt   An experienced black belt who is used as an organizational resource, trainer, and specialist.

matrix diagram   A brainstorming tool that can be used in a group to show the relationships between ideas or issues.

mean time between failures (MTBF)   The overall average time between product breakdowns. Usually expressed in terms of operating hours.

mean time to failure (MTTF)   The average time that has historically lapsed between product or system failures.

mean time to repair (MTTR)   The average time it takes before a product needs to be repaired.

measure phase   Six Sigma phase for collecting data.

measurement system analysis (MSA)   A set of tools used to determine the accuracy of measurements.

median chart   Control chart for monitoring variation in process central tendency when it is difficult to compute averages.

meeting management   A term that refers to the effective conducting of meetings in an organization.

mission   The central thrust of an organization; its raison d'être.

moment of truth   In a service context, the phrase "moment of truth" refers to the point in a service experience at which the customer expects something to happen.

mourning   The final stage of the team life cycle, in which team members regret the ending of the project and the breaking up of the team.

MR chart   (1) A chart for plotting variables when samples are not possible; (2) A moving range chart.

muda   A Japanese term for waste.

multilevel approach   Term used to depict state quality award programs that include two levels: a top level based on the full-Baldrige criteria and a second level based on the Baldrige-lite approach.

multiple-skills systems   A method for developing employees so that they can perform more than a single task.

multiuser CAD systems   Computer-aided design systems that are networked so multiple designers can work on a single design simultaneously.

$N = 2$ technique   An acceptance sampling approach that involves inspecting the first and last items in a shipment.

natural work groups   A term used to describe teams that are organized according to a common product, customer, or service.

new seven (N7) tools   Managerial tools that are used in quality improvement.

noise factors   Factors or variables that exhibit random variation.

nonrandom variation   Controllable variation.

norming   The third stage of team development, in which the team becomes a cohesive unit and interdependence, trust, and cooperation are built.

np chart   An attributes chart used to monitor the number of items defective.

offline experimentation   A method for determining the best configurations of processes. Usually uses a design of experiments (DOE) format such as the Taguchi method or Plackett-Burman experiments.

on-the-job training   Training that an employee receives at work during the normal workday.

operating characteristic (OC) curve   An assessment of the probability of accepting a shipment, given the existing level of shipment quality.

operating results   Measures that are important to monitoring and tracking the effectiveness of a company's operations.

operational auditing   Modern auditing practices that focus on operational efficiencies.

optimal levels   The best levels or settings of control variables in a Taguchi experiment.

ordinal data   Ranked information.

organic organization   An organization characterized by a focus on employee development and people-based decision making.

organizational design   The process of defining the best structure to meet company objectives.

organizational learning   The sum of the changes in knowledge among the employees of a firm.

orthogonal arrays   Experimental design tools that ensure independence between iterations of an experiment.

outbound logistics   Associated with the movement of products to the customer.

over-the-wall syndrome   Difficulties that arise when different types of engineers work in totally different departments in the same firm.

p chart   A chart used to monitor proportion defective.

PAF paradigm   Refers to prevention, appraisal, and failure costs of quality.

paper prototypes   A series of drawings that are developed by the designer on CAD systems and are reviewed by decision makers prior to acceptance.

parallel processing in focused teams   Performing work simultaneously rather than sequentially.

parallel reliability   This involves the use of backup or redundant components in a system.

parameter design   Designing control factors such as product specifications and measurements for optimal product function.

Pareto analysis   An economic concept identified by Joseph Juran that argues the majority of quality problems are caused by relatively few causes. This economic concept is called Pareto's law or the 80/20 rule. Juran dichotomized the population of causes of quality problems as the vital few and the trivial many.

Pareto chart   Chart used to identify and prioritize problems to be solved.

Pareto's law (the 80/20 rule)   States that 80% of the problems are a result of 20% of the causes.

parking lot   A term used in meetings that refers to a flipchart or whiteboard where topics that are off-the-subject are "parked" with the agreement that these topics will be candidates for the agenda in a future meeting.

partnering   An approach to selling in foreign markets that involves the collaborative effort of two organizations.

passive data gathering   Occurs when the customer initiates the data gathering for a firm such as filling out a customer complaint card or sending an e-mail. The firm provides the mechanism for feedback, and the customer must initiate the use of the mechanism.

passively solicited customer feedback   A method of soliciting customer feedback that is left to the customer to initiate, such as filling out a restaurant complaint card or calling a toll-free complaint line.

payback period   The amount of time required to recoup an investment. Usually associated with projects where costs are saved.

pay-for-learning programs   Programs that involve compensating employees for their knowledge and skills rather than singularly for the specific jobs they perform.

perceived quality   A dimension of quality identified by David Garvin that refers to a subjective assessment of a product's quality based on criteria defined by the observer.

performance   A dimension of quality that refers to the efficiency with which a product performs its intended purpose.

performance attributes   Attributes having to do with the functioning of a product such as horsepower, signal-to-noise ratio, or decibel output.

performance benchmarking   A type of benchmarking that allows initiator firms to compare themselves against benchmark firms on performance issues such as cost structures, various types of productivity performance, speed of concept to market, and quality measures.

performing   The fourth stage of team development, where a mutually supportive, steady state is achieved.

physical environment   The geographic area that is in the proximity of an organization.

plan–do–check–act (PDCA) cycle   A process for improvement pioneered by W. E. Deming.

poka-yoke   Mistake proofing.

ppk   Process capability index.

presidential audits Annual quality audits led by the president of a firm.

prevention costs Costs associated with preventing defects and imperfections from occurring.

preventive maintenance Maintaining scheduled upkeep and improvement to equipment so equipment can actually improve with age.

prioritization grid A tool used to make decisions based on multiple criteria.

process benchmarking A type of benchmarking that focuses on the observation of business processes, including process flows, operating systems, process technologies, and the operation of target firms or departments.

process chain diagram (PCN) A tool for adapting and improving service delivery processes (developed by Dr. Scott Sampson).

process charts Tools for monitoring process stability.

process decision program chart A tool that is used to help brainstorm possible contingencies or problems associated with the implementation of some program or improvement.

process improvement teams Teams that are involved in identifying opportunities for improving select processes in a firm.

process map A process flowchart with responsibilities.

producer's risk The risk associated with rejecting a lot of material that has acceptable quality.

product A tangible good that is produced for a customer.

product-based The context of Garvin's quality dimensions.

product benchmarking A type of benchmarking that firms employ when designing new products or upgrades to current products.

product data management (PDM) A method for gathering and evaluating product-related data.

product design and evaluation Activities that include the definition of the product architecture and the design, production, and testing of a system (including its subassemblies) for production.

product design engineering A form of engineering that involves activities associated with concept development, needs specification, final specification, and final design of a product.

product idea generation The process of generating product ideas from external and internal sources.

product liability The risk a manufacturer assumes when there is a chance that a consumer could be injured by the manufacturer's product.

product manufacture, delivery, and use Stages of the supply chain.

product marketing and supply chain The process of developing the marketing-related activities associated with a product or service.

product traceability The ability to trace a component part of a product back to its original manufacturer.

productivity ratios Ratios that are used for measuring the extent to which a firm effectively uses its resources.

profound organizational learning Quality-based learning that occurs as people discover the causes of errors, defects, and poor customer service in a firm.

project charter A document showing the purposes, participants, goals, and authorizations for a project.

project risk assessment A method for determining the propensity for a Six Sigma project to achieve desired results.

prototyping An iterative approach to design, in which a series of mock-ups or models is developed until the customer and the designer come to agreement as to the final design.

Pugh matrix A method of concept selection used to identify conflicting requirements and to prioritize design trade-off.

pull production The flow of production is regulated by customer need. Parts or products are not released at any stage of production until the immediate customer or stage of the process has a need for them.

QMS Quality management system that relates to ISO 9000 requirements.

QS 9000 A supplier development program developed by a Daimler Chrysler/Ford/General Motors supplier requirement task force. The purpose of QS 9000 was to provide a common standard and a set of procedures for the suppliers of the three companies.

quality assurance Those activities associated with assuring the quality of a product or service.

quality at the source A method of process control whereby each worker is responsible for his or her own work and performs needed inspections at each stage of the process.

quality audits Studies performed by auditors, quality specialists, or top managers to observe the quality practices within an organization.

quality circles Brainstorming sessions involving employees of a firm whose goal is improving processes and process capability.

quality control (QC) The process relating to gathering process data and analyzing the data to determine whether the process exhibits nonrandom variation.

quality dimensions Aspects of quality that help to better define what quality is. They include perceived quality, conformance, reliability, durability, and so on.

quality function deployment (QFD) QFD involves developing a matrix that includes customer preferences and engineering product attributes. A QFD matrix allows a firm to analyze quantitatively the relationship between customer needs and design attributes.

quality improvement system The result of the interactions between the various components that define the quality policy in a firm.

quality loss function (QLF) A set of Taguchi functions that determines economic penalties that society incurs as a result of producing a nonconforming product.

quality management The management processes that overarch and tie together quality control and quality assurance activities.

quality maturity analysis (QMA) A study in which a firm's level of maturity relating to quality practices is assessed.

quality measures Ratios that are used to measure a firm's performance in the area of quality management.

R **chart** A variables chart that monitors the dispersion of a process.

random variation Variation that is uncontrollable.

reactive customer-driven quality (RCDQ) A state that is characterized by a supplier "reacting" to the quality expectations of a customer rather than proactively anticipating customer needs and expectations.

readiness Used in a leadership context, the term refers to the extent to which a follower has the ability and willingness to accomplish a specific task.

ready–fire–aim A method that focuses on getting new technology to market and then determining how to sell the products.

recall procedures Steps for taking defective products from market. For example, Tylenol and Firestone Wilderness AT tires used these procedures to recall their products.

redundancy A technique for avoiding failure by putting backup systems in place that can take over if a primary system fails. For example, many redundant systems are used on the space shuttle to protect the crew if a primary system fails.

reengineering (1) A method for making rapid, radical changes to a company's organization and processes; (2) taking apart a competitor's products to see how they are designed and then designing similar products.

reinventing government Clinton administration effort to reduce government waste.

relationship management A method for developing long-term associations with customers.

reliability Propensity for failure of a product or component.

replications Number of runs of an experiment.

responsiveness   A dimension of service quality that refers to the willingness of the service provider to be helpful and prompt in providing service.

reverse engineering   The process of dismantling a competitor's products to understand the strengths and weaknesses of the designs.

robust design   Designing so that an increase in variability will not result in defective products.

RUMBA   Acronym for realistic, understandable, measurable, believable, actionable.

s **chart**   Standard deviation chart for monitoring changes in process variation.

sample   A part representing a whole.

sampling plan   A determination of how data are to be gathered and evaluated.

scatter diagram   A scatter plot used to examine the relationships between variables.

seiketsu   A term that refers to standardization.

seiso   A term that suggests that a highly productive workplace should be clean.

seiton   A term that refers to neatness in the workplace.

selection   The process of evaluating and choosing the best-qualified candidate for a particular job.

selective services packages   Service packages that can be selected from a menu of options.

self-directed work teams   Work teams that have a considerable degree of autonomy.

self-direction   A term that refers to providing autonomy to employees (or other recipients of training) in terms of facilitating their own training needs.

selri   A term that refers to organizing or throwing away things you do not use.

sensory attributes   Attributes having to do with our physical senses, such as fragrance, taste, or feel.

sequential or departmental approach to design   An approach to design that requires product designers, marketers, process designers, and production managers to work through organizational lines of authority to perform work.

series reliability   A system in which the failure of any single component causes the failure of the entire system.

service   A mix of intangibles and tangibles that are delivered to the customer.

service reliability   A dimension of service quality that refers to the ability of the service provider to perform the promised service dependably and accurately.

service transaction analysis (STA)   A process for understanding how a firm interacts with customers. For customer service improvement.

serviceability   A dimension of quality that refers to a product's ease of repair.

services blueprinting   A chart that depicts service processes and potential fail points in a process.

SERVQUAL   A survey instrument designed to assess service quality along five specific dimensions: tangibles, reliability, responsiveness, assurance, and empathy.

shitsuke   A term that refers to the discipline required to maintain the changes that have been made in a workplace.

signal factors   Factors in a Taguchi experiment that are not under control of the operator. Examples include small variations in ambient temperature and variability in material dimensions.

single source purchasing   An approach to purchasing that requires long-term agreements with few suppliers.

single sourcing   Using only one supplier for a single component.

SIPOC   Acronym for supplier-inputs-process-outputs-customer diagrams.

situational leadership model   A model of leadership proposed by Hersey and Blanchard that clarifies the interrelation between employee preparedness and effectiveness in leadership.

Six Sigma   An approach to process and product design improvement that emphasizes rapid results and payoffs.

social environment   The part of an organizational culture that defines the human condition.

societal environment   The portion of a firm's environment pertaining to cultural factors such as language, business customs, customer preferences, and patterns of communication.

soft costs   Savings that result in increased organizational slack, but not actual cost savings.

soft data   Data that cannot be measured or specifically quantified, such as survey data that ask respondents to provide their "opinion" about something.

sole-source filters   External validation measures of quality programs such as the Baldrige criteria and ISO 9000.

spider charts   Charts used for tracking *n* metrics in a two-dimensional space.

stability   The likelihood that a process will be random.

statistical process control (SPC)   A technique that is concerned with monitoring process capability and process stability.

statistical thinking   Deming's concept relating to data-based decision making.

storming   The second stage of team development, in which the team begins to get to know each other but agreements have not been made to facilitate smooth interaction among team members.

strategic alliances   An association between two firms by which they agree to work together to achieve a strategic goal. It is often associated with long-term, supplier-customer relationships.

strategic benchmarking   A type of benchmarking that involves observing how others compete. This type of benchmarking typically involves target firms that have been identified as "world class."

strategy   (1) The art of planning military operations; (2) what a firm does; (3) a firm's long-term plan for attaining objectives.

stretch target   A challenging goal or objective requiring significant effort to achieve.

structural attributes   Attributes having to do with physical characteristics of a product such as power steering or red paint.

structural measures   Measures that include objectives, policies, and procedures that are followed by a firm.

superordinate goals   Goals that transcend individual needs to reflect group objectives.

supplier alliances   A term used to characterize the relationship between suppliers and customers when a high degree of linkages and interdependencies exist.

supplier audit   The auditing portion of supplier development programs.

supplier certification or qualification programs   Programs designed to certify suppliers as acceptable for a particular customer.

supplier development   The process of improving supplier performance.

supplier development programs   Training and development programs provided by firms to their suppliers.

supplier evaluation   A tool used by many firms to differentiate and discriminate among suppliers. Supplier evaluations often involve report cards in which potential suppliers are rated based on different criteria such as quality, technical capability, or ability to meet schedule demands.

supplier filters   Hurdles that suppliers must pass in order to be considered by a potential customer.

supplier qualification   The process of grading suppliers. Usually associated with single sourcing.

supply chain   A network of facilities that procures raw materials, transforms them into intermediate subassemblies and final products, and then delivers the products to customers through a distribution system.

supply chain quality management (SCQM)   A systems-based approach to performance improvement that leverages opportunities created by upstream and downstream linkages with suppliers and customers.

surveying   Generating a list of strengths and weaknesses in a firm in a generic internal assessment.

sustainability The capability of a firm to be environmentally friendly or green.

system availability The proportion of time a system is available.

system reliability The probability that components in a system will perform their intended function over a specified period of time.

systems view A management viewpoint that focuses on the interactions between the various components (i.e., people, policies, machines, processes, and products) that combine to produce a product or service. The systems view focuses management on the system as the cause of quality problems.

Taguchi method An approach to quality management developed by Genichi Taguchi. The Taguchi method provides (1) a basis for determining the functional relationship between controllable product or service design factors and the outcomes of a process, (2) a method for adjusting the mean of a process by optimizing controllable variables, and (3) a procedure for examining the relationship between random noise in the process and product or service variability.

tangibles A dimension of service quality that refers to the physical appearance of the service facility, the equipment, the personnel, and the communications material.

target firm The firm that is being studied or benchmarked against.

task environment The portion of a firm's environment pertaining to structural issues, such as the skill levels of employees, remuneration policies, technology, and the nature of government agencies.

task needs assessment The process of assessing the skills that are needed within a firm.

team A group of individuals working to achieve a goal with activities requiring close coordination.

team building A term that describes the process of identifying roles for team members and helping the team members succeed in their roles.

teamware Computer software that is used in making group decisions.

technology development for process selection The act of choosing or developing technologies during the design process.

technology feasibility statement A feasibility statement used in the design process to assess a variety of issues such as necessary parameters for performance, manufacturing imperatives, limitations in the physics of materials, and conditions for quality-testing the product.

technology selection for product development The process of selecting materials and technologies that provide the best performance for the customer at an acceptable cost.

temporal attributes Attributes relating to time such as on-time performance and meeting delivery schedules.

360-degree evaluation A method for evaluating performance with input from supervisors, peers, and employees.

three spheres of quality Quality management, assurance, and control.

three Ts The task, treatment, and tangibles in service design.

tiger teams Teams with a specific defined goal and a short timeframe to attain the goal.

tolerance design The act of determining the amount of allowable variability around parameters.

total quality human resources management (TQHRM) An approach to human resources management that involves many of the concepts of quality management. The primary purpose of this approach is to provide employees a supportive and empowered work environment.

training needs analysis The process of identifying organizational needs in terms of capabilities, task needs assessment in terms of skill sets that are needed within the firm, and individual needs analysis to determine how employee skills fit with company needs.

training needs assessment A process for gathering organizational data relative to finding areas where training is most needed.

training program design A term that describes the process of tailoring a course or set of courses to meet the needs of a company.

trait dimension   A view of leadership that states leadership potential is related to the "traits" of an individual, such as height.

transactional analysis   A method for studying the interaction between customers and service providers to help improve service.

transcendent   A definition of quality that states quality is something we all recognize but we cannot verbally define.

tree diagram   A tool used to identify the steps needed to address a particular problem.

TS 16949   ISO standard for supplier development and management.

u **chart**   A chart used to monitor the number of defects in sequential production lots.

undeveloped events   A term used in fault-tree analysis. Undeveloped events are faults that do not have a significant consequence or are not expanded because there is not sufficient information available.

unified theory for services management   A set of propositions relative to managing services.

unique services packages   Services packages tailored for a specific customer need.

upstream   Processes that are closer to raw materials.

user-based   A definition of service or product quality that is customer centered.

value-added   A customer-based perspective on quality that is used by services, manufacturing, and public sector organizations. The concept of value-added involves a subjective assessment of the efficacy of every step in the process for the customer.

value-based   A definition of quality relating to the social benefit from a product or service.

value chain   A concept developed by Michael Porter that decomposes a firm into its core activities.

value-chain activities   Porter's chain of activities, including inbound logistics, production, and outbound logistics.

value stream mapping   Flowcharts used in process improvement.

value system   A network of value chains.

variable   A measurement.

variety   The range of product and service choices offered to customers.

vertical deployment   A term denoting that all of the levels of the management of a firm are involved in the firm's quality efforts.

virtual teams   Teams that do not physically meet, but are linked together through intranets and the Internet.

voice of the customer   A term that refers to the wants, opinions, perceptions, and desires of the customer.

voluntary services   Services that are sought by customers of their own volition.

working prototype   A functioning mock-up or model of a product.

X **chart**   A chart used to monitor the mean of a process for population values.

$\bar{x}$**-bar chart**   A chart that monitors the mean of a process for variables.

XY **matrix**   A matrix used to demonstrate and quantify the strength of relationships between dependent and independent variables.

$Y = f(X)$ A formula used in Six Sigma to illustrate the relationships between dependent and independent variables.

yellow belt   Someone who has completed yellow-belt Six Sigma training.

INDEX